PRICE THEORY
AND APPLICATIONS

PRICE THEORY AND APPLICATIONS

FIFTH EDITION

JACK HIRSHLEIFER
University of California at Los Angeles

AMIHAI GLAZER
University of California—Irvine
Carnegie–Melon University—Pittsburg

Prentice Hall, Englewood Cliffs, NJ 07632

Library of Congress Cataloging-in-Publication Data

Hirshleifer, Jack.
    Price theory and applications / Jack Hirshleifer, Amihai Glazer. —
5th ed.
      p.   cm.
    Includes index.
    ISBN 0-13-714296-X
    1. Prices. I. Glazer, Amihai. II. Title.
HB221.H62 1992
338.5—dc20   91-13866
                                                                   CIP

Freelance coordinator: Patrick Reynolds
Editorial/production supervision and
   interior design: Proof Positive/Farrowlyne Associates, Inc.
Acquisitions editor: Whitney Blake
Cover design: Thomas Nery
Pre-press buyer: Trudy Pisciotti
Manufacturing buyer: Bob Anderson
Scheduler: Liz Robertson
Editorial assistant: Diane DeCastro
Cover art: Genigraphics Corp.

© 1992 by Prentice-Hall, Inc.
A Simon & Schuster Company
Englewood Cliffs, New Jersey 07632

Printed in the United States of America

10 9 8 7 6 5 4 3 2

ISBN 0-13-714296-X

Prentice-Hall International (UK) Limited, *London*
Prentice-Hall of Australia Pty. Limited, *Sydney*
Prentice-Hall Canada Inc., *Toronto*
Prentice-Hall Hispanoamericana, S.A., *Mexico*
Prentice-Hall of India Private Limited, *New Delhi*
Prentice-Hall of Japan, Inc., *Tokyo*
Simon & Schuster Asia Pte. Ltd., *Singapore*
Editora Prentice-Hall do Brasil, Ltda., *Rio de Janeiro*

CONTENTS

PREFACE

Theory is useless unless it leads to applications. The opposite side of the coin is that real world problems are a buzzing, blooming confusion if no systematic theory puts them in some intellectual order. Earlier editions of this book have pioneered, we believe, in weaving theory and applications in a way that shows how microeconomic analysis casts light on both intellectual questions and policy issues. The dozens of brief boxed examples throughout the book direct attention to a host of specific applications. These discussions, which usually describe recent research published in scholarly articles and books, also instruct the student about the scientific work that professional economists actually do. (Given the media picture of economists as a squabbling band of rival soothsayers—some of them saying business will be good, others predicting doom—students may be surprised to find that there are scientifically validated results in economics.) In addition, appropriate places in the text provide more extensive discussions of such applied topics as rationing in wartime, alleged monopolistic suppression of inventions, and minimum wage laws.

We made an effort to address two other methodological points. First, economics is not a body of facts or propositions to be memorized, but is instead a way of thinking. There are diligent students who say, "Prof, just tell me what pages you want me to learn and I guarantee I'll know every word." However, memorization is not enough; economic insight and intuition must also be cultivated. The wide variety of applications discussed throughout the text are designed to train the student's intuition, which is not so much a matter of knowing economic propositions as it is applying the proper propositions in a specific context. On the other hand, not everything can be left to inspiration. Insight and intuition must be earned by hard intellectual labor.

Second, traditional economic theory has been guilty of tunnel vision in focusing so strictly on rationalistic individual behavior and on market interactions. But economics is really a universal science. An economic problem arises whenever the constraint of resource scarcity impinges upon life. Among the human decisions subject to the law of scarcity, and therefore amenable to economic analysis, are social choices (how many children to have, whether to live in the city or the suburbs, whom to seek as friends) and political ones (our nation must strike a balance, for example, between affluence and defense, between relief for persons unable or unwilling to work versus incentives to those who are productive, between regulation of improper behavior and greater freedom of the individual). Not all choices take place in a market context, and we all know that many of our decisions do not meet a high standard of rationality. We have therefore made an effort to incorporate materials from scientific work in anthropology, psychology, political science, social biology, and other fields, wherever convenient for illustrating economic principles. To cite one instance, students object that businesspeople never engage in anything as subtle or complex as marginal analysis. But biologists have discovered that marginal analysis explains many aspects of the behavior of birds and bees, or of animals generally (see "Birds Do It! Bees Do It!" in Chapter 2), and businesspeople are surely more clever than birds and bees.

In terms of technique, only recently has the classic scientific method—the use of experimentation—begun to play an important role in economic research. This is an exciting development. Accordingly, we present several examples on experimental studies. One important instance: while the conditions of perfect competition are never fully satisfied in the real world, experiments have shown that even highly imperfect markets may produce results close to the competitive ideal (see Chapter 13).

As to coverage and level of difficulty, this is not a minimal "thin gruel" book. Our aims are to meet the needs of a range of users and build in growth potential: the text can serve as reference and guide for readers pursuing additional self-study or coursework beyond the intermediate level. But perhaps the main reason for the breadth of coverage is simply the wealth of fascinating applications and extensions of the basic theory. In consequence, there is more in this text than can usually be handled in a one-term microeconomics course. To meet the needs of instructors and students in more compact courses, a shorter book-within-the-book exists in the series of Core Chapters (Chapters 1 through 8 and 11 through 13). Also, if time pressures so dictate, several advanced or tangential discussions (indicated by asterisks in the Contents) can be omitted with little or no loss of continuity. Most of the text can be covered within a two-term undergraduate price theory course.

We made a special effort to provide three expository aids. First, detailed descriptive legends accompany the diagrams. The analytical high points of a chapter can often be efficiently reviewed by rereading these legends in sequence. Second, each chapter ends with a summary and two groups of questions—a first group for straightforward testing of recollection and recall, and a second group providing challenges for further thought and discussion. Third, the text includes many numerical exercises, with answer solutions.

Users of the previous edition will find that the organization of chapters remains substantially as before. However, the text has been completely rewritten in the interest of clarity. In addition, since this book is increasingly used in schools of business administration and management as well as departments of economics, we include topics of significance for business policy, such as the discussion of the Capital Asset Pricing Model in Chapter 14. Among the many other topics and applications covered in new or revised fashion in this edition are auctions (Chapter 8), the principal-agent problem (Chapter 8), product quality (Chapter 9), efficiency wages (Chapter 12), signaling in labor markets (Chapter 12), and the Coase Theorem (Chapter 15).

This text uses the exciting new analytical technique of game theory; our emphasis is on applications rather than on abstract theorems. Game theory is employed, in particular, when we address such topics as oligopoly, principal-agent problems, and free-riding in the provision of public goods. The vital and rapidly growing field of law and economics is covered at several points; in particular the discussion of product liability in Chapter 9 and the Coase Theorem in Chapter 15.

Several additional features of this book represent, we claim, improvements upon conventional textbook coverage:

1. Traditional intermediate texts offer no price-theoretic explanations for money. In Part Five the analysis of exchange as a costly economic activity provides the foundations

for understanding how a monetary commodity works. And even earlier, Part Three indicates that business firms exist because of the costliness of exchange.

2. "Monopolistic competition" is covered in Part Three under a more general heading—variation of product. This part also takes up equilibrium of product quality and equilibrium product assortment.

3. Saving and investment are tied to the underlying theory of intertemporal choice and equilibrium in Part Six. The coverage here provides a bridge to macroeconomics and to the business-finance literature.

4. Our discussion of political economy first treats the traditional normative issues of welfare economics in Chapter 15. The final Chapter 16 gives a positive analysis of government. Two views of the state, a voluntarist or public-choice model versus an exploitative or conflict model, are contrasted.

As in previous editions, calculus is used only in marked mathematical footnotes. However, the delta (Δ) notation used in defining marginal concepts will be readily interpreted in derivative or differential terms by students who know calculus. The instructor should of course warn students that further command of college math is needed for study of economics beyond the intermediate level.

Whether a proper balance has been struck between coverage and simplicity, between theory and application, between technical accuracy and intuitive suggestion, only the reader can judge. We will be grateful for guidance on this point from instructors and students, and also for specific corrections where errors appear. As in past editions, the Teacher's Manual for this fifth edition of *Price Theory and Applications* is available to instructors, upon request, from the publisher. The Teacher's Manual and the Study Guide have both been prepared by Michael Sproul.

In its several editions this text has had the benefit of helpful reviews by many colleagues, by now too many to be individually named here. We are particularly grateful to the teachers, students, and other readers who have independently taken the trouble to send valuable corrections and comments. We also thank research assistants over the years, who have worked mainly on the boxed examples and the questions and answers for the various chapters. Once again the number has grown too large for a complete listing, but we would especially like to name Charles Knoeber for his outstanding assistance on the initial edition of the book.

CHAPTER 1

THE NATURE AND SCOPE OF ECONOMICS

EXAMPLES

Economics concerns decisions. To reach good decisions you must recognize that action has pros and cons, pluses and minuses, benefits and costs. For example, tennis may trim your figure and improve your disposition, but it will take time from your studies and could damage your joints. If you drop out of college now to earn money on a job, you will likely have lower income later in life. Similarly decisions in business and government—whether made by the corner grocer putting a price tag on potatoes or Congress voting on a declaration of war—will encounter arguments for and against. Faced with such opposed arguments, what criteria should individuals, firms, or governments use to choose among them? Economics shows how to determine the *best* action, through a systematic assessment of the pros and cons.

Economics also emphasizes that decisions are not made in a vacuum. Other people are likely to change their behavior in response to what you do. If a grocer raises the price of potatoes, customers may decide to buy less. So a higher price may not increase the grocer's profits after all. The same holds for social problems. When the likely responses of all the people affected are taken into account, the outcome is often much less attractive than it first appeared. Consider a law that aims to help the poor by requiring all grocers to cut food prices in half. Before concluding that this is a good idea we would need to know the reactions of the grocers and of their suppliers. Will they provide the groceries at the lower prices, or will shoppers find the store shelves bare? A law forcing sellers to cut prices in half may seem unlikely, but something similar occurs when rent-control legislation freezes apartment rents during a period of general inflation. If incomes and most other prices double, but the rent is fixed, then in *real* terms the rent has fallen by 50%.

Economics has been called the "dismal science" because economists often bring bad news. They point out that a superficially appealing project may turn out not to be such a great idea once the responses of all the affected individuals are considered.

Let's look at and consider some other examples. Table 1.1 lists a number of social problems with possible solutions. Notice that sometimes the same problem has diametrically opposed solutions. Take a moment to think of possible objections to each solution listed in the table. Then note the somewhat less obvious adverse consequences mentioned for each solution.

How many of these adverse consequences did you think of? Are there others that should be added? Finally, why are such consequences so often overlooked? Often it is because these consequences involve something not directly visible, *changes* in people's behavior as they react to the imposed solution.

Because people committed to one side of the question generally do not want to listen to contrary arguments, learning to think like an economist may not make you very popular. But it will make your private decisions more effective, and your views on social issues more balanced.

The economist is the opposite of the *advocate* who gives only arguments favoring his or her side of a question. There is a time and a place for advocacy. A person on trial for murder would probably not want his or her lawyer to present evidence for guilt with the same enthusiasm as the evidence for innocence. There is a time and place for balancing the pros and cons, and a time and place for action. And we all know people who can never stop saying "But on the other hand . . . ," when they should be taking action. Nor can economists replace prophets and poets who inspire us with ideals and goals. Society needs prophets and poets, men and women of action, and even advocates. But it also needs economists.

TABLE 1.1   Finding Solutions to Social Problems

Social Problems	Possible Solutions	Consequences
1. Our country's steel producers are threatened by competition from imports.	Impose a tariff on imported steel.	a. Since the price of steel will rise, steel-using industries will have higher costs and will have to raise prices to consumers. b. Foreigners, since they will be selling less steel to us, will buy less of our country's exports.
2. Apartment rents are rising, putting decent housing out of reach for the poor.	Freeze apartment rents.	a. Landlords will skimp on upkeep and repair of apartments. b. In the longer run, fewer rental units will be constructed.
3. Women's wages are less than men's.	Adopt "comparable worth" laws requiring equal pay for men and women doing comparable jobs.	a. Employers will become less willing to hire women. b. Costly bureaucratic and judicial proceedings will be involved in setting wages.
4. Commercial fishing for tuna kills large numbers of dolphins.	Require domestic fishermen to use special nets that let dolphins escape.	a. Consumers will have to pay more for tuna. b. Foreign fishermen not subject to our laws will take over more of the tuna trade.
5. Medical costs are very high.	Require government to pay a share of medical bills, especially for the poor.	a. Doctors' bills and hospital charges will rise even more than they have previously. b. Taxes will have to rise.
6. Many people are addicted to drugs.	Toughen enforcement of narcotics laws.	a. Street prices of narcotics will rise, forcing addicts to steal to feed the habit. b. Huge financial stakes in the narcotics trade will lead to more corruption of the police and judiciary.
7. Many people are addicted to drugs.	Abandon enforcement of narcotics laws.	Increased availability and lower prices of narcotics will increase usage and addiction.

1.1 ECONOMICS AS A SOCIAL SCIENCE

The economist has essentially the same outlook as the scientist. And indeed this text presents economics as a science: as a body of models (theories) that explain the real world. More specifically, economics is a *social* science; it aims to explain how human beings interact with one another.

Is Economics a Science?

Is economics really a science? One cynic might offer this opinion: "Anyone who reads the papers knows that economists always disagree with one another—that doesn't give me much confidence that economics has arrived at scientific truth. Furthermore, if economists can scientifically predict financial and commercial events, why aren't they all rich?"

It is easy to misinterpret how much economists disagree, because the mass media rarely discuss issues on which economists largely agree. The findings that are subject to wide agreement—price controls lead to shortages, free trade improves the international division of labor, firms will not invest if they are not allowed sufficient profits—make for little drama on a television show. Nor do differences among economists necessarily mean that economics is unscientific. All sciences advance through disagreement. In astronomy the geocentric model of Ptolemy was opposed by the new heliocentric model of Copernicus. In chemistry Priestley supported the phlogiston theory of combustion while Lavoisier supported the oxidation theory. And in biology creationism was countered by Darwin's theory of evolution. It is not universal agreement but rather the willingness to examine evidence that characterizes science. For Galileo's opponents to challenge the theory of Jupiter's moons was not unscientific of itself; it was unscientific for them to refuse to look through his telescope and see. The important issues of economics—for example, the monetarist versus fiscalist hypotheses in macroeconomics and the effectiveness of centralized planning for achieving economic growth—are under continuous scientific evaluation. Scientists may disagree because the problems are complex or the investigators incompetent, but there will always be unresolved issues in any living science.[1]

Observers often exaggerate not only the extent of disagreement among economists but also the degree to which the natural sciences have been mastered. In applied physics few topics have been so well studied as strength of materials. Yet engineers, after making their calculations, commonly add a huge safety factor (50 percent or even 100 percent) before building a bridge or a dam. And even so, bridges still collapse and dams wash away. If economists predicting the rate of inflation were permitted a safety factor as wide as engineers, they would rarely go astray.

EXAMPLE 1.1 Hydrology Versus Economics

In 1955 the New York City Board of Water Supply projected that the city's future rate of water use would reach 1,320 MGD (million gallons per day) as of 1960, rising further to 1,500 MGD by 1970. The city's hydrologists confidently estimated the "safe yield" from existing water sources to be 1,550 MGD. With only a thin safety margin ($1550 - 1500 = 50$ MGD) anticipated by 1970, the Board of Water Supply decided to acquire a new water source.

A team of economists reviewed this decision in 1960. They concluded that the Board's projections of water use were much too high; the economists predicted that actual water use in New York City would surely not reach 1,500 MGD by 1970, if ever. Since the "safe yield" supposedly guaranteed by hydrologic science already equaled 1,550 MGD, the economists concluded that an enormously expensive new supply was not warranted.

After 1960, the economists' prediction about actual use was confirmed. Water consumption in New York City stabilized well below 1,300 MGD, far under the Board's projected rate of 1,500 MDG, and never approached the supposed "safe yield" of 1,550 MGD. So

---

[1]*Scientific* consensus need not imply general agreement about *policy*, however. See the section on "Positive Versus Normative Analysis," p. 9

all should have been well. Instead, the city was hit by a catastrophic water shortage. What had happened? Throughout the early 1960s the actual yield of water sources was far below the hydrologists' "safe yield." In the four successive years (1962–65), the highest actual water yield was only 1,204 MGD. Economics, one of the social sciences, thus proved to be immensely more reliable than one of the vaunted natural sciences.[a]

COMMENT In making policy recommendations, the economist may have to evaluate the reliability of other sciences as well as his own.

[a]See J. Hirshleifer and J.W. Milliman, "Urban Water Supply: A Second Look," *American Economic Review*, v. 47 (May 1967), pp. 169–78.

What about the charge that if economics were truly a science, economists would all be rich? Several answers can be offered. It is sometimes argued that scientific knowledge of economics need not lead to financial success. If Hank Aaron had studied the aerodynamic equations governing the motion of spheroidal missiles, would that have helped him beat Babe Ruth's home-run career record? This argument should not be pressed too far, however. After all, what is the use of economics (or of aerodynamic knowledge, for that matter) if it does not lead to some *practical* result? Economics is useful, certainly, for understanding market phenomena; such knowledge ought to lead to higher cash income. Although most people can hardly be expected to match the life achievements of geniuses like Hank Aaron or J. Paul Getty in their respective fields, there ought to be some observable effect of economics training upon income. And, as Example 1.2 shows, to some degree there is.

EXAMPLE 1.2 **Salaries**

This table shows salaries for individuals with college or graduate degrees in different fields in 1984.

Mean Monthly Earnings (1984)

Field	Mean Monthly Earnings	Field	Mean Monthly Earnings
Business/Management	$1,986	Law	$3,338
Economics	2,366	Math/Statistics	1,855
Education	1,211	Medicine/Dentistry	3,060
Engineering	2,258	Psychology	1,350
English/Journalism	1,184		

Source: *Statistical Abstract of the United States,* 1989, p. 159.

COMMENT Economists have high salaries in the United States (third highest in this table). Only law and medicine, which require professional degrees, yield higher incomes.

Nevertheless, the data in Example 1.2 do not prove that economics training leads to higher incomes. There are other possible explanations. Perhaps the higher salaries that economists earn are only normal rewards for those exceptional talents necessary to understand economics in the first place. Aristotle (384–322 B.C.), in discussing his predecessor Thales, expressed such a view.

> Thales . . . was reproached for his poverty, which was supposed to show the use-lessness of philosophy; but observing from his knowledge of meteorology (so the story goes) that there was likely to be a heavy crop of olives, and having a small sum at his command, he paid down earnest-money, early in the year, for the hire of all the olive presses in Miletus and Chios; and he managed, in the absence of any higher offer, to secure them at a lower rate. When the season came, and there was a sudden and simultaneous demand for a number of presses, he let out the stock he had collected at any rate he chose to fix, and making a considerable fortune he succeeded in proving that it is easy for philosophers to become rich if they so desire, though it is not the business which they are really about. (Aristotle, *Politics,* I)

Thales was renowned not only as a meteorologist but as an astronomer, mathematician, and statesman. Still, we may doubt Aristotle's assertion that "it is easy for philosophers to become rich if they so desire," unless, like Thales, a philosopher happens to be a pretty good economist as well.

The Scope of Economics

Economics is not the only social science. Sociology, anthropology, political science, social psychology, and sociobiology also help us understand human behavior. But where does economics stop and these other sciences begin? The boundaries are rather indistinct, which provides a healthy intellectual situation, because the approaches of different disciplines can then compete over bordering territories. But economics has a definite focus, one that covers a limited range of human activity: *rational behavior* and *market exchange.*

What is rational behavior? At least two meanings are in common use (and are often confused). The first meaning refers to *method,* the second to *result.* In terms of method, rational behavior is action selected on the basis of logical thought rather than habit, prejudice, or emotion. In terms of result, rational behavior is action that achieves the desired goals. The two are not the same. In the first place, good methods can lead to bad results: "The best laid schemes o' mice and men/Gang aft a-gley" (Robert Burns). Actually, the seemingly inferior methods available to creatures with very limited capacity for thought often work very well. Chase a fly with a swatter and you quickly realize that the insect, despite its tiny brain, may easily defeat you. But in general, on the human level we expect that considered thought will (at least on average) lead to better action.

Everyone behaves irrationally to some extent—out of passion, thoughtlessness, mental defect, or just plain perverseness. Some who behave very irrationally are institutionalized for their own or others' protection. With the prevalence of human irrationality, how can rationality be assumed in economics? Clearly, postulating rationality is justifiable only to the extent that doing so correctly predicts how people will behave. Economists have found that theories assuming rationality function better than theories that do not. And yet economics as a science is not irrevocably wedded to the rationality postulate. When a more useful alternative comes along, it will be adopted instead.

EXAMPLE 1.3 **Rational Psychotics?**[a]

With 44 female psychotics (primarily schizophrenics) as experimental subjects, the psychologists T. Ayllon and N.H. Azrin studied how patients in a mental institution responded to changes in rewards for their services. Patients could choose among a variety of tasks (laundry service, dietary service, etc.). Tokens served as the reward and could be exchanged for commissary articles (clothing, toiletries, cigarettes, etc.) or hospital privileges (e.g., privacy, leave from the ward).

During the first 20 days of the experiment patients were given tokens only upon completion of their tasks—a system the psychologists term contingent reinforcement. After 20 days it was announced that the same number of tokens as before would be paid to each patient automatically, whether or not the tasks were performed—in psychological jargon, a shift to a system of noncontingent reinforcement. On an average day in the first period of contingent reinforcement (that is, where patients were paid for services), the patients worked 45 hours in total, just a bit over one hour per patient per day. After the shift to noncontingent reinforcement (that is, to the free gift of tokens), the total number of hours worked by the patients declined to 35 on the first day and to 20 hours on the third. Shortly afterward the bottom dropped out, and very few hours were worked thereafter.

Then, at the end of the second period of 20 days, the earlier system of contingent reinforcement was reinstated. The total number of hours worked jumped immediately to 45 hours per day, and remained near that level to the end of the experiment 20 days later.

COMMENT   The experimental subjects may have been psychotic, but they were not stupid. They adapted to rewards in their society. When working was necessary to earn these rewards, they worked; if the rewards came without working, they chose not to work.

[a]Discussion based upon T. Ayllon and N.H. Azrin, "The Measurement and Reinforcement of Behavior of Psychotics," *Journal of Experimental Analysis of Behavior,* v. 8 (November 1965).

So psychotics can be pretty rational, at least at times. How do they compare with college students?

EXAMPLE 1.4   **Rational Economics Students?**

In recent years economists have made increasing use of experimental techniques that are extremely successful in the natural sciences. Such experiments usually test how well individuals make economically sound decisions. But making rational decisions can involve hard thinking. Not everyone is inclined to work hard, physically or mentally, purely in the interests of advancing economic science.

David M. Grether conducted a number of experiments with UCLA economics students. Half the students were given $7 for participating in the experiment, regardless of their performance. (This was like noncontingent reinforcement in the experiments on psychotics.) The other subjects were paid either $5 or $25, depending upon their success rate (equivalent to contingent reinforcement). The students were presented with several possible gambles and asked to choose the one that had the greatest win probability. Figuring out the best gamble required students to make some complex mathematical calculations. The table indicates some of the results obtained. The first row shows, for example, that 33 of the 48 students who were offered payment contingent on success made no errors. But only 17 of the 49 students not receiving rewards succeeded in avoiding errors.

Evidently, the UCLA students behaved rationally; they were more careful and correct in their decisions when they derived some financial benefit from doing so.

Incentives and Performance

Errors	With Rewards	Without Rewards
0	33	17
1	5	6
2	3	10
3	3	3
4	1	4
5	1	1
6	1	2
7	1	1
8 or more	0	5
Totals	48	49

Source: Calculated from charts in David M. Grether, "Financial Incentive Effects and Individual Decisionmaking," California Institute of Technology Social Science Working Paper 401 (September 1981), p. 11.

Rationality is an instrumental concept. It requires the prior existence of goals. In the traditional view, economics does not ask how goals are formed. Only the net results of this process—the patterns called tastes, wants, or preferences—are relevant for economics. From the economist's point of view, goals are arbitrary. In one society individuals may protect children but eat cattle; another society may protect cattle but permit infanticide. Either way, the scientific economist is prepared to predict the social consequences of the given preferences.

Of course, goals and preferences are not determined randomly. Psychologists explain them in terms of primitive instincts, as reinforced or suppressed by socialization. Anthropologists analyze the relevance of culture for goal formation; sociologists examine the role of class or of other group identification. Social biologists argue that human tastes and preferences are the product of evolution over the long period in which the human species developed. Partly stimulated by this line of scientific work, economists have more recently begun to study the cultural and biological sources of preferences.[2]

The economist treats preferences as *stable* factors underlying human choices. If a tax

[2]For an example, Paul H. Rubin and Chris W. Paul II have examined the bioeconomic sources of the "taste for risk," as evidenced by the higher auto accident rates of young males in "An Evolutionary Model of the Taste for Risk," *Economic Inquiry*, v. 17 (October 1979).

on liquor is imposed, economists usually assume that the desire to drink is just as great, but that the tax makes it more expensive to indulge the desire. This represents a possible blind spot. For example, the remarkable temperance campaign of Father Matthew around 1850 in Ireland succeeded in cutting the consumption of spirits from 12,000,000 to 5,000,000 gallons per annum (but only temporarily). Nor is the assumption of unchanging tastes very helpful for analyzing fashion and style in consumption. More importantly, many of the great social changes in human history followed shifts in people's goals. Indeed, the economist may trivialize these fundamental values and goals by suggesting that they are merely arbitrary "tastes." From the prophets of ancient Israel, to the ministry of Jesus, to the modern decline of belief, the changes in the kinds of rewards that people seek from life have had an enormous effect upon Western society. The ethical messages of Buddha and Confucius have perhaps had similar impacts upon the civilization of the East. The aspects of human behavior that the economist fails to explain are therefore at least as important as those subject to economic analysis.

Critics sometimes say that economics assumes everyone is completely selfish. This is an uninformed accusation. It is true that, by observing facts, the economist ordinarily supposes that individuals seek their own advantage. "It is not from the benevolence of the butcher, the brewer, or the baker, that we expect our dinner, but from their regard to their own interest."[3] Nevertheless, charity is a factor; people have, in a sense, a taste for benevolence. Even so, the economist is likely to claim that if benevolence became less costly (for example, if larger tax deductions were allowed for charitable giving), we would surely see more of it. As another example, parental aid to children can hardly be explained by complete selfishness. But again, financial inducements would elicit more love and care by parents.

Economics focuses on rational behavior in a market setting. If a consumer wants bread from the baker, it may seem rational to get a job and earn the price of a loaf. But he or she might instead simply steal the bread. Alternatively, the consumer may support a political movement that would force bakers to give away their bread. Or, the consumer might attempt to persuade bakers that it is their charitable duty to do so. Any or all of these choices might be rational, in certain circumstances, but economics concentrates upon the first of these forms of interaction: voluntary exchange *through the market*. For the most part, crime has been left to sociology, the uses of state power to political science, and techniques of persuasion to psychology. But the vigor and rigor of economic science are proving increasingly useful in these related areas. Economics has tended, therefore, to overflow these boundaries.

EXAMPLE 1.5   Rational Criminals?

Crime sometimes does pay. It is perfectly rational for a criminal to steal rather than to work if he feels the gains are worth the risks. However, modern criminology (which until quite recently made no use of economic analysis) usually views criminals as individuals with "deviant" motivations. The solution to crime, according to this opinion, lies on the psychological level—for example, improving the mental health of potential criminals, or providing them with better role models. Economic analysis, without necessarily denying that criminals are psychologically "deviant" in some ways, suggests that criminals may still respond to incentives in a way that could be regarded as rational.

[3]Adam Smith, *The Wealth of Nations*, Book I, Chapter 2.

A study by Isaac Ehrlich asked whether commission of major felonies was affected by the punishments and rewards for crime in the different states of the United States.[a] As economists would expect, the crime rate tended to be lower the more effective the punishment. The rate of commission of robberies, for example, decreased about 1.3 percent in response to each 1 percent increase in the probability of punishment; robberies decreased about 0.4 percent for each 1 percent increase in the length of imprisonment. In another seemingly rational response, the property crime rate in a state tended to be higher where average income and inequality of income were both high. Presumably, in those states criminals were relatively poor individuals living in an environment containing many attractive targets.

Ehrlich's most controversial results concerned the effect of capital punishment in deterring murder. The standard view in criminology—emphasizing the abnormal psychology of murderers—asserts that murderers are surely too "deviant" to be deterred by the threat of execution. Yet Ehrlich's investigation indicated very big deterrent effects. According to one set of data each execution was associated with 7 to 8 fewer murders; another set claimed 20 to 24 fewer murders.[b]

In a study of crime rates in England and Wales, Kenneth Wolpin[c] also found evidence for the deterrent effects of punishment. A 1 percent increase in the proportion of crimes cleared by police led to a decline of about 0.8 percent in the number of criminal offenses; an increase in the proportion of the guilty who are imprisoned had similar effects. Indeed, a decline in the deterrent variables accounts for half of the increase in English crime over the period 1954–67. The largest single contributor among the deterrent variables was the fall in imprisonment rates, which contributed to a 44 percent increase in aggregate crime.

[a]I. Ehrlich, "Participation in Illegitimate Activities: A Theoretical and Empirical Investigation," *Journal of Political Economy,* v. 81 (May/June 1973).

[b]I. Ehrlich, "The Deterrent Effect of Capital Punishment: A Question of Life and Death," *American Economic Review,* v. 65 (June 1975), p. 414; "Capital Punishment and Deterrence: Some Further Thoughts and Additional Evidence," *Journal of Political Economy,* v. 85 (August 1977), p. 779.

[c]Kenneth Wolpin, "An Economic Analysis of Crime and Punishment in England and Wales, 1894–1967," *Journal of Political Economy,* v. 86 (October 1978).

These results suggest that economic analysis applies to other nonmarket interactions as well. And indeed, biologists have analyzed animal behavior in economic terms.[4] One important nonmarket form of interaction is politics, which will be examined from the economic point of view in Part Seven of this text.

Market interactions do, however, have characteristics that distinguish them from other forms of human transactions. The market relation is *mutual* and *voluntary*. Theft, a nonmarket interaction, is clearly *involuntary* on the part of the victim. Two plausible objections challenge this understanding. First, if H is hungry and B has bread, can their relation really be voluntary? Must not the H's of this world be "wage slaves" of the B's? Then how does the market differ from coercive dominance? Second, suppose some highwayman threatens his victim, "Your money or your life!" Isn't he offering a voluntary deal? Then how can criminal extortion be distinguished from market exchange?

[4]Martin L. Cody, "Optimization in Ecology," *Science,* v. 183 (March 22, 1974); David J. Rapport and James E. Turner, "Economic Models in Ecology," *Science,* v. 195 (January 18, 1977).

Explanations to these puzzles rely on the legal concept of *property*. First, the highwayman does propose a market deal: to "sell" the victim back his or her own life, in exchange for money. But under our legal system each person has property in his or her own life. The seemingly voluntary transaction proposed by the highwayman is based on his seizing power over something he has no right to—the victim's life. As for the "wage slave" contention, it is true that those endowed with more valuable property will be better off in the market than those possessing few resources. But there is a vast difference between a slave and a free laborer who can bargain with alternative employers for the best available terms. Slaves have no property; indeed, they are property. They cannot market or trade their labor, for it is not legally theirs to sell.

Positive Versus Normative Analysis: "Is" Versus "Ought"

In its scientific aspect economics is strictly *positive*. It answers the question "What is reality like?" But *normative* issues in public policy, which turn on the question, "What ought to be done?", also require economic analysis. Given a social objective, economists can use their knowledge of "what is" to analyze the problem and suggest ways of achieving "what ought to be."

Economists may disagree on policy issues because they seek different goals: one may be more concerned with social equality, another with individual freedom. Even complete scientific understanding of economic reality will not resolve such philosophical conflicts. But often disagreement among economists is over *means* rather than *goals:* over how to do it rather than what to do. Scientific progress in positive economics will, over time, tend to eliminate this source of disagreement.

EXAMPLE 1.6 **When Do Economists Disagree?**

A random sample of 600 members of the American Economic Association were asked their opinions on a variety of important issues. The questions represented a mixture of positive and normative issues. The table here summarizes results for six of the macroeconomic questions, divided equally between positive and normative.

Agreement Among Economists

Proposition	Generally Agree	Agree with Provisions	Generally Disagree	Index of Consensus*
Positive issues				
A minimum wage increases unemployment among young and unskilled workers.	68%	22%	10%	58
A ceiling on rents reduces the quantity and quality of housing available.	78	20	2	76
The fundamental cause of the rise in oil prices	11	14	75	64

Proposition	Generally Agree	Agree with Provisions	Generally Disagree	Index of Consensus*
of the past three years is the monopoly power of the large oil companies.				
Normative issues				
The distribution of income in the United States should be more equal.	40	31	29	11
Antitrust laws should be used vigorously to reduce monopoly power from its current level.	49	36	15	34
The economic power of labor unions should be significantly curtailed.	32	38	30	2

*The column labeled "Index of Consensus" was constructed from the original data by comparing "Generally Agree" with "Generally Disagree," subtracting the smaller of these from the larger. ("Agree with Provisions," the middle position, was omitted.) As can be seen, the amount of scientific consensus on the *positive* issues is impressive; note the much larger range of opinion on the *normative* issues.

Source: Adapted from J.R. Kearl, Clayne L. Pope, Gordon C. Whiting, and Larry T. Wimmer, "A Confusion of Economists," *American Economic Review,* Papers and Proceedings, v. 69 (May 1979), p. 28.

1.2 THE INVISIBLE HAND

As astronomy has Newton's principle of universal gravitation, and biology has Darwin's principle of evolution through natural selection, economics also has a great unifying theme. Its discovery was, like Newton's and Darwin's, one of the important intellectual achievements of humanity.

Adam Smith's *The Wealth of Nations* appeared in 1776. The following quotation conveys a key idea:

> But it is only for the sake of profit that any man employs [his] capital. . . . He will always, therefore, endeavor to employ it in the support of that industry of which the produce is likely to be of the greatest value, or to exchange for the greatest quantity either of money or of other goods. . . . He is in this, as in many other cases, led by an invisible hand to promote an end which was no part of his intention. Nor is it always the worse for the society that it was no part of it. By pursuing his own interest he frequently promotes that of the society more effectually than when he really intends to promote it.[5]

[5]Smith, Book IV, Chapter 2.

In more familiar terms, a person is led by self-interest to put his or her resources to use wherever those resources earn the most. To earn, you must produce something that people want to buy. Consequently, seeking your own advantage automatically leads you to produce goods or services that others desire.

Does this seem obvious? Two centuries ago people commonly believed (and a great many today still do believe) that the only way to help others is by benevolence—by "doing good." More sophisticated individuals know, as did Adam Smith, that you often help others more by trade than by direct aid. Nevertheless, it is not so easy to understand just how untrammeled selfishness avoids mutual harm or even total chaos. How is it that New York City can be regularly fed by converging food shipments from all corners of the earth without any governing plan to make sure that the Kansas farmer, the New England fisherman, and the Florida orange grower actually deliver food to the city? Though none of its suppliers need be motivated by any particular love and concern for New Yorkers, the city is fed. Kansas farmers simply find it more profitable to ship their wheat to New York than to consume the crops themselves, and similarly for the others.

Adam Smith also stated that "in civilized society [man] stands at all times in need of the cooperation and assistance of great multitudes, while his whole life is scarce sufficient to gain the friendship of a few persons."[6] The "invisible hand" leads an individual to work for the good of persons practically unknown to him, in an orderly economy that has arisen without anyone having planned it that way.

Adam Smith's object in composing *The Wealth of Nations* was largely policy-oriented or normative; he opposed the then politically dominant "mercantilists,"[7] arguing instead in favor of a policy of "natural liberty."[8] But it is not his policy recommendations that will mainly concern us. Another key concept was that the economy follows scientifically determinable laws. In early times, some people thought the planets were pushed in their courses by angels. The development of astronomy eventually led to the scientific idea of gravitation to explain planetary motions. Similarly today, many people find it utterly incomprehensible that (for example) water is cheap and diamonds are expensive. We attribute to Adam Smith the scientific idea of the market economy as a mechanism, driven by the self-interest of participants, yet integrated so that each is led to serve the desires of others. We shall see later in this text how this leads to cheap water and expensive diamonds.

1.3 ELEMENTS OF THE ECONOMIC SYSTEM

After learning that there is an economic system—that there are laws of economics—we can survey some of the basic elements of the economic system.

Decision-Making Agents in the Economy

There are three main types of decisionmakers: individuals, firms, and governments. Individuals are the basic units of social systems. (The consumption decisions of individuals will be discussed in Part Two. Actually, recognizing the mutual support and cohesiveness of the family, some economists consider the "household" to be the effective consumption unit.

---

[6]Smith, Book I, Chapter 2.

[7]The mercantilists believed that a nation's well-being required the accumulation of gold and silver, and that government should therefore encourage exports and restrain imports.

[8]Smith recommended free trade among nations and laissez faire within.

Except where otherwise specified, the individual here will be understood as making decisions for his or her family or household.

The business firm is an artificial unit; it is ultimately owned by or operated for the benefit of individuals. Surprisingly, this fact is often overlooked. It is sometimes argued, for example, that corporations can be taxed without cost to "the people." But of course taxing a corporation will hurt some people: the company's owners will earn lower profits, its workers may receive lower wage increases, its customers may have to pay higher prices. At the same time, taxes paid by a corporation allow government to assist other people. As usual, every choice of policy involves both costs and benefits. The economist finds it convenient to think of the firm as an aggregation of individuals for the purpose of production, that is, for the conversion of resource inputs into desired goods as outputs. (Firms are discussed further in Part Three.)

Individuals and firms are not the only economic decisionmakers. A third type of decisionmaker is government. Governments, like firms, are artificial groupings. Governments, unlike firms, have the legal right to take property without consent (as by taxation). From the economic point of view, governments produce a variety of goods and services, as determined by a political rather than a market process. Perhaps even more important, governments establish the legal framework within which the entire economy works. (The role of government is examined in Part Seven.)

In complex modern economies there are still other decision-making units. Trade unions and cartels are organizations of sellers in markets. Also of economic importance are voluntary associations like clubs, foundations, and religious institutions, through which individuals combine for certain collective consumption choices.

Scarcity, Objects of Choice, and Economic Activities

The source of all economic problems is *scarcity*. People always want more than they can have. Even if all desired goods were present in unlimited quantities, we would not have enough time to enjoy them all. And, in addition, we all desire things apart from material commodities: power, love, prestige. There can never be enough of these commodities. Scarcity thus forces us to make economic decisions; that is, we produce and/or trade with a view to obtaining desired goods.

The objects of economic choice are called *commodities,* or *goods and services.* (The term *goods* is usually understood to include services as well as physical wares or merchandise.) Services represent a flow of benefits over a period of time, derived either from physical goods (like the shelter provided by a house) or from human activities (like the entertainment provided by concert performers).

Consumption is one of the main economic activities. In their consumption decisions, individuals choose the goods they like best, given their incomes and the prices of the goods. We shall say that goods are the objects of choice for the consumption decision.

Production by individuals and firms is another main economic activity. We usually think of production as changing inputs into outputs, transforming resources into consumable goods. More fundamentally, production is any activity that adds to the social totals of some goods (which necessarily means giving up the opportunity to produce other goods with the same resources). Production can change physical form, as in the conversion of leather and human labor into shoes, but not necessarily so. Production may simply mean transforming goods over space (shipment of oranges from Florida to Maine) or over time (storing potatoes after harvest to distribute consumption over the year).

Of course, to be economically rational, production should represent a conversion from a less desired to a more desired configuration. Burning an antique Chippendale chair for heat is production, but would be ill-advised under ordinary conditions. (On the other hand, a person in danger of freezing to death might find the conversion from chair to warmth exceedingly advantageous.)

The third main economic activity is *exchange* (to be discussed in Part Five). For the individual, exchange is also a kind of conversion—a trade of some objects for others. But from the social point of view, exchange is distinguished from production in that the totals of commodities are unaffected; goods and services are reshuffled in trade, but wherever one person has less someone else must have more. Thus, exchange is a kind of transfer. But it is a mutual and voluntary transfer; *all* parties involved must be satisfied or they would not have traded in the first place.

The Circular Flow

In a simplified world with only two types of economic agents, individuals and business firms, the relations between them can be pictured as in Figure 1.1 (p. 16). Individuals and firms have dual aspects, and thus transact with one another in two distinct ways. Individuals *consume goods,* while firms *produce goods.* Thus, the diagram shows a "real" flow of consumption goods (solid upper channel) from firms to individuals. To permit production there must be a "real" flow of productive services (solid lower channel), from individuals who *own resources* to firms that *employ resource services.*

In a command economy these flows of goods and resources might be directly ordered by a dictator. But in a private-enterprise economy the relations are based on exchange and so must be mutual and voluntary. Hence, the "real" flows are offset by reverse "financial" flows of claims that normally take the form of money payments. The consumers' financial expenditures on goods (dashed upper channel) become the receipts or revenues of the firms. The exchange of consumption goods between individuals and producing firms in return for financial payments takes place in the "product market." (Actually, there will of course be a host of separate product markets, one for each distinct consumption good.)

The revenues received from sales to consumers provide firms with the wherewithal to buy productive services from resource-owners (dashed lower channel). This closes the circle; the firms' payments for productive services become income to the individuals, available once more for spending on consumer goods. Purchase and sale of productive services take place in the "factor market," again, really a number of distinct markets for the various types of productive services.

Production, the physical transformation of resources into products, takes place within the box representing the firms as economic agents. Within the box representing individuals, *consumption* of the produced goods takes place. Here again, the circle is closed by the fact that consumption is necessary to recreate the main productive resource—labor power—for the next cycle.

1.4 MICROECONOMICS AND MACROECONOMICS

A distinguished professor of logic, deploring the division of the subject between deductive reasoning and inductive reasoning, once declared: "In our textbooks on deduction we explain all about logical fallacies; in our textbooks on induction, we then commit them." Economic

FIGURE 1.1   The Circular Flow of Economic Activity

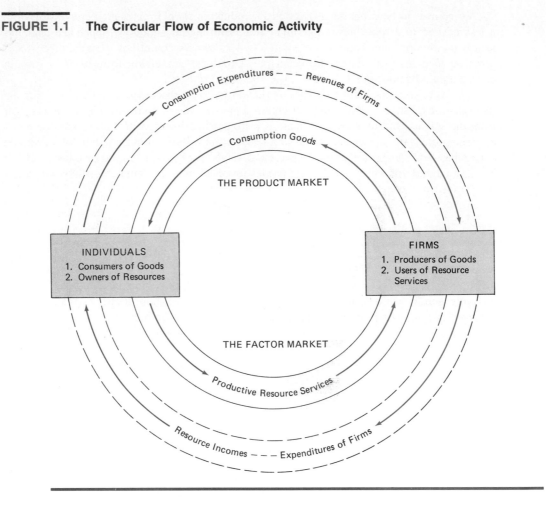

theory has a similar split between microeconomics and macroeconomics. In microeconomics we see how and why the Invisible Hand operates (how and why self-interest leads people to serve one another in a spontaneous system of productive cooperation); in macroeconomics we examine why coordination through the "invisible hand" may break down.

Microeconomics mainly concentrates on equilibrium in particular markets, presuming an equilibrium of the market system as a whole. But often the equilibrium of the market system is not robust. The overall circular flow of economic activity may become disrupted, perhaps leading to inflation or to large-scale unemployment. These malfunctions of the system as a whole comprise macroeconomics studies.

For some time, starting in the 1930s, macroeconomists attempted to develop modes of reasoning largely independent of any microeconomic foundation. Some theorists even dismissed classical microeconomics as obsolete or irrelevant. It is now generally recognized that this attempt failed. Significant progress in macroeconomics has been made by improving the logical connection of the subject with the microeconomic theories of production, consumption, and exchange. So the study of microeconomics is necessary for proper understanding of macroeconomics.

SUMMARY

Economics is a social science that concentrates on the *rational behavior* of individuals and firms as they interact with one another through *market exchange*. Rational behavior is the appropriate choice of means for achieving given ends, requiring the comparison of benefits and costs and the advantages and disadvantages of alternative courses of action. Economists do not ordinarily ask why people have certain tastes, wants, or desires, but instead treat these as facts to be explained by the other social sciences. Individuals can try to satisfy their desires in a number of ways, for example, by persuasion, by force, by theft, or by calling upon government assistance. But economics mainly studies market relations, in which people seek to achieve their aims through voluntary exchange.

Adam Smith's principle of the Invisible Hand shows how persons who are interested only in their own welfare are nevertheless led to cooperate with one another through market exchange. The market economy is a spontaneous order, an unplanned yet integrated arrangement whose behavior follows scientifically determinable laws.

The main agents in the economic system are individuals (possibly acting on behalf of their families or households), firms, and governments. Individuals are the only agents who consume. Though individuals may also produce goods and services, in modern economies most production takes place through business firms—artificial agents created by individuals for that purpose. Production must be distinguished from exchange. *Production* transforms the physical shape, location, or availability of commodities, whereas *exchange* merely reshuffles the existing goods and services among the economic agents.

The circular flow of economic activity summarizes the market interactions among economic agents. In the *product market,* individuals as consumers purchase consumption goods from firms; in the *factor market,* individuals as resource-owners provide productive services to firms. The "real" circular flow has resources moving from individual owners to firms, converted by firms into consumption goods, whereupon the goods return to the individuals to complete the circle. In the "financial" circuit, funds are paid out by firms as they hire resources, thus providing individuals with an income for purchase of consumption goods; these purchases circulate the funds back once again to the firms, allowing the next cycle to begin.

QUESTIONS

For Review

*1. a. In what respects can economics be considered a science?
   b. Give an example of a prediction that modern economic science can confidently make.
   c. Are there predictions that economic science has not yet shown itself competent to make?
*2. a. What is rational behavior?
   b. Give examples of rational and irrational behavior.
   c. Can the economist's postulate of rationality be useful even when irrational elements strongly influence behavior?

*The answers to starred questions appear at the end of the book.

3. Does the economist assume stable preferences? Give an example of a change in preferences that has had important economic effects.

4. Does the economist assume that everyone is selfish? Give an example of unselfish behavior which has important economic consequences.

5. Market transactions are said to be both *mutual* and *voluntary*. Give an example of a nonmarket interpersonal transaction that is not voluntary and an example of one that is voluntary but not mutual.

6. What are positive issues in economics? What are normative issues? Give an example of each.

*7. a. How does the Invisible Hand lead individuals in a market economy to cooperate for mutual advantage even without any intention on their part to do so?
   b. Would self-interested behavior lead to mutual advantage in a monastic economy where all income is equally divided?
   c. In a dictatorship where the political authorities confiscate the lion's share?
   d. In an economy with no property, so that any person could take what he or she needs from any other persons?

*8. a. In the circular flow of economic activity, distinguish between the real and financial circuits of flow. What is the relation between the two?
   b. Distinguish between the "product market" and the "factor market." How are these connected?

9. "The principle of the Invisible Hand asserts that self-interested behavior on the part of resource-owners leads inevitably to chaos." True or false, and why?

10. What is the difference between production and exchange?

For Further Thought and Discussion

*1. a. Other things being equal, would you expect the murder rate to be lower in jurisdictions applying capital punishment?
   b. If the income-tax exemption granted for each child were increased, would you expect the birth rate to rise?

*2. The psychiatrist T. S. Szasz argues that mental illness is the result of rewarding people for disability. Not only is the patient motivated to become "ill," but there is a financial advantage to the healing professions in declaring personal problems to be "illnesses." How could mental illness be made less "rewarding"? Would doing this reduce mental illness?

3. If government were to increase relief payments to the unemployed, would you expect unemployment to rise?

4. In terms of the circular flow of economic activity, explain why some individuals are wealthy (in a position to consume a great deal in the product market) and others are poor.

*5. If the Invisible Hand leads individuals to serve their own interests by serving others, why are some people led to a life of crime? Why do some corrupt politicians find it advantageous to serve themselves at the expense of their constituents? Why are dictators motivated to seize power? [*Hint:* Does the principle of the Invisible Hand apply to all kinds of social interactions, or does it hold only when individuals interact in a particular way?]

*6. Would an effectively enforced law requiring drivers to wear seat belts tend to reduce driver deaths? pedestrian deaths?

*7. Dr. Samuel Johnson said "There are few ways in which a man can be more innocently employed than in getting money." Charles Baudelaire declared "Commerce is satanic, because it is the basest and vilest form of egoism." What do you think each had in mind?

8. Classify each of the following statements or propositions as either *positive* or *normative*. (Does the classification "positive versus normative" have any bearing upon truth or falsity?)
   a. Smoking in enclosed public spaces should be banned.
   b. Prohibiting smoking in public places would reduce the demand for cigarettes.
   c. Legislation to limit the places where smoking is permitted would be opposed by the tobacco industry.
   d. Nonsmokers' rights to breathe clean air are more important than smokers' rights to pollute the air.
   e. Antismoking laws will have no effect on sales of cigarettes because smokers will light up just as much as before but confine their puffing to legal areas.

9. It may soon become possible to predict the place and time of earthquakes, weeks or even months before their occurrence. Some influential writers have argued that such predictions should be kept secret, or even that investigations leading to such predictions should be banned. Allegedly, the panic caused by predicting an earthquake would be more damaging than the earthquake itself. What does this view imply about individual rationality? Would you favor or oppose a ban on earthquake prediction?

CHAPTER 2
WORKING TOOLS

E X A M P L E S

L et's start with some good news. Most of the analysis in this book, and throughout economics generally, makes use of only two analytical techniques: (1) *finding an optimum* and (2) *finding an equilibrium*. Facing any question, your first step should be to ask "Is this an optimization problem or an equilibrium problem?"

How can you tell which is which? Without getting into technical definitions, Table 2.1 will give you the main idea.

Notice that optimization problems take the following form: "Is it better for me (or for my business, or my nation, or even humanity as a whole) to do this or that?" In short, what is the best action to take? The second type, the equilibrium problems, ask instead "What explains the observed facts? And more particularly, what explains prices and quantities in markets?"

Optimization problems are encountered in all domains of life. An engineer may ask if titanium is better than stainless steel for a girder, an army general may have to decide whether to attack or retreat, and a physician may consider whether to prescribe an antibiotic or a placebo. Economics provides a systematic way of analyzing optimization problems that will be valid for any of these fields of application.

In solving equilibrium problems, it is essential to understand how the behavior of each person or firm interacts with the decisions made by others. To predict whether a strike will increase wages we must consider not only the desires of the workers, but also the resistance of management, the ease with which the firm's customers can switch to competing products, and so forth.

Each of these techniques uses a characteristic working tool. The analysis of optimization problems requires understanding the relations among *total, average,* and *marginal magnitudes*. The primary technique used to solve equilibrium problems is *supply-demand* analysis. This chapter reviews and illustrates these two techniques.

2.1 EQUILIBRIUM: SUPPLY-DEMAND ANALYSIS

Equilibrium of Supply and Demand

The supply-demand diagram of Figure 2.1 should be familiar, but let's review some of the details. The horizontal axis represents the quantity Q of some particular good, for example, grain (in tons).[1] The vertical axis represents price, P, per ton of grain. We usually think of prices in terms of money, but more fundamentally a price is a *ratio of quantities:* it signifies

List of Notation

AC	Average Cost		*MR*	Marginal Revenue
AR	Average Revenue		*P*	Price
C	Total Cost		*Q*	Quantity
MC	Marginal Cost		*R*	Total Revenue

---

[1] In accord with the idea that the economy represents a continuing circular flow of activity, it is sometimes important to think of quantity as a rate per unit time: for instance, tons per month or per week. Throughout the book it should be understood that quantities represent flows over time.

TABLE 2.1   Optimization and Equilibrium Problems

Optimization Problems	Equilibrium Problems
1. Should I buy a new car, or keep my old one a while longer?	1. Are new car prices likely to be lower next year?
2. Will I be happier working, or should I drop out of the rat race and live on handouts?	2. Would generous "welfare" benefits for the unemployed raise the unemployment rate?
3. Should I buy a condo, or live in a rental apartment?	3. What determines the ratio between the annual rental of an apartment and its purchase price as a condominium?
4. Should narcotics laws be made stricter or more lenient?	4. If use of narcotics were decriminalized, would drug usage increase?
5. Should our union go on strike or had we better accept management's offer?	5. Do strikes raise the wages of workers?

the amount of some other commodity that must be given to obtain a unit of the desired good. Thus, if a bushel of grain costs $5.00, while a quart of milk costs $0.50, we could say that the bushel of grain costs ten quarts of milk. For now, let us think in terms of money prices. Consequently, the vertical axis (price axis) of Figure 2.1 is labeled $/Q (dollars per ton of grain). The horizontal axis (quantity axis) measures tons of grain.

The demand curve DD shows the quantity that consumers want to buy at each price P. This curve traces the amount that consumers would purchase if the price of grain is P dollars

FIGURE 2.1   Demand and Supply   The quantity consumers wish to purchase equals the quantity sellers wish to sell at the equilibrium point E, where price is P^* and quantity is Q^*.

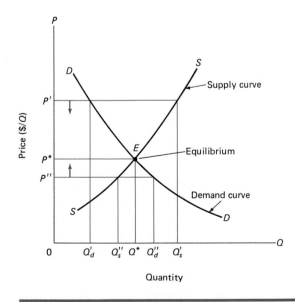

per unit and consumers could buy as much grain as they wanted to at that price. The demand curve does not tell us what the price actually is, but rather how much consumers will want to purchase at each possible price.

The negative slope of the demand curve reflects the fact that buyers would want to purchase more as the price decreases. [Stores often try to attract customers by claiming to offer unusually low prices. Do sellers ever try to attract customers by asserting that their prices are exceptionally high?] Similarly, the positive slope of the supply curve indicates that sellers normally offer more of the good the higher the price.

In Figure 2.1 market equilibrium is represented by the point E where the supply and demand curves intersect; the equilibrium quantity is Q^* and the equilibrium price is P^*.[2]

How do we know this is an equilibrium? Suppose the market price were, momentarily, at a price higher than P^*—for example, at P' in the diagram. At that price, suppliers would want to sell the quantity Q_s' while consumers only want to buy the quantity Q_d'. This means that some suppliers will not be able to sell as much as they want to. What will then happen? Some suppliers may find it profitable to quote a price slightly lower than that quoted by competitors, and thereby dispose of previously unsold stocks of goods. So there is downward pressure on price, as indicated in the diagram by the arrow pointing downward.

What if the market price were initially lower than P^*? At P'' in Figure 2.1, the quantity that consumers want to purchase, Q_d'', exceeds the quantity that suppliers offer, Q_s''. Here there is upward pressure on price.

Clearly, one or the other process will always be at work so long as price is not at the equilibrium P^*. Only at P^* does the quantity that consumers want to purchase match the amount suppliers want to sell. When Q_d equals Q_s, we have the market equilibrium quantity Q^*.

CONCLUSION: The intersection of the demand curve and the supply curve determines the equilibrium values of price and quantity.

This equilibrium is not necessarily desirable; it is simply a prediction of what price and quantity will appear in the market. There is an equilibrium price and quantity of good things (like housing) and an equilibrium price and quantity of bad things (like heroin). *Positive* economics (see Chapter 1) simply predicts, without making value judgments.

How realistic is this picture of equilibrium? We are dealing here with a *model* of reality, not reality itself. It is a model (as will be explained later) of perfect competition among buyers and sellers interacting in a perfect market. The question of scientific interest is not the literal truth of the model, but rather its usefulness. That is the subject of the next section.

How Changes in Supply and Demand Affect Equilibrium

Equilibrium is determined, as in Figure 2.1, by the intersection of given supply and demand curves. But what about changes in supply and demand? What happens, for example, if costs of production fall, or if consumers' incomes rise? Such changes affect the supply curve, or the demand curve, or both.

Suppose that, perhaps as a result of increased income or altered preferences, buyers suddenly want to consume more grain than before. This is called an *increase of demand*.

---

[2]Asterisks will generally be used in the text to designate solution values, such as equilibrium or optimum positions.

As shown in Figure 2.2, the demand curve shifts *to the right* (from D_1D_1 to D_2D_2). The old equilibrium price was P_1^* and quantity Q_1^*; the new equilibrium price and quantity are P_2^* and Q_2^*.

How does the change of the equilibrium come about? Suppose the price momentarily remained unchanged at P_1^* after the demand curve shifted to D_2D_2 in Figure 2.2. Then consumers would want to buy Q_d', *but at price P_1^** suppliers would still want to sell only the quantity Q_1^*. So there would be upward pressure on price. In a free market, price will respond to this pressure and increase to P_2^*.

This description of price-quantity adjustment is not entirely free of problems. For example, some sales may take place at "wrong" prices (before P_2^* is reached), and these "wrong" transactions may affect the supply or demand curves. In other words, the final equilibrium reached may depend on the path that is followed. Analyzing such issues of economic dynamics requires more advanced techniques than we can use in this text. Instead, to analyze changes in supply or demand, we will simply compare the initial and the final equilibrium situations. This is called the method of *comparative statics*. Our basic technique, then, in analyzing some change in economic circumstances is to ask, Does the change shift supply or shift demand (or, possibly, both)?

It will be immediately evident from Figure 2.2 that an increase in demand leads to an increase in both equilibrium price and equilibrium quantity.

What about an increase in supply? In Figure 2.3 (p. 26) an increase in supply is shown as a shift of the supply curve to the right (from S_1S_1 to S_2S_2), since at each price suppliers would want to sell more than before. (*Warning:* A common slip is to think of an increase

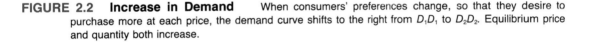

FIGURE 2.2 **Increase in Demand**   When consumers' preferences change, so that they desire to purchase more at each price, the demand curve shifts to the right from D_1D_1 to D_2D_2. Equilibrium price and quantity both increase.

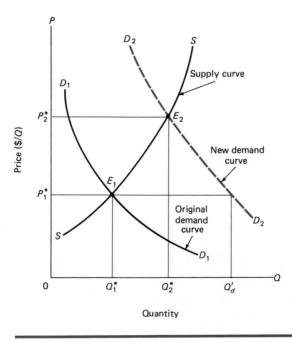

FIGURE 2.3 **Increase of Supply** When a change in conditions induces sellers to offer more at each price, the supply curve shifts down and to the right from S_1S_1 to S_2S_2. Equilibrium quantity increases, but equilibrium price falls.

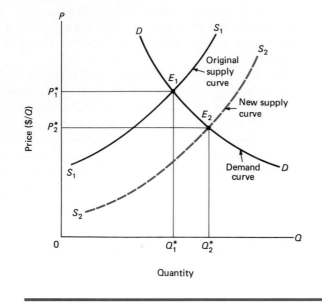

of demand or supply as an *upward* shift of the corresponding curve; this is correct for the demand curve but incorrect for the supply curve. To avoid error, always interpret an increase as a rightward shift of the curve.) The new equilibrium is at E_2, with price P_2^* and quantity Q_2^*. An increase in supply thus leads to an increase in equilibrium quantity, but to a decrease in equilibrium price. [*Question:* What can be said if both supply and demand increase?]

PROPOSITION: If demand increases, equilibrium price and quantity both rise. If supply increases, equilibrium quantity rises but equilibrium price falls.

What forces may cause the demand or supply curves to shift? It is sometimes useful to distinguish between changes that originate outside and inside the economic system. The outside sources of variation include (1) *changes in tastes* (a news report about the dangers of cholesterol may make some people avoid butter); (2) *changes in technology* (Eli Whitney's invention of the cotton gin vastly increased the supply of cotton); (3) *changes in resources* (an important oil discovery will enlarge the world's supply of petroleum); and (4) *changes in legal rules* (decriminalization of marijuana can be expected to increase both the market supply and the market demand for that substance). All these changes can be regarded, to some degree at least, as originating autonomously from outside the economic system.

Shifts of supply and demand curves may also stem from movements inside the economic system. Such inside variations can include:

1. *changes in prices (or quantities) of goods related in demand* (an increase in the price of butter raises the demand for margarine)

2. *changes in prices (or quantities) of goods related in supply* (an increase of beef production necessarily increases the supply of hides)
3. *changes in income* (the higher incomes recently received by petroleum-exporting countries raised their demands for consumption goods)[3]

The following examples should help develop your intuition about the effects of outside or inside sources of economic changes upon equilibrium prices and quantities.

EXAMPLE 2.1 **Catholics and Fish**

For over one thousand years the Roman Catholic Church forbade eating meat on Fridays. The Church abolished this requirement for American Catholics as of December 1966 (except for Fridays falling within Lent). Frederick W. Bell studied the effect of this liberalization on the price of fish in New England (whose population is approximately 45 percent Catholic). The study compared a ten-year period before the liberalization with the nine-month period just after (excluding Lenten months). To isolate the effects of the change in Church rules, Bell had to control a number of other variables, including imports of fish, prices of closely competitive foods (poultry and meat), and personal income. As shown in the table, prices received for fish of all seven species were lower after the liberalization than before.

Prices of Fish, Monthly Data, 1957–67

Species	Percent Change Due to Liberalization (%)
Sea scallops	−17
Yellowtail flounder	−14
Large haddock	−21
Small haddock (scrod)	−2
Cod	−10
Ocean perch	−10
Whiting	−20

Source: F.W. Bell, "The Pope and the Price of Fish," *American Economic Review,* v. 58 (December 1968), p. 1348.

Bell's example illustrates a decrease in demand for fish. (The demand curve for fish shifted leftward, rather than rightward as in Figure 2.2.) The source of the variation would seem to lie outside the economic system, since the modification in Church regulations was not in any evident way a response to market factors.

[3]There is no hard-and-fast rule to distinguish "outside" from "inside" elements. Although the text speaks of changes in resources as an "outside" source of variation, prospecting for mineral resources is itself a business that would surely be affected by mineral prices, by tax policies, and so forth. Even population size is likely to respond to economic incentives—for example, if governments subsidize large families. The pace and direction of technological change also vary with the financial inducements offered to inventors. (When the British government in the eighteenth century announced a prize for an accurate chronometer, inventors made significant advances.)

EXAMPLE 2.2   **Potatoes**

Vegetables are cheapest at harvest time. Although potato production continues throughout the year, the major crop is harvested in the fall. The following table shows the average U.S. prices and production of potatoes in various seasons of the year during the period from 1968 to 1970.

Prices and Production of Potatoes, 1968–70

Season	Average Production (CWT)	Average Price Received by Farmers ($/CWT)
Fall	237,391	1.90
Winter	3,765	2.09
Early spring	5,154	2.48
Late spring	20,977	2.71
Early summer	13,483	2.73
Late summer	29,790	2.07

Source: Data from U.S. Department of Agriculture, *Agricultural Prices, 1970 Annual Summary*, p. 22; *Crop Production,* July 9, 1971, p. A2; July 10, 1969, p. 2.

During the fall potato harvest season, supply increases (the supply curve shifts right). The table shows that quantity sold is greatest, and price is lowest, in that season. Are you surprised that despite the enormous production swings over the year there is so little variation in price? The main reason is that potatoes are stored from harvest on. Therefore, in the winter season, when there is very little production, price is still relatively low since this is just after the fall harvest. As potatoes stored earlier are gradually consumed, price rises steadily over the year, until the new crop begins to arrive in the late summer.

The original source of agricultural supply variation over the year is the outside element of God-given seasonal climate. But the inside element of storage greatly modifies the force of the external factors. Other economic activities, such as improvements in transportation, changes in agricultural practices, and development of new seed varieties, also help stabilize price over the year despite the huge seasonal variation of supply.

EXAMPLE 2.3   **Heating Oil**

The supply of petroleum is quite constant over the year, but demand varies substantially over the seasons. Gasoline is used heavily in the summer for vacation travel; during the winter gasoline consumption falls, but demand for heating oil greatly increases.

The second column of the table is an index of monthly consumption of distillate fuel oil, which is largely used for heating, for the years 1984 and 1985. (The index figure of 100 represents average consumption over the entire year.) A slight adjustment has been made to account for the differing numbers of days in the months. The third column is a similar index of the monthly prices of a gallon of heating oil at retail. Here an adjustment has been made in the data to eliminate the effect of continuing inflation, which tends to make all end-of-year prices higher than beginning-of-year prices.

Indexes of Retail Sales and Prices, Distillate Fuel Oil, in the United States, 1984–85

Month	Index of Average Consumption (adjusted for number of days in month)	Index of Average Price (per gallon, retail, adjusted for inflation)
January	119	102.7
February	114	107.0
March	109	107.2
April	101	100.3
May	92	98.6
June	91	95.3
July	85	93.5
August	90	93.5
September	93	96.7
October	97	100.1
November	99	102.2
December	106	102.9

Source: Indexes calculated from data in American Petroleum Institute, *Petroleum Facts and Figures, 1986 ed.,* p. 486; and U.S. Department of Commerce, *Survey of Current Business,* January 1984 through December 1985.

Consumption of fuel oil varies widely over the year. Evidently, demand is highest in December through March (the demand curve is farthest to the right). Increased demand is also accompanied by higher prices. As before, it may seem surprising that the prices change so little over the seasons. Here, once again, the main explanation is storage from low-consumption to high-consumption months. In addition, refineries adjust their operations to extract larger fractions of heating oil and smaller fractions of gasoline from their petroleum input in winter months. So a rightward shift of heating oil supply partially offsets the larger winter demand. Storage also explains why the price index lags slightly behind the quantity index. December is a high-consumption month, but price is still moderate because stocks are ample. In February, consumption has begun to decline, but prices are high since inventories have been drawn down to their lowest levels.

EXAMPLE 2.4 **Brides**

Among the Sebei in Uganda, husbands purchase wives. The anthropologist Walter Gold-schmidt analyzed bride prices paid by husbands in two communities: the cattle-herding district of Kapsirika and the farming district of Sasur.

The Kapsirika herders pay higher prices for brides than do the Sasur farmers, even though the herders are not generally wealthier. The rate of polygyny (several wives) is also higher among the Kapsirika; the wife/husband ratio is 1.52, whereas among the Sasur farmers it is only 1.17.[a] Intermarriage is common, but it takes entirely the form of herder husbands buying farmers' daughters. Thus, the herders' demand curve for brides seems to be higher; they pay more, and so they get more.

[a]Walter Goldschmidt, "The Brideprice of the Sebei," *Scientific American,* v. 229 (July 1973).

In Examples 2.2 and 2.3 supply and demand changed over time. Example 2.4 shows how demand can vary across communities at a single point in time. The herders' demand curve for brides can be regarded as greater than (lying to the right of) the farmers' demand curve. The source of the difference might be the outside factor of different preferences for brides by males in the two communities. An alternative inside explanation is that wives are more productive assets for herders than for farmers. One interesting question is why any bride-price difference persists: If Kapsirika herders and Sasur farmers compete to buy wives, why don't they end up paying about the same price? The answer appears to be that inter-marriage takes only the form of the Kapsirika "importing" wives; it seems that the "importers" must pay a premium to overcome the reluctance of brides to move (or of their families to let them move) from one community to the other.

EXAMPLE 2.5 **Electricity**[a]

During most of the nineteenth century steam power was the dominant energy source in manufacturing. This era came to an abrupt end in 1882 when Thomas Edison introduced the first commercial electric generating plant. At first used primarily for lighting, electricity gradually came to be the standard source of power in factories. In 1902, electricity accounted for only 4 percent of all power used in manufacturing, but by 1920 this figure had risen to over 50 percent.

Over the years the cost of generating electricity fell dramatically. In 1902, 7.3 pounds of coal were needed to produce one kilowatt hour of electricity; by 1932 only 1.5 pounds were required. Thus, at any given price for electricity, generating companies were able to profitably sell larger and larger quantities. As the supply curve shifted to the right, the price of electricity fell by more than 50 percent between 1900 and 1929. At the same time wholesale prices in general approximately doubled, so that in real terms (that is, after adjusting for inflation) the cost of electricity in 1929 was about one-fourth of its cost in 1900.

[a]This discussion is based on Arthur G. Woolf, "Energy and Technology in American Manufacturing: 1900–29," *Journal of Economic History,* v. 42 (March 1982).

In Example 2.5, technological advances caused an increase in supply—a rightward shift of the supply curve—leading to an increase in quantity and a fall in price. At the same time, firms found new applications for electricity, so that the demand curve also shifted to the right. These shifts make the drastic reduction in price all the more remarkable, since the demand shift considered separately would have caused the price of electricity to increase.

Algebra of Supply-Demand Analysis

We saw that the equilibrium price and quantity can be determined in a graph by the point where the supply curve and the demand curve intersect. The same solution can also be obtained with algebra. The supply curve can be described by an equation that relates price to quantity. The demand curve can be described by a different equation that also relates price to quantity. We thus have two equations and two unknowns (price and quantity). Solving the two equations simultaneously determines the equilibrium price and quantity.

The solution is especially easy to find when the demand and supply curves are both straight lines, as pictured in Figure 2.4. Panel (a) shows a demand curve with the equation $P = 10 - Q$. The supply curve is $P = 1 + Q/2$. (These equations apply only for this particular example.) To find the equilibrium, we can set either the prices or the quantities equal. Here it is more convenient to equate the prices. By setting the right-hand sides of the equations equal we obtain the equilibrium condition $10 - Q = 1 + Q/2$. Solving, we get $Q = 6$. Now insert $Q = 6$ into the demand equation to find the equilibrium price: $P = 10 - 6 = 4$. (Or we can obtain the same price by substituting $Q = 6$ into the supply equation: $P = 1 + 6/2 = 4$.)

Exercise 2.1

As before, let the equation for the demand curve be $P = 10 - Q$, and the supply curve $P = 1 + Q/2$. Find the equilibrium price and quantity by equating quantities rather than prices.

Answer: Rewrite both equations to put Q on the left-hand side. The demand curve becomes $Q = 10 - P$ and the supply curve $Q = 2(P - 1)$. Setting the two quantities equal to each other leads to the equilibrium condition $10 - P = 2(P - 1)$, so that the solution is $P = 4$. To find the equilibrium quantity, substitute $P = 4$ in the supply or the demand equation to obtain $Q = 6$.

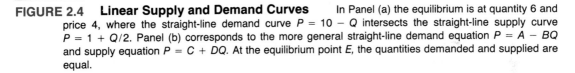

FIGURE 2.4   Linear Supply and Demand Curves   In Panel (a) the equilibrium is at quantity 6 and price 4, where the straight-line demand curve $P = 10 - Q$ intersects the straight-line supply curve $P = 1 + Q/2$. Panel (b) corresponds to the more general straight-line demand equation $P = A - BQ$ and supply equation $P = C + DQ$. At the equilibrium point E, the quantities demanded and supplied are equal.

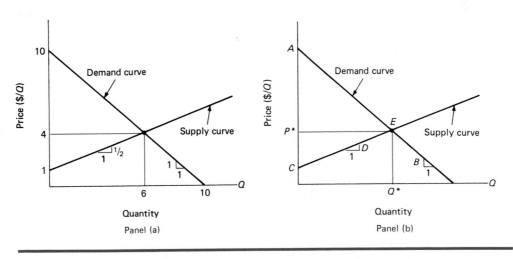

The general demand equation (assuming it is a straight line) can be written $P = A - BQ_d$, where Q_d is the quantity demanded and A and B are positive constants. Geometrically, A is the intercept of the demand curve with the vertical price axis (the price so high that purchases are zero); $-B$ is the slope of the demand curve. The supply curve has the equation $P = C + DQ_s$, where Q_s is the quantity supplied. Here the positive constant C is the intercept of the supply curve on the vertical axis (the price so low that none of the good will be supplied); the positive constant D represents the slope of the supply curve.

The condition of equilibrium can be written as follows:

$$Q_d = Q_s \tag{2.1}$$

Since $Q_d = Q_s$, we can drop the subscripts and just use Q. So we have two simultaneous equations.

$$\begin{cases} P = A - BQ \\ \\ P = C + DQ \end{cases} \tag{2.2}$$

Equations (2.2) can be solved algebraically to yield the solution values.

$$Q^* = \frac{A - C}{B + D} \text{ and } P^* = \frac{AD + BC}{B + D} \tag{2.3}$$

Exercise 2.2

For demand and supply curves that are not straight lines, this exercise extends the previous technique. Suppose the demand curve is described by the equation $Q_d = 12 - P^3$. The supply curve is $Q_s = P^2$. Find the equilibrium price and quantity.

Answer: At the equilibrium price $Q_d = Q_s$. By inspection we see that $P = 2$ satisfies the equation $12 - P^3 = P^2$. Let's make sure that the quantities demanded and supplied are equal. $Q_d = 12 - 2^3 = 4 = Q_s = 2^2$. So $P = 2$ and $Q = 4$ is the solution.

We now turn to the algebra of comparative static analysis. A shift in the demand curve can take many forms: a parallel shift that does not change the slope (an increase or decrease in the intercept A in Equation (2.2)), a change in the slope that does not change the intercept (a change in B in Equation (2.2)), a change in both the intercept and the slope, or even a change that transforms a demand curve into one of a different shape altogether.

Exercise 2.3

Consider an upward parallel shift of the linear demand curve used in Exercise 2.1, so that the new equation is $P = 15 - Q$ instead of $P = 10 - Q$. The supply curve is the same as before, $P = 1 + Q/2$. Find the new equilibrium price and quantity.

Answer: Solving the equation $15 - Q = 1 + Q/2$, we obtain the solution $Q = 9\ 1/3$, and $P = 5\ 2/3$. The equilibrium price has increased from $P = 4$ to $P = 5\ 2/3$. Note that the increase in the equilibrium price, $1\ 2/3$, is less than the vertical shift, 5, of the demand curve.

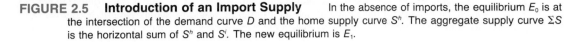

FIGURE 2.5 **Introduction of an Import Supply** In the absence of imports, the equilibrium E_0 is at the intersection of the demand curve D and the home supply curve S^h. The aggregate supply curve ΣS is the horizontal sum of S^h and S^i. The new equilibrium is E_1.

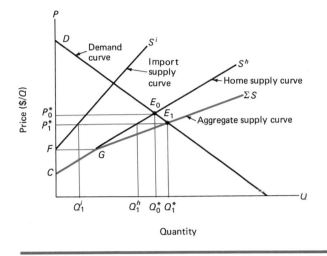

An Application: Introduction of a New Supply Source

Let's take up a more challenging problem. Using Figure 2.5, suppose a country that had previously barred imports of grain now permits them. The demand curve is D. The "home" supply curve (S^h) shows the amount of grain domestic firms would want to sell at any specified price. The "import" supply curve, or the quantities foreign firms would offer, is S^i. With no imports, the equilibrium E_0 is at the intersection of the D and S^h curves. When imports are allowed, the new equilibrium E_1 is determined by the point where the demand curve intersects the aggregate or *summed* supply curve. In Figure 2.5, the curve labeled ΣS is the *horizontal* sum of the S^h and S^i curves. (The Greek letter Σ is the equivalent of the English letter S representing sum). Allowing imports to enter reduces the equilibrium price (from P_0^* to P_1^*) and raises the equilibrium quantity (from Q_0^* to Q_1^*). Note one slightly tricky feature. At any price below the "choke price" F no foreign goods are imported. Therefore at prices below F the ΣS curve is identical with S^h. At prices above F, ΣS diverges to the right of S^h by the amount of imports. [*Question:* What would happen if the initial equilibrium price P_0^* was below the import choke price F?]

Exercise 2.4

Let demand be $P = 300 - Q_d$. Let the home supply curve be $P = 60 + 2Q_s^h$. The initial equilibrium E_0 where $300 - Q_d = 60 + 2Q^h$, has $P_0^* = 220$ and $Q_0^* = 80$. Let the new import supply curve be $P = 80 + 4Q_s^i$. Find the new equilibrium price, the amount sold by domestic firms, and the amount imported.

Answer: Note that the import choke price, 80, is lower than the original equilibrium price, $P_0^* = 220$. Since foreign firms will wish to enter the market, we have to sum the amount that foreign and domestic firms intend to sell at any particular price. To perform this summation we first put Q on the left side of the foreign and domestic supply equations. [*Warning:* Do not put P on the left side of the equations and then sum; this would be adding the prices, and we want to sum quantities.] By rewriting the home supply curve, we have $Q^h = (P - 60)/2$. For imports, we have $Q^i = (P - 80)/4$. The sum of the two is $Q = Q^h + Q^i = 3P/4 - 50$. The demand curve is $Q_d = 300 - P$. The equilibrium solution has $300 - P = 3P/4 - 50$, so $P^* = 200$ and $Q^* = 100$, of which $Q^h = 70$ and $Q^i = 30$.

An Application: Effects of a Tax on Price and Quantity

When government taxes a good, the price that the consumer pays differs from the amount the seller receives. The imposition of such a tax can be interpreted as causing a shift of the demand curve or of the supply curve. Applying simple demand-supply analysis to taxes leads to a surprising conclusion—a tax will usually cause price to increase by less than the amount of the tax.

Commodity taxes can take many forms. The tax can be a fixed amount for each unit of the good sold, a percentage of the price, or else a value-added tax levied on the difference between the cost of the firm's inputs and the value of its output. The simplest tax to consider is the fixed tax per unit sold. Either the seller or the buyer has the legal obligation to pay the tax. In either case, taxes create a gap between the price paid by the buyers (the *gross* price P^+) and the amount received by the sellers (the *net* price P^-). Surprisingly, it turns out the results are the same regardless of who bears the legal obligation to pay. But for concreteness we assume that it is the seller who has the legal obligation to pay the tax collector.

Suppose a seller faces the demand curve DD shown in Panel (a) of Figure 2.6. The government now imposes a tax of $2 on every unit sold. Before the $2 per unit tax, suppose the seller could have received $7 per unit when he sold three units. He can still sell three units after the tax is imposed, at a *gross* price of $7, but the *net* (after-tax) price he receives will now be only $7 - $2 = $5. In the eyes of the seller, therefore, the tax caused the demand curve to shift down by the amount of the tax, in this case by $2. (As an exercise, calculate the gross and net prices for 4, 6, and 9 units.) If the tax is T we can write the following, where P^+ is the gross price and P^- the net price:

$$P^+ = P^- + T$$

By assuming that the seller is legally obligated to write the check to the tax collector, we see that the tax only changes the demand curve *as seen by the seller;* he sees the net-of-tax demand $D'D'$. The tax does not change consumers' desires or incomes, so the demand curve that describes the behavior of consumers remains DD.

To find the after-tax equilibrium, notice point E' where the after-tax demand curve $D'D'$ intersects the supply curve SS in Panel (b). You can see that quantity falls from Q^* to Q'. To determine the consumers' cost (the new *gross* price P^+), go from Q' up to the gross demand curve DD. To find what the seller gets (the new *net* price P^-), go from Q' up to the net demand curve $D'D'$.

PROPOSITION: A tax on transactions reduces the equilibrium quantity sold, raises the *gross* price paid by consumers, but lowers the *net* (after-tax) price received by sellers.

What if the legal obligation to pay the tax collector falls on the buyer instead of the seller? We could follow an analysis similar to that used before: shift the demand curve and

FIGURE 2.6 **A Tax on Sales**   A sales tax of $T per unit shifts the demand curve (*net* of tax) downward to D'D'. The original DD is the *gross* demand curve. As shown in Panel (b), the tax causes a decline in the equilibrium quantity from Q* to Q'. The tax increases the equilibrium gross price (inclusive of tax) paid by consumers from P* to P⁺; the net price received by sellers declines to P⁻

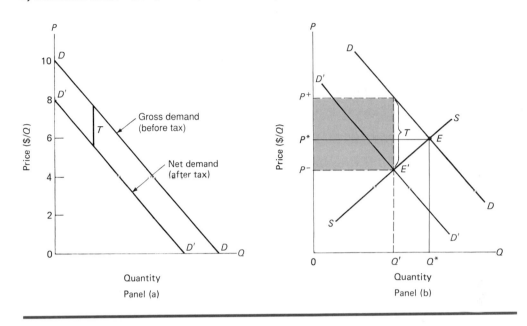

Panel (a)   Quantity

Panel (b)   Quantity

find the new equilibrium. But sometimes in economics it is simpler to guess at an answer, and then prove that the answer is correct. Suppose that in the previous equilibrium the price paid by the consumer is $10, that the tax per unit is $2, and therefore the seller keeps $8 per unit after he pays the tax collector. Since this solution is an equilibrium, the amount that consumers intend to buy at a price of $10 per unit will be identical to the amount sellers want to sell when they receive a net price of $8 per unit. Let this equilibrium amount be, say, 1,000 units.

Suppose now that the gross price paid by the consumer is $10 per unit, of which a consumer pays $2 to the tax collector for each unit bought, while the seller receives $8 per unit. Since sellers effectively receive $8 per unit, they will want to sell the same quantity as before (when they effectively received $8 per unit by receiving $10 from the consumer and paying $2 to the tax collector). That is, supply at a price of $8 is 1,000 units as before. The effective price paid by consumers is $10 ($8 plus the $2 paid the tax collector). But the previous paragraph stated that when consumers effectively pay $10 per unit, they wish to purchase 1,000 units. Thus, the quantity consumers wish to purchase is identical to the quantity sellers wish to sell. We conclude that in equilibrium the effective (gross) price paid by consumers and the effective (net) price received by sellers is exactly the same where the seller rather than the buyer has the legal obligation to pay the tax collector. Moreover, the reasoning used here is not limited to the particular numbers used in the illustration. Instead, the reasoning implies that it makes no difference whether a tax on transactions is legally levied upon buyers or upon sellers.

For an algebraic proof with linear demand and supply functions, assume as before that the seller is legally obligated to pay the tax collector the tax due: the consumers must pay the gross price, while the suppliers receive only the net price. There are three simultaneous equations:

$$P^+ = A - BQ \text{ (demand equation)} \tag{2.4}$$

$$P^- = C + DQ \text{ (supply equation)}$$

$$P^+ = P^- + T \text{ (tax equation)}$$

The solution is found by solving the three equations simultaneously. Skipping over the algebraic details, the solution values are as follows:

$$Q' = \frac{A - (C + T)}{B + D}, \quad P^+ = \frac{AD + B(C + T)}{B + D} \quad P^- = \frac{(A - T)D + BC}{B + D} \tag{2.5}$$

Comparing Equations (2.5) to Equations (2.3) (where there was no tax) we see that Q' here is less than Q^*; the tax reduces the volume of transactions. The new gross price P^+ is greater than the old price P^*, and the new net price P^- is less than P^*, thus confirming the geometrical result. We also see that if we plot P^+ as a function of T, we get a straight line with slope $B/(B + D)$, which is less than 1. A one-cent increase in the tax causes the price of the good to consumers to rise by less than one cent.

Exercise 2.5

Suppose that in the absence of any taxes the demand function is $P = 300 - Q_d$ and the supply function is $P^- = 60 + 2Q_s$. An excise tax $T = 15$ is imposed. Find the new equilibrium.

Answer: Equations (2.4) become, numerically $P^+ = 300 - Q$, $P^- = 60 + 2Q$ and $P^+ = P^- + 15$. Substituting from the third equation, the second equation can be rewritten as $P^+ - 15 = 60 + 2Q$. We now have the first and second equations in terms of two variables P^+ and Q. Solve to obtain the solutions $Q = 75$ and $P^+ = 225$, from which it follows that $P^- = 210$. As expected, the tax reduces the quantity exchanged (from 80 to 75), raises the *gross* price (from 220 to 225) but lowers the *net* price (to 210).

EXAMPLE 2.6 The Effect of a Sales Tax on Retail Cigarette Prices

The analysis just presented predicts that a sales tax will increase the retail price of the good by somewhat less than the amount of the tax. Michael Sumner and Robert Ward[a] tested the theory by examining the retail prices of cigarettes in 45 states over the period 1954–76. They found that, on average, a one-cent rise in the tax per pack raised the retail price by 0.9 cents. In contrast, a one-cent increase in the wholesale price of cigarettes increased the retail price by one cent.

It is somewhat surprising that increases in the sales tax and the wholesale price have different effects. According to economic theory, a one-cent increase in either the wholesale price or in the tax shifts the supply curve up and to the left by one cent. One possible explanation is interstate competition. For example, changes in wholesale prices will affect New Hampshire and Massachusetts similarly. But if the tax is increased in Massachusetts only, retailers there may have to limit price increases or risk losing customers willing to cross the border to make purchases. The authors also found that retail firms do not usually increase prices immediately after an increase in tax or wholesale cost. Such behavior makes

Interferences with Equilibrium

Government action may sometimes be necessary for efficient operation of the market. For example, the judicial system enforces private contracts, making it easier for people to trade. (Compare this to a system where it is up to each person to enforce any agreement he or she makes with others.)

Government interventions, however, may prevent prices from reaching equilibrium. Supply-demand analysis can be used to predict the consequences of such interventions.

Recent years have seen attempts to repress inflation by "freezes" or other forms of maximum wage-price controls. During the deflationary period of the 1930s in the United States, in contrast, the National Recovery Administration imposed *minimum* wage-price controls. Whether such price ceilings or price floors can cure a general inflation or a general deflation is a question in macroeconomics that does not concern us here. Instead, our interest is in the effects of price controls on particular markets.

Figure 2.7 depicts a meaningful ceiling price P'. (To be meaningful, the ceiling must

FIGURE 2.7   A Price Ceiling   An effective price ceiling $P' < P^*$ reduces the quantity traded from Q^* to Q'_s.

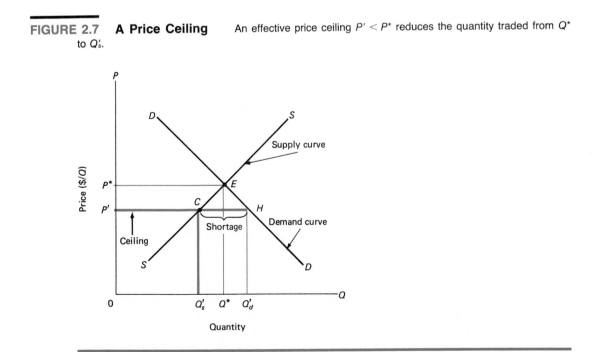

be *lower* than the equilibrium price $P*$.) At the ceiling price the quantity demanded Q_d' exceeds the quantity supplied Q_s', so there is upward pressure on price, indicated by the upward-pointing arrow. However, the arrow is blocked by the fixed ceiling at P'. (We do not consider here the possibility of illegal trading at higher prices—black markets.)

What about the actual quantity traded? There is a fundamental maxim of markets, "It takes two to tango"; that is, exchange requires willing buyers *and* willing sellers. At the ceiling price P' the buyers want Q_d', but the sellers offer only Q_s', so Q_s' is the amount that will be traded. (Notice that the amount traded is not some compromise between the desired purchases and the desired offers; rather it is always the *smaller* of the two.) So the final outcome is at point C in the diagram. The distance CH represents the shortage—the excess of the demand quantity over the supply quantity at the legal ceiling price.

EXAMPLE 2.7 **Repressed Inflation and Trekking**

During and after World War II all the major powers suffered from inflation. Heavy war spending led to enormous budget deficits, covered largely by printing new money. At the same time, governments froze consumer prices at low ceiling levels, so there was strong upward pressure on prices. In these circumstances city-dwellers would leave town for a day and scour the nearby countryside for food, make private black-market deals with farmers or sometimes simply steal. The more governments controlled prices in the legitimate markets, the more this abnormal system of trekking flourished. On one day, it was reported, over 900,000 persons trekked from Tokyo to the countryside.[a] In Germany, the Erhard reforms of 1948 abolished price freezes and thus eliminated trekking. A curious and unexpected consequence was a financial crisis for the state railroads. Short-haul railroad passenger traffic dropped immediately to less than 40 percent of its pre-reform volume, demonstrating the massive trekking that had previously been occurring.[b]

[a]Jerome B. Cohen, *Japan's Economy in War and Reconstruction* (Minneapolis: University of Minnesota Press, 1949), p. 378.
[b]Lucius D. Clay, *Decision in Germany* (Garden City, N.Y.: Doubleday, 1950), p. 191.

A meaningful price *floor* is pictured in Figure 2.8. At the legal floor P'' the quantity offered by sellers, Q_s'', exceeds the quantity Q_d'' desired by buyers. There is downward pressure on price. The government, however, will not permit such a price decrease. The effective price is thus higher than the unregulated price $P*$, but the quantity traded Q_d'' is again *lower* than the equilibrium $Q*$. Once more, "It takes two to tango." Although price ceilings and price floors have opposite effects upon price, they have parallel effects on the quantity traded; in either case, the quantity exchanged is less than in the unregulated market. (Again, a black market may come into existence, permitting the trading of somewhat larger quantities at illegally low prices.)

The picture changes when price floors are supported. Support takes the form of a "buyer of last resort"—the federal government in the case of agricultural price supports in the United States. As Figure 2.8 shows, private buyers are only willing to take Q_d'' at the high floor price P''. But now suppose the government agrees to buy as much of the goods as suppliers offer but cannot otherwise sell. At the supported price suppliers want to sell Q_s'',

FIGURE 2.8 A Price Floor   An effective price floor $P'' > P^*$ reduces the quantity traded from Q^* to Q''_d. However, if the floor is "supported" by government purchases, the amount Q''_s will actually be supplied. The government must absorb the "surplus," the difference between Q''_s and Q''_d.

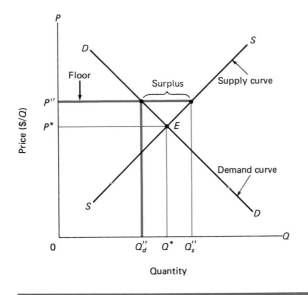

consumers purchase Q''_d of this quantity, and the "surplus" bought by the government would be the difference. Suppliers will sell the quantity Q''_s. There is no black-market problem with a supported floor, because no supplier would sell for less than the floor price. Instead, there is a problem of surplus disposal, since the buyer of last resort must accumulate larger and larger unwanted stocks.

EXAMPLE 2.8 **Agricultural Parity Prices**

The U.S. government has attempted since the 1930s to maintain parity prices for agricultural products. *Parity* means the relationship between agricultural and nonagricultural prices obtained during the years 1910 to 1914, a period of farm prosperity. Throughout the 1950s and 1960s parity was primarily attained by price supports of farm products. A federal agency, the Commodity Credit Corporation (CCC), would buy any otherwise unsold quantities of supported crops at the support level—usually 90 percent of the parity price.

The "surpluses" purchased by the CCC were mostly kept in storage; the federal government intended to sell them on the market in years of small crops. But almost every year the amount harvested was greater than the amount consumers wished to purchase at the artificially high prices guaranteed by the government. By 1960 the CCC held in storage as much wheat as that year's entire crop.

To reduce the cost of holding such huge stores, Congress passed food stamp and school lunch programs that lowered the price some consumers had to pay for food. More importantly, under a system of acreage limitation farmers were paid *not* to produce. In addition, the price support levels were adjusted downward.

CONCLUSION: Meaningful ceilings hold down prices; meaningful floors keep them up. In either case, the quantity exchanged is *less* than in unregulated equilibrium. If, however, the floor is *supported*, quantity supplied will be greater than under the unregulated equilibrium, but the "buyer of last resort" must accumulate inventories.

2.2 OPTIMIZING: TOTAL, AVERAGE, AND MARGINAL MAGNITUDES

The second major type of economic analysis is *optimizing,* finding the most advantageous action among the choices available. Economists use a method, marginal analysis, for solving optimization problems that does the work of the mathematical calculus without requiring any formal knowledge of it. Think of how to pack a suitcase for a trip. The more clothes you take, the greater your pleasure once you arrive. On the other hand, a heavy suitcase is a large burden. One way to determine the optimal quantity is to consider all possible combinations and choose the best one. Or, you could start packing the most important things, and add more items until you find that the added weight causes more burden than benefit. Similarly, for the production decisions of a firm, a producer should rationally increase output as long as the added benefit (revenue) is greater than the added burden (cost).

Here we consider the general relations that must logically hold among Total, Average, and Marginal magnitudes. To be specific, we will analyze these concepts in relation to a firm's *revenue* and *cost*. Consider Figure 2.9, which shows the market demand curve for some good. Numerical data for this demand curve are shown in the first two columns of Table 2.2.

FIGURE 2.9 **Demand Curve and Average Revenue**   The demand curve, which shows price as a function of quantity, can also be regarded as an Average Revenue curve since $P = R/Q = AR.$

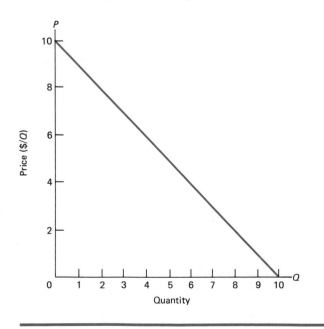

TABLE 2.2   Total, Average, and Marginal Revenue

Quantity (Q)	Price or Average Revenue (P ≡ AR)	Total Revenue (R ≡ PQ)	Marginal Revenue (MR)
0	10	0	
			$9 - 0 = 9$
1	9	9	
			$16 - 9 = 7$
2	8	16	
			$21 - 16 = 5$
3	7	21	
			$24 - 21 = 3$
4	6	24	
			$25 - 24 = 1$
5	5	25	
			$24 - 25 = -1$
6	4	24	
			$21 - 24 = -3$
7	3	21	
			$16 - 21 = -5$
8	2	16	
			$9 - 16 = -7$
9	1	9	
			$0 - 9 = -9$
10	0	0	

By definition, Total Revenue (or, simply, Revenue) is price P times quantity Q.[4]

$$R \equiv PQ \tag{2.6}$$

Total Revenue is tabulated in the third column of Table 2.2, and the corresponding data are plotted in the upper diagram of Figure 2.10 (p. 42).

Revenue is a *total* magnitude, whereas price can be regarded as an *average* magnitude. In Table 2.2, for example, at quantity $Q = 2$ Total Revenue is 16. The Average Revenue received when $Q = 2$ is $16/2 = 8$, which is, of course, nothing but the price along the demand curve for that quantity. Formally, Equation (2.7), which defines Average Revenue *(AR),* follows immediately from equation (2.6).

$$AR \equiv \frac{R}{Q} \equiv P \tag{2.7}$$

Note that price is measured in dollars per unit quantity ($\$/Q$), whereas Revenue is measured in dollars.

---

[4]The triple equality sign $\equiv$ represents a mathematical identity. This symbol will be used in the text where it is desired to emphasize that the two sides of the equality are equivalent by definition.

FIGURE 2.10 **Derivation of Average and Marginal Magnitudes from Total Function: Revenue**   The upper diagram illustrates the derivation of Average Revenue *(AR)* and Marginal Revenue *(MR)* when $Q = 4$, $P = 6$, and Total Revenue $= 24$. The height of the *AR* curve in the lower diagram at $Q = 4$ corresponds to the slope of the bold line in the upper diagram, so that $AR = 24/4 = 6$. The height of the *MR* curve in the lower diagram equals the slope *along* the Total Revenue curve in the upper diagram. At $Q = 4$, this slope is approximated by averaging the slopes of the dotted lines *LN* and *NM*. Thus $MR = (1/2)[(24 - 21) + (25 - 24)] = 2$.

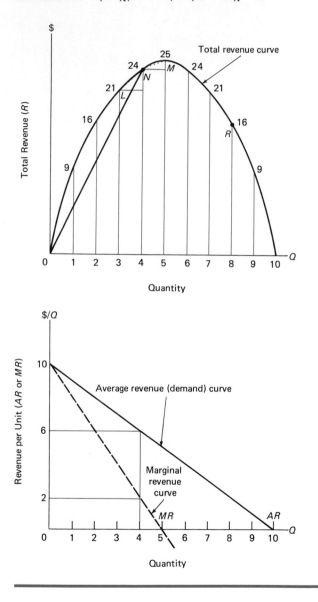

Marginal Revenue *(MR)* is shown in the fourth column of Table 2.2. It is defined as the change in Revenue per unit change in output. As with price, *MR* is measured as dollars per unit quantity ($/Q$). [*Warning:* The vertical axis of the upper diagram of Figure 2.10 is scaled in dollars ($). The lower diagram is scaled in dollars per unit ($/Q$). A total magnitude (like Revenue) should never be plotted on the same axes as average or marginal magnitudes (like Average Revenue and Marginal Revenue), since the magnitudes are different.]

We can define *MR* in symbols as follows, where ΔR stands for the change in Revenue and ΔQ stand for the change in quantity.[5]

$$MR \equiv \Delta R / \Delta Q \tag{2.8}$$

For example, if the supplier sells 2 units instead of 1, Table 2.2 shows that Revenue increases from 9 to 16; over this interval $MR = 16 - 9 = 7$. If output were increased further to 3 units, *MR* would be 5, and so on.

The value of Marginal Revenue can be quite well approximated without calculus, but there is one tricky point to keep in mind. When we calculate the effects upon Revenue of an increase in output from, say, $Q = 1$ to $Q = 2$, we must define *MR* to apply "between" these two quantities of output. In Table 2.2, for example, we have $MR = 7$ "between" $Q = 1$ and $Q = 2$; while $MR = 5$ "between" $Q = 2$ and $Q = 3$. To find *MR* "at" some output (say, at $Q = 2$), we should interpolate. Since $MR = 7$ between $Q = 1$ and $Q = 2$, and $MR = 5$ between $Q = 2$ and $Q = 3$, we can average these to get an estimate of $MR = 6$ at $Q = 2$. You should check, by similar reasoning, that $MR = 2$ at $Q = 4$, that $MR = 0$ at $Q = 5$, and so on.

It is a common error, and often a numerically substantial one, to ignore this distinction, and confuse the Marginal Revenue "between" two outputs with the Marginal Revenue "at" one of those outputs. In our example, it would be poor practice to determine the *MR* "at" $Q = 2$ by taking the added revenue received when output increases from $Q = 1$ to $Q = 2$, implying that $MR = 7$. We saw earlier that the answer obtained by interpolation is $MR = 6$. While finding the exact Marginal Revenue generally requires the use of calculus, for a linear demand curve (like that shown here) the method we recommend always yields the exact answer.[6] If the demand curve is not a straight line, there may be some error, but the recommended method almost always gives a more accurate answer than the incorrect method described above.

Exercise 2.6 _____

For the nonlinear demand curve $P = 100 - Q^2$, compare the recommended with the incorrect method for approximating *MR* at $Q = 4$.

Answer: Since Revenue = Price $\times$ Quantity, the Total Revenue equation becomes $R = (100 - Q^2)Q = 100Q - Q^3$. At $Q = 3$, R is 273, and at $Q = 4$, R is 336; *MR* "between" $Q = 3$ and $Q = 4$ is $336 - 273 = 63$. Since at $Q = 5$ we have $R = 375$, *MR* "between" $Q = 4$ and $Q = 5$ is $375 - 336 = 39$. To estimate *MR* "at" $Q = 4$, we interpolate by calculating $(39 + 63)/2 = 51$. (Using calculus, we find *MR* by taking the derivative of the revenue function at $Q = 4$ getting the exact figure as $MR = 52$.) The incorrect method described above, taking the *MR* "between" $Q = 3$ and $Q = 4$ for the *MR* "at" $Q = 4$, would lead to the estimate $MR = 63$, which is far off.

_____

[5]*Mathematical Footnote:* For small changes, Marginal Revenue can be interpreted as the derivative dR/dQ.

$$MR \equiv dR/dQ \equiv \lim_{\Delta Q \to 0} \Delta R / \Delta Q.$$

[6]*Mathematical Footnote:* The demand-curve equation underlying Table 2.1 is $P = 10 - Q$. Then Total Revenue is $R = PQ = 10Q - Q^2$. Taking the derivative, Marginal Revenue is $MR = dR/dQ = 10 - 2Q$. At $Q = 2$, therefore, $MR = 6$. Thus, the recommended method is exactly correct.

To understand the geometrical relations between total, average, and marginal magnitudes, you should remember two main principles:

1. *The marginal magnitude is the slope of the total function.*
2. *The average magnitude is the slope of a ray from the origin to the total function.*

The first principle is demonstrated in the upper diagram of Figure 2.10. Corresponding to Table 2.2, the parabolic-shaped curve shows Total Revenue R for each level of output Q. You can see that as Q rises from 3 to 4, R rises from 21 to 24, so MR is $24 - 21 = 3$ between $Q = 3$ and $Q = 4$. A good approximation to the slope of this curve at any point is obtained by looking at the slope of a straight line that connects two points on the curve near the point of interest. Look, for example, at the dotted chord LN. The slope of LN is its "rise over run." It is approximately equal to the slope of the Revenue curve on that interval. The rise is 3 and the run is 1, so the slope of LN is 3—the same as Marginal Revenue. This is no coincidence. The rise of LN is the change in Total Revenue (i.e., ΔR), and the run is the change in quantity (i.e., ΔQ). So when we find the slope of LN by dividing "rise over run" we find $\Delta R / \Delta Q$, which is the definition of Marginal Revenue. Try this again between $Q = 4$ and $Q = 5$. Over that interval MR is $25 - 24 = 1$, and similarly the slope of the chord NM is also 1. As before, the estimated MR at $Q = 4$ is the average of MR between 3 and 4 and between 4 and 5; that is $MR = (3 + 1)/2 = 2$.

The second rule states that Average Revenue at any given output is determined by the slope of a line that connects the origin to the point on the Revenue curve that corresponds to the output level chosen. Look again at the upper diagram in Figure 2.10. When $Q = 4$, $R = 24$. Divide Revenue by Quantity to obtain $AR = 24/4 = 6$. Geometrically, look at the ray ON. The slope of ON is the "rise" 24 divided by the "run" 4, which is Average Revenue. The rise is equal to Total Revenue and the run is equal to Q. So dividing rise over run is the same as finding R/Q, which is the definition of Average Revenue.

The lower panel of Figure 2.10 depicts the Average Revenue and Marginal Revenue curves which correspond to the Revenue function shown in the upper panel. Both AR and MR in this panel fall throughout. Referring back to the upper panel, we can see that MR is falling because the graph relating revenue to quantity is less steep the further we move to the right. Note that the slope is initially positive, becomes zero at $Q = 5$ (where the Revenue curve reaches its maximum) and is negative thereafter. Similarly, AR must fall throughout because the slope of the ray from the origin to a point along the Revenue curve falls steadily as we move to the right. Thus the slope of line OM is less than the slope of line ON. Note that at $Q = 10$ the line from the origin to the Revenue curve is flat. Its slope is zero, so AR is zero at the output where the demand curve intersects the horizontal axis.

As long as Total Revenue rises when Q increases, the slope along the Revenue curve is positive. Hence Marginal Revenue, though declining as seen above, remains positive. In the region past the peak of the Revenue curve, however, the slope along the curve is negative, and so MR is also negative. Thus from the geometry we have the following propositions concerning the total and marginal functions:

PROPOSITION 2.1a: When a total magnitude is rising, the corresponding marginal magnitude is positive.

PROPOSITION 2.1b: When a total magnitude is falling, the corresponding marginal magnitude is negative.

But when Revenue reaches a maximum (or a minimum), the Revenue function is neither increasing nor decreasing; it is level. Drawing the obvious inference, we have another proposition.

PROPOSITION 2.1c: When a total magnitude reaches a maximum or a minimum, the corresponding marginal magnitude is zero.[7,8]

These principles are used over and over again in economics. They formalize the intuition used in packing a suitcase: the optimal number of items to pack is that number such that an additional shirt or skirt yields no net benefit. Similarly, Total Revenue is maximized at that level of output where Marginal Revenue is zero; profits are maximized at that level of sales where selling an additional unit neither increases nor decreases profits. It is important to note that maximizing a total magnitude does *not* correspond to maximizing the *average* magnitude. Instead, maximizing a total requires, as stated above, that the *marginal* magnitude be zero.

EXAMPLE 2.9   **Birds Do It! Bees Do It!**

Critics of economic theory often argue that solving optimization problems is too intricate for most people. Supposedly, for example, business firms do not consider anything as subtle as marginal concepts when determining the price to charge or the output to produce.

Biologists, in contrast, have recently discovered that the decisions of animals can often be interpreted in marginal terms. Consider a bird foraging for seeds or insects that are distributed in patches. The bird must decide when to leave its current patch and fly off to look for another. As it continues to exploit the current patch, food becomes sparser and sparser there; the bird's marginal "revenue" (energy intake) per unit of time spent in the patch is falling. But if the bird abandons its current patch, it loses energy intake in the dead time before it locates a fresh patch. Bioeconomic reasoning in this situation says that the bird should continue to exploit its current patch until the *marginal* "revenue" per unit of time spent there falls to equality with the *average* "revenue" it can attain elsewhere, allowing for the dead time between patches.[a]

Field studies confirm that foraging birds do indeed behave as if they solve this economic problem. Under more controlled laboratory conditions, Richard Cowie was able to study in more detail the foraging behavior of the great tit *(Parus major)*.[b] These birds were able to estimate quite precisely the marginal and average "revenue" (energy intake) of time spent in different patches of the environment.

And what birds can do, bees can too. C.M. Hodges and L.L. Wolfe[c] studied nectar consumption of bumblebees feeding on flowers containing, on average, 6.09 microliters of nectar. If the bees obeyed correct marginal principles, they calculated, a flower would be abandoned when its remaining nectar fell to 1.0 microliters. The actual measured amount

[7]*Mathematical Footnote:* When $dR/dQ > 0$, the Total Revenue function R is increasing; when $dR/dQ < 0$ it is decreasing; when $dR/dQ = 0$, we have a stationary value of the function.

[8]Some technical qualifications should be made to these assertions. Not all minima or maxima are "flat." In the upper diagram of Figure 2.10, R has an interior maximum at $Q = 5$, where $MR = 0$. But it also has minima at $Q = 0$ and $Q = 10$ (where revenue is zero). But the curve is not flat at those points, that is, $MR \neq 0$. In this book we will deal almost always with flat minima or maxima, so that Proposition 2.1c holds.

The lower diagram in Figure 2.10 illustrates another proposition:

PROPOSITION 2.2a: When the average magnitude is falling, the marginal magnitude must lie below it.

Think of the average weight of people in a room. If someone walks in and the average weight falls, it must be that the *marginal* weight (the weight of the person who walked in) was less than the average weight. In Figure 2.10 each new unit lowers Average Revenue (*AR* is always falling), hence the Marginal Revenue curve *MR* lies below it.

What if the average magnitude is not falling but rising? Then we have the following analogous proposition:

PROPOSITION 2.2b: When the average magnitude is rising, the marginal magnitude lies above it.

And, of course, Propositions 2.2a and 2.2b together imply

PROPOSITION 2.2c: When an average magnitude is neither rising nor falling (at a minimum or maximum), the marginal magnitude equals the average magnitude.[9]

The lower diagram of Figure 2.10, with its falling Average Revenue curve, illustrates Proposition 2.2a. To illustrate Propositions 2.2b and 2.2c as well, we need to look at average functions that rise over some range and decline over other ranges. Such a function is shown in Figure 2.11. The upper diagram shows a firm's Total Cost curve *C*. Total cost is positive at an output of zero (that is, the vertical intercept of the curve is positive) because of fixed costs (such as the rent on a building that must be paid even if nothing is produced).

[9]*Mathematical Footnote:* Let us verify Proposition 2.2a of the text, and specifically that *MR* is below *AR* when *AR* is falling. For *AR* to be falling

$$\frac{d(AR)}{dQ} = \frac{d(R/Q)}{dQ} = \frac{Q(dR/dQ) - R}{Q^2} < 0$$

Since the numerator in the last term must be negative, this directly implies that $dR/dQ < R/Q$, or $MR < AR$. Similar proofs apply for Propositions 2.2b and 2.2c.

FIGURE 2.11   Derivation of Average and Marginal Magnitudes from Total Function: Cost

The lower diagram derives Average Cost *(AC)* and Marginal Cost *(MC)* from the Total Cost function *C* in the upper diagram. At the quantity where the slope along the Total Cost function is least, *MC* is at a minimum. Where the slope of the line drawn from the origin to the curve is least (point *L* in the upper diagram), *AC* is at a minimum. When *AC* is falling, *MC* lies below it; when *AC* is rising, *MC* lies above it.

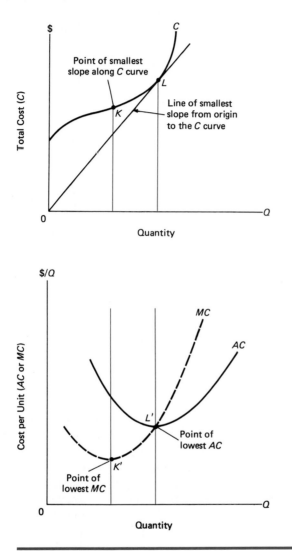

To derive Marginal Cost *MC* from the Total Cost function shown, remember that *MC* is the slope of *C*. The slope along the cost curve in the upper diagram falls as we move to the right up to point *K*. After that the cost curve becomes steeper. Correspondingly, in the lower diagram *MC* falls until we reach *K'*, then starts rising.

To derive the Average Cost curve AC, we use the rule that AC at any output is given by the slope of a ray from the origin to the point on the cost curve corresponding to that output: the rise (cost C) at that point divided by the run (output Q). As we move to the right along the cost curve, the slope of the ray out of the origin falls until point L. Then the slope rises as we move farther to the right. So, in the lower diagram, AC falls until point L', and rises after that. This means that AC is at its lowest value when output is L'. (Note that when $Q = 0$, $AC \equiv C/Q$ is infinite, if fixed costs are positive.)

In the upper diagram, anywhere to the left of L a ray from the origin to the cost curve is steeper than the slope of the cost curve itself. Since the slope of the ray is greater than the slope of the cost curve, AC is greater than MC for any output level in this range. This confirms Proposition 2.2a: when AC is falling, MC lies below it.

To the right of L, a ray from the origin to a point on the cost curve is flatter than the cost curve itself at that point, so AC is less than MC. This confirms Proposition 2.2b: at those values of Q for which Average Cost is rising, Average Cost is less than Marginal Cost.

Finally, the ray from the origin to point L along the cost curve has the same slope as the cost curve itself at point L. This means that here Marginal Cost = Average Cost, and Proposition 2.2c is confirmed.

The unintended effects of government policy illustrated in Example 2.10 stem from a failure to distinguish between average and marginal concepts. Sometimes marginal and total concepts may also be confused, as indicated in Example 2.11.

EXAMPLE 2.10 **The Oil Entitlement Program**

In the period 1973 to 1974 the Organization of Petroleum Exporting Countries (OPEC) cut back production of oil, and caused the world price of crude oil to increase from about $2 to almost $12 per barrel (see "The OPEC," Example 8.7 in Chapter 8). The U.S. government, concerned about its balance of payments, tried to reduce oil imports. At the same time, United States policymakers wanted to eliminate inequitable windfall gains to the domestic producers of crude oil, who were profiting from the higher prices of crude. Unfortunately, the method chosen to achieve the second objective tended to defeat the first.[a]

To prevent domestic producers from reaping windfall gains, the U.S. government froze the price of *domestic* crude oil. (It was impossible, of course, to freeze the price of imported oil.) This immediately caused a problem, because some refiners had access to the limited supply of artificially cheap domestic crude while others did not. Again in the interests of equity, the Entitlement Program was undertaken. The basic idea was that every refiner was entitled to buy, at the low frozen price, the nationwide average fraction of cheap domestic oil. This program forced refiners having better access to cheap domestic crude to compensate refiners who made more-than-average use of expensive imported crude. The unanticipated effect was to encourage rather than discourage imports.

From the point of view of the nation as a whole, the Marginal Cost of crude oil was a rising function, the highest-cost step being the imported crude at $12 per barrel. Had refiners

[a]This is necessarily a very simplified discussion of the enormously complicated and ever-changing details of U.S. oil policy. In particular, the legal distinction between so-called *new domestic oil* and *old domestic oil* has been omitted here.

been required to pay this world price for imported crude, they would have had a strong incentive to reduce dependence upon OPEC supplies. But, under the Entitlement Program, each barrel imported entitled the importer to a great bargain: the right to obtain an equivalent amount of domestic crude at the artificially cheap frozen price. In effect, all refiners were "equitably" treated by being able to obtain crude at the nationwide *Average* Cost. As a result, no refiners were discouraged from using imported crude even though that source represented the highest *Marginal* Cost for the nation as a whole.[b]

[b]Many discussions of the oil entitlement program are available. See, for example, C.E. Phelps and R.T. Smith, *Petroleum Regulation: The False Dilemma of Decontrol* (Santa Monica, Calif.: RAND Corporation, 1977).

EXAMPLE 2.11   **Taxes**

The table here shows the personal income tax schedule for single taxpayers in the tax year 1989. For any "Taxable Income"[a] bracket on the left-hand side of the table, the right-hand side shows the Marginal Tax for increments of income within the bracket, the Total Tax at the bottom of the bracket, and the Average Tax at the bottom of the bracket.

The following fallacy is sometimes encountered. An employee's taxable income is $18,550, so he is at the top of the 15% Marginal Tax bracket, and liable for a Total Tax of $2,783. His employer offers him a raise of $100, but the worker refuses the raise because it would put him in a higher tax bracket! The worker may think that in moving up to a higher *marginal* tax rate (28% instead of 15%) he will be taxed the extra 13% on *all* his income, ending up worse off than before. This is incorrect. The worker's additional tax would be only 28% of $100, or $28. Accepting the raise would increase his after-tax income by $100 − $28 = $72. His loss from refusing the raise is one of the costs that arise from ignorance of the marginal concept of economics.

Personal Income Tax Schedule

Taxable Income		Marginal Tax Rate	Tax at Lower End of Bracket	
Over	But not over		Total	Average
$0	$18,550	15%	0	—
$18,551	$44,900	28%	0.15 · $18,550 + 0.28($1) = $2,783	$2,783/$18,551 = 15%
$44,901	$93,130	33%	$2,783 + + 0.28(44,900 − 18,551) + 0.33(1) = $10,161	$10,161/$44,901 = 23%
$93,131	or more	28%	$10,161 + 0.33 · ($93,130 − $44,901) + 0.28 · $1 = $26,077	$26,077/$93,131 = 28%

[a]"Taxable Income" is earned income minus the exemptions, deductions, etc., provided in the tax law.

Marginal reasoning can even be applied to driving, as Example 2.12 shows.

EXAMPLE 2.12 Traffic Congestion

Additional cars on a congested road cause other cars to slow down. On uncongested freeways the Total Flow per hour past a given point increases with added traffic. This means that the Marginal Flow (defined as the change in traffic flow resulting from one more car per one-mile stretch of lane) is positive. Beyond a certain point, however, as additional cars enter the freeway the Marginal Flow may become negative because of the slowing of traffic.

The following table shows a typical speed-density relationship for a single lane of U.S. four-lane freeways. Density is measured as the number of cars per one-mile section of one lane. You can see that as density rises from 38 to 39, traffic flow increases by 11. Thus Marginal Flow is 11. However, when density rises from 43 to 44, the additional congestion causes so much slowing that traffic flow actually falls by 3. This congestion phenomenon is the bane of traffic engineers. It means that eventually the attempt of more people to use the freeway results in a reduction in transportation service.

Traffic Density, Speed, and Flow (one lane of a four-lane freeway)

Density (cars/mile)	Speed (miles/hour)	Total Flow (cars/hour)	Marginal Flow (cars/hour/car)
38	45.8	1,740	
			1,751 − 1,740 = 11
39	44.9	1,751	
			1,760 − 1,751 = 9
40	44.0	1,760	
			1,771 − 1,760 = 11
41	43.2	1,771	
			1,781 − 1,773 = 8
42	42.4	1,781	
			1,785 − 1,781 = 4
43	41.5	1,785	
			1,782 − 1,785 = −3
44	40.5	1,782	
			1,778 − 1,782 = −6
45	39.5	1,778	
			1,771 − 1,778 = −7
46	38.5	1,771	
			1,772 − 1,771 = 1
47	37.7	1,772	

Source: California Highway Research Board, *Highway Capacity Manual* (1965), pp. 49–50.

Marginal analysis suggests that it may be advisable to reduce access to the freeway at rush hours, for example, by a blinking traffic signal that feeds cars onto the road at a limited rate. Such a control will delay cars at the point of entry, but this may be warranted by the higher speed achieved once on the freeway.

This chapter discussed two main topics: (1) supply-demand analysis and (2) the relations among total, average, and marginal magnitudes.

Supply-demand analysis is the main working tool for solving problems of *equilibrium*. Equilibrium price and quantity are determined by the intersection of a supply curve and a demand curve. Changes in demand or supply are represented by shifts in the positions or shapes of one or both of these curves. An increase in demand (rightward shift of the demand curve) raises both equilibrium price and equilibrium quantity in the market; an increase in supply (rightward shift of the supply curve) raises equilibrium quantity but lowers equilibrium price. A tax on transactions reduces the quantity exchanged; it raises the *gross price* (the price paid by buyers) but lowers the *net price* (price received by sellers).

Price ceilings or floors, if effective, prevent markets from reaching equilibrium. In such cases the quantity exchanged is always the *smaller* of the amounts demanded and supplied. (Exceptions arise when government intervenes to support the price floor by buying unsold quantities.)

The relations among total, average, and marginal magnitudes are essential for understanding problems of *optimization*. Regardless of the variable involved (whether revenue, or cost, or utility, or other), the marginal magnitude is positive, zero, or negative depending on whether the total magnitude is rising, level, or falling. And the marginal magnitude is below, equal to, or above the average magnitude depending on whether the average magnitude is falling, level, or rising.

QUESTIONS

For Review

*1. Which of the following are optimization problems? Which are equilibrium problems? [*Note:* You're not asked for the answers, but you might think about them.]
   a. Is it more profitable for a business to offer occasional special sales at reduced prices, or to stick with moderate prices year-round?
   b. Would a gold discovery in Hawaii raise apartment rents on the island?
   c. If the punishment for murder were made more severe, would there be fewer murders?
   d. As a military commander, should I attack now when the enemy doesn't expect it or wait for my reinforcements, even though the enemy will then be alerted?
   e. Over the year, why is the price of strawberries more variable than the price of potatoes?
   f. If my spouse and I have had three girl babies in a row, should we give up or try again for a boy?

2. Is supply-demand analysis the key tool for equilibrium or for optimization problems? For what class of problem is the relation among total, average, and marginal quantities the key tool?

*3. In what sense is price a "ratio of quantities"?

*The answers to starred questions appear at the end of the book.

4. Explain why market equilibrium is determined by the *intersection* of the supply curve and the demand curve.

5. How does an "increase in demand" shift the demand curve? How does an "increase in supply" shift the supply curve? Does an increase in demand affect the equilibrium price and quantity in the same direction? What about an increase in supply?

*6. In the analysis of a $T per unit tax, we shifted the demand curve downward by $T to find the new equilibrium. Would the same result have been achieved if instead the supply curve were shifted upward by $T? Explain.

7. Draw supply and demand diagrams, with upward sloping supply curves and downward sloping demand curves, to illustrate the following possibilities:
   a. A large demand increase may have little effect on equilibrium price.
   b. A demand increase may raise price substantially, while an equal supply decrease would hardly affect price.
   c. A small demand decrease may produce a large drop in equilibrium quantity.
   d. Supply changes may have no effect on the dollar values of total sales.

*8. In each of the following cases, state whether an excise tax will raise the (gross) price *paid* by consumers, or lower the (net) price *received* by sellers, or both.
   a. Supply curve slopes upward and demand curve slopes downward.
   b. Supply curve horizontal, demand curve slopes downward.
   c. Supply curve vertical, demand curve slopes downward.
   d. Supply curve vertical, demand curve horizontal.

9. Suppose the government pays a $5 per unit *subsidy* on sales of flags. What would be the effect on the quantity exchanged? on the gross and the net price?

*10. a. What is a "meaningful" price ceiling or price floor?
   b. Why do both meaningful floors and ceilings *decrease* the quantity traded?
   c. What happens, however, if a price floor is supported?

11. Starting from a given Total Revenue function show how the Average Revenue function is derived. Show how the Marginal Revenue function is derived.

12. Starting from a given Total Cost function, show how the Average Cost function and the Marginal Cost function are derived.

*13. The Lackawanna Social Club, which has twenty resident members, keeps a refrigerator stocked with soda. Each can is obtained from a local distributor for thirty cents per can. Each member has free access to the refrigerator and can consume as many cans as he likes. At the end of each month, the total cost of the soda is divided equally among the members.
   a. What is the marginal cost to a member of drinking a can of soda?
   b. What is the marginal cost to other members?

*14. In terms of the general relations among total, average, and marginal quantities, which of the following statements are *necessarily* true, and which are not?
   a. When the total function is rising, the marginal function is rising.
   b. When the total function is rising, the marginal function is positive.
   c. When the total function is rising, the marginal function lies above it.
   d. When the marginal function is rising, the average function is also rising.
   e. When the average function is falling, the marginal function lies below it.
   f. When the marginal function is neither rising nor falling, the average function is constant.

For Further Thought and Discussion

*1. Suppose the supply curve for gold is very steep (positively sloped, but almost vertical).
   a. Would a $T tax tend to have a relatively large or a relatively small effect upon the quantity exchanged in the market? Would there tend to be a relatively large or a relatively small effect upon the gross price paid by buyers? upon the net price received by sellers?
   b. Explain in terms of the underlying economic meaning.

2. Analyze correspondingly the case where the demand curve is very steep (negatively sloped, but almost vertical).

*3. a. If the price of gasoline rises as a result of a reduction in petroleum supplies, what effect would you anticipate on the price of automobiles?
   b. upon the relative price of small, light cars versus large, heavy cars?

*4. a. What assumptions underlie "the method of comparative statics"?
   b. Will these assumptions ever be met in the real world?

5. The British government in World War II imposed a ceiling price on bread. Explain why there was upward pressure upon the price of bread. What consequences of the upward pressure would you anticipate, given continuing enforcement of the ceiling? To help reduce this upward pressure, the British government took fresh bread off the market; all bread sold had to be at least one day old. Would you expect this regulation to achieve the desired effect?

6. Gregory Peck International Airport wishes to limit the number of daily airplane departures to one hundred. (The airlines are eager and willing to provide two hundred flights a day.) Two methods of doing so are proposed: (1) arbitrarily pick the one hundred flights that will be allowed to operate, and impose no special fees on these flights or (2) auction off the rights to use the terminal, thus in effect imposing departure fees. Will the price of airline tickets be higher under the second method than under the first?

*7. In the year 302, the Roman emperor Diocletian "commanded that there should be cheapness." His edict declared

   > Unprincipled greed appears wherever our armies, following the command of the public weal, march, not only in villages and cities but also upon all highways, with the result that prices of foodstuffs mount not only fourfold and eightfold, but transcend all measure. Our law shall fix a measure and a limit to this greed.

   a. Why do you think Diocletian found food prices higher wherever he marched with his armies?
   b. What result would you anticipate from the command that "there should be cheapness"?

*8. The table below gives a partial tabulation of a demand function. Estimate Marginal Revenue at $Q = 3$.

Quantity	Price
0	30
3	20
6	12

9. The following is part of a price schedule, showing the quantity discounts offered by a printing shop. Does something peculiar happen as the size of your order approaches the upper limit in a given price range? Explain in terms of Marginal Revenue to the printing shop. Can you think of a more sensible way for the printing shop to offer quantity discounts?

Size of Your Order	Your Price ($)
1–10 units	.50 each
11–20 units	.40 each
21–50 units	.35 each
Over 50 units	.30 each

CHAPTER 3

UTILITY AND PREFERENCE

EXAMPLES

The previous chapter emphasized that economists basically use only two methods of analysis: *finding an optimum* and *finding an equilibrium*. Part Two applies the first of these methods to analyze the optimum of the consumer—determining the bundle of goods a consumer would wish to purchase. You may think that you are already an expert in this area. After all, you are a consumer and you make choices all the time. Why, then, do you have to learn how economists analyze these choices? Why can't the economist simply ask a consumer what choices he or she would make?

There are two main reasons. First, a more formal analysis (using, for example, statistical techniques) may derive results that the consumer is not aware of, or might even deny! Consumers often claim, for example, that they would buy something regardless of its price, but there is evidence to refute this. Second, when the economist proposes a model (a theory) of consumer behavior, predictions derived from it can be measured against the facts. This process leads to the construction of better and better theories.

3.1 THE DECISION PROBLEM OF THE INDIVIDUAL

People in a market economy face two main types of optimizing choices: how to earn an income and how to spend it. Part Two considers how income is spent, taking the earning decision as given. Later in the text, Chapter 12 analyzes decisions relating to sources of income.

The economist describes the process of choosing the best decision as the *maximization of utility*. Utility as an index for preference will be the central topic of this chapter.

3.2 LAWS OF PREFERENCE

Scientific analysis uses theories (or models) as simplified pictures of reality. Irrelevant details are stripped away to concentrate on essentials. The economist's simplified picture or theory of preferences is based on two axioms.

1. *Axiom of Comparison*—Each individual can compare any two distinct baskets *A* and *B* of commodities. Such a comparison must lead to one of the three following results: *A* is preferred over *B*, *B* is preferred over *A*, or the consumer is indifferent between *A* and *B*.
2. *Axiom of Transitivity*—Consider any three baskets *A*, *B*, and *C*. If the consumer prefers *A* to *B*, and prefers *B* to *C*, then he or she must prefer *A* to *C*. Similarly, a person who is indifferent between *A* and *B*, and also indifferent between *B* and *C*, must be indifferent between *A* and *C*.

The Axiom of Comparison is an idealization of reality. Note that it does not permit an individual to say "I just can't decide." Nor is he or she supposed ever to say, "Two-thirds of the time I prefer *A*, but the other one-third of the time I prefer *B*."[1]

The Axiom of Transitivity is also an idealization, since violations of it no doubt take place. (See Example 3.1.) But suppose someone were to tell you, "I prefer apples to bananas

---

[1]A number of economists have developed models of behavior that attempt to allow for limited ability to make comparisons. But as yet there is no general agreement as to how to deal with this complex problem.

EXAMPLE 3.1 **Transitivity and Age**

Arnold A. Weinstein administered a questionnaire asking people for preference rankings over ten commodity bundles, offered as pairs in random order. Among the bundles, all having a market value of about $3 at the time, were the following items: (1) $3 in cash; (2) the three latest Beatles 45-rpm phonograph records; (3) three men's clip-on bow ties, all with red polka dots, one brown, one blue, one gray; (4) a brush-stroke print of El Greco's "View of Toledo"; (5) two glasses of vanilla malted milk per day for ten days.

The intent of the experiment was to detect possible intransitivities of preference over triads of offerings. An intransitivity would occur if, for example, a particular person chose cash over malted milk, malted milk over bow ties, but bow ties over cash. The great majority of the triads showed consistent transitive preferences. An interesting result obtained was that transitivity tended to increase with age, as indicated in the table.

Transitivity Experiment Results*

Group	Transitive responses (%)
52 children aged 9–12	79.2
36 teenagers aged 14–16	83.3
46 high-school seniors aged 17–18	88.0
18 mature adults (mostly teachers)	93.5

***Source:** Table compiled from data reported in Arnold A. Weinstein, "Transitivity of Preference: A Comparison among Age Groups," *Journal of Political Economy,* v. 76 (March/April 1968), p. 310.

The experimenter concluded that transitivity in preference ordering is an acquired skill, hence more difficult for younger people to achieve. More arguably, he concluded that his results lent some support for placing legal restrictions upon the choices of young people.

COMMENT   As an alternative explanation, younger persons are more likely to make choices that seem inconsistent only because they are exploring alternatives. "Don't knock it until you've tried it" is a dangerous maxim, but one with some appeal. If all possibilities are to be tried by actual consumption, some seeming intransitivities of choice are inevitable. Consider the three possibilities: cash, malted milk, and bow ties. If a person chooses cash over malted milk, and malted milk over bow ties, the only way he can try out the bow ties is to choose them when offered—even over cash. Since the Laws of Preference presume an already well-settled pattern of consumer desires, it is not surprising to find more violations of them among younger persons who are still exploring their needs and tastes.

and bananas to cherries," and were then to add, "but I'll always take cherries over apples!" Surely you would regard that person as rather odd.

In fact, a clever confidence man could exploit someone whose preferences violate the Axiom of Transitivity. Suppose Smith intransitively prefers apples to bananas, bananas to cherries, and cherries to apples, and imagine that he initially possesses only cherries. Since Smith prefers bananas to cherries, he will be willing to pay the confidence man some small bonus x to get bananas instead of cherries. Now holding bananas, Smith would be willing to pay another bonus, $y,$ to obtain apples in place of the bananas. Finally, holding only

FIGURE 3.1
FIGURE 3.1 **Alternative Consumption Baskets** Points *A, B, C,* and *D* represent different combinations, or baskets, of commodity *X* and commodity *Y*. If *X* and *Y* are both *goods,* then basket *A* is preferred to any of the other marked points.

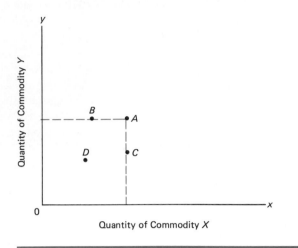

apples, he would be willing to pay a third bonus, *z,* to obtain cherries instead. But Smith is now back where he started, with cherries, except that he is poorer by the amount *x + y + z*! The confidence man can then repeat the process until Smith has paid out all his wealth. [Query for the student: Could a confidence man exploit someone who violates the Axiom of Comparison?]

The Axiom of Comparison and the Axiom of Transitivity taken together lead to the

PROPOSITION OF RANK ORDERING OF PREFERENCES: All conceivable baskets of commodities can be consistently ranked in order of preference by the individual. This ranking is called "the preference function."

Exercise 3.1 ─────────────────────────────────────

John prefers the basket consisting of one beer and one taco to either a basket consisting of two beers alone or to a basket consisting of two tacos alone. Comparing the last two baskets, he would rather have two beers over two tacos. Do the facts just stated indicate that the Axiom of Comparison and the Axiom of Transitivity apply for John, at least among the three combinations described? If they do apply, what is his rank ordering of preferences?

Answer: As to the Axiom of Comparison, yes, the stated facts show that John can compare all three consumption baskets. As to the Axiom of Transitivity, the answer again is yes. Transitivity would tell us that if John prefers the mixed basket over two beers, and two beers over two tacos, he should prefer the mixed basket over two tacos. And, we are told, in fact, that he does. His rank ordering is, clearly: first the mixture, then the two beers, then the two tacos.

Suppose you are choosing between two different quantities of the two commodities, *X* and *Y.* The amounts *x* and *y* are scaled along the axes in Figure 3.1.[2] Four possible baskets

─────────

[2]Capital letters *X* and *Y* here designate the commodities; lowercase letters *x* and *y* indicate particular quantities of each.

are represented by the points *A, B, C,* and *D.* The Laws of Preference tell us only two things about this situation: (1) you can rank all four baskets; and (2) if, for example, you prefer *A* over *B* and prefer *B* over *D,* then you must also prefer *A* over *D.*

X and *Y* are called *goods* (as opposed to *bads* such as garbage and pollution) when more of each is preferred to less. If *X* and *Y* are goods, point *A* in the diagram is the most preferred of the four points and *D* the least preferred, while *B* and *C* are intermediate.

DEFINITION: A *good* is a commodity for which more is preferred to less.

3.3 UTILITY, PREFERENCE, AND RATIONAL CHOICE

The term *utility* was introduced by the British philosopher Jeremy Bentham. Bentham declared:

> Nature has placed mankind under the governance of two sovereign masters, *pain* and *pleasure.* . . . The *principle of utility* recognizes this subjection. . . . By the principle of utility is meant that principle which approves or disapproves of every action whatsoever, according to the tendency which it appears to have to augment or diminish the happiness of the party whose interest is in question.[3]

For Bentham, then, the maximization of utility simply means that human beings avoid pain and seek pleasure or happiness.

The modern economic theory of choice is not based on the arguable premise that humans seek only to gain pleasure and avoid pain. Economists today simply say that individuals tend to make consistent choices: the Laws of Preference of the preceding section, while undoubtedly idealized, do generally describe actual behavior. Since the Laws of Preference are really rules of rational choice, this reduces to the postulate of rationality discussed in Chapter 1.

What modern economists call *utility* reflects nothing more than rank ordering of preference. The statements "John prefers Basket *A* over Basket *B*" and "Basket *A* has higher utility for John than Basket *B*" mean the same thing. They both lead to the empirical prediction: If John is offered a choice between Basket *A* and Basket *B,* each available for free or at the same price, then John will choose Basket *A.*

CONCLUSION: Utility is the variable whose relative magnitude indicates direction of preference. In finding the most preferred position, the individual is said to maximize utility.

3.4 UTILITY: CARDINAL OR ORDINAL MAGNITUDE

Early economists thought utility could be measured quantitatively like length or temperature. They would have regarded it as perfectly reasonable to construct a diagram like the upper part of Figure 3.2 (p. 60), where an individual's utility is shown as a function of the quantity of a consumption good. Some even believed it possible to add up these "util" numbers interpersonally: 5 of John Doe's utils could be added to 7 of Richard Roe's to give a total

---

[3]J. Bentham, *An Introduction to the Principles of Morals and Legislation* (1823 edition), Chapter 1.

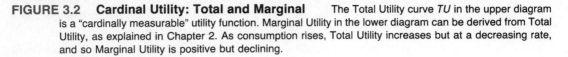

FIGURE 3.2 **Cardinal Utility: Total and Marginal** The Total Utility curve *TU* in the upper diagram is a "cardinally measurable" utility function. Marginal Utility in the lower diagram can be derived from Total Utility, as explained in Chapter 2. As consumption rises, Total Utility increases but at a decreasing rate, and so Marginal Utility is positive but declining.

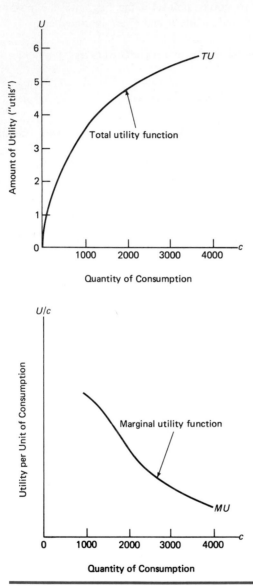

of 12 utils for the pair. On this basis, it was thought that public policies—for example, how severely the state should punish crime, whether the rich should be taxed more or less heavily than the poor—could be determined by summing the utils of everyone involved. (This seems to be what Bentham meant in recommending public policies designed to achieve "the greatest good of the greatest number," a mystifying though noble-sounding expression.)

Modern economists do not share these views. Economists today generally believe that comparing or summing the utilities of different people is meaningless, and cannot be used as a basis for economic policy.

Cardinal Versus Ordinal

What do we mean when we say that a variable is "quantitatively measurable"? This needn't imply that there is only a *single* way of measuring or scaling it. Temperature is certainly quantitatively measurable, but there are alternative measures. For example, 32° Fahrenheit is 0° Celsius, and each degree up or down of Celsius corresponds to 1.8 degrees up or down of Fahrenheit. The two scales differ, but only in zero point and unit interval. Similarly, altitude could be measured from sea level or from the center of the earth (shift of zero-point) and in feet or meters (shift of unit interval). Both temperature and altitude are more technically called *cardinal* magnitudes. These are variables that have the following property: regardless of shift of zero-point and unit interval, the relative magnitudes of *differences* remain the same. Consider altitude: there's a bigger difference between the heights of the base and crest of Mount Everest than between the ground floor and roof of even the tallest building. This remains true whether we scale altitude in feet or in meters, and whether we measure from sea level or from the center of the earth.

Figure 3.2 assumes that utility is cardinally measurable. As just indicated, it does not matter where we place the zero-point or what unit interval we choose for U. The real assertion is that *magnitudes of utility differences* can be compared. For example, regardless of how we might shift the zero-point and the unit interval of the U scale along the vertical axis in the diagram, it remains true that moving from 1,000 to 2,000 consumption units yields a bigger utility improvement than moving from 2,000 to 3,000 units.[4]

Exercise 3.2 ——————————————————————————————

Suppose an alternative "new-util" scale were adopted such that the "old-util" zero-point shown in the diagram is assigned the new-util value 10, and each unit up or down on the old scale would be 2 units on the new. (Thus the "new-util" measure U' is related to the old-util measure U by the formula $U' = 10 + 2U$.) In the upper panel of Figure 3.2, verify that the utility difference between $c = 2,000$ and $c = 1,000$ remains greater than the utility difference between $c = 3,000$ and $c = 2,000$.

Answer: A visual estimate indicates that the old-util difference between $c = 2,000$ and $c = 1,000$ is approximately $4.8 - 3.6 = 1.2$, while the corresponding difference between $c = 3,000$ and $c = 2,000$ is approximately $5.4 - 4.8 = 0.6$. So the first utility difference is the larger, in fact about twice as big. On the new-util scale the first difference would be around $19.6 - 17.2 = 2.4$, while the second difference would be about $20.8 - 19.6 = 1.2$. Evidently, the first difference remains larger.

---

[4]*Mathematical Footnote:* Two utility scales U and $\hat{U}$ are cardinally equivalent if measurements along the two scales are related by the linear equation:

$$\hat{U} = a + bU \text{ (for } b > 0)$$

The constant a here represents the shift of zero-point, and the constant b the change in unit interval. Consider three quantities U_1, U_2, and U_3 along the U scale, where the difference $U_3 - U_2$ exceeds the difference $U_2 - U_1$. Then $\hat{U}_3 - \hat{U}_2$ also exceeds $\hat{U}_2 - \hat{U}_1$, as can be verified by direct substitutions. So the *ranking of differences* is unchanged for all cardinally equivalent scales.

Utility in the upper diagram of Figure 3.2 is a *total* function of consumption *C*. The corresponding *Marginal Utility* function, defined (as described in Chapter 2) as the slope, or rate of change, of the Total Utility function, is shown in the lower panel of Figure 3.2. Since the slope of Total Utility is positive, Marginal Utility is positive. But since Total Utility in the upper diagram is increasing *at a decreasing rate,* the Marginal Utility curve in the lower diagram declines as consumption increases. This property is called *diminishing Marginal Utility.*[5] In commonsense terms, we usually get more of a thrill from our first million than from our tenth.

EXAMPLE 3.2 **Does Money Buy Happiness?**

While most economists do not believe that there is a valid cardinal scale for utilities, the economist Julian Simon disagrees. He proposed to measure utility, among other ways, by asking people, "Are you happy?"[a] Psychologists have surveyed people, asking them to classify themselves as very happy, pretty happy, or not too happy. The results in the table were obtained from a survey of residents in four small Illinois towns reported in 1965.

Income and Happiness*

Income	Responses (%)			Score
	Very Happy	Pretty Happy	Not too Happy	
Less than $3,000	14	55	31	−0.17
$ 3,000–3,999	21	63	16	+0.05
$ 4,000–4,999	27	61	12	+0.15
$ 5,000–5,999	26	64	10	+0.16
$ 6,000–6,999	24	65	10	+0.14
$ 7,000–7,999	30	60	10	+0.20
$ 8,000–9,999	29	63	7	+0.22
$10,000 or more	38	54	8	+0.30

***Source:** N. M. Bradburn and D. Caplovitz, *Reports on Happiness* (Chicago: Aldine, 1965), p. 9.

To interpret the first four columns we still need a numerical utility (happiness) scale. Let us count "very happy" as +1, "pretty happy" as 0, and "not too happy" as −1. The average for each income group is then shown by the column headed "Score." If plotted, the score data would show (despite some irregularities) a picture not too different from Figure 3.2.

[a]Another suggested measure is based on the suicide rate. See Julian L. Simon, "Interpersonal Welfare Comparison Can Be Made—And Used for Redistribution Decisions," *Kyklos,* v. 27 (1974).

[5]*Mathematical Footnote:* Let utility be a function of consumption, *c*. Since $\hat{U} = a + bU$, and *b* is positive, positive Marginal Utility according to the *U* scale ($dU/dc > 0$) implies positive Marginal Utility according to the $\hat{U}$ scale ($d\hat{U}/dc = bdU/dc > 0$). Note that a change in zero-point *a* does not affect Marginal Utility at all, and a change in unit interval *b* changes it only by the same positive multiplicative constant everywhere. *Diminishing* Marginal Utility according to the *U* scale ($d^2U/dc^2 < 0$) similarly implies diminishing Marginal Utility according to the $\hat{U}$ scale.

EXAMPLE 3.3 **The Weber-Fechner Law**

The psychologists E.H. Weber (1846) and G.T. Fechner (1860) theorized that subjective ability to discriminate is a function of proportionate change in the magnitude of stimulus.

Applying this to utility, an individual's subjective satisfaction can be regarded as sensitive to proportionate changes of income. For example, if an increase in income from $10,000 to $12,000 (i.e., by 20 percent) is valued as a "one-util" improvement, it would take a further 20 percent increase (from $12,000 to $14,400) to add a second util and still another 20 percent increase (from $14,400 to $17,280) for a third util. The Weber-Fechner law implies that utility is a logarithmic function of income. The graph of such a function would resemble Figure 3.2, and in particular would imply diminishing Marginal Utility.

Despite the discussions in the Examples 3.2 and 3.3, most modern economists do not believe that utility can be given a *cardinal* measure. If people can state that they prefer two million to one million—but not by how much—their utility is said to be an *ordinal* magnitude. Put another way, if Total Utility is an ordinal magnitude we cannot say anything about the *size* of Marginal Utility, though we can still say whether Marginal Utility is positive or negative. As will be seen at the end of the next section, ordinal utility is all that is needed for the analysis of consumption decisions.

Utility of Commodity Baskets

Let us now consider the utilities of *combinations,* or baskets, of goods. With just two goods X and Y, the utility function is $U(x,y)$.

Figure 3.3 presents a possible cardinal function $U(x,y)$. The quantities x and y are scaled along the horizontal axes. Utility in utils is measured in the upward direction, as the height above the base plane. When $x = x_1$ and $y = y_2$, for example, utility is the height TT'. If the quantity of Y is held constant at $y = y_1$, we can see how utility varies with x. This is shown by the curve PQR lying on the utility surface; note that Total Utility rises as x increases. If Y is held constant at $y = y_2$ instead, we get a similar curve STU; or if Y is held constant at $y = y_3$, we see the curve BVG. Each curve rises (Total Utility increases) as x increases, and so Marginal Utility of X is positive. Similarly, the Marginal Utility of commodity Y remains positive as y increases.

In terms of the satisfaction obtained, there is likely to be some interdependence between the goods. A consumer's incremental satisfaction from an additional pound of butter normally depends on the current rate of consumption of other commodities like margarine (a substitute) or bread (a complement).[6] In the illustration here, the Marginal Utility of X at the point T (i.e., when $x = x_1$ and $y = y_2$) is shown by the slope at point T along the curve STU; it is not necessarily the same as the Marginal Utility of X at the point V (where $x = x_1$ but $y = y_3$), which is the slope at V along BVG. So we see that the Marginal Utility of X may depend on the quantity of Y, and vice versa.

---

[6]*Mathematical Footnote:* Where Utility $U(x,y)$ is a function of amounts consumed of both X and Y, the Marginal Utilities are defined as *partial derivatives:* $MU_x \equiv \partial U/\partial x$ and $MU_y \equiv \partial U/\partial y$. In general, each Marginal Utility will be a function of both x and y, that is, the cross-derivative $\partial^2 U/\partial x \partial y$ will not ordinarily be zero.

FIGURE 3.3 **A Cardinal Total-Utility Function of Two Goods** Utility is measured up from the page, and the horizontal axes *x* and *y* represent quantities consumed of commodities *X* and *Y*. The curves *OA, PR, SU,* and *BG* along the surface show how Total Utility changes as *x* increases, holding *y* constant (at a different level for each curve). Similarly the curves *OB, WV,* and *AG* show how Total Utility changes as *y* increases, holding *x* constant.

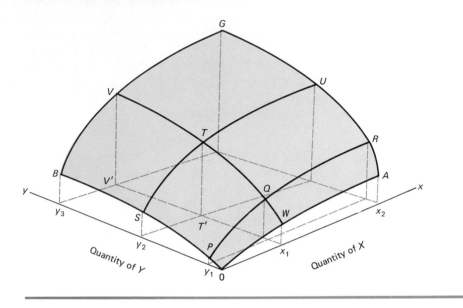

Figure 3.4 is a different representation of the same utility function as Figure 3.3. The curves drawn here on the surface (*CC, DD,* and *EE*) are level curves or contours connecting points of equal height on the "utility hill"; in effect, they show slices into the hill at fixed heights. These contours therefore are *curves of constant utility.* They were first employed by Edgeworth (1881),[7] who called them *indifference curves.*

If we look at the contours of Figure 3.4 from above we see a picture like Figure 3.5. The contours remain visible, but we no longer see the hill itself. Geometrically, the axis pointing up has been deleted so that we see the indifference curves in two dimensions. This step was taken by Pareto (1906).[8] Since *X* and *Y* are both goods, "More is preferred to less." Hence a consumer is certain to prefer point *A* to point *B* if point *A* lies above and to the right of point *B;* note the preference directions indicated by the arrows in the diagram. Any indifference curve that can be reached by moving northward or eastward from another is higher on the invisible utility hill. The indifference curves and the preference directions are all we need to know to determine how a consumer ranks baskets of goods.

The geometrical step of deleting the utility dimension of Figure 3.4 corresponds to the shift from a *cardinal* to an *ordinal* utility concept. On an ordinal scale the only meaningful comparisons are whether two magnitudes are equal or, if not equal, how they are ranked.[9]

---

[7]Francis Y. Edgeworth, British economist, 1845–1926.

[8]Vilfredo Pareto, Italian economist and sociologist, 1848–1923.

[9]*Mathematical Footnote:* If the two utility scales are only ordinally equivalent, all we can say is that $\hat{U} = F(U)$ and $d\hat{U}/dU = F'(U)$, where $F'(U) > 0$. The positive derivative $d\hat{U}/dU$ always preserves rankings of *magnitudes:* If $U_1 \geq U_2$, the associated $\hat{U}_1 \geq \hat{U}_2$. Since the second derivative $d^2\hat{U}/dU^2 = F''(U)$ has indeterminate sign, however, the ranking of *differences* according to the $\hat{U}$ scale need no longer correspond with their ranking on the *U* scale.

FIGURE 3.4 **Cardinal Utility and Indifference Curves**   The surface here is the same as in the preceding diagrams, but the curves *along* the surface *(CC, DD, EE)* are contours that connect points with equal heights (levels of utility). The projections of these curves onto the base plane (the dashed *C'C'*, *D'D'*, *E'E'*) are indifference curves.

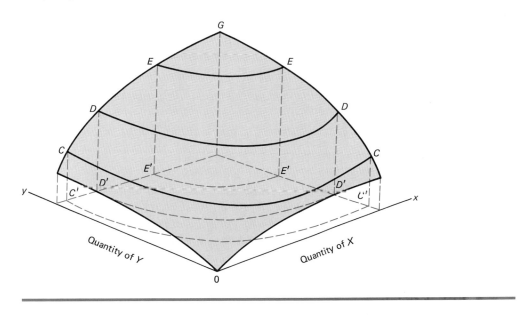

FIGURE 3.5   Indifference Curves and Preference Directions: Ordinal Utility   Here the cardinal scaling of utility has been stripped away, and we are left with the indifference curves. These indifference curves, together with the preference directions, give us all the information needed to rank alternative consumption baskets in terms of *ordinal* utility.

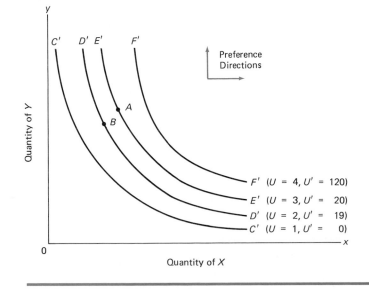

The two different cardinal preference scales U and $\hat{U}$ attached to the indifference curves of Figure 3.5 are equivalent in the ordinal sense, since they give the same answers as to which baskets are equal in utility (lie along the same indifference curve) and as to how baskets that are unequal in utility should be ranked (preference directions).

3.5 CHARACTERISTICS OF INDIFFERENCE CURVES FOR GOODS

Most of the analysis in this book considers only *goods,* commodities for which more is preferred to less. Indifference curves, then, have four crucial properties.

1. *Negative slope*—For simplicity, assume there are only two goods X and Y. We plot their quantities as before in the x,y-plane (the commodity space). Since more is preferred to less, in Figure 3.6 a consumer would prefer all points above and to the right of any point like A over the basket represented by point A. Similarly, the consumer would prefer point A to all points that lie below and to the left of A. It follows that all points *indifferent* to A must lie either below and to the right of A (like points R and Q), or else above and to the left of A (like points S and T). Thus an indifference curve passing through A cannot lie within either the $+$ or $-$ region shown in Figure 3.6. Any indifference curve must have a negative slope, more or less like U_1 or U_2 in the diagram.[10]

2. *Indifference curves cannot intersect*—Employing Figure 3.6 again, assume tentatively that two indifference curves like U_1 and U_2 can actually intersect at point A. Indifference curve U_1 states that the consumer is indifferent between baskets A and Q. Indifference curve U_2 states that the consumer is indifferent between A and R. By transitivity, the consumer must therefore be indifferent between Q and R. But R represents more of both goods than Q, so the consumer certainly prefers R over Q. Thus the assumption that indifference curves intersect leads to a contradiction. Hence indifference curves cannot intersect.

3. *Coverage of indifference curves*—An indifference curve passes through each point in commodity space; between any two indifference curves another can always be drawn. A corresponding property is possessed by the real number system. For example, between any two numbers like 17.4398 and 17.4399 we can always find another number like 17.43987 larger than the first and smaller than the second. The coverage property is equivalent to the Axiom of Comparison, which said that it is always possible to compare any baskets of commodities. Hence, any basket must lie on some indif-

---

[10]*Mathematical Footnote:* In terms of calculus, along any indifference curve utility $U(x,y)$ is constant. So

$$0 = dU \equiv \partial U / \partial x \, dx + \partial U / \partial y \, dy$$

Then the slope along the indifference curve is

$$\left. \frac{dy}{dx} \right|_U = \frac{-\partial U / \partial x}{\partial U / \partial y}$$

Since $\partial U / \partial x$ and $\partial U / \partial y$ are both positive (X and Y are both *goods* with positive Marginal Utilities), the slope is negative.

FIGURE 3.6 **Properties of Indifference Curves**   The preference directions indicate that every point in the + region is preferred to *A*; *A* is preferred over every point in the − region. It follows that any indifference curve through *A* must have negative slope. There can be only one indifference curve through *A*, since intersecting indifference curves violate transitivity of preference.

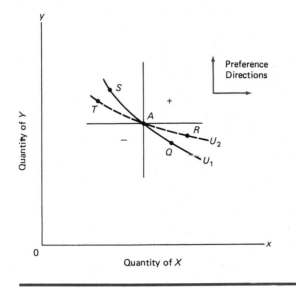

ference curve. (Empirically, however, this is an idealization rather than a literal description of reality.[11])

  This coverage property can cause confusion. A diagram can never show all indifference curves; if it did, the picture would be solid black. The diagrams in this book thus show only some selected indifference curves, those that are typical or else of some special importance.

4. *Indifference curves are convex to the origin*—In the two panels of Figure 3.7 we see the curvatures defined as convex and concave to the origin. The convex curve of Panel (a) represents the standard shape. A curve is convex if the straight line that connects any two points on it lies above the curve. For example, the line segment *BC* in Figure 3.7(a) would lie above the indifference curve. A curve is concave if the straight line that connects any two points on it lies below the curve. In contrast with the previous three properties (negative slope, nonintersection, and coverage), convexity cannot be proved from the postulates of rational choice. Rather, it is based on the well-established empirical principle of diversity in consumption (to be discussed in Chapter 4).

[11]Psychological experiments indicate that below a minimum threshold sensations cannot be distinguished from one another. This suggests that indifference curves have some "width" in actuality, which would not fit very conveniently into our picture. But this is no more disturbing than the fact that Euclid's "lines" (straight curves with no breadth) cannot be observed in the world, since the best we can do in drawing a line leaves some crookedness and some breadth.

FIGURE 3.7 **Convexity and Concavity** Between two goods, indifference curves must have negative slope. Curvature may be "convex to origin" as in Panel (a), or "concave to origin" as in Panel (b). The convex case is normally observed, even though concavity would not necessarily violate the axioms of rational choice.

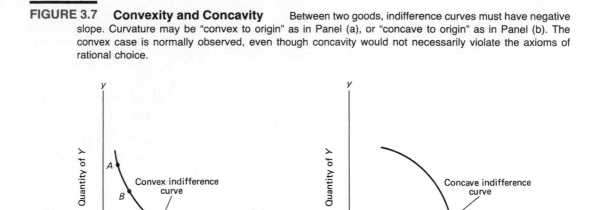

A commonsense justification for convexity is illustrated in Panel (a) of Figure 3.7. Suppose X stands for food and Y for entertainment.[12] At point A the person has plenty of entertainment but little food. We would reasonably expect him to be willing to give up a lot of entertainment for only a little food. The diagram shows him just as willing to move from A to B, giving up 3 units of entertainment Y for just 1 unit of food X. At B his consumption is more diversified. Therefore he would not be quite as willing as before to give up entertainment for more food. This time he is willing to give up only 2 units of Y for 1 unit of X. Finally, from C to D, he is willing to give up only 1 unit of his now scarce entertainment Y for 1 unit of food X. Convexity means, therefore, that the less you possess of good Y relative to good X, the more reluctant you are to give up additional units of Y for X. Thus, the picture of Panel (a) of Figure 3.7 seems to fit our normal patterns of preference, while the picture of Panel (b) does not.

Exercise 3.3 _____

(a) Someone claims that the two equations $xy = 100$ and $x + y = 20$ can both be valid indifference curves for some single individual. Is this correct? (b) What about the curves corresponding to the equations $xy = 100$ and $xy = 200$?

Answer: (a) No. Algebraically it may be determined that the curves corresponding to these two equations intersect at $x = 10$, $y = 10$. This violates the condition that indifference curves

_____

[12]Food and entertainment are aggregations, rather than simple commodities, but this does not affect the point at issue.

cannot intersect. (b) The curves $xy = 100$ and $xy = 200$ do not intersect, but we should also check the other properties. Use algebra or plot the functions to satisfy yourself that the curves have negative slope (property 1) and are convex toward the origin (property 4). So these two curves could both be valid indifference curves for some person.

Example 3.4 suggests something about the shape of parents' indifference curves between numbers of sons and daughters, regarded as "goods." (These goods happen to be of a kind ordinarily produced at home rather than purchased in the market, but how goods are acquired is a different matter from the preferences individuals might have.)

EXAMPLE 3.4 Preferences for Children: Number and Sex

In the table below, the two "goods" are sons and daughters. As is typical for baskets of goods, parents seem to prefer diversity. The table shows that parents who had either all boys or all girls were more likely to go on and have another child than parents who already have a mixture of boys and girls. For example, among two-child families with all boys or all girls, 56 percent of the parents went on to have another child. But for the two-child families with one boy and one girl, only 51 percent had another. The difference means that the parents with one boy and one girl were relatively more satisfied and therefore less likely to try again.

This pattern of preferences means that parents' indifference curves—apart from the fact that fractional children are not possible!—are convex. With two children, for example, the combination (1,1) is preferred to (on a higher indifference curve than) either (2,0) or (0,2). This implies that parents' indifference curves bulge toward the origin, as in Panel (a) of Figure 3.7.

Families Who Had Another Child (by number and sex of children)

Number of Children	Number of Boys	Number of Families	Families Who Had Another Child (%)
2	2	35,674	56
	1	64,585	51
	0	31,607	56
3	3	10,431	47
	2	26,497	44
	1	24,897	45
	0	8,948	48
4	4	2,619	40
	3	8,260	40
	2	11,489	38
	1	7,527	40
	0	2,241	41

Source: 1970 Census data reported in Yoram Ben-Porath and Finis Welch, *Do Sex Preferences Really Matter?*, The RAND Corporation Paper Series, P–5560 (December 1975), p. 7.

3.6 GOODS, BADS, AND NEUTERS

Not all commodities are *goods;* some are *bads*. Consider pollution. If two bundles are identical except that one involves consumption (breathing) of more polluted air, a reasonable person would surely prefer the bundle with clean air.

An important application of utility theory in recent years has been the problem of portfolio selection—the balancing of an individual's wealth over assets like stocks, bonds, real estate, and so forth. (This will be discussed in greater length in Chapter 14.) Portfolio analysts construct utility functions that treat r, the average percent yield of the portfolio as a desired feature or good; the riskiness s of the return enters as an undesired feature or bad. Figure 3.8 illustrates the indifference map of a typical investor. Note that the preference directions here are up and to the *left*. For the "good" r, more is preferred to less. But for the "bad" s, less is preferred to more. These preference directions imply that the indifference curves have *positive* slopes as shown in the diagram.

Everyday experience also tells us that a commodity can be a good up to a point of satiation, beyond which it becomes a bad.

EXAMPLE 3.5 **Ballpoint Pens and French Pastries**

K.R. MacCrimmon and M. Toda[a] conducted experiments on patterns of indifference curves. The first choice offered was between money (which we may interpret here as the equivalent of a generalized consumption commodity) and ballpoint pens. The subjects' indifference curves all showed negative slopes. The next choice offered was between money and French pastries, with the proviso that the pastries had to be eaten on the spot. Not surprisingly, French pastries became a bad after the first one or two; the subjects would eat more only if paid more money for doing so. Consequently, these indifference curves had normal negative slope only in the region marked as Zone 1 in Figure 3.9, to the left of the curve drawn through the lowest points of the successive indifference curves. In Zone 1 the preference directions are up and to the right as usual. In Zone 2, to the right of the dividing curve, French pastries have become a bad; the preference directions are up and to the left, and the indifference curves take on a positive slope.

[a]Kenneth R. MacCrimmon and Maseo Toda, "The Experimental Determination of Indifference Curves," *Review of Economic Studies*, v. 37 (October 1969).

Sometimes the quantity of a commodity can leave a person entirely unaffected; he or she simply doesn't care about having more or less. We all, perhaps, know someone who feels that way about soap. Such a commodity is called a *neuter,* neither adding to nor detracting from utility. Then the indifference-curve picture will be as in Figure 3.10 (p. 72).

Exercise 3.4 _____

For each of the following algebraic utility functions, assuming that x and y are always positive, indicate whether each commodity is a good, a bad, or a neuter: (a) $U = xy$. (b) $U = x/y$. (c) $U = 2xy/y$.

FIGURE 3.8 **Indifference Curves Between a Good and a Bad**   Mean Return r on assets is a good, but Riskiness of Return s is a bad. The preference directions are therefore up and to the left, so that the indifference curves slope upward.

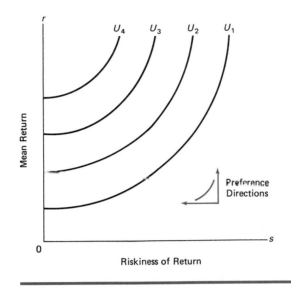

Mean Return

Riskiness of Return

FIGURE 3.9   **Satiation**   In Zone 1 both commodities, money and French pastries, are goods, so that the indifference curves have negative slope. Zone 2 is the region of satiation for French pastries; in this region the preference directions are up and to the left, and the indifference curves have positive slope. In this region an individual would have to be paid to eat another pastry.

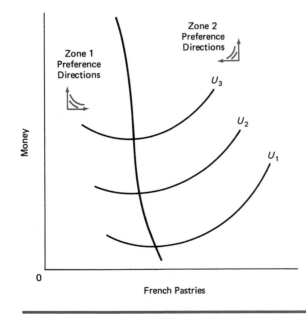

Money

French Pastries

FIGURE 3.10

FIGURE 3.10 **A Neuter Commodity** *Y* is a good, but *X* is a neuter commodity. The consumer does not care whether he has more or less of *X*. The only preference direction is up, and so the indifference curves are horizontal.

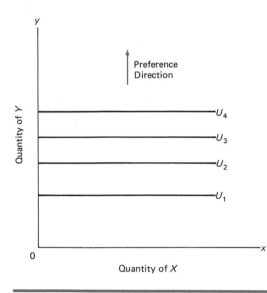

Answer: (a) Since utility *U* increases as *x* and *y* increase, both *X* and *Y* are goods. (b) Here *U* rises with *x* but falls as *y* increases, so *X* is a good while *Y* is a bad. (c) Note here that *y* cancels out, to leave the function $U = 2x$. So *X* is a good, and *Y* is a neuter (since utility does not depend at all upon *y*).

An Application: Charity

The following observations, among others, can be made about charity: (1) not everyone makes charitable contributions, (2) some people do, and (3) those who give charity almost always give to persons poorer than themselves. The problem is to construct an indifference-curve picture or pictures consistent with these observations.

One approach is as follows. Figure 3.11 has axes "My Income" and "His Income." We are thinking solely of "my" preferences, so the feelings of the other individual are not involved in the picture. Imagine first that I am completely uninterested in whether he has any income or not. Then "His Income" is a neuter commodity for me; I do not care at all about movements up or down. This is the situation pictured in Panel (a) of Figure 3.11. Since "My Income" is surely a good for me, the only preference direction shown is to the right, and my indifference curves are vertical.

If my preferences were as pictured in Panel (a), would I give charity to the other person? At the initial situation at *E* in Panel (a), I would have 1,000 units of income and he would have zero. Suppose that by reducing my income I can transfer income dollar for dollar to him. In the diagram, this means that I could attain any point along the line *EF* of slope −1. But any such movement from point *E* puts me on a lower indifference curve. So I

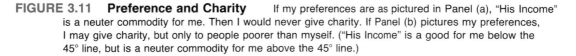

FIGURE 3.11 **Preference and Charity** If my preferences are as pictured in Panel (a), "His Income" is a neuter commodity for me. Then I would never give charity. If Panel (b) pictures my preferences, I may give charity, but only to people poorer than myself. ("His Income" is a good for me below the 45° line, but is a neuter commodity for me above the 45° line.)

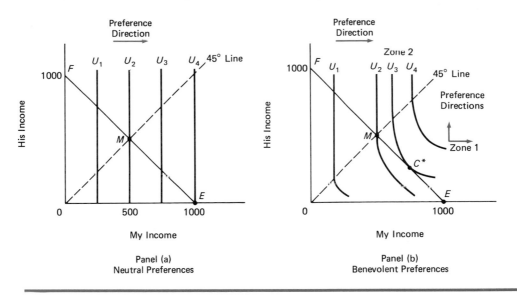

Panel (a)
Neutral Preferences

Panel (b)
Benevolent Preferences

would not give charity. Notice that I am in no way malevolent to the other individual here, but I am not benevolent either.

Panel (b) of Figure 3.11 is a more interesting case. Suppose I am benevolent only to people poorer than myself. The points where the other person is poorer than me lie below the dashed 45° line (Zone 1 in the diagram). Only in Zone 1 am I benevolent, so that the indifference curves have their usual negative slopes. If I were initially at E, I would transfer just enough income to attain point C^*. (Why? Because C^* is a point of tangency on indifference curve U_3, my highest level of utility attainable along line EF.) If, on the other hand, I were initially at a point like M, any charity on my part would make him richer than me (would put me in Zone 2, above the 45° line). But by assumption I do not give charity under these circumstances. Therefore, my indifference curves in this range must be vertical.

3.7 THE SOURCES AND CONTENT OF PREFERENCES

Why do people want some things and not others? Why are our desires for some goods easily satiated, and for others not easily satiated? Can anything be said about how preferences vary with age, ethnic origins, and circumstances?

As indicated in Chapter 1, economists ordinarily take individuals' goals as given; the nature and formation of goals are thought to fall in the province of other social sciences. Yet, in some cases, the forces involved are clear enough. It is not hard to predict that iced drinks will be more popular in Georgia than in Alaska; that diapers will not be a big merchandising item in a retirement community; that bagels will sell best in Jewish neighborhoods, and soul food in Harlem. But what are the bases for these commonsense judgments? The economist who intends to apply his discipline should have some knowledge of the deeper forces determining preferences.

On a very primitive level, human beings are animals that normally favor (and so can be said to have preferences for) survival and comfort. We like to keep our skins intact, our body parts connected, and our blood temperatures not very far from 98.6° Fahrenheit. Physical considerations like these broadly explain the desires for food, shelter, and protection against injury. But cultural and personal elements are clearly involved in translating these very general desires into more specific preferences for commodities like three-piece suits or Levi's, pizza pies or *pâté de foie gras,* split-level houses or mobile homes.

EXAMPLE 3.6 **Demand for Housing**

An important determinant of the demand for housing is age. N. Gregory Mankiw and David N. Weil[a] found a sharp jump in the demand for housing between the ages of 20 and 30. People below 20 have little effect on the demand for housing, and the demand for housing appears to decline after age 40 by about one percent per year.

A changing age distribution in the population can therefore cause changes in the demand for, and prices of, housing. In 1960 only 24 million people, or 13.3 percent of the U.S. population, were between the ages 20 and 30. In 1980 the corresponding number was 44.6 million, or 19.7 percent of the population, so we would expect a large increase in housing demand in the 1980s compared to the 1960s.

Mankiw and Weil used these demand estimates and the age distributions of the population in the United States to estimate a 1.84 percent increase in the demand for housing from 1940 to 1950; a 1.16 percent increase from 1950 to 1960; a 1.31 percent increase from 1960 to 1970; and a 1.66 percent increase from 1970 to 1980. Further estimates show that a one percent increase in the demand for housing leads to a 5.3 percent increase in the real price of housing. Thus, a large part of the inflation in housing prices in the 1980s can be explained by the sharp rise in the number of persons with ages associated with peak demands for housing. The aging of the Baby Boomers, they predicted, should cause a decline in housing prices in the 1990s.

[a]N. Gregory Mankiw and David N. Weil "The Baby Boom, The Baby Bust, and The Housing Market." Harvard Institute of Economic Research Discussion Paper No. 1414, December 1988.

As people grow richer they go beyond physiological needs and indulge their tastes for esthetics, social distinction, or novelty. These nonmaterial "goods" therefore are more significant for the affluent than for the poor. To explain behavior as overall wealth increases, economics must consider these nonmaterial tastes and drives.

An essential element in society is the aid that individuals give one another, as in the charity behavior discussed earlier. One observation has been offered to explain the "taste" for providing this kind of help: people often give charity to those poorer than themselves, but only rarely to those richer than themselves. Another fact about the taste for helping others is even more obvious: people help their own children more than they help almost anyone else. This last fact suggests a biological evolutionary explanation. Organisms that choose to help their own offspring rather than others' offspring have tended to leave more descendants over the generations.[13]

Sometimes, however, what looks like altruistic behavior can be explained on other grounds. Thus consider a father who has a son and a daughter. The son and daughter are perfectly selfish. The father is altruistic and will divide a $1,000 gift between them. Since the father loves his children equally, he will want to allocate the $1,000 to make the benefits conferred upon his two children as equal as possible. Suppose the son can incur an expense of $10 that increases the utility of his sister by the equivalent of $500. The son would want to do this, because the added utility of his sister would induce the father to give more money to the son and less to the sister. We thus would find behavior that looks like altruism between the brother and sister, even if both are driven totally by selfishness.

SUMMARY

A person choosing his or her preferred consumption basket is said to maximize utility. We postulate that preferences follow two laws: (1) the Axiom of Comparison (a person can compare all possible pairs of consumption baskets) and (2) the Axiom of Transitivity (a person who prefers basket A to B, and prefers B to C, will prefer A to C). These two laws together imply that the individual can rank all conceivable consumption baskets in order of preference.

If utility is quantifiable in the sense of being "cardinally" measurable, statements can be made about the shape of the Marginal Utility curve. But for most purposes in modern economics it suffices if utility is only "ordinally" measurable. If one basket is preferred to another the utility of the former is simply greater—how much greater does not matter.

In choosing baskets of two or more commodities, cardinal utility would be represented by a quantifiable "utility hill." The ordinal utility interpretation lets us suppress the utility dimension and portray preferences in terms of *indifference curves*—contours connecting consumption baskets yielding equal utility—together with an indication of the *preference directions* (that indicate the way up on the invisible utility hill). For a *good,* utility increases as the amount consumed increases. For a *bad,* utility decreases with the amount consumed. For a *neuter,* utility is unaffected by the amount consumed.

Indifference curves have three properties that follow from the laws of rational choice: negative slope, nonintersection, and coverage. There is also a fourth property, convexity to the origin, that is based on the observation that individuals tend to diversify the commodities they consume.

---

[13]Sociobiologists have gone even further, to quantify the degree of altruism on the basis of kinship. A person shares half of his or her genes with a child or a full sibling, a quarter with a grandchild, an eighth with a first cousin, and so forth. Thus, it has been suggested, evolution should have selected individuals who were willing to give up their own lives to save two brothers or sisters, four grandchildren, eight cousins, and so on! See J.B.S. Haldane, "Population Genetics," *New Biology,* v. 18 (1955); W.D. Hamilton, "The Genetical Evolution of Social Behavior," *Journal of Theoretical Biology,* v. 7 (1964). How this prediction squares with the evidence remains unclear.

For Review

*1. An individual is offered a choice between a ski trip to Aspen and four cases of Cutty Sark whiskey. Which of the following possible responses violate the laws of preference?
   a. "They're so different, I can't choose."
   b. "I don't care, you choose for me."
   c. "Whichever I choose, I know I'll be sorry."

2. Name a commodity that is a good for many people, but is a bad for you. Name a commodity that is a good for you, but only up to a point; after that it becomes a bad.

3. Draw possible indifference maps between the following:
   a. Two goods.
   b. A good and a bad.
   c. A good and a neuter.
   d. A good and a commodity that is a good up to a point, but then becomes a bad.

*4. What do modern economists mean by the term *utility?*

5. Given a "cardinal" (quantitatively measurable) Total Utility function, show how a corresponding Marginal Utility function is derived.

*6. What can be said about the Marginal Utility function if Total Utility is given only in "ordinal" terms?

7. What are the four essential properties of indifference curves between two goods? Explain the justification for each of the four properties.

*8. Which of the following requires only *ordinal* utility, which requires *cardinal* utility, and which requires *interpersonal comparability* of cardinal utilities?
   a. Indifference curves can be drawn.
   b. A Marginal Utility function can be used to see numerically how Total Utility changes as consumption of a good increases.
   c. It can be determined which person is most desirous of receiving a particular prize.

For Further Thought and Discussion

*1. Is it possible to give an exact meaning in utility terms to the expression "greatest good of the greatest number"?

2. In suppressing the "cardinal" dimension of the utility hill so as to picture preferences only in terms of indifference curves, why is it necessary also to indicate the preference directions?

*3. An example of an ordinal measure is the military rank system. A sergeant has more authority than a private, a lieutenant more than a sergeant, and so on. Give another example of an ordinal scale of magnitude.

4. Since you probably would not want to eat pickles and ice cream together, does it follow that your indifference curves between these two goods are concave rather than convex?

*5. For "His Income" and "My Income" regarded as goods, what shape for the indifference curves would correspond to the Golden Rule ("Love thy neighbor as thyself")?

*The answers to starred questions appear at the end of the book.

*6. In surveys of income and happiness, a puzzling discrepancy has been noted. While higher income is associated with higher reported happiness *at a moment in time,* this conclusion does not seem to hold for comparisons *over time.* Even though wealth has risen over the years in the United States all across the scale, so that both rich and poor have higher incomes than before, reports on happiness do not average higher than before.[14] The most natural explanation of this paradox is that happiness is more powerfully affected by relative income status than by absolute income. The poor consume more than before, but are still on the bottom of the heap and so still feel just as unhappy. How would you draw the preference map to picture this situation?

---

[14]See R.A. Easterlin, "Does Economic Growth Improve the Human Lot? Some Empirical Evidence," in P. David and M. Reder, eds., *Nations and Households in Economic Growth; Essays in Honor of M. Abramovitz* (New York: Academic Press, 1974).

CHAPTER 4

CONSUMPTION AND

DEMAND

EXAMPLES

T his chapter analyzes the optimizing decisions of consumers. We will see how the choices among consumption goods depend on individual preferences (as discussed in the preceding chapter) together with market opportunities. Opportunities depend, in turn, upon income and market prices. We will also learn how consumption choices respond to changes in people's tastes, in their incomes, or the prices they face.

4.1 THE OPTIMUM OF THE CONSUMER[1]

The Algebra and Geometry of Consumer Choice

In Figure 4.1 the shaded triangle shows all baskets consisting of two goods, X and Y, that a consumer with given income can afford. This is called the *opportunity set,* or more specifically the *market opportunity set.*[2] The upper boundary of the opportunity set, the *budget line KL,* shows the baskets a person could purchase if spending all income on X and Y. In this chapter we will usually assume that all income is spent and none saved. This is not as unrealistic as it seems since saving is, in effect, spending for future consumption.

Suppose John's income is $I = \$100$, and market prices are $P_x = \$2$ and $P_y = \$1$. If John spent all his income on X, he could buy $100/2 = 50$ units of X. This would put him at point L in the diagram. If he spent all his income on Y, he could purchase $100/1 = 100$ units of good Y (point K). He could also afford any combination of goods lying on the straight line between K and L. This line is his budget line or (as it is sometimes called) his *budget constraint.*

In a modern economy, prices are generally quoted in money terms, but here we want to "pierce the veil" of money and discuss the underlying *real* magnitudes. We thus concentrate on the real meaning of cost, which is always opportunity cost: the true cost of buying more apples is having less of the other good or goods. Think of prices and income as measured in terms of some standard real good called a *numeraire.* Then P_x, the price of X, is the

List of Notation

I	Income	MU_X	Marginal Utility of X
IEP	Income Expansion Path	PEP	Price Expansion Path
MRS_C	Marginal Rate of Substitution in Consumption	P_X	Price of Good X
MRS_E	Marginal Rate of Substitution in Exchange		

---

[1] The optimum of the consumer is sometimes carelessly called, by textbook authors and others, the *equilibrium* of the consumer. Such wording blurs the distinction between the two key analytical concepts—equilibrium and optimum. An optimum is the best possible choice for a decisionmaker. An equilibrium represents a balance of forces—for example, the outcome when many buyers and many sellers interact in a market. Here we deal with the optimizing decision of a single consumer.

[2] Other types of consumption opportunity sets can also exist. Robinson Crusoe, for example, could be regarded as having an opportunity set in terms of the fish and bananas available on his island. Crusoe's consumption opportunity set would depend entirely upon his own isolated efforts, and in no way upon the possibility of transactions in markets.

amount of the standard good that must be paid for a unit of X. P_y is the amount that must be paid for a unit of good Y; income is the total amount available for spending.

Since each unit of good X costs P_x, the cost of x units of good X is $P_x x$. If a consumer spends all his income on goods X and Y, the following equation holds:

$$P_x x + P_y y = I \qquad (4.1)$$

This equation, which corresponds to the budget line KL in Figure 4.1, can also be written as $y = (I - P_x x)/P_y$. The vertical intercept of KL is the value of Y when $x = 0$. Substituting $x = 0$ in the equation $y = (I - P_x x)/P_y$, we obtain $y = I/P_y$; this is the number of units of Y obtained by spending all income on Y. The horizontal intercept is obtained by setting $y = 0$ and solving for x; we obtain I/P_x, which is the number of units of X the individual could purchase by spending all income on commodity X. Any mixed basket containing positive quantities of both goods lies along the line between the two intercepts. The shaded opportunity set in Figure 4.1 is also bounded by the horizontal and vertical axes, since a consumer cannot purchase negative quantities of goods.

We can express the possibility that a consumer does not spend all his income purchasing goods with the following condition:

$$P_x x + P_y y \leq I \qquad (4.1')$$

The more general expression (4.1'), together with the nonnegativity assumptions, describe the entire shaded opportunity region of Figure 4.1.

In a market situation only the budget line (the upper boundary of the opportunity set) constrains the consumer. Why? Because the consumer can get to any position in the *in-*

FIGURE 4.1 **Optimum of the Consumer** The shaded region *OKL* is the consumer's market opportunity set; it is bounded by the horizontal and vertical axes and by the budget line *KL*. The optimum is the point on the budget line *KL* that lies on the highest attainable indifference curve (point *C** on indifference curve U_2).

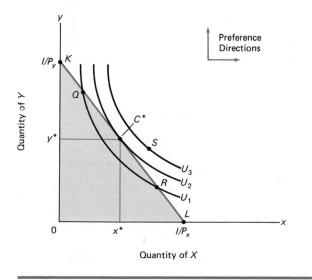

terior of the shaded region, starting from a point on the budget line, simply by throwing away some X or some Y or both. But since X and Y are goods, no one would ever want to do so.[3]

We will frequently refer to the *slope* of curves or lines drawn in two dimensions. The slope will be symbolized as $\Delta y/\Delta x$, the change in y per unit change in x along the curve. For a straight line the slope is the same at every point on the line. The slope of the budget line, symbolized $\Delta y/\Delta x|_I$, is seen from the equation $y = (I - P_x x)/P_y$ to be $-P_x/P_y$. (The symbols $|_I$ mean that income (I) is being held constant.) Another way of obtaining this result is to observe that the slope of the budget line is the value of the vertical intercept (I/P_y) divided by the negative of the horizontal intercept (I/P_x).

$$\left.\frac{\Delta y}{\Delta x}\right|_I = \frac{-I/P_y}{I/P_x} = -\frac{P_x}{P_y} \tag{4.2}$$

Along the budget line the slope is negative, since an increase in x is associated with a decrease of y.[4]

Algebraically, Equation (4.2) tells us that the slope of the budget line is equal to the price ratio P_x/P_y, with the sign reversed. If commodity X is wine at \$3 a quart, and commodity Y is a soft drink at \$1.50 a quart, then a consumer who purchased one less quart of wine would have 3 more units of the numeraire with which to purchase soda. This means that the consumer could purchase an additional $3/1.50 = 2$ quarts of soda; the slope of the budget line would be -2.

Exercise 4.1 ——————————————————————

Suppose the price of apples is $P_a = 10$ and the price of beer is $P_b = 2$; income is $I = 100$. (a) With beer on the vertical axis, what is the equation of the budget line, and what are the intercepts on the two axes? What is the slope? (b) Describe what happens if, with income unchanged, the price of apples were cut in half. (c) Describe what happens if, with the original prices unchanged, income were to double.

Answer: (a) The equation of the budget line $P_a a + P_b b = I$ becomes, after substituting $P_a = 10$, $P_b = 2$, and $I = 100$, $10a + 2b = 100$. The a-intercept is $100/10 = 10$; the b-intercept is $100/2 = 50$. The slope is $-50/10 = -5$. (b) If P_a were cut in half, the new equation of the budget line would be $5a + 2b = 100$. The a-intercept becomes 20 instead of 10; the b-intercept is unchanged. So the budget line swings to the right, with a flatter slope equal to $-50/20 = -2 1/2$. (c) If, with the original prices, income doubled, the equation of the budget line becomes $10a + 2b = 200$. Both intercepts double. So the budget line has the same slope as before: $-100/20 = -5$. In this case the line moves outward, parallel to itself.

With the data on preferences and opportunities, we can determine the consumption bundle that maximizes the consumer's utility. Figure 4.1 shows that the consumer's best choice along the budget line *KL* (and, therefore, the best position attainable within the shaded

---

[3]Later on we will see that the imposition of additional constraints upon the consumption decision, such as rationing, may force the individual into the interior of his market opportunity set.

[4]*Mathematical Footnote:* Let the budget line be $P_x x + P_y y = I$. The slope is found as the derivative.

$$dy/dx|_I = -P_x/P_y$$

Since this derivative is a constant, it equals the ratio of finite increments $\Delta y/\Delta x|_I$ in Equation (4.2).

market opportunity set) is point C^*—the consumption basket containing x^* units of commodity X and y^* units of commodity Y. Any point that gives the consumer more utility than point C^* lies above line $KL,$ and therefore represents an expenditure greater than the consumer's income. Thus, point C^* represents the point on the budget line that lies on the highest indifference curve. Another way to describe this point is to say that at point C^* budget line KL has the same slope as the indifference curve, U_2, that goes through point C^*. That is, the indifference curve is *tangent* to the budget line at C^*.

Nontangency points like Q and R in the diagram (which lie on indifference curve U_1 at the points where U_1 cuts the budget line) must necessarily be less desirable than the tangency point C^* on indifference curve U_2. In terms of the invisible "utility hill" of Chapter 3, Q and R lie along a lower contour than C^*; the highest contour attainable is the one that can just barely be reached at the single tangency point C^*. It is true that a point like S on indifference curve U_3 would be superior to C^*, but basket S is not attainable since all points on indifference curve U_3 lie outside the opportunity set.

CONCLUSION: The optimum of the consumer is found at the tangency between the budget line and a convex indifference curve (if such a tangency exists).

In Chapter 3, we found that convexity of indifference curves did not follow from the logic of the Laws of Preference but rather from observation of behavior in the world. This point can now be demonstrated. Imagine indifference curves that are concave instead of convex, as in Figure 4.2. The preference directions, shaded opportunity set, and budget line KL remain as in the previous diagram. Here the tangency point T is not the optimum. Instead, T is the least preferred point on the budget line, lying as it does on U_2, the lowest indifference curve reached along KL. With the concave indifference curves shown here, the optimum is

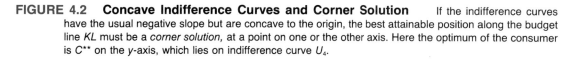

FIGURE 4.2 **Concave Indifference Curves and Corner Solution**   If the indifference curves have the usual negative slope but are concave to the origin, the best attainable position along the budget line KL must be a *corner solution,* at a point on one or the other axis. Here the optimum of the consumer is C^{**} on the y-axis, which lies on indifference curve U_4.

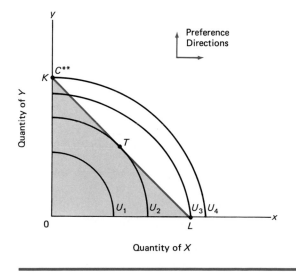

at C^{**}, where the consumer spends all his income on Y. This is called a *corner solution,* as opposed to the *interior solution C^** in Figure 4.1. But in the actual world people diversify their consumption, purchasing a mixture of many different commodities. Since concave indifference curves are inconsistent with diversified consumption, we can rule them out and assume that indifference curves are convex.

It is true, however, that among the vast numbers of commodities that consumers recognize as goods, many are not actually purchased. The price is too high. You may enjoy the flavor of Beluga caviar, be able to afford at least a small quantity of it, and yet not be willing to pay the steep price required. Thus, you are at a corner solution with regard to the "caviar axis" of your utility function.

However, as Figure 4.3 illustrates, corner solutions for some goods can arise with convex indifference curves. Here, no tangency exists. The consumer's best consumption bundle is at C^{**}, which shows no consumption of X. Convexity can thus explain both corner solutions and interior solutions.

GEOMETRICAL OPTIMUM PRINCIPLE: The optimum of the consumer is the point on the budget line that touches the highest attainable indifference curve. With convex indifference curves, the optimum may be an *interior solution* at a point where the budget line is tangent to the best attainable indifference curve. Or it may be a *corner solution* where the budget line reaches the highest attainable indifference curve along an axis.

Optimum of the Consumer: Marginal Analysis

This section re-interprets the optimum of the consumer using marginal concepts. If utility were a "cardinal" variable measured in utils, it would be meaningful to speak of the magnitude

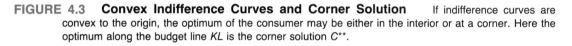

FIGURE 4.3   Convex Indifference Curves and Corner Solution   If indifference curves are convex to the origin, the optimum of the consumer may be either in the interior or at a corner. Here the optimum along the budget line KL is the corner solution C^{**}.

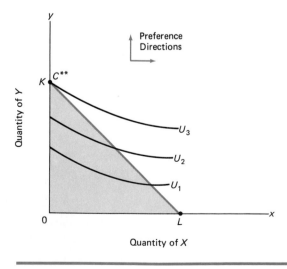

of Marginal Utility. Then the consumer is at an (interior) optimum when the following Consumption Balance Equation is satisfied:[5]

$$\frac{\text{Marginal Utility of } X}{\text{Price of } X} = \frac{\text{Marginal Utility of } Y}{\text{Price of } Y} \qquad \begin{array}{l} \text{Consumption} \\ \text{Balance} \\ \text{Equation} \\ \text{(Interior} \\ \text{Solution)} \end{array} \qquad (4.3)$$

The explanation is immediate: for any good, Marginal Utility divided by price is Marginal Utility per dollar spent on that commodity. At the optimum, the last dollar must yield the same satisfaction when spent on X as on Y. If this were not the case, the consumer would buy more of the commodity whose Marginal Utility per dollar was high, and less of the commodity whose Marginal Utility per dollar was low. He would continue this process until Marginal Utilities per dollar become equal over all commodities purchased.

Exercise 4.2

An apple costs 50 cents and an orange 25 cents. A consumer initially purchases 10 apples and 5 oranges. The Marginal Utility of an apple is then 3 utils and of an orange 1 util. Is the consumer at an optimum?

Answer: For an interior optimum, the Marginal Utility per dollar spent must be equal for all goods. In terms of equation (4.3) we see that $3/\$0.50 = 6 > 1/\$0.25 = 4$; the Marginal Utility per dollar is higher for apples than for oranges. Thus, the consumer could increase his utility by purchasing somewhat fewer oranges and somewhat more apples; in giving up one orange the consumer would sacrifice one util, but would have 25 more cents to spend on apples. At a price of 50 cents an apple, the 25 cents buys half an apple, yielding $3/2 = 1.5$ additional utils in place of the 1 util sacrificed. Since this is an improvement, the consumer was not initially at an optimum.

---

[5]*Mathematical Footnote:* Optimization problems in economics are often solved using the method of Lagrangian multipliers. Specifically, in the present case we seek to maximize a cardinal utility function $U(x,y)$ subject to the constraint $P_x x + P_y y = I$, where P_x, P_y, and I are constants. The technique involves setting up an artificial maximand in the following form:

$$\max_{(x,y,\lambda)} L = U(x,y) + \lambda(P_x x + P_y y - I)$$

Take the derivative of L with respect to x, y, and λ to obtain the first-order conditions for a maximum.

$$\partial L/\partial x = \partial U/\partial x + \lambda P_x = 0$$
$$\partial L/\partial y = \partial U/\partial y + \lambda P_y = 0$$
$$\partial L/\partial \lambda = P_x x + P_y y - I = 0$$

The first two conditions imply

$$\frac{\partial U/\partial x}{P_x} = \frac{\partial U/\partial y}{P_y}$$

This is, of course, the Consumption Balance Equation (4.3). The technique works because by taking the partial derivative with respect to λ we obtain $P_x x + P_y y - I = 0$. This guarantees that the budget equation is met, and also assures that the maximum of the artificial variable L is the same as the desired maximum of U. (The second-order conditions for a maximum are omitted here.)

The marginal utilities of X and Y generally change as the consumer changes his consumption bundle. The benefit of an added apple may be low when a consumer eats 10 apples a day, but high if he eats only 1 a day. Condition (4.3), which says that the consumer should consume those quantities of X and Y that make the values of MU_x and MU_y equal, is valid when the marginal utilities are both declining.

What about the possibility of a corner solution? Suppose that, for some commodity like Beluga caviar, the Marginal Utility per dollar remains lower than that of the other commodity even when no caviar is purchased. Then we would have a corner optimum, which can be expressed (letting X represent caviar which is not consumed) as the following inequality:[6,7]

$$\frac{MU_x \text{ (when } x = 0)}{P_x} < \frac{MU_y \text{ (when } y > 0)}{P_y} \qquad \begin{array}{c} \text{Consumption} \\ \text{Balance Inequality} \\ \text{(Corner Solution)} \end{array} \qquad (4.3')$$

So, at the optimum either the Consumption Balance Equation (for an interior solution) applies or else the Consumption Balance Inequality (for a corner solution) applies. In addition, the consumer has to meet the budget-line condition (4.1) that constrains expenditure to equal income.

Exercise 4.3

Let the Marginal Utility of bread, MU_b, be given algebraically by the expression $MU_b = 40 - 5b$. Similarly, let the Marginal Utility of wine be $MU_w = 30 - w$. [Note the special assumption that MU_b depends only on the quantity b, and MU_w depends only on the quantity w. This property, called "absence of complementarity," will be discussed shortly below.] (a) Let the prices be $P_b = 5$ and $P_w = 1$, and let the consumer's income be $I = 40$. Find the optimum of the consumer. (b) What if income is 10 instead of 40?

Answer: (a) The budget equation (4.1) is $5b + w = 40$. If there is an interior solution, it must satisfy the Consumption Balance Equation.

$$\frac{40 - 5b}{5} = \frac{30 - w}{1}$$

Solving the two equations simultaneously, we obtain $b^* = 3$, $w^* = 25$ (verifying that there is indeed an interior solution). (b) The budget equation here is $5b + w = 10$. Solving simultaneously with the Consumption Balance Equation we obtain $b^* = -2$, $w^* = 20$, which is impossible. So there is no interior solution. The correct corner solution is $b^{**} = 0$, $w^{**} = 10$.

This is very direct and simple. But, as we saw in Chapter 3, only with "cardinal" utility is quantitative measurement of Marginal Utility possible. (With "ordinal" utility, we can

---

[6]If there were many commodities, there might be corner solutions for some pairs of goods and interior solutions for others. For three goods, the solution might take the form

$$\frac{MU_x(x = 0)}{P_x} < \frac{MU_y(y > 0)}{P_y} = \frac{MU_z(z > 0)}{P_z}$$

Here positive amounts of commodities Y and Z, but not of commodity X, are being purchased.

[7]*Mathematical Footnote:* Since a corner solution is generally not at a tangency, calculus techniques involving equality of derivatives are not applicable. The optimum is not at a point where the indifference-curve slope equals the budget-line slope.

only determine whether Marginal Utility is positive, zero, or negative.) The next step is to rework the solution without using measurable Marginal Utility.

Think now of the ratio at which the individual is just willing to substitute a small amount of Y for a small amount of X in his consumption basket. This ratio is called the Marginal Rate of Substitution in Consumption, denoted MRS_C. The expression "just willing to substitute Y for X" means the same as "a substitution of Y for X that leaves the consumer indifferent." So MRS_C corresponds geometrically to the slope of the indifference curve (in absolute value). Mathematically, we can write

$$MRS_C \equiv -\left.\frac{\Delta y}{\Delta x}\right|_U \qquad (4.4)$$

(Since MRS_C is defined as positive, while the indifference curve has a negative slope, the ratio on the right-hand side has to be preceded by a minus sign.[8] The symbols $|_U$ mean that the ratio is evaluated for a given level of utility, or along a given indifference curve.)

We can also think of MRS_C as the Marginal Value of good X in terms of good Y. Indeed, if we think of Y not as a single good but as "all other goods," the Marginal Rate of Substitution is the marginal value to the consumer of good X in terms of goods in general: it describes how much of "all other goods" the consumer is willing to give up to obtain an additional unit of good X.

Consider Figure 4.4 (p. 88). At point A the individual holds the basket $x = 3$, $y = 15$. He is contemplating consuming instead the basket $x = 5$, $y = 10$ represented by point B. He is indifferent between baskets A and B, since they lie on the same indifference curve. In moving from A to B, the change in Y is -5 and the change in X is 2. The numerical ratio $5:2$ approximates the Marginal Rate of Substitution in the neighborhood of points A and B. It is also the numerical slope of the line connecting points A and B, and a close approximation of the slope of the indifference curve at points A or B. The smaller the changes considered, the better the approximation. In the limit, then, the Marginal Rate of Substitution is the numerical slope of the indifference curve.

We now know the ratio at which the consumer is *willing* to substitute Y for X in his consumption basket. The next question is, at what ratio can he trade in the market? This second ratio is called the Marginal Rate of Substitution in Exchange, denoted MRS_E, and is simply the price ratio.

$$MRS_E = P_x/P_y \qquad (4.5)$$

In Figure 4.4, the assumed prices are $P_x = 5$ and $P_y = 3$. In other words, the individual is able to exchange 5 units of Y in the market for 3 units of X. This consumer is in a happy position. He is willing to give up 5 units of Y for just 2 units of X, but for 5 units of Y the market will give him 3 units of X. Geometrically, he is willing to move from A to B but his market opportunities permit a move to G, on a higher indifference curve. He will obviously make the trade.

---

[8]*Mathematical Footnote:* The definition of MRS_C in the text was expressed in terms of finite differences Δx and Δy. In terms of derivatives it becomes

$$MRS_C \equiv -dy/dx|_U$$

FIGURE 4.4 **Marginal Rate of Substitution in Consumption (MRS_C) and Marginal Rate of Substitution in Exchange (MRS_E)** MRS_C at point A is the absolute value of the slope of indifference curve U at that point. It is approximated by the ratio $AD/DB = 5/2$. MRS_E, which here is also the price ratio P_x/P_y, is the slope of the budget line (with the sign changed). In the diagram it is given by the ratio $AD/DG = 5/3$. The inequality of MRS_C and MRS_E at A shows that A cannot be an optimum for the consumer.

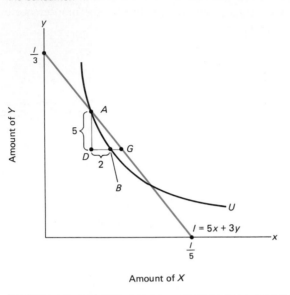

EXAMPLE 4.1 **Prisoners of War: Tea Versus Coffee**

The economist R.A. Radford had the unfortunate opportunity of studying, from the inside, social behavior in prisoner-of-war camps in Germany and Italy during World War II. He found that highly active economies functioned in these camps, particularly under the relatively favorable conditions that prevailed in the earlier war years.

Cigarettes served generally as the *numeraire* (or standard good) in terms of which prices were quoted. Coffee might go for about 2 cigarettes per cup, a shirt might cost 80 cigarettes, washing service 2 cigarettes per garment, and so on. In the English camp section, tea was definitely preferred to coffee. In the French section, coffee was preferred to tea. A regular smuggling trade permitted prisoners in each section to adjust their consumption choices to the price ratio reflecting the overall supply-demand balance in the camp as a whole.[a]

COMMENT The two panels of Figure 4.5 illustrate the situations of typical English and French prisoners. In both camp sections prices were quoted, in cigarettes, for coffee (P_c), and for tea (P_t). The efficient smuggling trade between sections equalized prices in the two sections. Therefore, the Marginal Rate of Substitution in Exchange, MRS_E = P_c/P_t, was the same for both groups of prisoners. But for the English prisoners, the tangency point C^{**}, where $MRS_C = MRS_E$, was well over toward the tea axis, while for the French prisoners the optimum at C^* lay toward the coffee axis.

[a]R.A. Radford, "The Economic Organization of a P.O.W. Camp," *Economica*, v. 12 (1945). In his enforced period of stay Radford made many other striking observations, some of which will be mentioned later in the text.

FIGURE 4.5 **Coffee Versus Tea in a P.O.W. Camp**   English and French P.O.W.'s had different tastes for tea relative to coffee. An efficient smuggling system equalized the price ratio P_c/P_t, so the two groups of prisoners faced the same Marginal Rate of Substitution in Exchange. For the French prisoners, the optimum C^* had a large consumption of coffee relative to tea; the English prisoners, consuming at C^{**}, drank a relatively large amount of tea.

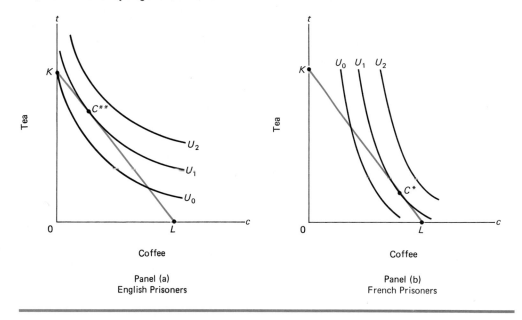

Panel (a)
English Prisoners

Panel (b)
French Prisoners

To summarize the discussion, in an interior solution (with positive consumption of both commodities) the consumer is at an optimum only if the rate at which he is *willing* to make small substitutions in his consumption bundle *(MRS_C)* equals the rate at which he *can* trade in the market *(MRS_E)*. Mathematically, we can express this as the Substitution Equivalence Equation which must hold for the consumer to be at an interior optimum.

$$MRS_C = MRS_E \quad \text{or} \quad -\frac{\Delta y}{\Delta x}\bigg|_U = \frac{P_x}{P_y} \qquad \begin{array}{c}\text{Substitution}\\\text{Equivalence}\\\text{Equation}\\\text{(Interior Solution)}\end{array} \qquad (4.6)$$

What about corner solutions? The corresponding condition is the Substitution Equivalence *Inequality*, which must take one or the other of the two following forms:

$$\begin{array}{c}MRS_C > MRS_E \quad \text{when } y = 0\\\text{or}\\MRS_C < MRS_E \quad \text{when } x = 0\end{array} \qquad \begin{array}{c}\text{Substitution}\\\text{Equivalence}\\\text{Inequality}\\\text{(Corner Solutions)}\end{array} \qquad (4.6')$$

[*Question:* Which of the inequalities holds for the corner solution in Figure 4.3?]
    We can sum up as follows:

ANALYTICAL OPTIMUM PRINCIPLE: If the optimum of the consumer is at an interior solution, where he purchases positive amounts of both commodities, then (1) the consumer must be spending all his income (i.e., he must be on his budget line) and (2) his Marginal Rate of Substitution in Consumption (MRS_C) must equal the Marginal Rate of Substitution in Exchange $(MRS_E$, or the price ratio $P_x/P_y)$. These conditions correspond to the geometrical tangency of the budget line and indifference curve. If no tangency exists, then MRS_C and MRS_E cannot be set equal. They are brought as near to equality as possible by going to a corner solution, reducing consumption of some commodity to zero.

One important implication of this analysis is that, despite differences of taste, at an interior solution everyone places the same preferences for *marginal* changes in consumption of the two goods (that is, all individuals have the same Marginal Rate of Substitution in Consumption). In our prisoner-of-war example, French prisoners preferred coffee and English prisoners preferred tea. Nevertheless, once each group had adapted to the ruling prices, a French prisoner was no more willing than an English prisoner to give up a unit of tea for a unit of coffee. Thus, even though utility is "subjective," as a result of trade the "objective" price ratio between two goods in the market measures the *marginal* preference ratio for all the individuals who consume both goods.

In terms of the Marginal Value terminology, where the price of Y was set to 1 and interpreted as the price of a unit of all other goods, the Substitution Equivalence and Inequality take the forms

$$MV_x = P_x \text{ when } x > 0 \tag{4.7}$$

$$MV_x < P_x \text{ when } x = 0 \tag{4.7'}$$

Re-interpreting the Analytical Optimum Solution, the consumer increases his purchases of good X as long as its subjective Marginal Value to him (MV_x) is greater than its price (measured in terms of the price of "all other goods").[9]

If indifference curves are convex as in Figure 4.1, rather than concave as in Figure 4.2, then the absolute value of the slope of any indifference curve decreases as we move to the right along that indifference curve. That is, decreasing Marginal Rate of Substitution in Consumption (falling Marginal Value) is required to guarantee that the Substitution Equivalence Equation (4.6) really determines the consumer's optimum.[10]

---

[9]*Mathematical Footnote:* The Substitution Equivalence Equation (4.6) yields the same results as the Consumption Balance Equation (4.3). Equation (4.3) can be rewritten as $MU_x/MU_y = P_x/P_y$. Along an indifference curve,

$$0 = dU \equiv \partial U/\partial x \, dx + \partial U/\partial y \, dy$$

Then

$$-dy/dx \bigg|_U \equiv \frac{\partial U/\partial x}{\partial U/\partial y}$$

That is, MRS_C equals the ratio of the Marginal Utilities of X and Y, so that at the optimum $|dy/dx| = P_x/P_y$.

[10]*Mathematical Footnote:* We are dealing here with the *second-order* conditions for a maximum. The condition for indifference-curve convexity is $d(MRS_C)/dx < 0$.

4.2 COMPLEMENTS AND SUBSTITUTES

Certain commodities go well together and tend to be consumed jointly: bread and butter, shoes and socks, tennis rackets and tennis balls. The more you have of one, the more you desire the other. Such pairs of goods are called *complements*. Other commodity pairs go poorly together and tend to be used to the exclusion of one another; examples are butter and margarine, brown shoes and black shoes, tennis racquets and badminton racquets. Such pairs are called *substitutes* or *anticomplements*. Pairs of goods that are unrelated in people's preferences are said to be *independent* in consumption.

Consider two commodities that consumers regard as *perfect substitutes*. A person may be completely indifferent between 2 nickels and 1 dime, 200 nickels and 100 dimes, and so on. Then the preference map will have the appearance of Panel (a) of Figure 4.6: the indifference curves are parallel straight lines. For two goods that are close but not perfect substitutes, the indifference curves would be nearly linear, showing some convex curvature, as in Panel (b) of Figure 4.6. For close substitutes, such as Jonathan and Macintosh apples,

FIGURE 4.6 **Substitute Commodities** The indifference curves of Panel (a) are parallel straight lines, indicating that the two commodities (nickels and dimes) are perfect substitutes. If the price ratio in the market, represented by the slope of the budget line, differs from the slope of the indifference curves, the consumer will go to a corner solution. In Panel (b) the indifference curves have a slight degree of normal convex curvature, indicating that the two commodities (Macintosh apples and Jonathan apples) are good though not perfect substitutes. A relatively small change in the price ratio (from the slope of line SS' to the slope of line FF') causes a relatively large change in consumption (from S^* to F^*), but not a total switch from one good to the other.

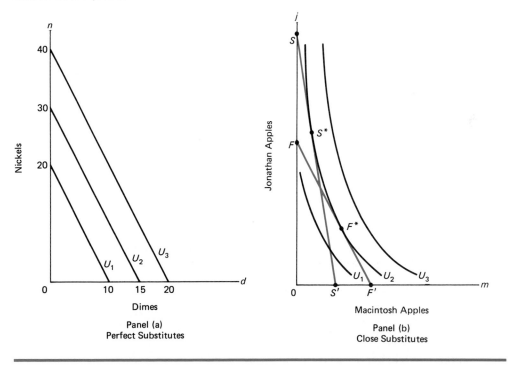

a small change in relative prices causes large changes in consumption. Consider a steep budget line such as SS'. This represents a high price of Macintoshes relative to the price of Jonathans. The consumer's best consumption bundle is S^*, where he purchases mostly inexpensive Jonathans. A slightly flatter budget line, FF' (representing a lower relative price of Macintosh apples) leads the consumer to a drastically different consumption bundle, F^*, where he consumes mostly Macintoshes. [*Query:* If the goods are perfect substitutes, will the individual almost always choose a *corner* solution—buying one good to the absolute exclusion of the other?]

The extreme opposite case is *perfect complementarity*. Here the consumer wants to buy goods in some fixed ratio (such as one left shoe for each right shoe). Extra right or left shoes are useless. Panel (a) of Figure 4.7 shows the right-angled indifference curves implied by perfect complementarity; the slope of the dashed line through the "elbows" represents the desired ratio of the two commodities. For two goods that are strong (but not perfect) complements, the indifference map would be as in Panel (b) of Figure 4.7. Other examples of highly complementary pairs are bacon and eggs, electricity and appliances, highways and automobiles. For complements, large changes in price ratios lead to only small shifts in relative quantities purchased. As can be seen in Panel (b) of Figure 4.7, along the steeper budget line SS' the tangency solution S^* is close to the optimum F^* along the flatter budget line FF'.[11]

Exercise 4.4

Suppose the Marginal Rate of Substitution in Consumption for wine and bread is $MRS_C = w/b$. For another commodity pair, roses and daisies, $MRS_C = (r/d)^2$. Which pair are better complements (poorer substitutes)?

Answer: Plotting a few points, we can determine easily that the roses versus daisies indifference curves are less tightly "curled" than the wine versus bread indifference curves. Thus, roses and daisies are closer substitutes.

EXAMPLE 4.2 **Rats**

A team of psychologists and economists investigated how rats responded to changes in "price ratios" of desired goods.[a]

In the first experiment, rats had unlimited amounts of water and rat chow, but could obtain two other commodities—root beer and Collins mix—only by pressing one of two

---

[11]*Mathematical Footnote:* The most commonly used measure of substitutability is called the *elasticity of substitution* (symbolized as σ). Along any indifference curve, the degree of curvature can be expressed as the rate of change in the absolute value of the slope of an indifference curve as y/x varies. Thus, curvature can be represented as $d(MRS_C)/d(y/x)$, remembering that $MRS_C \equiv -dy/dx|_U$. But as the degree of substitutability is inversely related to the curvature of the indifference curves (substitutability being greater the closer these curves approach linearity), we are interested in the reciprocal derivative $d(y/x)/d(MRS_C)$. The final step is, as in all elasticity measures, to deal with *proportionate* rather than absolute changes, in both numerator and denominator. The result becomes

$$\sigma \equiv \frac{d(y/x)}{(y/x)} \Big/ \frac{d(MRS_C)}{MRS_C}$$

Using the condition that at the consumer's optimum $MRS_C = P_x/P_y$, it can be verified that if σ is large, then a small change in P_x/P_y will be associated with a large change in y/x along a given indifference curve.

levers. "Income" was the total number of lever presses allowed a rat each day. The "price" of a good was the number of times a rat had to press a lever to receive a milliliter of fluid. The price ratio was varied by increasing one price and simultaneously reducing the other, so as to hold "real income" approximately constant. Root beer and Collins mix proved to be rather good substitutes for these experimental rats; the consumption ratio changed markedly, in the expected direction, when the price ratio changed even by a small amount.

In a second experiment, "free" food and water were no longer provided. Instead, to obtain them a rat had to pay a price by pressing the appropriate lever. When the price ratio was varied (again holding "real income" approximately constant), the rats did not greatly change their consumption of the goods. Food and water, it appears, were strong complements for these rats.

COMMENT   In the second experiment, drastic changes in the prices of food and water led to what the authors termed "disruptive" behavior. The rats sometimes failed to spend all their "income," and began to lose weight. This kind of irrational response to change may be found among humans as well, though not allowed for in standard economic theory.

[a]J.H. Kagel, H. Rachlin, L. Green, R.C. Battalio, R.L. Basmann, and W.R. Klemm, "Experimental Studies of Consumer Demand Behavior Using Laboratory Animals," *Economic Inquiry,* v. 13 (March 1975).

FIGURE 4.7   Complementary Commodities   The right-angled indifference curves of Panel (a) indicate that the two commodities (right shoes and left shoes) are perfect complements. A change in the price ratio has no effect on the quantity ratio chosen, which will always be 1:1 at the best attainable "elbow" point. In Panel (b) the indifference curves are nearly but not quite right-angled: the commodities (electricity and electrical appliances) are strong though not perfect complements. Here a relatively large change in the price ratio (from the slope of line *SS'* to the slope of line *FF'*) induces only a relatively small change in the quantity ratio (from *S** to *F**).

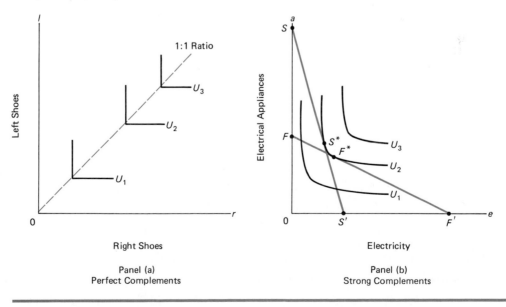

Panel (a)
Perfect Complements

Panel (b)
Strong Complements

4.3 THE CONSUMER'S RESPONSE TO CHANGING OPPORTUNITIES

If *preferences* do not change, the optimum of the consumer can vary only in response to changes in *opportunities*. The consumer's market opportunities, we have seen, depend on two elements: income and commodity prices. This section examines the predictions of consumer theory about changes in consumption following changes in income and prices.

Income Expansion Path and Engel Curve

Suppose, to begin with, that income I increases while all prices remain unchanged. Then, in a simplified world of only two commodities X and $Y,$ we can picture the situation as in Figure 4.8. The original optimum is at point $Q,$ where the budget line KL is tangent to the indifference curve $U_0.$ (This position corresponds to point $C*$ in Figure 4.1.) Now let income rise from I to $I'.$ This causes the budget line to shift outward from KL to $K'L'.$ The slope of the budget line depends only upon the price ratio $P_x/P_y,$ so the shift does not change the *slope* of the budget line. The new optimum position is shown as point $R,$ where the budget line $K'L'$ is tangent to the higher indifference curve $U_1.$

FIGURE 4.8 Derivation of the Income Expansion Path   As income increases from I to I' to $I'',$ with prices P_x and P_y held constant, the budget line shifts outward from KL to $K'L'$ to $K''L''.$ The tangency defining the consumer optimum correspondingly shifts from Q to R to $S.$ The Income Expansion Path (IEP) shows all the optimum consumption bundles for the consumer as I varies, with prices remaining the same. For a smaller price ratio P_x/P_y (with corresponding budget lines which are flatter) the IEP lies further down and to the right, as indicated by the dashed IEP$'$ curve.

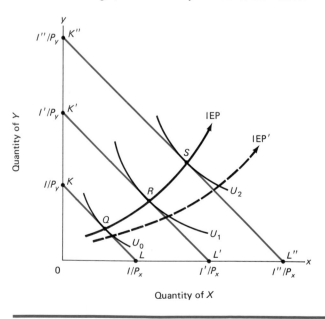

A further increase in income from I' to I'' causes the budget line to shift further outward to $K''L''$. Here the optimum is the tangency position S on indifference curve U_2.

More generally, if income varies while prices and tastes remain unchanged, an entire curve—the Income Expansion Path (IEP)—is traced out that connects all the different optimum positions like Q, R, and S in Figure 4.8. The Income Expansion Path indicates the response of the rational consumer to changes in income alone with prices held constant.

Since the Income Expansion Path curve reflects the effect of changing income given some particular price ratio P_x/P_y, it follows that each different price ratio generates a different IEP curve. In particular, Figure 4.8 shows how a smaller ratio P_x/P_y (implying flatter budget lines) is associated with an IEP that lies below the original IEP. (*Query:* Can two IEP curves drawn for the same individual ever cross?)

Exercise 4.5

Suppose an individual's Marginal Rate of Substitution in Consumption is given by the equation $MRS_c = y/x$. Let the market prices be $P_x = 5$ and $P_y = 1$. (a) What is the equation of the IEP and what does it look like? (b) How would the IEP change if P_x fell to $P_x = 4$?

Answer: (a) The Substitution Equivalence Equation (4.6) tells us that $MRS_c = y/x = P_x/P_y = 5/1 = 5$. So the equation for the Income Expansion Path is $y = 5x$. It is a ray out of the origin with slope 5. (b) If P_x fell to $P_x = 4$, the equation of the new IEP is $y = 4x$ (a flatter ray out of the origin, with slope 4).

What shapes are possible for the Income Expansion Path? Consider the three panels of Figure 4.9 (p. 96). In all three cases the original optimum is at point Q, where indifference curve U_0 is tangent to budget line KL. Now let income increase, so that the budget line shifts to $K'L'$. In Panel (a) the new tangency point, R, lies above and to the right of Q, so the IEP has positive slope. This means that the consumer purchases more of both X and Y following a rise in income; in this case X and Y are called *normal* goods.

In Panel (b) the new tangency R lies above and to the left of Q. The consumer buys more Y but less X; the slope of the IEP is negative. A commodity like X whose consumption falls when income rises is called an *inferior* good.

Economists have no standard term for the other commodity Y in this case. The expression "superior good" refers to any good that is not inferior, that is, whose consumption rises with income. Hence Y would be called superior in the situation of either Panel (a) or Panel (b). Let us adopt the term *ultra-superior* for the good that is a "partner" of an inferior good. Then Y is ultra-superior in Panel (b). Since less of an inferior good is purchased when income increases, it follows that more than 100 percent of the increase in income is devoted to additional purchases of the associated ultra-superior good.

Finally, Panel (c) shows the opposite situation, where Y is inferior and X is ultra-superior. The IEP has a negative slope, but in contrast to Panel (b) the consumption optimum associated with the higher income lies below and to the right of the original point.

In all three cases, the IEP has been drawn with an arrowhead pointing in the direction of rising utility (upward on the invisible utility hill). The arrow is convenient for distinguishing between the X-inferior [Panel (b)] case and the Y-inferior [Panel (c)] case.

CONCLUSION: A positively sloped Income Expansion Path, for two goods X and Y, indicates that consumption of both goods rises as income grows. Then X and Y are both normal superior goods. If the IEP has a negative slope, one of the goods must be inferior. The other good must

FIGURE 4.9   Income Expansion Paths: Three Cases   In all three diagrams the outward shift of the budget line (from *KL* to *K′L′*) represents an increase in income *I*, with prices held constant. In Panel (a) the Income Expansion Path (IEP) points up and to the right. Here both *X* and *Y* are normal superior goods. In Panel (b) the IEP points up and to the left; here *X* is an inferior good, and *Y* is an ultra-superior good. Panel (c) is the opposite case, where the IEP points down and to the right; here *Y* is inferior, and *X* is ultra-superior.

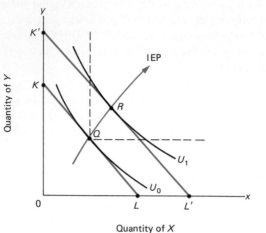

Panel (a)
X and *Y* normal

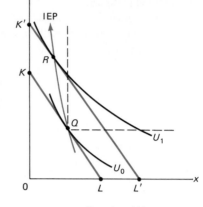

Panel (b)
X inferior, *Y* ultra-superior

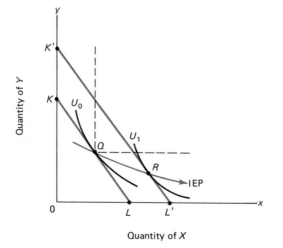

Panel (c)
Y inferior, *X* ultra-superior

of course be superior, but more specifically may be called ultra-superior because it accounts for more than 100 percent of the increment of income.

EXAMPLE 4.3 Luxuries Versus Necessities in a P.O.W. Camp

Goods that are predominantly purchased by wealthy people are commonly called luxuries. Correspondingly, goods that account for a large portion of the consumption budget of poor people are sometimes termed *necessities*. Standard items of food like bread are generally considered necessities. For, while richer people can afford to and generally do buy more loaves of bread per person than poorer people (i.e., bread is not an inferior good), the *proportion* of the budget spent on bread falls as income rises.

In the prisoner-of-war economy mentioned in Example 4.1, R.A. Radford[a] also made interesting observations about necessities and luxuries. Toward the end of the war, prisoners suffered severe privation as the Germany economy deteriorated. In August 1944 rations, primarily for food and cigarettes, were cut in half. Unexpectedly, cigarettes proved to be more of a "necessity" (by the standard definition just presented) than food. Despite the presence of many nonsmokers, in the market as a whole there was a net attempt to trade food for cigarettes. As a result, the price of food (in terms of cigarettes) decreased.

COMMENT Figure 4.10 (p. 98) shows the implied shape of indifference curves between cigarettes C and food F at the higher income level (point $Q°$) and the lower income level (point Q'). The Marginal Rate of Substitution in Consumption, $MRS_c \equiv -\Delta c/\Delta f$ is less (the indifference curve is flatter) at the lower real-income point.

[a]R.A. Radford, "The Economic Organization of a P.O.W. Camp," *Economica*, v. 12 (1945).

The Income Expansion Path shows the effect of income on consumption *baskets*. We can also use the Income Expansion Path to determine the effect of a change in income on the consumption of any particular good included in a basket. For any single good such as X, the relation between income and consumption is conveniently summarized by the *Engel Curve*.[12] A portion of a typical Engel Curve is shown in Figure 4.11 (p. 99). In the case illustrated, the quantity of X consumed rises as income rises; that is, X is a superior good.

In practice we are not so interested in specific single commodities but rather in broader categories like food, clothing, vacation travel, and so forth. There is, however, no natural quantity unit for a broad commodity grouping like food or clothing. To handle this, we can

[12]Ernst Engel (1821–96), German statistician.

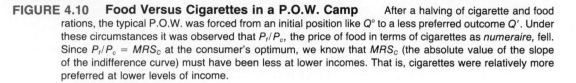

FIGURE 4.10   Food Versus Cigarettes in a P.O.W. Camp   After a halving of cigarette and food rations, the typical P.O.W. was forced from an initial position like $Q°$ to a less preferred outcome Q'. Under these circumstances it was observed that P_f/P_c, the price of food in terms of cigarettes as *numeraire,* fell. Since $P_f/P_c = MRS_c$ at the consumer's optimum, we know that MRS_c (the absolute value of the slope of the indifference curve) must have been less at lower incomes. That is, cigarettes were relatively more preferred at lower levels of income.

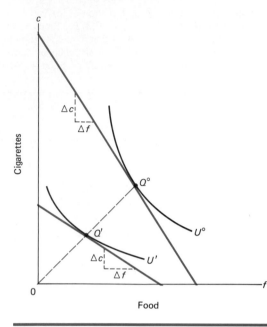

replace the quantity of X on the vertical axis of the Engel Curve diagram of Figure 4.11 with consumer *expenditure* on X. If X is a single good, expenditure on it is price times quantity purchased, or $P_x x$. And if X represents a group of consumption goods $X_1, \ldots, X_G$, expenditure is $P_1 x_1 + P_2 x_2 + \ldots + P_G x_G$. The income-consumption relation in terms of expenditures is called the *Engel Expenditure Curve.* Both the simple Engel Curve and the Engel Expenditure Curve represent the same data as the Income Expansion Paths of Figures 4.8 and 4.9, but translated onto different axes. For the simple Engel Curve, the *consumption* of a good is plotted as a function of income; for the Engel Expenditure Curve, *expenditure* on a good or a set of goods is plotted as a function of income.

DEFINITIONS: The *Engel Curve* relates consumption of a good to income. The *Engel Expenditure Curve* relates expenditure on a good (that is, price times quantity) to income.

The Engel Expenditure Curve has the advantage over the simple Engel Curve of directly displaying the difference between a normal superior good and an ultra-superior good. The Engel Expenditure Curves in the three panels of Figure 4.12 (p. 100) correspond to the three cases of Figure 4.9. To interpret Figure 4.12, first note the dashed 45° line from the origin. An Engel Expenditure Curve that lies along this 45° line would imply that the consumer's expenditure on the commodity or grouping equals his income, or, in other words, that the consumer spends his entire income on the purchase of the commodity or grouping

FIGURE 4.11 **Engel Curve**   For any good *X*, the Engel Curve shows the quantity purchased as a function of income. For a superior good, the Engel Curve has positive slope as shown here.

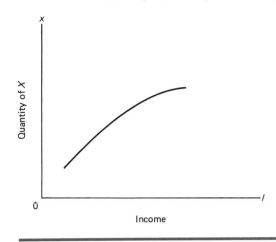

depicted on the vertical axis. Hence the 45° line constitutes an upper limit for the Engel Expenditure Curve.

Panel (a) shows that expenditures on *X* rise as income increases. But the curve is not as steep as the 45° line. This means that expenditures on *X* rise by *less* than the rise in income; that is, some of the increase of income is spent on a good or goods other than *X*. Hence this corresponds to the "normal" case in Panel (a) of Figure 4.9.

Jumping to Panel (c) of Figure 4.12, in the range between *I′* and *I″* the Engel Expenditure Curve rises more sharply than the 45° line. It follows that in this range a dollar increase in income causes the consumer to increase his spending on *X* by more than one dollar. This means that *X* is ultra-superior, as in Panel (c) of Figure 4.9. Finally, in the middle Panel (b) of Figure 4.12, expenditures on *X* decline as income rises. Since the price of *X* is constant, the consumer spends less on *X* as his income increases; hence *X* is inferior, as in Panel (b) of Figure 4.9.

EXAMPLE 4.4   **Engel Expenditure Curves**

David E.A. Giles and Peter Hampton[a] determined how expenditures on different types of goods changed as income changed. Each number in the table shows the percentage change in expenditure on the good or service for a 1 percent change in income. The data are based on a sample of 3,487 households in New Zealand surveyed in the period 1981–82.

Estimated Effect of Income on Expenditures

Category	Lowest Income Group	Highest Income Group
Food	0.63	0.84
Housing	1.22	1.80
Household operation	0.66	0.85

FIGURE 4.12 **Engel Expenditure Curves** An Engel Expenditure Curve shows $P_x x$—expenditures on good X as a function of income I with price P_x held constant. If the curve touched the 45° line, at that point *all* of income would be spent on X. In Panel (a), $P_x x$ rises with income but diverges from the 45° line, indicating that as income rises more is spent on other goods as well. In Panel (b) less is spent on X as income rises, so X must be inferior. In Panel (c), as income rises the curve approaches the 45° line, which means that less is spent on other goods, so these other goods are (in aggregate) inferior.

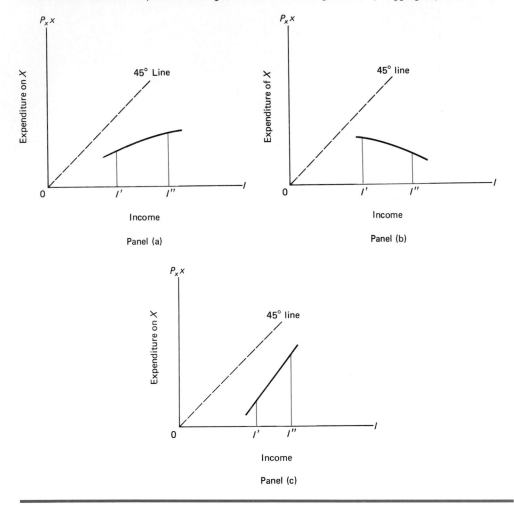

Category	Lowest Income Group	Highest Income Group
Clothing	1.29	0.98
Transportation	1.50	0.90
Tobacco and alcohol	2.00	0.85
Other supplies	0.92	0.89
Other services	0.94	0.85

The Engel curve refers to the change in a consumer's behavior as his income changes. If we look at different people at the same time, we may capture, however, not the effects of changes in income, but differences in the tastes of different persons. For example, on average rich people have more years of education than poor people. It is therefore difficult to say whether the consumption patterns of the rich differ from those of the poor because of differences in income, or differences in tastes caused by education. This problem of interpretation is common in cross-sectional studies.

COMMENT   It is somewhat surprising that the demands for food and housing are more sensitive to income for the rich than for the poor. Part of the reason is a difference in the quality of the goods consumed; the rich may not eat more, but they may substitute expensive ready-made foods for homemade meals. The data also suggest that food (which shows relatively little sensitivity to income) is a necessity, and that housing is a luxury.

[a]David E.A. Giles and Peter Hampton, "An Engel Curve Analysis of Household Expenditures in New Zealand." *Economic Record*, v. 61 (March 1985). For a more complete survey see H. Houthakker, "An International Comparison of Household Expenditure Patterns, Commemorating the Centenary of Engel's Law," *Econometrica*, v. 25 (October 1957).

Price Expansion Path and Demand Curve

The previous section analyzed changes in income. This section discusses the effects of changes in prices. It is convenient to let Y be the *numeraire* commodity (all other goods) whose price is held constant at $P_y = 1$. Thus only the price of X varies. Here again the change in price affects the market opportunity set, or more specifically the budget line. But whereas a rise in income moves the budget line outward parallel to itself, a change in price tilts the budget line.

In Figure 4.13 (p. 102), the optimum is initially at Q where the budget line KL is tangent to indifference curve U_0. Now let the price of X fall. The intercept of the budget line with the vertical Y-axis is unchanged at I/P_y. But the intercept of the budget line with the horizontal X-axis is at I/P_x, so the fall in P_x causes the budget line to become flatter, with a new position like KL'. This tilting reflects a decline in the price of good X which allows the consumer to buy more of that good. The consumer's new optimum is at point R where the new budget line KL' is tangent to a higher indifference curve, U_1. A further decline in P_x leads to further outward tilting of the budget line, to the position KL''; here the optimum is at S on the still higher indifference curve U_2.

FIGURE 4.13 **Derivation of the Price Expansion Path**   A fall in the price of good X (with income I and the price of the other good held constant) tilts the budget line outward (from KL to KL' to KL''). The optimal consumption bundle shifts from Q to R to S. The Price Expansion Path (PEP) connects all such optimum positions; the arrowhead on the PEP curve indicates the direction of utility improvement.

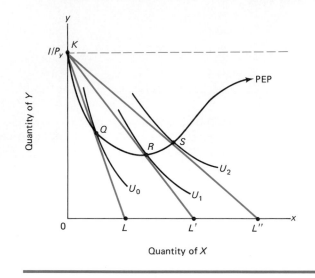

We can draw a curve that connects all the optimum positions like Q, R, and S that correspond to different values of P_x. This curve is the Price Expansion Path (PEP), which indicates the response of a rational consumer to changes in P_x alone, with income and the prices of all other goods held fixed.

Just as there is a different Income Expansion Path for each different price, there is a different PEP for each different income. Specifically, if goods X and Y are normal goods, an increase in income tends to shift the PEP upward and to the right. [Check this to verify your understanding of the PEP.]

Exercise 4.7 _____

Let Smith have $MRS_C = y$, income $I = 120$, and assume that $P_y = 1$. (a) What is the equation for the Price Expansion Path and what is its shape? (b) How would it change if income increased to $I = 150$?

Answer: (a) The Substitution Equivalence Equation (4.6) here is $y = P_x/P_y$. Since $P_y = 1$, this simplifies to $y = P_x$. The budget line is $P_x x + P_y y = I$ or numerically $P_x x + y = 120$. Thus we have two simultaneous equations: (1) $P_x = y$ and (2) $P_x x + y = 120$. Substitute (1) in (2) to obtain the equation of the Price Expansion Path as $yx + y = 120$, or, in more convenient form, $y(x + 1) = 120$. This PEP has a y-intercept of 120. Like the PEP of Figure 4.13, it slopes down from the y-intercept; unlike that curve, it never curls up again but approaches (without ever intersecting) the horizontal axis. (b) If income is $I = 150$, the equation of the PEP is $y(x + 1) = 150$. The intercept on the y-axis is higher and the curve shifts generally upward and to the right.

The Price Expansion Path has the following additional geometrical characteristics:

1. As the price of good X, say wine, falls, the consumer obtains greater utility. Thus, the arrowhead shows the direction of rising utility along the PEP in Figure 4.13. The

FIGURE 4.14 **Price Expansion Path: Giffen Case**   The Price Expansion Path (PEP) can have a segment where it curls back up and to the left (as in the circled region): less of *X* is purchased as its price declines. In this range *X* would be called a "Giffen good."

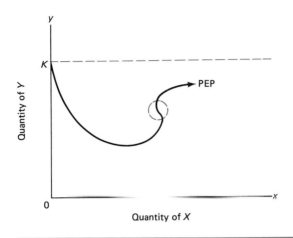

level of satisfaction increases since, with income held constant, a fall in the price of wine allows the consumer (in the worst case) to purchase the same amount of other goods as before, but to enjoy more wine.

2. When the PEP curve has negative slope, as in the range between *Q* and *R* along the curve in Figure 4.13, a decrease in the price of wine causes the consumer to choose more wine and less *Y*. Where the PEP has a positive slope, as in the range between *R* and *S* in the diagram, a decrease in the price of wine causes the consumer to purchase more of both goods.

3. If there is a "choke price" for wine such that the consumer purchases no wine at all, then at that price (or any higher price) the optimum of the consumer is a *corner solution* on the *Y*-axis, as in Figure 4.3. If this condition holds, the PEP has a terminating point on the *Y*-axis (point *K* in Figure 4.13). But no matter how low the price of wine falls (so long as it does not become negative), the budget line must lie below the dashed horizontal line at height *K* in the diagram, and so the PEP must also lie everywhere below this line.

4. The PEP may have a section that curls upward and to the left, as in the circled region in Figure 4.14. In this region, a fall in the price of wine causes the consumer to purchase less wine! When this condition applies, the commodity is called a "Giffen good"[13] for this consumer. But the Giffen property can only hold over a limited range. With negatively sloped indifference curves and positive preference directions, the PEP cannot move up and to the left very long and still enter regions of higher utility. (Giffen goods are discussed further in Chapter 5.)

Finally, we can replot the data summarized by the PEP to show the relation between the quantity of wine consumed and the price of wine, as in curve *dd* in Panel (a) of Figure 4.15. This curve represents, of course, the individual's demand for wine.

---

[13]Sir Robert Giffen, British statistician and economist (1837–1910).

Exercise 4.7 derived the Price Expansion Path $y(x + 1) = 120$ for an individual with $MRS_C = y$, income $I = 120$, and assuming that $P_y = 1$. What is the individual's demand curve associated with this PEP?

Answer: The Substitution Equivalence Equation here, we saw in Exercise 4.7, is $y = P_x$. The demand curve shows X as a function of P_x, so that we need to rewrite the equation for the PEP in terms of X and P_x. Substituting $y = P_x$ in $y(x + 1) = 120$ yields $P_x(x + 1) = 120$, or $x = 120/P_x - 1$. This is the equation for the demand curve. [*Query:* What happens at $P_x = 120$, or any higher price? *Hint:* $P_x = 120$ is the "choke price" for good X.]

If there is a range in which the Price Expansion Path curls up and to the left (the circled region in Figure 4.14), then there will be a corresponding positively sloped range along the demand curve (the circled region in Panel (b) of Figure 4.15). In this range the demand curve has the "Giffen property" that at lower prices a smaller quantity is demanded. The Law of Demand states that demand curves always (or almost always) have negative slope (i.e., that the Giffen case rarely if ever occurs). This principle, like convexity of indifference curves, does not follow from the pure logic of choice. Its justification is empirical observation of the world.

EXAMPLE 4.5 The Law of Demand: Animals and Humans

In 1978 the psychologist S.E.G. Lea[a] reviewed a wide variety of demand studies including animal experiments, retailing experiments, and econometric investigations. The following summary shows the number of instances that either support or contradict the Law of Demand, or represent mixed or uncertain results.

Studies of the Law of Demand

	Law of Demand Supported	Law of Demand Contradicted	Mixed or Uncertain
Animal experiments* (18)	15	1	2
Retailing experiments**(9)	7	1	1
Selection of econometric studies***(25)	25	0	0

*Estimated visually from Lea, Figure 1 (p. 447).

**Estimated visually from Lea, Figure 2 (p. 448).

***Estimated visually from Lea, Figure 3 (p. 449).

[a]S.E.G. Lea, "The Psychology and Economics of Demand," *Psychological Bulletin,* v. 85 (1978).

Common sense tells us that downward sloping demand curves describe the great majority of ordinary consumption decisions. But what about exceptional situations, like the demand for narcotics by addicts or the demand for liquor by alcoholics? Even then, income is limited. Suppose an addict were to spend all of his income on drugs, regardless of price. Then he *must* buy less as price rises. It is true that to support his habit as price goes up, the addict may try to increase his income by stealing, begging, or working. But the more income needed, the harder the effort involved, and the Law of Demand still tends to hold. So we

FIGURE 4.15 **Demand Curves: The Law of Demand Versus the Giffen Case**   Panel (a) pictures a negatively sloped individual demand curve, satisfying the Law of Demand: as the price falls, more of *X* is purchased. In Panel (b) the demand curve has the exceptional "Giffen" property. In the small circled region (corresponding to the circled region in Figure 4.14) more of *X* is purchased as P_x rises. The Giffen property can hold, if at all, only over a limited range of prices.

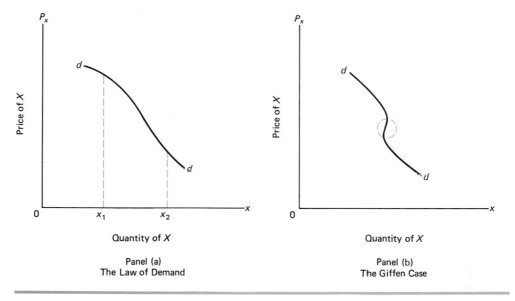

Panel (a)
The Law of Demand

Panel (b)
The Giffen Case

are not surprised to read, for example, that when the effective street price of liquor in the United States rose during Prohibition, there was a decline in liquor consumption.

EXAMPLE 4.6   **Shocking Alcoholics**

As a portion of an experiment conducted by M.B. Sobell and L.C. Sobell,[a] forty alcoholics who had admitted themselves to Patton State Hospital in California were randomly assigned to an experimental or a control group. The twenty patients assigned to the experimental group attended special sessions in which liquor was freely available, except that "inappropriate" drinking behavior was punished by an electric shock. Shocks were administered if the patient ordered a drink straight, took too large a sip, ordered drinks less than 20 minutes apart, or ordered more than three drinks in a session. During three of the thirteen sessions, however, no shocks were administered. The overall results were as follows:

Shocks and Behavior

Sessions	Average Inappropriate Behaviors*
With shocks	2.2
Without shocks	18.7

*Calculated from Sobell and Sobell, p. 39.

Note that this was a case without a fixed constraint on purchasing power. A patient could always "earn" the right to take another drink by undergoing an electric shock. Nevertheless, drinking declined as its price increased.

COMMENT   An interesting point regarding the nature and stability of "tastes" (as discussed in Chapter 3) was observed in follow-up studies. Individuals in the experimental group seemed more successful in remaining sober afterward than did individuals in the control group. This evidence suggests that life experiences can indeed change attitudes. While this is not an astonishing conclusion, it is at odds with the standard economic assumption of unchanging preferences. A possible explanation is the following. It seems likely that admission to the hospital, which was voluntary, indicated a willingness on the part of these alcoholics to engage in exploratory behavior (like the children of Example 3.1), suggesting that they did not feel confident about their true preferences for being alcoholics. The shock treatment seemed to induce more effective exploration of nonalcoholic lifestyles.

[a]Mark B. Sobell and Linda C. Sobell, *Individualized Behavior Therapy for Alcoholics: Rationale, Procedures, Preliminary Results, and Appendix,* California Mental Health Research Monograph No. 13 (1972).

Figure 4.16 shows the effect of a change in income on the demand curve. If X is normal or ultra-superior, a rise in income causes the demand curve to shift up and to the right. If X is an inferior good (economy cars, for example) then a rise in income causes the demand curve to shift down and to the left.

FIGURE 4.16   The Demand Curve: Effect of Income Changes   If X is a superior good (whether normal or ultra-superior), a rise in income implies larger purchases of X at a given price P_x—the demand curve shifts to the right (from dd to $d'd'$). But if X is an inferior good, as income increases *less* is purchased at a given price; the demand curve shifts to the left (from dd to $d''d''$).

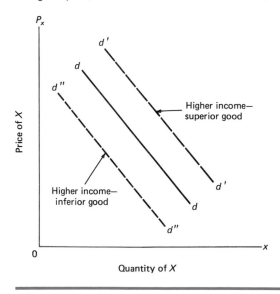

Exercise 4.9

For the individual of Exercise 4.8, how would the demand curve shift if income rose from $I = 120$ to $I = 150$? Is X a superior good?

Answer: With $I = 120$ the demand equation was $P_x(x + 1) = 120$, or equivalently $x = 120/P_x - 1$. With $I = 150$, the same technique yields $x = 150/P_x - 1$. The demand curve for X has shifted to the right. Thus, commodity X must be a superior good.

4.4 INCOME AND SUBSTITUTION EFFECTS OF A PRICE CHANGE

Economists have found it useful to distinguish two effects of a price change on a consumer's demand.

1. A fall in price increases the consumer's *real* income. Since he can purchase the same bundle of goods as before with less outlay, he is effectively richer and will therefore change his consumption choices. This is called the *income* effect.
2. At a lower price of good X, the consumer would buy more even at the same level of real income. This is called the pure *substitution effect* of the price change.

Figure 4.17 (p. 108) pictures what is known as the Hicks[14] decomposition of the income and substitution effects. (Figure 4.17 shows the effect of a fall in the price of X, but a similar analysis applies for an increase in P_x.)

Suppose a consumer is at an initial optimum point Q on indifference curve U_0. When the price of good X falls, the new optimum is at S on indifference curve U_1. Since he is on a higher indifference curve than before, the price reduction has effectively raised his real income. Now, keeping the lower price P_x, imagine taking away just enough income to leave the consumer on his old indifference curve U_0. This leads to the dashed budget line MN parallel to KL' but just touching indifference U_0, at point R. The movement from point Q to point R eliminates the change in real income and therefore isolates the *pure substitution effect* of the price change. In terms of the quantity of X, the substitution effect is the distance $x_R - x_Q$.

The *income effect* of the price change is the remainder, the movement from R to S. In terms of quantities of X, the income effect is $x_S - x_R$. Thus the overall change from Q to S has been decomposed into two movements: from Q to R (the substitution effect) and then from R to S (the income effect).

A key point is that the substitution effect is always negative. Quantity and price always change in opposite directions. This must be the case since the pure substitution effect involves movement along an indifference curve, and indifference curves have negative slopes.

The income effect is ambiguous. A fall in the price of beer always raises real income; higher income leads to greater consumption of beer if beer is a superior good, as pictured for X in Figure 4.17. If beer had been inferior, the new optimum S would lie above but to the left of R instead of to the right (for example, people may substitute relatively expensive wine for some beer if a deep cut in the price of beer makes them feel richer). An abnormal

---

[14]Sir John R. Hicks, contemporary British economist.

FIGURE 4.17 **Income and Substitution Effects: Hicks Decomposition** A fall in price P_x, with income and P_y held constant, shifts the budget line from KL to KL' so that the consumptive optimum changes from Q to S. Since S lies on a higher indifference curve, there has been an increase in real income. The "income effect" of the price change can be separated from the pure "substitution effect" by constructing an artificial budget line MN that is parallel to KL' and tangent to the original indifference curve U_0. At the tangency point, R, utility is the same as at Q. The income effect of the price change is therefore $x_S - x_R$; the pure substitution effect of the price change is $x_R - x_Q$.

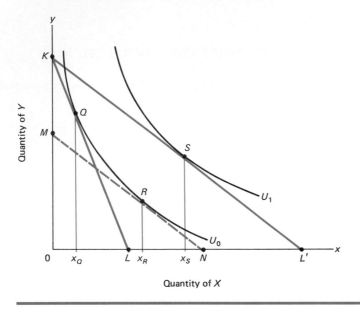

Quantity of X

(negative) income effect might even outweigh the normal substitution effect. If this occurs a fall in price would lead to a net fall in quantity purchased; this is the "Giffen case" to be discussed further in Chapter 5.

4.5 FROM INDIVIDUAL DEMAND TO MARKET DEMAND

The *market demand curve* shows the aggregate quantity demanded by all consumers together, as a function of the price. Geometrically, the market demand curve is obtained by summing the individual demand curves horizontally, as illustrated in Figure 4.18.

Suppose the market has only two consumers, with demand curves d_1 and d_2. At the price P_x the first consumer will buy x_1 units and the second x_2 units. The quantity demanded in the market is thus $x_1 + x_2$, which corresponds to point A on the market demand curve. Repeating this process for every possible price traces the entire market demand curve D. More generally, for any number of consumers:

$$X = \sum_{i=1}^{N} x_i \tag{4.8}$$

FIGURE 4.18   Individual and Aggregate Demand   Here d_1 and d_2 are the demand curves for two individuals. If these are the only two potential purchasers of the good, the overall market demand curve D is the horizontal sum of d_1 and d_2.

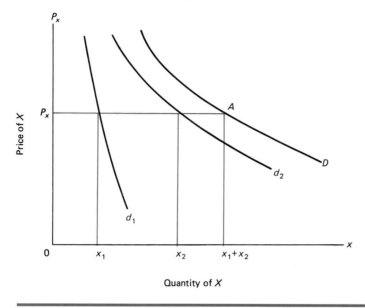

Quantity of X

The market demand X is the sum of the demands of all N individuals in the market, where i indexes the individuals from 1 to N. (The aggregate market quantity here is symbolized by an uppercase letter—a convention we usually follow throughout the text.)

Note that the market demand curve in Figure 4.18 has a much flatter slope than the individual demand curves. This tells us that, if price falls, the increase in the market quantity will ordinarily be much greater than the increase in quantity consumed by any single individual. However, the *percent* increase in X along the aggregate demand curve D need not be any greater than the *percent* increase along the individual demand curves. This point will be considered further when we take up the concept of elasticity in the next chapter.

An implicit assumption of the foregoing analysis is that all individuals pay the same market price P_x. Where this assumption is not appropriate, a market demand curve in the ordinary sense cannot be constructed.

CONCLUSION: The market demand curve is the *horizontal* sum of the individual demand curves.

Exercise 4.10 _____

Let Adam have the demand curve $x_a = 10 - 2P_x$ for commodity X, and let Betty have the demand curve $x_b = 10 - 3P_x$. If these are the only two consumers in the market, what is the market demand curve? Compare the individual demand slopes and the market demand slope.

Answer: Remember that we must sum the quantities demanded (not the prices). So the market demand equation is $X = x_a + x_b = 20 - 5P_x$. Price is on the vertical axis, so that the slopes are given by $-\Delta P_x / \Delta x$. The slope of Adam's demand curve is $-1/2$, the slope of Betty's demand curve is $-1/3$, while the slope of the market demand curve is $-1/5$. Thus, as in the diagram of Figure 4.18, the market demand curve is notably flatter than any of the individual demand curves. [This market demand equation is invalid if $P_x \geq 10/3$. Why? (*Hint:* What is the choke price for each individual?)]

4.6 AN APPLICATION: SUBSIDY VERSUS VOUCHER

Governments often try to encourage people to consume more of a particular good, for example, education. One method is to subsidize producers or consumers of education. (Free public education is of course an extreme kind of subsidy.) Voucher schemes represent a somewhat different technique.

In Figure 4.19, E represents education and Y "all other goods." Panel (a) shows the effect of a *subsidy*. The original (unsubsidized) tangency optimum is at Q on indifference curve U_0. A subsidy acts like a reduction in price; it rotates the budget line from KL outward to KL'. The new optimum is at R, on indifference curve U_1. Apart from the unlikely possibility that education is a Giffen good in this range, the subsidy increases the consumer's purchases of education. In the diagram, the increase is the distance $e_1 - e_0$ on the horizontal axis.

FIGURE 4.19 **Subsidy Versus Voucher** In Panel (a) a subsidy to consumption of education reduces its price; the budget line shifts from KL to KL'. At the new consumptive optimum, R, the quantity of education purchased will be greater (unless it is a Giffen good in this range, which is highly unlikely). In Panel (b), the "voucher" amount KK' is a gift of income that is spendable only on education. The budget line shifts to the right, from KL to $K'L'$, except that the consumer cannot consume in the range between K' and K'' (since the full amount of the voucher would not then be spent on education). The new optimum at S will involve increased purchases of education, so long as it is not an inferior good.

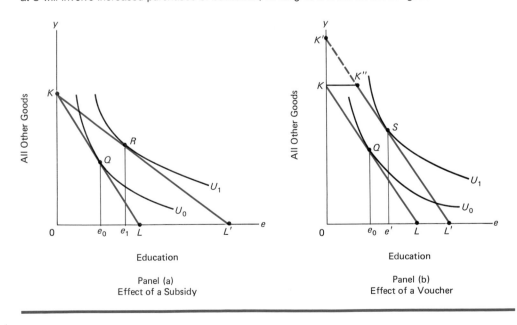

Panel (a)
Effect of a Subsidy

Panel (b)
Effect of a Voucher

Panel (b) of Figure 4.19 shows the effect of a *voucher*. The initial optimum Q on indifference curve U_0 is the same as before. The "voucher" is a gift of income spendable only on education. The distance KK' on the vertical axis represents the amount of the gift, so that the consumer's budget line shifts outward from KL to $K'L'$. But since the gift can only be spent on education, the consumer cannot consume on the dashed segment $K'K''$. Therefore his effective new budget line is the kinked line $KK''L'$. In Panel (b) of Figure 4.19 the new optimum is at S, on indifference curve U_1. The voucher will increase purchases of education ($e' > e_0$) whenever education is a superior good. (But it may decrease purchases of education if education is inferior.)

So far there appears to be little difference between a subsidy and voucher. The subsidy works through a price change, the voucher through an income change. But the voucher does have a certain special power for a consumer who would otherwise take very little or no education. Consider Figure 4.20. Here the individual is initially at a corner solution. The optimum is at point K on indifference curve U_0, where he or she consumes no education. Even a fairly substantial subsidy, which rotates the budget line outward, might have little or no effect upon his or her consumption of education. But the voucher displaces the entire budget line outward to $K'L'$ (of which only the solid range $K''L'$ is effective). The new optimum is at K'' (not at K' which is outside the opportunity set). At K'' the individual spends the entire voucher amount on purchases of education, and spends the same amount on other goods as before. We see that a voucher for a good like education almost always increases its consumption by a person who had previously not consumed it at all, or who consumed an amount less than the voucher amount. The only exception would be if education

FIGURE 4.20   **Corner Solution and Voucher**   The initial consumptive optimum is the corner solution at K; no education is purchased. A voucher gift of income in the amount KK' leads to a new consumptive optimum at K''. (The consumer would still prefer a corner solution at point K', but this is unattainable.) The voucher leads to increased consumption of education, provided only that education is a good rather than a bad for this individual.

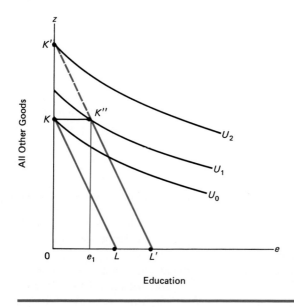

is a bad rather than a good for the individual. (If so, a voucher spendable only on education would simply remain unused.)

However, at least two flaws exist in this analysis. First, the market price of education was assumed to remain unchanged throughout. This assumption would be reasonable if a single person received a subsidy or voucher; then increased consumption would have a negligible effect on market price. But if, as is normally the case, the benefit is granted to a large class of consumers, the increase in demand due to a subsidy or voucher would tend to increase the market price of education, which we have not allowed for. Second, the analysis failed to indicate the source of funds needed to finance the subsidy or voucher. Collection of these funds via taxes would reduce the spendable income of some or all consumers. So our discussion does not tell the whole story.

SUMMARY

The optimum of the consumer involves the interaction of his or her *preferences* (indifference curves) with *market opportunities* (budget line). The optimum position is where the budget line bounding the opportunity set touches the highest attainable indifference curve. There are two types of optimum positions: (1) for an interior solution, the optimum occurs at a tangency point and (2) if no interior tangency exists, the highest indifference curve attainable is found at zero quantity for some commodities (corner solution). In the real world both situations are observed; we consume mixtures of commodities, but do not purchase positive amounts of every possible good. Convex indifference curves are consistent with both corner and interior solutions.

Analytically, the budget equation for an individual whose income is I, with goods X and Y available at prices P_x and P_y, is

$$P_x x + P_y y = I$$

For cardinal utility the optimum condition at an interior solution is expressed by the following Consumption Balance Equation:

$$\frac{MU_x}{P_x} = \frac{MU_y}{P_y}$$

That is, Marginal Utility per dollar (the utility of the last dollar) spent on either commodity is the same. If good Y is "all other goods," then the condition states that at the optimum the consumer will purchase good X up to the point where its Marginal Value equals its price. The Consumption Balance Equation implies the Substitution Equivalence Equation.

$$MRS_C = MRS_E$$

This form is more general, because it does not require that utility be cardinally measurable. MRS_C corresponds to the slope of the indifference curve, and MRS_E to the slope of the budget line. The equality of the two, together with the equation for the budget line, determine the optimum (interior solution) of the consumer.

Goods which are strong complements, like bread and butter, tend to be consumed together. Consequently, a large change in the price ratio between them will cause only a small change in the ratio in which they are consumed. Close substitutes, like Hondas and Toyotas, tend to be consumed to the exclusion of one another. Hence, even a small price shift may lead to a big change in the ratio in which they are purchased.

As income increases, with prices held constant, the budget line shifts parallel to itself and outward from the origin. The optimum positions attained, for given prices P_x and P_y, are shown by the Income Expansion Path (IEP). If both X and Y are normal superior goods, the IEP has positive slope (with utility increasing up and to the right). If either good is inferior (in which case the other good is ultra-superior), the IEP has negative slope. The data described by the IEP can also be plotted as an Engel Curve showing how the quantity of X purchased varies as income increases. An Engel Expenditure Curve shows how $P_x x$, expenditure on good X, varies as income increases.

As price P_x falls, with I and P_y held constant, the budget line tilts outward while retaining the same intercept on the y-axis. The optimum positions attained are represented by the Price Expansion Path (PEP). The direction of increased utility along the PEP is (almost always) toward the right. When the data represented by the PEP are plotted on x, P_x axes as a demand curve, we normally find that more of X is purchased as P_x falls (the Law of Demand). But the Law of Demand may fail over a limited range of prices (the Giffen case).

A fall in P_x, with I and P_y held constant, implies an increase in *real* income (higher level of utility). It is possible to separate the income effect of the price change from the pure substitution effect of the price change. The substitution effect is always in the normal direction; when P_x falls more of X will be purchased. But the direction of the income effect depends upon whether X is superior or inferior. The Giffen case results when the substitution effect is overbalanced by an inferior-good income effect.

Market demand is aggregated from individual demands by summing, at each price, the quantities purchased by all the consumers.

Subsidies and vouchers can change an individual's consumption. A subsidy works like a change in price, while a voucher works like a change in income. A voucher is especially effective in the case of someone who would otherwise have consumed very little of the good or none at all.

QUESTIONS

For Review

1. What is the meaning of the expression "the optimum of the consumer"?
2. In a situation with just two goods, how does the amount of income affect the shape of an individual's market opportunity set? How do the prices of the two goods affect the shape?
*3. a. What is the "budget line"?
   b. What is its equation?
   c. What determines the slope of the budget line?
*4. What is the geometrical condition for the optimum of the consumer? (Distinguish between a corner solution and an interior solution.)
5. If indifference curves were concave, why would the consumer's optimum never be in the interior?

---

*The answers to starred questions appear at the end of the book.

*6. a. What is the Consumption Balance Equation that expresses the optimum of the consumer? Relate this to the Substitution Equivalence Equation.

   b. Do the equations hold for an interior solution, a corner solution, or both?

7. Explain the relation between Marginal Value and Marginal Rate of Substitution. What are the differences between them?

8. Give examples of pairs of goods that are strong complements, versus pairs that are close substitutes. What observable market characteristic distinguishes them?

9. Characterize a normal good, an inferior good, and an ultra-superior good. Give examples of each. For two goods, which of the above must they be if the Income Expansion Path has positive slope? What can you say if the Income Expansion Path has negative slope?

10. Prove that if X and Y are goods rather than bads, the Income Expansion Path never points down and to the left.

*11. a. A positively sloped Income Expansion Path implies what shape for the Engel Curve?

   b. For the Engel Expenditure Curve?

   c. What can you say about the Engel Curve for an inferior good?

12. Show how an individual's demand curve can be derived from the Price Expansion Path.

13. Is there a utility-increasing direction along the Income Expansion Path? along the Price Expansion Path?

*14. What does the Law of Demand say about the shape of the Price Expansion Path?

15. How does the Hicks decomposition separate the "income effect" and the "substitution effect" of a price change?

16. Using the Hicks decomposition, show that the Giffen condition (a price decrease reduces consumption of the good) can hold only for an inferior good.

17. How is the market demand curve derived from knowledge of individuals' separate demand curves? Can individual demand curves be determined from knowledge of the market demand curve?

*18. "As compared with a simple subsidy, the voucher scheme is particularly effective for consumers who would otherwise have chosen little or none of the commodity." Illustrate and explain.

For Further Thought and Discussion

*1. a. Describe an experiment that might reveal an individual's Marginal Rate of Substitution in Consumption between two goods.

   b. Describe how it might reveal Marginal Utility for either good.

2. Why is diminishing Marginal Utility necessary if the Consumption Balance Equation is to express an optimum? Why is decreasing Marginal Rate of Substitution in Consumption necessary if the Substitution Equivalence Equation is to express an optimum? Is decreasing Marginal Utility also necessary?

*3. a. Why can the Giffen condition hold only over a limited range of the Price Expansion Path?

   b. Could the Price Expansion Path ever circle around and rejoin itself at its starting point on the y-axis?

*4. a. How does a change in the price of a good tend to shift the position of the Income Expansion Path?

b. How does a change in income tend to shift the position of the Price Expansion Path?

5. Let an individual's demand curve cut the vertical price axis at some finite "choke price" P_x^o. Show the equivalent situation in terms of the individual's indifference curves and budget line. Must the consumer's optimum then be a corner solution at price P_x^o?

6. "I think I could be a good woman if I had five thousand a year"—Becky Sharp, in Thackeray's *Vanity Fair*. Following are two possible interpretations:
   a. "Being a good woman" is a good for Becky, but one she can't afford until her income gets up to five thousand a year.
   b. Becky regards "being a good woman" as unpleasant (a bad, like hard labor). But for a fee (like wages for hard labor) of five thousand a year she would be a good woman.

   Which interpretation is correct? Can you imagine a test that would distinguish which of the two Becky meant?

*7. Consider a pair of commodities like bread and butter, which are strong complements, versus another pair like butter and margarine, which are close substitutes. Which pair is more likely to have a member that is an inferior good? Explain.

*8. Let there be three goods X, Y, and Z, where Y is the numeraire. Suppose that X and Z are complements. What happens to demand for X when the price of Z falls? How would this change affect the derivation of the Price Expansion Path on the x, y axes, as in Figure 4.13?

*9. Why is the income effect of a price change usually small compared to the substitution effect?

10. "Since 1900, real income has increased tremendously, yet the average number of children per family has decreased." Consider the following possible explanations, and illustrate in terms of market opportunity sets and indifference curves of families between number of children and "all other goods."
   a. Children are an inferior good; since we're richer now, we want fewer of them.
   b. Children are not an inferior good; however, it has become more expensive to bear and raise children.
   c. Children are not an inferior good, nor have they become relatively more expensive. What has happened is that tastes have changed; couples today want smaller families than couples did in 1900.

*11. In the comparison of subsidy versus voucher in the text, it was assumed that the price of the good remained unchanged. Would it be correct to anticipate some change of price? In which direction is this likely to go? Show the effect upon the market opportunity set.

12. Still another consideration is that government expenditures on subsidies or vouchers must ordinarily be financed by taxes, say on income. Show the effects upon a consumer's market opportunity set of a tax-financed subsidy and of a tax-financed voucher.

*13. The following is sometimes given as an example of a Giffen-good situation. A person with only $100 available must make a 1,000-mile train trip. He prefers first-class travel to coach travel, but his first priority is to complete his trip. Suppose first-class travel costs 20 cents per mile and coach costs 5 cents per mile. Then it can be verified that he will travel 333 1/3 miles in first class and 666 2/3 miles in coach. Now let the price of coach travel rise to 10 cents per mile. Then the traveler cannot afford any first-class miles at all if he is to complete his trip, so the amount of coach travel will rise from 666 2/3 to 1000 even though its price has doubled!

  a. Is coach travel an inferior good here? (What would happen if the travel budget were to rise above $100?)

  b. Under what circumstances will the traveler choose a corner solution with only coach travel? with only first-class travel?

*14. a. If two commodities are perfect substitutes, is it true that the consumer's optimum will almost always be a corner solution?

  b. Will it ever not be?

*15. At a given price ratio, variations in income generate an Income Expansion Path (IEP). If the price ratio were different, we know that a different IEP curve would be generated. For the same individual, could these two IEP curves ever cross?

*16. Exercise 4.8 showed that for an individual with $MRS_C = y$, income $I = 120$, and $P_y = 1$, the demand curve is $x = 120/P_x - 1$.

  a. What happens when $P_x = 120$?

  b. Is the equation above valid for prices $P_x > 120$, and if not, what is the correct equation in that price range?

17. Suppose a gasoline tax is imposed, taking the form of a fixed number of cents per gallon (the same for regular and for premium gas). Consider the following arguments. (1) While we would expect the quantity demanded of both premium and regular gasoline to fall after the tax is imposed, there should be a *relatively smaller* effect for the premium quality, since a fixed number of cents is a smaller *proportionate* tax for the premium gas. (2) On the contrary, we'd expect a *relatively bigger* effect for the premium quality, because premium gasoline is more of a "luxury" good, and regular gasoline more of a "necessity" good. Is one or the other of these arguments totally wrong, or is it a matter of which of two valid arguments is the stronger? Analyze each argument separately and explain.

CHAPTER 5

APPLICATIONS AND EXTENSIONS OF DEMAND THEORY

EXAMPLES

A gasoline tax will raise prices to consumers and, by the Law of Demand, it will reduce consumption—but by how much? Similarly, a decrease in consumer incomes discourages gasoline usage, but to what extent? This chapter describes the measures economists use to *quantify* how consumption responds to changes in income and to changes in price.

5.1 THE ENGEL CURVE AND THE INCOME ELASTICITY OF DEMAND

The most direct measure of the effect of a change in income I on consumption of some good X is the ratio $\Delta x/\Delta I$. For small changes Δx and ΔI, this ratio is the slope of the Engel Curve.[1] Figure 5.1 shows portions of a number of possible Engel Curves with different slopes.

A difficulty with the simple ratio $\Delta x/\Delta I$ is its sensitivity to the units of measurement. If commodity X were butter, the numerical value of the ratio would vary depending on whether we measured butter in ounces or tons; a $1,000 increase in income will cause demand for butter to increase by very few units if measured in tons, but by many more units if measured in ounces. The ratio will also be different depending on whether income is expressed in dollars or in cents. To eliminate the difficulty, the ratio can be converted into an elasticity. *Elasticity* is a ratio of proportionate changes; both the numerator and denominator are expressed in percentage terms. Specifically here, the proportionate response of quantity purchased to a proportionate change in income is called *the income elasticity of demand*.

DEFINITION: The income elasticity of demand is the proportional change in the quantity purchased divided by the proportional change in income.

We shall use the notation ϵ_x for the income elasticity of demand for commodity X (ϵ is the Greek letter *epsilon*). This definition is represented by the first ratio in Equation (5.1).[2] The other two ratios shown are equivalent algebraic forms that are also useful.

$$\epsilon_x \equiv \frac{\Delta x/x}{\Delta I/I} \equiv \frac{\Delta x/\Delta I}{x/I} \equiv \frac{\Delta x}{\Delta I}\frac{I}{x} \tag{5.1}$$

List of Notation

η_x	Price elasticity of demand for good X	I	Income
ϵ_x	Income elasticity of demand for good X	P_x	Price of good X

---

[1]*Mathematical Footnote:* We can write this slope as $\partial x/\partial I$. (The partial derivative symbol indicates that other independent variables, such as the price P_x, are being held constant.)

[2]*Mathematical Footnote:* In terms of partial derivatives

$$\epsilon_x = \frac{\partial x/x}{\partial I/I}$$

FIGURE 5.1 **Engel Curves and Income Elasticity of Demand** Four possible Engel Curves relating consumption of X to income are shown. Income elasticity is the ratio of the slope *along* an Engel curve to the slope of a ray drawn from the origin *to* the curve. So curve I has an income elasticity of one, II less than one, and III greater than one. Curve IV has negative income elasticity.

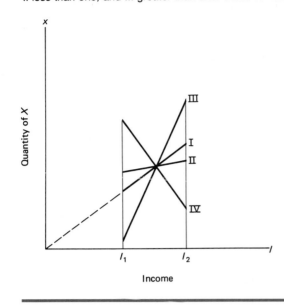

The income elasticity does not give any new information not already shown in the Engel curve. It merely presents the information in a different and useful way.

Exercise 5.1

The following table shows a consumer's income and purchases of butter B and apples A over two successive years. Compute the income elasticities.

	Year 1	Year 2
Income	$10,000	$11,000
Apples purchased	100	116
Butter purchased	20 oz.	22 oz.

Answer: The change in income is $\Delta I = \$1,000$. Since the income elasticity formula also requires a value for income, the question arises whether to use \$10,000 or \$11,000. The simplest approximation is to use the value halfway between: $I = \$10,500$. Similarly for apples, $\Delta a = 116 - 100 = 16$ and $a = (100 + 116)/2 = 108$; for butter $\Delta b = 2$ and $b = (20 + 22)/2 = 21$. Substituting into the last ratio in Equation (5.1) yields the income elasticities.

$$\text{Apples: } \epsilon_a = \frac{16}{1000} \frac{10,500}{108} = 1.56 \qquad\qquad \text{Butter: } \epsilon_b = \frac{2}{1000} \frac{10,500}{21} = 1$$

So a 1 percent rise in income would increase purchases of apples by about 1.56 percent and increase purchases of butter by about 1 percent.

Income elasticity is illustrated geometrically in Figure 5.2. Consider the Engel Curve depicted by the straight line *ADB* drawn through the origin. By the geometry of similar triangles, the percentage increase in income between points *A* and *B* is associated with the same percentage increase in the amount of good *X* consumed. Thus, by Equation (5.1), the income elasticity anywhere along the line *ADB* is 1.

Now consider the Engel Curve represented by curve *CDE*, which lies above the line-segment *AB* but is tangent to it at point *D*. Along *CDE* the income elasticity of demand does not remain constant at different levels of income. Nevertheless, at the specific tangency point *D*, we can think of very small changes Δx and ΔI along *CDE* as approximated by movement along the line *ADB*. Thus, the Engel Curve *CDE* has income elasticity $\epsilon_x = 1$ in the neighborhood of point *D*.

Returning to Figure 5.1, we see that Engel Curve I is like *ADB* in Figure 5.2: it lies on a line through the origin and so has income elasticity equal to 1. Engel Curve II has positive slope, but it does not go through the origin and is flatter than curve I. This means that as income rises by 1 percent, consumption of good *X* increases by less than 1 percent, that is, $\epsilon_x < 1$. By reversing the argument, we see that the steeper Engel Curve III represents an income elasticity $\epsilon_x > 1$. What about Engel Curve IV? This one has a *negative* slope. Here demand for good *X* *decreases* as income rises, so *X* must be an inferior good. Its income elasticity is negative, that is, $\epsilon_x < 0$.

PROPOSITION: Income elasticity is positive when the Engel curve has positive slope. It is greater than, equal to, or less than 1 depending on whether the slope *along* the Engel Curve is greater than, equal to, or less than the slope of a ray drawn from the origin *to* the curve. If the Engel Curve has negative slope, income elasticity is negative.

FIGURE 5.2   Engel Curve and Unitary Income Elasticity   The straight-line Engel Curve *ADB* has income elasticity of 1, since the slope *along* the curve is the same as the slope of a ray from the origin *to* any point on the curve. The nonlinear Engel Curve *CDE*, tangent at point *D* to *ADB*, therefore also has an income elasticity of 1 for small changes in the neighborhood of point *D*. In the range *CD* the slope *along* curve *CDE* is less than the slope of a ray from the origin *to* the curve, so $\epsilon_x < 1$. Correspondingly, $\epsilon_x > 1$ in the range of *CDE* between *D* and *E*.

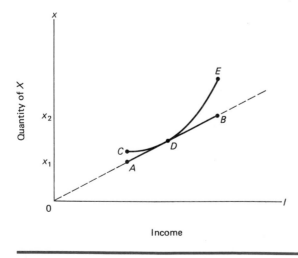

Notice that *any* Engel Curve that is a straight line through the origin with positive slope has income elasticity of 1, but such lines can be drawn from very nearly vertical to very nearly horizontal. It is not simply the steepness of an Engel Curve at a particular point that indicates elasticity, but rather the steepness *as compared with a line through the origin*.

Exercise 5.2 _____

The following four equations describe possible Engel Curves (a) $x = I/8$; (b) $x = 5 + I/10$; (c) $x = -75 + I/2$; (d) $x = 30 - I/40$. Determine the slope and the income elasticity for each at the point $I = 200$, $x = 25$. In which of these cases is the commodity an inferior good? (e) What if the Engel Curve were $x = 5 + I/8$?

Answer: (a) The slope $\Delta x/\Delta I$ all along the curve $x = I/8$ is evidently $1/8$. The income elasticity is $(\Delta x/\Delta I)(I/x) = (1/8)(200/25) = 1$. (b) The slope of $x = 5 + I/10$ is $1/10$, and so $\epsilon_x = (1/10)(200/25) = 0.8$. (c) Slope is $1/2$, $\epsilon_x = (1/2)(200/25) = 4$. (d) Slope is $-1/40$, $\epsilon_x = (-1/40)(200/25) = -0.2$. [Note that the four curves correspond generally to those pictured in Figure 5.1.] Commodity X is inferior only in case (d), where the income elasticity is negative. (e) We tried to trick you here. The equation given is perfectly possible for an Engel Curve, but the specific point $I = 200$, $x = 25$ does not lie on the curve so the question cannot be answered.

5.2 DEMAND CURVE AND PRICE ELASTICITY OF DEMAND

Income elasticity measures the response of consumption to changes in *income*. Consider next the response of consumption to changes in *price*. Again, an obvious measure is the ratio $\Delta x/\Delta P_x$.[3] For small changes Δx and ΔP_x, the ratio $\Delta x/\Delta P_x$ corresponds to the reciprocal of the slope of the demand curve.[4] The alternative demand curves labeled I, II, III, IV in Figure 5.3 (p. 122) illustrate flatter and steeper slopes. The steeper the curve, the smaller the absolute magnitude of $\Delta x/\Delta P_x$.

The measure $\Delta x/\Delta P_x$ is affected by changes in units of measurement in the numerator (e.g., changes from pounds to tons) or in the denominator (e.g., changes from dollars to cents). To avoid this difficulty, once again we measure elasticity as the ratio of *proportionate* changes; this ratio is the *price elasticity of demand*. (The expression *elasticity of demand* is always understood to refer to the price elasticity of demand.)

Since the slope of a curve depends on units of measurement, it would not be informative to assert, for example, that the demand curve for wheat is steeper than, say, the demand curve for haircuts. The demand curve for wheat could be made as steep or flat as desired by converting from tons to pounds to ounces as quantity units, or from dollars to cents as price units. But it is meaningful to say that the demand for wheat is less elastic than the demand for haircuts; if that were the case, we could validly conclude that the demand for wheat is less responsive to price changes than the demand for haircuts.

DEFINITION: The price elasticity of demand is the proportional change in the quantity purchased divided by the proportional change in price.

_____

[3]*Mathematical Footnote:* In terms of derivatives, this is $\partial x/\partial P_x$.

[4]Since economists conventionally draw demand curves with price P_x on the vertical axis, the slope of the demand curve is $\Delta P_x/\Delta x$. To measure the effects of price changes upon quantity consumed, we need to take the reciprocal of the slope in the diagram.

FIGURE 5.3 **Alternative Demand-Curve Slopes**   The four demand curves represent different responses of quantity purchased to changes in price. Since demand curves are conventionally drawn with price on the vertical axis, a greater response is represented by a flatter demand curve. Curve IV has a region that represents the exceptional Giffen case.

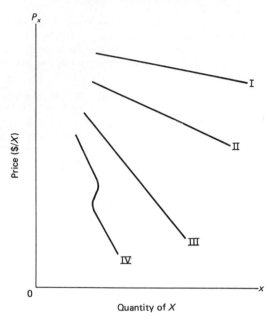

As with income elasticity, price elasticity of demand can be expressed in several ways. These are shown in Equation (5.2), where price elasticity is symbolized by η_x (η is the Greek letter *eta*). The definition of elasticity is algebraically represented by the first ratio in Equation (5.2).[5]

$$\eta_x \equiv \frac{\Delta x/x}{\Delta P_x/P_x} \equiv \frac{\Delta x/\Delta P_x}{x/P_x} \equiv \frac{\Delta x}{\Delta P_x} \cdot \frac{P_x}{x} \tag{5.2}$$

When the demand curve is negatively sloped (as required by the Law of Demand), Δx and ΔP_x have opposite signs. Thus, the price elasticity of demand η_x is normally negative. Conventionally, when we speak of a "high" elasticity we mean large in absolute value (a large negative number, for example -10, rather than -0.5); "low" elasticity means small in absolute value. Writing the absolute value of elasticity as $|\eta_x|$, demand is elastic if $|\eta_x| > 1$, while demand is inelastic if $|\eta_x| < 1$. [*Warning:* Since elasticity is usually changing along

[5]*Mathematical Footnote:* In terms of derivatives,

$$\eta_x = \frac{\partial x/x}{\partial P_x/P_x}$$

a demand curve, it is generally wrong to identify a demand curve as elastic (or inelastic); it would be correct to say that in the neighborhood of some given price, the demand is elastic (or inelastic)].

Exercise 5.3

The following linear equations represent different possible demands for commodity X: (a) $x = 240 - 30P_x$; (b) $x = 320 - 50P_x$; and (c) $x = 20 + 25P_x$. What are the associated price elasticities at the point $x = 120$, $P_x = 4$? Which is a Giffen good?

Answer: From Equation (5.2) $\eta_x = (\Delta x/\Delta P_x)/(x/P_x)$. In each case, the denominator ratio is $x/P_x = 120/4 = 30$. Inserting the appropriate numerator ratio we have (a) $\eta_x = -30/30 = -1$; (b) $\eta_x = -50/30 = -5/3$; and (c) $\eta_x = 25/30 = 5/6$. Since the price elasticity is positive in the last case, the Law of Demand fails and (c) represents a Giffen good. [We saw in Chapter 4 that a good could have the Giffen property only over a limited range; therefore, an equation like (c) could not be valid over the whole range of prices.]

Suppose the price elasticity is $\eta_x = -1$ (unitary elasticity) What is the effect of a small decrease in the price of good X upon total *spending* on that good? (A price decrease normally increases the quantity demanded, but it is not obvious whether total spending will go up or down.) From the first ratio in Equation (5.2) we know that when $\eta_x = -1$ the proportionate increase in quantity $\Delta x/x$ equals the proportionate decrease $\Delta P_x/P_x$ in price. But since the consumer's expenditure on good X is $P_x x$, the proportionate increase of x just offsets the proportionate decrease of P_x. So with unitary elasticity total expenditure remains unchanged as price rises; Marginal Revenue to the seller or sellers is zero.

If the price elasticity is greater than one ($|\eta_x| > 1$, or elastic demand), the proportionate increase in quantity is larger than the proportionate decrease in price—total expenditure $P_x x$ increases when price falls. So Marginal Revenue is positive. By a similar argument, if demand is inelastic, a decrease in P_x leads to a less-than-offsetting rise in x so total expenditure $P_x x$ decreases (Marginal Revenue is negative).[6]

PROPOSITION: If the demand for X is elastic, a reduction in price P_x increases a consumer's expenditures $P_x x$ on commodity X. A price reduction decreases $P_x x$ if demand is inelastic, and leaves $P_x x$ unchanged if the elasticity is -1.

As with the income elasticity of demand, the price elasticity gives no information not already available from the demand curve itself. But it provides a succinct measure of the sensitivity of demand to price.

[6]*Mathematical Footnote:*

$$\frac{\partial(P_x\,x)}{\partial x} = P_x + x\,\frac{\partial P_x}{\partial x} = \left(1 + \frac{x}{P_x}\frac{\partial P_x}{\partial x}\right)P_x = P_x\left(1 + \frac{1}{\eta_x}\right)$$

This tells us that

$$MR = P_x\left(1 + \frac{1}{\eta_x}\right)$$

Recall that the sign of η_x is negative, so Marginal Revenue is positive, zero, or negative depending on whether $|\eta_x|$ is greater than, equal to, or less than 1.

Exercise 5.4

A consumer's demand curve for good X is given by the equation $x = 100 - 2P_x$. (a) What is the elasticity of demand at the point $x = 20$, $P_x = 40$? (b) If price falls from $P_x = 40$ to $P_x = 35$, what happens to total expenditure $P_x x$ and what does this imply about the elasticity of demand? (c) Compute the elasticity to verify the answer.

Answer: (a) Along the demand curve $100 - 2P_x$, the ratio $\Delta x/\Delta P_x$ is a constant equal to -2. Using the second expression for η_x from Equation (5.2), we have

$$\frac{\Delta x/\Delta P_x}{x/P_x} = \frac{-2}{20/40} = -4$$

(b) At $P_x = 40$, $x = 100 - 2(40) = 20$, and total expenditure is 800. At $P_x = 35$, $x = 100 - 2(35) = 30$, and so total expenditure is 1,050. Since expenditure is greater at the lower price, demand is elastic. (c) Over the interval, $\Delta x/\Delta P_x$ equals -2. Taking the midpoint values for x and P_x, the elasticity is $-2/(25/37.5) = -3$, confirming that demand is elastic in this interval.

5.3 THE CROSS-ELASTICITY OF DEMAND

The amount of butter consumers want to purchase depends not only on the price of butter, but also to some extent on the prices of related goods like bread or margarine. Once again, it is convenient to use a unit-free elasticity measure called the *cross-elasticity of demand*. The definition is as follows:[7]

$$\eta_{xy} \equiv \frac{\Delta x/x}{\Delta P_y/P_y} \equiv \left(\frac{\Delta x}{\Delta P_y}\right)\left(\frac{P_y}{x}\right)$$

Bread and butter are of course complements in demand (see Chapter 4) since having more of either makes the other more desirable. A higher butter price tends to reduce consumption of butter (the Law of Demand), thus lowering the desirability of bread (negative cross-elasticity between bread and butter). In contrast, as the price of butter rises, consumers will demand more margarine; thus, between substitutes like butter and margarine the cross-elasticity of demand is positive.

EXAMPLE 5.1 Elasticities of Electricity Demand

How the demand for electricity varies with prices and consumer income is an important question for national economic policy. A study of electricity demand over the period 1946 to 1972 used three determining variables: (1) electricity price, (2) income, and (3) the price of a competing commodity—gas. It was found convenient to classify the data according to residential, commercial, and industrial use.

[7]*Mathematical Footnote:* In terms of derivatives:

$$\eta_{xy} = \frac{\partial x/x}{\partial P_y/P_y}$$

Elasticities of Electricity Use*

With Respect to:	Electricity Price	Income	Gas Price
Residential	−1.3	+0.3	+0.15
Commercial	−1.5	+0.9	+0.15
Industrial	−1.7	+1.1	+0.15

***Source:** D. Chapman, T. Tyrrell, and T. Mount, "Electricity Demand Growth and the Energy Crisis," *Science,* v. 178 (November 17, 1972), p. 705.

The elasticities of electricity demand with respect to its own price were found to be negative and in the elastic range ($|\eta_x| > 1$), showing a more than proportionate response of consumption to price change. This was the most important result of the study, running counter to the common but uninformed opinion that people have needs for electricity regardless of price. The positive income elasticities show that electricity is a normal good. And the positive cross-elasticities with respect to gas price show that gas and electricity are substitutes.

COMMENT   The results here refute the crude techniques for projecting future electricity demands often employed in energy crisis debates. Government planners, industry insiders, and outside critics sometimes argue as if purely mathematical extrapolations, which simply extend historically observed rates of demand growth into the indefinite future, represent valid estimates of what will happen. They are surely mistaken; the demand for electricity *strongly* responds to price. And the price of electricity is bound to increase as fuels become more expensive and as requirements for environmental protection add to cost. (Indeed, since the period of the study electricity prices *have* increased sharply, with the anticipated discouraging effect upon electricity use.)

5.4 AN APPLICATION: FITTING A DEMAND CURVE

To test theories and to predict future demands, economic statisticians ("econometricians") use historical data to estimate or "fit" demand curves. Any such fitted curve is more or less artificial; a statistician can only approximate the true demand function.

Constant-Slope Versus Constant-Elasticity Functions

To keep the statistical problems manageable, the econometrician often assumes that the demand curve has either *constant slope* or *constant elasticity*. Figure 5.4 (p. 126) compares two such curves. The constant-slope demand curve is a straight line on X, P_x axes;[8] the constant-elasticity demand curve is convex (bowed toward the origin).

Consider the straight-line demand curve DD' illustrated in Figure 5.5 (p. 126). First of all, recall the definition of price elasticity.

---

[8]The uppercase symbol X in equations indicates that we are now dealing with *aggregate* consumption or demand in the market.

FIGURE 5.4 **Linear and Constant-Elasticity Demand Curves**   Simple functional forms are ordinarily assumed in attempting to estimate (to "fit") a demand curve to observed data shown as heavy dots in the diagrams. The functional forms most commonly used are linear demand as in Panel (a) and constant-elasticity demand as in Panel (b).

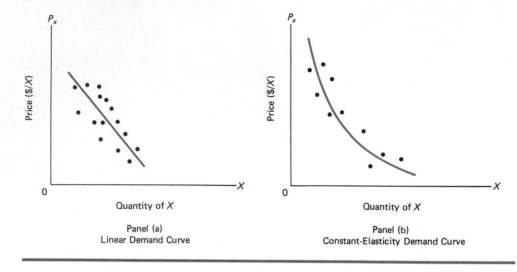

Panel (a)
Linear Demand Curve

Panel (b)
Constant-Elasticity Demand Curve

FIGURE 5.5   **Graphical Measure of Elasticity**   Elasticity at a point T along a linear demand curve DD' is the slope of the demand curve divided by the slope of the ray OT (which connects the origin to the demand curve). In the situation pictured, OT is steeper (its slope is larger in absolute value) than DD', so the demand elasticity at T is greater than one. Elasticity always equals one at the midpoint M along a linear demand curve like DD' (since OMD' is an isosceles triangle). For a nonlinear demand curve like FTF', the demand elasticity at point T is identical with the elasticity at T along the tangent straight-line demand curve DD.

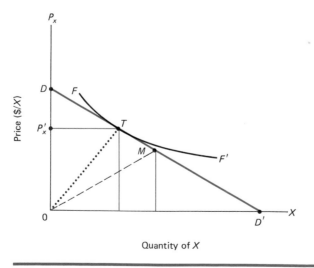

Quantity of X

$$\eta_x \equiv \frac{\Delta X / X}{\Delta P_x / P_x} \equiv \frac{\Delta X}{\Delta P_x} \frac{P_x}{X}$$

From this we see that elasticity of demand must be zero at D' (the intersection with the horizontal axis) since P_x is zero there. Similarly, elasticity is infinite at D (the intersection with the vertical axis) since X is zero there. So evidently, elasticity rises (in absolute value) as we move left along a straight-line demand curve.

Several geometrical methods can be used to find the elasticity of demand at any point like T along the linear demand curve DD'. Perhaps the simplest is to divide the slope of a ray from the origin to the curve by the slope of the curve itself. Mathematically, we use the definition of elasticity in the following form:

$$\eta_x \equiv \frac{P_x / X}{\Delta P_x / \Delta X}$$

The denominator here represents the (ordinarily negative) slope *along* the curve—the constant slope of DD' in Figure 5.5. The numerator P_x / X is the (necessarily positive) slope of the ray OT from the origin *to* the curve. To find the elasticity at the point T, divide the slope of OT by the slope of DD'. In the diagram OT is steeper (in absolute value terms) than DD', so at T the elasticity of demand is greater than one.

Another way of demonstrating that elasticity is not constant along a linear demand curve is to examine Marginal Revenue at different points. In Figure 5.6 (p. 128) let the quantity sold be initially X_1, at a price of P_1. Total revenue is P_1 times X_1, or the area of rectangle OX_1CP_1. Consider a small increase in sales, from X_1 to X_1'. If this greater amount is sold, then the price must decrease from P_1 to P_1'. Total revenue is then X_1' times P_1', or the area of rectangle $OX_1'C'P_1'$. The change in total revenue is the difference between the areas of the two rectangles; this is the area of rectangle $X_1X_1'C'A$ minus the area of rectangle $P_1'ACP_1$. Since the first rectangle is larger than the second, total revenue is greater when output is X_1' than when output is X_1; Marginal Revenue is positive. Put another way, a decrease in price from P_1 to P_1' caused an increase in total expenditures, which means that demand is elastic near point C.

Consider Marginal Revenue or elasticity around point D. When output is X_2 and price is P_2, total revenue is the area of rectangle OX_2DP_2. At a slightly lower price, P_2', the quantity sold is X_2'. The change in total revenue is the area of rectangle $X_2X_2'D'B$ minus the area of rectangle $P_2'BDP_2$. Since the first rectangle is smaller than the second, total revenue must have declined and Marginal Revenue is negative. The decline in price from P_2 to P_2' caused a decrease in total expenditures, which means that the elasticity of demand is less than 1. Since near point C demand is elastic, whereas near point D demand is inelastic, the price elasticity of demand cannot be constant along a linear demand curve.

Exercise 5.5

Consider the demand curve $P_x = 30 - X/4$. What is the elasticity of demand when $x = 60$? when $x = 120$? when $x = 0$?

Answer: The slope of this linear demand curve is $-1/4$, so elasticity at any point is equal to $(P_x/x)/(-1/4)$ or $-4P_x/x$. At $x = 60$, $P_x = 30 - 60/4 = 15$, so elasticity is $-4(15/60) = -1$. At $x = 120$, $P_x = 0$ and so elasticity is zero. At $x = 0$, elasticity is negative infinite.

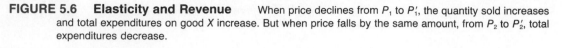

FIGURE 5.6 Elasticity and Revenue   When price declines from P_1 to P_1', the quantity sold increases and total expenditures on good X increase. But when price falls by the same amount, from P_2 to P_2', total expenditures decrease.

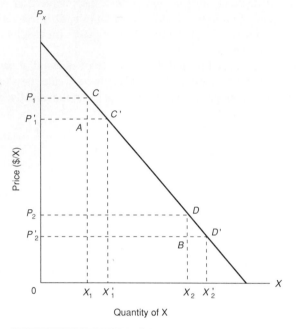

In Figure 5.7 the demand curve EE' has constant elasticity. This means that the slope of the ray OF divided by the slope of the demand curve at F equals the slope of the ray OG divided by the slope of the demand curve at $G;$ the equality also holds at every other point on the demand curve. As we have seen before, when elasticity is -1 the Marginal Revenue is zero. So, for a constant-elasticity demand curve with $\eta_x = -1$, like EE' in the diagram, consumers will spend the same amount of dollars on X no matter what the price. [*Query:* What is the fixed dollar expenditure associated with demand curve EE'?] This constant-expenditure property holds only for demand curves with constant elasticity equal to -1. If the elasticity were constant but equal to -2 instead, every 1 percent fall in price would cause a 2 percent increase in quantity. Then expenditure would steadily rise moving downward along the demand curve.

A demand curve with a constant slope is a straight line. We can write it as a linear equation.

$$X = A + BP_x \tag{5.3}$$

Here A and B are constants; B is normally negative according to the Law of Demand. When we take into account other variables that affect demand, such as income I and the price of a related good Y, we obtain a generalized demand function in linear form.

$$X = A + BP_x + CI + DP_y \tag{5.4}$$

FIGURE 5.7 **Constant-Unit-Elasticity Demand Curve** *EE'* is a demand curve with a constant elasticity of −1. At all points like *F, G, H* along *EE'*, consumer expenditures P_xX equal 400.

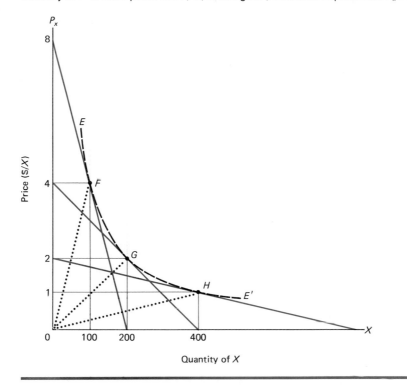

Here, *A, B, C,* and *D* are all constants. *B* is again normally negative. *C,* the coefficient on income, is the slope of the Engel Curve, and is only negative when *X* is an inferior good. The sign of *D* is positive if *X* and *Y* are substitutes and negative if they are complements.

When an econometrician statistically fits a linear demand function to the data, the equation is valid only within a limited range. Taken to extremes, it may give absurd results. For example, interpreted literally, Equation (5.4) says that people will buy some *X* even if they have zero income *I*. This is of course impossible.[9]

A better statistical fit is often obtained with a demand curve of constant elasticity rather than of constant slope. The equation for such a demand curve is

$$X = aP^b \qquad (5.5)$$

Here *a* is a positive constant and *b* a negative constant. We can readily verify that Equation (5.5) represents a constant-elasticity demand curve. The inverse slope of this function is

[9]It is true, however, that allowing for borrowing and lending would make it possible for consumption expenditures in any single time period to diverge from income *of that period*. This topic will be taken up in Chapter 14.

$\Delta X/\Delta P = abP^{b-1}.$[10] The elasticity is $(\Delta X/\Delta P)\cdot(P/X) = abP^{b-1}P/aP^b = b,$ which is a constant.

A particularly simple form of a demand function with constant elasticity is $X = 1/P$ (here $a = 1$ and $b = -1$). This equation can be transformed into $PX = 1$, which means that total expenditures equal 1 at all prices; this implies an elasticity of -1.

Equation (5.5) is sometimes expressed in logarithmic form.[11]

$$\log(X) = \log(a) + b\log(P) \tag{5.6}$$

This equation is easily generalized, paralleling the generalized linear demand function of Equation (5.4), to become

$$\log(X) = \log a + b\log(P_x) + c\log(I) + d\log(P_y) \tag{5.7}$$

It is easy to see that the coefficients of the variables are elasticity measures: b is the own-price elasticity, c is the income elasticity, and d the cross-elasticity.[12]

EXAMPLE 5.2 Demand for Coffee

Coffee demand is relatively stable over time, whereas the supply can shift drastically because of crop fluctuations in the major producing countries, especially Brazil. These changes in supply produce a scatter of price-quantity combinations over the years that provides data for estimating the demand function.

Cliff J. Huang, John J. Siegfried, and Farangis Zardoshty examined the U.S. demand for coffee from 1963 to 1977.[a] For regular coffee (but not instant coffee), they found that the elasticity of demand was nearly the same at high prices as at low prices. This similarity justified a logarithmic (constant-elasticity) equation form. The equation that best fit the data for regular coffee was

$$\log X = -.16 \log P + .51 \log I + .15 \log P_t - .009T + \text{constant}$$

Here X represents the quantity of coffee demanded, P is its price, I is income, P_t is the price of tea, and T is time. (Some seasonal factors were omitted here.) As seen above, in logarithmic form the coefficients of the variables are elasticities. So the price elasticity for coffee is $-.16$, the coefficient on the variable $\log P$, which means that the demand is quite inelastic. The income elasticity is .51, so coffee is a normal superior good. Since the cross-elasticity of .15 is positive, tea, as expected, is a substitute for coffee. Finally, the time coefficient is negative, indicating that consumption of regular coffee was subject to a declining trend.

For instant coffee, the researchers found rather different results. First of all, the logarithmic form of the equation was inappropriate since the elasticity of demand proved not to

---

[10]The (inverse) slope is the derivative $dX/dP = abP^{b-1}$.

[11]Taking logarithms of both sides of the equation $X = aP^b$ we obtain $\log X = \log a + \log(P^b) = \log a + b\log P$.

[12]Concentrating only on price elasticity, the definition is $\eta_x = (dX/X)/(dP/P)$. Note that $d\log(X)/dX = 1/X$, and $d\log(P)/dP = 1/P$. This means that $\eta_x = d\log(X)/d\log(P)$. But this derivative is b in Equation (5.7). The same technique applies for the income and cross elasticities.

be constant. Elasticity was high at high prices and low at low prices (which is what occurs with a linear demand curve). The price elasticities for instant coffee ranged from $-.89$ at the highest prices down to $-.02$ at the lowest prices during the period. There was no time trend, suggesting that the increasing convenience value of instant coffee (due, among other things, to the rising fraction of married women working away from home) nearly offset the overall decline in coffee consumption.

COMMENT   One rather surprising result was that substitution between regular and instant coffee was not important in explaining the demand for either. This seems hard to believe, but the explanation remains a problem for future research.

[a]Cliff J. Huang, John J. Siegfried, and Farangis Zardoshty, "The Demand for Coffee in the United States, 1963–77," *Quarterly Review of Economics and Business*, v. 20 (Summer 1980).

5.5 DETERMINANTS OF RESPONSIVENESS OF DEMAND TO PRICE

Why is demand for some commodities highly sensitive to price, while demand for others is not? There are a number of explanations.

1. *The availability of substitutes makes demand elastic.* Demand for a commodity will be more elastic the more numerous and the closer the available substitutes. This effect is based on the substitution effect of the price change (see Chapter 4). Panel (a) of Figure 5.8 (p. 132) shows two goods that are close substitutes, like butter and margarine. Here a fall in the price of good X, which tilts the budget line from KL to KL', leads to a relatively large change in the quantity of X demanded (x_1 is considerably greater than x_0). For close substitutes like butter and margarine, as the price ratio changes people shift their purchases substantially to buy more of the cheaper commodity. Panel (b) shows two goods that are close complements, like tennis balls and tennis rackets. Here we see that at the lower price the new quantity x_1 is only a little larger than x_0. For close complements like balls and rackets, people will still want to buy the goods in about the same proportions, regardless of the price ratio.

2. *The demand for luxuries is more elastic than demand for necessities.* Recall that a luxury is a strongly superior good, so that a great deal more is purchased as income rises. A necessity is a good with low income elasticity so that an increase in income causes only a small increase in consumption. Thus the argument runs in terms of the income effect of a price change. A fall in the price of a good tends to enrich the consumer, and this enrichment leads to a greater increase in the consumption of a luxury good than of a necessity.

3. *The demand for high-priced goods is more elastic than demand for low-priced goods.* What is a "high" price? The natural interpretation is that a high price for a given consumer is one near the choke price, the vertical intercept of his or her demand curve. If the demand curve actually intercepts the vertical axis, elasticity is indeed infinite at that point. And at an intercept with the horizontal axis, elasticity must be zero. But it is also possible to have a constant-elasticity demand curve, for which elasticity remains constant however closely the axes are approached. (Of course, such a demand curve cannot actually *intersect* either axis.) So the logic of the argument here is not compelling.

FIGURE 5.8   Closeness of Substitutes and Demand Elasticity   In Panel (a) the two goods are close substitutes. A fall in P_x shifts the budget line from KL to KL' and leads to a relatively large change in consumption of X (from x_0 to x_1). In Panel (b) the two goods are poor substitutes (strong complements): a fall in P_x leads to only a small change in the amount of X purchased.

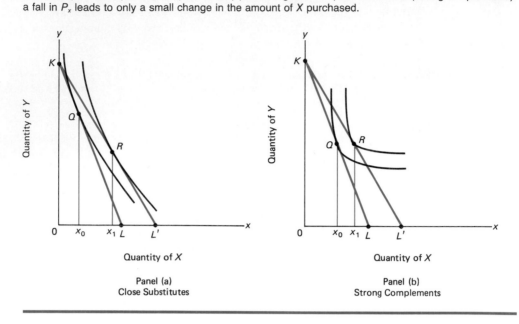

Panel (a)
Close Substitutes

Panel (b)
Strong Complements

As a fourth possible explanation, some economists claim that a commodity that is unimportant for the consumer—that is, one accounting for only a small fraction $P_x x / I$ of his budget—tends to have inelastic demand. For example, if the price of salt fell, you are unlikely to buy much more salt. It would follow, of course, that a commodity that is important tends to have elastic demand. Once again, the argument here is based on the income effect: If the price of an important commodity falls, the consumer is, in effect, a lot richer and can buy considerably more of the commodity. But this argument is wrong. Indeed, if X is an important commodity for some consumer and its price falls, we can expect the *absolute* increase in his consumption, Δx, to be large. But elasticity concerns *proportionate* changes, not absolute changes. Since for an important commodity the individual's consumption x was large to begin with, the percentage change $\Delta x / x$ need not be particularly large.[13] The inelastic demand for salt is not due to its "unimportance" in consumers' budgets but probably to the fact that salt is a necessity with no close substitutes.

5.6   AN APPLICATION: GIFFEN GOOD

The Giffen case refers to a possible situation violating the Law of Demand—a lower price *decreases* the quantity demanded. It follows that the elasticity η_x has a positive rather than the normal negative sign.

---

[13]Consider the special case of an "all-important" commodity, accounting for 100 percent of the consumer's budget. For such a commodity the price elasticity of demand is not extraordinarily large. Indeed, the elasticity must be exactly -1.

FIGURE 5.9 **Conditions for Giffen Good** At the initial high potato price the budget line is *KL* and the consumptive optimum is at *Q*. A fall in the price of potatoes shifts the budget line to *KL'*. The consumer is sufficiently enriched to prefer buying fewer potatoes and more bread, at point *R*. The movement from *Q* to *R* consists of a small substitution effect (*Q* to *S*) and a large negative income effect (*S* to *R*). For this Giffen result to occur, potatoes must be strongly inferior.

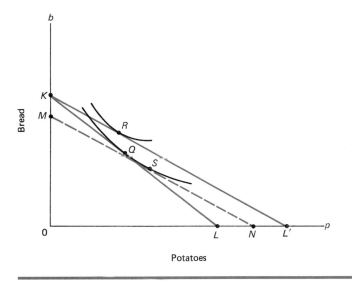

Here is an example commonly given. Suppose poverty forces you to live mainly on potatoes (the cheapest source of calories), and to consume little bread (a more desired but more expensive food). Since you spend most of your income on potatoes, a fall in the price of potatoes makes you richer. But when you are richer you can afford to buy more bread, so your consumption of potatoes might actually fall.

A Giffen good must have the following two properties:

1. It must be inferior, so that the income effect of a price change is negative.
2. It must account for a large fraction of the budget. This property creates a large income effect—large enough to overcome the normal substitution effect of a price change.

These properties are illustrated in Figure 5.9. Initially the consumer consumes at *Q*. The price of potatoes falls and the pure substitution effect moves him to *S* along the artificial dashed budget line *MN* (as in Figure 4.17). But the inferior income effect (compare Figure 4.9) leads him to reduce consumption of potatoes so much as to overwhelm the substitution effect. At the new optimum *R*, he consumes fewer potatoes at the lower price.

EXAMPLE 5.3 **Was Bread a Giffen Good?**

The idea of a Giffen good was first suggested by historians to describe the behavior of rural laborers in England at the end of the eighteenth century. Here wheat bread was supposedly a Giffen good, and meat was supposedly an important substitute.

A study by Roger Koenker[a] casts doubt on this example. In the late eighteenth century, the very limited transportation network in Britain permitted considerable local price differences to develop among communities. These differences, as well as changes over time, provided data for estimating typical demands for bread as price varied.

Using a linear (constant-slope) assumption, a demand function for English rural laborer households was estimated as follows:

Bread = .40 + .41 *Family size* +
.024 *Weekly expenditures* −
.35 *Bread price* + .57 *Meat price*

Here bread quantity is measured in loaves per week, bread price in pence per loaf, the meat price in pence per pound. Weekly expenditures in pence per week (for all food items) were the best available measure of overall income.

The negative coefficient for bread price refutes the contention that bread was a Giffen good for these consumers. In fact, the positive coefficient for weekly expenditures (income) shows that bread was a normal and not an inferior good. (Recall that only an inferior good *may* be a Giffen good; a normal or superior good cannot be.) The positive coefficient for meat price does however support the historians' contention that bread and meat were substitutes. And, as would be expected, it turned out that meat was a high-income-elasticity or luxury good in comparison with bread.

[a]Roger Koenker, "Was Bread Giffen? The Demand for Food in England circa 1790," *Review of Economics and Statistics,* v. 59 (1977).

5.7 MULTIPLE CONSTRAINTS

In "The Optimum of the Consumer," Chapter 4, the *budget line* was introduced as the upper boundary of the market opportunity set. The familiar equation of the budget line, for two commodities X and $Y,$ is

$$P_x x + P_y y = I \tag{5.8}$$

The market opportunity set as a whole is the shaded region of Figure 5.10. Mathematically, it is the set of points satisfying the inequalities.

$$\begin{cases} P_x x + P_y y \leq I \\[2mm] x \geq 0 \\[2mm] y \geq 0 \end{cases} \tag{5.9}$$

The last two conditions specify that a person cannot consume a negative quantity of either good.

Rationing as an Additional Constraint on Consumption

Governments sometimes ration goods—in wartime, for example. Even though a consumer may have enough income to buy more of the good, he or she may not be legally allowed to do so.

FIGURE 5.10

FIGURE 5.10 **Market Opportunity Set** The normal market opportunity set is the shaded area bounded by the budget line $P_x x + P_y y = I$ and the vertical and horizontal axes.

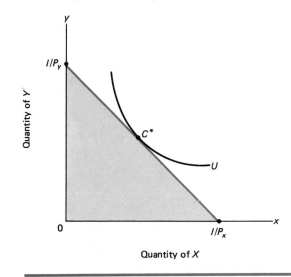

Figure 5.11 (p. 136) illustrates three cases. In Panel (a) the ration limit is indicated by the vertical dashed line at the quantity $x = R_x$. Here the ration limit is so large that it is ineffective for this consumer. In Panel (b) the ration limit R_x is potentially binding; it truncates the market opportunity set (it reduces the size of the shaded area). However, given the individual's preferences, the ration limit is not *actually* binding at C^*, since he does not want to consume as much of X as the ration permits. Only in Panel (c) is the ration limit R_x actually binding. In the absence of rationing the consumer would consume at C^*. With the ration constraint, the best achievable point is T. Notice that a *binding* ration will always reduce utility.

Exercise 5.6 _____

Suppose an individual's preferences are represented by a Marginal Rate of Substitution $MRS_C = 2y/x$, that prices are $P_x = 3$ and $P_y = 1$, and that income is $I = 180$. (a) What is the optimal consumption basket? (b) What happens if a ration limit $R_x = 50$ is applied to commodity X? (c) What if the ration is tightened to $R_x = 20$? (d) Returning to the original ration limit $R_x = 50$, what would happen if income had doubled to $I = 360$?

Answer: (a) Utility-maximization requires that $MRS_C = P_x/P_y$. Letting Y be the *numeraire* so that $P_y = 1$, we have $2y/x = P_x$ or $2y = P_x x$. Then the budget equation $P_x x + P_y y = 180$ can be written $2y + y = 3y = 180$. The solution is $y = 60$, $x = 40$. (b) If $R_x = 50$ the X-ration is potentially binding (since the individual might have purchased as many as $I/P_x = 180/3 = 60$ units of X). But, since he preferred to buy only $x = 40$, the ration is not actually binding and the optimum is unchanged. (c) If $R_x = 20$ the ration limit is binding: he will obviously want to purchase his full allowed ration, so $x = 20$. With the remaining income $I - P_x x = 180 - 60$ he will buy $120/P_y = 120$ units of commodity Y. (d) It is easy to verify that when $I = 360$ the unconstrained optimum is $x = 80$, $y = 120$. Then the ration limit $R_x = 50$ would be binding, and he would have to choose $x = 50$, $y = 210$.

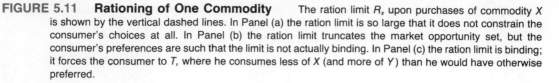

FIGURE 5.11 **Rationing of One Commodity** The ration limit R_x upon purchases of commodity X is shown by the vertical dashed lines. In Panel (a) the ration limit is so large that it does not constrain the consumer's choices at all. In Panel (b) the ration limit truncates the market opportunity set, but the consumer's preferences are such that the limit is not actually binding. In Panel (c) the ration limit is binding; it forces the consumer to T, where he consumes less of X (and more of Y) than he would have otherwise preferred.

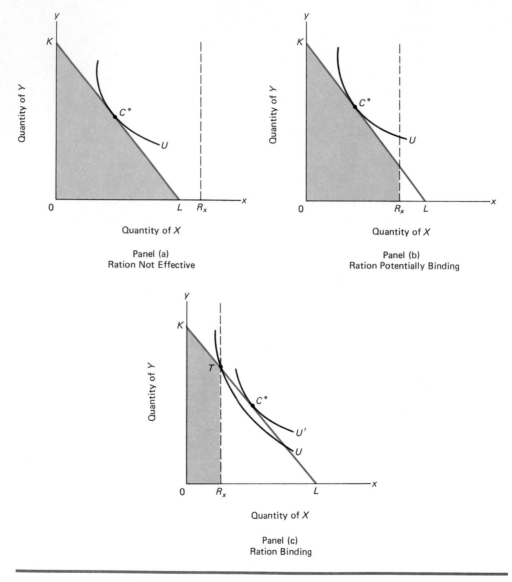

What if commodities X and Y were *both* rationed? In Figure 5.12 (p. 138) we see only the more interesting situations where both of the ration limits R_x and R_y are at least *potentially* binding, where the market opportunity set is truncated at both ends. Panel (a) shows that even when both ration limits are potentially binding, neither may *actually* be effective at the consumptive optimum position C^*. In Panel (b), only the ration limit R_y for commodity Y is actually binding; it forces the individual to a position T inferior to the tangency optimum C^* that he would otherwise choose. (There would of course be an opposite case, not diagrammed here, in which only the ration limit R_x is binding.) Panel (c) shows the case in which *both* ration limits are actually binding. Here the budget constraint is *not* binding. This would correspond to the situation of a wealthy person who is unable to legally spend all of his or her income because of severe rationing.

Mathematically, the constraints defining the consumption opportunity set under rationing can be written as follows:

$$
\left\{
\begin{array}{ll}
P_x x + P_y y \leq I & \text{Income Constraint} \hspace{2cm} (5.10) \\[1em]
0 \leq x \leq R_x & \\[0.5em]
& \text{Ration Constraints} \\[0.5em]
0 \leq y \leq R_y &
\end{array}
\right.
$$

Rationing is usually imposed under conditions of special scarcity, as in wartime, to assure that poor people can buy at least minimal quantities of essential goods.[14] But simple quantity rationing is a crude technique. It does not guarantee that poor people will receive goods; it only limits the consumption of the rich in the hope there will be more left over for the poor. However, when a good is rationed in demand, there is correspondingly less profit in producing it, so overall supply is likely to fall. Another problem is that goods do not go where they are wanted most. Someone who doesn't like tea would have no use for a tea ration, while a tea-lover will probably get a tea ration that is too small.

In the later years of World War II, several countries adopted more sophisticated point rationing schemes aimed at giving consumers a wider choice. Instead of an absolute ration limit, people were granted a *ration-point income (N)* to be spent as they chose within their limited cash income *(I)*. Rationed goods were assigned point prices (p_x and p_y) and money prices (P_x and P_y). To buy an item, the consumer had to pay the money price and also the point price. Thus, the maximum amount of X the consumer could purchase was the smaller of N/p_x and I/P_x.

Three possible shapes of the opportunity set under point rationing are shown in Figure 5.13 (p. 139). In Panel (a) point income is so large relative to ordinary income that only the income constraint is binding. This might be the situation of a poor person. Panel (b) represents the opposite case: a rich person for whom ordinary income is so ample that only the point constraint is binding. And finally, Panel (c) pictures a situation in which over a certain range ordinary income is binding, but elsewhere point income is binding.

Formally, the opportunity set under point rationing is determined by the following inequalities:

---

[14]This may not be the only purpose of rationing. In Nazi Germany, for example, smaller rations were assigned to Jews than to Aryans. Similarly, during the period 1917–21 in revolutionary Russia, members of the former upper and middle classes were allowed smaller rations than individuals of proletarian origin.

FIGURE 5.12 **Rationing of Two Commodities** X and Y are subject to ration limits R_x and R_y (vertical and horizontal dashed lines). In Panel (a) neither ration limit is binding. In Panel (b) R_y is binding, forcing the consumer to choose less of Y (and more of X). In Panel (c) both ration limits are binding, so that the consumer cannot spend all his income.

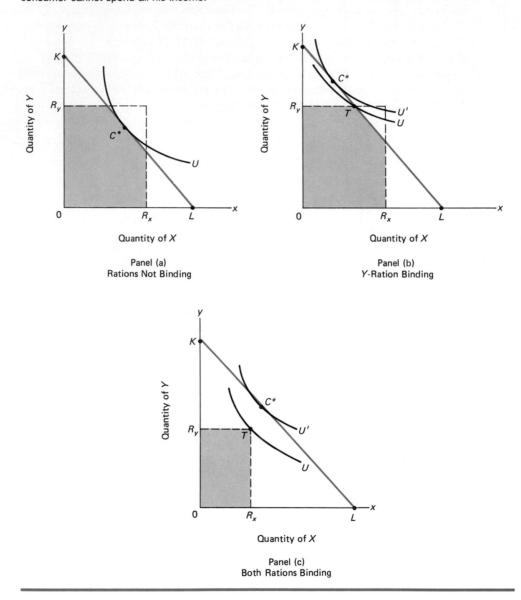

Panel (a)
Rations Not Binding

Panel (b)
Y-Ration Binding

Panel (c)
Both Rations Binding

FIGURE 5.13 **Point Rationing**   Consumption is subject to an income constraint I and also to a ration point constraint N. Commodity X is more expensive in terms of income, and commodity Y more expensive in terms of points, so the income budget line KL is steeper than the point budget line GH. In Panel (a) "point income" is so large that only money income is binding; Panel (b) represents the opposite case. In Panel (c) each constraint is binding over a certain range.

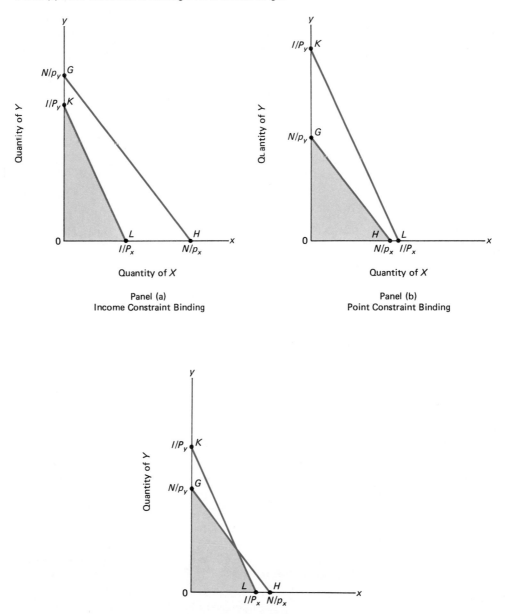

Panel (a)
Income Constraint Binding

Panel (b)
Point Constraint Binding

Panel (c)
Both Constraints Binding

$$\begin{cases} P_x x + P_y y \leq I & \text{Income Constraint} \qquad (5.11) \\[2mm] p_x x + p_y y \leq N & \text{Point Constraint} \\[2mm] x \geq 0, \, y \geq 0 & \text{Non-Negativity conditions} \end{cases}$$

In Figure 5.13 the income budget line KL was drawn to be steeper than the point budget line GH; that is, $P_x/P_y > p_x/p_y$. Commodity X is therefore (by assumption) comparatively more expensive in terms of ordinary income, and commodity Y is more expensive in terms of points. It follows that consumers who like commodity X would tend to find the income constraint binding; those more interested in Y would tend to find the point constraint binding.

EXAMPLE 5.4 **Wartime Point Rationing**

Cheese and canned fish were among the commodities rationed by points during World War II in the United States. The following table compares the 1942 (pre-rationing) purchases of different income groups with the quantities purchased during 1944 when rationing was effective.

Average Weekly Purchases by Housekeeping Families in Cities (lb.)

Income	$1000 or Less	$1000– 2000	$2000– 3000	$3000– 4000	Over $4000
1942					
Cheese	0.26	0.57	0.64	0.81	1.03
Canned fish	0.21	0.36	0.56	0.44	0.37
1944					
Cheese	0.24	0.33	0.44	0.49	0.52
Canned fish	0.06	0.12	0.17	0.22	0.18

Source: L.A. Epstein, "Wartime Food Purchases," *Monthly Labor Review*, v. 60 (June 1945), p. 1148.

This table compares the binding power of income versus points at different income levels. Looking only at the three highest income groups (last three columns), we see that their consumption patterns in 1944 were almost identical. Consumers in this income range were in the situation pictured in Panel (b) of Figure 5.13. Consumption of cheese and canned fish was almost entirely limited by points, and higher income made little difference. An important fact about this period is that the money price of canned fish relative to cheese approximately doubled between 1942 and 1944. The fish/cheese consumption ratio for the lowest income group consequently fell from $0.21/0.26 = 0.81$ in 1942 to $0.06/0.24 = 0.25$ in 1944, showing strong sensitivity to the price change (fish and cheese were evidently close substitutes). But for the highest income group the 1942 fish/cheese consumption ratio ($0.37/1.03 = 0.36$) remained almost unchanged ($0.18/0.52 = 0.35$) in 1944. The reason was that, owing to the rationing, the dollar prices were simply not binding for them.

SUMMARY

The *income elasticity* of demand for commodity X, denoted ϵ_x, represents the *proportionate* change of quantity purchased in response to a proportionate change in income. The first ratio that follows represents the definition; the others are useful alternative algebraic forms.

$$\epsilon_x \equiv \frac{\Delta x/x}{\Delta I/I} \equiv \frac{\Delta x/\Delta I}{x/I} \equiv \frac{\Delta x}{\Delta I}\frac{I}{x}$$

Income elasticity is positive for superior goods, negative for inferior goods.

The *price elasticity* of demand for X, denoted η_x, represents the proportionate change of quantity in response to a proportionate change in the price P_x. The first ratio that follows represents this definition; the others are useful alternative algebraic forms:

$$\eta_x \equiv \frac{\Delta x/x}{\Delta P_x/P_x} \equiv \frac{\Delta x/\Delta P_x}{x/P_x} \equiv \frac{\Delta x}{\Delta P_x}\cdot\frac{P_x}{x}$$

The Law of Demand implies that price elasticity is negative. Demand is elastic or inelastic depending upon whether the absolute value of η_x is greater or less than 1. If demand is elastic, a reduction in price leads to an increase in consumer expenditures P_xx; if demand is inelastic, a reduction in price leads to a fall in P_xx.

The *cross-elasticity* of demand η_{xy} is the proportionate change in quantity demanded of some good X in response to a proportionate change in the price of *another* commodity P_y. The definition and an alternative algebraic form are as follows:

$$\eta_{xy} \equiv \frac{\Delta x/x}{\Delta P_y/P_y} \equiv \frac{\Delta x}{\Delta P_y}\cdot\frac{P_y}{x}$$

If the cross-elasticity is positive, the two goods are called *substitutes*. If η_{xy} is negative, the two goods are called *complements*.

Demand functions are commonly estimated (fitted) from data by using either a linear or a constant-elasticity form. Along a linear demand curve the price elasticity of demand increases (in absolute value) as we move up and to the left along the line. A constant-elasticity demand curve, correspondingly, cannot be a straight line.

There are several possible causes of high price elasticities of demand. First, if a commodity has close substitutes, the large substitution effect of a fall in the price of the good leads to a large increase in consumption. Second, if a commodity is a luxury (a strongly superior good), the large income effect of a price decrease causes a big increase in consumption. Third, if the demand curve is approximately linear, elasticity tends to be large at high prices (that is, where the consumer is taking very little of the good). But since demand curves need not have a linear form, this generalization is not strongly grounded.

Finally, it is sometimes thought demand tends to be inelastic for a commodity that accounts for only a small proportion of the consumer's budget demand. However, the argument is fallacious, since the small response of an unimportant commodity to a price change need not be small in *percentage* terms.

Under normal conditions, the consumer's purchases of goods are constrained only by his or her income. In some circumstances other constraints are applicable, such as rationing in wartime. Point rationing allows greater freedom of choice than simple quantity rationing, but all forms of rationing are effective only when actually binding upon consumer choices.

QUESTIONS

For Review

1. What is the general definition of all elasticity measures? Why is the income elasticity of demand considered a more useful measure than the simple slope along an Engel Curve? Why is the price elasticity of demand considered a more useful measure than the simple slope along a demand curve? Are elasticity measures always better than the simple measures? (See the question following.)

*2. Consider this paradox: Income elasticity is supposed to measure the responsiveness of consumption to changes in income. But income elasticity is unity along *any* Engel Curve that is a straight line through the origin, whether very steep or very flat. Since Engel Curves of different steepness surely show different responses of consumption to income, how can they all be characterized as having the same income elasticity?

3. True or false: "Income elasticity is unity at any point along an Engel Curve such that the tangent at that point extends through the origin." Explain.

4. True or false: "Since income elasticities must average out to unity, any commodity accounting for a very large fraction of income expenditure cannot have an income elasticity very far from unity." Explain.

*5. a. What is meant by elastic demand and inelastic demand?
   b. How can elasticity at a point along a linear demand curve be determined by inspection?
   c. Along a nonlinear demand curve?

*6. Let the demand curve be $P = A - BX$, where A and B are positive constants.
   a. What is the elasticity at $X = 0$?
   b. At $X = A/B$?
   c. At $X = A/(2B)$?

7. If the demand curve is $PX = 100$, what is the price elasticity of demand at $X = 10$? At $X = 50$? At $X = 100$?

8. What is the analytical form of a demand function that is *linear* in both income and price? What is the analytical form of a demand function that has *constant elasticities* with respect to both income and price? Explain the economic meaning of each form.

*9. If there is a single "all-important" commodity that absorbs all of the individual's income, what is its price elasticity? income elasticity?

*10. Gasoline rationing was proposed in 1973 and again in 1979 as a remedy for the energy crisis. If all persons are given identical rations, compare the opportunity sets of a wealthy and a poor consumer for gasoline consumption versus "all other goods." Show typical indifference maps if automobile usage is a luxury. Would permitting sale of coupons be a good idea?

*The answers to starred questions appear at the end of the book.

For Further Thought and Discussion

*1. "On average over all goods, income elasticity must be unity." Prove this proposition.

*2. a. Consider the demand curve $PX = 100$. What happens to the elasticity of demand as price falls? What happens to "importance" (share of the consumer budget spent on X) as price falls?

    b. Apply the previous questions for the demand curve $P^2X = 100$.

    c. For the demand curve $P^{1/2}X = 100$.

    d. What can you infer about the relation between elasticity and "importance"?

*3. The American economist Irving Fisher argued in 1891 that a poor community will hardly distinguish quality grades of a commodity like beef, while a rich community would.

> In the country districts of "the West" all cuts of beef sell for the same price (about 10 cents. per lb.). In the cities of the West two or three qualities are commonly distinguished, while in New York a grocer will enumerate over a dozen prices in the same beef varying from 10 to 25 cents per lb.[15]

    a. Construct the implied indifference curves, at low and high levels of income, between low-quality beef and high-quality beef.

    b. Why should different beef qualities be better substitutes at low incomes than at high incomes? What would you anticipate about the price elasticity of demand for low-quality beef? For high-quality beef?

4. Name some goods you expect to have elastic demand and some with inelastic demand. Justify your choices.

*5. Tickets to a sports match are available only on a black-market basis. Professor X, calling from out of town, gives purchasing instructions to his secretary: "If the price is $30 each, buy one ticket for me; at $20 each, buy two; if it is $10, buy three." The secretary says: "Prof, there must be something wrong here. You're saying you'd be willing to pay more in total for two tickets than for three!" Is the secretary correct? Explain.

*6. For a commodity with snob appeal, consumers might be willing to buy more at a higher price than at a lower price (violation of the Law of Demand). Is this possible or likely? Explain.

*7. If uninformed consumers judge quality by price, they may also be willing to buy more at a higher than at a lower price. Is this possible or likely? Explain.

*8. In wartime rationing situations it is generally illegal to buy another person's ration allowances for cash, or to exchange ration coupons.

    a. Is there any justification for this?

    b. Are there adverse consequences of forbidding such exchanges?

---

[15]Irving Fisher, *Mathematical Investigations in the Theory of Value and Prices* (New Haven: Yale University Press, 1925), p. 74.

CHAPTER 6

THE BUSINESS FIRM

EXAMPLES

P art Two of this text focused on the consuming *individual*. Part Three concentrates on the *business firm*, and on the collection of firms in a given market that we call the *industry*. This chapter is devoted specifically to the business firm. The following chapter explains the behavior of firms in a given industry under perfect competition; later chapters take up imperfect competition and its consequences.

6.1 FIRMS AND THE CIRCULAR FLOW OF ECONOMIC ACTIVITY

Figure 1.1 showed the circular flow of economic activity. Two types of economic agents were shown: individuals or households, and business firms. Individuals or households constitute the demand side of the product market—the market for consumption goods and services discussed in previous chapters. Although economic analysis usually takes the number of people in a society as a factor determined "outside" the economic system, population size does respond to economic conditions and incentives, as has been recognized since the time of Malthus.[1] Good or bad harvests, and business conditions more generally, affect birth rates and death rates, as well as immigration and emigration.

Business firms, on the other hand, are artificial entities that people create in response to economic incentives. Specifically, firms exist to produce goods and services. Of course, some production still takes place within households. Despite this, we say for simplicity that, as pictured in Figure 1.1, firms constitute the supply side of the product market and individuals the demand side.

6.2 WHY FIRMS? ENTREPRENEUR, OWNER, MANAGER

If individuals and households can (and to some extent do) produce goods and services, why do firms exist? There are two interrelated reasons: to take advantage of team production, and to reduce contracting costs.

Team production is a fact of economic life. Many goods simply cannot be produced without a team of workers, each trained for a specific task (clerk, assembly-line worker,

List of Notation

AC	Average Total Cost	*MC*	Marginal Cost
AR	Average Revenue	*MR*	Marginal Revenue
AVC	Average Variable Cost	*P*	Price
C	Total Cost	*Q*	Quantity
F	Fixed Cost	*R*	Total Revenue
LRAC	Long-Run Average Cost	*SRTC*	Short-Run Total Cost
LRMC	Long-Run Marginal Cost	*VC*	Variable Cost
LRTC	Long-Run Total Cost	*Π*	Profits

[1]T.R. Malthus (1766–1834) was an English clergyman and economist. Malthus maintained that population would always tend to expand to the limits of subsistence. His views had an important influence upon Charles Darwin's thinking that culminated in the theory of biological evolution.

inspector, foreman, etc.). But the advantages of team production do not of themselves explain why the business firm exists. Individuals who own different resources could contractually arrange to cooperate in production. In creating a motion picture the producer, director, actors, camera operators, and so forth might agree on a contract specifying the types and quantities of inputs each party would contribute at stated times to making the film. The contract would also indicate, of course, each person's financial obligations and rewards. Such multilateral arrangements are rare because of the high costs of negotiating and enforcing them. When a firm is set up to produce a motion picture, in contrast, only *bilateral* contracts are involved. The resource-owners do not have to come to an agreement with every other participant, but instead only with the firm itself.

In actuality, however, the "firm" is an abstraction. People can really deal only with other human beings. Therefore some person or group (management) must have authority to make decisions in the name of the firm. Management may simply be the owner or owners of the firm, those who receive the residual return after all contractual payments are made. But here again, especially with large firms, a division of labor tends to emerge. Owners contract only with management, while management makes and enforces contracts with all the other resource-suppliers.

EXAMPLE 6.1 Effectiveness of Management

Using "predelinquent" boys in a youth home as experimental subjects, the psychologist E.L. Phillips[a] conducted experiments to evaluate the effectiveness of payment systems for the performance of various tasks. Task completion was reinforced by the awarding of points, which could be converted into desired commodities or privileges. One of the experiments involved cleaning bathrooms.

Among the experimental setups examined were the group condition and the manager condition. In the group condition, responsibility was collective. All boys received the same reward or fine, which depended on the group's overall performance. In the manager condition, a weekly auction determined which boy became the manager. The manager could assign tasks and distribute rewards or fines based on his judgment of the work performed. The manager's reward or fine depended on the overall level of achievement.

Results under the group condition typically showed completion of about 6 of the 16 tasks involved in cleaning. Under the manager condition, in contrast, about 14 of the 16 tasks were usually completed.

COMMENT Under the group condition each boy failing to complete any task suffered only a portion of the overall penalty (which was assessed upon *every* boy in the group). So the incentive to work rather than shirk was weak. The manager, in contrast, was paid solely in terms of the group achievement, so he had a strong incentive to make the others toe the mark. (The question of how to arrange for efficient collective action will be discussed in more detail in Part Five, as a problem of political economy.)

[a]E.L. Phillips, "Achievement Place: Token Reinforcement Procedures in a Home-Style Rehabilitation Setting for 'Pre-delinquent' Boys," *Journal of Applied Behavior Analysis,* v. 1 (Fall 1968).

Who monitors the manager? Ultimately, it is up to the owner or owners to perform this task themselves. This inescapable decision-making aspect of firm ownership is called *entrepreneurship*. Firms are created, we have seen, to achieve certain transaction economies.

But unavoidably there must be a contract among the owners (if there is more than one) that sets up the firm, and a contract between the owners and the manager of the firm (if those two functions are not combined). The execution and enforcement of these contracts pose considerable difficulties.

The invention of the corporate form has greatly simplified contracting among multiple owners of a firm. By doing business as a corporation, large groups of people can combine their resources to exploit large and risky multiperson projects. The key features of the corporation are limited liability and transferable shares. Limited liability means that the contractual obligations of the corporation cannot be brought home to the personal accounts of the individual owners. A supplier whose bill is not paid, for example, can sue the corporation but cannot sue any individual stockholder. In contrast, if the firm were a sole proprietorship or a partnership, the owner or owners could be sued personally.

Thus, under corporate ownership shares may become valueless (at worst), but the rest of the stockholder's assets are safe. And an individual stockholder who needs cash, or who is dissatisfied with the policies of the manager or of the other owners, can easily sell his shares. Consequently, a corporation can raise far more money than can a partnership.

The corporate form is obviously to the advantage of the owners of the firm, but the creditors of the firm (banks that lend money, consumers who make advance payments, or workers paid only at the end of the month) may well be concerned about the money owed them. Indeed, though you may not often think of yourself as such, you may be a creditor of such firms as General Motors and Delta Airlines. If you purchase a new automobile from General Motors, you expect the firm to perform warranty service when needed. If you purchase an airline ticket, you expect the airline to accommodate you on the date of the flight. But should the firm be bankrupt at the time you need service, the warranty or the airline ticket may be worthless. It may therefore appear that suppliers and consumers would prefer to deal with firms that have unlimited, rather than limited, liability; though the firm may close down, a creditor could still seek compensation from the former owners.

While this inference is true, it is somewhat misleading. No one is actually forced to do business with corporations on limited-liability terms. Banks, for example, often require owners of a corporation to assume personal liability for a loan made to the corporation. People contract with a corporation on limited-liability terms only because on balance they believe they get a good deal. Put another way, the corporate form improves efficiency to such an extent that corporations can offer very favorable terms, enough to make their suppliers and customers willing to accept the risk associated with limited liability.

As a related point, under unlimited liability there would be a tendency for businesses to be owned by individuals with few assets available to be seized. This leads to the more general question of what types of persons, or which categories of resource-owners, become the entrepreneurs or owners of the firm and thus take their income in the form of residual profit rather than fixed contractual payments.

In farming, the landowner may be the entrepreneur who hires labor at a fixed wage. Or, the working farmer (supplier of labor input) may be the entrepreneur instead, leasing land for a fixed rental payment. Sometimes the supplier of land and the supplier of labor share the uncertainty of profit and loss; this is called share-cropping. In general, we would expect the entrepreneurs to be best able to bear risk. Another consideration is the need for monitoring. Inputs that are more easily monitored will tend to be purchased or rented, while inputs for which monitoring of performance is more difficult tend to be provided by owners. For example, in a small restaurant the cashier or even the chef is more likely to own the business than is the landlord of the building or the supplier of the silverware.

6.3 ECONOMIC PROFITS DIFFER FROM ACCOUNTING PROFITS

Individuals maximize utility, but what do firms maximize? Economists usually assume that the firm maximizes *profits*—the difference between *total revenue* and *total cost*.

Revenue is receipts from sales. In the simple case where the price charged for each unit is the same, revenue is price times quantity sold. *Cost* is a more complicated concept. The economic cost of any activity is the value of the *best foregone alternative*. To attract the resources or inputs necessary for production, the firm must pay the owners of resources amounts sufficient to induce them to sacrifice their best alternatives, whether these alternatives be finding employment elsewhere or leisure.

Accountants treat costs in a different way, and so economic profits may diverge from accounting profits. Economic profits compare the firm's current activities to the next best alternative. If profits are positive the uses of resources within the firm yield higher returns than the best alternative uses. So the firm should continue in its current business. But if profits are negative, the firm would do better by shutting down or undertaking another line of business. In contrast, accounting numbers have other purposes: they control fraud, allow creditors or investors to determine whether to invest in the firm, tell management how well it is doing, and, very importantly, are required by the tax authorities to determine the tax liability of the firm.

We will not delve here into the definitions used in accounting. We merely note some of the important differences between accounting profits and economic profits.

Accounting profits do not deduct *all* the costs of operating the firm. Accountants mostly consider costs to be those expenses that the firm paid for in a measurable way. In particular, these costs do not include the alternative values of the owners' self-supplied services. Consider a butcher who owns a shop. His accountant says that the profit for the year, that is, the difference between sales and measurable expenses, was $33,000. Suppose, however, that a local supermarket would have paid the butcher $20,000 per year for his services, and that the butcher could have rented the shop to another merchant for $10,000 net of all expenses. The true "economic profit" is therefore only $33,000 − $20,000 − $10,000 = $3,000. If the butcher's accounting profit had instead been $5,000, then his business would have an economic loss of $25,000. (We set aside here any extra satisfaction he may enjoy from running his own business.)

Similarly, if a firm developed a highly successful new technology, the accountant would value the technology at the cost of developing it, not at the amount someone else would be willing to pay for it. Or suppose the firm had bought a building at a low cost many years ago, and now this building is at the heart of a booming shopping center. The accountant would calculate as cost the depreciation in terms of the historical purchase price, not in terms of the current market price. So we could find that the firm's accounting profits are very high, but its economic profits may be negative: the owner might do better selling the building to someone who could use it to far greater advantage.

Thus, economic profits adjust accounting profits by subtracting the highest alternative return on all inputs contributed by the owner or owners. Put another way, economic profit is revenue minus economic cost, not revenue minus accounting cost.

6.4 THE GOALS OF THE FIRM

Some critics deny that firms aim to maximize (economic) profits, claiming that the separation of ownership and control in large modern corporations causes these firms to pursue goals other than profit maximization.

For very large firms, where no single stockholder accounts for more than a tiny fraction of the shares outstanding, management may (it is contended) be in a position to run things without significant monitoring by owners. Of course, there are limits. If the shareholders were literally powerless, management could do whatever it wished, even dissipate the value of the firm by enormous executive salaries and expense accounts. But, of course, managers do not have a license to steal. Shareholders can and do sue management, indicating that at least some owners monitor corporate managers.

In addition, and perhaps more significantly, outsiders are often eager to come in and take over the firm. Suppose those currently managing the corporation are self-serving or inefficient. Then the low earnings now and in prospect reduce the market value of the corporate shares. An alternative management group has an incentive to buy shares, at their current low prices, with the hope of obtaining enough to win control. Or the new group may instead try to win the votes of existing shareholders in a proxy contest.

The challenge to the profit-maximizing model need not go so far as to claim that shareholders have no power. The critics may concede that management must provide some minimum level of profits, to reduce the likelihood of lawsuits or takeover contests. But beyond this level, the contention is, managers pursue their own goals rather than those of owners. Managers may seek power (empire-building), publicity in the form of a corporate image, amenities like luxurious offices, or a stable environment without risk of unpleasant surprises.

Suppose then that a manager of a firm owned by stockholders gets some non-pecuniary benefits from running the firm. To be concrete, suppose the manager values working in a prestigious office building at $10,000 a year. This means that, other things equal, a manager would be willing to accept a salary of roughly $10,000 a year less if he or she has the right to choose the company's offices. But the cost of an office at a prestigious address may be an extra $100,000 a year. If so, allowing such a manager to choose the firm's office will impose a net cost of $90,000 on the stockholders. Since it may cost more than $90,000 for stockholders to monitor the manager's office location decision, there may be some room for a manager to pursue policies that do not maximize the firm's profits.[2]

Notice, however, that to get as much as possible of these amenities, the manager must maximize the firm's profits before his or her outlandish expenses are considered: he or she would prefer to have a million dollars to play with than only half a million. The amenity-maximizing manager therefore has the same incentives as a profit-maximizing manager to buy raw materials at a low price, to obtain as large a revenue as possible from any output sold, and so on.

---

[2]Such problems could be avoided if the manager himself were the owner. And indeed, for most small firms the owners are the managers. But the corporate form, we have seen, allows a great many different people to share ownership and such multiple owners are not in a position to manage the firm themselves.

EXAMPLE 6.2   Are Managers Compensated for Good Performance?

Managers will be especially likely to attempt to increase profits if their compensation is tied to the firm's performance. Robert Gibbons and Kevin Murphy[a] examined this connection. Between the mid-1970s and the mid-1980s, a Chief Executive Officer (CEO) typically received a pay increase of 6.8 percent in a year when shareholders' returns in the firm and in the overall stock market were both zero. Managers of firms that performed better got larger increases. For example, on average, the CEO in a firm generating a shareholder return of 10 percent, when the overall stock market return was zero, received an extra pay increase of 1.8 percent. In a different study, Michael Jensen and Kevin Murphy[b] found that a $1,000 increase in the value of a firm's shares increases the total compensation (through salary, stock options, and the like) of a CEO by only $3.25. A critical, though unanswered question, is whether more closely tying managerial compensation to performance would improve management.

[a]Robert Gibbons and Kevin J. Murphy "Relative Performance Evaluation for Chief Executive Officers." NBER Working Paper No. 2944, 1989.

[b]Michael C. Jensen and Kevin J. Murphy "Performance Pay and Top-Management Incentives." *Journal of Political Economy*, v. 98 (April 1990).

Under some conditions, profit maximization may not be the sole goal of stockholders. For example, stockholders have mixed incentives if they also purchase the good produced by the firm. As recipients of dividends they may prefer high prices, as consumers they prefer low prices. (This consideration is unlikely to be important in practice, however.) Also, a stockholder in one firm who also owns shares of other firms is concerned with the aggregate profits of all the firms in which he has invested. If, for example, Coca-Cola and Pepsi Cola were by and large owned by the same investors, then the investors would not necessarily want Coca-Cola to take market share away from Pepsi Cola.

No doubt managers sometimes serve their own interests at the expense of the owners, and shareholders are not always concerned exclusively with the firm's profits. But are these problems significant enough to make the profit-maximization hypothesis unworkable? That is a question for empirical investigation. So far at least, for purposes of economic analysis the standard concept of the profit-maximizing firm has proven more useful and insightful than alternative assumptions about the goals of the business firm.

Do monitoring and threats of takeover keep managers' activities in line with shareholders' interests? Examples 6.3 and 6.4 give illustrative evidence.

EXAMPLE 6.3   The Separation of Ownership and Control

Harold Demsetz and Kenneth Lehn studied the concentration of ownership in a sample of 511 very large U.S. corporations.[a] Their view was that higher concentrations of ownership, as measured by the proportion of stock in each company controlled by the five largest ownership interests, should lead to more effective monitoring of management by owners.

On average, in these corporations the five largest ownership interests controlled over 25 percent of the shares in 1980. Furthermore, individuals and families owning large fractions of a particular firm typically did not own significant numbers of shares in *other* firms. This makes sense if large stockholders are concerned about effective monitoring. Since overseeing management is costly and difficult, other things equal, wealthy individuals and families will prefer to specialize their holdings in a single firm that they can supervise closely. On the other hand, an investor who concentrates wealth in a single company loses the advantages of diversification.

Monitoring will be needed more, Demsetz and Lehn believed, the more unstable the environment in which the corporation finds itself. Among their measures of instability were (1) the variation in monthly rates of return on corporate shares and (2) the variability from year to year of accounting profit rates. For all the measures of instability, it was found that the greater the instability, the larger the concentration of ownership. This evidence supports the thesis that large holdings are associated with monitoring, since otherwise an individual would want to hold a *smaller* proportion of his or her wealth in a very risky stock.

Demsetz and Lehn also found that, other things equal, in percentage terms larger corporations had less concentration of ownership. This is logical in view of the greater cost of acquiring any given fraction of the shares, but also because a smaller percentage is more effective as a controlling interest in larger corporations where the bulk of the shares tend to be widely diffused. Regulated industries also tended to have smaller concentration of ownership, presumably because government regulation provides some outside monitoring that reduces the need for owners to monitor management. As a final point, Demsetz and Lehn found significantly greater concentration of ownership in media firms and sports firms. The reason offered is that each of these industries offers significant amenities to owners. Owners of sports firms may enjoy being in the public eye and associating with celebrities; owners of newspapers and magazines may enjoy influencing public opinion. Thus, ownership and supervision of management may be desired for nonprofit goals as well as for higher profit.

[a]Harold Demsetz and Kenneth Lehn, "The Structure of Corporate Ownership: Causes and Consequences," *Journal of Political Economy*, v. 93 (December 1985).

EXAMPLE 6.4 Owners Versus Managers

When managers of a corporation do not perform as well as they might in terms of profit, this fact will be reflected in a lower stock price. Outsiders who believe they can run the company more profitably are then in a better position to take it over—by buying a controlling number of shares in the market, by winning shareholder support in a proxy fight, or by negotiation with the existing management.

If in fact the new management will run the company more profitably, or at least if that is the general market opinion, then a successful takeover will lead to a jump in the stock price. Michael C. Jensen and Richard S. Ruback reviewed a considerable number of studies of this question. Adjusting for such effects as general movement of the stock market, they calculated the abnormal effects attributable to the takeover itself. The following table represents a summary of their evidence, averaged over a large number of successful and unsuccessful takeover attempts.

The tender offer and the proxy contest represent ways of taking over a corporation against the will of existing management. Merger, by contrast, is a voluntary arrangement. (However, such agreement may be due to the threat of involuntary takeover.) In either case, stockholders evidently profited substantially from successful takeovers, suggesting that previous management had not maximized profit for the shareholders. Share-holders did not do particularly well after unsuccessful takeovers. This might have been due to market disappointment that a potentially more effective management had failed to gain control. On the other hand, the takeover attempts may have failed because existing management had really been, in the opinion of the stockholders, doing as well as possible.

While the data summarized here might be taken as evidence that American corporate managements quite commonly fail to maximize profits for corporate shareholders, this conclusion is really not warranted. After all, the great majority of American companies have not been the targets of takeover attempts.

COMMENT An interesting sidelight is the fact that *bidder* companies, as opposed to the target corporations, gained very little on average from the takeover efforts—whether successful or unsuccessful. This suggests either that there might have been "nonprofit amenities" such as empire-building or power-seeking involved in motivating takeover efforts, or, alternatively, that the takeover business is so competitive that large profits cannot be earned, at least on average.

Abnormal Stock Price Changes

Takeover Technique	Price Change (%)
Successful takeovers	
tender offers	30
mergers	20
proxy contests	8
Unsuccessful takeovers	
tender offers	−3
mergers	−3
proxy contests	8

Source: Michael C. Jensen and Richard S. Ruback, "The Market for Corporate Control: The Scientific Evidence," *Journal of Financial Economics*, v. 11 (1983).

6.5 THE OPTIMUM OF THE COMPETITIVE FIRM

We shall assume that the firm aims to maximize profit, which is defined as the difference between total *revenue* and total (economic) *cost*. This chapter deals with the *competitive* or price-taking firm. Any such firm is assumed to view the market price P as constant, regardless of the firm's own level of output. (While never literally true, this approximates reality.) Total Revenue R is then, by definition, price P times quantity q (that is, $R = Pq$); this is plotted in the upper panel of Figure 6.1 as a ray through the origin with slope P. Total Revenue is zero when output q is zero; since price is constant, R increases thereafter proportionately with q. The vertical axis in the upper panel of Figure 6.1 (p. 154) is scaled simply in dollars, since dollars are the units in which revenue is measured.[3]

---

[3]Why money is used as a medium of exchange will be covered in Chapter 13.

FIGURE 6.1 **Optimum of the Competitive Firm** The profit-maximizing output is q^* in the upper diagram, where the vertical difference between the Total Revenue curve R and the Total Cost curve C is maximized. The maximized profit is Π^*. At q^* the slopes along curves R and C are equal, so in the lower diagram the Marginal Revenue curve MR and the Marginal Cost curve MC intersect at output q^*. At output q' in the upper diagram, a ray from the origin is tangent to the Total Cost curve, so Average Cost equals Marginal Cost; in the lower diagram q' lies at the intersection of the MC and AC curves, so at output q' Average Cost is at a minimum.

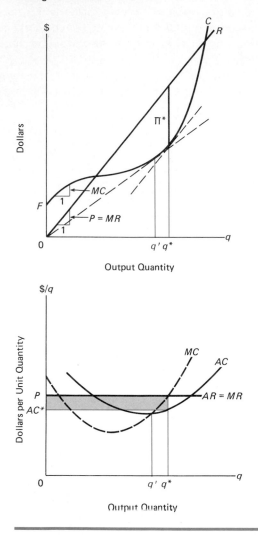

Total Cost is shown by curve C in the upper panel of the diagram. Typical Total Cost curves have the following three main features:

1. The vertical intercept, F, represents the Fixed Cost, such as the rent which must be paid for use of a building even if the occupant produces nothing. Thus even when output is zero, C may be positive.

2. At low outputs, C increases slowly with an increase of output owing to the advantages of large-scale production.
3. At high outputs, however, C rises at an increasing rate, reflecting the Law of Diminishing Returns.

By definition, profit is Revenue minus Cost. In symbols, $\Pi = R - C$. In the upper panel, profit is at a maximum when output and sales are q^*; at this point the difference between the R and C curves is greater than at any other level of output. This maximum level of profit, Π^*, is shown as the vertical bold line-segment. As is geometrically evident, the profit maximum occurs where the Total Cost curve C is parallel to (has the same slope as) the Total Revenue curve R. (The parallelism is suggested by the dashed tangent drawn along the C curve at $q = q^*$.) This fact provides the key to the connection between the solution in total units as shown in the upper panel of Figure 6.1 and the solution in average-marginal units portrayed in the lower panel.

The relations among total, average, and marginal magnitudes were explained in Chapter 2. We saw there that (1) a *marginal* function corresponds to the rate of increase along a total function and (2) an *average* magnitude is the total function divided by the underlying variable (which here is quantity of output, q).

Marginal Revenue MR was formally defined in Chapter 2 as follows:[4]

$$MR \equiv \frac{\Delta R}{\Delta q} \tag{6.1}$$

As with all marginal concepts, the Δ notation in $\Delta R / \Delta q$ indicates that we are dealing with small changes in each case. Geometrically, MR is the *slope* of the Total Revenue curve. (Note the small triangle drawn along the R curve in the upper panel of Figure 6.1.) For the competitive firm pictured in the diagram, this slope is a constant equal to the market price P. For example, when a furniture store sells one more chair, it keeps whatever revenue it had before, and gets an additional P dollars from the sale of this new chair; Marginal Revenue is therefore P. (We shall later see that for a monopolist, in contrast, Marginal Revenue is less than price.) Since MR, the addition to receipts from producing and selling one more chair, is constant here and equal to P, it can be plotted in the lower panel as a horizontal line of height P. Note that the vertical axis of the lower panel is scaled in units of $\$/q$, the dimensions of price.

Average Revenue AR is defined as Total Revenue divided by output, or R/q. But since $R \equiv Pq$, by definition it is always true that $AR \equiv P \equiv R/q$—so the AR curve in Panel (b) must also be a horizontal line at the level of P. Thus, for a price-taking firm the AR curve and the MR curves coincide as a horizontal line at height P. (This is an example of Proposition 2.2c: When the average function is constant, the marginal function is equal to it.)

Exercise 6.1 ———————————————————————————————

A firm faces market price $P = 25$, independent of its own level of output q. What are the equations for its Total Revenue, Marginal Revenue, and Average Revenue?

---

[4]*Mathematical Footnote:* The calculus definition would be: $MR \equiv \lim_{\Delta q \to 0} \Delta R / \Delta q$. This is, of course, the derivative dR/dq.

Answer: The equation for Total Revenue is $R = 25q$. Since $\Delta R / \Delta q$—the increase in R per unit increase in q—is always 25, we know that Marginal Revenue is a constant, with equation $MR = 25$. And, since $R/q = 25$, Average Revenue is also constant with equation $AR = 25$.

Marginal Cost, MC, is defined as[5]

$$MC \equiv \frac{\Delta C}{\Delta q} \qquad (6.2)$$

Again, the notation $\Delta C / \Delta q$ will be used with the understanding that we are dealing with small increments Δ. Geometrically, in the upper panel of Figure 6.1 MC is the slope along the Total Cost curve (note the small triangle drawn along the C curve). This slope is not a constant but instead has different values at different levels of q. The slope is first positive but decreasing (corresponding to the region where C rises at a decreasing rate) and then positive and increasing (corresponding to the region where C rises at an increasing rate).

Average Cost, AC, is total cost divided by output, or C/q. In the upper panel it is represented by the slope of a ray drawn from the origin to the C curve. At $q = 0$, this ray is vertical, so AC is infinite at the vertical axis. As output increases, the slope of the ray falls until output reaches q', which is the point of minimum AC. Thereafter, the slope of the ray rises as q increases further.

The lower panel shows the Average Cost curve AC and Marginal Cost curve MC. From Propositions 2.2a-c we know that when AC is falling, MC lies below it; when AC is rising, MC lies above it; and when AC is constant (at a minimum), $MC = AC$. The lower panel of Figure 6.1 shows that MC lies below AC for outputs less than q', then MC cuts AC at its minimum at q', and finally MC is greater than AC for outputs greater than q'.

In the upper panel we saw that profits are maximized at q^*, where Total Revenue R and Total Cost C have the same slope. Since MR is the slope of the R curve, and MC is the slope of the C curve, it follows that in the lower panel MR and MC are equal at q^* (where the MR and MC curves intersect). That is, the firm maximizes profits by choosing the level of output where Marginal Revenue = Marginal Cost.

The intuition behind this result is as follows. If in selling one more chair a store increases revenue more than it increases costs $(MR > MC)$, then the additional chair should be sold. If instead $MR < MC$, the last chair sold increases costs more than revenue, and so output should be reduced. For profit to be at a maximum the condition $MR = MC$ must hold. And since we are dealing with competitive (price-taking) firms for which $MR =$ Price $= AR$, this condition takes on the specific form:

$$MC = MR = P \qquad \text{Maximum-Profit Condition, Competitive Firm} \qquad (6.3)$$

One complication is worth noting. The output at which $MC = MR$ is an optimum only if the MC curve cuts the MR curve from below. In the lower panel of Figure 6.1 the MR and MC curves intersect at two points. But at the left-hand intersection, MC cuts MR *from above*. This means that just to the right of that intersection, we have $MR > MC$. And so

---

[5]*Mathematical Footnote:* The calculus definition would be: $MC \equiv \lim_{\Delta q \to 0} \Delta C / \Delta q$. This corresponds to the derivative dC/dq.

economic logic tells us that it pays to produce more units until the right-hand intersection is reached[6] where *MC* cuts *MR from below*.[7]

PROPOSITION: The profit-maximizing output for the firm occurs where Marginal Cost equals Marginal Revenue, provided that the Marginal Cost curve cuts the Marginal Revenue curve from below.

Exercise 6.2 ————————————————————————————————————

A firm faces a price $P = 38$ that is independent of its output q. Marginal Cost is $MC = 2 + (q - 10)^2$. (a) At what output level or levels does $MC = MR$? (b) Where does the *MC* curve cut the *MR* curve from below? (c) What is the most profitable level of output?

Answer: (a) Marginal Revenue here is $MR = P = 38$. Solving for $MC = MR$, or $2 + (q - 10)^2 = 38$, leads to two solutions: $q = 16$ and $q = 4$. The *MC* and *MR* curves intersect at both of these output levels. (b) By plotting some points we can verify that *MC* cuts *MR* from below only at the larger output, $q = 16$. (c) The most profitable level of output is $q = 16$.

——

The *size* of economic profit at the profit-maximizing output q^* was represented in the upper panel of Figure 6.1 as the bold vertical line-segment Π^* between the Total Revenue and the Total Cost curves. In the lower graph, we see that profit *per unit* is the vertical distance between Average Revenue and Average Cost. Then total profit is $(AR - AC)q$. That is, profit equals the difference between Average Revenue and Average Cost, multiplied by the level of output. So, in the lower panel maximum profit is shown as the shaded rectangle whose area is $(P - AC^*)q^*$.

Table 6.1 (p. 158) illustrates a hypothetical set of revenue and cost data for a competitive profit-maximizing firm. Price is constant at $P = 60$, so the Total Revenue column (R) is simply $R = 60q$. The cost function is assumed to be $C = 128 + 69q - 14q^2 + q^3$. This formula was used to compute values in the Total Cost column C. Plotting these points would show Total Revenue and Total Cost functions with the general shapes pictured in the upper panel of Figure 6.1; the average and marginal functions would resemble those in the lower panel.

Three different Marginal Cost concepts, described in Chapter 2, are represented by separate columns in the table. Suppose we wanted to estimate the Marginal Cost at $q = 7$. The poorer approximation MC_1 is calculated from the additional cost incurred by increasing output from $q = 6$ to $q = 7$; that is, it is the cost of the last unit produced. Thus $MC_1 = 268 - 254 = 14$ is taken as the Marginal Cost at $q = 7$. The better approximation MC_2 takes this same cost increment, 14, but regards it as providing an estimate of *MC* not at $q = 7$, but halfway between $q = 6$ and $q = 7$—specifically, $MC_2 = 14$ at $q = 6\ 1/2$. To obtain the better approximation MC_2 at $q = 7$, we also estimate *MC* at $q = 7\ 1/2$; this is the cost difference $296 - 268 = 28$ incurred by increasing output from $q = 7$ to $q = 8$. Thus, the better approximation MC_2 at $q = 7$ is the average of 14 and 28, or

[6]The left-hand intersection of *MC* and *MR* in the lower panel corresponds to a *minimum*-profit (or maximum-loss) output.

[7]*Mathematical Footnote:* We are maximizing $\Pi = R - C$ with respect to q. Differentiating and setting equal to zero, we have as the *first-order* condition for a maximum: $dR/dq = dC/dq$, or $MR = MC$. The *second-order* condition for a maximum is $d^2\Pi/dq^2 < 0$, or $d^2R/dq^2 < d^2C/dq^2$. This says that *MR* must be falling relative to *MC*, i.e., that *MC* must be cutting *MR* from below.

TABLE 6.1   **Hypothetical Revenue and Cost Functions: Competitive Firm**
$P = 60$, so $R = 60q$
$C = 128 + 69q - 14q^2 + q^3$

q	P	R	C	Approximation to Marginal Cost (poorer)	(better)	MC (exact)	AC	VC	AVC
0	60	0	128	—	—	69	∞	0	—
1	60	60	184	56	45	44	184.0	56	56
2	60	120	218	34	26	25	109.0	90	45
3	60	180	236	18	13	12	78.7	108	36
4	60	240	244	8	6	5	61.0	116	29
5	60	300	248	4	5	4	49.6	120	24
6	60	360	254	6	10	9	42.3	126	21
7	60	420	268	14	21	20	38.3	140	20
8	60	480	296	28	38	37	37.0	168	21
9	60	540	344	48	61	60	38.2	216	24
10	60	600	418	74	—	89	41.8	290	29

21. The averaged or interpolated estimates, for integer values of q, are shown in the "better approximation" column.

Finally, the *true* Marginal Cost at integer values of q is shown by the column labeled "*MC* (exact)." These numbers were computed using the equation $MC = 69 - 28q + 3q^2$, which was derived by calculus.[8]

With $P = 60$, setting the true MC equal to price leads to the profit-maximizing solution $q^* = 9$. (Using MC_2 and interpolating would yield a very close approximation, while using MC_1 would lead to a substantial error.) At $q^* = 9$, Total Revenue is 540 and Total Cost is 344; hence the maximized profit is $\Pi^* = 196$.[9]

Exercise 6.3

Suppose Total Revenue remains $R = 60q$ as in Table 6.1, but the Total Cost function is $C = 10 + 5q^2$. (a) How does this Total Cost function differ from that pictured in the upper panel of Figure 6.1? (b) How does Marginal Cost differ from that pictured in the lower panel of Figure 6.1? (c) What is the profit-maximizing output, and what is the amount of the maximized profit?

Answer: (a) Plotting several points and sketching, we can see that the C curve here always rises at an increasing rate, whereas in Figure 6.1 in an initial range the C curve rose at a decreasing rate. (b) Using the better approximation method of the text, the points obtained fit the equation $MC = 10q$. (This is also the exact Marginal Cost that can be obtained by calculus.) Unlike the MC curve in the diagram, here MC is a straight line of positive slope through the origin. (c) Since $MC = 10q$ and $MR = P = 60$, setting $MC = MR$ leads to a profit-maximizing

---

[8]*Mathematical Footnote:* $C = 128 + 69q - 14q^2 + q^3$. Then $MC \equiv dC/dq = 69 - 28q + 3q^2$.

[9]There is also a false solution (where MC cuts MR *from above*) at $q = 1/3$. At this output $R \equiv Pq = 60(1/3) = 20$, while the fixed cost alone is 128, so profit is negative.

solution at output $q* = 6$. (There is only a single intersection of the MC and MR curves.) At this output, $R = 6 \cdot 60 = 360$ and $C = 10 + 5 \cdot 6^2 = 190$, so profit is $\Pi* = 360 - 190 = 170$.

The last two columns of Table 6.1 show *Total Variable Cost VC* and *Average Variable Cost AVC*. Total Variable Cost is defined as Total Cost less Fixed Cost: $VC \equiv C - F$. Average Variable Cost is, correspondingly, $AVC = VC/q = (C - F)/q$. The relations between Total Cost and Total Variable Cost are shown geometrically in the upper panel of Figure 6.2 (p. 160). Note that VC is everywhere lower than C by a constant vertical distance equal to the amount of the Fixed Cost, F.

The relations among Marginal Cost *(MC)*, Average Cost *(AC)*, and Average Variable Cost *(AVC)* are shown in the lower panel of Figure 6.2. AC and AVC are vertically farthest apart at the vertical axis since, at $q = 0$, AC is infinite. As q rises, AC and AVC converge. The reason is that Fixed Cost becomes a smaller fraction of Total Cost as q rises. Mathematically, $AC \equiv (F + VC)/q \equiv F/q + AVC$. As q rises, the F/q term gets smaller, so AC and AVC approach each other. Marginal Cost was originally defined as the slope of the Total Cost curve C, but at any given output the VC curve has the same slope as the C curve, so that MC is also the slope of the VC curve. In other words, the level of fixed costs does not affect Marginal Cost.

Following are some other important features of Figure 6.2:

1. At $q = 0$, $MC = AVC$. In Table 6.1, note that as q approaches zero, MC and AVC approach one another.[10]
2. MC is related to AVC in the same way as to AC. That is, when AVC is falling, $MC < AVC$; when AVC is rising, $MC > AVC$, and when AVC is constant (at its minimum level), $MC = AVC$.
3. AVC is at a minimum to the left of the minimum of AC. This results from the fact that MC has a positive slope and cuts the minimum points of both AC and AVC.

In the table, both MC and AVC are 20 when $q = 7$; hence this is the minimum of AVC. The table indicates that both MC and AC are 37 at $q = 8$; this is the minimum of AC.[11]

The maximum-profit condition for the competitive firm, Marginal Cost = Marginal Revenue = P (Equation 6.3), is valid even if the firm is suffering a loss (in which case it becomes a minimum-loss condition) and provided that the firm does not shut down instead. When should the firm shut down? There is a shutdown condition for the short run (when the firm's fixed costs are positive) and a different condition for the long run (when the firm can adjust its activities so that fixed costs are zero). In the short run a firm should continue to produce as long as Total Revenue exceeds Total Variable Cost.

$$R > VC \text{ or equivalently } P > AVC \quad \text{No-Shutdown Condition} \quad (6.4a)$$
$$\text{(short run)}$$

---

[10]*Mathematical Foonote:* At $q = 0$, $AVC = 0/0$ is indeterminate. But applying L'Hôpital's Rule, $\lim_{\Delta q \to 0} VC/q = \lim_{\Delta q \to 0} [dVC/dq]/[dq/dq] = MC$. So MC and AVC coincide at $q = 0$.

[11]*Mathematical Footnote:* To find the minimum of AVC, differentiate $AVC = q^2 - 14q + 69$ and set equal to zero. The solution is $q = 7$. To find the minimum of AC, differentiate $AC = q^2 - 14q + 69 + (128/q)$. A cubic equation is obtained, but the only root in the relevant range is $q = 8$.

FIGURE 6.2   The Cost Function   In the upper diagram, Total Cost C rises with output, first at a decreasing rate but ultimately at an increasing rate. The curve VC showing Total Variable Cost lies below the curve C by the amount of the fixed cost F. In the lower diagram the Marginal Cost MC curve cuts first through the low point of Average Variable Cost AVC, and then through the low point of Average Cost AC. The firm will shut down if in the long run price is less than P_C. If price is below P_V, the firm produces nothing even in the short run.

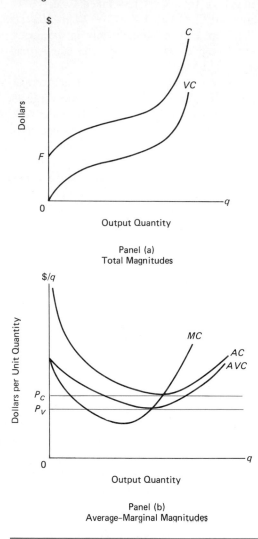

Panel (a)
Total Magnitudes

Panel (b)
Average–Marginal Magnitudes

The minimum price meeting the short-run No-Shutdown Condition is shown as P_V in Figure 6.2.

In the long run, a firm should continue to operate only if *all* its costs are covered, so the long-run No-Shutdown Condition is

$$R \geq C \text{ or equivalently } P \geq AC \quad \text{No-Shutdown Condition} \qquad (6.4b)$$
$$\text{(long run)}$$

FIGURE 6.3 **Short-Run Versus Long-Run Shutdown**   When price P = $15, the short-run optimal output (where $MC = P$) is 10 shirts per day. Since Average Cost AC equals $17 at that output, the firm loses $20 (area $ABCF$). In the long run the firm would shut down unless conditions improved. But since P = $15 exceeds Average Variable Cost AVC = $10, the firm would continue operating in the short run.

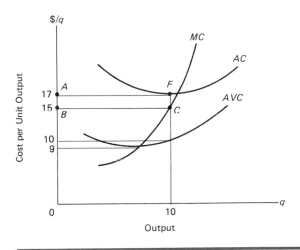

The minimum price meeting the long-run No-Shutdown Condition is shown as P_c in Figure 6.2.

These conditions are illustrated further in Figure 6.3. A firm sells 10 shirts per day at a price of $15. Suppose Average Variable Cost AVC at this output is $10 per shirt, and Average Cost (which includes fixed costs) is $17 per shirt. This means the firm loses 10($17) − 10($15) = $20, which is the area $ABCF$ in the diagram. What if the firm were to shut down? It would then receive no revenue, while in the short run the fixed costs continue to run on; for example, the firm must pay rent on the factory even if it produces nothing. In this case these fixed costs equal ($17 − $10)(10) or $70 in total. So the firm might as well produce as long as it can cover its variable costs. But if price fell below $9, the minimum of the Average Variable Cost curve, the firm would lose less by producing zero.

In the long run, any price below $17 is incompatible with production. The firm cannot lose money indefinitely, so it will dispose of its fixed plant and shut down if price remains permanently below Average Cost.

PROPOSITION: A competitive (price-taking) firm maximizes profit by choosing that level of output where Marginal Cost = Marginal Revenue = P, provided that P > Average Variable Cost in the short run and P > Average Cost in the long run.

An Application: Division of Output Among Plants

Consider a firm that can divide output between two plants, one in Albany (plant a) and another in Buffalo (plant b). Then, by extension of Equation (6.3), the firm's optimizing rule is

$$MC_a = MC_b = MR \equiv P \tag{6.5}$$

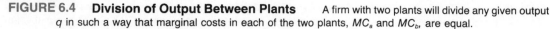

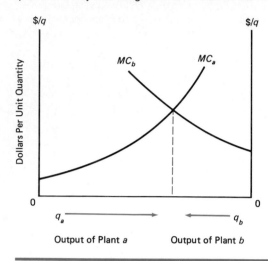

FIGURE 6.4 **Division of Output Between Plants** A firm with two plants will divide any given output q in such a way that marginal costs in each of the two plants, MC_a and MC_b, are equal.

That is, the firm should so divide its production to bring into equality the Marginal Costs in the different plants; furthermore, the total output should be such that this level of Marginal Cost equals Marginal Revenue. (For a price-taking firm, of course, Marginal Revenue is identical with price P.)

Figure 6.4 depicts the division of output between two plants. The given total level of output, $q_a + q_b = q$, is indicated by the horizontal distance between the two vertical axes. The output in Albany, q_a, is measured in the usual way, as the distance to the right of the left-hand axis. Output in Buffalo, q_b, is measured in the opposite direction, as the distance to the left of the right-hand axis. This construction is convenient since the optimal division of output, where $MC_a = MC_b$, is then at the intersection of the two Marginal Cost curves (both assumed rising throughout).[12] The *total* output of the firm is optimal at that level where $MC_a = MC_b$ so determined is also equal to Marginal Revenue.

What if the MC_a and MC_b curves, each an increasing function of its own plant output, do not intersect at all? This means that for the specified total output, one plant's Marginal Cost is *always* higher than the other's. The plant with the lower Marginal Cost should produce all the output.

Exercise 6.4 _____

(a) Suppose the Marginal Cost functions for the two plants are $MC_a = 5 + 2q_a$ and $MC_b = 40 + q_b$. If the total output is $q = 25$, how should the outputs be divided? (b) What if the total output were $q = 15$?

Answer: (a) Setting the Marginal Costs equal, we have $5 + 2q_a = 40 + q_b$. Making use of $q_a + q_b \equiv q = 25$ and substituting, we obtain the solution $q_a = 20$ and $q_b = 5$. (b) For $q = 15$, if we try to set the Marginal Costs equal as before, a negative output would be indicated

---

[12]There are interesting complications if one or both of the plant MC curves are falling rather than rising functions of output, but these topics cannot be pursued here.

for plant b. This is impossible. The explanation, which can be verified by sketching, is that the MC_a and MC_b curves do not intersect if the total output q is only 15. The best solution is to assign all output to the plant in Albany; that is, to set $q_a = 15$ and $q_b = 0$. At $q_a = 15$ the Albany plant's Marginal Cost is still only 35, while for the plant in Buffalo Marginal Cost is *never* less than 40.

Economies of Scope

We have assumed so far that the firm produces only one product. Suppose that a firm can produce two products, say shirts and dresses (symbolized by s and d), and that the firm owns two plants. Economies of *scope* are said to exist when it is less expensive to combine the production of *both* dresses and shirts in each plant, rather than have one plant specialize in dresses and the other specialize in shirts.

To illustrate, let the cost function at each plant be $C = (s + d)^2 + sd$. Let total output of shirts and dresses be s and d, respectively. If one plant produces only shirts, and the other produces only dresses, then total costs are $s^2 + d^2$. If, instead, each of the two plants produces $s/2$ shirts and $d/2$ dresses then total costs will be $2(s/2 + d/2)^2 + 2sd/4$. Algebraic manipulation shows that there are economies of scope—both plants should produce both dresses and shirts—if and only if $(s - d)^2 > sd$. For example, if $s = 100$ and $d = 100$, then producing 100 dresses in one plant and 100 shirts in the other costs $20,000; producing 50 shirts and 50 dresses in each of the two plants costs more, $25,000. So here there are diseconomies of scope. In contrast, if $s = 100$ and $d = 26$, then it is cheaper not to specialize production, but to produce both shirts and dresses in each of the two plants.

The example suggests that economies of scope are likely to arise when the outputs of the two products are very unequal—the resources at one plant can then be used in producing the small-scale product without greatly diminishing their productivity for the large-scale product. When outputs are more equal, it appears, there is more of a tendency to construct plants of efficient scale for each product separately.

6.6 SHORT RUN VERSUS LONG RUN

In the short run some costs are fixed; in the long run all costs are variable. This is the fundamental difference between the long run and the short run. The distinction is a matter of degree. The longer the length of time contemplated, the greater the range of costs considered variable rather than fixed.

Consider a manufacturing firm. Toward the variable cost end are expenses for such inputs as electric power, supplies of materials, and ordinary labor services; toward the fixed end are costs associated with ownership or leasing of real estate and machinery. Suppose an interruption of supplies or a breakdown of machinery calls for a very short, say hour-long, reduction in output. Some electric power would be saved in the slowdown, and the firm could use less materials, but little else would be changed. If output were to be cut back over a period as long as a day, some labor might also be laid off. Over a period like a month more workers could be furloughed (their wages would become a variable cost), and perhaps some leased equipment like trucks could be dispensed with. Finally, if the reduction in output is permanent, the firm may sell off machinery and scale down its real estate commitments.

In the discussion that follows "long run" means that *all* costs are variable; the "short run" means that only some costs are variable. The relations between total short-run and long-run costs under this assumption are shown in Figure 6.5. The single Long-Run Total Cost curve *LRTC* (shown in the upper panel) goes through the origin, since there are no long-run fixed costs. So at zero output $LRTC = 0$. The Long-Run Total Cost function shows the *lowest cost* of producing any given level of output. Why the lowest cost? Because, when *all* costs are variable, at any output q the firm is free to choose the best (most economical) mix of all resources employed.

Three different Short-Run Total Cost functions are shown in the upper panel. First, $SRTC_1$ is associated with a low level of fixed cost F_1. This level is assumed optimal for the relatively small rate of output q_1. If the lowest cost of producing output q_1 is with the fixed

FIGURE 6.5   Short-Run and Long-Run Cost Functions   In the upper diagram, *LRTC* is the Long-Run Total Cost function showing the cost of producing any output q when all inputs are allowed to vary. The Short-Run Total Cost curve $SRTC_1$ applies when the fixed input is held constant at a level appropriate for small-scale production (q_1); similarly, $SRTC_2$ and $SRTC_3$ are associated with the higher levels of fixed cost appropriate for medium-scale production (q_2) and large-scale production (q_3). The corresponding average and marginal curves are shown in the lower diagram. At output q_1, $SRAC_1 = LRAC$ (the curves are tangent) and $SRMC_1 = LRMC$ (the curves intersect); similar conditions hold for output levels q_2 and q_3. At any output, the Total Cost curves and the Average Cost curves are *never* higher in the long run than in the short run. (Note that no such statement can be made for the Marginal Cost curves.)

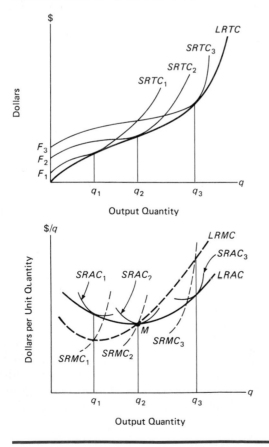

cost F_1, then the Short-Run Total Cost as given by curve $SRTC_1$ at q_1 must be equal to the Long-Run Total Cost at q_1. Any other level of output will call for a different level of optimal fixed cost. The Short-Run Total Cost curve $SRTC_1$ must therefore lie above the Long-Run Total Cost for all levels of output other than q_1. A concise way of stating this result is to say that the curve $SRTC_1$ is tangent to $LRTC$ at output q_1.

Operating along $SRTC_1$ is fine for small outputs. But at larger outputs the curve $SRTC_1$ rises steeply and increasing production beyond q_1 becomes very costly. Curve $SRTC_2$ reflects short-run costs corresponding to a level of fixed costs most suitable for a higher rate of output, q_2. Moderately large levels of production are cheaper along $SRTC_2$ than along $SRTC_1$. Finally, $SRTC_3$ represents a level of fixed cost F_3 that is optimal for the large output q_3. It represents the best of the three situations for high production, but the worst for low production.

The following example describes a common confusion. In the short run a retail store cannot increase the amount of space it leases, but in the long run it can. Since short-run adjustments are made by increasing only *some* of the inputs, say the number of salespeople hired but not the floorspace, while long-run adjustments may involve increases in *all* inputs, short-run costs are supposedly less than long-run costs. Isn't it cheaper to increase sales by expanding only the workforce than by expanding both the workforce and the floorspace? Expressed this way, the fallacy is evident. The store may choose a higher fixed cost because doing so is less costly (involves a more economical mix of salespeople and floorspace) than expanding output by increasing variable cost (salespeople) alone.

Let us now translate from the total units in the upper panel of Figure 6.5 to average-marginal units in the lower panel. Since $SRTC_1$ lies above $LRTC$ everywhere except at the tangency point q_1, it follows that the corresponding Short-Run Average Cost curve $SRAC_1$ lies above the Long-Run Average Cost curve $LRAC$ except at q_1.[13] A similar argument applies for the relation between $SRTC_2$ and $SRAC_2$, and so forth. The upshot is that the $LRAC$ is a lower envelope of the $SRAC$ curves, just as $LRTC$ is a lower envelope of the $SRTC$ curves.

There is a famous puzzle about the relation of the Short-Run Average Cost curves to the Long-Run Average Cost curve. $SRAC_1$ is tangent to $LRAC$ at a point where both have a downward slope, and so the minimum of the $SRAC_1$ curve lies to the right of (at a greater output than) the tangency point q_1. For $SRAC_3$ the situation is reversed, and the minimum of $SRAC_3$ is to the left of q_3. This seems strange; you may wonder why the points of tangency with $LRAC$ do not all occur at the minimum points of the $SRAC$ curves.

Experimenting with the curves will show that it is geometrically impossible to draw an $LRAC$ curve through the minimum points of the $SRAC$ curves and still have $LRAC$ lie everywhere *below* these curves. For $LRTC$ we really want to know the lowest unit cost of producing any given level of output, not the output which minimizes $SRTC$. Thus, $LRTC$ is the lower envelope of the $SRTC$ curves, and a point on this envelope is not generally the lowest-cost output for any given level of fixed cost.

Consider now the short-run and long-run Marginal Costs. At the tangencies of the $SRTC$ and $LRTC$ curves in the upper panel of Figure 6.5, not only the levels but also the slopes of the curves in contact are equal. But the marginal function is always the slope of the corresponding total function. It follows that at output q_1, Short-Run Marginal Cost,

---

[13]$SRTC_1 > LRTC$ implies $SRTC_1/q > LRTC/q$. But $SRTC_1/q \equiv SRAC_1$ and $LRTC/q \equiv LRAC$, so $SRTC_1 > LRTC$ evidently implies $SRAC_1 > LRAC$. At the point of contact itself, at output q_1, the equality $SRTC_1 = LRTC$ implies the equality $SRAC_1 = LRAC$.

$SRMC_1$, equals Long-Run Marginal Cost, $LRMC$; at q_2, $SRMC_2 = LRMC$; and at q_3, $SRMC_3 = LRMC$. This leads to the relation among the various short-run and the long-run marginal curves shown in the lower panel. Note that the slope of the $LRMC$ curve is generally flatter than the slopes of the $SRMC$ curves. This feature will play a role in the distinction between the short-run and long-run supply functions of the firm, to be discussed in the next chapter.

Exercise 6.5 _____

A firm has a Long-Run Total Cost curve given by $LRTC = q^2$. Its Short-Run Total Cost curve is $SRTC = 2B + q^4/8B$, where B represents the level of the input "fixed" in the short run, for example the number of machines. Suppose $B = 4$, so that $SRTC = 8 + q^4/32$. Then it can be shown by calculus (or approximated by tabulating) that the associated Marginal Costs are $LRMC = 2q$ and $SRMC = q^3/8$. (a) At what output are $LRTC$ and $SRTC$ tangent? (b) Are the Average Cost functions, $LRAC$ and $SRAC$, also tangent at this output? [The answer here requires use of calculus.] (c) What can you say about the Marginal Cost functions, $LRMC$ and $SRMC$, at this output? (d) How does the overall picture here differ from the cost function diagrammed in Figure 6.5?

Answer: (a) At a point of tangency the curves must touch and have equal slopes. If $LRTC$ and $SRTC$ touch, it must be that $LRTC = SRTC$. So we can set $q^2 = 8 + q^4/32$. The solution is $q = 4$. We now must verify that the slopes are equal at that output. Since the marginal functions correspond to the slopes of the total functions, we need to verify that $LRMC = SRMC$ at $q = 4$. Direct substitution in the $LRMC$ and $SRMC$ equations shows that indeed $2 \cdot 4 = 4^3/8$. So the $LRTC$ and the $SRTC$ curves associated with $B = 4$ are indeed tangent at $q = 4$. (b) Since $LRTC = SRTC$ at $q = 4$, it is obvious that $LRTC/q \equiv LRAC = SRAC \equiv SRTC/q$ at $q = 4$. To show that the *slopes* are equal, we must use calculus. The derivatives of both curves equal 1 at $q = 4$, and so the curves are indeed tangent. (c) We have already seen, in (a) above, that $LRMC = SRMC$ at $q = 4$. By calculus or by plotting we can show that $SRMC$ is steeper; $LRMC$ and $SRMC$ intersect at $q = 4$, but are not tangent to one another. (d) The main difference is that the $LRTC$ curve here rises throughout at an increasing rate. This implies that both $LRAC$ and $LRMC$ are positively sloped throughout, rather than U-shaped as in the diagram. The short-run $SRAC$ curves all have the usual U-shape, however.

_____

A difficulty with the concept of fixed costs now ought to be faced. Common sense tells us that a firm that stops production for an hour will not sell its buildings and machinery with the intent of buying them back when output picks up again. How is this consistent with our analytical models? Why should a firm continue to incur any needless "fixed" costs? Why not sell off the buildings not needed today? It is sometimes said that "fixity" arises from previous contractual arrangements—for example, a mortgage on an owned building or a long-term lease on a rented one. But mortgages and leases can be renegotiated; any losses thereby incurred are attributable to past errors of judgment, and are in no way costs of current production.

Fixity is in part due to the costs of transactions discussed earlier in the chapter. The difficulty of negotiating and executing complex contracts makes it unprofitable to sell and repurchase a factory building for a production shutdown of an hour. But a second element may also be involved: the specialization of resources to the firm.

Many different types of resources may be specialized to the firm. Machinery can be made to order and buildings can be partitioned or remodeled. Workers may have specific training useful only within the firm. Highly specialized assets owned by the firm will be of little use to other firms and thus have little or no resale value. Hence, the firm cannot profitably sell such assets to meet a temporary reduction of output. Also, knowing that the resale value will be low, the firm is less ready to acquire more of such a resource merely to temporarily increase production. Even if the firm leases rather than purchases such specialized resources, the cost of canceling the lease will tend to be high. The owner of a building to be remodeled for a particular tenant, for example, will surely protect himself by insisting upon steep cancelation penalties. And a specialized worker must be paid a higher wage or else given long-term job protection.

In the absence of transaction costs, and if only unspecialized resources were used in production, there would be only a single cost function—the distinction between long run and short run would be meaningless. But with specialized resources a firm can respond in short-run or long-run ways to a decline in demand. In the short-run response, appropriate for a *temporary* reduction of output, the firm holds specialized resources fixed and continues to count their cost as a cost of doing business. Thus, a loss may be incurred in the short run (Average Cost may exceed price), meaning that it is rational for the firm to accept a temporary loss rather than dispose of a specialized resource that would shortly have to be repurchased or rehired. The long-run response, appropriate for a *permanent* decline in output, is to dispose of the specialized resources. Hence their cost is no longer "fixed." (Any accounting loss suffered in the disposition of specialized inputs is a "sunk" cost, the result of a past error of judgment and thus not relevant for any current decision.)

Corresponding considerations apply to an *increase* in demand. A firm that views the increase as temporary will be cautious about incurring the cost of hiring additional specialized workers, in view of the likely cancellation penalties when the time comes to lay them off. If the firm believes the demand change is permanent, however, it will want to incur additional fixed costs in order to efficiently produce large rates of output.

CONCLUSION: Inputs may be held fixed in the face of a temporary demand fluctuation for two reasons: (1) to save the costs of specializing inputs to the firm; (2) to avoid round-trip transaction costs associated with purchase and resale (or sale and repurchase, or hiring and firing) of inputs. In holding inputs fixed the firm makes a *short-run* response to the fluctuation in demand. The firm will want to make a *long-run* response, varying the amounts of all inputs, if it regards the demand change as permanent.

6.7 RISING COSTS AND DIMINISHING RETURNS

Throughout this chapter both Marginal Cost and Average Cost are pictured as eventually rising functions of output q. These characteristics must apply if the firm actually operates under competitive price-taking conditions.

What if Marginal Cost MC instead falls throughout? The profit-maximizing condition $MC = MR =$ Price is valid only if the MC curve cuts the MR curve *from below*. Since competitive conditions dictate a horizontal MR curve, the MC curve cannot cut MR from below for levels of output where MC is falling. So if MC declines for all levels of output, a competitive optimum cannot be found.

Exercise 6.6 —————————————————————————————

What would happen if a publisher's Marginal Cost of producing calendars were falling throughout—for example, if $MC = 20 + 8/(1 + q)$? Let the fixed cost be F, and suppose the market price is $P = 22$.

Answer: Setting $MC = MR = P$, the algebraic solution is $q = 3$. But clearly MC exceeds $P = 22$ for all $q < 3$, so at $q = 3$ the publisher suffers a loss, even without allowing for the fixed cost F. On the other hand, as output exceeds $q = 3$ the publisher earns a profit on each unit, and this profit increases with output forever! The publisher would then try to produce an infinite output, which is obviously impossible. (If it were to try to expand output indefinitely, eventually the market price P would decline, which means that competitive conditions would no longer apply.)

What if *Average* Cost were falling throughout? Then one publisher with very large output could always produce more cheaply than any number of smaller publishers adding up to the same output; the smaller competitors would be driven out of business. A falling Average Cost curve is a possible source of what is called *natural monopoly,* a topic to be discussed in Chapter 8. [*Question:* Was it necessary to discuss falling Marginal Cost and falling Average Cost separately? If Marginal Cost declines with output does it follow that Average Cost falls with output? If Average Cost falls everywhere, must Marginal Cost also fall? *Answer:* Verify that, for some Total Cost curves, Average Cost falls with increasing output but the corresponding Marginal Cost curve does not have negative slope at all levels of output. On the other hand, if Marginal Cost has negative slope everywhere, then the corresponding Average Cost curve also has negative slope throughout.]

Marginal and Average Cost curves that eventually rise are associated with the famous Law of Diminishing Returns, a topic to be covered in more detail when the theory of production is discussed in Chapter 11. The law is actually a technological principle, intended to explain, for example, why all the world's food could not be grown in a flowerpot. More formally, the principle can be stated as follows: if one or more productive inputs are held fixed, then additional production requires that the other (variable) inputs be increased at an increasing rate. Thus, holding constant the amount of soil in the flowerpot, the attempt to grow more flowers—if successful at all—requires ever-rising additions of labor, fertilizer, and so forth. Of course, rising amounts of inputs imply rising levels of cost. Thus, diminishing returns (marginal and average) translate into rising costs (marginal and average).

The Law of Diminishing Returns clearly applies in the *short run,* which (we have just seen) is defined by the condition that one or more inputs are held fixed by the firm. But in Figure 6.5 not only are the Short-Run Marginal Cost and Short-Run Average Cost curves shown as eventually rising, but so are the Long-Run Marginal Cost and Long-Run Average Cost curves. Can this be justified? If it were literally the case that in the long run *all* inputs were variable, the Law of Diminishing Returns would not apply. It would be possible to choose the best combination of inputs, and then to proportionately increase or decrease all inputs. The Long-Run Average Cost curve *(LRAC)* would be horizontal, in which case the Long-Run Marginal Cost curve *(LRMC)* would also be horizontal and equal to *LRAC* (Proposition 2.2c). But it is not really possible to vary all inputs together. One or more inputs, and in particular entrepreneurship, may not be readily expandable by the firm. Also, the very nature of the firm may be associated with some unique productive opportunity. A mining company, for example, may exploit some particular body of ore. It could try to obtain more output by increasing the use of labor and machines and other variable inputs, but the firm cannot duplicate the ore body itself. The existence of fixed inputs thus explains why, in any economically possible long run, the Law of Diminishing Returns ultimately applies: the Long-Run Marginal and Average Cost curves must eventually rise.

EXAMPLE 6.5   **Diminishing Returns in Emissions Control**

In 1970 the U.S. Congress enacted legislation requiring a 95 percent reduction in certain harmful emissions from auto exhausts. Critics, especially from the automobile industry, questioned the economic rationality of such an extreme goal. They contended that it is disproportionately more costly to go to higher and higher levels of emissions control, just as it is harder and harder to squeeze the last few drops from an orange.

A later government study tended to support this objection. In the table, note how sharply the increments of cost begin to rise after 80 percent emissions reduction has been achieved.

Costs of Emissions Reductions

Reduction in Emissions (%)	Cost per Car
50	$45
55	55
60	62
65	70
70	80
75	90
80	100
85	200
90	375
95	600

Source: *Cumulative Regulation Effect upon the Cost of Automotive Transportation*, Office of Science and Technology RECAT Report, February 28, 1972.

The fact that rising levels of emissions control are increasingly expensive does not tell us how far society should or should not continue in this direction. So the data do not tell us that the Congress was wrong, although it might raise a question in our minds. We shall consider the principles that guide such social decisions in Chapter 15, under the heading "Welfare Economics."

EXAMPLE 6.6   **Electricity: Short-Run and Long-Run Costs**

Many studies of the long-run costs of electricity production conclude that economies of scale exist; the Long-Run Average Cost curve is a declining function of output.[a] Thus, electric power firms appear to use levels of capacity (i.e., sizes of fixed plants) that let them operate to the left of the minimum of the *LRAC* curve in the diagram of Figure 6.5. This means, in particular, that Long-Run Marginal Cost *(LRMC)* is less than *LRAC*.

The main technological source of economies of scale is in power generation; almost without exception, the larger the generating plant capacity, the cheaper the power output. The opposite effect appears in power transmission: the greater the concentration of power generation in a single plant of huge capacity, the higher are the transmission losses when power is carried to geographically dispersed customers.

In the short run, however, average and marginal costs are surely rising. A power system must provide for large variations in usage even within short periods like a single day; since electricity is nonstorable, in peak hours far more power must be produced and delivered than in off-peak quiet hours. Of course, it would be absurd to expect generating firms to respond by adjusting fixed capacity up and down within the day. And in any case, since these demand fluctuations are obviously temporary, the firm would not want to do so. So the Marginal and Average curves appropriate for contractions and expansions of short-run output will look like $SRAC_1$ and $SRMC_1$ in Figure 6.5. In particular, with capacity held fixed, the firm's Average and Marginal costs will increase with output, at least at the high outputs required to meet peak demands.

Technologically, there are two main reasons for rising short-run costs. Pieces of electrical equipment generally have a rated "capacity." This is not an absolute limit; capacity can be temporarily exceeded. But doing so leads to losses from overheating, risk of breakdowns, and so forth. Also, any power system has various plants, and generating units within plants, of differing "technical efficiency" (output/fuel ratio). Rationality dictates that the most efficient equipment carry the "base load." As demand grows, increasingly less efficient units are started up, so that average costs rise. (The less efficient units may be obsolescent equipment close to replacement, but not necessarily. An electrical system can benefit by investing in units with relatively poor fuel efficiency, provided that such units possess other desirable properties such as low capital costs, rapid startup, and so on.)

[a]A review of studies is contained in D. Huettner, *Plant Size, Technological Change, and Investment Requirements* (New York: Praeger, 1974), pp. 29–39.

SUMMARY

Individuals organize business firms for the purpose of efficient production—converting resource services into consumption goods. Firms supply goods in the product markets and demand inputs in the input markets.

Production can take place without firms, since multilateral contracts can be arranged among all the resource-owners involved. But the costs of negotiating and enforcing multilateral contracts may make it advantageous to set up a firm as an artificial entity that contracts *bilaterally* with each separate resource-supplier. The owners of firms (the entrepreneurs) take ultimate responsibility, by agreeing to receive only the residual rewards that remain after making contractually agreed payments to other resource-suppliers. The owners, either directly or through a hired manager, must monitor the resource-suppliers. If a manager is hired, his performance must also be monitored.

Standard economic theory postulates that the business firm attempts to maximize economic *profit*—the difference between revenue and economic cost. Economic costs differ from accounting costs. Economic costs include not only contractual payments made to hire resources but also implicit charges that represent the best alternative employments of resources self-supplied to the firm by owners.

For a competitive (price-taking) firm in the product market, Total Revenue $R \equiv Pq$ is simply proportionate to output q. The constant price P is equal both to Average Revenue and to Marginal Revenue.

The Total Cost function of the competitive firm rises throughout, starting possibly from some positive level of fixed cost. It is usually assumed to rise first at a decreasing rate (falling Marginal Cost MC) but eventually at an increasing rate (rising MC). Economic profit is the difference between Total Revenue and Total Cost or equivalently it is the output quantity q multiplied by the difference between price P and Average Cost AC; that is, $\Pi \equiv q(P - AC)$.

The output level that maximizes profit (or minimizes loss) for the competitive firm is given by the following condition provided that the MC curve cuts the Marginal Revenue MR curve from below:

$$MC = MR \equiv P$$

(Here, since the MR curve is horizontal, this condition applies if MC is rising.) The firm will set output to zero in the short run if the market price is less than the minimum of the Average Variable Cost, that is, if Total Revenue at the best positive level of output fails to cover Total Variable Costs. The firm will shut down in the long run if market price is less than the minimum of Average Cost, that is, if at the best level of output Total Revenue fails to cover Total Cost.

The short-run and long-run cost functions differ. In the short run, some inputs are held fixed that become variable in the long run. At any level of output, Short-Run Total Cost is at least as great as Long-Run Total Cost (and, similarly, Short-Run Average Cost is at least as great as Long-Run Average Cost). This raises the problem of how it can be rational to respond to a demand change by moving along a short-run cost function. The answer is that short-run responses, which hold some inputs fixed, are appropriate for demand changes expected to be only temporary. The amount of a fixed input does not continually vary in response to temporary price changes because of transaction costs and because inputs may have been specialized to the firm and so have little value in alternative uses.

The eventually rising Average Cost and Marginal Cost functions that characterize the price-taking firm have their source in the Law of Diminishing Returns. When one or more inputs are held constant, additional output eventually requires increasing increments of the variable inputs. Since by definition in the short run one or more inputs are fixed, rising Short-Run Marginal and Average Costs are directly explained by this technological law. But even in the long run, not all inputs can be varied. The very nature of the firm dictates that entrepreneurship, and/or the unique production opportunity exploited by the firm, cannot be expandable without limit. Therefore, even the Long-Run Average Cost and Marginal Cost curves are eventually rising.

QUESTIONS

For Review

1. Why is most productive activity carried out by firms rather than simply by individuals who contract mutually with one another?

2. Partnership firms are generally small and managed directly by their owners. Why? How does the corporate form facilitate the organization of larger enterprises?

*3. a. What is meant by economic profit?
   b. Is profit maximization an appropriate goal for owners? for managers?
   c. What tends to happen if owners are not also managers?

4. What would be the effect upon the firm's decisions of a 50 percent tax upon economic profit? upon accounting profit?

5. How will an increase in a firm's fixed costs affect its Marginal Cost curve? What will be the effect of such an increase in fixed costs on the firm's supply curve?

*6. Consider a firm with Marginal Cost curve $MC = 10 + 5q$, Average Variable Cost curve $AVC = 10 + 2.5q$, and fixed costs of $250.
   a. What is the firm's total cost function?
   b. If the market price for the firm's output is $50 per unit, what is the firm's profit-maximizing output?
   c. Is it making an economic profit?

*7. a. If Marginal Cost falls throughout, does Average Cost necessarily fall?
   b. If Average Cost falls throughout, does Marginal Cost necessarily fall?

8. If Marginal Cost MC is rising throughout, will the Average Cost curve AC necessarily be rising? If AC is rising throughout, is MC necessarily rising?

*9. When will a firm respond to changes in economic conditions by a short-run adjustment? when by a long-run adjustment?

10. Show why no Long-Run Average Cost curve satisfies both of the following conditions:
   a. It shows the lowest cost at which any given output can be produced (i.e., it is a lower envelope of the Short-Run Average Cost curves).
   b. It shows the lowest-cost output at any given level of the fixed input (i.e., it goes through the minimum points of all the Short-Run Average Cost curves).
   Which of the two conditions is the correct one?

For Further Thought and Discussion

1. What types of production that take place in the household are not delegated to firms?

2. A mafia leader was on trial for directing his enforcers to break the legs of anyone defaulting on a debt owed him. The leader readily admitted the fact, but explained.

> We provide a valuable service to borrowers who do not have good enough credit standing to obtain loans from banks. In the interests of full disclosure, we always inform our borrowers that we will break their legs if they default. We have found that borrowers would very likely fail to exercise due diligence in their use of the borrowed funds if we allowed them to walk away from their loans whenever unable to pay. Indeed, it would be impossible to carry on our business if we allowed something like a declaration of bankruptcy to cancel the debts owed us.

Answer the following, and explain briefly in each case.
   a. Is this type of business a "valuable" service to borrowers?
   b. Would it be efficient to permit contracts in which borrowers agree in advance that their legs will be broken if they fail to repay?
   c. Does it follow that bankruptcy laws are not a good idea?

*The answers to starred questions appear at the end of the book.

*3. In railroading, about two-thirds of costs are said to be fixed and only one-third variable. If so, *AVC* is approximately one-third of *AC*. It would therefore always be financially advantageous for railroads, it has been argued, to take on *additional* traffic even at a price lower than Average Cost. Is this argument valid? Explain.

*4. a. Why will a firm ever keep *any* inputs fixed in the face of changing economic conditions?
   b. What determines which inputs are held fixed, and which varied?

5. Compare the effect upon a competitive firm's output of a tax of $1 per unit upon output versus a license fee of $200 payable each year regardless of output.

6. Is the firm's Total Cost curve necessarily rising, or can it have a falling range? Is the firm's Average Cost curve necessarily U-shaped, or can it be rising throughout (or falling throughout)? What about the Average Variable Cost curve? For each allowable shape of the Average Cost and Average Variable Cost curves, show the implied shape of the Marginal Cost curve.

7. Consider the most efficient way of dividing output between two plants (as in electricity load dispatching). If the Marginal Cost curves are rising, when will one of the plants not be operating? What can be said if one or both of the Marginal Cost curves are falling?

*8. What is wrong with the following reasoning on the part of a factory manager:

> My plant is working steadily at its most efficient output. Nevertheless, I could always meet a short-run surge in demand simply by running the machines a little faster and deferring maintenance. So in the short run my Marginal Cost is practically zero.

9. Electric utilities commonly keep their most modern and efficient generating equipment, characterized by a low ratio of fuel input to power output, working around the clock. Older equipment still on hand is used only to meet periods of higher load. What does this imply about the shape of the Short-Run Marginal Cost curve for generation of electricity? Why doesn't the firm always use only the most modern equipment?

*10. An urban rapid-transit line runs crowded trains (200 passengers per car) at rush hours, but nearly empty trains (10 passengers per car) at off hours. A management consultant makes the following argument:

> The cost of running a car for one trip on this line is about $50 regardless of the number of passengers. So the per-passenger cost is about 25 cents at rush hour but rises to $5 per passenger in off hours. Consequently, we had better discourage off-hour business.

   a. Is there a fallacy in the consultant's argument?
   b. "Commutation tickets" (reduced-price, multiple-ride tickets) sold by some transit systems are predominantly used in rush hours. Are such tickets a good idea?

CHAPTER 7

EQUILIBRIUM IN THE PRODUCT MARKET-COMPETITIVE INDUSTRY

EXAMPLES

T he preceding chapter examined an *optimization* problem: how do firms in a competitive industry maximize profits? The answer (apart from certain qualifications associated with the possibility of not producing at all) was to choose the output level where Marginal Cost equals price. A textile manufacturer selling in a world market, for example, would adjust production until the additional cost of producing one more shirt equalled the price received. In this chapter the emphasis shifts to the *equilibrium* problem. Looking now at the market for shirts, when will the price be high and when will it be low? How do high and low prices relate to the quantities produced and consumed?

The answer to an equilibrium problem depends, of course, upon supply and demand. We will see in this chapter how the decisions of the different firms lead to an *industry supply function*. Market equilibrium is determined by the interaction of the industry supply function with the *consumers' demand function* (which was analyzed in Chapter 4).

Later in the chapter, the concepts of Consumer Surplus and Producer Surplus will be introduced. These provide ways of measuring the benefits of market exchange to the demanders and suppliers of a commodity.

7.1 FROM FIRM SUPPLY TO MARKET SUPPLY: THE SHORT RUN

The competitive firm, by definition, takes market price P as a factor beyond its control. It cannot sell any units at a higher price, and would not want to charge a lower price. So the firm maximizes profits by choosing that output at which Marginal Cost = Marginal Revenue = P.

At each different possible price P the relation between P and q is the firm's *supply curve* pictured as s_f in Figure 7.1. In the diagram, one point on the firm's supply curve is point A (price P^o and quantity q^o), another is point B (price P' and quantity q').

Consider more specifically the firm's short-run supply curve. (In the short run the firm cannot avoid paying fixed costs on its plant, equipment, and so on.) Recall the qualification expressed in Equation (6.4a): When market price is less than P_V, which is the minimum level of Average Variable Cost AVC, the optimal short-run output for the firm is zero. Thus, the competitive firm's short-run supply function s_f may have a discontinuity, as illustrated in Figure 7.1. First, s_f runs along the vertical axis from the origin up to the price P_V, indicating that at any price lower than P_V the output supplied is zero. The supply curve then skips to the right (dotted line) and thereafter follows the rising branch of MC above the point K. [*Query:* Why do we say that the supply function "may" have such a discontinuity? *Hint:* Is it logically necessary for Average Variable Cost to have an initial falling range?]

List of Notation

AC	Average cost	*MR*	Marginal Revenue
C	Total cost	*q*	Output
LRAC	Long-Run Average Cost	*SRAC*	Short-Run Average Cost
LRMC	Long-Run Marginal Cost	*SRMC*	Short-Run Marginal Cost
LRTC	Long-Run Total Cost	*SRTC*	Short-Run Total Cost
MC	Marginal Cost		

FIGURE 7.1 **Supply Function of a Competitive Firm: Short Run**   At product prices less than P_V, the minimum of Average Variable Cost AVC, the firm will supply zero (the firm's supply curve s_f runs along the vertical axis). Above this price, s_f coincides with the Marginal Cost curve MC.

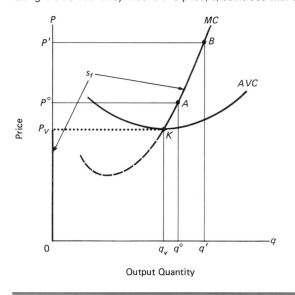

Output Quantity

Exercise 7.1

Consider the firm's cost function of Table 6.1: $C = 128 + 69q - 14q^2 + q^3$. Find the supply function of the firm, using the exact formula for Marginal Cost: $MC = 69 - 28q + 3q^2$.

Answer: The firm's supply curve is based on the rule $MC = P$, which implies $P = 69 - 28q + 3q^2$. However, this equation is valid only for $P \geq P_V$, where P_V is the minimum of Average Variable Cost AVC. From the equation for C it follows that $AVC = (C - F)/q = 69 - 14q + q^2$. The minimum of this expression could be found by calculus. Or else, making use of the rule that MC and AVC intersect at the minimum of AVC, we can set $MC = AVC$ or $69 - 28q + 3q^2 = 69 - 14q + q^2$. Solving algebraically, MC and AVC intersect at $q = 7$, where $MC = AVC = 20$. So the supply function can be written as follows:

$$P = 69 - 28q + 3q^2, \text{ for } P \geq 20$$

$$q = 0, \qquad\qquad \text{for } P < 20$$

Since firms often specialize, any given good is typically produced only by a limited group of producers; this group of firms is called the *industry* associated with that good. So the economy-wide aggregate of the firm supply curves for a particular product is called the *industry supply curve*. (Note the similarity with *demand* aggregation in Chapter 4; there the separate demands of the individual consumers were horizontally summed to obtain the overall market demand curve.)

Exercise 7.2

Suppose an industry consists of 100 identical firms, each having the cost function of Exercise 7.1, $C = 128 + 69q - 14q^2 + q^3$. What is the industry supply curve?

Answer: The industry output is $Q \equiv 100q$, where q is the output of each firm. Going directly to the supply function of Exercise 7.1 and substituting from the above, we have:

$$\begin{cases} P = 69 - 28\left(\dfrac{Q}{100}\right) + 3\left(\dfrac{Q}{100}\right)^2, & \text{for } P \geq 20 \\ \\ Q = 0, & \text{for } P < 20 \end{cases}$$

There is one complication, however. In Chapter 6, by definition each competitive firm viewed the *product price* as fixed. It was also implicitly assumed that the competitive firm views *input prices* as fixed. The individual firm is so small that expansion of its output would not significantly drive up the prices of the resources it hires. For example, a single coal mine may be able to hire more workers without significantly affecting the wages of coal miners. But if many of the firms in the coal-mining industry simultaneously try to expand output, wages of coal miners are likely to rise.

This effect is shown in Figure 7.2. Suppose the initial price of a ton of coal is P' and industry aggregate output is Q'; this price and quantity determine one point on the industry supply curve S. Initially each firm has a Marginal Cost curve, like MC in Figure 7.1, which (for prices $P > P_V$) is the supply curve of the firm. It might then be thought that the effect of a product price increase from P' to P'' can simply be found by moving along the curve

---

FIGURE 7.2   Industry Supply Function: Input-Price Effect   At price P' firms in the industry would want to sell the quantity Q', as one point on the industry supply curve S. When actual industry output is Q', the aggregate of the supply curves visualized by the separate firm is $\Sigma s_f'$. But if product price increases to P'', the consequent increase in industry output causes the prices of inputs to increase. This raises costs to the firms, shifting their separate supply curves upward so that aggregate supply is represented by $\Sigma s_f''$. Thus, the effective industry supply curve, S, is steeper (less elastic) than the aggregate of the firms' supply curves.

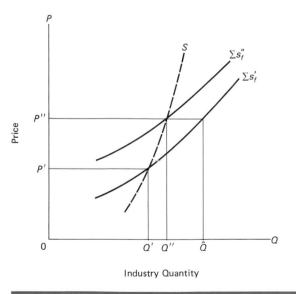

Industry Quantity

$\Sigma s_f'$ in Figure 7.2—which is the horizontal sum of the firm's supply curves—to the output level $\hat{Q}$.

But if the collective expansion of industry output affects input prices (as of mine workers), *the industry as a whole* cannot expand output along $\Sigma s_f'$. Increased industry output tends to raise the prices of inputs used by the industry. With higher input prices, at any level of output the Marginal Cost curve of each firm shifts up, and therefore the supply curve of each firm also shifts up. So when product price rises from P' to P'', the new quantity supplied by the industry will not be $\hat{Q}$ along $\Sigma s_f'$ in Figure 7.2. The correct quantity Q'' lies along a somewhat higher summation curve $\Sigma s_f''$, which reflects the higher Marginal Cost curves at the higher level of *industry* output. In other words, each firm's supply curve depends on what other firms do—the more coal the other firms produce, the higher the wages they must all pay miners. An observer who failed to take this "input-price effect" into account would predict too big a supply response of the industry to variations in output price P.

CONCLUSION: The short-run supply curve of a competitive *firm* is identical to its *MC* curve (above the minimum of its *AVC* curve). The short-run supply curve of a competitive *industry* is the horizontal sum of the firms' supply curves, but only after allowing for the input-price effect that raises or lowers the *MC* curves as industry output expands or contracts. The input-price effect reduces the magnitude of the supply response to changes in output price; that is, it makes the industry supply curve steeper.

Just as the elasticity of demand measures how the quantity demanded responds to changes in price, the *elasticity of supply* measures how the quantity supplied responds to a change in price.

DEFINITION: The elasticity of supply, symbolized as κ, is the proportional change in the quantity supplied, $\Delta Q/Q$, divided by the proportional change in price, $\Delta P/P$.

$$\kappa \equiv \frac{\Delta Q/Q}{\Delta P/P} \equiv \frac{\Delta Q}{\Delta P} \cdot \frac{P}{Q}$$

In contrast to elasticity of demand, the elasticity of supply is normally positive.[1]

Since elasticity is defined in terms of proportionate changes, it is independent of units of measurement. As explained in Chapter 5, this makes it meaningful to compare supply elasticities for different goods. We can also compare a firm's elasticity of supply to the supply elasticity of the industry as a whole:

PROPOSITION: The input-price effect normally makes the industry's short-run supply curve *less* elastic than the separate firms' short-run supply curves.

---

[1]Just as with demand, the cross-elasticity and the income-elasticity of supply can be defined. The cross-elasticity of supply would be relevant for two goods related in production—for example wool and mutton. The income elasticity of supply may be significant when higher individual incomes lead to a withdrawal of labor from the market (the income elasticity would be negative). But attention will be limited here to the direct price elasticity of supply.

7.2 LONG-RUN AND SHORT-RUN SUPPLY

Figure 7.1 shows a short-run firm supply function. The *MC* curve represents the Short-Run Marginal Cost for some given quantity of a fixed input. For a coal mine, the number of shafts in use may be a fixed input in the short run. As explained in earlier chapters, a firm that sees a temporary change in price may not find it profitable to open new shafts or close existing ones, even as it varies output. This is the short-run response. But if the firm believes the price has permanently fallen, it will want to adjust all of its inputs (including those fixed in the short run) and move to the left along its Long-Run Marginal Cost curve (not pictured in Figure 7.1).[2]

The competitive firm's long-run supply function Ls_f is shown as the broken bold curve in Figure 7.3. It is identical to Long-Run Marginal Cost *LRMC* except that, below the minimum of Long-Run Average Cost (point *M*), the supply curve lies along the vertical axis. This means that if price were to fall *permanently* below P_C the firm would shut down.

Suppose price is initially $P°$, so that the firm produces $q°$ (the level of output at which *LRMC* equals $P°$). Now let the market price jump to P'. If the firm believes the price change

FIGURE 7.3 Firm's Long-Run Supply Function   The firm's long-run supply function Ls_f runs along the vertical axis (zero quantity supplied) up to P_C, the minimum level of the Long-Run Average Cost curve *LRAC*. Above this price, the supply function coincides with the Long-Run Marginal Cost *LRMC*.

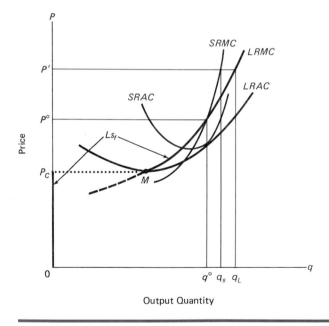

Output Quantity

---

[2]How *rapidly* it pays to move from the overexpanded to the correct level of the fixed factor depends upon the durability and the resale value of the "excessive" fixed equipment specialized to the firm. If resale value is relatively high, the firm may sell off the excess equipment and move to the correct scale almost immediately. But if resale value is very low, it may pay the firm to retain the equipment until it wears out. Note that it may or may not take a long period of *calendar* time to make a long-run scale adjustment.

is temporary, it will choose the level of output q_S, where $SRMC = P'$. If the firm believes the change in price is permanent, it will choose output q_L, where $LRMC = P'$. Of course, there will be various degrees of "temporary" and "permanent" price changes. In addition, firms may differ in their estimates as to the permanence of the price changes. So within any industry we would typically expect to observe some *mixture* of short-run and long-run responses to a price change.

Exercise 7.3 ——

Using the information in Exercise 6.5 of the preceding chapter, suppose Long-Run Total Cost $= q^2$ and Short-Run Total Cost $= 2B + q^4/(8B)$, where B is the amount of the "fixed" input. It can be shown by calculus that $LRMC = 2q$ and $SRMC = q^3/(2B)$. (a) If $B = 4$, find the short-run supply curve. (b) Find the long-run supply curve. (c) At what price and output do these supply curves intersect, and what is the significance of this intersection? (d) What would happen if price rose to $P = 27$, and were interpreted as either a temporary change or a permanent change?

Answer: (a) The short-run supply curve is given by the condition $SRMC = P$, or $P = q^3/8$. (b) The long-run supply curve is $P = 2q$. [*Note:* We did not have to allow here for any discontinuity in either the long-run or short-run supply curve. Why?] (c) The curves intersect at $q = 4$, $P = 8$. At this point use of the fixed input ($B = 4$) is optimal, since the short-run supply curve and long-run supply curve dictate the same output of 4. (d) If price rose to $P = 27$ and the firm regarded the change as temporary, it would respond along the $SRMC$ curve, setting $q^3/8 = 27$. The short-run optimal output would be $q = 6$. If the firm regarded the price change as permanent, it would make a long-run response and choose output at 13 1/2 where $LRMC = 2q = 27$. Evidently, the long-run output response is greater; that is, the long-run supply curve is more elastic.

EXAMPLE 7.1 Cotton Spindles[a]

Cotton spinning in the United States is generally regarded as a good approximation of a competitive industry. The industry is mostly concentrated in New England and the South. The table shows, for each region, the average variation (by calendar quarters over the period 1945 to 1959) in "spindle hours." Spindles as fixed equipment are of course an essential element of spinning, so that spindle hours can be regarded as measuring output. "Changes in Hours per Spindle" may be interpreted as an index of the firms' short-run adjustment to the price changes taking place quarter by quarter. "Changes in Active Spindles" represents a long-run adjustment—variation in the amount of fixed equipment.

Changes in Cotton Spinning, per Quarter, 1945–59

Area	Changes in Hours per Spindle	Changes in Number of Active Spindles (%)
Southern states	90.5	9.2
New England	76.5	21.8

Source: U.S. Census data cited in G. J. Stigler, *The Theory of Price*, 3rd ed. (New York: Macmillan, 1966), p. 144.

Evidently, the quarterly price changes in this period were predominantly interpreted by firms as temporary, since they led only to small changes in the quantities of fixed equipment.

The difference between the two regions appears to be due to the fact that the industry, while relatively static in the South, was declining in New England. In periods of low prices the higher-cost New England firms were more likely to make long-run adjustments, gradually disposing of their fixed spindle equipment.

[a]Discussion based upon G. J. Stigler, *The Theory of Price,* 3rd ed. (New York: Macmillan, 1966), pp. 143–44.

EXAMPLE 7.2 **Preclusive Buying of Wolfram**[a]

The Allied powers' "preclusive buying" program in World War II provides a striking example of the responsiveness of supply to price. In this program the United States and Great Britain attempted to buy supplies of strategic materials to prevent their shipment to enemy nations.

Wolfram is an ore of tungsten, a vital alloying metal for steel. It was produced in Spain and Portugal, neutral countries that were potential suppliers to Germany and Italy. In August 1940, before the commencement of preclusive buying, the market price of wolfram in Portugal and Spain was $1,144 per ton. Since the Allies tried to buy up literally *all* the wolfram that would otherwise have gone to Germany and Italy, the price was rapidly driven to unprecedented levels. By October 1941 it had reached $20,000 per ton. Portugal reacted by controlling the price and allotting the wolfram supply between the Axis and the Allies. Spain, however, chose to let the market process operate unhindered (to the advantage of the Spanish wolfram miners).

The program succeeded in the sense that Germany eventually (in July 1943) quit bidding for Spanish wolfram, making do with substitutes for tungsten alloy. But before this occurred, wolfram production in Spain had increased to ten times its prewar level. In undertaking the program, the Allies seriously underestimated the long-run supply elasticity of wolfram production.

[a]Discussion based on D. I. Gordon and R. Dangerfield, *The Hidden Weapon* (New York: Harper & Brothers, 1947), pp. 105–16.

The *industry* long-run supply curve, like the industry short-run supply curve, is the horizontal sum of the supply curves of all firms in the industry. As before, allowance must be made for the effect of industry-wide output changes upon input prices, as shown in Figure 7.2. For both short-run and long-run supply, the industry supply curve is less elastic when this effect is taken into account than when it is not.

Two additional elements operate in the long run: *entry* and *exit*. In long-run equilibrium every firm in the industry must earn non-negative economic profits, which means that price must cover Long-Run Average Cost: $P \geq LRAC$. If firms cannot make a profit at any level of output, at least some of them will eventually go out of business (the entrepreneur will shift to a new industry or take a non-entrepreneurial job). And if an outside firm—whether newly organized, or already in existence but operating in some other industry—can earn a profit within the industry, it will eventually enter. If there were an indefinitely large number of essentially identical firms standing ready to enter or leave, an industry's long-run supply curve would be effectively horizontal (infinitely elastic).[3] But this is unlikely. Some firms will have a cost advantage in one industry, other firms will have a cost advantage in other industries. Those firms already in an industry will tend to be the ones with the lowest costs. New firms will typically have higher costs, ruling out a horizontal long-run supply curve. (This fact docs not necessarily mean that the new firms are "inefficient"; it may only be that their alternatives elsewhere are relatively more attractive.)

We have seen that an increase in the price of coal leads to a larger supply reaction when each coal-mining firm adjusts along its Long-Run Marginal Cost curve (i.e., when firms believe the price change to be permanent) than when each adjusts only along the Short-Run Marginal Cost curve (i.e., when firms believe the price change is only temporary). Entry and exit work in the same direction. A high price leads in the long run not only to each firm mining more coal, but also to an increase in the *number* of coal-mining firms; a low price leads in the long run not only to output reductions by each firm, but also to a decrease in the *number* of firms.

Figure 7.4 shows the effect of "length of run" on the supply-demand equilibrium. The initial equilibrium is represented by price $P°$ and quantity $Q°$ along demand curve DD. Now

---

[3]*Qualification:* For this to hold, external economies and diseconomies (see below) must also be absent.

FIGURE 7.4   Market Response to Change in Demand   The initial demand curve is DD and equilibrium is at point F (price $P°$ and output $Q°$). In the "immediate run" an upward shift in the demand curve from DD to $D'D'$ has no effect on output since by assumption the quantity $Q°$ cannot be immediately changed (the supply curve is the vertical line IS); the entire effect is therefore upon price, which rises to P_I. In the "short run" (that is, if firms can vary output but believe the demand change is temporary), the upward sloping supply curve SS is relevant; aggregate quantity increases to Q_S and price declines from P_I to P_S. In the "long run" (if firms believe the demand change is permanent), the relevant supply curve is LS; quantity sold increases to Q_L, and the price falls from P_S to P_L.

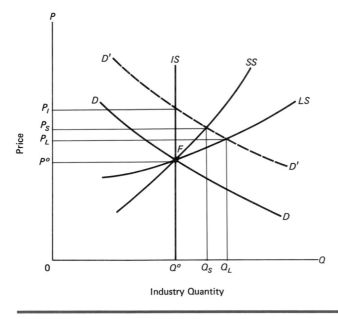

Industry Quantity

suppose demand for coal shifts upward to $D'D'$. The vertical curve labeled IS is the "immediate-run" supply function. It is supposed to represent a period of time so momentary that production has no chance to respond. Since by assumption the quantity sold is fixed, price is determined by the intersection of supply curve IS with demand curve $D'D'$ at the level P_I. If the demand change lasts long enough for coal mines to adjust their variable inputs (for example the number of miners), there will be some quantity response as indicated by the positive slope of the short-run supply curve SS. In the new *short-run* equilibrium, price P_S is higher than the initial price $P°$, but lower than the immediate-run price P_I. Finally, the long run supply LS (which allows firms to open new shafts, acquire new equipment, and so on) is still more elastic. So, in *long-run* equilibrium, price declines from P_S to P_L, which is still higher, however, than $P°$.

CONCLUSION: As the industry responds to an increase of demand, in moving from the immediate run to the short run to the long run, the upward effect on the equilibrium price is progressively reduced while the upward effect on the quantity produced is increased. (The corresponding implications of a decrease in demand are left to the reader.)

7.3 EXTERNAL ECONOMIES AND DISECONOMIES

Industry supply is determined by (1) effects *internal* to the separate firms of the industry; (2) effects *external* to the separate firms (but still "internal" to the industry as a whole).

Internal effects are reflected in the firms' short-run and long-run cost functions. *Internal diseconomies* of scale dictate rising short-run supply curves for each firm in an industry. And, although supply is more elastic in the long run, the Law of Diminishing Returns must eventually apply. So the competitive firm's long-run supply curve also slopes upward.

External economies and diseconomies can be either *pecuniary* or *technological*. In both cases, the externality arises when changes in the output of the industry as a whole affect the cost function of its member firms.

Figure 7.2 showed an *external diseconomy* of scale. The diseconomy arises, for example, when increased output by many farmers causes an increase in the prices of inputs they use (such as fertilizer or seed). This diseconomy makes the supply curve of the industry less elastic than the simple horizontal sum of the separate firms' supply functions. Since only input prices are affected, this is a pecuniary diseconomy.

A technological externality, in contrast, occurs when changes in some firms' outputs directly affect other firms' physical possibilities of production—their production functions. Consider marshy land devoted to agriculture. Farmer A must drain his land to produce crops. But pumping water out of his marshy soil also drains the lands of neighboring farms B, C, D, and so forth. Since their lands are less marshy than before, A's actions confer a real benefit upon his neighbors: their Average Costs and Marginal Costs are lower. So this is a *technological external economy*. Similarly, any drainage efforts by neighbors B, C, D, and so forth shift AC and MC downward for farmer A. When all farmers expand output by draining more land, the situation is as shown in Figure 7.5. The original industry price-quantity equilibrium is at point P', Q'. With a rise in price to P'', the $\Sigma s_f'$ curve (the horizontal sum of the firms' s_f' curves) would indicate industry output $\hat{Q}$. But since the technological external economy here shifts the firms' MC curves downward, the curve $\Sigma s_f'$ shifts down to $\Sigma s_f''$ so that the new equilibrium is at Q''. The industry supply curve S is thus more elastic than the separate supply curves of its component firms.

FIGURE 7.5   Industry Supply Function: External Economy   An "external economy" makes each firm's costs of production fall as industry output expands, and so flattens the industry supply curve. (Note that the picture here is the reverse of Figure 7.2.)

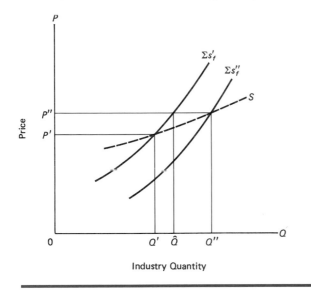

Industry Quantity

Now consider a *technological external diseconomy*. Suppose the farm lands are too dry rather than too wet. To irrigate, each farmer must pump water from underground wells. Doing so drains water from neighbors' wells, thus increasing their Average Costs and Marginal Costs. Here the true industry supply curve S is steeper than the horizontal sum of the firms' supply curves, as in Figure 7.2.

Can a favorable externality be so powerful as to make the industry supply curve actually slope downward? That is, can the *external economies* be so great as to override *internal diseconomies* of scale? The answer is yes. Such a possibility is illustrated in Figure 7.6. Starting from an initial equilibrium at F, demand increases from D' to D''. As firms expand output, the resulting increase of industry output sharply reduces costs of production owing to a strong technological external economy. Point G shows the ultimate result: in response to an upward shift of demand, equilibrium quantity increases and price decreases. Thus, the industry supply curve has negative slope. Notice however that each *firm's* supply curve is still positively sloped.

Exercise 7.4

The plum-producing industry in a small island consists of 100 identical farms, each with Marginal Cost $MC = 10 + 8q - Q/10$, where q is the farm's own output and Q is the total plum output. (a) Is this an external economy or diseconomy? (b) What is the equation for the industry supply curve? (c) Which diagram in the text pictures this situation?

Answer: (a) From the equation for MC, larger industry output Q reduces Marginal Cost. So this situation represents an external economy. (b) Since each farm sets $MC = P$, its supply function is given by $P = 10 + 8q - Q/10$. Substituting $Q \equiv 100q$, the industry supply curve is $P = 10 + 8Q/100 - Q/10$, or simplifying: $P = 10 - 0.02Q$. (c) The situation is like the picture in Figure 7.6: the supply curve has a negative slope.

FIGURE 7.6   Negatively Sloped Supply Function Due to External Economies   The initial demand curve is D' and the industry supply curve is $\Sigma s'_f$; the equilibrium is at point F. An upward shift in the demand curve to D'' temporarily raises price; firms begin to respond along their individual supply curves. But the external economy means that increased industry output reduces firms' costs of production, shifting the sum of the firm's supply curves downward from $\Sigma s'_f$ to $\Sigma s''_f$. If the external economy is sufficiently strong, as shown here, the new equilibrium at G represents larger quantity at lower price. Thus, the industry's supply curve S is negatively sloped.

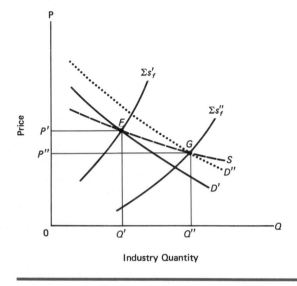

CONCLUSION: In a competitive industry, the *internal* determinants (effects of a firm's own output on its costs) are predominantly diseconomies that tend to make the industry supply curve upward-sloping. But this effect is less strong in the long run. The *external pecuniary* effects, which are due to changes in input hire-prices as the industry output changes, also are normally diseconomies. But *external technological* effects, which work through changes in production functions, can be either economies or diseconomies. Such external economies may even lead to a downward-sloping industry supply curve.

7.4 FIRM SURVIVAL AND THE ZERO-PROFIT THEOREM

Competition tends to reduce economic profits to zero. Wherever profit exists, new firms enter, industry output grows, and product prices fall. Simultaneously, resource prices are forced upward. Profit is thus squeezed from above and from below.

Where does this process end? Entry stops (long-run equilibrium is attained) when no firm still outside the industry can see its way to earning a profit within. It follows that the marginal firm, the one just on the borderline of entering or leaving the industry, can earn only negligibly more within the industry than outside. Thus, its economic profit (excess of revenues over the best alternative foregone) is essentially zero.

Does it follow that the established firms, which typically have lower costs, earn positive economic profits in long-run equilibrium? Surprisingly, though accounting profits may be high for these firms, economic profits are zero in the long run. The reasoning is that if an established firm earns positive economic profit, its Average Cost must be lower than the

Average Cost of the marginal firm. Some unusually productive resource must be responsible for its unusually low cost of production. All firms in the industry will bid for that special resource, and so in the long run its hire-price is driven upward to eliminate the profit.

A clear case occurs in mining. Suppose the demand for copper rises, so that the long-run equilibrium price of copper is higher than before. New firms enter to develop copper ore bodies previously too lean to work. If the marginal firm working a very thin ore just breaks even, it might be thought that an established firm exploiting a richer ore must be making a handsome profit. And indeed it may, in the short run. But in the long run all firms in the industry will bid for the right to work the richer ore. Consequently, the owner of the resource, i.e., the owner of the richer body of ore, will be able to charge a higher price that will recapture any economic profit that might have existed. What if the mining firm itself owns the richer ore deposit? Here the distinction between economic profit and accounting profit (see Chapter 6) is essential. The accounting profit of a firm controlling a rich ore body may indeed be high. But that firm could lease or sell the deposit to another firm. It should therefore charge itself, as an economic cost of its mining operations, the highest bid an outsider would make for the right to exploit its ore. In this way, its economic profit as a mining firm also becomes zero in long-run equilibrium.

PROPOSITION: In the long run, economic profit for any firm in a competitive industry is zero.

Of course, in an ever-changing world the long run may never actually arrive. Something almost always happens to change the conditions of long-run equilibrium before that state is achieved. But the *tendency* toward zero economic profit, due to downward pressure on product price and upward pressure on input prices, is always in operation.

EXAMPLE 7.3   **Economies of Scale and the Survivor Principle**

The continuing pressure upon firm survival provides a source of information about efficient scale of production. Firms that choose wrong levels of fixed inputs have higher production costs. In the long run, if they are to survive in the industry, such firms must shift to a more appropriate scale. The *survivor principle* looks at changes in the proportions of industry output generated by large and small firms for evidence concerning typical cost functions in the industry.

The survivor principle was applied to medical practice by H. E. Frech III and P. Ginsberg, who compared the market shares of physicians engaged in solo versus joint practice for the years 1965 and 1969. A later study by William D. Marder and Stephan Zuckerman extended the results through 1980. As can be seen from the table, the share accounted for by solo or two-physician practices declined, whereas larger-sized groups gained steadily in market share between 1965 and 1980. But it seems that by 1980 the decline in one or two-physician practices tapered off.

Market Share by Group Size, Medical Practice*

Group Size	1965	1969	1975	1980
1–2	84.69%	78.25%	68.67%	67.45%
3–7	8.37	11.53	13.31	13.14
8–25	4.30	5.09	8.53	7.78

Market Share by Group Size, Medical Practice* (cont.)				
Group Size	1965	1969	1975	1980
26–99	1.33	3.00	5.08	4.66
100+	1.31	2.12	4.42	6.97
Total	100%	100%	100%	100%

The data in the table can be interpreted quite differently depending on whether a static or dynamic viewpoint is adopted. From the static point of view, even in 1980 the great bulk of the market was accounted for by single-physician or two-physician groups. This strongly suggests that small size must indeed be the most efficient in medical practice. On the other hand, it is precisely this size that declined relative to all others. So it appears that, on the margin, firms of moderate and large size have been more profitable. New entrants find it advantageous to form groups of moderate or large size, while exiting firms must have come disproportionately from the small one-to-two physician class.

A possible explanation is that in any period there is an efficient mixture of firm sizes. Even though the small one-to-two physician firm may on the whole be most efficient in medical practice, it appears that there has been in recent years relatively too many in this size class. So we observe the market shares shifting in favor of the larger groups.

Sources: H. E. Frech III and P. Ginsberg, "Optimal Scale in Medical Practice: A Survivor Analysis," *Journal of Business,* v. 47 (January 1974), p. 30 and William D. Marder and Stephan Zuckerman, "Competition and Medical Groups: A Survivor Analysis," *Journal of Health Economics,* v. 4 (June 1985), p. 167.

7.5 THE BENEFITS OF EXCHANGE: CONSUMER SURPLUS AND PRODUCER SURPLUS

One of the most important principles of economics is the *Fundamental Theorem of Exchange:*

PROPOSITION: Trade is mutually beneficial.

In other words, voluntary exchange increases utility for all parties involved. An alternative and mistaken view is the *exploitation theory,* which claims that in exchange one side's gain is the other's loss. The proof of the Fundamental Theorem of Exchange, and disproof of the exploitation theory, is elementary. Since exchange is voluntary, a rational person will trade *only* if he or she expects to gain.

In practical applications it is very helpful to measure the benefits of trade, scaled in objective units that do not depend on individuals' subjective utilities. *Consumer Surplus* and *Producer Surplus* are such measures.[4]

In Figure 7.7, the market supply-demand equilibrium is at price P^* and quantity Q^*. Consumer Surplus is represented by the upper shaded area, lying beneath the demand curve

---

[4]The names of these measures are, unfortunately, somewhat misleading. The benefits stem from *trading* (buying or selling), not from consuming or producing.

FIGURE 7.7   Consumer Surplus and Producer Surplus   At the transaction quantity Q^* Consumer Surplus is the area that lies below the demand curve D and above the equilibrium price P^*. It is the difference between the aggregate willingness to pay for the quantity Q^* (the roughly trapezoidal region $OABQ^*$) and the amount actually paid (the rectangle OP^*BQ^*). The Producer Surplus is similarly the area above the supply curve S and below the price P^*.

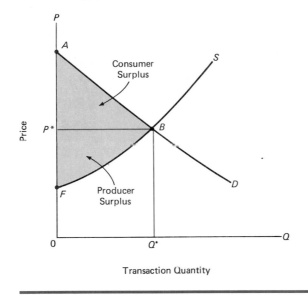

Transaction Quantity

D and above the horizontal line P^*B. The general intention is to show the net advantage to consumer-buyers of being able to buy at price P^*, even though they would have been willing to pay higher prices (as shown by the height of the demand curve) for smaller numbers of units. Producer Surplus is the corresponding lower shaded area, lying above the supply curve S and below the horizontal line P^*B. It shows the net gain to producer-sellers of receiving a price as high as P^* for *all* units sold even though they would have been willing to supply some units at lower prices.

The concepts of *demand price* (height of a demand curve at any quantity) and *supply price* (height of a supply curve at any quantity) are useful here. The demand price at any quantity can also be regarded as the *Marginal Value* of the good at that price. For the very first unit purchased in Figure 7.7, the demand price or Marginal Value is OA. But the price charged is only P^*—hence a Consumer Surplus of $OA - OP^* = AP^*$ is gained on the first unit bought. Now extend this argument to all successive units. Then, at the aggregate transaction quantity $Q = Q^*$, the sum of successive demand prices or Marginal Values (the consumers' aggregate *willingness to pay* for quantity Q^*) is the roughly trapezoidal area $OABQ^*$. But the amount that consumers actually pay is only the rectangle OP^*BQ^*. So the upper shaded (roughly triangular) area AP^*B is the Consumer Surplus—the difference between aggregate willingness to pay and aggregate actual payments. A corresponding argument applies to Producer Surplus, which can be regarded as the difference between sellers' aggregate receipts OP^*BQ^* and the minimum aggregate payment $OFBQ^*$ they would accept—the area FBP^*.

Producer Surplus has two main elements: (1) economic profits of firms in the industry, and (2) payments to the suppliers of resource services, over and above the minimum these suppliers would have been willing to accept in offering the resources to the industry. In long-run equilibrium, since economic profits are zero, Producer Surplus would consist entirely of these extra payments to owners of resource services. (These payments, sometimes called "economic rents," are discussed further in Chapter 12.)

EXAMPLE 7.4 **Freeze-Dried Coffee**[a]

Freeze drying was introduced prior to World War II primarily as a biomedical laboratory procedure; it was first used on a large scale in the production of blood plasma for the military during World War II. A commercial application of the method appeared in 1965 with freeze drying of coffee. This process improved the quality of instant coffee, increased consumers' willingness to pay for it, and thus shifted the demand curve to the right—as suggested in Figure 7.8. The change in Consumer Surplus is the shaded area shown; this is the value of the innovation to consumers (if price remains unchanged).

To estimate this benefit, Susan B. Vroman and Louise B. Russell compared demand for coffee in the United States before and after the introduction of freeze drying. To control for other effects, their demand equation adjusted for consumer income and for the price of regular coffee. Their estimates of the annual addition to Consumer Surplus caused by freeze drying are shown in the table. (The values are in millions of 1967 dollars; in 1967 a dollar had about 3.5 times the purchasing power of a dollar in 1989.)

Annual Gain in Consumer Surplus from Freeze-Dried Coffee

Year	Millions of 1967 Dollars
1971	150
1972	153
1973	158
1974	168
1975	160
1976	153
1977	150

[a]Discussion based on Susan B. Vroman and Louise B. Russell. "The net social benefits of a product improvement: the case of freeze dried coffee." *Applied Economics*, v. 19 (January 1987).

An Application: Membership Fees at Discount Stores

Individuals are often offered the opportunity to pay a supplier some fixed membership fee or up-front cost entitling them to buy goods afterward at lower prices. Examples include student cooperative bookstores and many health maintenance organizations. We can even think of house prices in this way. Someone who buys a house in Hawaii effectively purchases the right to subsequently go surfing at a low cost per day. (A person who lives in Kansas can also surf, but must bear the large expense of an airplane ticket each time he does so.)

FIGURE 7.8 **Consumer Benefits from Freeze-Dried Coffee**   Consumers desire freeze-dried coffee more than regular coffee. At the same price *P**, demand increases from *Q'* to *Q"*. The increase in Consumer Surplus, if price remains unchanged, is shown by the shaded area.

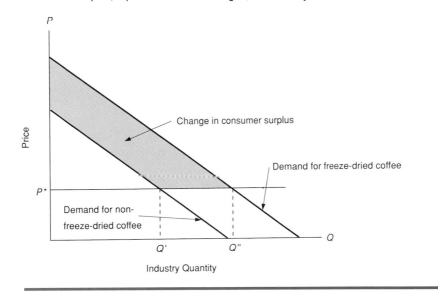

The question is, when should a consumer be willing to pay such a fee? Suppose Adam considers buying at most one biology textbook and one economics textbook. His demand price or Marginal Value for the biology book is $75; his demand price for the economics book is $60. A bookstore charges $80 for the biology book and $50 for the economics book, but will give a discount of 20 percent for members who pay an annual fee of $25. If Adam does not become a member, he would purchase only the economics book (since the price of the biology book is greater than its Marginal Value.) So Adam ends up with a Consumer Surplus of $60 − $50 = $10 from purchasing the economics book.

If Adam purchases the membership, the price of the biology textbook becomes $80(0.8) = $64. The price of the economics book becomes $50(0.8) = $40. Adam would now buy both books, obtaining a Consumer Surplus of $75 − $64 = $11 from the biology book, and $60 − $40 = $20 from the economics book. His total Consumer Surplus would be $31, except that he must still pay the membership fee of $25—leaving him with a net Consumer Surplus of only $6. So he is better off not buying the membership, paying full price for the economics book and obtaining the Consumer Surplus of $10.

An Application: The Water-Diamond Paradox

Many people cannot understand why a vital commodity like water is very cheap, while diamonds—satisfying relative insignificant human needs—are so dear. They conclude that there is something wrong with a market system that makes the frivolous commodity, diamonds, so much more expensive.

To explain the paradox we must consider supply as well as demand. If water were as scarce as diamonds, it would be far more valuable. (See Figure 7.9.) Using some common

FIGURE 7.9 **The Water-Diamond Paradox**   Water is "more valuable" than diamonds in the sense that consumers' aggregate willingness to pay (total area under the demand curve) is greater. But the supply of water is so enormous, in comparison to demand, that the *market value* of water (rectangle of width Q_w and height P_w) is small. Purchasers of water therefore derive a huge Consumer Surplus (shaded region). For diamonds the quantity on the market is tiny relative to the demand. Compared to the area under the demand curve, the market value of diamonds (rectangle of width Q_d and height P_d) is large and so Consumer Surplus is small.

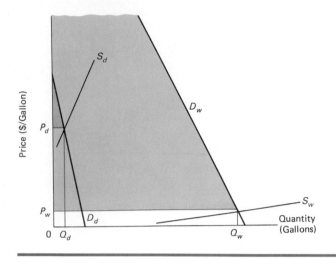

physical unit (e.g., weight) for equivalent quantities the demand curve for water, D_W, is surely far higher than the demand curve for diamonds, D_d. But at the actual tremendously disparate quantities, the market price of water is lower. Municipal water typically costs about $100 per acre-foot, or 3 cents per hundred gallons. At this price water consumption is commonly about 150 gallons (five-eighths of a ton) per capita per day. Diamond quantities are measured in carats (one-fifth of a gram), and gem-quality prices run upward from $1,000 per carat. At such prices (on the order of $20,000,000 per *gallon*) the weight of diamonds demanded per day (or even per year or per lifetime) is small.

The Consumer Surplus derived from water purchases must then be enormous in comparison with the actual market value of water bought and sold. This market value, $P_W \cdot Q_W$, is represented in the diagram by the very low rectangle lying just above the horizontal axis. The enormously greater area above this rectangle but below the demand curve D_W approximates the Consumer Surplus. Using the instructive terminology of Adam Smith, the *value in use* of water (its total worth to consumers, or their total willingness to pay) is very large in comparison with its *value in exchange;* the difference between the two is Consumer Surplus. For diamonds, on the other hand, Consumer Surplus is only the small dark area under the D_d curve and above P_d. Thus, for diamonds the market value represents the great bulk of the value in use; Consumer Surplus is small.

Hindrances to Trade

Chapter 2 demonstrated that a tax imposed on buyers (which shifts the demand curve) has the same effects as a tax imposed on sellers (which shifts the supply curve). Figure 7.10

FIGURE 7.10

Effects of a Transactions Tax on Consumer Surplus and Producer Surplus A unit tax on transactions shifts the supply curve from S to S' and lowers the quantity exchanged from Q^* to $Q°$. The gross price paid by consumers rises from P^* to P^+; the net price received by sellers falls from P^* to P^-. The upper shaded area is a transfer from Consumer Surplus and the lower shaded area is a transfer from Producer Surplus; the two transfers together constitute the amount of tax collections. The small dotted areas represent losses of Consumer Surplus and Producer Surplus that are not balanced by tax collections.

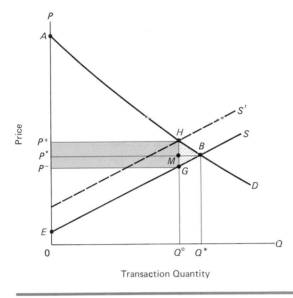

Transaction Quantity

illustrates a tax imposed on sellers. The effect on quantity traded is clear: it falls from Q^* to $Q°$. But there are two prices to consider: a *gross price* P^+ inclusive of tax and a *net price* P^- exclusive of tax. Buyers pay the gross (demand) price, whereas sellers receive only the net (supply) price. We see in the diagram that the tax makes the gross price P^+ higher than the pre-tax equilibrium price P^*, while the net price P^- is lower. (It is often said that taxes raise prices. This is true only for P^+; it is more accurate to say that a transaction tax raises the price to the buyer but lowers the price received by the seller.)

We can use Consumer and Producer Surplus to analyze how a tax affects the gains from trade. In Figure 7.10, when the price paid by buyers rises to P^+, Consumer Surplus falls by the area P^+HBP^*. Since the price received by sellers falls to P^-, Producer Surplus is reduced by the area P^*BGP^-. The combined loss of Consumer and Producer Surplus is therefore the entire shaded area P^+HBGP^-. This amount does not represent a total loss to society. The payments received by the government have not been lost. (Taxes can be understood as payment in kind not money; if a consumer who purchases a bicycle must deposit a can of food into a box, which is then turned over to the government, these cans do not disappear. The government may turn them over to the poor, trade them to a foreign nation, or use them for any other purpose.) Since the government has acquired the rectangle P^+HGP^- as tax revenue, this area represents a *transfer* from buyers and sellers to the government. Canceling this transfer leaves the dotted triangle HBG as the net loss to society from having imposed the tax. The loss is due, of course, to the reduction in mutually beneficial exchange.

This inevitable "deadweight loss" seems to imply that the costs of a tax are always greater than the benefits. The tax revenue, however, may be spent on a project that citizen-taxpayers regard as valuable enough to outweigh the loss of the triangle *HBG*. For example, the tax receipts may buy essential national defense. From a cost-benefit standpoint, then, to determine whether or not a tax should be imposed we must know the benefits from the projects financed with the tax revenue.

PROPOSITION: Taxes imposed on transactions reduce both Consumer Surplus and Producer Surplus. Some of the loss is a transfer from consumers and producers to the beneficiaries of government expenditures. But there is also a deadweight or efficiency loss due to the reduction in the volume of trade.

Exercise 7.5

Let the market demand curve for caviar be $Q = 300 - P$, and the market supply curve $Q = (P - 60)/2$. The initial solution is $Q^* = 80, P^* = 220$. (a) If a tax of $T = 15$ is imposed on each jar of caviar, what is the new equilibrium? (b) What is the loss of Consumer Surplus? What is the loss of Producer Surplus? (c) What is the amount of the transfer (tax collections)? (d) How great is the efficiency loss?

Answer: (a) We can verify that the new equilibrium quantity is $Q^\circ = 75$, that the gross price (paid by purchasers) rises to $P^+ = 225$, and the net price (received by sellers) falls to $P^- = 210$. At a price of $P^- = 210$ sellers want to sell $(210 - 60)/2 = 75$, and at a price of $P^+ = 225$ consumers want to purchase the same quantity, $300 - 225 = 75$. (b) The original Consumer Surplus corresponds to the area ABP^* in Figure 7.10. Since the supply and demand curves here are linear, the area is an exact triangle with size $(300 - 220)(80)(1/2) = 3,200$. The new Consumer Surplus is the smaller area AHP^+ or $(300 - 225)(75)(1/2) = 2,812.5$. So the loss of Consumer Surplus is 387.5. Similarly, the old Producer Surplus (area EBP^*) was $(220 - 60)(80)(1/2) = 6,400$; the new Producer Surplus (area EGP^-) is $(210 - 60)(75)(1/2) = 5,625$; the loss of Producer Surplus is $6,400 - 5,625 = 775$. (c) The transfers or tax collections (the rectangular area P^+HGP^-) equal $(225 - 210)(75) = 1,125$. (d) The remainder of the summed losses of Consumer Surplus and Producer Surplus is the efficiency loss, corresponding to the small dotted triangle HGB. Numerically it is $387.5 + 775 - 1,125 = 37.5$.

Taxes reduce trade through their effect on *prices,* by driving a "wedge" between the gross price P^+ paid by buyers and the net price P^- received by sellers. *Quantitative* restrictions on trade—rations or quotas—may also be analyzed in terms of Consumer Surplus and Producer Surplus.

Using Figure 7.11, suppose government regulations dictate that only a fixed *quota Q′* (less than the equilibrium quantity Q^*) of the good can be supplied to the market. The government, for example, may set a quota on imports of foreign computer memory chips. (We leave open the question of how much each supplier is allowed to sell.) The reduced quantity $Q′$ is sold at "whatever price the market will bear," which is $P′$ as determined along the demand curve D. We want to compare this outcome with the unregulated equilibrium at price P^* and quantity Q^*. Rectangle $P′BGP^*$ is a loss of Consumer Surplus that now goes to the suppliers of memory chips rather than to the government. (And, of course, the suppliers retain the lower shaded area, P^*GDE.) It follows that suppliers *may* benefit from the quota: they will do so if their transfer gain (upper shaded area $P′BGP^*$) is larger than their deadweight loss from the reduced sales (lower dotted area GCD). The buyers of memory chips, on the other hand, suffer both a transfer loss *(P′BGP*)* and a deadweight loss *(BCG)*. Thus, the buyers are surely worse off.

Unfortunately, the geometry of Figure 7.11 shows only a part, sometimes a small part, of the efficiency loss from quotas. There is an additional loss of Producer Sur-

FIGURE 7.11

Effects of a Supply Quota Upon Consumer and Producer Surplus   Market supply is limited to the quota Q', so price rises from $P*$ to P'. Consumer Surplus is reduced by area $P'BCP*$. Producer surplus increases by the area $P'BGP*$ minus the area GCD. If this difference is positive, sellers benefit from imposition of the quota. But buyers and sellers, considered together, lose by the amount of area BCD, which represents the combined efficiency losses.

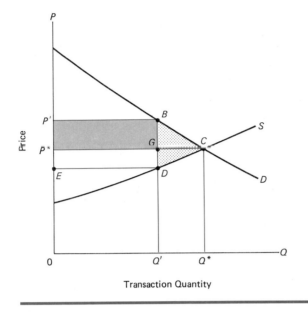

Transaction Quantity

plus if the firms allowed to sell the good are not the ones that could produce it at the lowest cost. The total costs of producing the quantity sold would be higher than they need be, and therefore Producer Surplus would be lower than that depicted in the figure.

EXAMPLE 7.5   **Sugar Quotas**

Except for the years 1974–81, the United States has restricted the import of sugar since 1948. The U.S. market price for sugar was consequently higher than the world price: by 35 percent in 1960, 61 percent in 1968, and 40 percent in 1970. Since 1981 the price differential has become enormous, reaching a maximum of 776 percent in June 1985.

The effects of the quotas were studied by Ilse Mintz for the year 1970, when the premium was relatively moderate; the figures here are based upon her "low" estimates.[a] The situation is pictured in Figure 7.12. Panel (a) shows the free-market equilibrium that would have occurred in the absence of quotas. The world price is 5.5 cents per pound, and the domestic price would equal this. United States domestic production along the supply curve S_{US} is 2.9 million tons at this price, and imports are 8.7 million, making up a total of 11.6 million tons along the curve S_w showing world supply (inclusive of domestic supply) to the United States. Since this is an equilibrium, the U.S. demand curve D intersects S_w at this price. Producer Surplus of the *domestic* producers is the small lower shaded area in Panel (a); the U.S. Consumer Surplus is the large upper shaded area.

The effects of the quotas are shown in Panel (b). The quota assignments (6.0 million tons of domestic supply, 5.2 million tons of imports) aggregate to only a little less than the 11.6 million tons that would have been supplied annually under free markets. But because demand is highly inelastic (price elasticity of -0.1, according to the "low" estimate), the U.S. domestic price is sharply higher, P_{US} instead of P_w.

The deadweight loss of Consumer Surplus (area 5) is estimated to be $10,280,000 per year. But the most obvious feature of the situation is the tremendous cost increase to consumers. This amounts to $575,680,000 annually.

The increased cost to U.S. consumers, all at the expense of Consumer Surplus, is broken down into four numbered areas in Panel (b). Area 1 is the transfer from domestic consumers to foreign producers, calculated on the basis of the higher price received for the 5.2 million tons they continue to deliver to the U.S. market. This amounts to $267,280,000 per year. Area 2 is the transfer to domestic producers, calculated on the 2.9 million tons they would have delivered in either case. This amounts to $149,060,000 per year. Areas 3 and 4 are equal (assuming for simplicity that the domestic supply curve S_{US} is linear), and add up to the remaining $159,340,000. However, they are conceptually quite different. The upper area 3, like area 2, is a transfer from Consumer Surplus to domestic Producer Surplus. But the lower area 4 is a deadweight loss, which represents increased cost of production (higher supply price) on sugar produced domestically that could have been obtained more cheaply from foreigners. This is the type of deadweight loss, described in the text above, that is due to a *non-ideal distribution* of quantitative restrictions upon trading.

If we regard the transfers as canceling out, the aggregate of the deadweight losses to the United States (the "efficiency loss" due to the sugar quotas) amounts to $89,950,000 per year.

A more recent study by Keith E. Maskus[b] showed much larger losses for later years, about $1.3 billion annually. The quotas have indeed, as intended, reduced the amount of sugar sold in the U.S. by foreign producers. But foreign producers made extraordinary gains on the amount of sugar they have been permitted to sell: $1.1 billion in 1982–83, and $390 million in 1987–88 (in the latter year, the United States relaxed the quotas to permit more imports). Had the United States imposed tariffs rather than quotas on imports, this money would have accrued to the U.S. Treasury rather than to the exporting countries. A major beneficiary of the quotas were producers of sugar substitutes, particularly high-fructose corn syrup: in 1986, corn sweeteners accounted for 53 percent of caloric-sweetener consumption in the U.S., up from 32 percent in 1980.

[a]Ilse Mintz, *U.S. Import Quotas: Costs and Consequences* (Washington, D.C.: American Enterprise Institute for Public Policy Research, February 1973).

[b]Keith E. Maskus, "Large Costs and Small Benefits of the American Sugar Program." *World Economy*, v. 12 (1989).

An Application: Comparable Worth

Some proponents of "equity" propose that workers be paid equal wages for jobs requiring comparable levels of skill, education, effort, and so on.

If workers in two types of jobs are equal in all respects, except that past training makes it difficult to switch from one job to another, then in a competitive market any difference

FIGURE 7.12 **Sugar Supply and Demand** S_{US} is the supply curve of domestic producers; S_w is the supply curve from foreign producers. In Panel (a), in the absence of quotas the price is P_w. The small lower shaded triangle is the annual Producer Surplus of U.S. suppliers; the large upper shaded area is the annual Consumer Surplus of U.S. purchasers. In Panel (b), imposition of a quota smaller than the equilibrium market quantity raises price in the United States to P_{US}. Consumer Surplus falls by the amount of the five numbered areas. U.S. Producer Surplus rises by the amount of the areas 2 and 3; these represent transfers from domestic consumers. Area 1 is a transfer from domestic consumers to foreign producers. Area 4 is an efficiency loss due to displacement of low-cost foreign production by high-cost domestic production. Area 5 is an efficiency loss due to reduced consumption.

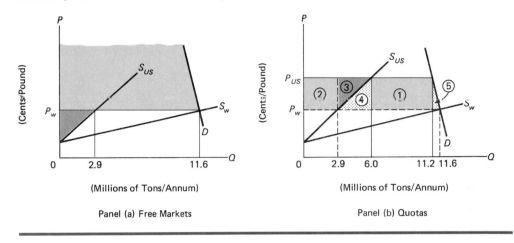

Panel (a) Free Markets

Panel (b) Quotas

in wages must be due to differences in demand. Suppose that teaching English and teaching computer science are jobs of the same skill level, so that the supply curves to the two employments are identical. But imagine that the demand curve is higher for computer scientists. The equilibrium wage will therefore be higher for computer scientists.

Suppose now that universities are not allowed to pay higher wages in one field than another. If the wage is set at the equilibrium wage for computer scientists, P_0 in Figure 7.13 (p. 198), universities will presumably respond by hiring fewer English professors: at a wage of P_0 universities will want to hire Q_C computer science professors and only Q_e English professors. One consequence may be that universities will be more selective in the hiring of English professors, so that the average quality of employed English professors (as measured perhaps by teaching effectiveness, number of publications, or grades in graduate school) ends up higher than of computer science professors.

So while comparable worth attempts to thwart the market forces that led to English professors and computer science professors of equal qualifications being paid different wages, these forces continue to operate in a disguised way. When wage rates are equalized, only relatively higher-quality English professors will be demanded. Before comparable worth, people of equal quality received different wages; under comparable worth, people of unequal quality receive equal wages. Thus, if the situation before comparable worth could validly be regarded as discriminatory against English professors, the same would be true of the situation after comparable worth. And, what is probably more important, English professors will suffer reduced employment. So not only the computer science professors but even the

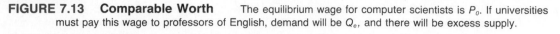

FIGURE 7.13 **Comparable Worth** The equilibrium wage for computer scientists is P_0. If universities must pay this wage to professors of English, demand will be Q_e, and there will be excess supply.

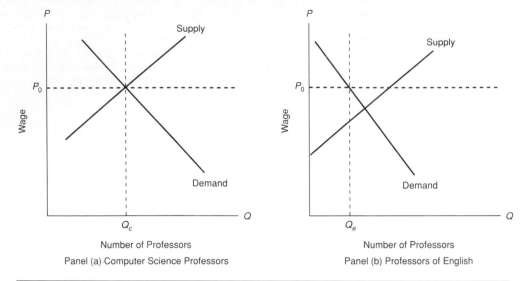

Panel (a) Computer Science Professors

Panel (b) Professors of English

supposed beneficiaries of comparable worth, the English professors, may find themselves worse off.

An Application: Managing a Shortage

Prices are always changing. A flood in Brazil will cause the price of coffee to rise; good farming weather in the Midwest will lead to a fall in the price of wheat; advances in technology steadily lower the price of computers. If enough people are drastically affected by the price change the government may decide to do something about it—whether wisely or unwisely. Rising apartment rents lead to calls for rent control, falling wheat prices lead to pressure for agricultural price supports, and so forth.

Legislation that sets the price of a good below its market-clearing level creates a shortage.[5] A *shortage* is not the same as *scarcity*. Scarcity simply means that not all desires can be satisfied; scarcity is always present. Diamonds are scarce, but there is no shortage; anyone willing to pay the price of a diamond can buy one. A shortage exists when goods are unavailable to some people willing to pay the price. In a city with rent controls, newcomers may be unable to rent an apartment at all, regardless of their willingness to pay. Thus, faced with a supply shift or a demand shift dictating a higher equilibrium price, consumers are bound to lose one way or the other—either from the higher price if the market adjustment proceeds unimpeded, or from the "shortages" that follow when government interventions keep the price low.

---

[5] In the opposite case, where government enforces a price *above* the equilibrium level, commodity surpluses are generated.

EXAMPLE 7.6 **Two San Francisco Housing Crises**[a]

In the 1906 earthquake and fire, the city of San Francisco lost more than half its housing facilities in three days. Nevertheless, the first post-disaster issue of the *San Francisco Chronicle* did not report a housing shortage! Indeed, the newspaper's classified advertisements carried 64 offers of houses or apartments for rent, and only 5 advertisements for apartments or houses wanted. Of course, prices of accommodations rose sharply.

In contrast, in 1946 San Francisco was gripped by the national postwar housing shortage. In the first 5 days of 1946 newspapers carried only 4 advertisements offering houses or apartments for rent, but around 150 advertisements by persons seeking rentals. The explanation is that in 1906 the catastrophic reduction in the housing stock led to a sharp rise in rents. But in 1946, rents frozen below the market-clearing price left an excess of quantity demanded over quantity supplied.

COMMENT In the physical sense, housing supply was clearly much scarcer, relative to population, after the 1906 earthquake and fire than in 1946. The 1946 shortage was an outgrowth of the general price freeze aimed at controlling inflation during and after World War II. Actually, housing supply had not decreased at all in the wartime period. But rising money incomes, the return of war veterans, and a growing number of families led to an upward shift in demand for housing. With rents frozen, a shortage ensued.

[a] Discussion based on M. Friedman and G. J. Stigler, *Roofs or Ceilings?* (Irvington-on-Hudson, N.Y.: The Foundation for Economic Education, September 1946).

We use the concepts of short-run and long-run supply developed earlier in the chapter to trace the consequences of a governmental ceiling on prices. In Figure 7.14 (p. 200) the ceiling holds price at its old equilibrium P° after demand shifts upward from D to D'. At the price P°, there is a perceived shortage equal to the distance $\hat{Q} - Q^\circ = H$. If the price were free to rise, it would jump to P_I in the "immediate run" but would eventually come down to the long-run equilibrium at P_L. The market would eliminate the shortage—in the short run primarily by a high price choking off demand, and in the long run by inducing more supply. At the new long run equilibrium price P_L in Figure 7.14, the interval ΔD is the long-run reduction in demand quantity; ΔS is the long run increment of supply.

Exercise 7.6

Suppose demand is described by the equation $P = 300 - Q$. Let the long-run supply curve be $P = 60 + 2Q$, and the short-run supply curve $P = -180 + 5Q$. Verify that the market is in long-run and short-run equilibrium at quantity $Q^\circ = 80$ and price $P^\circ = 220$. Now suppose the demand curve shifts to the right, so that it is described by $P = 360 - Q$. (a) What happens in the immediate run? (b) What is the new short-run price-quantity equilibrium? (c) What is the new long-run equilibrium? (d) What would be the perceived "shortage" if a price ceiling prevented price from rising?

Answer: (a) In the immediate run, quantity would be unchanged at $Q_I = 80$. The new equilibrium price is found by using the new demand condition: $P_I = 360 - Q_I = 280$. (b) In the new short-run equilibrium, $360 - Q = -180 + 5Q$, so $Q'_s = 90$, $P'_s = 270$. (c) In the new long-run equilibrium $360 - Q = 60 + 2Q$, so $Q'_L = 100$, $P'_L = 260$. (d) If price could not rise above $P = 220$, the quantity supplied would remain $Q = 80$ but the quantity demanded would be $Q = 360 - P = 140$. The perceived shortage would be $140 - 80 = 60$.

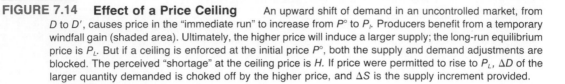

FIGURE 7.14 **Effect of a Price Ceiling**   An upward shift of demand in an uncontrolled market, from D to D', causes price in the "immediate run" to increase from $P°$ to P_I. Producers benefit from a temporary windfall gain (shaded area). Ultimately, the higher price will induce a larger supply; the long-run equilibrium price is P_L. But if a ceiling is enforced at the initial price $P°$, both the supply and demand adjustments are blocked. The perceived "shortage" at the ceiling price is H. If price were permitted to rise to P_L, ΔD of the larger quantity demanded is choked off by the higher price, and ΔS is the supply increment provided.

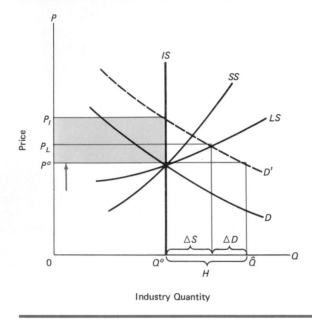

Industry Quantity

What are the effects of a price ceiling upon Consumer Surplus and Producer Surplus? Initially, you may think that in the *immediate run* there is only a transfer from sellers to buyers. Thus, it is sometimes claimed that a rent ceiling means only that landlords do not make a "windfall" gain at the expense of renters. The argument is wrong. Under rent control the households who get apartments are not necessarily the households who value those accommodations the most. It is quite possible that apartments will be rented to people who are only willing to pay $P°$ instead of to people willing to pay P_I or more. So even in the immediate run a price ceiling can reduce Consumer Surplus.

Price ceilings may also encourage inefficient competition among consumers to acquire desired commodities: waiting in line, fighting, using political influence, and so forth. These forms of competition can be extremely wasteful, because what the consumer gives up (for example, time spent waiting in line) is not reflected in any benefit that the seller acquires in exchange.

Summarizing this discussion, price ceilings cause two types of loss in the immediate run: (1) the "wrong" (less highly valued) demands may be the ones satisfied, and (2) non-price competition to acquire the good may itself waste resources. And, of course, in the short run and increasingly in the long run, the price ceiling reduces both Consumer Surplus and Producer Surplus by discouraging additional supply to the market.

EXAMPLE 7.7   Gasoline Waiting Lines

Gasoline crises occurred in 1973 and again in 1979 when the cartel of oil-producing nations—the Organization of Petroleum Exporting Countries (OPEC)—reduced the supplies available to importing nations. In the United States, price ceilings on gasoline prevented the price from rising to a market-clearing level. Instead, long lines of cars had to wait at filling stations in the hope of getting some of the limited supplies.

A study by H.E. Frech III and William C. Lee[a] examined the losses of Consumer Surplus during these crises. The authors used statistical estimates of demand elasticities in the two periods to determine what the market price would have been without the price ceilings. Even though the actual dollar price was frozen below the equilibrium price, consumers paid the difference in the form of a waiting-time price—the value of time wasted standing in line. The authors found that rural users tended to pay higher waiting-time prices (i.e., they waited in line longer). Perhaps rural demand is less elastic, since possible substitutes for auto travel (buses, subways, etc.) are less available. Or else, suppliers may have found it profitable to divert gasoline to the more accessible and concentrated urban markets. The table indicates the waiting-time prices in peak months of the earlier (1973 to 1974) and the later (1979) crises, in cents per gallon (adjusted to 1989 dollars).

Waiting-Time Prices in Two Gasoline Crises (Adjusted to 1989 Dollars)

	March 1974	May 1979
Urban users	66.1¢	46.7¢
(as percentage of money price)	(49.7)	(33.2)
Rural users	111.8¢	44.1¢
(as percentage of money price)	(84.0)	(31.3)

The authors estimated the losses in Consumer Surplus due to this waiting-time cost and also to the reduced volume of transactions resulting from the discouragement of supply. Calculated by this method, the total losses in California were $587 million for the December 1973 to March 1974 period, and $237 million from May to June 1979.

COMMENT   These estimates failed to allow for one additional loss of Consumer Surplus—diversion of gasoline from higher-valued to lower-valued uses. It is true that gasoline went to the consumers most willing to wait in line, but willingness to wait the longest is not necessarily the same as willingness to pay the most. A busy physician might have been willing to pay a very high price for gasoline, but be forced out of the waiting-line game by the high value of his or her time.

[a]H. E. Frech III and William C. Lee, "The Welfare Cost of Rationing-by-Queuing Across Markets: Theory and Estimates from the U.S. Gasoline Crises," *Quarterly Journal of Economics,* v. 102 (February 1987).

Price ceilings have some less visible consequences. Firms that cannot raise prices openly may use subtler strategies. They may eliminate discounts or seasonal sales, reduce the quality, variety, and convenience of their offerings, or concentrate production in product lines that happen to have received a better break from the price-control authorities. Supplies may be sold abroad, leaving even less available for domestic consumers. Black markets may develop. In extreme cases, legitimate trade may disappear. In this connection, we can learn much from the great inflationary episode associated with World War II and its aftermath.

EXAMPLE 7.8   **Repressed Inflation in Postwar Germany**[a]

Germany, like most of the belligerent countries in World War II, had financed her war effort by inflationary expansion of money and credit—in effect, by printing money. Simultaneously, price freezes limited inflation. By the time the war ended in 1945 the German money supply had risen about tenfold, while prices were still largely at the levels frozen by the Nazi government back in 1936. War bombing had smashed Germany's cities and industries. Germany also faced the special problems of a defeated nation—divided, occupied, and subjected to punitive reparations.

In the early postwar years, the Allied occupation authorities in Germany continued the wartime price freeze. (This was not a special attempt to punish Germany, but reflected the "conventional wisdom" of the period; the victorious nations followed similar policies in their own domestic economic programs.) But prices were so drastically out of line with supply-demand reality that over most of the economy production for legal sale could take place only at financial loss. Industrial production in the first half of 1948 was only 45 percent of the 1938 amount, despite a larger population.

Observers were puzzled, however, that the black market accounted for only 10 percent of transactions. This figure was so low because in Germany the term black market was given a very narrow definition: outright trading of goods for cash at illegal prices. Black market professionals were a specialized class of disreputable individuals. In contrast, *everybody* engaged without moral taint in a form of transaction known as bilateral exchange or compensation trade. Such trade took place at entirely legal prices in money, with one catch: no one could acquire goods or services for money alone. In addition to the money price, every buyer had to provide compensation in real goods and services. Estimates are that one-third to one-half of all transactions took this form. Even the occupation authorities engaged in it; the noon meal provided to German employees of the occupation administration was often a more important attraction than the monetary salary. Money was effectively eliminated as a medium of exchange, and the economy suffered the inefficiencies of barter (a topic discussed in Chapter 13).

While some of the frozen prices were more out of line than others, the overwhelming fact was that almost *all* money prices were too low. The Erhard policy of June 1948 was correspondingly double-barreled: (1) a drastic currency reform, exchanging new marks for old, cut down the money supply by a factor of about ten, and (2) price controls were removed. The effect was dramatic. According to one observer: "It was as if money and markets had been invented afresh as reliable media of the division of labor."[b] The German postwar economic miracle was under way.

[a]Discussion based on J. Hirshleifer, *Disaster and Recovery: A Historical Survey,* The RAND Corporation, Memorandum RM-3079-PR (April 1963), pp. 83–112.

[b]H. Mendershausen, "Prices, Money and the Distribution of Goods in Postwar Germany," *American Economic Review,* v. 39 (June 1949), p. 646.

SUMMARY

The supply curve of the competitive firm is derived from the profit-maximizing condition $MC = P$, subject to a qualification that Total Revenue must cover Total Variable Cost in the short run and cover Total Cost in the long run. As a result of these qualifications, the short-run and long-run supply curves of the firm may each have a discontinuity. For the short-run supply curve s_f, zero quantity will be offered at any price lower than the minimum of Average Variable Cost; above that price, s_f is identical with the Short-Run Marginal Cost curve. For the long-run supply curve Ls_f, output is zero for price less than the minimum of Average Cost; above that price, Ls_f is identical with the Long-Run Marginal Cost curve.

To find the industry supply curve, at each price we must add the quantities offered by all firms. However, it is necessary to allow for the external effects on firms' costs, due to changes in industry-wide output, and also to allow for entry into or exit from the industry.

External *economies* reduce firms' costs as industry output rises; external *diseconomies* do the opposite. The external effects may be *pecuniary* (a change in industry-wide output may affect the prices of inputs) or *technological* (a change in industry output may affect firms' production functions). Pecuniary external effects are normally diseconomies, since increases in industry output generally drive up the prices of inputs used in that industry; these make the industry supply curve less elastic. Technological external effects can go either way. It is even possible for *external economies* to override *internal diseconomies* of scale, so that the industry supply curve may have a negative slope.

In the immediate run, quantity produced by the industry is constant (the supply curve is completely inelastic), so that a shift in demand affects only price. Allowing *short-run* adjustment of firms' outputs leads to an industry supply curve that is usually upward-sloping. So in the short run the price increase will not be as great as in the immediate run, owing to the positive quantity response. In the *long run,* the industry supply curve is even more elastic because Long-Run Marginal Cost curves are less steep than Short-Run Marginal Cost curves, and because new firms will enter in response to price increases (or old firms will exit in response to price decreases).

Competition puts pressure on firms' profits. Positive profits attract the entry of new firms. The expansion of industry output tends to reduce product price (pressure from above) and to raise prices of inputs (pressure from below). In long-run equilibrium the *marginal* firm makes zero economic profit. But even established firms earn only zero profit in the long run. Since different firms in the industry compete for any especially desirable input responsible for the low costs leading to positive profit, in the long run that input will command a price so high that its owner captures the entire benefit.

Voluntary trade is mutually beneficial; this is the Fundamental Theorem of Exchange. Consumer Surplus is a measure of the benefit of trade to purchasers, and Producer Surplus a measure of the benefit to suppliers. Consumer Surplus is the difference between buyers' aggregate willingness to pay and what they do pay in the market for the good. Similarly, Producer Surplus is the difference between sellers' aggregate market receipts and the minimum terms at which they would have been willing to offer the good.

A hindrance to trade (like a tax or a quota on supply) has two effects: redistributions between Consumer Surplus and Producer Surplus which are mere *transfers*, and uncompensated reductions of Consumer Surplus and/or Producer Surplus that represent *efficiency losses* to the economy.

A price freeze, following a demand increase or a supply decrease, creates a shortage—an excess of quantity demanded over quantity supplied. By not having to pay a higher price, consumers reap a transfer gain at the expense of suppliers. But the supply response that would have occurred in the long run is blocked; this is a source of efficiency loss to both producers and consumers. There are also losses of Consumer Surplus and Producer Surplus due to non-ideal distribution of the limited supplies available, and to the wasteful techniques (like standing in line, or using political influence) that consumers will employ in order to acquire the good at its artificially low price.

QUESTIONS

For Review

*1. At any rate of output, the industry *long-run* supply curve tends to be less steep than the *short-run* supply curve. Is it also necessarily more elastic? Explain.

*2. "In the long run, a firm could always produce twice as much simply by doubling the amount of every input employed. So in the long run there must be constant returns to scale." Evaluate.

3. Does elasticity of supply for an industry tend to be large or small if the firms' Marginal Cost curves are sharply upward-sloping? What is the effect on elasticity of supply if higher industry output greatly increases the hire-prices of inputs employed in the industry?

*4. If there are *N* identical firms and no "external" effects on input hire-prices, is the *industry* supply curve more or less steep than the *firm* supply curve? more or less elastic?

5. Explain the distinction between *internal* and *external* economies or diseconomies.

*6. a. In long-run equilibrium, why does the marginal firm (the highest-cost firm in the industry) earn zero economic profit?

   b. Why do the other "infra-marginal" firms earn zero economic profit?

7. Consider the exceptional case of an industry with a downward-sloping supply curve. Starting from an initial equilibrium, will a decline in demand lead to a rise or a fall in price? to a rise or a fall in output? Explain.

8. If a tax is imposed upon some commodity, indicate the areas of the following: loss of Consumer Surplus, loss of Producer Surplus, tax collections (transfers of Consumer Surplus and Producer Surplus to government), and efficiency losses.

For Further Thought and Discussion

*1. "In a competitive industry, for any firm there may be internal economies of scale over a certain range. But each firm must operate in the region where internal *diseconomies* of scale dominate." True or false? Explain.

2. Under what circumstances would you expect a rise in demand for an industry's product to be met primarily by a short-run output response by existing firms? by a long-run response by existing firms? by entry of new firms?

*The answers to starred questions appear at the end of the book.

3. Which of the following is a pecuniary effect, which a technological effect? Which is internal to the firm, which external to the firm (but internal to the industry)?
   a. As the number of films produced rises, actors' salaries go up.
   b. As fishing activity intensifies, each fisherman finds fish scarcer.
   c. As new retail shops open, existing shops find customers scarcer.
   d. Steel mills along a river use the water for cooling. But the greater the use, the warmer the water gets, so that the river becomes less effective for cooling.

*4. If at a certain equilibrium price every firm in the industry earns zero economic profit, doesn't that imply that a fall in market price would cause all firms to fail? Explain.

5. A number of techniques are available to cope with increased scarcity and higher world prices of petroleum. Analyze the following in terms of supply-demand responses in the short run and long run.
   a. Price freeze and "rationing by queue" (waiting in line for gasoline).
   b. Price freeze and rationing by coupon (nonsalable).
   c. Rationing by coupon (nonsalable) without a price freeze.
   d. A tax on all petroleum used.
   e. A tariff on imports of petroleum.

*6. In policy (c) (rationing by coupon without a price freeze), suppose consumers were permitted instead to sell ration coupons to one another.
   a. Would this tend to elicit more supply?
   b. Would the limited supplies be reallocated to those with greater willingness to pay?
   c. Explain the consequences in terms of Consumer Surplus.

*7. If a price ceiling is imposed on some good X, is it possible that assigning (nonsalable) ration tickets blocks all trade in X? What if the tickets were made salable?

8. Apartments in New York City are subject to rent control. Apartment owners there often require tenants to purchase their furniture from them. Why? Use a diagram to explain your answer.

9. Suppose that, after a decline in demand for a product, a *floor* is placed under its market price. Then the problem arises of managing a surplus instead of a shortage. What are the disadvantages of a price floor? Would the disadvantages tend to increase over time, as in the case of managing a shortage? Would black markets tend to develop?

*10. Recent petroleum regulations in the United States froze prices of "old oil" coming from existing wells. The justification was that while producers had to be offered more to induce them to drill new wells, the output from existing wells would be forthcoming even at low prices. Is this argument correct?

11. In the longer run, the presence or even the threat of price freezes may induce firms to integrate vertically (to merge with "upstream" supplier firms or with "downstream" customer firms). Explain why.

*12. a. Analyze the effects upon Consumer Surplus and Producer Surplus of a *subsidy*.
   b. If a tax which hinders trade causes an efficiency loss, does it follow that a subsidy which encourages trade causes an efficiency gain?

CHAPTER 8

MONOPOLY

EXAMPLES

A monopoly is said to exist when an industry contains only a single firm. If that firm can drive out competitors because its costs of production are lower, the situation is termed *natural monopoly*. Not all monopolies are natural, however. A government can create a monopoly by granting an exclusive privilege—for example, a public utility franchise or a patent on an invention. At the other extreme from monopoly is the large-numbers or "competitive" case. Actually, the number of firms is economically significant only as a clue to behavior. Large numbers usually lead to *price-taking behavior:* each firm acts as if it can sell as much as it wants at the going market price. (But, as we shall see when we examine cartels later in this chapter, large numbers of firms can sometimes behave like a collective monopolist.) In contrast, the output of a monopolist does affect the price of the product. Geometrically, a competitive firm faces a horizontal demand curve, whereas a monopolist faces a downward-sloping demand curve.

Where there are more than one but only a very few firms in an industry, the market structure is called *oligopoly*—competition among the few. Under oligopoly each single firm's output noticeably affects the demand faced by the other firms. Recognizing that their decisions interact in this way, firms may engage in strategic rather than price-taking behavior, as will be explored in Chapter 10. Another important market structure is *monopolistic competition,* which arises when different firms produce distinct products that nevertheless compete closely with one another—for instance, brands of toothpaste. Monopolistic competition is covered in Chapter 9. This chapter examines the cases of a single-firm monopolist and a cartel of firms acting collectively as a monopoly.

8.1 MONOPOLY AND NONPROFIT GOALS

It has been contended that monopoly firms, being sheltered from competition, give special weight to *nonprofit* goals (as discussed in Chapter 6). In pure competition, firms must always struggle for survival in the face of downward pressures on the price of the product they sell and upward pressures on the prices of the inputs they buy. A monopolist firm, in contrast, may have some freedom of choice. The management of a monopolist may pursue such nonprofit goals as building empires, supporting charitable institutions, granting favors to friends and relatives, and discriminating against unpopular ethnic groups.

However, it is by no means clear that monopolies are *especially* inclined to pursue nonprofit goals. Owners of a monopolistic firm, like owners of a competitive firm, want managers to maximize profit. Consider a monopoly organized as a corporation. The value of the corporation's stock will depend on the firm's present and future profits. If a monopoly earns less than it otherwise could, the loss will be borne by shareholders—who can be

List of Notation

AC	Average Cost	*Q*	Output
C	Total Cost	*R*	Total Revenue
MC	Marginal Cost	η	Elasticity of Demand
MR	Marginal Revenue		

expected to complain, to sue in the courts, or to support takeover attempts.[1] In this chapter, we assume that profit maximization remains the operative goal, even for monopolistic firms.

8.2 MONOPOLY PROFIT-MAXIMIZING OPTIMUM

Price-Quantity Solution

Figure 8.1 (p. 210) illustrates the price-quantity optimum for the monopolistic firm. The upper panel shows the solution in terms of the Total Cost curve C and the Total Revenue curve R. The lower panel shows the solution in terms of the corresponding average and marginal curves.[2] The bold line-segment labeled Π^* in the upper panel is the maximized profit—the excess of Total Revenue over Total Cost at the optimal output Q^*. At this optimal output the R and C curves are farthest apart; in other words their slopes are parallel, as suggested by the dashed tangent lines drawn at the points R^* and C^*. Consequently, in the lower panel Marginal Revenue MR (representing the slope of the R curve) and Marginal Cost MC (representing the slope of the C curve) intersect at this same output Q^*. The maximized profit Π^* is represented in the lower panel by the shaded rectangle; the base of the rectangle is the optimum quantity Q^* and its height is Price − Average Cost, or $P^* - AC$.

The difference between the competitive and monopoly solutions lies on the revenue side. For the competitive firm of Figure 6.1, price was constant so that the Total Revenue curve R was a ray out of the origin. But for the monopolistic firm, price falls as unit sales increase. Consequently, the R curve in the upper panel of Figure 8.1 rises (at a decreasing rate) up to some maximum point and then falls.

Geometrically, we know that Marginal Revenue MR is the slope along the Total Revenue curve R. Along the R curve in the upper panel, slope is decreasing throughout, which means that MR is always falling. In the range where R rises, MR in the lower panel is positive. At the level of output where R reaches its maximum, MR equals zero. And for levels of output where R falls, MR is negative. Since the demand curve D is identical to the Average Revenue curve AR, Average Revenue is also falling throughout.

In the lower panel, Marginal Revenue always lies below Average Revenue. This is, of course, an instance of Proposition 2.2a: When the average magnitude is falling, the marginal magnitude must lie below it.

> [*Warning:* It is important to distinguish the *price* charged for the last unit sold from the *Marginal Revenue, MR*. Note the two shaded areas in Figure 8.2. As sales increase from Q to $Q + 1$ units, the demand curve D shows that price must fall slightly from P' to P''. We can think of P'' as the price received for the last unit, represented by the thin, tall rectangle of width $\Delta Q = 1$ and height P''. But we must

---

[1] If *owners* insist on maximizing profits, does that mean that empire-building, nepotism, group prejudice, and the like will not occur? Such a conclusion is unwarranted. Even if the owners are uninterested, it may be that suppliers of resource services will accept a lower hire-price to achieve such goals. A manager might serve at lower pay if he or she is able to hire relatives, for example. Or men might work for less if women are (or, perhaps, are not) also employed.

[2] The capital letter Q has previously been used to signify *industry* output. Since the monopolist is a single-firm industry, Q can be used to denote the output of a monopolist firm.

FIGURE 8.1 **Monopoly Profit-Maximizing Solution**   Maximum profit Π* occurs at output Q*, where the vertical difference between the Total Revenue curve R and the Total Cost curve C in the upper diagram is greatest. At this output the slopes of the R and C curves are equal (note the dashed tangent lines). In the lower diagram, the curves of Marginal Revenue MR and Marginal Cost MC intersect at output, Q*. Profit in the lower diagram is represented by the shaded area, equal to Q* times the difference between price P* and Average Cost AC* at that output.

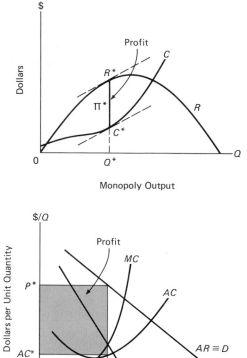

Monopoly Output

Monopoly Output

remember that price has fallen from P' to P'' *on all the other units* sold. The effect of this price reduction is represented by the flat, thin rectangle of width Q and height $\Delta P = P' - P''$. Marginal Revenue is approximately equal to the area of the tall rectangle minus the area of the flat rectangle.]

So both positive and negative elements enter into the Marginal Revenue of a monopolist. The positive element is the price P received for the last unit (the revenue gained). The negative element is the price reduction on all the other units (the revenue lost). Marginal Revenue can therefore be expressed as the algebraic sum[3]

[3]This equation is strictly valid only if Marginal Revenue is defined as the *limit* of the ratio $\Delta R/\Delta Q$ for small changes in quantity. But if the "better approximation" MR_2 for Marginal Revenue (see Chapter 2) is used, Equation (8.1) will be found to hold almost exactly.

FIGURE 8.2 **Marginal Price Versus Marginal Revenue**   Marginal *price*, the price of the last unit sold, corresponds in revenue terms to the area of the tall shaded rectangle of width one and height P''. To calculate Marginal Revenue we must deduct from this amount the thin wide rectangle of height $P' - P'' \equiv \Delta P$ and width Q. This rectangle corresponds to the loss of receipts due to the reduced price on units that could have been sold at P'.

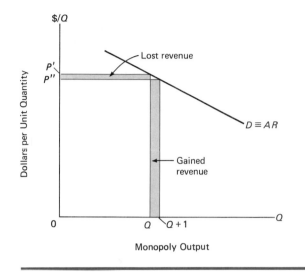

$$MR \equiv P + Q\,\frac{\Delta P}{\Delta Q} \tag{8.1}$$

$\Delta P/\Delta Q$ is the slope along the demand curve. Since a demand curve that is not perfectly elastic has a negative slope, it follows that the last term is negative. Thus, Equation (8.1) shows that MR is always less than P for a downward sloping demand curve.

The cost functions for the monopolistic firm (Total Cost, Average Cost, and Marginal Cost) have the same appearance as for the competitive firm, except that the monopolistic firm is likely to produce at a relatively large scale.[4]

Where both Total Cost *(C)* and Price *(P)* are functions of output *(Q)*, the monopolist's optimizing problem is to

$$\text{Maximize } \Pi \equiv R - C \equiv PQ - C \tag{8.2}$$

---

[4]There may be one underlying difference due to this larger scale of operation. The competitive firm was assumed in Chapter 6 to be a price-taker with respect not only to the product market but also to the prices of inputs it hires; in consequence, the competitive firm's cost function does not allow for any effects on input prices. Only after turning to the supply function of the competitive industry in Chapter 7 was the input-price effect encountered (as an external diseconomy). But the single monopolistic supplier is itself an entire industry. Hence, any input-price effect would be displayed within the cost function of the monopolist firm. Since an increase in industry output tends to raise input prices, the input-price effect tends to make the monopolist firm's cost functions—total, average, and marginal—all rise more sharply as output increases.

As usual, the condition of optimality (maximum of profit or minimum of loss) is the equality of Marginal Cost and Marginal Revenue.[5]

$$MC = MR \equiv P + Q\,\frac{\Delta P}{\Delta Q} \quad \text{Maximum-Profit Condition, Monopolist Firm} \quad (8.3)$$

As in Chapter 6 for the competitive firm, profits are at a maximum only if the Marginal Cost curve cuts the Marginal Revenue curve from *below*. If Marginal Cost cuts Marginal Revenue from *above*, profit is a *minimum* (or loss is a maximum) at that output.[6] The "No Shutdown" conditions of Chapter 6 also apply: the firm will produce a positive output in the short run only if Total Revenue is at least as great as Total Variable Cost; it will produce in the long run only if Total Revenue is at least as great as Total Cost.

As explained in Chapter 6, this maximum-profit condition, $MC = MR$, holds for competitive firms as well. For the competitive firm, which takes product price P as a constant, the ratio $\Delta P/\Delta Q$ would be zero in (8.3) so that $MC = MR$ reduces to $MC = P$.

The price elasticity of demand was defined in Chapter 5. In the notation of this chapter, elasticity of demand is

$$\eta \equiv \frac{\Delta Q/Q}{\Delta P/P} \equiv \left(\frac{\Delta Q}{\Delta P}\right)\left(\frac{P}{Q}\right) \tag{8.4}$$

(Recall that η is ordinarily negative.) We can use Equations (8.1) and (8.4) to obtain an important expression connecting Marginal Revenue MR and price elasticity η. First, from (8.1)

$$\frac{MR}{P} = 1 + \frac{Q}{P}\frac{\Delta P}{\Delta Q} = 1 + \frac{1}{\eta}$$

This relation between Marginal Revenue and elasticity of demand is usually written in the following form.

$$MR \equiv P\left(1 + \frac{1}{\eta}\right) \quad \text{or} \quad MR \equiv P\left(1 - \frac{1}{|\eta|}\right) \tag{8.5}$$

Since elasticity η is ordinarily negative, we see again that Marginal Revenue is less than Price.

Recall that along a given demand curve the elasticity need not be constant, but instead may have different values at different prices or at different levels of output. In fact, along

---

[5]*Mathematical Footnote:* Taking derivatives of profit Π as defined in Equation (8.2) and setting equal to zero

$$\frac{d\Pi}{dQ} = \frac{dR}{dQ} - \frac{dC}{dQ} = 0$$

Marginal Revenue dR/dQ is $P + Q(dP/dQ)$, and Marginal Cost is of course dC/dQ, so $MR = MC$ follows directly.

[6]*Mathematical Footnote:* The second-order condition for a maximum of Π is $d^2R/dQ^2 < d^2C/dQ^2$. That is, MR must be falling relative to MC, or MC must cut MR from below.

a straight line demand curve, elasticity varies from $-\infty$ to 0. It was noted in Chapter 5 that when demand is elastic ($|\eta| > 1$), a decline in price is associated with an increase in consumer expenditure $(P \cdot Q)$ on the good. *Consumer expenditure* is, of course, *Revenue* to the firm. So for levels of output at which demand is elastic, *MR* is positive. Similarly, for levels of output at which demand is inelastic, *MR* is negative. Since *MC* is never negative, the condition $MC = MR$ dictates that the monopolist produce where Marginal Revenue is positive—that is, in the range of *elastic* demand. (In the limiting case where *MC* is zero, the monopolist will choose an output such that $MR = 0$, which implies that demand is unit-elastic, or $\eta = -1$.)

PROPOSITION: A profit-maximizing monopoly firm always chooses a price-quantity solution in the region of elastic demand along the market demand curve.

Monopolistic Versus Competitive Solution

Table 8.1 illustrates a hypothetical set of revenue and cost data for a monopolist firm. The cost data are identical to those shown for a hypothetical competitive firm in Table 6.1. But on the revenue side, the monopolist's demand function is assumed here to be $P = 132 - 8Q$: price is a declining function of output.

In the table, the Marginal Cost column is the *exact* Marginal Cost of Table 6.1. The Marginal Revenue column has been calculated according to the numerical method of Chapter 2 (Table 2.1). This corresponds to the better approximation technique for finding Marginal Cost shown in Table 6.1. Thus, the revenue increment in moving from $Q = 1$ to $Q = 2$ is $232 - 124 = 108$, so $MR = 108$ at $Q = 1\ 1/2$. Similarly, moving from $Q = 2$ to $Q = 3$ increases revenue by $324 - 232 = 92$, so $MR = 92$ at $Q = 2\ 1/2$. Interpolating, $MR = 100$ at $Q = 2$. [*Note:* Since the demand curve here is linear, the better approximation

TABLE 8.1 **Revenue and Cost Functions: Monopolist Firm[7]**

$P = 132 - 8Q$, or $R = 132Q - 8Q^2$, and $MR = 132 - 16Q$
$C = Q^3 - 14Q^2 + 69Q + 128$, and $MC = 3Q^2 - 28Q + 69$

Q	P	R	MR	C	MC	η
0	132	0	—	128	69	$-\infty$
1	124	124	116	184	44	-15.5
2	116	232	100	218	25	-7.25
3	108	324	84	236	12	-4.5
4	100	400	68	244	5	-3.125
5	92	460	52	248	4	-2.3
6	84	504	36	254	9	-1.75
7	76	532	20	268	20	-1.36
8	68	544	4	296	37	-1.06
9	60	540	-12	344	60	-0.83
10	52	520	—	418	89	-0.65

[7]*Mathematical Footnote:* If $P = 132 - 8Q$, then $R \equiv PQ = 132Q - 8Q^2$. Differentiating we get $MR \equiv dR/dQ = 132 - 16Q$.

for Marginal Revenue is identical to the exact Marginal Revenue that can be found by applying calculus.]

The monopolist could, of course, behave like a competitive firm and set output at the level where $MC = P$ (at $Q = 9$). But doing so would sacrifice some profit. A profit-maximizing monopolist would instead choose the output where $MC = MR$, and so $MR < P$ (Equation 8.3). In Table 8.1 the profit-maximizing output is $Q = 7$ where MC and MR both equal 20. The corresponding price is $P = 76$. Total Revenue is 532 and Total Cost is 268, so the maximized profit is $\Pi^* = 264$.

It is easy to prove the following.

PROPOSITION: Given any linear demand $P = A - BQ$, the Marginal Revenue function is $MR = A - 2BQ$. Geometrically, the MR curve starts at the vertical intercept of the demand curve on the P-axis; it then falls twice as fast as the demand curve. This can be proven with Equation (8.3), $MR = P + Q(\Delta P/\Delta Q)$. By definition $\Delta P/\Delta Q$ is the slope of the demand curve, which is constant when the demand curve is a straight line. Given the demand equation $P = A - BQ$, this slope is equal to $-B$. Substituting on the right hand side of Equation (8.3): $MR = (A - BQ) + Q(-B) = A - 2BQ$.

COROLLARY: If the demand curve is a straight line, the Marginal Revenue curve bisects the horizontal distance between the vertical axis and the demand curve.

It was stated above that the monopolist's optimum lies in the elastic range of demand— that is, where $|\eta| > 1$. The last column of Table 8.1 shows the demand elasticity at various levels of output. The computation is based on the relation $\eta \equiv P/(MR - P)$, derived by solving Equation (8.5) above for η. Note that the competitive rule $(MC = P)$ yields $Q = 9$ in the table, where $|\eta| < 1$. We see that it is quite possible for a *competitive* industry's price-quantity equilibrium, but not for a monopolist's price-quantity optimum, to be in the inelastic range of demand. In other words, a competitive industry produces too much for its own good but, of course, the consumers end up better off.

PROPOSITION: The monopoly output solution occurs where Marginal Cost = Marginal Revenue $< P$. Since competitive firms produce where Marginal Cost $= P$, a monopolized industry charges a higher price and produces a smaller output than a competitive industry with the same cost and industry demand curves.

Exercise 8.1 ───

Suppose the demand equation is $P = 10 - Q$. (a) What is the equation for Marginal Revenue? (b) If Marginal Cost is given by $MC = 1 + Q$, what is the profit-maximizing price-quantity solution? (c) What is the elasticity of demand at this solution?

Answer: (a) Since the demand curve is a straight line with the equation $P = A - BQ$, we can use the Proposition that $MR = A - 2BQ$. Specifically here, $MR = 10 - 2Q$. (b) Setting $MC = 1 + Q$ equal to $MR = 10 - 2Q$, the solution is $Q = 3$, $P = 7$. (c) Since the slope of the demand curve is $\Delta P/\Delta Q = -1$, the elasticity of demand is

$$\frac{P}{Q}\frac{\Delta Q}{\Delta P} = \frac{7}{3}(-1) = -\frac{7}{3}$$

As expected, this answer is in the elastic range.

This analysis of the monopolist's price-setting decision is subject to serious qualification. At the beginning of the chapter we distinguished between natural monopoly (which arises when a firm can produce at a lower cost than any potential competitor) and monopoly created by an exclusive privilege granted by law. The governmentally protected monopolist need not fear entry of competitors, but may be subject to governmental regulation (as will be discussed in the section entitled "Regulation of Monopoly"). On the other hand, a natural monopolist cannot ignore the threat posed by potential competitors. In particular, a monopolist who wants to deter entry must set a price below the minimum Average Cost of the lowest-cost potential entrant. (If the monopolist were willing to tolerate entry of a small number of additional firms, the situation would become one of *oligopoly,* which will be covered in Chapter 10.)

EXAMPLE 8.1 Specialists on the New York Stock Exchange

Each security listed for trading on the New York Stock Exchange (NYSE) is assigned to a member of the Exchange who becomes the specialist for that stock. The specialist's function is to "make a market" in the stock by always standing ready to buy or sell. Of course, a specialist can make money only if, on average, his selling price exceeds his buying price. The difference between the two, or "bid-ask spread," reimburses the specialist for taking on the market-making function.

Only one specialist is assigned to a security listed on the New York Stock Exchange and so each such specialist has a monopoly position for dealings on the NYSE. But the NYSE does not necessarily monopolize trades for a given security; some stocks are listed on other organized exchanges as well as on the NYSE. A study by S.M. Tinic showed that competition worked in the expected direction. The bid-ask spread on the New York Stock Exchange was lower, other things equal, for those securities traded on other exchanges as well as on the NYSE.[a] The Stock Exchange's specialist has a monopoly on that exchange, but competitors (firms offering similar services) on other organized exchanges reduce the specialist's monopoly power.

[a]S.M. Tinic, "The Economics of Liquidity Services," *Quarterly Journal of Economics,* v. 86 (February 1972).

EXAMPLE 8.2 Gas and Electric Utilities

Public utility corporations generally have exclusive (monopoly) franchises to serve a particular locality. Among such public utilities are companies providing gas and electricity. In some areas these are provided by the same company, while in other communities the services are separately supplied. Gas and electricity are close *substitutes* in many cases, for example, for cooking, home heating, and operating clothes dryers. So a company providing only one of them would have to be concerned that by raising price it would lose business to the other energy source.

Bruce M. Owen made a comparative study of companies providing combined versus separated gas and electricity services.[a] He found that private companies supplying both gas and electricity services charged on average about 6 percent more for electricity and provided about 15 percent less output, in comparison with companies supplying electricity only. On the other hand, there seemed to be no significant effect of combined versus separated service upon *gas* prices. Perhaps demand for natural gas is quite elastic for reasons apart from availability of electricity as a substitute.

COMMENT   Privately owned public utility corporations are almost always regulated (as we will discuss later in the chapter); the prices they charge must be approved by a government agency. This evidence of a corporation's apparent ability to exploit monopoly power suggests that regulation may have been ineffective.

[a]Bruce M. Owen, "Monopoly Pricing in Combined Gas and Electric Utilities," *The Antitrust Bulletin,* v. 15 (Winter 1970).

CONCLUSION: A natural monopoly, if it is to prevent entry of competitors, cannot charge a price higher than the minimum Average Cost of the lowest-cost potential entrant into the industry.

An Application: Author Versus Publisher and the Principal-Agent Problem

In the publishing industry, book prices are usually set by the publisher. But, of course, authors could negotiate with publishers over the price to be set. The question is, does the author want a lower price for the book than the publisher? For simplicity, we assume that authors' royalties are a straight percentage of the publisher's revenues from sales of the book.

Since normally there is only one seller of any single text, the theory of monopoly is applicable. Suppose the author's royalty is 10 percent of Total Revenue. Denote his royalty as $R_a = 0.1R$. The net revenue to the publisher is then $R_p = 0.9R$. In Figure 8.3, the Total Revenue R received from customers is divided between the dashed R_p (publisher's revenue) and the dotted R_a (author's revenue). The publisher prefers the output Q_p^* where the *slopes* along R_p and along the Total Cost curve C are equal; profit π_p^* at that output is indicated by the height of the upper bold line-segment.

The publisher's preferred output is not ideal for the author, however. *Since the author incurs no cost of production,* his preferred output is Q_a^*, where R_a (and R_p) is greatest. That is, the author prefers the price that maximizes Revenue without regard to cost. The largest possible royalty income for the author is shown by the bold line-segment π_a^*. The upshot of the analysis is that the publisher prefers a higher price (implying a smaller number of books sold) than the author.

Exercise 8.2

The demand function for a certain text is given by $P = 20 - 0.0002Q$; the publisher's Marginal Cost is $MC = 6 + 0.00168Q$. The author's royalty is 20 percent of Total Revenue. What is the publisher's preferred price-quantity solution? the author's?

Answer: The publisher wants to set $MR_p = 0.8MR$ equal to Marginal Cost. Since $MR = 20 - 0.0004Q$, eight-tenths of this is $MR_p = 16 - 0.00032Q$. Equating MR_p to MC, the publisher's optimum is $Q = 5,000$ and $P = 19$. The author wants to maximize royalty

FIGURE 8.3

FIGURE 8.3 **Author Versus Publisher**   Total Revenue from customers is shown by the R curve. Of this revenue, 10 percent goes to the author (R_a curve) and 90 percent to the publisher (R_p curve). Output Q_a^* maximizes the author's royalty income. The publisher's maximum profit Π_p^* occurs at output Q_p^*, where the distance between the R_p curve and the Total Cost curve C is at a maximum. The publisher prefers a smaller output (wants to set a higher price) than the author.

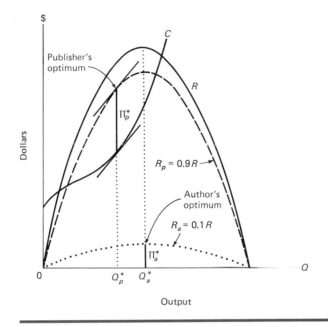

income, which requires that $MR = 0$, or that $20 - 0.0004Q = 0$. The solution is $Q = 50,000$, and $P = 10$. Note the large difference between the two solutions.

We now consider a more difficult problem, which is an example of more general principal-agent problems. Given that the publisher sets the price of the book, what royalty rate should the author negotiate for? The tricky feature here is that the price the publisher sets will depend on the royalty rate the author receives.

The author wishes to maximize his income, $(1 - f)R$, where $(1 - f)$ is the author's royalty rate and R is Total Revenue. To simplify the analysis, suppose the demand function is $P = A - BQ$, and that the Marginal Cost function is $C = G + HQ$; A, B, G and H are given constants. The Marginal Revenue that corresponds to this linear demand function is $MR = A - 2BQ$.

For any given royalty rate, $1 - f$, the publisher's revenue is fR. So the publisher chooses the level of output Q that satisfies $(f)(MR) = MC$. In terms of our linear demand and cost functions, Q must satisfy $(f) (A - 2BQ) = G + HQ$. Solving for Q we obtain $Q = (Af - G)/(2Bf + H)$. Substitute $Q = (Af - G)/(2Bf + H)$ in $(1 - f)R = (1 - f)(A - BQ)Q$ to obtain the *author's* revenue as a function of f. For each value of f there is a corresponding level of royalty income for the author.

Rather than develop the algebraic solution, let us work with a numerical illustration. Suppose, as before, that $MR = 20 - 0.0004Q$, and that $MC = 6 + 0.00168Q$ (that is, we assume $A = 20$, $B = 0.0002$, $G = 6$ and $H = 0.00168$). We find that the author maximizes his royalty income when $1 - f = 0.37$; the corresponding value of Q is 3,416, and the unit price is \$19.32; the author's revenue is $(0.37)(3,416)(\$19.32) = \$24,418$.

Ignoring fixed costs, the Total Cost function corresponding to the Marginal Cost used here is $6Q + 0.00084Q^2$. The publisher's profit is $[(0.63)(3,416)(\$19.32)] - [6(3,416) + 0.00084(3,416)^2] = \$11,280$. This level of f, which maximizes the author's royalty income, does not maximize the publisher's profits. The publisher's profits are maximized when $f = 1$; the publisher would then choose $Q = 6,730$ and obtain a total profit of \$47,115. Notice that the publisher's profit would increase by $\$47,115 - \$11,280 = \$35,835$ if the author took no royalty.

The publisher should therefore be willing to pay the author \$35,835 for giving up royalty rights. Since \$35,835 is greater than the \$24,418 the author earns when his royalty rate is 37 percent, it would appear that the author and the publisher should mutually agree to a lump-sum payment instead of a percentage royalty arrangement.

Book contracts, however, only rarely take this form nowadays. The usual arrangement is a straight percent royalty, or a combination of a lump-sum payment and a percentage royalty. Why is this the case? The probable explanation is the incentive problem. Only the author, usually, is in a position to know how hard he has worked to write the book. If his receipts will be a lump-sum independent of sales, he is less motivated to make the effort necessary to generate large sales. So the two sides agree on a contract that provides better incentives to the author. On the other hand, in earlier times, authors like Trollope and Dickens commonly received only lump-sum payments for each book. The royalty system was slowly developing, perhaps because authors were more risk-averse than publishers—recognizing that publishers may go bankrupt and fail to deliver the promised percentages.

There is a surprising similarity between an author who seeks royalty income from a book and a state that seeks tax income from racetrack betting.

EXAMPLE 8.3 Racetrack Betting

In several jurisdictions in the United States, racetrack betting is an important source of tax income. Of the total amount wagered by bettors (the *handle*), a certain percentage (the *takeout*) is withdrawn from the pari-mutuel pool and not paid out in winnings. From the point of view of the bettors, the takeout percentage is the price paid for the privilege of wagering. This takeout is divided, in varying proportions depending on the specific regulations of each state, between taxes to the state and revenues for the racing industry (payments to the track management, horse owners, etc.) Another source of receipts called *breakage*, is usually computed by rounding down winnings to the next lower 10 cents. If the pari-mutuel odds would have paid off \$5.18 on a winning \$2.00 bet, for example, the state presumes that the bettor does not want to bother with the extra 8 cents. So the state kindly retains the odd amounts. For simplicity we can assume here that breakage is part of the takeout.

The position of the state with regard to the takeout percentage resembles the position of an author with regard to the price of the book: neither incurs any production costs. So, in accordance with the earlier analysis, the state, like the author, would prefer simply to maximize revenue (to set $MC = MR = 0$). But whereas the author is not usually in a position to set the price of a book, a state can and normally does fix the takeout percentage.

A state that seeks to maximize its revenues should fix the takeout percentage where the demand for wagering has an elasticity of -1. The evidence for this statement is mixed. A study by Arthur Gruen[a] indicated that the takeout percentage could advantageously be lowered at New York racetracks (demand was in the elastic range). This was actually attempted for a sixty-five-day trial period but without success. The overall handle did indeed increase but not by enough to offset the lower percentage take. Perhaps the experiment did not last long enough for bettors to recognize the more favorable takeout percentage.

A study by Donn R. Pescatrice,[b] using different methods of analysis, arrived at somewhat opposed results. He found the demand elasticity at New York tracks to be close to -1, suggesting that the takeout percentage was about right. More typically around the country, demand appeared to be in the inelastic range, indicating that an increase in the takeout percentage would have been profitable. In fact, almost all changes in the takeout rate in recent years have been increases rather than decreases. Identifying specific instances where states had increased the takeout percentage, Pescatrice found that the anticipated gains in state revenues were achieved in twenty of twenty two cases.

COMMENT   We cannot simply assume that the state's goal was to maximize revenues. Bettors are politically influential, and they favor a low rather than a high takeout percentage. It seems reasonable to believe that political decision-makers would strike some balance between having more revenue versus not angering the bettors excessively. The tendency toward higher takeout rates in recent years suggests that the need for more tax revenue has been politically more urgent than preserving the goodwill of bettors. (Political decision processes will be studied in detail in Chapter 16.)

[a]Arthur Gruen, "An Inquiry into the Economics of Race-Track Gambling," *Journal of Political Economy,* v. 84 (February 1976).

[b]Donn R. Pescatrice, "The Inelastic Demand for Wagering," *Applied Economics,* v. 12 (1980).

8.3 MONOPOLY AND ECONOMIC EFFICIENCY

Monopoly, as compared to perfect competition, leads to higher price and lower output. Is this good or bad? Though a high price is bad for customers, it is good for the owners of the monopoly firm. Recall, however, the Fundamental Theorem of Exchange—*trade is mutually beneficial*. We can use the concepts of Consumer Surplus and Producer Surplus to show that monopoly hinders trade. It therefore leads to an efficiency loss, apart from whatever transfer gain the monopolist obtains at the expense of consumers.[8]

Figure 8.4 illustrates the monopoly profit-maximizing solution and compares it to the competitive solution. A competitive industry with supply curve S would produce where the supply and demand curves cross at Q_c, P_c. Now, without introducing any changes in costs of production, suppose the industry is monopolized. The competitive supply curve S then

[8]However, we cannot therefore conclude that monopoly should be abolished. (Any more than we could conclude in Chapter 7 that taxes, which also reduce Consumer Surplus and Producer Surplus, should be abolished.) There may be other considerations to be balanced against the efficiency loss.

FIGURE 8.4 **Monopoly and Efficiency Loss**   If there are no *productive* losses or gains from organization of the industry into a single large firm versus competing small firms, the supply curve *S* of the competitive industry is identical with the Marginal Cost curve *MC* of the monopolist. The competitive equilibrium is at price P_c and quantity Q_c; the monopoly optimum is at the higher price P_m and the smaller quantity Q_m. In comparison with the competitive outcome, the shaded area is a transfer from consumers to the monopolist supplier (equal to the price difference times the quantity still produced). The upper dotted area is the loss of Consumer Surplus due to the reduction in quantity traded. The lower dotted area is the analogous loss in Producer Surplus on the amount $Q_c - Q_m$ not produced.

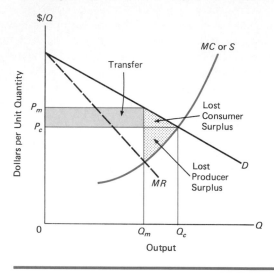

becomes the Marginal Cost curve of the single large firm.[9] The monopolist chooses the level of output where Marginal Cost = Marginal Revenue and sells Q_m at price P_m. (Notice that price is *not* the height of the point where *MC* and *MR* intersect. The price P_m is determined by the height of the *demand curve* at the quantity Q_m.)

Monopoly thus raises price from P_c to P_m. The shaded area labeled Transfer was part of Consumer Surplus under competition and is now captured by the monopolist as Producer Surplus. In addition, monopoly brings about an efficiency loss due to the reduced volume of production and exchange, measured by the Consumer Surplus and Producer Surplus from those units of the good no longer produced. The lost Consumer Surplus is the upper dotted triangle; the lost Producer Surplus is the lower dotted triangle. Overall, consumers lose both the shaded rectangle (transfer) and the upper dotted triangle (efficiency loss). The monopolist, on the other hand, gains the shaded rectangle (transfer) but loses the lower dotted triangle (efficiency loss). Canceling out the transfer, the total efficiency loss is the dotted area in the diagram.

CONCLUSION: In comparison with the competitive outcome, monopoly involves a transfer from consumers to suppliers. There is also an efficiency loss, which is the sum of the reductions in Consumer Surplus and Producer Surplus due to reduced trade.

[9]As explained in an earlier footnote, any "input-price effect" is incorporated within the monopolist's *MC* curve.

EXAMPLE 8.4   **Monopoly Efficiency Loss**

A.C. Harberger[a] estimated the aggregate efficiency loss due to monopoly in the United States from 1924 to 1928. He made a number of heroic assumptions, in particular, that Marginal Cost was constant for all industries, and that the price elasticity of demand was −1 everywhere. Identifying monopolized industries on the basis of high average profit rate on assets, he obtained a surprisingly low estimate of the loss: only around 0.1 percent of national income.

G.J. Stigler[b] criticized Harberger's results on several grounds. First, Stigler claimed that a rational monopolist will always produce in the range where elasticity is *greater* than one (as we have seen). Second, reported profit rates for monopolists may omit monopoly returns in the form of such disguised costs as patent royalties and executive salaries. Finally, monopoly firms may count intangible items among assets, so as to reduce the reported profit as a percentage of assets.

A number of later studies examined different sets of data, allowing in various ways for Stigler's objections. D.R. Kamerschen[c] studied the period 1956 through 1961, using assumptions quite different from Harberger's. For example, he included royalties, intangibles, and advertising expenditures with the monopoly returns. He obtained demand-elasticity estimates by industry, averaging around −2 or −3. On this basis Kamerschen concluded that the annual welfare loss due to monopoly is around 6 percent of national income. Still later, D.A. Worcester, Jr.,[d] studied the period 1965−69, using *firm* rather than *industry* data for added precision. Taking account of the Stigler objections in a variety of ways, and using an overall elasticity figure of −2, he still obtained low maximum defensible estimates of the welfare loss due to monopoly, in the range of 0.5 percent of national income. Example 10.2 in Chapter 10 offers further evidence that the welfare loss due to monopoly power is quite small.

Data from France yield similar results.[e] Under the assumption that the price elasticity of demand is −1 in all industries, the welfare loss due to monopoly is about 0.13 percent to 1.18 percent of GNP between 1967 and 1970. Allowing elasticity of demand to differ across industries leads to much larger estimates, as high as 7.39 percent.

COMMENT   As this very condensed report suggests, we have an unresolved economic controversy, involving issues of both theory and statistical data. Even if the low estimates prove correct, it would be wrong to infer automatically that antimonopoly activities of government should be suspended. Perhaps the low monopoly losses are to be attributed to the success of those very activities.

[a]A.C. Harberger, "Monopoly and Resource Allocation," *American Economic Review*, v. 54 (May 1954).

[b]G.J. Stigler, "The Statistics of Monopoly and Merger," *Journal of Political Economy*, v. 64 (February 1956).

[c]D.R. Kamerschen, "An Estimation of the 'Welfare Losses' from Monopoly in the American Economy," *Western Economic Journal*, v. 4 (Summer 1966).

[d]D.A. Worcester, Jr., "New Estimates of the Welfare Loss to Monopoly, United States: 1956−1969," *Southern Economic Journal*, v. 40 (October 1973).

[e]Frederic Jenny and Andre-Paul Weiss, "Aggregate Welfare Loss Due to Monopoly Power in the French Economy: Some Tentative Estimates," *Journal of Industrial Economics*, v. 32 (December 1983).

There may be an additional efficiency loss not considered here: *the cost of getting or keeping the monopoly*. (This is an example of rent-seeking, to be discussed further in Chapter 15.) If a drug manufacturer's monopoly profits are $5,000 per day, then the monopolist would be willing to spend up to $5,000 per day to acquire and retain the monopoly position. Geometrically, in Figure 8.4, to maintain a monopoly the firm would, if necessary, spend any amount up to the value of the monopoly gain (the transfer rectangle minus the lower dotted triangle of lost Producer Surplus). Several firms contending for the monopoly would in aggregate be willing to spend an amount more or less equal to the potential monopoly gain.[10]

Whether the costs of contending for the monopoly position are an efficiency loss depends on the nature of the contest. Suppose the monopoly privilege is simply auctioned off by the government. Then the additional efficiency loss can be negligible, since an auction is not itself a very resource-consuming process. (Of course, the winning bidder will have to pay his bid, but this amount is a transfer to the government, not a net loss to society.) Cable TV franchises are usually awarded in this way: local governments offer an exclusive franchise to whichever cable company makes the most attractive bid. However, in some cases the struggle for a monopoly is very costly. For example, Chicago-style gang wars were attempts to gain monopoly over crime—evidently, a highly destructive process for all concerned. Less picturesque, entirely lawful, but still often quite expensive, are contests in which prizes are awarded by a government authority at its discretion. The Federal Communications Commission awards broadcasting channels, the Patent Office grants patents, and so on. Here the proceedings typically involve elaborate documentary submissions, hearings at which highly paid lawyers and consultants make their cases, and perhaps very large costs secretly incurred to bring political or other pressures to bear.[11]

These costs of achieving monopoly rights resemble the costs involved in acquiring or defending any rights in our society. Rights to property, rights to sue in court, and even civil rights like freedom of speech can often only be gained or exercised at considerable cost.

An Application: Import Quotas Under Monopoly

In Chapter 2 ("An Application: Introduction of a New Supply Source") and in Chapter 7 ("Hindrances to Trade") we discussed the effects of import quotas in a competitive industry: a restriction of imports necessarily raises the price, which leads to increased output by the domestic producers. That conclusion need not apply under monopoly.

In Figure 8.5, the demand curve is D and the domestic monopolist has a Marginal Cost curve MC. When imports are unrestricted, we assume that the supply by foreign producers to the domestic market is perfectly elastic at price P_0. The domestic monopolist can charge no more than this price, so he will sell the quantity Q^* (where $MC = P_0$); the remaining amount Q^*Q_0 comes from imports.

Suppose instead that imports are restricted to Q^*Q_0 as a quota. The monopolist now faces a demand curve D', which is curve D shifted left by the amount of the foreign quota.

---

[10]Estimates of the expenses incurred to achieve monopoly positions in a number of industries are provided in R.A. Posner, "The Social Costs of Monopoly and Regulation," *Journal of Political Economy*, v. 83 (August 1975).

[11]What if the prize were simply awarded to the contestant offering the highest bribe? This is like an auction, so that (to a first approximation, at least) there would be no efficiency loss. Only a transfer is involved, in this case going to the private purse of the corrupt official rather than to the government treasury. Note that illegal or immoral methods may involve an efficiency loss (gang war) or may not (bribery), just as legal and moral methods may or may not. (This suggests that efficiency ought not be the sole criterion for social judgments.)

FIGURE 8.5   **Import Restrictions**   Initially the supply curve of imports is perfectly elastic at the price P_0, and so the domestic monopolist charges P_0. An import quota of Q^*Q_0 shifts the demand curve as viewed by the monopolist to D'; the corresponding Marginal Revenue curve is MR'. The monopolist will now choose output Q' and price P'.

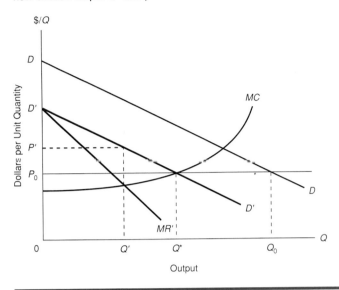

The corresponding Marginal Revenue curve is MR'. The domestic monopolist's profit-maximizing output is now Q', where $MR' = MC$. The price charged at this output is P', as read from the demand curve D'. The new solution has the monopolist producing a *smaller* output—Q' instead of Q. Thus, the quota can cause the monopolist to reduce output (and most likely employment as well), increase price, and increase profits. Surprisingly, the monopolist benefits from a quota, even when the quota is large enough to leave the amount of imports unchanged. Consumers, of course, are worse off because price has increased. [*Query to the student:* Can you verify that the sum of Producer Surplus and Consumer Surplus has decreased as well?]

8.4 REGULATION OF MONOPOLY

Monopoly, we have seen, can lead to economic inefficiency. In addition, excessive monopoly profits are commonly regarded as unfair to consumers. Policies for dealing with monopoly range from laissez faire or tolerance at one extreme to trust-busting at the other. Another possibility is to have government own monopolistic enterprises, as is common in Europe for railroads and telephone service. The policy discussed here is government *regulation* of the monopoly's price, quantity, or quality of service. In the United States regulation is standard practice for privately owned public utilities, which provide goods and services usually thought to be natural monopolies—electric power, water, telephone, and transportation among them.

Regulation usually aims to limit the monopolist to a *normal profit*. Normal profit is supposed to be just adequate to attract needed capital and other resources into the business, but not so high as to exploit consumers. As explained in Chapter 6, normal profit in the accounting sense corresponds to *zero economic profit*. And, we saw, zero economic profit characterizes long-run equilibrium in perfect competition. So, in a sense, regulation aims at achieving the result that would have occurred had competition been possible.

Figure 8.6 shows a monopoly firm with rising Average Cost and Marginal Cost curves. The figure repeats the monopoly solution (Q_m and P_m) and the competitive solution (Q_c and P_c), and adds the zero-profit regulatory solution (Q_z and P_z). Zero economic profit is equivalent to setting a price and associated output (determined along the consumers' demand curve) such that Average Cost = Average Revenue. In the situation pictured the unregulated monopoly solution had too small an output and too high a price compared to the efficient competitive outcome; here the regulatory correction overshoots the competitive solution. Output is too high and price too low.

Figure 8.6 illustrates the striking feature that in the range of output greater than Q_c, Marginal Cost exceeds the demand price or Marginal Value (the consumers' "marginal willingness to pay"). In this range, therefore, the cost of producing additional units is greater than the value to buyers. To produce these units, the firm employs resources that have more highly valued uses elsewhere. Geometrically, when output rises from Q_c to Q_z, the cost incurred on the additional output is *ABDE*—the area under *MC*. The benefit to consumers is only *ACDE*—the area under the demand curve. So the dotted area represents a net efficiency loss in comparison with the competitive ideal. However, in comparison with unregulated monopoly the result is indeterminate. The unregulated monopoly here produces too little, the regulated monopoly produces too much, and we cannot say which is the more efficient.

FIGURE 8.6   Regulation of Monopoly: Increasing Cost   The regulatory solution, fixing price so that the monopolist receives zero economic profit, is the price-output combination P_z, Q_z where the Average Cost *AC* and Average Revenue *AR* curves intersect. If this occurs in the range where *AC* rises, regulated output Q_z will be even greater than the competitive equilibrium output Q_c. In comparison with the competitive solution, the shaded rectangle is a transfer from suppliers to consumers. The dotted area *ABC* is an efficiency loss due to excessive output.

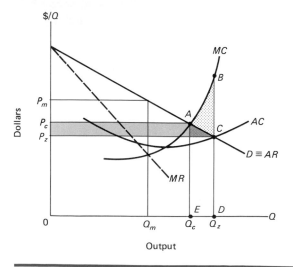

The usual argument offered for regulation does not apply to the rising Average Cost curve of Figure 8.6. Proponents of regulation usually think in terms of natural monopoly, with an Average Cost curve AC that falls throughout the relevant range,[12] as pictured in Figure 8.7.[13] If all the firms have this cost function, any one firm that produced more than the others would have a lower Average Cost. The cost advantage grows as the output lead increases, and so the ultimate outcome is likely to be a single surviving firm.

Since in Figure 8.7 Average Cost AC falls throughout, Marginal Cost MC always lies below it (Proposition 2.2a). It follows that, as shown in the diagram, the regulatory solution where $AC = AR$ (at output Q_z and price P_z) lies between the monopoly solution (output Q_m and price P_m) and the competitive solution (output Q_c and price P_c). So, in this case, the regulatory solution is definitely an improvement over unregulated monopoly; it comes closer

FIGURE 8.7 Regulation of Monopoly: Decreasing Cost The regulatory solution that imposes zero economic profits occurs at P_z, Q_z where Average Cost AC equals Average Revenue AR; this happens to occur in the range where Average Cost is falling. In this "natural monopoly" situation the regulated output Q_z is greater than the profit-maximizing monopoly output Q_m, but less than the ideally efficient output Q_c where Marginal Cost $MC = AR$. In comparison with the efficient outcome, the dotted areas represent losses of Consumer Surplus and Producer Surplus due to insufficient output.

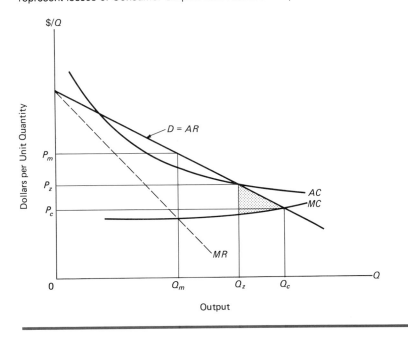

[12]Any firm that can produce at lower Average Cost AC than its competitors, as its scale grows large, has a natural monopoly. This *may* be due to a falling AC curve, where operation at a larger scale gives the firm a cost advantage. But there may also be a natural monopoly with rising AC, if the firm's Average Costs remain lower than its competitors' even at large outputs.

[13]The Average Cost curve cannot fall forever, since that would violate the Law of Diminishing Returns. But it may continue to decline throughout the range of practical interest.

to the ideal. The dotted triangle shows the efficiency loss that still remains, due to the regulated output that is still "too small."

There is a paradox here, however. At Q_c (the output that maximizes the sum of Consumer Surplus and Producer Surplus) Marginal Cost < Average Cost. Thus Average Cost exceeds price, violating the long-run No-Shutdown Condition (the firm would be losing money). It seems unreasonable to regard as ideal a situation in which the utility would have to suffer a financial loss. The answer to the paradox is that, from the efficiency point of view, it would indeed be better to have the utility produce the larger output despite the financial loss.[14] In principle, the loss could be covered by a lump-sum transfer of funds to the firm that would leave the amounts of Producer Surplus and Consumer Surplus unaffected.[15]

We have seen that an unregulated monopoly with a rising Average Cost function (as in Figure 8.6) could not charge the profit-maximizing price if it faced potential competition from outsiders. To prevent entry of competitors, the firm must charge a price below the minimum Average Cost of the lowest-cost potential entrant. The same applies if the Average Cost curve is falling, as assumed here. A falling Average Cost curve means that it is always cheaper to produce at a larger than at a smaller scale, so that only a single firm can ultimately survive in the industry. But different firms may compete to be the single supplier. Such situations are described as competition "for the field" instead of competition "in the field," or more concisely as "contestable markets."[16]

An interesting current example is long-distance telephone service in the United States. American Telephone and Telegraph (AT&T) once had a legally protected monopoly, but the Federal government now allows several firms to compete for the consumers' favor. If indeed the Average Cost function is declining, one of the contenders—very likely AT&T, because it is now the largest—will eventually be able to drive out the others. But the ever-present threat of "competition for the field" is likely to prevent the winner from earning any great monopoly profit.

CONCLUSION: With a rising Average Cost curve, the regulatory zero-profit solution increases output beyond the profit-maximizing solution but goes too far—leading to output that is "too large" rather than "too small." With a falling Average Cost curve, the zero-profit rule increases welfare by increasing output, but the regulation does not go far enough. However, the supposed problem of underproduction in the case of natural monopoly may be exaggerated. The pressure of outsiders anxious to enter the industry may prevent the monopolist from exploiting consumers by charging the profit-maximizing price.

There is a further problem with regulation, one not visible in Figures 8.6 and 8.7. Regulated firms may have little incentive to reduce costs. Indeed, if regulators always maintained the zero-profit condition $AC = P,$ a utility would have no incentive to control costs. Any increase in its costs will lead the regulator to raise the price ceiling, maintaining

[14]The justification is as follows. At the regulatory solution, $AC = P$, so there is no financial loss. Now we ask, speaking in efficiency terms, should output be expanded from Q_z to Q_c? The answer is yes, since in the region between Q_z and Q_c the demand price always exceeds Marginal Cost. The amount consumers are willing to pay for the *additional* units exceeds the cost of providing those units.

[15]Where would the funds come from? Perhaps, from a government subsidy. Or the consumers themselves might be willing to subsidize the firm, or to pay lump-sum fees up front, to allow it to remain in business while still charging the efficient low prices.

[16]See Harold Demsetz, "Why Regulate Utilities?", *Journal of Law & Economics*, v. 11 (April 1968) and William J. Baumol, "Contestable Markets: An Uprising in the Theory of Industry Structure," *American Economic Review*, v. 72 (March 1982).

the normal profit of the firm. In practice, however, there is *regulatory lag*. When costs rise or fall, some time passes before regulators adjust prices. In addition, regulators may punish a firm that conspicuously fails to keep its costs under control. So the incentives to reduce costs are not totally absent for regulated firms, though they are indeed seriously weakened.

8.5 MONOPOLISTIC PRICE DISCRIMINATION

Until now we assumed that the monopolist quotes a single price at which customers can buy any quantity they want. Sometimes, however, a monopolist may *discriminate* by using more complex pricing schemes. A monopolist may be able to divide the market and offer different prices to different buyers *(market segmentation)*. Or, for any given buyer, the monopolist might be able to charge different prices for different quantities *(multi-part pricing)*. In the extreme a different price can be charged to each consumer for each unit he or she buys; this is called *perfect price discrimination*. (Note that price discrimination cannot exist under pure competition. No consumer would pay more than the market-determined competitive price, and no firm would have a reason to sell for less.)

Market Segmentation

Suppose the monopolist divides the customers into two or more separate portions and charges "whatever the market will bear" in each. Japanese auto manufacturers have been accused, for example, of charging more for their cars in Japan than abroad, since the overseas car market is more competitive than the highly protected Japanese market. Note that the two markets must be kept separate for the scheme to work. If cars are priced at $10,000 in Japan and $7,000 in the United States, and if shipping costs are less than $3,000 per car, Americans could ship their $7,000 cars back to Japan and sell them for $10,000. Any price difference in excess of the shipping cost would tend to disappear.[17]

We suggested earlier that sellers would charge a lower price in the more competitive market segment. More precisely, the monopolist maximizes profits by charging a lower price in the segment with more elastic demand. ("Dumping abroad," as in the Japanese car example, occurs because demand is generally more elastic in the competitive world market than in a firm's protected home market.) Imagine a manufacturer of specialty automobiles who sells in countries 1 and 2, charges prices P_1 and P_2, and generates Marginal Revenues mr_1 and mr_2 (we shall ignore transportation costs here). To maximize profits the firm must set $mr_1 = mr_2$. (If not, profit could be increased by withdrawing automobiles from the country with low Marginal Revenue and selling them in the country with high Marginal Revenue.) Furthermore, the firm will set Marginal Cost equal to $mr_1 = mr_2$. In other words, it will operate where the extra cost of producing one more unit is equal to the extra revenue gained from selling in either market. Thus[18]

$$MC = mr_1 = mr_2 \qquad \text{Market-Segmentation} \qquad (8.6)$$
$$\text{Optimality Condition}$$

---

[17]However, the insulation of the two segments need not be total. The monopolist could accept some "leakage" and still remain ahead.

[18]The technical qualification earlier, that *MC* must cut *MR* from *below*, here takes the following form: *MC* must cut the horizontal sum of the *mr* curves (see Figure 8.8) from below.

From Equation (8.5), and knowing that $mr_1 = mr_2$, we see that

$$P_1\left(1 - \frac{1}{|\eta_1|}\right) = P_2\left(1 - \frac{1}{|\eta_2|}\right) \tag{8.7}$$

It follows that if, for example, $|\eta_1| > |\eta_2|$ (demand in country 1 is the more elastic), then $P_1 < P_2$. Thus, as asserted above, the monopolist sets a lower price in the country with more elastic demand.

Figure 8.8 gives a geometrical illustration. The key device is the curve labeled Σmr, the *horizontal sum* of mr_1 and mr_2. This horizontal sum tells us the level of Marginal Revenue (in either country) for a given level of total output. The intersection of the firm's Marginal Cost curve MC with Σmr at the point W establishes the optimal total output $Q = q_1 + q_2$. Drawing a horizontal line from W shows the optimal quantities for the separate countries. The intersection T determines q_1, and the intersection U determines q_2. The associated prices P_1 and P_2 are found along the respective demand curves d_1 and d_2. [*Challenge to the reader:* Show that the lower price corresponds to the *more elastic* demand.]

In addition to dumping abroad, there are other examples of market segmentation. Movie theaters and buses may offer discounts to the elderly or to children (markets segmented by age). There may also be price variation according to season at resorts, and by time of day at restaurants or places of entertainment. (But some of these price variations may be due to

FIGURE 8.8   **Market Segmentation**   The market consists of two segments with independent demand curves d_1 and d_2; the corresponding Marginal Revenue curves are mr_1 and mr_2. The Σmr curve represents the horizontal sum of these separate Marginal Revenue curves. At the profit-maximizing output Q, $MC = MR = mr_1 = mr_2$. Of this total output, amount q_1 is sold to the first sector at price P_1 and q_2 is sold to the second sector at price P_2.

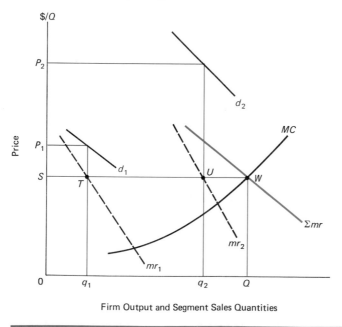

Firm Output and Segment Sales Quantities

differing costs of serving the different types of customers, so we cannot always be sure they are instances of monopolistic price discrimination.) The discount coupons offered by supermarkets are another possible example, since they let the store charge lower prices to those people willing to take extra time and trouble. The discounts appear to be aimed at poorer customers, who presumably have lower demand prices (less willingness to pay). But we have to be careful here, since profit-maximizing market segmentation does not depend on the *heights* of the demand curves but upon the demand *elasticities*. [*Challenge to the reader:* In each of the instances cited, can you show that the discounts are offered to the more elastic market?]

Exercise 8.3

A monopolist has its domestic market protected by law from import competition. The domestic demand curve for its product is $P_d = 120 - q_d/10$. The firm can also sell in the more competitive world export market, where the price is $P_e = 80$ independent of the quantity q_e exported. (That is, this firm is a price-taker so far as the world market is concerned.) Marginal Cost is $MC = 50 + Q/10$, where $Q \equiv q_d + q_e$. (a) Find the profit-maximizing total output and its division between the two markets. (b) Compare the prices and demand elasticities in the domestic market versus the world market.

Answer: (a) The firm maximizes profits by setting total output and sales in each of the two markets so that the Marginal Revenues in the two markets, mr_d and mr_e, equal each other and also equal Marginal Cost. Since the domestic demand curve is linear, we have $mr_d = 120 - q_d/5$. And since the export demand curve is horizontal: $mr_e = P_e = 80$. Equating the Marginal Revenues: $120 - q_d/5 = 80$, which implies $q_d = 200$. Equating Marginal Cost to mr_e leads to $50 + Q/10 = 80$, which implies $Q = 300$. Since $Q - 300$ and $q_d = 200$, it follows that $q_e - 100$. (b) The export price is $P_e = 80$, and demand elasticity in that market is minus infinity. In the domestic market, $q_d = 200$ implies $P_d = 100$. The demand elasticity is

$$\eta_d = \frac{P_d \Delta q_d}{q_d \Delta P_d} = \frac{100}{200}(-10) = -5$$

The price is of course higher in the less elastic domestic market.

Multi-Part Pricing

Whereas in market segmentation the seller charges different prices to different customers, in *multi-part pricing* the seller charges different prices to a single customer. For example, a one-pound package of detergent might sell for $1.00, while a two-pound package sells for $1.50. The seller thus charges a customer $1.00 for the first pound bought and $0.50 for the second.

Figure 8.9 shows the demand curve of a single consumer. Suppose that without price discrimination the monopolist would charge P^* for each unit sold. Consumer Surplus would equal the entire shaded triangle. However, the monopolist could charge as much as P_1 for the first q_1 units sold and then sell an additional q_2 units at the lower price P^*. The monopolist could thereby capture the dark-colored rectangle as revenue, rather than leaving it as Consumer Surplus. The rectangle is thus a transfer from the consumer to the monopolist.

A qualification is needed, however. The monopolist would not ordinarily be able to do quite this well. The high initial price reduces the consumer's disposable income, reducing his demand for additional units (due to the income effect of a price change, as discussed in Chapter 4). Only if the income elasticity of demand is zero will the demand curve be totally

FIGURE 8.9 Two-Part Pricing   The monopolist faces the demand curve d for a typical consumer. P^* is assumed to be the profit-maximizing simple price for a monopolist. The monopolist can do better by charging a higher price P_1 on an initial block quantity B and charging $P_2 = P^*$ thereafter. This two-part pricing scheme allows the monopolist to capture the portion of Consumer Surplus represented by the rectangle lying within the shaded area.

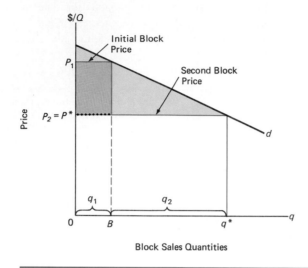

unaffected by multi-part pricing.[19] Multi-part pricing, therefore, cannot capture quite as much additional revenue for the monopolist as indicated in Figure 8.9.

Differences among consumers may also limit the profitability of multi-part pricing. Ideally, the monopolist would like to use a different multi-part price schedule for each buyer. But this is usually impractical. If the same price schedule is used for all, some consumers may be charged too high a price and others too low a price for maximizing the firm's profit. As another practical difficulty, multi-part pricing entails higher transaction costs for the seller.

It may appear that discrimination by multi-part pricing is very common. Electric and water utilities, for example, normally charge a high price for the first block consumed in any period, and a lower price thereafter. The price schedules often have four or five parts (blocks), and market segmentation of different classes of customers as well. Printing shops and furniture movers also commonly use declining-block prices. Indeed, wherever quantity discounts are encountered, multi-part price discrimination may be suspected.

The suspicion, however, is not conclusive; the pricing scheme may be due not to discrimination but to the costs incurred in serving different classes of customers. Electric utilities, for example, may incur a lump-sum cost in connecting a consumer to the main power line, a cost that is essentially independent of the number of kilowatt hours consumed. Similarly, for printing jobs there is normally a lump-sum cost per transaction (such as the cost of setting up the type for a printing order) and a variable cost representing the actual

---

[19]It follows from this that the geometrical picture of Consumer Surplus we have been using, as an area under the ordinary demand curve (the demand curve applicable with single pricing), is not quite correct. But we will not pursue this point further here.

run of the press. Ideally, then, charges to consumers should have a lump-sum and a variable component. For a variety of reasons, it may be more convenient to bill the consumer for the cost of the lump-sum component by charging an extra-high price on the first few units taken. Thus, what appears to be discriminatory multi-part pricing may really represent a "cost-justified" quantity discount.

Perfect Discrimination

Under the logical extreme of *perfect price discrimination,* the monopolist charges a different price for each additional unit bought by each consumer. If this were feasible the monopolist could extract the full amount the consumer is willing to pay, effectively capturing all of the Consumer Surplus.

Figure 8.10 shows a four-part pricing schedule, an extension of the two-part schedule in Figure 8.9. As in the previous analysis, we assume for simplicity that the income elasticity of demand is zero. Then the quantities taken at the lower prices are unaffected by the higher amounts paid out for earlier units. As can be seen, such a multi-part schedule can transfer large portions of the Consumer Surplus to the seller; in Figure 8.10, only the small shaded areas remain as Consumer Surplus.

If this process is carried to the limit, with different prices for each successive infinitesimal unit, *all* the Consumer Surplus is transferred from the buyer to the seller. So a perfectly discriminating monopolist can gain for itself all the advantages of trade.

Despite the apparent inequity that gives the seller all the benefits from trade, perfect price-discrimination leads to an efficient outcome; there are no efficiency losses, only transfers. For the last infinitesimal unit purchased by each consumer, the monopolist charges a price equal to Marginal Cost. Thus, under perfect price discrimination, as under perfect

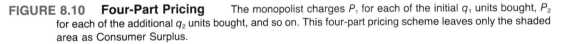

FIGURE 8.10   **Four-Part Pricing**   The monopolist charges P_1 for each of the initial q_1 units bought, P_2 for each of the additional q_2 units bought, and so on. This four-part pricing scheme leaves only the shaded area as Consumer Surplus.

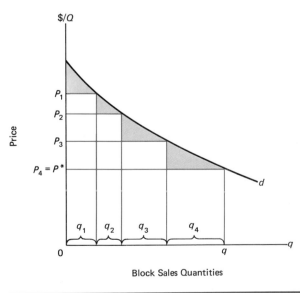

competition, the firm sets Marginal Cost = Price. Since each buyer's Marginal Value (demand price) then equals the seller's Marginal Cost of production, there can be no efficiency gain from producing either a larger or a smaller output.

Auctions

So far, we have supposed that the only way a monopolist can sell goods is to post prices and make sales to all consumers willing to pay those prices. Often, however, goods are sold by auction. Examples include Sotheby's selling an old master painting, a bank selling a foreclosed house, or the government selling oil-drilling rights. What can be said about the bids rational participants in an auction should make, and about the price the seller can expect to get?

Consider a seller who wishes to dispose of a famous painting. Different potential buyers place different values on the painting. Suppose each of the N participants in the auction knows how much he or she values the painting, but does not know how much others value it. For simplicity, imagine that bids must be made in increments of $100, in the familiar oral ascending-bid (or English) auction. What is the best bidding strategy for each participant? At what price will the good be sold?

The answer is surprisingly simple. Suppose I value the painting at $10,000, and that it is about to be sold to someone else who has bid $9,000. If I don't raise the bid, I will not get the painting: I won't pay anything, but then neither will I get any benefit. So my Consumer Surplus would obviously be zero. What happens if I bid $9,100? One of two events must occur. Either $9,100 will be the highest bid and I win the painting, or else someone bids more than $9,100. Consider the first possibility. If I bid $9,100 and win, then I get the painting at that price, and gain a Consumer Surplus of $10,000 − $9,100 = $900. Clearly I am better off than had I not topped someone else's bid of $9,000.

The second possibility is that someone tops my bid of $9,100, say to $9,200. Then, by the same logic as before, I should raise again, to $9,300 rather than see the painting go to someone else for less than $10,000. Ultimately, I either get the painting for less than $10,000, or else, if the bidding goes over $10,000, I would drop out and not get the painting. But I *certainly* would not have gotten it if I had not increased my bid. So if I value the painting more than the current high bid plus the minimum increment in the bid, then I should top the previous bid by that minimum increment. If I value the painting at less than the current high bid plus minimum increment, then I should drop out of the bidding.

If all bidders follow this strategy, the painting will be sold to the person who values it most highly. And the price will nearly equal its value to the person with the *second-highest* valuation, because the winning bidder will not bid up the price higher than that. (The price will *nearly* rather than *exactly* equal its value because of the slight inequalities introduced by the existence of the minimum increment.)

Now consider instead a sealed-bid auction, where each bidder writes down his bid and puts it in an envelope. The auctioneer opens the envelopes and sells the painting to the person who made the highest bid. In such an auction, the winner usually pays the auctioneer his actual bid. But suppose (as indeed sometimes occurs) the auction is conducted under the "second-price" auction rule that says the winner has to pay only the amount bid by the runner-up. For example, suppose Mr. A bid $10,000, Mr. B bid $9,000, and Mr. C bid $8,500. Then the good will be sold to Mr. A at a price of $9,000.

In such an auction, surprisingly perhaps, each person should rationally bid his exact true valuation of the painting. The price at which the good will be sold will then be the same—apart from slight inequalities due to the minimum increment—as under the English auction described above!

To illustrate a sealed-bid second-price auction, suppose I value the painting at $10,000. Should I ever bid any higher, say $10,100? I could only benefit if I become the highest bidder and win the painting. If no one else has bid as high as $10,000 it would make no difference if I bid $10,000 or $10,100. But if someone else has bid between $10,000 and $10,100, I will have to pay more than $10,000 for a painting worth only $10,000 to me. So I evidently cannot benefit by bidding more than my valuation of $10,000.

Should I bid less than $10,000, say $9,900? Two possibilities arise. Either my $9,900 is the highest bid or else it is not. If $9,900 is the highest bid, then so would $10,000, and by bidding either $9,900 or $10,000 I would win the auction. But since what I would pay is someone else's second-highest bid, in either case I would pay the same. Suppose instead that $9,900 is not the highest bid. For concreteness, suppose that $9,950 is the highest. Then in bidding $9,900 I would not get the painting. But had I bid $10,000 I would have won the painting, which is worth $10,000 to me, at a cost of only $9,950 (the second highest bid). I would then get a Consumer Surplus of $50. Thus, the best I can do is to bid my true valuation.

This reasoning demonstrates that the two types of auction (an oral auction and a sealed-bid second-price auction) lead to similar results. Moreover, they are both efficient in the sense that the person who most highly values the good is the one who gets it. [The more usual type case of a sealed-bid auction, where the winner must pay his full bid, is considerably more difficult to analyze.]

8.6 CARTELS

A cartel is a group of firms that aim to behave as a collective monopoly. Each firm in a cartel agrees to produce less than it would under unrestrained competition, in order to drive the price up so that all can earn higher profits.

Cartels have an Achilles heel. However desirable the arrangement to the firms as a group, it pays any single firm to "chisel" on the agreement. Consider a single firm in a cartelized industry that would otherwise be perfectly competitive. Figure 8.11 illustrates such a situation. At price $P°$ that would rule in perfect competition, $d°$ is the familiar horizontal demand curve *as viewed by* the competitive firm. Assuming that the No-Shutdown Condition is met, the firm maximizes profits by producing output $q°$ where $MC = P°$. If a cartel is to raise price, industry output must be cut back—for example, by fixing production quotas for each firm. Suppose this firm is assigned an output q', and suppose further the cartel successfully raises price to P'. The incentive to chisel is evident. The new demand curve *as viewed by* the firm is d'—effectively horizontal, just like the $d°$ curve before cartelization. This means that by charging a slightly lower price, any single firm can get as much business as desired, taking away sales from others. Even at the old competitive price $P°$ the firm would have liked to produce $q°$, more than the quota q'. (Cartel production quotas must be smaller than what competitive firms would have produced, or the price could not rise from $P°$ to P'.) But once the cartel has raised price, the incentive to chisel is that much greater. At price P' the firm would want to sell output q''. The additional profit available to a chiseler, assuming all the other firms faithfully abide by the cartel agreement, is indicated by the shaded area in the diagram.

FIGURE 8.11 **Incentive to Chisel Under a Cartel** If the competitive equilibrium price is P^o, a price-taking firm would produce output q^o. A cartel can drive price up only by forcing its members to cut back production. If this firm's assigned production quota were q', and the cartel succeeded in driving price up to P', the firm's gain from chiseling (increase in profit due to exceeding its quota) would be the shaded area. Note that, at the high price P', the firm would find it profitable to produce output q'', which is greater than its competitive output, q^o.

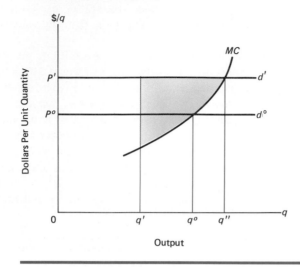

CONCLUSION: Cartels can only raise prices by cutting output. But at the higher prices, member firms are motivated to produce even more than at the competitive equilibrium. So the more successful the cartel, the greater the incentive to chisel.

Exercise 8.4

Suppose there are 100 identical firms in an initially competitive market. Market demand is given by $P = 10 - Q/200$ and market supply by $P = 1 + Q/200$. (a) Find the competitive equilibrium price, industry output, and firm output. (b) If the 100 firms formed an effective cartel, what would be the price-quantity solution for maximum aggregate profit? [Assume that the industry supply curve is simply the horizontal sum of the firm Marginal Cost curves.] (c) At this price, what production quota would be assigned each firm? How much would each firm like to produce?

Answer: (a) Equating supply and demand, we have: $10 - Q/200 = 1 + Q/200$. The solution is $Q^o = 900$, $q^o = 9$, and $P^o = 5\,1/2$. (b) Since the demand curve is linear, $MR = 10 - Q/100$. Marginal Cost for industry output as a whole is, by assumption, $MC = 1 + Q/200$. The profit-maximizing solution for the cartel, where $MR = MC$, is $Q' = 600$, $P' = 7$. (c) At this price the typical firm would have to limit output to $q' = 6$. But it would like to set its output so $MC = 1 + q/2 = P' = 7$, implying desired output of $q = 12$.

Cartels are most likely to be effective when they formally agree to set the price at the monopolistic level. In a number of countries the law treats a cartel agreement as a legally enforceable contract. Some jurisdictions take a neutral position: the cartel agreement is not unlawful, but the courts will not enforce it. Finally, as in the United States, government may outlaw cartels as "conspiracies in restraint of trade." In such a situation a formal cartel would require enforcement devices that are both effective and secret—an unlikely combination when any detected chiseler can complain to the authorities.

EXAMPLE 8.5 **Agricultural Marketing Orders**

Federal legislation in the United States allows growers of certain agricultural products to create an agreement to limit supply and assign marketing quotas. If two-thirds of the growers (by number or volume) vote for such an agreement, the Secretary of Agriculture is authorized to make it apply to *all* growers.

Quantities produced beyond the marketing quotas are "dumped" abroad, used in special government programs outside normal trade channels (e.g., school lunches), or simply destroyed. In effect, the cartel (representing the growers as an aggregate) buys excess production to limit supplies and thereby raises price in the primary market. However, this means that each individual producer has an incentive to produce more and more. In addition, as the price rises, growers of other commodities tend to shift over to the cartelized product. Consequently, we would expect to see an increasing percentage of the cartel crops diverted away from primary markets. This trend is illustrated in the table.

Annual Supply Diverted from Primary Markets Under Federal Marketing Orders

Crop	1960–64 Average	1965–68 Average
California raisins	28.2%	39.6%
California-Arizona lemons	55.2	62.5
California almonds	15.0	21.2
California-Oregon-Washington walnuts	0.8	7.5
Oregon-Washington filberts	21.8	27.5
California dates (Deglet Noor)	21.4	28.2

Source: John A. Jamison, "Marketing Orders and Public Policy for the Fruit and Vegetable Industries," *Food Research Studies in Agricultural Economics, Trade, and Development,* v. 10, no. 3 (1971), p. 347.

Some cartel agreements, we have just seen, are supported or even promoted by branches of government. As for the anti-cartel activities of other branches of government, it is not always clear whether these are well-designed or effective.

EXAMPLE 8.6 **Antitrust and Prices**

The Antitrust Division of the U.S. Department of Justice is responsible for prosecuting cartels engaged in illegal price fixing. If this activity is effective, detection of a price-fixing conspiracy and indictment of its members should be followed by lower prices.

Michael Sproul studied twenty-five accused industry cartels indicted between 1970 and 1985.[a] He found some evidence of more price declines than price increases in the 12-month period after indictment. However, when longer time spans of 24, 36, and 48 months were considered, price increases substantially outnumbered price decreases. The following table summarizes the data. Note also that the price increases were generally of larger magnitude than the price decreases.

Indicted Industry Cartels

Months after Indictment	Cases with Price Increases		Cases with Price Decreases	
	Number of Cases	Average Price Change	Number of Cases	Average Price Change
12	12	6.7%	13	−5.5%
24	17	8.2%	8	−7.4%
36	14	18.18%	11	−7.06%
48	17	14.3%	8	−6.4%

There are two possible explanations for these observations: (1) The government may have been harassing innocent firms, in which case prosecution merely raised operating costs or (2) penalties were not severe enough to force the firms to abandon the conspiracy. These two competing theories can be tested. Under new legislation passed in 1976, price fixing became a felony so that much more severe penalties could be imposed. When cases instituted prior to 1976 were compared with those after 1976, it was found that prices were even more likely to rise in the cases brought after 1976. Thus, greater severity only made the problem worse. The implication is that many (if not most) antitrust cases alleging cartel behavior are not in fact justified, at least so far as effects upon consumers are concerned.

[a]Michael F. Sproul, "The Effect of Antitrust Prosecution on Prices Charged by Firms Accused of Price Fixing," UCLA Ph.D. Dissertation, 1990.

The most successful cartel in history is the Organization of Petroleum Exporting Countries (OPEC).

EXAMPLE 8.7   The OPEC

In pre-OPEC days, before 1960, the international oil companies (such as Royal Dutch Shell and Standard Oil of New Jersey) were often accused of acting as a cartel. If their aim was to keep prices high they failed, as became evident later when the OPEC came into existence and greatly raised prices. In fact, it was the attempt of the major companies to cut oil prices that led the oil-exporting nations to establish the OPEC in 1960. (The U.S. State Department, at a low point for intelligent foreign economic policy, actively encouraged formation of the OPEC!) The subsequent history of the world petroleum market can be divided into five phases.

1. *Phase 1* (1960–73)—The OPEC nations, by requiring the private oil companies to reduce production levels, prevented prices from falling. Over most of this period the price for Arabian light crude was about $1.80 per barrel, rising to $2.59 by 1973.[a] Also during this period the exporting nations solidified their control over pricing and production, in effect expropriating the private oil concessions. Thenceforth, the private oil companies in OPEC

countries received only what amounted to fees for extraction and marketing services. For example, Saudi Arabia captured all but about $.60 of the price in effect on January 1, 1973.

2. *Phase 2* (1973–78)—In solidarity with the attack of Egypt and Syria upon Israel in late 1973, the Arab countries dominating OPEC reduced output. While the attempt to embargo shipments to Europe and America was unsuccessful, the cutback of production drove the price dramatically upward. By January 1, 1974 the price had more than quadrupled, to $11.65 per barrel. It says something about economic gullibility that the Shah of Iran, the King of Saudi Arabia, and other oil potentates succeeded in convincing a large part of the Western public that the high prices were due not to OPEC's production squeeze but to the machinations of the private oil companies. (These companies, in fact, typically received $.60 per barrel from their OPEC concessions, which is what they had earned before.)

The problem for the OPEC was and is to hold production down despite member countries' incentives to "chisel." Each separate exporting nation can gain by expanding output as long as the others are holding back. In fact, in the period from 1974 to late 1978 most of the member countries were probably not withholding supplies but were producing heavily. The cartel was viable in that period only because a few major producers, notably Saudi Arabia and Kuwait, held their production at a relatively low level. Nevertheless, OPEC's power gradually weakened. While the official price rose from $11.65 per barrel at the beginning of 1974 to $13.00 five years later (an increase of about 12 percent), the U.S. dollar depreciated about 38 percent over the same period. Thus, by January 1, 1979, the real price of OPEC crude oil was down substantially from its peak.

3. *Phase 3* (1979–82)—The turmoil in Iran paralyzed their production and permitted OPEC to start another round of price increases. Even after the Khomeini government took over, Iranian exports remained drastically less than before. The official OPEC price rose ultimately to $34 per barrel in late 1981. (And at the peak some OPEC suppliers demanded and received a premium of as much as $5 above the official price.) However, especially toward the end of the period, maintaining these high prices necessitated increasingly severe production cutbacks by the major OPEC producers—in particular, by Saudi Arabia. From the OPEC point of view these events had two adverse consequences. First, demand elasticity proved greater in the long run than in the short run. The continuing high price impelled consuming nations to use oil more economically, and to shift toward substitute fuels. Second, high prices encouraged non-OPEC oil exporters like Britain and Mexico to develop and expand their capacity. The combined effect of lesser demand and increased non-OPEC supply led to the next phase.

4. *Phase 4* (early 1982)—In this phase, OPEC attempted to maintain the high price of oil while coping with the "glut" that inevitably was created. The only way of doing so was for OPEC to cut back production. OPEC output fell from a 1979 peak of 32 million barrels per day (mbd) to less than half that amount by early 1983.[b] And within OPEC the brunt of the decline fell upon the largest producer, Saudi Arabia, which was forced to curtail its output from a peak of 10.2 mbd to less than 4 mbd. (Even so, the nominally fixed $34 per barrel price was slipping in real terms; the dollar depreciated about 5 percent between October 1981 and March 1983.) Bowing to economic reality, in March 1983 OPEC was finally forced to cut the dollar price to $29 per barrel.

5. *Phase 5* (late 1985)—Saudi Arabia finally followed through on its longstanding threat to expand production, in retaliation for the failure of other OPEC members to abide by their quotas. This meant that the Saudis were abandoning their role as the price stabilizer. In November 1985 the price of oil was $30 per barrel; by February 1986, the price had fallen to $15.[c] By August, the price had dropped further to $10. At this time, OPEC members

agreed to a production-limiting strategy, and, in fact, there was a reduction in OPEC output from more than 20 million barrels per day to less than 15 million barrels per day. The price of oil, after having rebounded to $17, by October settled at $14 per barrel.[d] It remains doubtful how long OPEC will be able to maintain even its reduced effectiveness as a cartel.

[a]Data on prices have been collected from several sources including *International Economic Report of the President,* Washington, D.C.: U.S. Government Printing Office, February 1974, pp. 110–11, and *Los Angeles Times* (March 15, 1983), p. 1.

[b]Production figures from S. Fred Singer, "What Do the Saudis Do Now?" *Wall Street Journal* (March 18, 1983), p. 20.

[c]Terri Thompson, "The Perils of Cheap Oil," *Business Week* (April 21, 1986).

[d]Sarah Miller, "OPEC Will Have to Run Hard Just to Stay in Place," *Business Week* (October 6, 1986).

SUMMARY

A monopoly exists when an industry consists of a single firm. This may be the result of a governmental license or franchise. A second possibility, *natural monopoly,* is said to occur when one firm can produce more cheaply than any larger number.

Monopolists, like ordinary firms, are assumed to maximize profit. This requires setting output (or price) such that Marginal Cost = Marginal Revenue. For the monopoly firm, in contrast with the price-taking firm, Marginal Revenue *MR* is less than price *P*. The relation between these two variables involves the demand elasticity η.

$$MR = P(1 + 1/\eta)$$

The ability of a firm to charge a price higher than Marginal Cost tends to decrease with the number of firms in the industry, and with the consumers' elasticity of demand for the product. The extent to which a single firm in an industry can earn a monopoly profit is also limited by the competitive threat from outsiders. Unless protected by an exclusive legal franchise, a firm will not be able to charge a price higher than the Average Cost at which an outsider could enter and produce.

Assuming the firm can exploit its monopoly position, output will be less and price higher than under pure competition. There is an efficiency loss (reduction in Consumer Surplus and Producer Surplus) due to the smaller volume of production and exchange, and also a pure transfer from consumers to the monopolist seller. There may also be an additional efficiency loss if resources are expended in the struggle to gain and maintain a monopoly position.

Monopolies, and in particular franchised public utilities, are often regulated. The goal of regulation is commonly to reduce price to the lowest level that attracts and retains the resources employed in the industry. Since no economic profits are then earned, Average Revenue and Average Cost must be equal. If the monopolist's Average Cost curve is rising, the intersection of Average Cost and Average Revenue overshoots the competitive equilibrium; there will be an efficiency loss due to excessive production in this industry. On the other hand, for levels of output where Average Cost is falling, the regulated solution lies between the monopolist's profit-maximizing output and the competitive outcome.

Price discrimination may allow a monopolist to earn higher revenue (that is, to capture more of what would have been Consumer Surplus). Under *market segmentation,* the monopolist sets overall Marginal Cost of production equal to the Marginal Revenue in each segment. It follows from the equation relating price, Marginal Revenue, and elasticity that higher prices will be charged in segments with less elastic demands. *Multi-part pricing*— an alternative form of price discrimination—captures some of Consumer Surplus with a price schedule that charges different unit prices for different quantities sold. Such discrimination is most effective if an individualized schedule can be offered to each consumer. *Perfect* discrimination is a limiting case in which each consumer is charged the maximum he or she would be willing to pay for each unit, so that no Consumer Surplus remains. Surprisingly, there is no efficiency loss under perfect discrimination.

Cartels are associations of firms in an industry that act collectively like a monopolist. Since raising price requires reducing production, output quotas typically have to be imposed upon members of a cartel. Each member is therefore motivated to "chisel" (produce beyond quota). In addition, potential producers outside the cartel have an inducement to enter the industry. As a result, cartels have historically been fragile except where supported by government power.

QUESTIONS

For Review

*1. Why will a monopolist's profit-maximizing rate of output always be in the region of elastic demand?

*2. A monopolist initially maximizes profits by selling 1,000 panes of glass a year. A salesman then offers to rent a machine that reduces the firm's Marginal Cost by $10 at each level of output. Should the firm be willing to pay more or less than $10,000 rent per year?

3. Why is monopoly power over price smaller as elasticity of demand increases?

*4. "Monopoly is a bad thing for consumers, but a good thing for producers. So, on balance, we can't be sure that monopoly is responsible for any loss in economic efficiency." Analyze.

5. A competitive industry may have its equilibrium in the range of inelastic demand. Then the industry would receive more revenue if its output were smaller. Does it follow that such a competitive industry is producing "too much" of the good in terms of efficient use of resources?

*6. Monopoly firms are accused of pursuing "nonprofit goals" to a greater degree than competitive firms. Why might a monopolist be any less interested in profit than a firm in a competitive industry?

7. Compare the profit-maximizing conditions for simple monopoly, market-segmentation monopoly, and perfect-discrimination monopoly. Why is only the last of these said to be efficient?

*8. In making efficiency comparisons between a monopolized and a competitive industry, the Marginal Cost function of the monopolist was said to correspond to the supply function of the competitive industry. Explain why.

*The answers to starred questions appear at the end of the book.

9. When will zero-profit regulation of a monopoly lead to too high a price from an efficiency point of view? too low a price?

10. Show how behavior of a cartel's members may threaten its survival. Show how behavior of outsiders may threaten it.

For Further Thought and Discussion

*1. Explain whether there is a contradiction between the following assertions: (1) the oil industry is an effective monopoly (cartel), and (2) higher prices for petroleum products will do little to discourage demand?

2. Is it better (more efficient) to have a monopolized industry, or no industry at all?

*3. a. In comparison with a simple monopolist, does a perfectly discriminating monopolist *possibly* or *necessarily* produce more output?
   b. Does a market-segmentation monopolist?
   c. A multi-part pricing monopolist?

*4. Market segmentation tends to be more common in the sale of services (e.g., discrimination by income for medical services, by age for transportation services) than in the sale of manufactured goods. Why?

*5. Movie theaters often offer price discounts to the young.
   a. Is there likely to be a "leakage" problem in this form of market segmentation?
   b. Can the discount be explained in terms of differing elasticities of demand?

*6. a. Are supermarket discount coupons a form of market segmentation?
   b. If so, how is "leakage" controlled?
   c. Do consumers who choose to use the coupons have a more elastic demand for grocery products? Explain.

7. Physicians often charge poorer customers lower fees for medical services. They usually explain this as a charitable gesture. Alternatively, can this be an example of market segmentation?

8. It has been alleged that sellers' cartels are more effective in dealing with government as a buyer because of the existence of public records of all transactions in which government engages. Explain. How might the contention be tested?

9. Governments sometimes auction off the right to monopolize a commodity. (The *gabelle,* or salt monopoly, of pre-Revolution France, was an example.) Show diagrammatically the maximum amount the government might expect to acquire by auctioning off a monopoly. Is this likely to generate more or less income for the government than the most lucrative excise tax the government might impose?

*10. If an organization like the Mafia effectively monopolized illegal activity, would you expect to observe less crime than under competitive free entry into this "industry"?

E X A M P L E S

S o far we have discussed the firm's choice of the *quantity* to produce. This chapter focuses on the *characteristics of the product* offered to the consumers. We will distinguish between two questions: the problem of *variety* and the problem of *quality*. Variety is a matter of taste. Some people like red roses, some pink, some white. Some people like conservative cars, others prefer flashy ones. Quality, on the other hand, is something everyone can agree on. Durability, strength, reliability, and the like, are things that everyone desires.

9.1 MONOPOLISTIC COMPETITION—PRODUCT VARIETY

In the market structure known as *monopolistic competition,* it is assumed that—as in pure competition—firms do not collude on price or quantity, and that free entry into the industry (or exit from it) is possible. The monopolistic element in monopolistic competition is *product differentiation:* each firm has its own unique variety of product. Each enterprise has a clientele that prefers the firm's product even if another firm offers a similar product at a lower price. A particular city, for example, may have a dozen supermarkets. They may closely compete in some respects but each has some monopoly power due to geographical location or other special features that make it the favorite of some customers. The crucial proposition to be demonstrated is that a group of monopolistically competitive firms produces more and charges less than a monopolist able to produce the same range of products the same way.

Consider first a monopolist with N plants. The industry demand faced by the monopolist is shown as D_N in Figure 9.1. Marginal Revenue is MR_N. Each of the plants is assumed to serve a fraction $1/N$ of the total demand, so that each plant's pro-rata share of the overall demand is $D_n \equiv D_N/N$. Marginal Revenue for each plant is $MR_n \equiv MR_N/N$. If $N = 4$, the D_n and MR_n curves would represent one-fourth of the quantities along the corresponding D_N and MR_N curves. With the assumed constant Marginal Cost $MC = B$, the profit-maximizing solution is Q_N^* for the entire monopolist firm and q_n^* for each of its separate plants. The same price P_m is arrived at either way.

Now suppose the industry structure changes from simple monopoly to monopolistic competition: each *plant* becomes a separate *firm*. Then, and this is the key point, each independent firm would produce more output than a monopolist would allow its plant to produce.

As shown in Figure 9.2 (p. 244), the independent firm's *perceived* demand curve d_n is more elastic (flatter) than the monopolist's per-plant demand curve D_n. The curve d_n is more elastic than D_n because, by lowering price relative to its neighbors, each firm figures that it can win some customers away from them. (The monopolist, of course, would not permit

List of Notation

D_N	Industry demand	P_n	Price for unit of physical output charged by firm n
D_n	Demand curve faced by each of n plants of a monopolist	q_n	Physical output of firm n
d_n	Demand curve faced by each of n separate firms in industry	s_n	Output, in terms of service level, of firm n
P_s	Price for unit of service output	z_n	Units of the quality present in each unit of firm n's output

FIGURE 9.1   **Monopoly Solutions: Aggregate and Plant**   For a given number of plants *N*, the monopolist's effective *aggregate* demand curve is D_N. Curve $D_n \equiv D_N/N$ is the pro-rata *plant* demand curve. MR_N and $MR_n \equiv MR_N/N$ are the associated Marginal Revenue curves. Marginal Cost is assumed to be constant at the level *B*. The profit-maximizing aggregate output is Q_N^* (where $MC = MR_N$), and plant output is q_n^* (where $MC = MR_n$). Of course, $Q_N^* = Nq_n^*$. For either the plant or the firm solution, the same profit-maximizing price P_m is found along the associated demand curve.

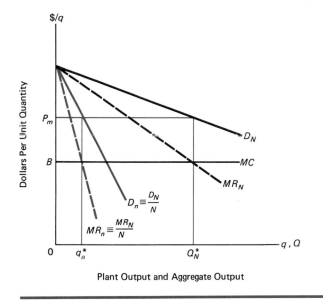

Plant Output and Aggregate Output

its separate plants to cut price at one another's expense.) Corresponding to the more elastic firm demand curve d_n is a higher perceived Marginal Revenue curve mr_n.[1] The firm in Figure 9.2 therefore maximizes profits by producing output q_n' where $mr_n = MC$. Since output q_n' is greater than the monopoly output q_n^*, price P' will be less than the monopoly price P_m.

Figure 9.2 shows that the output of a firm under monopolistic competition is greater than the per-plant output of an ordinary monopolist. But Figure 9.2 does not depict the equilibrium solution. The solution with output q_n' sold at the price P' along demand curve d_n is not possible as an overall equilibrium of the industry. With a fixed number *(N)* of firms, at any price each firm can sell no more than its pro-rata share of demand $D_n \equiv D_N/N$. The flatter demand curve d_n in the diagram is therefore an illusion (like the illusion of the horizontal demand curve faced by the firm in pure competition). If only one firm cuts price it can indeed expand output along d_n. But *N* identical firms must all end up choosing the same price. In trying to sell output q_n' at price P' each firm will find that sales expand less than expected; each firm faces the steeper pro-rata demand curve D_n in the diagram rather than the "illusory" d_n curve.

When all the independent firms cut price (as compared with the monopoly solution), the new equilibrium must lie at a point on the pro-rata demand curve D_n, like *S* in Figure

---

[1]Since $MR \equiv P(1 - 1/|\eta|)$, when the demand elasticity η is greater (in absolute value) the Marginal Revenue is higher.

FIGURE 9.2 **Monopoly Plant Versus Monopolistic-Competition Firm, at Monopoly Solution**   The solution for the monopoly plant, where $MC = MR_n$ at output q_n^* and associated monopoly price P_m, is the same as in the preceding diagram. But once the monopoly plant becomes an independent firm, at price P_m the *perceived* demand curve would be d_n. This curve is more elastic than the pro-rata demand curve D_n, since the firm can win customers from its neighbors if it lowers its price. The firm will therefore attempt to achieve the solution H at output q_n' where Marginal Cost MC cuts the curve mr_n.

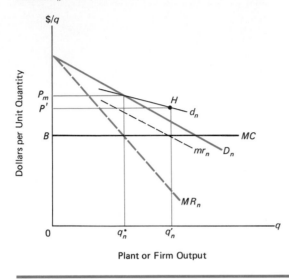

Plant or Firm Output

9.3. Each firm produces quantity q_n'', and the price is P''. Once again the firm *perceives* a flatter demand curve d_n; however, the d_n in Figure 9.3 has the property that each firm's optimal price-quantity choice lies along the pro-rata demand curve. The solution on the firm level is now consistent with its pro-rata share of the overall consumer demand. At this solution each firm's output is greater than what the monopoly plant would produce $(q_n'' > q_n^*)$. And the price to consumers is of course lower $(P'' < P_m)$.

One more element must be considered to determine the *long-run* equilibrium for monopolistic competition: changes in the *number* of firms. Depending on the fixed costs, in the short-run equilibrium shown in Figure 9.3 each firm may either earn economic profits (inducing new firms to enter) or make an economic loss (forcing some old firms to exit). Let us assume that the short-run equilibrium is profitable, and that new firms do enter. As a result, the true pro-rata demand curve $D_n = D_N/N$ shifts down and the illusory d_n as viewed by an existing firm also shifts down.[2]

---

[2]This shift is due to dividing the aggregate demand curve (D_N) horizontally by a larger N. There is a countervailing factor, however, since a larger number of varieties to choose from means there will be a better matching of consumer desires. In Figure 9.3, as N rises, D_N would also tend to rise. However, in the ratio D_N/N that defines the D_n curve, the numerator tends not to rise as fast as the denominator. When the number of firms increases from two to three, there is a 50 percent increase in N but not in general such an enormous increase in consumers' demand price. So, despite this countervailing factor, the D_n curve must, at least eventually, shift inward as N rises. The same holds, of course, for the d_n curve.

FIGURE 9.3 **Monopoly Plant Versus Monopolistic-Competition Firm, at Monopolistic-Competition Equilibrium**   Curve mr_n is the Marginal Revenue associated with the *perceived* (flatter) firm demand curve d_n. With N firms, point S in the diagram represents a monopolistic-competition equilibrium. Each firm is maximizing profit since $MC = mr_n$. This outcome is consistent with equilibrium of the industry as a whole, since the combination of output q_n'' and price P'' constitutes a point on the pro-rata demand curve D_n. Price is lower and output greater than in the monopoly case.

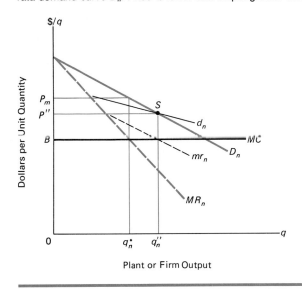

Plant or Firm Output

The long-run solution for the representative firm is shown at point L in Figure 9.4 (p. 246). Here all three equilibrium conditions are satisfied: (1) each firm chooses the level of output that maximizes profits $(MC = mr_n)$; (2) the aggregate quantity that firms want to supply equals the quantity consumers demand: the firm's price-output combination is consistent with the pro-rata demand curve D_n; and (3) no firms want to enter or exit the industry: each firm earns zero economic profit. This zero-profit condition is represented in the diagram by the tangency at point L of the firm's perceived demand curve d_n with its Average Cost curve AC_n. So the equilibrium output is q_n''' and price is P'''. At this equilibrium, total industry output is greater than what a monopolist who owned all the different plants would produce; price, of course, is correspondingly lower.

A second important question is, Does monopolistic competition, as compared with multi-plant monopoly, offer consumers more variety? In other words, would the number of independent firms (each serving its own clientele) under monopolistic competition be greater than the number of separate plants under monopoly? The result can go either way. We have just seen that when the plants operated by a monopolist become independent competing firms, the per-plant profit is less than before. But if the profits are still positive, new firms will enter—so that variety would increase. On the other hand, it could be that what was a positive per-plant monopoly profit turns into a loss when the separate plants become independent firms that compete by cutting price. Then some firms would exit and variety would decrease.

FIGURE 9.4 **Long-Run Equilibrium: Representative Firm in Monopolistic Competition**
The short-run equilibrium conditions of the preceding diagram continue to hold: $MC = mr_n$, and the representative firm's price-output combination at L lies on the true pro-rata demand curve D_n. The additional long-run condition is that entry or exit takes place until the representative firm earns zero profit (price equals Average Cost AC_n).

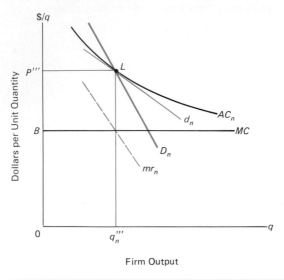

Firm Output

CONCLUSION: In comparison with multi-plant monopoly, under monopolistic competition aggregate output is greater and product price lower. In long-run equilibrium, each firm earns zero economic profit. But there may be a larger or smaller number of plants. Thus, while consumers benefit from a lower price, they may or may not find more varieties.

EXAMPLE 9.1 **Advertising and Prices**[a]

A firm may have monopoly power because consumers are not aware that other firms sell very similar products at lower prices. We would therefore expect that a deterioration of consumers' information makes the demand curve facing any firm less elastic, so that each firm can charge a higher price. A natural experiment to test this hypothesis arose in New York in 1979. Because of a strike, the three major newspapers in New York City (the *Times, Post,* and *Daily News*) suspended publication from August 10 to October 5. A major newspaper in neighboring Long Island, *Newsday,* continued publishing. This paper carried the usual food advertisements in which supermarkets listed prices for a number of products. Lacking their regular newspapers, shoppers in Queens County (one of the boroughs of New York City) had little access to supermarket food advertisements, while shoppers in neighboring Nassau county had a good deal of price information.

Amihai Glazer collected prices at 31 stores for 6 products (peaches, grapes, lettuce, watermelon, chicken, and ground beef). He found that over the period August 14–18, the first week of the strike, prices in Queens supermarkets increased by 3.4 percent more than in Nassau supermarkets. In contrast, over the period August 23–October 6, which saw the

9.2 EQUILIBRIUM QUALITY LEVEL: COMPETITION AND MONOPOLY

In the previous section we looked at the problem of *variety*. Here we consider *quality*. Suppose there is some single service characteristic that all consumers want from the product; for laundry detergent it would be cleaning power, for food products it may be calories or proteins.

There is one key idea to keep in mind. Although producers and consumers deal in quantities of *product Q* (e.g., hay), they are really interested in amounts of the *service (S)* provided (e.g., calories fed to cows). The price and quantity of the product (hay) will depend ultimately on the price and quantity of the service (calories) produced and consumed. Quality of a product is simply the amount of service provided per unit. Put another way, service is quantity times quality.

To begin with, let us assume a fixed number *(N)* of competitive firms. A firm produces q_n tons of hay; each ton contains z_n calories. So the firm's output of the service is

$$s_n = z_n q_n \tag{9.1}$$

Since users are really concerned about the service, the price P_n of the nth firm's physical product will (assuming that users are fully informed) directly reflect the implicit market price for the service (P_s).

$$P_n = z_n P_s \tag{9.2}$$

For example, if one firm's hay is known to yield 10 percent more calories than another firm's hay, and both types of hay are sold in the market, then the price of the higher-quality hay must be 10 percent higher.

What determines the price of the service, or P_s? As usual there will be an overall balance of supply and demand. Each separate firm will want to set its Marginal Cost of producing a calorie, MC, equal to the price of a calorie, P_s. But MC will generally depend on both the quantity and quality of hay it produces (that is, on both q_n and z_n). Panel (a) of Figure 9.5 (p. 248) shows an initial situation where the firm provides quantity $q_n = q_n^o$ and quality $z_n = z_n^o$, determining a calorie output $s_n^o = q_n^o z_n^o$. Three different Marginal Cost curves are shown: the dotted curve MC_q shows the cost of providing more calories by varying only *quantity* (i.e., holding quality constant at z_n^o). The dashed curve MC_z represents the marginal cost of calories by varying only the quality of the hay (holding quantity constant at q_n^o). These two Marginal Costs are equal at calorie output s_n^o, which means that the firm's choices

FIGURE 9.5 **Marginal Cost of Quantity Versus Quality**   In Panel (a) the dashed and dotted curves MC_z and MC_q show the Marginal Cost of producing more service output by increasing *quality* of product or *quantity* of product, respectively. Panel (b) shows market equilibrium at price P^o and service S^o. The industry supply curve, S, is the horizontal sum of the firms' marginal costs.

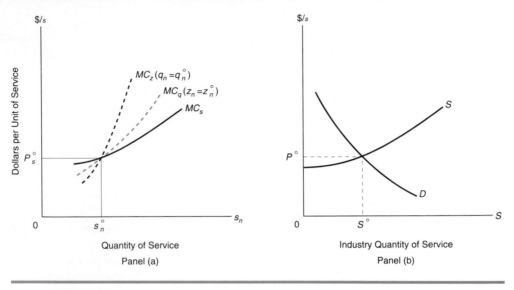

Quantity of Service

Panel (a)

Industry Quantity of Service

Panel (b)

of quality z_n and quantity q_n are optimal for that level of service output. Thus, it is generally cheaper to provide additional service output by a balanced increase of both quality and quantity rather than by increasing quantity alone or quality alone.

PROPOSITION: At any level of service output, the firm's quality and quantity choices are optimal when the Marginal Cost of expanding service by increasing quantity (MC_q) and the Marginal Cost of expanding service by increasing quality (MC_z) are equal.

Furthermore, the true Marginal Cost of the service must be the same as MC_q and MC_z when these are equal. So, in the diagram, s_n^o is the firm's profit-maximizing output of service at price P_s^o.

Balancing quality and quantity at each output of service permits us to construct the overall MC_s curve for each firm; notice that the MC_s curve is lower than either of the MC_q and MC_z curves separately. The upward-sloping branch of the curve is the firm's supply curve of calories contained in hay. The industry's supply of calories, curve S in Panel (b), is the horizontal sum of the firms' separate MC_s curves (adjusted for any input-price and exit-entry effects, as discussed in Chapter 7). The overall equilibrium would be at price P^o and service quantity S^o where industry supply equals consumer demand.

Competitive firms will not produce the same quality of hay if different firms have different cost functions with respect to quantity and quality. Some hay producers may have richer soil, others poorer soil, and so their hay may be of different quality. But the purchaser is really buying the valuable characteristic—calories or other nutrients—contained in the hay. So the firms will receive different prices for hay (P_n), but these all really reflect the single underlying price of calories (P_s) in accordance with Equation (9.2).

EXAMPLE 9.2   **The Demand for Efficient Automobiles**

In the eight years following the 1973 oil embargo, the price of gasoline increased by about 50 percent in real terms. This shift increased the value to consumers of fuel-efficient automobiles, implying that the market prices of cars with different fuel efficiencies should change accordingly. In estimating the effects of changing gasoline prices on automobile prices, James Kahn[a] had to estimate peoples' beliefs about the future trend of gasoline prices. He constructed two alternative possibilities: (1) static expectations (people expect future prices to equal current prices) and (2) dynamic expectations (people forecast future prices by extending the present average rate of change). The following table reports the estimated change in prices of a 12-mpg automobile relative to that of a 25-mpg automobile caused by the changed consumers' expectations about future prices of gasoline. The bigger the anticipated gasoline price, the more negative a number would be predicted on each line. All figures are in constant 1981 dollars.

Estimated Change in Price of Automobile Due to Fuel Efficiency

Year	Static Expectations	Dynamic Expectations
1973	− $39	− $52
1974	− 329	− 639
1975	109	314
1976	6	145
1977	− 30	82
1978	64	174
1979	− 239	− 262
1980	− 574	− 403
1981	− 16	131

Kahn found that, on average, an increase in gasoline prices that caused a $1.00 increase in the expected annual operating costs of using a car resulted in a decline of − $0.37 to − $0.50 in the price of such a car. This is a surprisingly small number, if we believe consumers are concerned only about the total costs of operating a car. For in purchasing a fuel-efficient car, a consumer had to pay less than $0.50 for each $1.00 in fuel savings in the year he purchased the car; he would also continue to enjoy such savings in future years. Presumably during the period studied, people also changed their preferences for other characteristics of automobiles, such as safety or comfort.

[a]James A. Kahn, "Gasoline Prices and the Used Automobile Market: A Rational Expectations Asset Price Approach." *Quarterly Journal of Economics*, v. 101 (May 1986).

EXAMPLE 9.3   **Price and Quality: Movie Theaters**

R.D. Lamson studied the relation between quality characteristics and the prices charged for movie admissions in a large metropolitan area during the period 1961 to 1964.[a] The adult evening admission price P (in cents) was estimated from the data by the following equation:

$$P = 4.13 + 31.46 \log_{10} U + 5.77L + 8.21T - 7.68D - 1.13F + 27.09S + 0.81R$$

The symbols used on the right-hand side represent several different quality variables.

U—average percentage of unused seating capacity per showing
L—theater location (1 if suburban, 0 if city center)
T—theater age (1 if less than 10 years since construction or major renovation, 0 otherwise)
D—type of theater (1 if outdoor, 0 if indoor)
F—parking (1 if provided, 0 otherwise)
S—screening policy (1 if first-run, 0 otherwise)
R—average film rental (cents per ticket charged by distributor)

The results were generally in the directions anticipated. For example, newer or renovated theaters charged an average of 8.21 cents more per admission. First-run houses charged 27.09 cents more. Each penny per ticket that was paid for film rental (a measure of film popularity) was associated with a 0.81-cent increment to admission price. The one puzzling result is the parking provision associated with a 1.13-cent reduction in price. This reduction is very likely due to a correlation of parking availability (a positive quality element) with remote or low rental location (an unfavorable element) not captured in the crude index L.

One interesting point concerns unused capacity (U). Unused capacity can be regarded as a quality measure of movie seating—uncrowdedness. The equation shows that a 10 percent increase in unused seating capacity (e.g., from 20 percent to 22 percent) is associated with a 1.30-cent increase in admission price. Notice that quality in the form of uncrowdedness automatically rises when quantity of sales decreases in response to a rise in admission price. So the true (quality-constant) elasticity of demand for movie admissions must be greater than that implicit in these data.

[a]R.D. Lamson, "Measured Productivity and Price Change: Some Empirical Evidence on Service Industry Bias, Motion Picture Theaters," *Journal of Political Economy*, v. 78 (March/April 1970).

Let us now consider the quality level that a monopolistic industry would provide. We saw in Chapter 8 that monopoly provides a smaller *quantity* of product than a competitive industry, but our analysis there did not take quality variations into account. The question here is, would a monopolist tend to offer consumers a lower *quality* of product? Consider laundry detergent, where a higher quality product might be one with more concentrated cleaning power. Two separate issues should be distinguished: (1) At a given industry output of service, would the monopolist produce a less concentrated detergent? (2) Since the monopolist will surely produce a smaller output of service, would this be associated with both lower quality (dilute detergent) and smaller quantity (fewer pounds of detergent)?

With regard to the first question, recall that the monopolist's Marginal Cost curve is essentially equivalent to the supply curve of the competitive industry; this curve, in turn, is the horizontal sum of the Marginal Cost curves of the competitive firms. It follows that in producing any given industry service output S, the monopolist would choose the same quality-quantity combination as the competitive industry (since that represents the least-cost way of producing). A manufacturer of detergents who sold the same service quantity as a competitive industry would use the same formula for detergents as the competitive industry.

If this principle were violated, the monopolist would be using an inefficient production process.

However, turning now to the second question, we know that the monopolist would not choose the same service output as the competitive industry, but would want to produce a smaller service output S to keep the price high. Since increases of service output tend to be provided by balanced increments of both quantity and quality, the smaller service output of the monopolized industry would normally involve some combination of reduced quantity and reduced quality: the monopolist would probably produce fewer pounds of less concentrated detergent.

CONCLUSION: A monopolist, producing a smaller service output S than a competitive industry, will generally do so by some combination of lesser quantity and reduced quality.[3]

EXAMPLE 9.4 **Cartels and Quality**

While a monopoly tends to produce a somewhat lower quality product than a competitive industry, the situation of a cartel is quite different. As shown in Chapter 8, when a cartel assigns production quotas each firm has a motive to "chisel"—to produce beyond quota. It is generally harder for a cartel to police the quality than the quantity of product. So members of a cartel, unable to expand quantity of output, may compete (chisel) by improving quality.

In 1981, following negotiations with the United States, Japanese auto firms agreed to voluntary export restraints limiting their shipments of cars to the United States. From the Japanese point of view, the agreement converted their auto industry into a highly profitable cartel, since regulations administered by Japan's Ministry for International Trade and Industry restricted the number of cars that each firm could export to the United States. The profitability of this action can be measured by the sharp increase in prices of corporate shares of Japanese auto companies—an average of around 24 percent in the month when the arrangement was announced. In the following two months a further 16 percent increase in share values occurred.[a]

Naturally, with reduced imports the prices of Japanese cars rose substantially in comparison with American-made cars. But apart from the obvious scarcity effect, there was also a quality effect. The cartelized Japanese exporters competed with one another to offer American consumers a higher-quality product. Since the export restraints constrained the number of cars exported, and not the size of cars or the number of options included, each firm could increase the value of its exports by selling more luxurious cars. According to a study by Robert C. Feenstra, the price index of Japanese cars in the United States rose by 48.3 percent in the period 1980–85 whereas the quality index rose 25.4 percent. Thus, the quality improvement offset around half of the observed price increase.[b]

[a]Arthur T. Denzau, "Made in America: The 1981 Japanese Automobile Cartel," Center for the Study of American Business, Washington University (August 1986).

[b]Robert C. Feenstra, "Quality Change Under Trade Restraints: Theory and Evidence from Japanese Autos," Department of Economics, University of California, Davis (May 1986).

[3]Thanks to S.J. Liebowitz, an erroneous treatment of this topic in some previous editions has now been corrected.

9.3 AN APPLICATION: SUPPRESSION OF INVENTIONS

Monopolists are sometimes accused of suppressing inventions. Let us define *invention* as a discovery permitting production of a higher-quality product at given cost or a given quality of product at lower cost.[4] Then it can be shown, under the key assumption that buyers are fully informed about the quality improvement, that suppression is *never* profit-maximizing.

Suppose there is a monopolist of gasoline, and that consumers are interested only in the service produced (mileage). The monopolist discovers a method of costlessly doubling the mileage per gallon (mpg) of its gasoline. The crucial point is that this quality-improving invention is also, from the firm's point of view, a cost-reducing invention, which it would surely be absurd to suppress.

Figure 9.6 shows how a cost-reducing invention affects a monopolist's output of service S (in the form of mileage offered to consumers). Suppose the invention doubles the quality (mpg) of the product with no effect on production cost. This development shifts the Total Cost curve from C^o to C'—a horizontal doubling (stretching) to the right. The key assumption, that consumers are fully informed, means that the Total Revenue curve in terms of service S remains unchanged. Consumers have no interest in gasoline as such; whether quality is high or low, they only pay for what concerns them—mileage.

FIGURE 9.6 **A Quality-Improving (Cost-Reducing) Invention**   A monopolist is considering adoption of an innovation that costlessly doubles the quality of its product. Since the horizontal axis represents amount of service S, the original Total Cost curve C^o shifts to C'—service output is doubled at each level of cost. Fully informed consumers are interested only in amount of service, and so the Total Revenue function R is unchanged. The monopolist will necessarily increase profits by adopting rather than suppressing the invention. In the situation pictured, the profit is $\Pi' > \Pi^o$. Consumers also benefit, since more service is produced to be sold at a lower price.

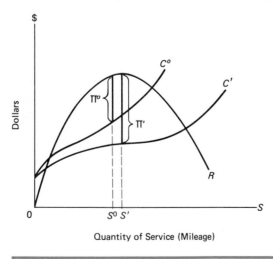

Quantity of Service (Mileage)

---

[4]Obviously, there is no problem in explaining the "suppression" of discoveries that lead to production of a *lower*-quality product at the same cost, or a constant-quality product at *higher* cost!

In Figure 9.6 the profit-maximizing level of service output is $S°$ *before the invention and S' after the invention. The maximum profit before the invention is $\Pi°$. Profits after the invention are necessarily higher, Π'. The diagram illustrates a normal case in which the monopolist's output of service increases as a result of the invention *($S' > S°$)* but by less than a doubling *($S' < 2S°$)*. This type of increase means that consumers benefit from having more service S (mileage) while the firm saves some cost by producing less physical quantity (gallons).

However if the Total Revenue curve rises almost linearly (i.e., if Marginal Revenue is almost constant), output of service S may more than double. The stretching of the Total Cost curve from $C°$ to C' reduces Marginal Cost in the relevant range. If throughout the doubling interval MC remains lower, while Marginal Revenue is nearly unchanged, the profit-maximizing output of service S will be *more than twice* the pre-invention amount. Here consumers would reap a very big benefit, while of course the firm gains as well.

Paradoxically, it is logically possible for the output of service at the post-invention solution to fall *($S' < S°$)*. In this case, while the invention will not have been suppressed, consumers are nevertheless worse off. How this might happen is visible in Figure 9.7, which is in Average-Marginal units rather than Total units. The invention does not change the demand curve D_s and Marginal Revenue curve MR_s, defined here in terms of units of service. The quality-improving invention reduces the Average Cost of producing any amount of

FIGURE 9.7   A Quality-Improving (Cost-Reducing) Invention Adverse to Consumers
A quality-improving invention is equivalent to a reduction in the Average Cost of producing the service, and so the new AC' curve lies everywhere below the original $AC°$ curve. Nevertheless, as shown here, *there may be a range in which the new Marginal Cost MC' is higher* than the original $MC°$. As a result, the new $MC' = MR$ intersection may determine a profit-maximizing level of service S' that is *smaller* than the initial level, $S°$. If so, consumers will be worse off for the invention.

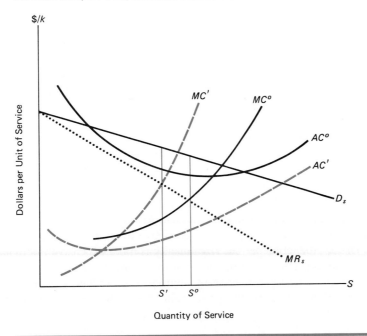

Quantity of Service

service. The new AC' curve (dashed) is, therefore, always lower than the original AC^o curve (solid). Nevertheless, as the diagram shows, there may be a range in which the Marginal Cost MC' associated with the new technology is higher than the original Marginal Cost MC^o. If, as shown here, the intersection of Marginal Cost with Marginal Revenue occurs in this range, the firm's profit-maximizing output of service will be smaller $(S' < S^o)$. This result implies that monopoly price will be higher, and so consumers must be worse off.

The assumption of full knowledge by consumers is essential to this analysis. If the invention really improves product quality but consumers do not believe it does, they would not be willing to pay any more for the higher-mileage gasoline. This unwillingness would, of course, reduce the monopolist's incentive to introduce the innovation. We should then, however, consider the cost of informing consumers as a part of the economic cost of invention. It is not really "suppression" when an invention, even though a genuine improvement, cannot be put on the market except at a cost that is too great (including the cost of spreading the information) in comparison with the benefit received.

Another possible motivation to suppress innovations emerges if the invention would destroy the monopoly. Suppose one firm had a monopoly of the only currently exploitable aluminum ore—bauxite. Imagine that the monopolist finds a cheap process for extracting aluminum from alumina instead. Since alumina is too abundant to be monopolized, the firm could lose its monopoly. Even here, the monopolist can in principle do better than by suppressing the invention. The exclusive knowledge of how to reduce alumina to aluminum is more valuable than the previous monopoly of bauxite. The monopolist could patent and license the new process, or alternatively use it while keeping the key steps a trade secret.[5]

CONCLUSION: Monopoly cannot validly be accused of *suppressing* inventions (assuming buyers are fully informed). But in some circumstances a monopolist may use inventions in such a way that consumers derive no benefit or are even made worse off.

9.4 QUALITY UNDER IMPERFECT CONSUMER INFORMATION

Consumers do not always know the quality of a product before they buy it: a software package may not work, a car may be a lemon, a computer may have unreliable components. What would induce a firm to provide high quality products then? After all, each firm can claim to have a high-quality product, so how are consumers to know which firms are telling the truth?

One important constraint on a firm arises from concern about its reputation. Assume for simplicity that the firm has to decide in the initial year what quality to produce (it may, for example, have to purchase different machinery for products of different quality). Customers are willing to pay a premium price for superior quality, but the firm's reputation is established in the first period. That is, in subsequent periods consumers believe that the quality produced by the firm is the same as in the first period.

The following table summarizes a possible set of conditions facing a monopolist; the numbers are for a single production period. High quality is more expensive to produce, but is more highly valued by consumers. A firm that aims to maximize the *sum* of profits earned in two periods would do better by producing the high-quality product. It would then earn $13 − $5 in each of the two periods, for a total gain of $16. In contrast, if the firm was

---

[5]In practice, however, there might be difficulties either with patenting or with maintaining secrecy.

able to fool consumers (perhaps because it had previously earned a reputation for producing good products) by selling a low-quality product in the first period, it would earn $13 − $4 in the first period, but only $4 − $4 in the second period; its total profit would be $9. In this case, it does not pay the firm to ruin its reputation. Since consumers know this, they can rationally rely upon the firm to continue supplying a high-quality product.

	Low Quality	High Quality
Cost of Production	4	5
Value to Consumer	4	13

Matters could differ if the firm could only charge a lower price, say $5.50, for a product it claimed to be high quality. Then, its profits in producing the high-quality product would be $5.50 − $5.00 in each of the two periods, for a sum of $1.00. By cheating in the first period, the firm would earn more, $5.50 − $4.00 = $1.50. Thus, consumers could rationally distrust a "bargain price," realizing that with a price so low, the firm would lower quality in the interests of short-term profits. A larger margin of profit is needed to make it worthwhile for a firm to produce high-quality goods.

Especially when consumers are not in a position to evaluate quality before purchase, a firm's primary motive for maintaining high quality is its desire to attract repeat business. The importance of repeat business may also explain why some services are provided by firms with multiple outlets—for example, Holiday Inns. Because consumers can more easily evaluate quality if they frequent many outlets, and because the chain realizes that bad service in one city may cause it to lose customers in other cities, the management of the chain has an incentive to build a good reputation and assure that each of its hotels gives good service.

What happens if, in contrast to the previous assumptions, firms can choose a *different* level of quality in each of the two periods? Even if the firm had a high-quality product in the initial period, customers in period two would fear a reduction in quality. If so, they might be willing to pay no more than $4 for the firm's product in period two. But then the firm would obtain no benefit from producing a high-quality product in period one.

A more interesting situation arises if (1) customers will only return to a store that had given high quality in the first period, and (2) some of the businesses always provide high quality products (perhaps because they are frequented by knowledgeable customers, or because they have a different production technology). We can use h to represent the proportion of stores that always sell high-quality products in the two periods and $(1 − h)$ to represent the proportion of stores that always cheat in period two.

Suppose the conditions shown in the table continue to apply and the market price is $5.50 in both periods. A firm that sold a low-quality product in period one would earn a profit of $5.50 − $4.00 = $1.50. If instead the firm provides a high-quality product in period one, but cheats in period two by supplying a low-quality product, it would gain $5.50 − $5.00 = $0.50 in period one and $5.50 − $4.00 = $1.50 in period two, for a total of $2.00. This exceeds the profit of $1.50 earned by a firm that sold only a low-quality product in period one. Thus, all firms that can vary quality will sell high quality in period one and low quality in period two.

But will a consumer find it worthwhile to purchase the good at all? In period one he will pay $5.50 and get a high-quality product, for a Consumer Surplus of $13.00 − 5.50 = $7.50. In period two he pays $5.50; with probability h he gets a high quality product, and therefore a Consumer Surplus of $13.00 − $5.50 = $7.50. With probability $(1 − h)$ the store he visits cheats him in period two, and the consumer pays $5.50 for a low-quality product; the Consumer Surplus is $4.00 − $5.50 = −$1.50. The consumer will find it worthwhile to shop for the good in period two only if $7.50h - \$1.50(1 - h) > 0$, or if $h > 1/6$. Thus, if $h > 1/6$, the consumer will purchase the good in both periods. If $h < 1/6$, the consumer will not purchase the good in period two, and dishonest stores would cheat him in period one. The consumer, therefore, would not even purchase the good in period one. Note the surprising feature that if $h > 1/6$ in this example, *all* stores provide high quality in period one. [*Query:* Suppose the price is \$6.00 in each period rather than \$5.50. What is the critical level of h that would induce consumers to purchase the good in period two?]

PROPOSITION: If consumers do not know the quality of a good until after they purchase it, then firms may find it profitable to produce only low-quality goods. This form of market failure can be overcome, however, if firms expect that a product of higher quality will generate more repeat business.

9.5 AN APPLICATION: PRODUCT SAFETY

As one quality dimension, the *safety* of a product often depends on both the producer and the user. Thus, a lawnmower is more likely to cause injury the less care the buyer uses, and the more faulty the product. The economic questions to determine are what level of built-in safety ("workmanship") will be provided by the seller, and what level of care will be taken by the buyer. We shall assume here, in contrast to the previous section, that the buyer has perfect information about the quality of the product.

Consider a perfectly competitive industry, so that price equals Marginal Cost. We shall suppose that the Marginal Cost of production is a constant that depends upon the workmanship of the product—the higher the quality the higher the Marginal Cost. Each of the "Iso-damage curves" in Panel (a) of Figure 9.8 depicts combinations of seller care and buyer care that yield equal levels of safety, defined as equal values of expected damages. The level of seller care is measured by expenditures on workmanship, and the buyer's level of care is measured by expenditures on safety precautions.

Each damage curve has a negative slope; the worse the workmanship, the more care the user must take to attain any given level of expected damages. The slope of each curve becomes flatter as we move to the right. This slope reflects the assumption of diminishing marginal returns of increasing buyer or seller care for a fixed level of the other. (That is, seller care and buyer care resemble *factors of production* in producing the product—lower damages.)

A given level of total expenditure E on care is depicted by a straight line of slope -1, such as KL. The equation of such a line is $S + B = E$, where S is the seller's expenditure on safety and B is the buyer's expenditure on safety. Each iso-expenditure line is defined by a different level of cost E. For each level of cost there exists a combination of S and B that maximizes safety. (Again, this problem resembles optimal factor balance in production.) Following familiar arguments we know that the optimal combinations of seller and buyer care are depicted by the points of tangency between the damage curves and the expenditure lines. Each such point represents a different total sum of spending on safety (determined by the expenditure line) and a different level of expected damages (determined by a damage curve). These pairs of values are plotted in Panel (b) as the curve AB; the axes are "Expected Damages" *(D)* and "Expenditures on Safety" *(E)*.

Economic efficiency requires minimizing the sum of (1) expected damages and (2) expenditures on safety. Different levels of total costs are represented in Panel (b) by lines

FIGURE 9.8 **Product Safety**   In Panel (a) the damage curves show combinations of seller care and buyer care that yield the same level of expected damages. The sum of damage and care costs is minimized at a point on a damage curve that is tangent to an expenditure line. Panel (b) shows the consumer's tradeoffs between expenditures on safety and damages. Each point on curve *AB* corresponds to a tangency point in Panel (a). The optimal solution is at point *G*. If the buyer takes no care, expected damages will be higher for a given level of expenditures on safety. The optimum will then be at point *H* on curve *AJ*.

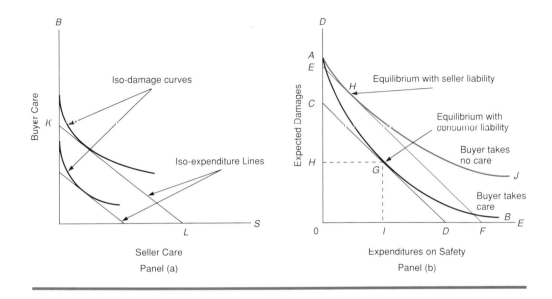

Panel (a)

Panel (b)

of slope -1 such as *CD* and *EF*. The optimal solution is the point on curve *AB* lying on the lowest total cost line—the tangency point *G*. The expected damage costs are then *OH* and the care costs are *OI*.

This is the solution when the buyer bears the full costs of accidents, the seller bearing no responsibility in the event of an accident. Notice that the consumer who aims to minimize only his own costs (the sum of the purchase price of the lawnmower, which varies with its workmanship, his own care, and the expected damages) ends up choosing levels of safety and care that minimize total costs of buyer and seller.

In contrast, suppose the seller is fully liable for damages. Having purchased the lawnmower, the buyer has no incentive to take any care at all. Any expenditures on safety are therefore made solely by the manufacturer. This typically means that any given level of safety will now require greater total expenditures *E*. (For example, rather than reduce the risk of an accident by having the manufacturer spend $10 on moderately strong bolts and the user spend $20 on maintenance, the same level of safety with no user maintenance might require the manufacturer to use extremely expensive bolts, which can withstand great abuse, at a cost of $40.) In Panel (b), the fact that the consumer spends nothing on maintenance means that the relation between expenditures on safety and expected damages shown by curve *AJ* lies above curve *AB*.

Though the seller must compensate the user in the event of an accident, the price charged for a lawnmower must reflect any such payments. The buyer, therefore, prefers to buy the quality lawnmower that minimizes total costs. This is point *H* on curve *AJ*. The associated cost is higher than the optimal point under consumer liability. Note also that in this example the seller produces a lower-quality product than he would under consumer liability. The effect can arise because under producer liability the consumer has no incentive to take any care at all, so that the marginal benefit of seller quality, given no consumer care, is very low.[6]

Exercise 9.1

Let the total cost of using a product of quality S and care B by the buyer be $S + B + 100 - SB$. S can be interpreted as the seller's expenditures on quality, B is the buyer's expenditures on care, and $100 - SB$ is the expected damage costs; we shall restrict attention to values of S and B that make $100 - SB$ non-negative. (a) What are minimum total costs under producer liability? (b) What are minimum total costs under consumer liability?

Answer: (a) If liability is placed on the producer, so that it must fully compensate the consumer for any accident costs that arise from use of the product, then the consumer has no incentive to take any care at all. The seller assumes that $B = 0$, and the seller's total cost per unit (including both production costs and expected damage costs) is $S + 100 - (S)(0) = S + 100$. Clearly, the seller will take no care, and his total costs per unit are 100. Assuming a competitive market, this is the price each consumer pays.

(b) In contrast, if the consumer is liable for all the costs of an accident, then he wants to choose care level B and purchase a product of quality S to minimize his total costs $S + B + 100 - SB$. Calculation shows that the consumer's optimal choice is to set $S = B = 10$. Total cost is then $S + B + 100 - SB = 20$, which is far lower than costs under producer liability.

SUMMARY

In previous chapters a firm could vary only the *amount* of output produced, and possibly (if it has monopoly power) also the *price*. In this chapter it is assumed that a firm can also change the characteristics of its own product. Under this general heading, two main topics are the problem of *variety* and the problem of *quality*.

The solutions for the profit-maximizing number of varieties (and for the associated price and quantity) were compared for two market structures: *monopoly* and *monopolistic competition*. Under monopoly, the separate producing locations (plants) are operated for the profit of the firm as a whole. Under monopolistic competition, each producing location becomes an independent firm working for its own profit. Each separate firm has some monopoly power; the competitive element is the presence of neighboring firms to whom customers can transfer their business. In comparison with ordinary monopoly, under monopolistic competition there will be greater aggregate output and lower price, but consumers may or may not have more variety to choose from.

The problem of *quality* applies when all consumers prefer larger amounts of some underlying service generated by the physical goods produced. Demand and supply ultimately determine an equilibrium price and quantity of the service. Each firm will produce the physical output and quality (amount of service per unit of commodity) that maximizes its profit. In general, because of differing production conditions, firms' outputs will be of differing qualities. If consumers are fully informed, however, they will pay only for the service contained in each firm's product. So the price of a firm's product must be simply

[6]In Chapter 15 we will encounter the *Coase Theorem* which states that if there are no transaction costs, all liability rules lead to efficient outcomes. Here, however, under seller liability we suppose buyers and sellers cannot negotiate to set the level of user care; users therefore take too little care.

proportional to its quality. In equilibrium, therefore, consumers are indifferent as to buying higher quality at a higher price or lower quality at a lower price.

A monopolist would tend to restrict service output, and would normally do so by a balanced reduction of both quantity and quality. But a rational monopolist would never suppress an invention that costlessly increases quality—since such an invention, when consumers are fully informed, is equivalent to one that reduces cost (of producing the service desired by consumers). By adopting the invention, the monopolist can always increase profit. The consumers usually gain as well from increased output of the service. It is, however, logically possible for the monopolist's profit-maximizing output of service to fall, in which case the consumers would be worse off after adoption of the invention.

If consumers do not know the quality of a good until after they purchase it, then no firm may have an incentive to produce a high-quality good. The cost of production is higher, but consumers cannot tell whether the product is really of high quality or not. This market failure can be overcome, however, if firms expect that a product of higher quality will generate more repeat business.

The service obtained from a product depends on decisions made both by the producer and the consumer. In particular, if product safety depends in part on the level of care taken by the consumer, then under the assumptions of perfect competition, efficiency requires consumer liability rather than producer liability. The consumer would then have the proper incentives to take care, and the producer would have proper incentives as well because consumers are willing to pay a higher price for a safer product.

QUESTIONS

For Review

1. How does monopolistic competition differ from pure competition? from pure monopoly?
2. In monopolistic competition, why is the firm's perceived demand curve flatter than the true demand curve?
3. Why is the firm's perceived demand curve in monopolistic competition analogous to the horizontal demand curve faced by the firm in pure competition?
*4. If a monopolist normally produces a smaller *quantity* of a product than a competitive industry, is it correct to presume that the monopolist would normally also offer a product of lower *quality?*
*5. a. Would a monopolist ever suppress an invention that lowered the cost of producing its product without reducing quality?
   b. Would it ever suppress an invention raising quality with no increase of cost?
   c. Will consumers in either case be necessarily better off if the invention is adopted?
6. What conditions make it more profitable for a firm to produce high-quality rather than low-quality products?

For Further Thought and Discussion

*1. Is there a reason to expect monopolistic competition (rather than pure competition) to emerge when the desired commodity is really a single "quality" characteristic contained in the marketed good? Explain.

*The answers to starred questions appear at the end of the book.

2. Would the price-quantity equilibrium under monopolistic competition tend to lie between that achieved under pure monopoly on the one hand, and pure competition on the other? Explain.

*3. In recent public policy debates, some analysts have asserted that there is "excessive competition" among hospitals. Allegedly, too many hospitals acquire expensive diagnostic machinery like CAT scanners, which remain idle much of the time. These analysts propose that in each community just one or a very few hospitals should obtain such devices; anyone validly needing to use them could be directed to those hospitals. Comment, in the light of the discussion in the text, about the quality of service likely to be provided by monopolized versus competitive industries.

4. Suppose that every peach looks good in the store, but some turn out to be uneatable. When half the peaches sold are uneatable, the demand curve is $P = 100 - 2Q$.
   a. What would the demand curve be if all peaches are good?
   b. Let a monopolist be the supplier of peaches, with a marginal cost of 30 if he sells only good peaches, and a marginal cost of 20 per peach when half the peaches he sells are bad. Assuming fixed costs are the same, does the monopolist make greater profits by selling only good peaches?

*5. Could a quality-improving invention in a *competitive* industry ever reduce consumer welfare?

*6. It is sometimes argued that only relatively high-quality products can "bear the cost" of shipment to distant locations. Thus, California oranges shipped to New York are (on average) of better quality than those consumed by Californians at home. Does this follow from the analysis in this chapter? [*Hint:* Does it cost much more to ship high-quality oranges than low-quality oranges?]

*7. Would imposition of a fixed per-unit tax (e.g., 10 cents per gallon of gasoline) tend to increase or decrease the equilibrium quality of gasoline (miles per gallon) offered on the market?

8. Mr. A says: "A monopolist will produce a product of higher quality, since cut-throat competition must lead to a decline in quality." Mr. B says: "A monopolist produces a smaller *quantity* of product than would a competitive industry, and by the same logic will also produce a product of lesser *quality*." Is either correct, or are they both wrong?

*9. In an attempt to reduce tobacco production and thereby raise prices received by tobacco farmers, a government program introduced in 1933 allotted quotas to farmers that fixed the number of acres that could be planted. Over the years production expanded anyway, since the farmers responded by applying more fertilizer, irrigating more intensively, etc. In 1965 the program was reformed, replacing acreage limitations with quotas that fixed the number of pounds that each farmer could sell. Would you expect the original and the reformed programs to have different effects upon the *quality* of tobacco produced by American farmers? Explain.

10. Suppose that in the initial period firms choose machinery and product design that commit them to a particular level of quality for five rather than two years. Explain why this increases the firm's incentives to produce a high-quality product.

11. A common rule of product liability is the *negligence* rule: the manufacturer is liable for damages if and only if its workmanship is below some specified standard. Suppose the standard is set to be identical to the level a firm would choose under perfect competition and no liability. What level of workmanship would the firm choose?

CHAPTER 10
OLIGOPOLY AND STRATEGIC BEHAVIOR

E X A M P L E S

O ligopoly is competition among the few. It therefore falls between pure competition (many firms) and monopoly (one firm). Whether the outcome is more like competition or more like monopoly depends on the degree to which the firms cooperate or compete. In Chapter 8 we saw that a cartel that attempts to raise price above marginal cost faces the problem of "chiseling." This chapter looks into the structure of cartels more closely, and describes conditions that allow a small number of firms to raise price above the competitive level.

10.1 STRATEGIC BEHAVIOR: PRISONERS' DILEMMA AND OTHER GAMES

A *strategic* situation exists when A's best course of action depends on what he expects B to do, and B in turn must consider what A will do. Earlier chapters analyzed problems in which only one side faced this problem. In Chapter 8, for example, a monopolist determined price based on consumers' demand, but no individual consumer could affect the decisions of the monopolist. When firms and individuals on both sides of the market must each consider how others will react, the concept of *optimizing*, of choosing a best outcome, can be hazy.

In market interactions the different parties have conflicting and common interests. The sellers have a common interest in keeping prices high, but a conflict of interest as to who gets more customers. The buyers have a common interest in keeping prices low, but a conflict of interest as to who gets to buy the low-priced goods. Sellers and buyers, of course, disagree over the price to be set, but (owing to the mutual advantage of trade) they share a strong interest in having exchange take place.

The theory of games provides a systematic way of exploring mixtures of such conflicting and common interests, and explicitly considers the interactions of different firms and individuals. Consider chiseling in cartels, which represents a type of game called the Prisoners' Dilemma. Let there be two firms, or "players," A and B. Suppose each firm can choose to produce either a "High" level of output or else a "Low" level of output. Table 10.1 depicts the problem each firm faces. Along the left side of the table we list the choices firm A can make. On the top we list the choices firm B can make. The four possible paired choices define four outcomes in terms of profits for the two firms. Each cell in the 2×2 "payoff matrix" shows two numbers. The first is the profit of firm A; the second is the profit of firm B.

For example, if A chooses low and B chooses high, then the cell in the bottom left-hand corner of the table shows that firm A will have a profit of 1, and firm B will have a profit of 4.

Given such a payoff matrix, what should each firm do? Notice that if A believes that B will produce a high output, then A maximizes its profit by producing a high output (profit of 2 instead of 1). And if firm A expects firm B to produce a low output, then A maximizes its profit by producing a high output (profit of 4 instead of 3). Thus, *regardless* of what A expects B to do, A maximizes profits by choosing a high output. Inspection of the table shows that the same applies for firm B: it maximizes profit by producing a high output

List of Notation

MC	Marginal Cost	MR	Marginal Revenue

TABLE 10.1   The Prisoners' Dilemma

		FIRM B High output	FIRM B Low output
FIRM A	High output	(2,2)	(4,1)
	Low output	(1,4)	(3,3)

regardless of what *A* does. It would thus appear that both firms will produce a high output, so that each will earn a profit of 2.

For the firms together, however, this outcome is undesirable. If they could some-how agree to produce a low output, each would earn 3 instead of 2. The difficulty is that once the firms reach an understanding to produce low, each has an incentive to chisel. Thus, if *A* expected *B* to abide by the agreement and produce low, then *A* maximizes its profit by producing high, thereby earning 4 instead of 3. It again appears that the only stable outcome has both firms producing a high output. This is called the Nash[1] equilibrium. It is an equilibrium since, once the choices are made, neither party has an incentive to change its action. Each is doing the best it can for itself, given the decision of the other.

In certain circumstances, however, one or both firms may be able to improve upon this equilibrium. Suppose the two firms will interact not only once, but indefinitely. And suppose *A* believes that *B* will be initially choosing low, and will continue to do so if and only if in all preceding periods *A* chose low. Firm *B* has similar beliefs about firm *A*. In effect, then, each believes that its competitor will respond favorably to a cooperative (low output) move, but unfavorably to an uncooperative (high output) move.

What is the equilibrium under these conditions? If *A* chooses low, it expects *B* to also choose low, and thus anticipates a profit of 3 in each period. If *A*, instead, chisels in the current period by choosing high, its current profits will be 4 instead of 3. But by assumption *B* will choose high in subsequent periods. Firm *A* will therefore also choose high in subsequent periods, earning 2 instead of 3. If the firm cares sufficiently about future profits, it would not find this tradeoff profitable, and would therefore not chisel in any period. The same applies to *B,* so the indicated equilibrium is that both firms choose low in each period. [*Query:* What happens if the firms expect to interact for only a finite number of periods? Suppose, for example, that the firms expect that period 5 is the last period in which both will be in business. Will they cooperate in period 5? Will they therefore cooperate in period 4 and earlier periods?]

In this equilibrium each firm believes the other uses a *trigger strategy*. Notice that the beliefs of the firms are mutually consistent, and are not violated by experience. If each believes that the other firm is following a trigger strategy, then both will choose low in each period, and neither will have any reason to change its beliefs about the other's strategy.

---

[1]J.F. Nash, contemporary American mathematician.

TABLE 10.2   The Entry-Deterrence Game

| | | INCUMBENT *(N)* | |
		Resist	Tolerate
POTENTIAL ENTRANT *(E)*	Enter	(−10,30)	(20,80)
	Stay out	(0,100)	(0,100)

Of course, we have not proven that firms *necessarily* collude. For one thing, firms may not think other firms will follow a trigger strategy. Thus we cannot be sure the firms will spontaneously move from a non-cooperative to a cooperative solution. But game theory has illustrated how, given certain beliefs, collusion can continue even without explicit agreement.

The game described in Table 10.1 was *symmetric*. Each player's situation was the mirror image of the other. Game theory can also be used to analyze *asymmetric* situations.

An important illustration of an asymmetric game is the problem of *entry deterrence*. Suppose an incumbent firm enjoys a monopoly yielding a profit of 100. A potential competitor threatens to enter the industry. If entry occurs, the former monopolist could resist by starting a costly price war to drive out the newcomer. Alternatively, the incumbent could tolerate the newcomer and settle for a share of the former monopoly profit. Table 10.2 shows three different asymmetries.

1. The assumed annual payoff numbers do not fall into the mirror-image pattern of the preceding table.
2. The strategy options of the players are not identical; the Potential Entrant can "Enter" or "Stay out" while the Incumbent can "Resist" or "Tolerate."
3. There is now a definite *sequence* of moves; the Potential Entrant makes his entry decision first, and then the Incumbent chooses a response.

To find the equilibrium here, first think of the choices facing the responding player, the incumbent *(N)*. If the potential entrant *(E)* chooses to stay out, *N* receives 100 in profits; no decision on his part is required. But if *E* enters, *N* does better to tolerate—where he gets a remaining profit of 80—rather than to resist, where he receives only 30. *E*, who knows that *N* reasons in this way, will therefore choose to enter. So the outcome is at the upper-right corner of the table, where the newcomer captures 20 of the monopolist's former 100 profit.

But suppose instead the incumbent threatens the newcomer as follows: "If you enter, I will resist and you will end up with −10 rather than +20. So you had better stay out." If this threat were credible, then *E* should stay out. But in the situation assumed the threat is not credible. Once entry has occurred, the incumbent can only lose by carrying out his threat.

10.2 AN APPLICATION: MICROMOTIVES AND MACROBEHAVIOR

We saw that in a competitive market the behavior of each firm leads to a result that none of them really wants—zero economic profits; in oligopoly a similar result may hold. The firms would certainly be happier if each firm charged a slightly higher price, so that all firms could earn higher profits. In *Micromotives and Macrobehavior,* Thomas Schelling discusses another example of how the behavior of individuals can lead to outcomes that no one intended or that no one wants.

Suppose that whites, though by no means racists, do not want to live in neighborhoods that are overwhelmingly black. Therefore, a white who finds that less than half of his neighbors are white will move away. Suppose also that blacks move away if less than a third of their neighbors are black. To see the effects of such behavior, draw a checkerboard grid. (The procedure can also be easily undertaken on a computer.) Write some Xs and Os at random in the squares. We can take Xs to represent whites and Os to represent blacks. Define each individual's neighborhood as the eight squares surrounding him or her. We will show that one person can cause a chain reaction that leads others to move.

An initial distribution of Xs and Os is given in Panel 1. The person in "Row" 7, "Column" 2 has only one-third of his neighbors X, so he moves, say one column to the right, as shown in Panel 2. Returning to Panel 1, the X in row 1, column 4 has both of his neighbors Os, so he moves, say to row 2, column 5. We now see that in Panel 2 the O at row 1, column 5 has all neighbors Xs, whereas he would like at least one-third to be Os. He therefore moves, say, to row 1, column 3. The X at row 1, column 1 has all his neighbors Os, so he moves, to row 1, column 5. Panel 3 still has two Os who want to move (at row 4, column 4, and at row 5, column 7); an equilibrium is shown in Panel 4. Note that the distribution in Panel 4 shows more segregation than the initial distribution. Indeed, in the final distribution no X has an O as a neighbor, and no O has an X as a neighbor!

So total segregation may result even though individuals are perfectly happy to have some neighbors of another type. Note also that there can be other equilibria. (In our discussion of a market we always were able to find a unique equilibrium; the uniqueness arises from the assumptions made in the model, and is not inherent in the definition of an equilibrium.) Panel 5 depicts a different equilibrium. Here 6 of the 9 Xs have an O neighbor, so that the degree of segregation is far less than in the totally segregated equilibrium shown in Panel 4.

These examples demonstrate that a meaningful equilibrium is *stable* in the face of small changes or shocks. What happens if one of the Xs or Os decides to move? Some moves by an X or an O will not affect the behavior of others; for example, the X in row 1, column 1 of Panel 5 could move to row 1 column 2, and no one else would see any need to move. So the situation is stable with respect to this change by one person. Suppose, however, that in Panel 5 the X in row 1, column 1 wants to move so that he has no X as a neighbor. Such a move would mean that the X in row 2, column 2 would have only an O as a neighbor, and this X would therefore also want to move: the equilibrium is not stable with respect to this change in the behavior of the X initially at row 1, column 1. Total segregation, as shown in Panel 6, is a stable equilibrium with respect to a change by any one individual. A change in the location of X to anywhere in the grid will not induce any other person to want to move; the same holds for a change in the location of any O. Thus, the segregation equilibrium is a highly stable one, which suggests that segregation is likely to persist even if no one prefers it.

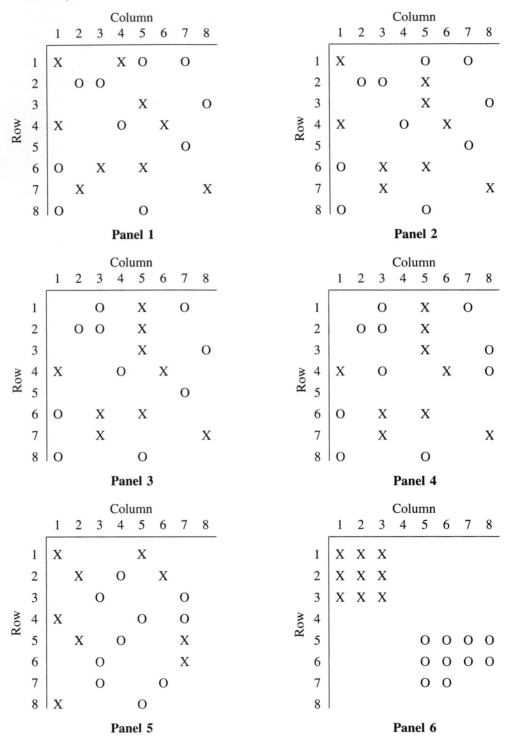

Panel 1

Panel 2

Panel 3

Panel 4

Panel 5

Panel 6

10.3 Duopoly with homogeneous products

This and the following sections of the chapter extend the analysis by distinguishing *homogeneous* from *heterogeneous* oligopoly. In the homogeneous case the products are identical. If firms choose prices rather than quantities, then even a slightly lower price quoted by one seller will capture all sales, and so the firms will have to charge the same price. In heterogeneous oligopoly, consumers can distinguish the firms' outputs, some preferring one firm's product and some another firm's. Since each firm has a "clientele," it can raise price somewhat without losing *all* of its customers.

Let us assume, only for simplicity, that (1) there are exactly *two* selling firms, so that oligopoly becomes the special case called *duopoly;* (2) the firms are identical; (3) production is carried on at zero cost (i.e., the Total Cost, Average Cost, and Marginal Cost functions are all zero throughout). For example, suppose each of two firms owns a mineral spring gushing forth costlessly and in unlimited volume forever. A monopolist, as we have discussed, can achieve the same optimum either by choosing the most profitable price or the most profitable quantity. But in oligopoly, it makes a difference whether the decisions run in terms of price or in terms of quantity.

Suppose quantity is the decision variable. Table 10.3 lists several different oligopoly (duopoly) solutions.[2] The table is based on an industry demand curve expressed by the equation $P = 100 - Q$, where the industry output Q is the sum of the two firm outputs: $Q = q_1 + q_2$.

The first solution shown in Table 10.3 is the Collusive outcome. Here the two firms act together as a collective monopolist or cartel, sharing the gain equally. A monopolist would want to set Marginal Revenue equal to Marginal Cost. Since production costs are assumed zero throughout, MC here is zero. The industry demand equation has the linear form $P = 100 - Q$, so industry MR is $100 - 2Q$.[3] The monopolist maximizes profits by setting $MR = 100 - 2Q$ equal to 0. The profit-maximizing industry output is $Q = 50$ and the associated price along the demand curve for the industry is $P = 100 - 50 = 50$. Total

TABLE 10.3 **Duopoly Solutions, with Industry Demand Curve**
$P = 100 - (q_1 + q_2)$

	q_1	q_2	Q	P	Π_1	Π_2
Symmetrical						
Collusive	25	25	50	50	1250	1250
Cournot	33 1/3	33 1/3	66	33 1/3	1111 1/9	1111 1/9
Competitive	50	50	100	0	0	0
Asymmetrical						
Stackelberg	50	25	75	25	1250	625
Threat	50	0	50	50	2500	0

[2]We make use here of a somewhat similar discussion in M. Shubik, "Information, Duopoly and Competitive Markets: A Sensitivity Analysis," *Kyklos,* v. 26 (1973), p. 748.
[3]Recall that if $P = A - BQ$, then $MR = A - 2BQ$.

Revenue is $PQ = 2500$ which, in the absence of any costs, is also the total profit Π. With equal division, each firm's profit under the Collusive solution will be $\Pi_1 = \Pi_2 = (50)(50/2) = 1250$.

This Collusive solution assumes that the problem of the Prisoners' Dilemma has somehow been solved. The two parties are maximizing joint profits. But what if the problem cannot be solved? Skipping to the third line of the table, the opposite extreme is the Competitive solution. It is based on two assumptions: (1) the firms do not cooperate but instead each operates in its own short-run selfish interest; (2) each firm acts as a price-taker. So each firm adopts the decision rule $MC = P$. Since $MC = 0$, a price-taking firm would be willing to produce indefinitely large amounts at *any* price P greater than zero. The result is the competitive equilibrium with $P = 0$. Combined output is 100, as dictated by the demand equation, but revenue and profits are zero for both firms.

On the second line of the table, lying between the Collusive and the Competitive outcomes, is the *Cournot solution*.[4] This solution is obtained by assuming that (1) as in the Competitive case, firms do not cooperate, (2) each firm knows that increasing its own output reduces the market price, and (3) each firm assumes that the other firm's output decision is *fixed*. The Cournot solution corresponds therefore to the Nash equilibrium in game theory: each decisionmaker does the best he can given the decision of the other. (This outcome is accordingly sometimes known as the Nash-Cournot solution.)

The analysis of the Cournot case goes as follows. For any output level q_1 chosen by the first firm, there is a profit-maximizing output q_2 for the second firm. In effect, firm 2 becomes a monopolist over the remaining demand not satisfied by the first firm's output q_1. Specifically, the demand equation for firm 2 becomes $P = (100 - q_1) - q_2$, with q_1 regarded as constant. Since this is a linear demand equation, firm 2's Marginal Revenue is $MR_2 = (100 - q_1) - 2q_2$. For example, if $q_1 = 10$ the condition $MR = MC$ for firm 2 leads to the equation $90 - 2q_2 = 0$, so that firm 2 would produce $q_2 = 45$. Plotting firm 2's choice of q_2 as a function of the given output of firm 1 yields a Reaction Curve, RC_2, like that shown in Figure 10.1. There is a corresponding Reaction Curve, RC_1, for firm 1. The Reaction Curves are mutually consistent only at the point of intersection, which is therefore the equilibrium solution. The equilibrium outputs are $q_1 = q_2 = 33\ 1/3$. This solution lies between the Collusive and the Competitive solutions.

A dynamic process that leads to this equilibrium is illustrated in Figure 10.1. Suppose firm 2 initially produces q_2^o. The RC_1 curve indicates that firm 1 will produce q_1' in response (point A in the diagram). But if firm 1 produces q_1', firm 2 reacts by moving to point B on its Reaction Curve RC_2 to produce q_2'. Firm 1 responds by moving to point C; firm 2 then moves to point D, etc. The result is that both firms end up at the intersection of the two Reaction Curves.[5]

Exercise 10.1

Find the equations for the Reaction Curves RC_1 and RC_2 in the numerical example above, and verify that their intersection is indeed the Cournot solution of Table 10.3.

---

[4]Antoine Augustin Cournot (1801–77), French mathematician and economist.

[5]There will be a stable equilibrium only if the dynamic process leads inward (as shown in the diagram) rather than outward. Geometrically, for example, if the labels of the two RC curves were interchanged, the process would take the form of an outward rather than an inward spiral. However, in duopoly problems the spiral will always be inward unless there are strongly increasing returns to scale (as in the case of natural monopoly).

FIGURE 10.1   **Duopoly Reaction Curves**   Given any output q_2 of the second firm, the first firm can determine its profit-maximizing output q_1. Considering all possible levels of q_2, a Reaction Curve RC_1 for the first firm is thereby defined. Similar reasoning (based on taking q_1 as given) leads to the construction of RC_2, the Reaction Curve of the second firm. The intersection of the two Reaction Curves determines the Nash-Cournot equilibrium.

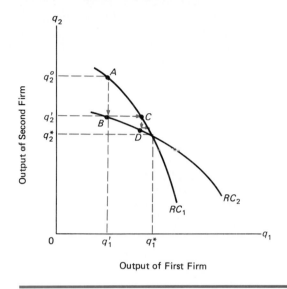

Answer: Firm 2 takes the output q_1 of firm 1 as given, so Marginal Revenue is $MR_2 = (100 - q_1) - 2q_2$. Marginal Cost MC_2 is zero, and so the firm sets $MR_2 = 0$, implying $q_2 = 50 - q_1/2$. This is the equation of RC_2. Similar reasoning yields the equation $q_1 = 50 - q_2/2$ for RC_1. Note that the curves are generally similar to those pictured in Figure 10.1—in particular, RC_1 is steeper than RC_2—except that here the two Reaction Curves are straight lines. Solving RC_1 and RC_2 simultaneously, the solution is indeed $q_1 = q_2 = 33\,1/3$.

The Cournot solution represents rather shortsighted behavior by the firms. Each reacts to the other's decision *without* allowing for the fact that the other firm will react in turn. A more justified interpretation of the Cournot solution runs in terms of each player's beliefs about the other. Suppose each firm has to decide on capacity or output before observing the other firm's choice. Once the capacity is built, the firms may compete in price, by each producing to the limit of its capacity. For example, each of two firms may have decided to build a plant to manufacture a newly discovered cancer drug. If it requires a long time to build a plant, one firm does not observe the other firm's capacity until after deciding on its own capacity; a firm's own decision cannot affect the other firm's decision. The Cournot model would make sense here: a Reaction Curve describes the capacity a firm would choose for any given belief about what the other firm would do, and the equilibrium condition is that each firm correctly anticipates the capacity choice that will be made by the other firm.

EXAMPLE 10.1 **Pioneering Oligopoly Experiment**

One of the first controlled economic experiments was conducted by the economist Lawrence E. Fouraker and the psychologist Sidney Siegel.[a] The experimental trials set up a duopoly situation. Each subject, acting as a seller, was asked to choose an output, but the profit to be received depended on the quantities offered by the two sellers together. In one case (complete information) each subject was informed of the other player's output choice and profit schedule; in the second case (incomplete information) each knew the quantity decision but not the profits of the other player.

There were 28 trials—14 for each of the two informational conditions. In the complete-information case, 5 trials most closely approximated the Collusive solution, 7 1/2 the Cournot solution, and 1 1/2 the Competitive solution. (The fraction represented a tie.) In the incomplete-information case, all 14 trials most closely approximated the Cournot solution.

COMMENT   These results suggest that the Cournot solution, in which each player takes as given the quantity decision of the other, successfully describes outcomes in oligopoly situations—especially under conditions of incomplete information. While the parties could have gained more by colluding, they were usually not able to achieve such an arrangement. On the other hand, each was sufficiently aware of his own impact on price so as to avoid, almost always, the disastrous Competitive solution.

The sensitivity of the experimental observations to the informational conditions was also an important finding. Later studies have shown that other details of the market process—for example, whether prices are secretly negotiated or openly posted—affect the extent to which the final outcome approaches the collusive or the competitive end of the spectrum of possibilities.[b]

[a]L. E. Fouraker and S. Siegel, *Bargaining Behavior* (New York: McGraw-Hill, 1963).

[b]See Charles R. Plott, "Industrial Organization Theory and Experimental Economics," *Journal of Economic Literature*, v. 20 (December 1982).

Let us now allow for *asymmetrical* behavior. In the lower portion of Table 10.3, firm 1 is assumed to be aggressive (a leader) while firm 2 is passive (a follower). The leader acts while the follower only reacts. An aggressive firm, if sufficiently knowledgeable, can make use of the other's Reaction Curve RC_2 to increase its profits.

The first solution in the lower part of Table 10.3 is called the *Stackelberg*[6] equilibrium. It involves pre-emptive behavior on the part of the firm that moves first. Knowing the follower's Reaction Curve, the leader (firm 1) picks an output level and commits itself not to modify that decision. If so, the best that firm 2 can do is to choose a point along its Reaction Curve RC_2. Of course, the leader will choose that output q_1 which, when combined with the follower's correctly predicted output q_2, leads to the most profitable outcome for itself.

Exercise 10.2 _____

Verify the Stackelberg solution shown in Table 10.3.

[6]Heinrich von Stackelberg, twentieth-century German economist.

Answer: Since firm 1 is the leader, it chooses the most profitable output for itself, knowing that firm 2 will respond along its Reaction Curve RC_2. In Exercise 10.1 we had found firm 2's Reaction Curve to be $q_2 = 50 - q_1/2$. Substituting in the industry demand curve, $P = 100 - q_1 - q_2$, firm 1's demand curve becomes $P = 50 - q_1/2$. Since this is linear, the Marginal Revenue equation for the Stackelberg leader is simply $MR_1 = 50 - q_1$. Setting $MR_1 = 0$, we obtain $q_1 = 50$. The other values shown in Table 10.3 for the Stackelberg solution can then be easily verified.

EXAMPLE 10.2   Monopoly Efficiency Loss Revisited

Example 8.4 (Chapter 8) discussed evidence showing that the welfare loss caused by monopoly is surprisingly small—about 0.5 percent of Gross National Product in the United States. That data assumed that an industry with a high concentration ratio was effectively monopolized. But most manufacturing production is generated by industries with concentration ratios lower than 50 percent, and these industries are often composed of many small firms that are price-takers. Micha Gisser[a] estimated welfare losses caused when a few firms sell a large fraction of total output, but where no firm has total monopoly power. He makes two different assumptions: (1) the four largest firms collude to act as price leaders (the Stackelberg solution); (2) the four leading firms act as Cournot competitors, that is, each of the leading firms sees a downward sloping supply curve, but assumes that the output of other firms is fixed. Using U.S. data for 1977, Gisser estimates that the upper limits on deadweight loss are 1.82 percent of GNP under collusion, and 0.11 percent of GNP under the Cournot assumption. Five industries account for 55 percent of this deadweight loss as shown in the table.

Five Industries and Deadweight Loss

Industry	4-Firm Concentration Ratio	Deadweight Loss in $Million
Motor vehicles and car bodies	93	994
Motor vehicle parts	62	90
Photographic equipment	72	43
Organic fibers	78	38
Tires	70	35

[a]M. Gisser, "Price Leadership and Welfare Losses in U.S. Manufacturing," *American Economic Review*, v. 76 (September 1986).

In the *Threat* solution, we suppose that if the follower dares enter the market at all, the leader will carry out a threat to make q_1 so big as to drive the price down to zero. The second firm will see no way to make a profit, and might as well stay out of the market entirely. So the leader does as well as if he had the sole monopoly of the industry.

We have been assuming that the firms compete by choosing *quantity*. Suppose instead they compete in terms of *price*. The key point is that, since the products are assumed identical, the firm that quotes the lower price attracts all the customers. Thus, if firm 1 selects any price P_1, then firm 2 will want to set its price P_2 a trifle lower. The only stopping point is where $P_1 = P_2 = 0$. Thus, when firms choose prices, the Cournot solution is the same as the Competitive solution.[7] If we allowed for nonzero Marginal Cost, and assumed firms chose prices, the Cournot equilibrium and the Competitive equilibrium are both $P_1 = P_2 = MC$.

What about the Stackelberg solution when price is the decision variable? Under our assumption of zero costs of production, it is evident that no firm will want to be the Stackelberg leader. Whatever price the leader announces, the follower will just undercut it. So, for any positive price the leader announces, it will end up with zero sales and zero profit. Alternatively, the leader could announce a price of zero, possibly achieving some sales, but still no profit.

In contrast, the asymmetrical Threat solution is still valid when price is the decision variable. Here firm 1 as leader announces that if firm 2 attempts to do any business at all by either matching or undercutting the leader's price, firm 1 will quote a price of zero and drive out its competitor. If this threat is believed, firm 2 might as well stay out of business completely. Firm 1 gains all the profit, as shown on the bottom line of Table 10.3.

EXAMPLE 10.3 Predatory Price-Cutting

The Threat solution of Table 10.3, but with price rather than output as the decision variable, corresponds to predatory price-cutting. A ruthless firm with the resources to carry out its threat might always stand ready to undertake a price war to drive out any competitors. Having achieved this reputation such a predator would not need to execute its threat often. Occasional punishment meted out to foolish interlopers would suffice to deter others.

John D. Rockefeller's old Standard Oil Company—dissolved in 1911 as a result of a landmark antitrust decision—is often described by historians as a predator. Standard Oil had achieved, before that date, a substantial degree of monopoly in oil refining through merger and acquisitions. It is widely believed that these mergers and acquisitions were mainly secured by threats of predatory price-cutting.

A study by John S. McGee demonstrated, surprisingly, that the tale is a myth.[a] Standard Oil rarely if ever started costly price wars to achieve its monopoly. Rather, it bought out competitors on relatively handsome terms.

[a] J. S. McGee, "Predatory Price Cutting: The Standard Oil (N.J.) Case," *Journal of Law and Economics*, v. 1 (October 1958).

10.4 HETEROGENEOUS PRODUCTS

In the preceding section we saw that, depending on the degree of rivalry among the sellers, there are a number of solutions for oligopolists selling a single or *homogeneous* product. The different solutions had one thing in common: the firms' identical products

[7] If Marginal Cost is positive at some constant level M, the leader would of course never quote a price less than M. When Marginal Cost is both positive and rising, a new consideration enters: rising Marginal Cost sets a limit upon the follower's incentive to undercut. Then the Stackelberg, Cournot, and Competitive solutions all coincide at $P_1 = P_2 = MC_1 = MC_2 = P^*$, where P^* is the competitive equilibrium price. This was the point of a famous attack upon the Cournot model by the French nineteenth-century mathematician Joseph Bertrand.

are sold in the market at the same price. But when oligopolists produce different or *heterogeneous* products, prices will usually *not* be identical. Nevertheless, the same underlying forces remain. Sellers would like to cooperate to earn monopoly profits, but each firm is tempted to benefit at the expense of the others by aggressive or rivalrous behavior.

The "Kinked" Demand Curve: A Partial Solution?

In the early part of the twentieth century, prices in the American steel industry were remarkably stable. The industry had few firms and so fit the pattern of an oligopoly. The theory of the kinked demand curve was proposed to explain the unusually stable prices in oligopolistic industries.

Given some initial equilibrium, it has been alleged, the demand curve for any single oligopolist has a kink at the point of equilibrium. Figure 10.2 pictures a single oligopolist firm charging an initial price of P^*. If that firm attempts to sell more by cutting price, then all the other oligopolists respond by meeting the price cut, so the original price-cutter can sell only a little more at the lower price. In other words, in the region below the initial equilibrium price P^* the firm's demand curve is steep. What if the firm raises its price? Then, assertedly, competing oligopolists would not meet the price increase, so that the firm loses a lot of sales. In other words, in the region above P^* the firm's demand curve is

FIGURE 10.2   Kinked Demand Curve: Heterogeneous Oligopoly   For oligopolists producing heterogeneous (nonidentical) products, suppose that in an initial equilibrium the firm produces output q^* at price P^*. If the firm cuts its price, the other oligopolists would meet the price reduction, so that the price-cutter's sales gain is small; if the firm raises price, the others do not follow the increase and the sales loss is large. These assumptions define a kink in the firm's demand curve d that is associated with a vertical gap in the Marginal Revenue curve MR. The profit-maximizing condition $MC = MR$ is therefore met at the initial equilibrium. The equilibrium price P^* will be relatively stable, since after small changes in the demand and cost curves the MC curve continues to cut through the vertical gap of the MR curve at output q^*.

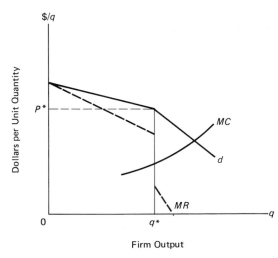

relatively flat. (Notice that the reasoning is the same as in the earlier discussion of "trigger strategies.")

This hypothesis is not a complete theory. It does not say how the original price P* was determined. But there is nevertheless an interesting implication: equilibrium prices arrived at by oligopolistic sellers will be relatively *stable*.

In Figure 10.2 note that the kink in the firm's demand curve generates a vertical jump in the corresponding Marginal Revenue curve. This is evident geometrically in the special case where the two branches of the demand curve are linear. For any linear demand curve, the *MR* curve bisects the horizontal distance from the demand curve to the vertical axis. With two separate linear branches of the demand curve, there must then be a vertical break or jump in the *MR* curve as shown.

For the price-quantity pair P*,q* to be a stable solution, *MC* must equal *MR* at q*. Geometrically, the *MC* curve must cut through the vertical jump of *MR*. If the *MC* curve shifts, but continues to intersect *MR* within the vertical gap in *MR*, the firm will continue to produce q* at price P*. Alternatively, consider a change in demand for the firm's output. Again we can see geometrically that if *MR* shifts slightly to the right or to the left, then *MC* will still cut through the vertical jump of *MR*. When this happens, output q* is unchanged, but price P* changes because of the shift in the demand function.

The competing oligopolists' behavior, on this hypothesis, is strongly rivalrous. How then did the initial equilibrium, which suggests some collusion, come about? One possible explanation is that the firms may have agreed on the initial price and also agreed to punish any firm that violates the agreement, by meeting its price cuts and not meeting its price increases.

EXAMPLE 10.4 Oligopoly and Price Rigidity

If oligopolists face kinked demand curves, demand and cost conditions can vary to some extent without changing the prices firms charge. A simple monopolist, on the other hand, will choose a new price following any shift of the *MC* or *MR* curves. Consequently, an implication of the kinked-demand hypothesis is that oligopoly prices should be relatively rigid.

This implication was tested by G. J. Stigler. The data in the table are typical of his findings. As can be seen, there is a strong indication that oligopoly prices are *less* rigid than monopoly prices. This is certainly true in terms of the number of monthly price changes, and tends to be confirmed by the quantitative measure of price change represented by the coefficient of variation (the standard deviation of monthly prices divided by their mean).

Price Flexibility (June 1929–May 1937)

	Number of Firms in Industry	Number of Monthly Price Changes	Coefficient of Variation of Prices
Oligopolies			
Bananas	2	46	16
Grain-binder	2	5	3
Plows	6	25	6
Tires	8	36	9

Price Flexibility (June 1929–May 1937) (cont.)

	Number of Firms in Industry	Number of Monthly Price Changes	Coefficient of Variation of Prices
Monopolies			
Aluminum	1	2	6
Nickel	1	0	0

Source: G. J. Stigler, "The Kinky Oligopoly Demand Curve and Rigid Prices," *Journal of Political Economy,* v. 55 (1947), p. 443.

A difficulty with Stigler's data is that they compare price changes across different industries. Business conditions vary from one industry to another, and it may be that the monopolized sectors would have had relatively rigid prices regardless of the number of firms. Another objection is that the definition of an industry can be arbitrary. Had aluminum and nickel been placed together in a single "nonferrous metals" category, they would have been classed as an oligopoly with heterogeneous products rather than as two separate monopolies.

Julian L. Simon[a] conducted a study less vulnerable to these objections. He examined prices quoted for business-magazine advertising, where the magazines had been classified into groups by the Standard Rate and Data Service (SRDS). Since all the groups fell into the business-magazine category, there was relative uniformity in conditions and methods of price quotation. And since the classification by SRDS was undertaken for the convenience of customers (advertisers), the grouping of magazines was presumably economically meaningful.

There were 148 groupings, ranging in size from 1 to 29 magazines. A magazine without competitors in its grouping could then be considered a monopolist. The data for two different periods, 1955–61 and 1961–64, once again suggested that the monopoly groups had *more* rigid prices than the oligopoly groups. Simon's test thus confirmed Stigler's previous negative conclusion as to the kinked-demand hypothesis. (However, the *quantitative* differences found by Simon were by no means as great as those reported by Stigler.)

COMMENT One explanation of the observations that would not contradict the kinked-demand hypothesis runs in terms of nonprofit goals. We saw in Chapter 8 that monopoly firms, sheltered from competition, may pursue goals other than economic profit. It might well be that an important nonprofit goal for monopoly firms is the easy life, avoidance of difficult decisions. Changing price, rather than just leaving things as they are, can be a difficult decision. Not only is sheer mental effort required, but "rocking the boat" is liable to attract unwanted attention and complaints. We might then expect monopoly and oligopoly prices to *both* be rigid, for different reasons: for oligopolists the kinked-demand hypothesis might be valid, while for monopolists the "easy life" goal might lead to even greater rigidity of prices.

[a]J. L. Simon, "A Further Test of the Kinky Oligopoly Demand Curve," *American Economic Review,* v. 59 (December 1969).

Variation of Product

Chapter 9 discussed product variety when each of many firms has some monopoly power. Here we consider oligopolists who can compete by changing not only price and quantity but also the product itself.

One type of variation is geographic location: a producer may be located close to or far from consumers. In Figure 10.3 consumers are assumed to be uniformly distributed along a line-segment scaled from 0 to 1, with midpoint $M = 1/2$. Suppose there is a constant per-mile transport cost t from any producing location to the consumer. Let P be the producer's price at some producing location R. The price at any other location is P plus the transportation costs. This delivered price is $P + ts$ at any distance s in either direction from point R, shown by the solid V-shaped lines. The dashed lines show the delivered prices if production is at the midpoint M. For example, M and R can represent two coal suppliers along a railroad. The price of coal at any point along the road, including transportation charges, is given by the height of the V-shaped line.

A curious solution to this problem was proposed by H. Hotelling.[8] Assume there are just two firms (duopoly), with identical costs of producing and delivering the commodity. Now suppose that consumers everywhere along the line segment want exactly one unit of the commodity, and are willing to pay any price for it. (Each person's demand is perfectly inelastic, but only for a single unit of the good.) Each consumer buys from whichever firm

FIGURE 10.3   **Delivered Price** P is the price at the producing location, t is the unit transportation cost, and s is the distance from a production point. The delivered price from that point to any consumer location is $P + ts$. The solid lines in the diagram show the delivered prices from a production locale at R; the dashed lines show the delivered prices from a production locale at the midpoint M.

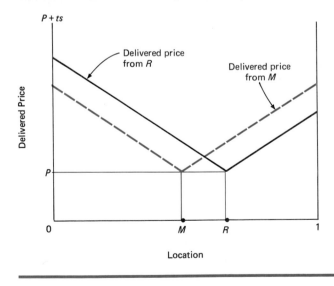

[8]H. Hotelling, "Stability in Competition," *Economic Journal*, v. 39 (March 1929).

has the lower delivered price at his location. Suppose one firm is located at the midpoint M in Figure 10.3 and the second firm at some other point R. Comparing the dashed and solid lines, we see that the firm located at M has an advantage: it can sell at a lower delivered price to the 50 percent of the market located to the left of M, and also to some of the consumers located to the right. So the firm at R has an incentive to move toward the midpoint M. Hotelling concluded that in equilibrium the duopolists would locate back to back, at either side of the midpoint M. In that way each is closer to half of the market, which serves as its clientele.

Interpreted in terms of product *variety*, the equilibrium here has the two firms supplying nearly identical products of middling character. Essentially no variety is offered to consumers at all! This model explains (so it has been claimed) why different companies' toothpastes and refrigerators are very much alike, why the political platforms of the Republican and Democratic parties converge toward a middle-of-the-road position, why Catholics and Protestants over time tend to minimize their theological differences, and so forth.

In the Hotelling equilibrium, suppliers offer too little variety. Put in locational terms, resources are wasted in transporting the good to consumers. When both firms are located at M the average distance between consumers and the nearest production point is $1/4$. If instead one firm were at the left quartile point and the other firm at the right quartile point, the average distance would be only $1/8$. Thus, by offering more variety the two firms would better satisfy consumer preferences at no extra cost.

Absolutely inelastic individual demand is of course a highly unreasonable assumption. (If this were really the case, the duopolists could earn an infinite profit by colluding to set price indefinitely high.) Once we allow some elasticity of consumer demand, the duopolists would be pulled away from the midpoint locations. In Figure 10.3, suppose there were initially two firms located back-to-back at M—the firm just to the right attracts all customers to its right, while the firm just to the left takes the rest. Suppose that the right-hand firm moved further to the right. Since delivered price would then be lower for most of its old clientele, it could sell more product to them—while losing to its competitor only a small fraction of its old clientele (those located in the immediate neighborhood of M). The other firm would behave similarly. So some variety would be offered to consumers after all. However, even if demand is quite elastic, the firms will not move as far as the ideal quartile locations.

The conclusions of the Hotelling model collapse when there are more than two suppliers. A third firm would want to locate at an infinitesimal distance on one or the other side of the initial pair. But then one of the original two would be boxed in, leaving it without any clientele at all. Such a firm would then surely "jump" to the outside, to be followed by the one now situated in the middle, and so on in an unending musical-chairs situation. So with more than two firms there cannot be a Cournot-Hotelling equilibrium.

The Hotelling conclusions also disappear if consumers are distributed uniformly around the circumference of a circle rather than along a line-segment. With downward-sloping demand, Cournot behavior in the circle model would lead to an efficient result. The first firm can choose any arbitrary location, in which case the second maximizes profit by locating 180° away at the opposite point around the circle. So transport cost is minimized. The circle model also generalizes easily to any number of firms, who are always motivated to spread themselves evenly around the circle. Whether the circle or the line-segment metaphor is more appropriate depends upon the actual situation.

10.5 OLIGOPOLY AND COLLUSION

What helps oligopolists collude? First and most obviously, firms can more easily police one another the fewer their number. Second, secret price cuts are more likely to be offered to large than to small buyers. A chiseling deal with a single big customer might be kept quiet; to try to get the same increase of business from ten small customers is stretching secrecy too far. Third, enforcement of collusion should be much easier where the product is homogeneous. Otherwise, price cuts can take the hard-to-penetrate guise of better quality. (Even where the physical commodity is homogeneous, a firm might still chisel by offering better credit terms or delivery.) Fourth, the more unstable the conditions of the industry, the harder it will be to negotiate and maintain agreements.

EXAMPLE 10.5 **Industry Concentration and Monopoly Power**

Collusion is easier when there are few firms. But at what point does an industry oligopoly become effectively collusive? Frederick Geithman, Howard Marvel, and Leonard Weiss examined this question using the four-firm concentration ratio—the percentage of a market served by the largest four firms in the industry. They found that collusion is not a problem in industries with a concentration ratio of less than 40 percent, that is, where the largest four firms serve less than 40 percent of the market. However, concentration ratios above this seemed to promote collusion, as evidenced by higher prices. Using data from gasoline retailing (1964–71) and grocery supermarkets (October 1974), they found that average prices tended to rise with the concentration ratio.

Prices and Concentration Ratios

Concentration Ratios (%)	Regular Gasoline ($/gallon)	Groceries (price of a standard grocery basket)
0–40	28.2	89.6
40–44	29.5	92.8
45–49	29.5	93.7
50–55	32.0	93.0
55–60	—	94.1
60–65	—	95.5
75–95	—	98.9

Source: Frederick Geithman, Howard Marvel, and Leonard Weiss, "Concentration, Price, and Critical Concentration Ratios," *Review of Economics and Statistics,* v. 63 (August 1981), pp. 349–350.

An Application: "Most-Favored-Customer" Clause[9]

To facilitate collusion, firms may offer price guarantees to purchasers. Imagine that only two firms, *A* and *B,* sell steel in a small country. For simplicity, assume that *A* considers

---

[9]This analysis is based largely upon Steven C. Salop, "Practices That (Credibly) Facilitate Oligopoly Coordination," in Joseph E. Stiglitz and G. Frank Mathewson, eds., *New Developments in the Analysis of Market Structures* (Cambridge, Mass.: MIT Press, 1986).

only two possible price quotations, High and Low. Similarly, *B* chooses between High and Low. The profit payoffs to each firm are given in Table 10.4. The duopolists here are once again caught in a Prisoners' Dilemma. If both choose High, each firm can attain its second-best outcome (numerically, a profit of 100). Yet for either firm a low price gives higher profits *regardless* of what the other does. So the two are likely to end up at their next-to-worst outcome—the Prisoners' Dilemma equilibrium strategy-pair (Low, Low) yielding a profit of 70 for each.

Each firm would surely agree to charge a High price provided the other did the same. If such agreement is illegal the same effect can be achieved by subtler means. Imagine that each duopolist "generously" guarantees its customers that no other customer will be offered a lower price. That is, should a later reduced price be offered to anyone else, earlier customers will get a rebate. (This is called a "Most-Favored-Customer" clause.)

It seems that buyers ought to be happy about the Most-Favored-Customer clause. But notice in Table 10.5 how this clause changes the duopolists' payoffs. Now when both firms choose High neither has any reason to change. If *B*, for example, cut its price, it would reduce its profits from 100 to 90. While it may gain new sales by cutting price, it will have to give rebates to its old customers.

A similar paradox is often encountered in strategic situations: it may pay to sacrifice an opportunity once the effect on other players' decisions is taken into account. Here the "sacrifice"—arranging to lose rather than gain profit by cutting price—guarantees that no firm will be a price-cutter.

A different arrangement with somewhat similar consequences is the Meet-or-Release clause. Here the seller guarantees a customer who has not yet taken delivery that any lower price on the market will be matched or the customer is released from his obligation to purchase. (The Most-Favored-Customer clause guarantees that buyers will get the advantage of the seller's *own* later price cuts, if any; Meet-or-Release guarantees that buyers will get

TABLE 10.4   The Prisoners' Dilemma: Oligopoly Profits

		FIRM B'S PRICE High	FIRM B'S PRICE Low
FIRM A'S PRICE	High	(100,100)	(−10,140)
FIRM A'S PRICE	Low	(140,−10)	(70,70)

TABLE 10.5   The "Most-Favored-Customer" Clause

		FIRM B'S PRICE High	FIRM B'S PRICE Low
FIRM A'S PRICE	High	(100,100)	(−10,90)
FIRM A'S PRICE	Low	(90,−10)	(70,70)

the advantage of *other firms'* lower prices.) Once again no firm has an incentive to charge a low price. The Meet-or-Release clause has the side-effect of encouraging the customer to report when competitors cut prices, thus reducing the likelihood of secret discounts and chiseling. [*Challenge to the reader:* Construct a payoff table corresponding to both firms' offering a Meet-or-Release clause.]

We should not, however, jump to the conclusion that the Most-Favored-Customer clause or the Meet-or-Release clause or similar arrangements are used only to keep prices high. They have other functions as well, for example, protecting buyers from price discrimination. Therefore, such clauses are not conclusive evidence of anticompetitive collusion.

SUMMARY

Oligopoly is competition among a small number of firms in an industry. With small numbers, decisionmakers are likely to recognize the interdependence of their choices: what is best for each depends upon what the others are doing. So the firms are required to make *strategic* decisions, a topic studied in the theory of games.

The Prisoners' Dilemma describes situations in which there are potential gains from cooperation. However, it is in the private interest of each party to behave selfishly so that, in what is called the *Nash equilibrium,* all lose. But when parties expect to interact repeatedly, as is often the case under oligopoly, they may be able to achieve a more cooperative outcome.

Oligopoly may be *homogeneous* (all the firms produce exactly the same product) or *heterogeneous* (the firms produce distinct, though similar, commodities). In the former case, no price difference between the firms can persist.

Under homogeneous oligopoly, either quantity or price may be the decision variable. When quantity is the decision variable, at one extreme firms *collude* to attain the monopoly outcome, and at the other extreme they act as *competitive* price-takers. If each simply reacts optimally to what is perceived as a fixed output decision of the other, the Cournot equilibrium (a special case of the Nash equilibrium) is attained, intermediate between the Collusive and Competitive outcomes. The key idea is that each firm chooses the best monopoly output for the remainder of the market, after subtracting the other firms' given production. If *asymmetric* behavior is allowed, on the other hand, the more aggressive firm may be able to gain more profit by forcing the other to an inferior position—and possibly driving the other out of the market entirely.

If firms set price rather than quantity, then each firm wants to barely undercut the price charged by the other. Here the Cournot outcome reduces to the Competitive one. Possibilities remain, however, for profitable symmetrical *collusion* on price, or for asymmetrical gain to a more aggressive firm.

In *heterogeneous* oligopoly a price difference between the firms may persist. Apart from this, the analysis of the symmetrical and asymmetrical outcomes is much the same. In particular, the Cournot solution remains intermediate between the Collusive and Competitive outcomes.

For oligopolists producing heterogeneous products, one particular type of assumed strategic interaction leads to a "kinked" demand curve for any single firm. If the other producers will meet any price cut, the firm's demand curve below the current price will be steep; if the others will not meet any price increase, above the current price the firm's demand curve will be flat. The effect is to discourage price changes. This theory does not explain how the equilibrium price was originally determined, but suggests that once equilibrium is attained price will be rather stable.

In heterogeneous oligopoly the firms also choose what product to offer consumers. The Hotelling model concludes that an oligopolistic industry would provide too little variety to consumers. This result depends, however, upon doubtful features of the model, in particular that each customer wants exactly one unit of the good and is willing to pay any price for it. Furthermore, the Hotelling model breaks down if there are more than two firms, or if consumers cannot be regarded as located along a line (rather than, say, along a circle).

Oligopolists find it difficult to enforce collusion; each is tempted to chisel (as in the Prisoners' Dilemma). Collusion is easier if the number of oligopolists is small, if no buyers are large, if the product is homogeneous, and if market conditions are stable. Certain contractual arrangements which at first appear to favor the buyers, such as Most-Favored-Customer clauses, may actually facilitate collusion and thus lead to higher prices.

QUESTIONS

For Review

1. What is strategic behavior? Why are suppliers more likely to engage in strategic behavior when there are only a few of them in the market?
*2. What is the "Prisoners' Dilemma"? Do the participants in this game have an unexploited mutual gain from trade, and if so, why?
*3. Distinguish oligopoly from monopolistic competition.
*4. Justify the statement in the text that the Cournot oligopoly outcome is a special case of the Nash equilibrium in the theory of games.
5. Explain the Cournot solution to the duopoly problem.
6. Why is collusion more likely if the firms expect to remain in the industry in the future?
7. Diagram the Reaction Curves for the asymmetrical Stackelberg and Threat cases (letting output be the decision variable).
*8. a. Why does a "kinked" demand curve tend to lead to rigid prices?
   b. How might a kinked demand curve for any single oligopolist result from the behavior of others designed to enforce a collusive agreement?

For Further Thought and Discussion

1. It seems somewhat strange that different duopoly solutions are obtained depending on whether price or quantity is the decision variable. Which outcomes are different, and why?
*2. Under the Cournot model, in making its output decision each duopolist firm assumes that the other's output is fixed. Over time, however, each would surely learn that this assumption about the other's behavior is not valid. What would then be likely to happen?
*3. In deterring entry, a monopolist faces the problem of making his threat—that he will always produce enough to drive out the entrant—*credible*. The difficulty lies in the fact that, once a newcomer has entered, it may be more profitable to share the market than to engage in a costly price war. How might a monopolist make his threat more credible?

*The answers to starred questions appear at the end of the book.

*4. Can a kinked demand curve arise under *homogeneous* duopoly? If so, what would be its shape?

5. Do small numbers inevitably imply cartel-like collusion?

*6. Some economists argue that "predatory price cutting" to enforce the Threat solution will almost never be observed. The reason given is that the symmetrical Collusive solution is typically better for both parties.

    a. Is this necessarily correct? Is it ever correct?

    b. Under what circumstances will predatory price cutting be likely to emerge, if ever?

7. Construct a payoff table in which two duopolist firms both offer consumers a Meet-or-Release clause. Show that this permits them to escape from the Prisoners' Dilemma so as to charge higher prices.

CHAPTER 11

DEMAND FOR FACTORS OF PRODUCTION

EXAMPLES

P revious chapters covered supply and demand in the *product market*—the markets for goods and services. Now we turn to the markets for resources used as inputs in producing goods and services. (These markets are sometimes called *input* or *factor* markets.) In terms of the circular flow diagram in Chapter 1, our attention shifts from the upper portion to the lower portion of the picture. This chapter surveys the demand side of the input market—that is, the decisions of firms about how much land, labor, or other productive services to hire. The following chapter takes up the supply side—the decisions of owners of resources about how much to offer to potential employers.

In the equilibrium of the input market, market structure (the degree of competition) continues to play an important role. A company in a large city may be a monopolist in its product market, but only one among many employers (and therefore a competitive or "price-taking" buyer) of a productive service like secretarial help. Conversely, a textile firm may face a highly competitive world market for its product and still be a "price-making" or monopsonist[1] employer of labor in a small town.[2]

11.1 SINGLE VARIABLE INPUT

The Production Function

Suppose a firm uses cloth, thread, labor, machinery, and so on to produce shirts. Quantities of the inputs A, B, C, . . . will be symbolized by a, b, c, ... The firm's production function is written as follows:

$$q = F(a, b, c, \ldots) \tag{11.1}$$

This expression simply means that there is some relation determining the maximum quantity of output given the input quantities a, b, c, ...

Let all inputs other than A be held fixed (we thus consider the "short run"). The production function can then be written more simply as

$$q = f(a) \tag{11.2}$$

List of Notation

aic_a	Average Input Cost per unit of input A	mp_a	Marginal Product of input A
mic_a	Marginal Input Cost per unit of A	MR	Marginal Revenue
		mrp_a	Marginal Revenue Product of input A
ap_a	Average Product of input A	tp_a	Total Product of input A
h_a	Hire price of input A	vmp_a	Value of Marginal Product of input A
MC	Marginal Cost		

---

[1]A monopolist is a sole *seller* in a market; a monopsonist is a sole *buyer*.

[2]Firms might also be *oligopolists* or *monopolistic competitors* in their respective product markets, as discussed in Chapters 9 and 10, but only pure competition and pure monopoly will be covered here.

The quantities of the fixed inputs $B, C, \ldots$ no longer directly appear in the equation, but they still have an effect. The amounts of the fixed inputs help determine the shape of the $f(a)$ function.

NUMERICAL ILLUSTRATION: Suppose the underlying production function is $q = 6a^{1/2}b^{1/4}$. This corresponds to Equation (11.1). If the quantity of input B is held fixed at $b = 1$, the equation corresponding to (11.2) would take the simpler form, $q = 6a^{1/2}$. If $b = 16$, Equation (11.2) becomes $q = 12a^{1/2}$.

We saw in Chapter 6 that the Law of Diminishing Returns explains why the Marginal Cost and Average Cost curves have positive slopes after some point. In this chapter the Law of Diminishing Returns is *defined* as a technological relation between inputs and output. That is, diminishing returns correspond to increasing costs.

THE LAW OF DIMINISHING RETURNS: If one input (or group of inputs), say labor, is increased while another input (or group of inputs) is held fixed, Total Product at first rises. But, eventually a point is reached where the rate of increase, the Marginal Product[3] $mp_a \equiv \Delta q / \Delta a$ of labor begins to fall; this is the point of diminishing *marginal* returns. With further increases in the use of labor, the Average Product $ap_a \equiv q/a$ also begins to fall; this is the point of diminishing *average* returns. As the amount of labor used rises still more, Total Product may fall. (That is, labor can become counterproductive, reducing Total Product.) This point represents diminishing *total* returns.

The Law of Diminishing Returns is illustrated in Figure 11.1. The upper panel shows the Total Product curve tp_a, which relates output quantity q to the quantity of input A used. The lower diagram shows the corresponding average function ap_a representing q/a, and the Marginal Product curve mp_a showing $\Delta q / \Delta a$. The general relations among the total, average, and marginal magnitudes, as first explained in Chapter 2, continue to hold. When tp_a is rising, mp_a is positive; at the level of output where tp_a is horizontal, mp_a is zero; at levels of output where tp_a falls, mp_a is negative (Propositions 2.1a, 2.1b, 2.1c). The Marginal Product curve mp_a lies above the Average Product curve ap_a for levels of output at which ap_a is rising; $mp_a = ap_a$ when ap_a is horizontal; mp_a is less than ap_a for levels of output at which ap_a is falling (Propositions 2.2a, 2.2b, 2.2c).

Exercise 11.1 —————————————————————————————

A firm's Total Product function for input A is given by the equation $tp_a \equiv q = 100a^2 - a^3$. The Average Product function is then $ap_a \equiv q/a = 100a - a^2$. It can be shown by calculus that the exact Marginal Product function is $mp_a \equiv \Delta q / \Delta a = 200a - 3a^2$. (a) When do diminishing *marginal* returns set in? (b) Diminishing *average* returns? (c) Diminishing *total* returns? (d) Verify that when Total Product reaches a maximum, Marginal Product is zero. (e) Verify that when Average Product reaches a maximum, Marginal Product equals Average Product.

---

[3]*Mathematical Footnote:* The Marginal Product is (like all marginal concepts) defined as a limit.

$$mp_a \equiv \lim_{\Delta a \to 0} \frac{\Delta q}{\Delta a} \equiv \frac{dq}{da}$$

(From this point on in the text, Mathematical Footnotes that simply translate marginal concepts into derivative notation will be omitted. Special notes will be provided only where points of difficulty may arise.)

FIGURE 11.1 **The Law of Diminishing Returns**   The upper panel shows the Total Product function for factor A, tp_a. The lower panel shows the corresponding Average Product function ap_a and Marginal Product function mp_a. Diminishing *marginal* returns set in first (the mp_a curve reaches its peak), then diminishing *average* returns set in (the ap_a curve reaches its peak), and finally diminishing *total* returns set in (the tp_a curve reaches its peak, at output $\bar{q}$).

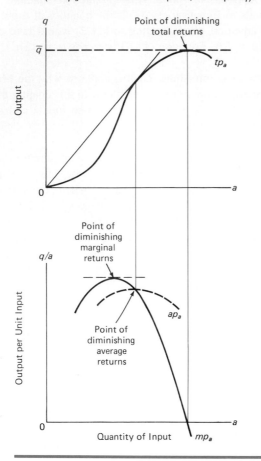

Answer: (a) It can be determined by calculus (or else by plotting the function) that Marginal Product reaches its maximum at $a = 33\ 1/3$. This is where diminishing *marginal* returns set in. (b) Average Product reaches a maximum (diminishing *average* returns set in) at $a = 50$. (c) Total Product reaches a maximum (diminishing total returns set in) at $a = 66\ 2/3$. (d) At $a = 66\ 2/3$, the formula for Marginal Product shows that $mp_a = 0$. (e) At $a = 50$, the formulas show that $ap_a = 2500 = mp_a$.

EXAMPLE 11.1   **Corn Yields**

In 1977 the University of Wisconsin Experimental Station at Arlington conducted an experiment in corn yields. Various levels of nitrogen fertilizer were tried, with other inputs held constant. The following table shows the resulting yields:

Corn Yields

Available Nitrogen (lbs./acre)	Total Yield (bushels per acre)	Marginal Yield (bushels per acre per pound N)
75	112	
		.679
131	150	
		.393
187	172	
		.250
243	186	
		−.089
299	181	
		−.089
355	176	

Source: Adapted from Ted F. Bay and Richard A. Schoney, "Data Analysis with Computer Graphics: Production Functions," *American Journal of Agricultural Economics*, v. 64, no. 2 (May 1982), p. 289.

The Marginal Yield column has been estimated here from the original source, by taking the difference between the Total Yields for successive rows and dividing by the nitrogen increment. Thus, the first Marginal Yield is calculated as $(150 - 112)/(131 - 75) = .679$. This number should be interpreted as an estimate of the Marginal Yield at the in-between nitrogen input of $(131 + 75)/2 = 103$ pounds per acre. Notice that in this experiment diminishing marginal returns applied throughout. Diminishing total returns set in somewhere around 250 pounds of nitrogen per acre.

From Production Function to Cost Function

This section shows how the properties of the production function explain the shapes of the various cost curves (Total Cost, Average Cost, Marginal Cost).

The firm can be regarded as buying the services of resources or factors, or equivalently as hiring the resources themselves.[4] Thus, we can think of a factory that rents a truck by the day or contracts with another firm to provide trucking services. (A firm that owns its own truck incurs expenses equivalent to those it would pay if it were to rent the truck.) If the input is used up in production (say, cloth used to produce shirts), the firm can be thought of as simply purchasing the input, and we need not distinguish between the "hire-price" of cloth and the price of the cloth itself. The "hire prices" of inputs A, B, . . . will be symbolized as h_a, h_b,. . . . We assume here that the firm is a "price-taker" in its input markets.

The firm's Total Cost for any given combination of inputs is

$$C \equiv h_a a + h_b b + h_c c + \ . \ . \ . \tag{11.3}$$

[4]In some cases a firm may be able either to hire or to buy. A business can rent office space or buy a building. Later on we will find it useful to distinguish the hire-price, h_a, of an input A from the price P_A of the input itself— of the *source* of the productive services used by the firm. But in this chapter we will deal mostly with the hire-price h_a, the price of the input's *services*.

When all inputs except A are held fixed, Total Cost can be divided into a fixed component F and a variable component V:

$$C \equiv F + V \equiv F + h_a a \qquad (11.3')$$

Here $h_a a$, the expenditure on input A, corresponds to the "variable cost" V; F corresponds to the "fixed cost" of all the other inputs B, C, etc.

As an example, Equation (11.3′) might show Total Cost as a function of the amount of cloth a shirt factory uses. If we want cost as a function of the number of shirts produced, we must determine how much cloth the firm requires to produce a given number of shirts, and then determine total expenditures on cloth. For example, let the production function (11.2) have the specific algebraic form $q = \sqrt{a}$. (Increased output may require a more than proportional increase in the amount of cloth because, for example, as more cloth is used less efficient machines are put into use that spoil more cloth during the production process.) The "inverted" relation is $a = q^2$, which says how much cloth the firm must use to produce q shirts. The firm's total cost of producing q shirts is then $C = F + h_a q^2$. More generally, the "inverted" production function can be expressed algebraically as

$$a = a(q) \qquad (11.4)$$

Then:

$$C \equiv F + h_a a(q) \qquad (11.5)$$

With a single variable input A, therefore, the Total Cost function depends upon the fixed cost F, the hire-price h_a, and the production function $q = f(a)$.

Geometrically, the upper panel in Figure 11.1 shows output as a function of input. But the diagram can also be read the other way—to each level of output there corresponds a quantity of input A required to produce that output. Multiply the hire-price of A by the amount of A required to produce a given output to find the Variable Cost of producing that output. This cost curve is shown in the upper panel of Figure 11.2. The Total Cost curve C lies above the Variable Cost curve V by the amount of the Fixed Cost F. The corresponding marginal and average curves are shown in the lower diagram in Figure 11.2.

Mathematically, the connection between Marginal Cost MC and the Marginal Product mp_a is

$$MC \equiv \frac{\Delta C}{\Delta q} \equiv \frac{h_a \Delta a}{\Delta q} \equiv \frac{h_a}{\Delta q / \Delta a} \equiv \frac{h_a}{mp_a} \qquad (11.6)$$

Since the hire-price h_a is assumed constant, this equation tells us that Marginal Cost increases as Marginal Product decreases. So, as already mentioned, it is the Law of Diminishing Returns that explains why the Marginal Cost curve eventually slopes upward. In particular, *rising* Marginal Cost corresponds to *diminishing* Marginal Product. (The expression h_a / mp_a on the right-hand side can be applied as follows. Suppose the Marginal Product of cloth is 5, which means that producing one more shirt requires an additional $1/5$ square yard of cloth. The marginal cost of producing one more shirt is therefore $1/5$ times the price, h_a, of a square yard of cloth.)

A corresponding inverse relationship holds between Average Product ap_a and Average Variable Cost $AVC \equiv V/q$.

FIGURE 11.2 **From Production Function to Cost Function** Multiplying the horizontal axis of the previous diagram by the constant hire-price h_a shifts the dimension from units of input *(a)* to units of Variable Cost *($h_a a$)*. Rotated 180° and flipped over, the tp_a curve of the previous diagram becomes the total Variable Cost V curve in the upper diagram. The mp_a curve of the previous diagram becomes the Marginal Cost curve MC in the lower diagram; the ap_a curve becomes the Average Variable Cost curve AVC.

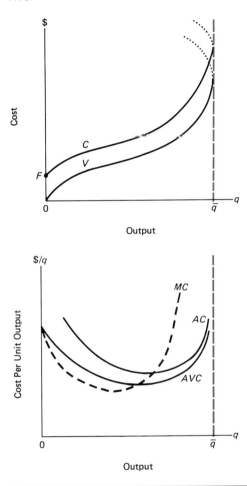

$$AVC \equiv \frac{V}{q} \equiv \frac{h_a a}{q} \equiv \frac{h_a}{q/a} \equiv \frac{h_a}{ap_a} \tag{11.7}$$

Because of the fixed cost term F, a slightly more complicated relation connects Average Cost AC and Average Product ap_a:

$$AC \equiv \frac{C}{q} \equiv \frac{F + h_a a}{q} \equiv \frac{F}{q} + \frac{h_a}{ap_a} \tag{11.8}$$

Exercise 11.2

Suppose the firm's short-run production function using Equation (11.2) is $q = 2\sqrt{a}$. This is also the Total Product function tp_a. The hire-price is $h_a = 4$ and the fixed cost is $F = 50$. (a) Find the Total Variable Cost function V and the Total Cost function C. (b) Relate Average Variable Cost AVC to Average Product ap_a. (c) Relate Marginal Cost MC to Marginal Product mp_a.

Answer: (a) The "inverted" function (Equation [11.4]) is $a = q^2/4$. Then $V \equiv h_a a = 4a = q^2$. And $C \equiv F + V = 50 + q^2$. (b) $AVC \equiv V/q = q^2/q = q$; $ap_a \equiv tp_a/a = 2\sqrt{a}/a = 2/\sqrt{a}$. Equation (11.7) tells us that $AVC \equiv h_a/ap_a$, which can be verified as follows: $h_a/ap_a = 4/(2/\sqrt{a}) = 2\sqrt{a} = q = AVC$. (c) Calculus or tabulation shows Marginal Cost to be $MC = 2q$. Similarly, Marginal Product is $mp_a = 1/\sqrt{a}$. Equation (11.6) tells us that $MC \equiv h_a/mp_a$, which we can verify: $h_a/mp_a = 4\sqrt{a} = 2q = MC$.

Now that we've seen how the underlying production function determines the shape assumed in Chapter 6 for the firm's cost function, we can return to the main business of this chapter—market demand for the productive services of inputs.

The Firm's Demand for Inputs

In its employment or hiring decisions, a price-taking firm in the input market faces an input supply curve that is a horizontal line drawn at the level of the hire-price h_a, as in Figure 11.3. Denoting the cost of hiring a units of input A by $C_a \equiv h_a a$, this supply curve can be

---

FIGURE 11.3 **Optimal Factor Employment: Price-Taking Firm in Both Factor Market and Product Market** The horizontal line, showing the supply curve s_a to the price-taking firm at hire-price h_a, is the curve of Average Input Cost (aic_a) and also of Marginal Input Cost (mic_a). If the firm is a price-taker in the product market as well, the Value of the Marginal Product (vmp_a) curve coincides with the Marginal Revenue Product (mrp_a) curve. The firm's demand curve d_a for input A is then the downward-sloping branch of the $vmp_a \equiv mrp_a$ curve.

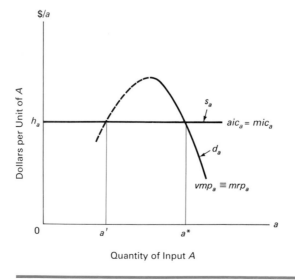

interpreted as Average Input Cost $(aic_a \equiv C_a/a)$. And, since the price per unit is constant, it is also a curve of Marginal Input Cost $(mic_a \equiv \Delta C_a/\Delta a)$.

To determine its optimal (profit-maximizing) use of input A, say cloth, the firm must balance the returns from using A against the price h_a. Two elements are involved in calculating these returns: (1) the physical productivity of cloth, and (2) the revenue gained from the shirts produced with the cloth.

With regard to the first element, only the Marginal Product is relevant. However great the contribution to Total Product may have been for earlier units of cloth, it is only the incremental yield from an additional unit that matters in deciding how much cloth to use. The Marginal Product mp_a curve, as in the lower panel of Figure 11.1, pictures this physical productivity.

Similarly, with regard to the second element, only Marginal Revenue matters. A firm in a competitive market is by definition a price-taker in the product market, so $MR = P$, where P is also taken as given. Valuing an input's physical productivity at this price P leads to the concept called *Value of the Marginal Product* of input A.

DEFINITION: Value of the Marginal Product vmp_a equals product price P times physical Marginal Product mp_a.

$$vmp_a \equiv P(mp_a) \tag{11.9}$$

Since price is assumed constant, the curve vmp_a showing Value of the Marginal Product in Figure 11.3 has the same shape as the Marginal Product curve in the lower panel of Figure 11.1. The only difference is in the vertical scale: it was output per unit of input (q/a) in Figure 11.1, but is dollars per unit of input $(\$/a)$ in Figure 11.3. Geometrically, the vertical scale of mp_a has been "stretched" by the multiple P.

The firm increases profits by using more of factor A (cloth) if the Value of the Marginal Product (that is, the shirt revenue obtained per additional unit of cloth) is greater than h_a, the cost of an additional unit of cloth. When vmp_a is less than h_a, the firm can increase its profit by using less cloth. In other words, the optimum condition for use of cloth by a price-taking firm is that quantity at which

$$vmp_a = h_a \tag{11.10}$$

Note, however, that, as shown in Figure 11.3, this equality may be satisfied at the two different levels, a' and a^*. So something more is needed to specify the optimum employment. A secondary condition for an optimum is that the vmp_a curve is falling relative to the horizontal curve depicting Average and Marginal Input Cost[5]; this holds only at a^* in the diagram.[6] To employ only a' units of cloth would be to forego the profitable range where the return from using an additional unit of cloth (vmp_a) exceeds the cost (h_a).

We conclude, therefore, that the demand curve for input A by a price-taking firm is the downward-sloping range of the Value of the Marginal Product curve.

---

[5]This condition corresponds to the technical qualification (see Chapter 6) that the output optimum for the firm occurs at $MC = MR$ provided that the MC curve cuts MR *from below*. Here the optimum occurs when vmp_a cuts h_a *from above*.

Exercise 11.3

Suppose the firm's Total Product function is $q = 2\sqrt{a}$ as in Exercise 11.2. Let the price of a shirt be $P = 60$, and the price of cloth be $h_a = 4$. (a) Find the Value of Marginal Product curve. (b) Find the optimal use of the input, a^*. (c) What is the associated output q^*? (d) What is the firm's demand curve for cloth?

Answer: (a) We saw in Exercise 11.2 that if $q = 2\sqrt{a}$, then $mp_a = 1/\sqrt{a}$. Thus, $vmp_a \equiv P(mp_a) = 60/\sqrt{a}$. (b) To find the optimal use of the input set $vmp_a = h_a$, or $60/\sqrt{a} = 4$, which implies $a^* = 225$. (c) The associated output is $q^* = 2\sqrt{a^*} = 30$. (d) Since vmp_a here is downward-sloping throughout, the demand curve is identical with the vmp_a curve. The equation of the demand curve is $h_a = 60/\sqrt{a}$.

Now suppose the firm is still a price-taker in the *input market* for cloth, but is a monopolist rather than a price-taker in the *product market* (shirts). As a result, the firm's revenues from increased use of cloth are adversely affected by a decrease in the price of shirts as the firm sells more. This condition is pictured in Figure 11.4. For a monopolist, the return on the margin from the use of an additional unit of cloth is not the *value* of the physical Marginal Product but rather the *revenue increment* obtained by sale of that Marginal Product. This leads to the concept known as *Marginal Revenue Product* of input A, denoted mrp_a.

$$mrp_a \equiv MR \cdot mp_a \tag{11.11}$$

DEFINITION: Marginal Revenue Product mrp_a equals Marginal Revenue MR times physical Marginal Product mp_a.

Returning to the competitive (price-taker) firm in the product market (Figure 11.3), we know that for such a firm MR equals price and does not vary with the firm's output. It follows immediately that for a competitive firm in the product market the vmp_a and mrp_a curves are identical for any input. (This was indicated by the labeling $vmp_a \equiv mrp_a$ in Figure 11.3.) For a firm with monopoly power in the product market, on the other hand, Marginal Revenue MR and product price P both decrease as output increases; furthermore the MR curve falls faster than the demand curve. So, for a monopoly firm, the mrp_a curve lies below the vmp_a curve, as in Figure 11.4. The profit-maximizing use of input A, a^* in this diagram, occurs where the mrp_a curve intersects the horizontal input supply curve s_a.[7] It follows that the monopoly firm's demand curve d_a for input A is given by the Marginal Revenue Product curve rather than by the Value of Marginal Product curve.

---

[6]*Mathematical Footnote:* The firm chooses the amount of A to maximize profit $\Pi \equiv R - C \equiv Pq - h_a a - F$ (where F stands for fixed costs representing expenditures on inputs other than A). Differentiating Π with respect to a and setting the derivative equal to zero, we have a first-order condition.

$$P\frac{dq}{da} = h_a \quad \text{or} \quad P(mp_a) \equiv vmp_a = h_a$$

This corresponds to Equation (11.10). Taking the second derivative of Π, the second-order condition for a maximum is

$$P\frac{d^2q}{da^2} < 0 \quad \text{or} \quad \text{(since } P \text{ is a positive constant)} \frac{d^2q}{da^2} < 0$$

This means that Marginal Product mp_a (and so the curve vmp_a) must be falling to have a profit maximum.

FIGURE 11.4 **Optimal Factor Employment: Monopolist in Product Market**   The firm is a price-taker or competitive purchaser in the input market, as indicated by the horizontal supply curve s_a at the level of the going hire-price h_a. But here the firm has monopoly power in the product market. Since at any output the product price exceeds Marginal Revenue, the curve vmp_a (Value of the Marginal Product) lies above the mrp_a (Marginal Revenue Product) curve. The firm's optimum is at the intersection of s_a and mrp_a, leading to employment a^* of input A. The downward-sloping branch of the mrp_a curve is also the firm's demand curve for input A.

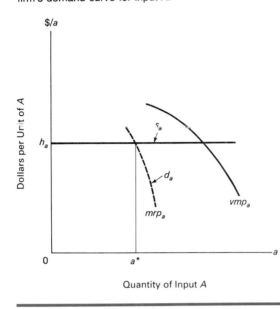

Exercise 11.4

Let the Total Product function be $q = 2\sqrt{a}$. Recall from Exercise 11.2 that the corresponding Marginal Product is $mp_a = 1/\sqrt{a}$. Assume the firm is a monopolist that faces the downward-sloping demand curve $P = 90 - q$. Let the hire-price be $h_a = 4$ as before. (a) Find the vmp_a and mrp_a functions, and verify that mrp_a lies below vmp_a. (b) What is the optimal input employment a^* and associated output q^*? (c) What is the monopoly firm's demand curve for input A? (d) Compare the solutions with those of Exercise 11.3.

Answer: (a) By definition, $vmp_a \equiv P(mp_a)$. Substituting $P = 90 - q$ and $mp_a = 1/\sqrt{a}$ we obtain $vmp_a = (90 - q)(1/\sqrt{a}) = (90 - 2\sqrt{a})(1/\sqrt{a}) = 90/\sqrt{a} - 2$. Since the product demand curve $P = 90 - q$ is linear, we know that the slope of the Marginal Revenue curve is double the slope of the demand curve, so $MR = 90 - 2q$. Then $mrp_a \equiv MR(mp_a) = (90 - 2q)$ $(1/\sqrt{a}) = 90/\sqrt{a} - 2(2\sqrt{a})/\sqrt{a} = 90/\sqrt{a} - 4$. We see that mrp_a is always less than

---

[7]*Mathematical Footnote:* The firm maximizes $\Pi = R - C = Pq - h_a a - F$ as before, but now recognizes that P is a decreasing function of output q—and so, indirectly, of input a. Differentiating and setting equal to zero, the first-order condition is

$$P\frac{dq}{dq} + q\frac{dP}{dq}\frac{dq}{da} = h_a \quad \text{or} \quad \left(P + q\frac{dP}{dq}\right)\frac{dq}{da} = h_a$$

The element in parentheses is Marginal Revenue. So the condition can be expressed as follows:

$$(MR)(mp_a) \equiv mrp_a = h_a$$

vmp_a. (b) Setting $mrp_a = h_a$ we have $90/\sqrt{a} - 4 = 4$, which implies $\sqrt{a} = 90/8 = 11.25$ or $a^* = 126.56$. The associated output is $q^* = 22.5$. (c) Since the mrp_a curve is everywhere downward-sloping, the demand curve for input A coincides with it. The demand-curve equation is $90/\sqrt{a} - 4 = h_a$, or $a = 8100/(h_a + 4)^2$. (d) The firm here could produce 30 units of output and sell them at the market price $P = 60$, as did the price-taking firm of Exercise 11.3. But, from (b) we saw that the monopolist produces only 22.5 units of output (and sells them at the higher price $P^* = 90 - q^* = 67.5$). Correspondingly, it employs fewer units of input A (126.56 instead of 225).

The general Factor Employment Condition for a firm that is a price-taker with respect to hire price h_a is

$$mrp_a = h_a \qquad \begin{array}{l} \text{Factor Employment Condition,} \\ \text{Price-Taking Firm in Input Market} \end{array} \qquad (11.12)$$

If the firm is in a competitive industry, the output price is constant and therefore $mrp_a = vmp_a$, so that Equation (11.12) reduces to Equation (11.10). Again, we have as a technical qualification that the mrp_a curve must cut the horizontal input supply curve *from above*.

CONCLUSION: For a firm facing a given hire-price h_a, the optimal use of input A occurs at that quantity where $mrp_a = h_a$ (in the downward-sloping range of the mrp_a curve). The firm's demand curve for A is therefore the Marginal Revenue Product curve, mrp_a, (in its downward-sloping range).[8] In Figure 11.3, which pictures a competitive firm in the product market, the input demand curve d_a coincides with the curve $vmp_a \equiv mrp_a$. In Figure 11.4, for a monopolist in the product market, the input demand curve d_a coincides with mrp_a (and *not* with vmp_a).

The separate discussions of the firm's *output* decision in Chapters 6 and 8 and of the *input-employment* decision in this chapter might suggest that these two choices are quite separate matters. However, the choice of how much of each input to use determines (through the production function) the firm's output. And, so long as we are dealing with a single variable input, the converse is also true: Choosing output necessarily determines the level of input.[9]

We can show the relation between the output decision and the input-employment decision by using the logical connection between Marginal Cost MC and Marginal Product mp_a derived earlier:

$$MC \equiv \frac{h_a}{mp_a} \qquad (11.13)$$

Dividing both sides by Marginal Revenue MR, we have

$$\frac{MC}{MR} \equiv \frac{h_a}{MR(mp_a)} \equiv \frac{h_a}{mrp_a} \qquad (11.14)$$

---

[8]Strictly speaking, this holds only for that portion of the downward-sloping range where the total expenditure $C_a \equiv h_a a$ on the variable input A is less than Total Revenue R.

[9]With several variable inputs, however, the determination of output still leaves a range of freedom for selection of the best resource combination to produce that output. This topic will be discussed in the next section.

So when the firm satisfies the Factor Employment Condition (11.12), $h_a = mrp_a$, the right-hand side of Equation (11.14) is 1, and the firm necessarily also satisfies $MC = MR$—which is the general Maximum-Profit condition of Chapter 8. The converse also holds, of course.

Exercise 11.5 ──

For Exercises 11.3 and 11.4, verify that the condition for optimal input *(mrp_a = h_a)* also implies optimal output *(MR = MC)*.

Answer: We saw in Exercise 11.2 that if $h_a = 4$ and Marginal Product is $mp_a = 1\sqrt{a}$, then Marginal Cost is $MC = 2q$. For a price-taking firm with $P = 60$, the Maximum-Profit Condition $MC = MR \equiv P$ says that $2q = 60$, or $q^* = 30$—which confirms the result obtained in Exercise 11.3 using the Factor Employment Condition $vmp_a = mrp_a = h_a$. For a monopolist firm facing the demand curve $P = 90 - q$, the Maximum-Profit Condition $MC = MR$ becomes $2q = 90 - 2q$, or $q^* = 22.5$—which confirms the result in Exercise 11.4.

───

11.2 SEVERAL VARIABLE INPUTS

When the firm can change its use of only one input it acts in the short run, whereas in the long run it can vary all inputs. When more than one input is variable the analysis of input demand is more complicated. To keep things simple we assume here just two variable inputs, A and B, say cloth and machinery.

The Production Function

In some ways, a firm that hires inputs resembles a consumer who purchases goods and services. Just as consumption goods can be regarded as generating utility, so inputs generate product. If there are just two variable inputs, the production function of Equation (11.1) can be written as follows:

$$q = F(a,b) \tag{11.15}$$

Diagrammatically, the production function is the three-dimensional "output hill" of Figure 11.5, which shows product quantity q as a function of the input amounts a and b.[10] Each contour, or *isoquant,* in the two-dimensional "contour map" of Figure 11.6 shows all the combinations of inputs A and B that produce a given quantity of output. Note also that, as with indifference curves, some isoquant goes through each point in the diagram; to make the diagram comprehensible we have, of course, depicted only a few of these isoquants.

Figure 11.7 illustrates the effect of changing either the amount of A or B separately. The different curves drawn along the surface of the output hill show how output quantity q changes as one input increases, the quantity of the other input held constant. These can be regarded as Total Product curves, like the tp_a curve defined for cloth in the previous section. But there are now Total Product curves for each of the two inputs—tp_a and tp_b.

─────────────────────────

[10]In contrast with the "utility hill" picture of Chapter 3, there is no "cardinal versus ordinal" problem here, since quantity has a natural cardinal (numerical) scale. We are not restricted, as we were in the case of utility, to merely ordinal comparisons of higher and lower.

FIGURE 11.5 **Output as a Function of Two Inputs**   Output *q*, measured vertically, is shown as a function of input quantities *a* and *b*. Curves *CC*, *DD*, and *EE* are contours of equal height (output) along the three-dimensional surface. The curves *C'C'*, *D'D'*, and *E'E'* are the projections of these contours in the base plane.

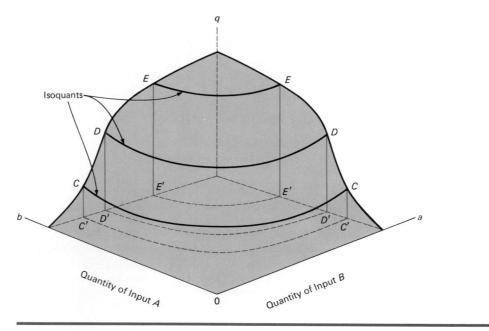

Indeed, for each input there is a family of such curves: the effect of using more cloth on the production of shirts depends on the amount of machinery available, and similarly the productivity of machinery depends on the amount of cloth used. In other words, both tp_a and tp_b depend on the amount of the *other* input. In the diagram the label $tp_a(b = b_0)$ indicates this is a Total Product curve for input *A*, with input *B* held fixed at $b = b_0$. The other labels have corresponding interpretations. Corresponding to each Total Product curve in Figure 11.7 is an Average Product curve and Marginal Product curve,[11] as in Figure 11.1.

Figure 11.8 (p. 299) shows in a different way the two families of Total Product curves. Here each curve has a form similar to the tp_a curve of Figure 11.1, as dictated by the Law of Diminishing Returns. In Panel (a) different Total Product curves for input *A* are shown for different levels of input *B*; the tp_a curve is highest when input *B* is used heavily (as in b_2); the tp_a curve is lowest when only small amounts of input *B* are used (as in b_0). Such shifts must occur if the other input is productive. Similar results apply for the other input in Panel (b).

---

[11]*Mathematical Footnote:* With two or more variable inputs, the Marginal Product of any single input such as *A* becomes a *partial* derivative:

$$mp_a \equiv \lim_{\Delta a \to 0} \frac{F(a + \Delta a,\ b) - F(a,b)}{\Delta a} \equiv \frac{\partial q}{\partial a}$$

FIGURE 11.6 **Isoquants of Output** The projections $C'C'$, $D'D'$, and $E'E'$ in the base plane of the previous diagram are shown here as isoquants (curves of equal output) in a contour map, without the overlying vertical dimension. Each isoquant is associated with a definite quantity of output (q_0, q_1, or q_2).

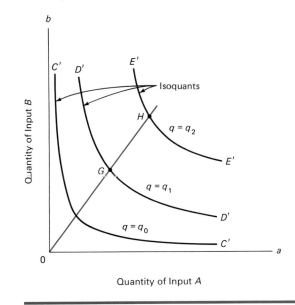

FIGURE 11.7 **Total Product Functions** Total Product curves are drawn along an output hill. The Total Product curves for input A, designated tp_a, hold constant the amount of the other input, B. However, the heights of the tp_a curves depend upon the specific constant values assumed for b in each case; similarly the tp_b curves depend on the values assumed for a.

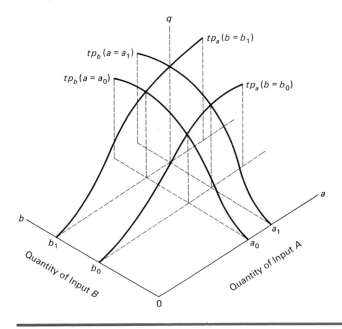

EXAMPLE 11.2 **Missouri Corn**

An agricultural experiment in Missouri reported by J. Ambrosius studied how corn yield (bushels per acre) changed as two inputs (number of plants per acre and pounds of nitrogen per acre) were varied. Reading across any single row, the table shows selected points on the Total Product curve tp_a for plants per acre—with nitrogen input per acre held constant along the row. Reading down any column, points are shown on the tp_b curve for nitrogen input—holding fixed the number of plants per acre. As expected, the entire tp_a curve shifts upward as b increases, and the tp_b curve shifts upward as a increases.

Bushels of Corn per Acre (Q)

	Number of Plants per Acre (a)				
Nitrogen per Acre (b)	9,000	12,000	15,000	18,000	21,000
0	50.6	54.2	53.5	48.5	39.2
50	78.7	85.9	88.8	87.5	81.9
100	94.4	105.3	111.9	114.2	112.2
150	97.8	112.4	122.6	128.6	130.3
200	88.9	107.1	121.0	130.6	135.9

Source: John Ambrosius, "The Effects of Experimental Size upon Optimum Rates of Nitrogen and Stand for Corn in Missouri," (1964), quoted in J. P. Doll, V. J. Rhodes, and J. G. West, *Economics of Agricultural Production, Markets, and Policy* (Homewood, Ill.: Richard D. Irwin, 1968), p. 89.

Diminishing returns apply here even to *proportionate variation* in both inputs together. For example, a doubling of both inputs from the combination 9000 and 50 to the combination 18,000 and 100 raises corn output from 78.7 to only 114.2.

The "Missouri Corn" example suggests a cause for diminishing returns to scale. Nitrogen and number of plants were varied in the experiment, but other inputs—notably, the number of acres—were held constant. Something like this will always be the case. Realistically, it is not usually possible to vary *all* inputs. So the condition that there be at least one fixed input for the Law of Diminishing Returns to hold will essentially always apply.

EXAMPLE 11.3 **Pigs**

E. O. Heady[a] reported an experiment that involved varying the amounts of corn (high in carbohydrate content) and soybean oil meal (high in protein content) fed to young pigs. The experiment was conducted on 302 pigs, carried from a weaning weight of 34 pounds to a market weight of around 250 pounds. The output measure was weight gain.

It was found that different production functions were appropriate for different weight ranges: the effects of carbohydrate versus protein upon weight gain tended to be different for younger (smaller) versus older (larger) pigs. The results obtained were as follows, where G is weight gain, P is input of soybean oilmeal (protein), and C is input of corn (carbohydrate)—all measured in pounds per pig.

$G = 1.60P^{.30}C^{.53}$, for weights from 34 to 75 pounds

FIGURE 11.8 Families of Total Product Curves

Here tp_a curves like those curves drawn along the output hill of Figure 11.7 are shown on q,a axes in Panel (a); the tp_b curves are similarly shown on q,b axes in Panel (b).

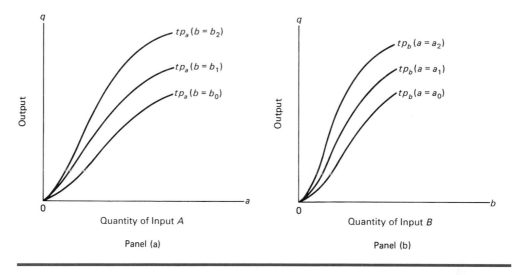

Panel (a)

Panel (b)

$G = 0.71P^{.14}C^{.77}$, for weights from 75 to 150 pounds
$G = 0.46 \, P^{.09}C^{.86}$, for weights from 150 to 250 pounds

The exponents of P and C in the different functions indicate, as is reasonable, that weight gain in young pigs responds relatively more to protein input while weight gain in older pigs responds more to carbohydrates.

COMMENT It can be shown that in functions of this "Cobb-Douglas" form there are increasing returns to scale (more than proportionate effect upon output for proportionate variation of both inputs) if the sum of the exponents exceeds unity. Constant returns to scale hold if the sum of exponents exactly equals unity, and decreasing returns to scale if the sum falls short of unity. Evidently, all three production functions here show decreasing returns to scale.

[a]E. O. Heady, "An Econometric Investigation of the Technology of Agricultural Production Functions," *Econometrica*, v. 25 (April 1957).

The Factor-Employment Decision: Geometry

Firms face two related production decisions: how much to produce and how to produce it. The question of how much to produce was answered in Chapter 6: the profit-maximizing firm chooses the level of output where Marginal Cost equals Marginal Revenue. This section answers the question of how to produce—that is, how much of each input to use. Naturally, the answer to one question affects the other.

Consider first what happens at a given level of Total Cost, say $100. Suppose the price of cloth input is $h_a = \$1$ and the hire-price of machinery is $h_b = \$2$. If the firm used only one or the other input it could afford 100 units of cloth or 50 units of machinery; total expenditures on the inputs would in either case be $100. These and other combinations of inputs A and B that $100 could buy are pictured by the *isocost* line labeled C' in Figure 11.9, with intercept C'/h_a on the horizontal axis and C'/h_b on the vertical axis.

> **DEFINITION:** An *isocost* curve shows all the combinations of two inputs that can be hired at a given total expenditure on inputs. When the hire-prices h_a and h_b are constant, the isocost curve is a straight line.

In Figure 11.9 the isocost line corresponds to a specific expenditure, or cost, level $C' = h_a a + h_b b$. A family of output isoquants q^0, q', q'', . . . are also shown in the diagram. Along the isocost line C', the highest isoquant that can be reached is q'. The firm maximizes output for a given level of costs by using input combination a', b'. Alternatively, the least expensive way of producing output q' is by using the input combination a', b': any other point on the isoquant q' lies on a higher isocost curve than point a', b'. We have thus determined the best input amounts at cost C' or output q'.

Figure 11.9 resembles the diagrams used in Chapter 4 to determine the consumer's optimum. Instead of indifference curves we have isoquants, and instead of a budget line we have an isocost line. But there is one important difference. A consumer has only a single budget line, determined by his income. But a firm is not restricted to a single isocost line. A firm *decides* how much cost to incur; the profit-maximizing level of cost is associated with the quantity that makes Marginal Cost equal Marginal Revenue. The production decision involves choosing the best level of expenditures as well as the best quantities of inputs to hire along the chosen isocost line; these decisions determine both how many shirts to produce and how to produce them.

Figure 11.10 pictures a family of isocost lines C^0, C', C'', . . . , and a family of production contours (isoquants) q^0, q', q^*, ... All the isocost lines have the same slope.

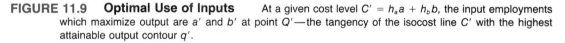

FIGURE 11.9 Optimal Use of Inputs At a given cost level $C' = h_a a + h_b b$, the input employments which maximize output are a' and b' at point Q'—the tangency of the isocost line C' with the highest attainable output contour q'.

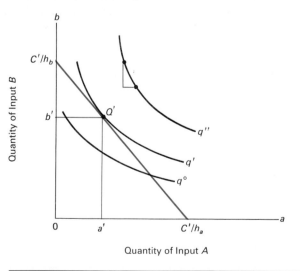

FIGURE 11.10 **Scale Expansion Path**   Along any isocost line, the tangency with an output isoquant represents the largest output attainable at that cost. Each such tangency shows the best factor proportions for that level of cost and output. The Scale Expansion Path (SEP) connects all these tangency positions.

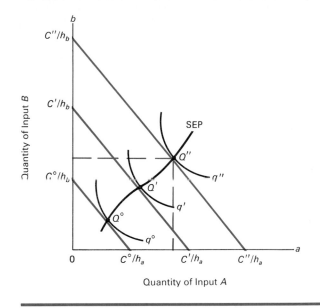

The curve drawn through the tangency points is called the Scale Expansion Path (SEP). It shows the best combination of inputs at each level of cost.

The firm will operate somewhere on the Scale Expansion Path—otherwise production would be inefficient. But exactly where? Note that output q^0 can be produced at a cost of C^0, output q' at a cost of C', and output q'' at a cost of C''. Plotting these data on $q, \$$ axes results in a Total Cost curve, C, as in Figure 11.11. To construct the Total Revenue curve we need corresponding data for output q and revenue R. But since $R \equiv Pq$, the only additional information required is the demand function, which relates price to quantity. Multiplying each quantity by the demand price determines R at each output q.[12] Putting Total Cost and Total Revenue together, we see in Figure 11.11 that profit is maximized at output q^*. Given this output, the Scale Expansion Path of Figure 11.10 tells us the best combination of inputs to use in producing it.

The Factor-Employment Decision: Analysis

We will now derive some propositions about the firm's hiring decisions that are equivalent to the previous geometrical development. From Equation (11.12) we know that profit-maximization requires that $mrp_a = h_a$ and that $mrp_b = h_b$. Since $mrp_a = MR(mp_a)$, and $mrp_b = MR(mp_b)$, these equations imply that $mp_a/mp_b = h_a/h_b$. Maximization of out-

---

[12]For a price-taking firm, of course, P is a constant and the revenue function $R \equiv Pq$ in Figure 11.11 would be a ray out of the origin.

FIGURE 11.11 **Total Revenue and Total Cost Functions**   Each point on the Scale Expansion Path of the previous diagram is associated with a particular level of cost and output. This information permits plotting the Total Cost curve C. Also, each level of output is associated with a level of revenue $R \equiv Pq$, given the firm's demand function. This information permits plotting the Total Revenue curve R. The profit-maximizing output, q^* in this diagram, also determines the firm's optimal factor employments in the preceding diagram.

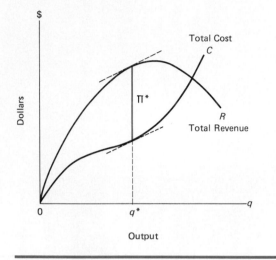

put for a given level of costs thus requires that the following Factor Balance Equation hold.[13]

$$\frac{mp_a}{h_a} = \frac{mp_b}{h_b} \qquad \text{Factor Balance Equation} \qquad (11.16)$$

That is, inputs are in balance when the Marginal Products *per dollar* spent are equal for each resource employed.

---

[13]*Mathematical Footnote:* We can use again the "method of Lagrangian multipliers" to maximize output $q = F(a,b)$ subject to a given level of cost $C = h_a a + h_b b$.

$$\begin{array}{c} Max \\ (a, b, \lambda) \end{array} \quad L = q + \lambda(h_a a + h_b b - C)$$

The first-order conditions are

$$\frac{\partial q}{\partial a} + \lambda h_a = 0, \ \frac{\partial q}{\partial b} + \lambda h_b = 0, \ \text{and} \ h_a a + h_b b - C = 0$$

It follows that

$$\frac{\partial q / \partial a}{h_a} = \frac{\partial q / \partial b}{h_b}$$

This is the Factor Balance Equation. (We omit discussion of the second-order conditions for a maximum.)

To get a feel for this condition, suppose input A is cloth and input B is labor. Let $mp_a = 6$ and $h_a = 2$; $mp_b = 18$ and $h_b = 6$. A firm that spent one less dollar on cloth would buy $1/2$ fewer square yards of cloth and produce $6/2 = 3$ fewer shirts. With this $1 in initial savings, the firm could hire $1/6$ additional hours of labor, and produce $18/6 = 3$ more shirts. Thus, if Equation (11.16) is satisfied, substituting labor for cloth or cloth for labor would not increase output for a given level of costs. If, instead, the firm chose levels of cloth and labor inputs where mp_a/h_a did not equal mp_b/h_b, the firm could increase output for the same level of cost by either using less cloth and more labor, or else by using more cloth and less labor.

Exercise 11.6

A firm's production function has the Cobb-Douglas form $q = a^{.5}b^{.5}$. Using calculus, the Marginal Product functions are then $mp_a = .5q/a$ and $mp_b = .5q/b$. The demand function is $P = 100 - q$. (Note that this firm has monopoly power in its market.) The input prices are $h_a = 4$ and $h_b = 1$. (a) Find the equation of the Scale Expansion Path. (b) Derive the Total Cost and Total Revenue equations. (c) Find the profit-maximizing output. (d) Find the optimal input employments a^* and b^*. (e) What is the magnitude of the maximized profit?

Answer: (a) The Factor Balance Equation can be written as follows:

$$\frac{.5q/a}{4} = \frac{.5q/b}{1}$$

From this it follows that $b = 4a$. This is the equation of the Scale Expansion Path. (b) Substitute the equation $b = 4a$ into the production function equation, to obtain $q = (a^{.5})(4a)^{.5} = 2a$. It follows that Total Cost $C = h_a a + h_b b = 4a + b$. Since $b = 4a$, we have $C = 8a$; and since $q = 2a$, $C = 4q$. (Notice that the cost function displays constant returns to scale.) The Total Revenue function is found by multiplying P in the demand equation by q, so that Total Revenue is $R = 100q - q^2$. (c) The Marginal Cost associated with the cost function $C = 4q$ is $MC = 4$. From the demand curve $100 - q$ we obtain $MR = 100 - 2q$. Setting MR equal to MC, the profit-maximizing output is $q^* = 48$. (d) Since $q = 2a$, it follows that $a^* = 24$. And since $b = 4a$, it follows that $b^* = 96$. (e) Total Cost is $C = 4q = 4(48) = 192$. Total Revenue is $100(48) - 48^2 = 2496$. So profit is $\Pi^* = 2304$.

EXAMPLE 11.4   Input Prices and Ocean Shipping

W. Y. Oi compared the relative input proportions used by shipping companies in Japan and Europe between 1952 and 1955. The important inputs of production were (1) capital (lease cost of vessel, or annualized construction expenses, plus ship maintenance), (2) fuel, and (3) labor (wages plus subsistence at sea). In the period studied, fuel prices were similar for all shippers. So the essential element was the ratio of labor cost versus capital cost. Labor costs were relatively cheapest for the Japanese shippers and most expensive for the continental Europeans, with the British in between.

One consequence of relatively high labor cost (or, equivalently, relatively low capital cost) is the use of fast ships. Faster ships are costlier to construct and maintain, but require less employee-hours on each trip. The table indicates that, as anticipated, the Japanese ships had the lowest and the continental European ships had the highest designed speed (measured in knots).

Median Design Speed		
	Small Ships (3000–9000 dwt)	Large Ships (over 9000 dwt)
Japanese Shippers	11.46	13.81
British Shippers	14.00	14.04
European Shippers	14.86	14.93

Source: W. Y. Oi, "The Cost of Ocean Shipping," in A. R. Ferguson *et al.*, eds., *The Economic Value of the United States Merchant Marine* (Evanston, Ill.: The Transportation Center at Northwestern University, 1961), p. 160.

We are now ready to derive the firm's demand curves for inputs A and B. First, using Equation (11.13) we have the following interpretation of the Factor Balance Equation:

$$\frac{h_a}{mp_a} = \frac{h_b}{mp_b} = MC \qquad (11.18)$$

That is, $h_a \equiv \Delta C / \Delta a$ divided by $mp_a \equiv \Delta q / \Delta a$ equals $\Delta C / \Delta q$ (Marginal Cost). Similarly, of course, for input B. When the firm uses the optimal input proportions as dictated by the Factor Balance Equation, it is equally costly to expand output by hiring a small extra amount of A, or of B, or any mixture of the two.[14]

Dividing through Equation (11.18) by MR, we have

$$\frac{MC}{MR} = \frac{h_a}{mrp_a} = \frac{h_b}{mrp_b} \qquad (11.19)$$

So when a firm maximizes profit by setting $MC = MR$, it automatically satisfies the following Factor Employment Conditions:

$$\left\{ \begin{array}{l} mrp_a = h_a \\ \\ mrp_b = h_b \end{array} \right. \qquad \begin{array}{c} \text{Factor Employment Conditions} \\ \text{(for Price-Taking Firm} \\ \text{in Input Markets)} \end{array} \qquad (11.20)$$

These equations correspond to Equation (11.12) that applied for a single variable input. But there is one important complication in the multi-input case: the Marginal Product mp_a,

---

[14]If D is some third input not actually employed at current input prices, its Marginal Product per dollar is related by an *inequality* condition to the others.

$$\frac{mp_a(a > 0)}{h_a} = \frac{mp_b(b > 0)}{h_b} > \frac{mp_d(d = 0)}{h_d}$$

For the optimal employment of D to be zero, its Marginal Product per dollar must be less than that of other inputs, even for the very first unit of D.

and therefore the Marginal Revenue Product mrp_a, may depend on the employment of the other input B. Similarly, of course, mp_b and mrp_b may depend on the amount of input A.[15]

Two inputs are said to be *complementary* if increased use of one raises the Marginal Product of the other.[16] Examples of complementary pairs are ships and sailors or land and fertilizer. If one input has no effect on the marginal product of the other, the two are said to be *independent*. Handcraftsmen and mass-production machines might be such a pair. A firm may hire both, but if so it is likely that the handcraftsmen work entirely apart from the machines so that there is no interaction between them. If increased use of one input actually reduces the Marginal Product of the other, the two are *anticomplementary*.[17] Inputs that are close substitutes for one another tend to be anticomplementary. Examples might be different grades of raw cotton for a textile firm, or male waiters versus female waitresses for a restaurant.

Figure 11.12 shows two complementary inputs A and B. The crucial point is that the mp_a curves shift up as the amount of input B increases from b_0 to b_1 to b_2; similarly, the mp_b curves shift up as A rises from a_0 to a_1 to a_2.

The Firm's Demand for Inputs: Geometry

If the firm has a single variable input, its demand curve for that input was given by (the downward-sloping part of) its Marginal Revenue Product curve mrp. However, with more than one input, matters are more complicated.

To derive the firm's demand curve for input A, suppose that at point G in Figure 11.13 the Factor Employment Conditions in Equations (11.20) are all met. At the initial hire-prices h_a^o and h_b^o, the firm hires a^o units of A and b^o units of B. Now let the hire-price of A fall from h_a^o to h_a'. If the quantity of the other input B remained unchanged, the diagram indicates that the firm would want to employ $\hat{a}$ units of input A—since that is where $mrp_a(b = b^o) = h_a'$. But suppose inputs A and B are complementary. If so, the increase from a^o to $\hat{a}$ is not the full adjustment. Increased use of input A increases the Marginal Product of input B, so mrp_b shifts up. This leads to increased use of input B, which makes input A more productive, which shifts mrp_a up, and so on. This "reverberation" process must have a limit, however. There must be some increased employment of *both* inputs that restores the equalities of Equation (11.20). The restored equalities can be expressed more explicitly as follows on the next page.

---

[15]*Mathematical Footnote:* If $q = F(a,b)$, the Marginal Products or partial derivatives $\partial q / \partial a$ and $\partial q / \partial b$ will in general both be functions of a and b. Geometrically, in Figure 11.7 we see that the slope along the Total Product curves tp_a in the a-direction ($\partial q / \partial a$) varies not only as a increases but also from one curve to the next as b increases. And similarly for the slope along the tp_b curves ($\partial q / \partial b$).

[16]*Mathematical Footnote:* The presence or absence of complementarity corresponds to the sign of the second cross-derivative of the production function. In the normal *complementary* case, $\partial(\partial q / \partial a) / \partial b \equiv \partial^2 q / \partial a \partial b$ is positive. *Independence* corresponds to a zero cross-derivative, and *anticomplementarity* to a negative cross-derivative.

[17]Anticomplementarity should be distinguished from what might be called *interference*, where the two inputs actually hamper each other. Thus, in some cases, hiring more females might actually reduce output of male workers and vice versa. Anticomplementarity means that employing more A reduces the *Marginal* Product of B; with interference, employing more A reduces the *Total* Product of input B. A firm would employ only one of two interfering inputs, to the exclusion of the other. But simultaneous employment of anticomplementary inputs is not uncommon.

FIGURE 11.12 **Complementary Inputs**   Marginal Product curves mp_a in Panel (a) are derived from the corresponding Total Product curves tp_a in Panel (a) of Figure 11.8. The mp_b curves in Panel (b) correspond similarly to the tp_b curves in Panel (b) of Figure 11.8. Only the ranges where the curves have negative slope (where the Marginal Product of each factor is a decreasing function of its own quantity) are illustrated here. The curves shift upward as the quantity of the *other* factor increases (the Marginal Product of each factor is an increasing function of the quantity of the other input). This illustrates the normal case of complementarity.

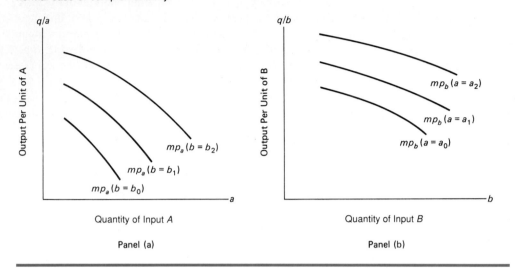

Panel (a)   Panel (b)

$$\begin{cases} mrp_a(b = b') = h'_a \\ mrp_b(a = a') = h^o_b \end{cases} \qquad (11.20')$$

Note that the hire-price of B is still at its original level; only the price of input A has changed.

The upshot is that in Figure 11.13 the demand curve d_a goes through points G and K, not through G and L. So the firm's demand curve for input A, when A and B are complementary, is flatter than the mrp_a curves.

If the inputs are *independent* rather than *complementary* in production, the interaction effect disappears. A change in the price of cloth affects the use of cloth but not the Marginal Product of machinery. The initial adjustment is the full adjustment.

What about anticomplementary inputs? You might think that if d_a is flatter than the mrp_a curves in the complementary case and is the same as the unique mrp_a curve when the inputs are independent, then d_a would be steeper than the mrp_a curves in the anticomplementary case (where an increase in one input reduces the Marginal Product of the other input). This is incorrect! In the anticomplementary as in the normal complementary case, the firm's demand curve for a factor is flatter than the mrp curves, as illustrated in Figure 11.13. [*Challenge to the student:* In Figure 11.13, after the initial adjustment from a^o to $\hat{a}$ in the anticomplementary case, do the mrp_b curves shift up or down? What is the direction of the effect upon the employment of B? Does that secondary effect shift the mrp_a curves up or down?]

FIGURE 11.13 **Firm's Demand Curve for an Input**   At the initial hire-price h_a^o the Factor Employment Conditions (11.20) are met by employments $a = a^o$ and $b = b^o$. Thus $mrp_a(b = b^o)$ equals h_a^o at G; this is one point along the firm's demand curve for input A. If the hire-price of A falls to h_a', increased employment of A to the amount $â$ would be indicated by a movement along $mrp_a(b = b^o)$ to point L. But this movement throws the employment condition for input B out of equality, if there is any complementarity (or anticomplementarity) between A and B. Restoring the equality for input B raises the Marginal Product of input A. The Factor Employment Condition can only be re-established at a point like K, where h_a' equals $mrp_a(b = b')$—with b' representing the increased amount of input B. The firm's demand curve d_a for input A is therefore flatter than the slope of the mrp_a curves.

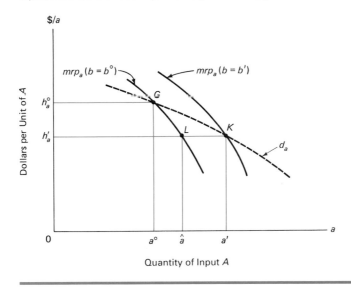

Quantity of Input A

CONCLUSION: Given complementarity or anticomplementarity between inputs, the demand curve for any input is flatter (more elastic) than the Marginal Revenue Product curves. One implication is that employment of a variable input tends to be more sensitive to price changes in the *long run,* when the amounts of the "fixed" factors can be varied.

EXAMPLE 11.5   Cost Function for Police

A cost function commonly used in empirical studies is the translog. In this function all variables are first transformed into their logarithms. Costs are then supposed to be linearly related to the sum of all outputs (the firm may produce more than one type of output), the sum of the prices of inputs, and the sum of all cross terms of input prices. Gyapong and Gyimah-Brempong[a] used this cost function for 130 Michigan State municipal police departments in 1984 and 1985. They represent output by the number of arrests for each of personal crimes (sum of murder and negligent manslaughter, rape, aggravated assault), robbery, burglary, larceny, motor vehicle theft, and arson. The inputs are sworn police officers, police employees, and police squad cars.

They find the following elasticities of input demand:

Another important result follows directly from this analysis: *factor demand curves always have negative slope*. That is, there can be no such thing as a Giffen factor. A lower hire-price h_a cannot lead to smaller employment of A, since mp_a is negatively sloped and any interaction with input B makes d_a flatter rather than steeper.

11.3 INDUSTRY DEMAND FOR INPUTS

Let us proceed from the *firm's* demand to the *industry's* demand for inputs. We begin with the assumption of a single variable input—the "short run" case.

Consider a monopolized industry (i.e., an industry composed of a single seller in the product market). Evidently, the demand by a monopolized industry for an input is identical to the demand of the monopolist firm itself.

Consider next an industry that consists of a large number of *competitive* producers in the product market. The two panels of Figure 11.14 show a typical firm and the competitive industry as a whole. Suppose that at the initial equilibrium the price of a unit of cloth is h_a^o and the price of the product, shirts, is $P = P^o$. Given the hire price h_a^o and the demand curve labeled $d_a(P = P^o)$ in Panel (a), each firm will use a^o units of cloth. For the industry as a whole, we sum these firm demand curves horizontally: total industry demand is the demand by firm one, plus the demand by firm two, and so on. We obtain the curve labeled $\Sigma d_a(P = P^o)$ in Panel (b). At the initial input price h_a^o, this horizontal sum yields total industry demand of A^o, shown by point K.

There is a complication, however, when we consider industry demand at different hire-prices. Suppose the hire-price falls to h_a'. In Panel (a) a typical firm first moves along the initial demand curve, $d_a(P = P^o)$, to use quantity $\hat{a}$ of cloth. The corresponding industrywide movement in Panel (b) would be to the aggregate employment level $\hat{A}$ (point N). But this is not the full solution. As the firms in the industry use more cloth, industry output increases, and therefore the equilibrium price of shirts falls, say to P'. And since $vmp_a = P(mp_a)$, each firm's vmp_a will shift down. So each firm's demand curve for cloth shifts down, as shown by the dashed demand curve $d_a(P = P')$.

FIGURE 11.14 **Demand for an Input: Competitive Firm and Industry, Product-Price Effect**   Panel (a) pictures a firm's demand for input A; Panel (b) pictures industry demand. At an initial hire-price h_a° and product price P°, point K in Panel (b) lies on the industry demand curve for input A. The associated firm demand curve is $d_a(P = P^\circ)$ in Panel (a). In Panel (b) the solid curve $\Sigma d_a(P = P^\circ)$ is the horizontal sum of these firm demand curves. When factor price falls to h_a', each firm aims to expand use of A from a° to $\hat{a}$—the corresponding industrywide summations in Panel (b) are A° and $\hat{A}$. But as firms use more of input A, industrywide output also rises, reducing product price to P'. Thus each firm's demand curve will fall to a position like the (dashed) curve $d_a(P = P')$ in Panel (a); the dashed summation curve in Panel (b) will move similarly. The new point on the industry factor demand curve in Panel (b) will be L. Thus, the product-price effect tends to make the industry demand curve for a factor more inelastic.

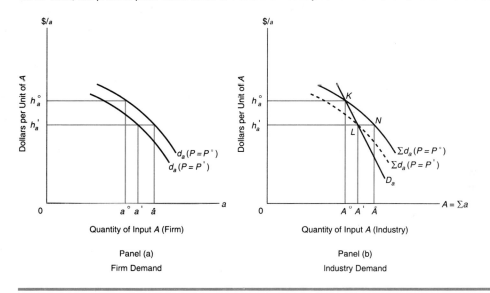

Panel (a)
Firm Demand

Panel (b)
Industry Demand

It follows that curve Σd_a, the horizontal sum of demands by firms, shifts down to the dashed line in Panel (b). The upshot is that at the hire-price h_a', a typical firm uses a' units of cloth, and total industry use of cloth is A' at point L in Panel (b). Note that the true demand D_a through points K and L is *steeper* (less elastic) than the simple horizontal sum of the firms' demand curves.

Exercise 11.7

Let the production function be $q = 2\sqrt{a}$ and let the initial price of shirts be $P = 60$. The price-taking firm's demand equation for input A was found in Exercise 11.3 to be $h_a = 60/\sqrt{a}$. Suppose the industry consists of 1000 identical such firms, and that the consumers' demand curve for shirts is given by the equation $P = 90 - Q/1000$. (a) What is the equation corresponding to the curve labeled $\Sigma d_a(P = P^\circ)$ in Figure 11.14? (b) What is the industry demand equation for input A? (c) Compare the effect on the firm and on the industry of a fall in the hire-price of A from 4 to 3.

Answer: (a) From the equation $h_a = 60/\sqrt{a}$ we obtain $a = 3600/h_a^2$. For 1000 identical firms, $A \equiv 1000a = 3,600,000/h_a^2$. (b) We now want to account for the effect of changes in h_a on the market price of the product, P. Since $Q = 1000q$, the consumers' demand curve $P = 90 - Q/1000$ can be written $P = 90 - q$. We know from Exercise 11.2 that $mp_a = 1/\sqrt{a}$. Since each price-taking firm sets $vmp_a = P(mp_a) = h_a$, we have $(90 - q)$ $(1/\sqrt{a}) = h_a$, or $a = 8100/(h_a + 2)^2$. Then, since $A \equiv 1000a$, the industry's demand equation can be written $A = 8,100,000/(h_a + 2)^2$. (c) Using the firm's demand function $a =$

$3600/h_a^2$, a decrease in h_a from 4 to 3 would cause desired employment to rise from $a^\circ = 225$ to $\hat{a} = 400$. But as industry hiring expands beyond $A^\circ = 225{,}000$, product price P falls. At the new equilibrium, using the function $a = 8100/(h_a + 2)^2$, employment is only $A = 324{,}000$ and not 400,000. (This can be confirmed with the industry demand equation.) Product price falls from $P^\circ = 60$ to $P' = 54$.

We must also consider entry and exit of firms. A decline in the price of cloth increases the profits of existing firms, and therefore attracts new shirt manufacturers into the industry. If existing firms are already operating in a region of sharply diminishing marginal returns, this price decline in cloth will not cause them to greatly increase output. The addition of new firms, however, can lead to a sharper rise in output, causing the sum of the firms' demand curves Σd_a to *rise,* and tending to make the true demand D_a *flatter.*

CONCLUSION: Industry demand for an input tends to be steeper (less elastic) than the horizontal sum of firms' demand curves so long as consumer demand for the product is downward-sloping. (This is the product-price effect.) On the other hand, if firms can easily enter or leave the industry, the industry demand for the input will tend to be flatter (more elastic) than the demand by any one firm. This is the entry-exit effect.

Finally, what if there are other variable inputs? A fall in the price of input A normally causes firms to expand output. If other inputs are complements to A, firms will use more of inputs B, C, ... Consequently, the market hire-prices h_b, h_c, . . . will rise; the price increases limit the demand for these inputs.

11.4 AN APPLICATION: MINIMUM-WAGE LAWS

The effects of minimum-wage laws in a competitive market are illustrated in Figure 11.15. The commodity is a certain grade or class of labor *(L)*, whose hire-price is the wage rate w. The competitive equilibrium wage is w_c and employment is L_c. Now suppose the government imposes a minimum wage w°, at a level higher than w_c. At wage w° the labor offered on the market is L_s but the labor demanded is only L_d. So the unemployment gap at the legal wage is the quantity BC or $L_s - L_d$. However, the reduction in employment due to the wage floor is the somewhat smaller amount FE or $L_c - L_d$. Thus, a minimum wage imposed on a competitive market reduces employment and causes an even larger degree of *unemployment*—provided only that the minimum wage is effective, that is, at a level higher than the pre-existing market equilibrium wage.

Exercise 11.8

Suppose the demand and supply functions for labor are $D = 240 - 2w$, and $S = -60 + 80w$, where w is the wage rate. (a) What is the equilibrium wage and the level of employment? (b) Suppose the minimum wage is set to \$5.00 per hour. Determine the level of unemployment, and the decline in employment.

Answer: Solving the equation $240 - 2w = -60 + 80w$ we obtain $w = 3.66$. The level of employment is found by substituting 3.66 for w in either the demand or supply equation; we obtain $D = S = 233$. (b) With a minimum wage of 5.00, $D = 240 - 2(5) = 230$. $S = -60 + 80(5) = 340$. Unemployment is therefore $340 - 230 = 110$. Employment fell from 233 to 230, or by 3.

FIGURE 11.15   Minimum Wage   The competitive equilibrium point E is associated with wage w_c and employment L_c. A wage floor or minimum wage at the level $w°$ reduces employment to L_d. The quantity FE is the reduction in employment. At the higher wage L_s units of labor seek employment, so the perceived "unemployment gap" is the larger quantity BC.

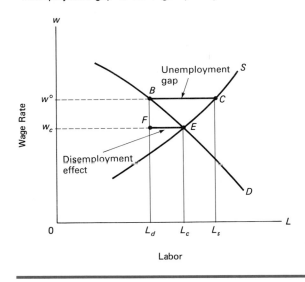

It is important to remember that there is a spectrum of labor skill and quality. Some workers will already be earning more than the minimum wage and others less. So we would expect minimum-wage laws to have quite different effects on high-wage and low-wage workers. Low-skilled (low-wage) workers would be affected as in Figure 11.15. Their wage rates would rise, but some previously employed workers would lose their jobs. For higher-skilled workers, in contrast, the equilibrium wage is likely to be already above the minimum wage and no direct effect is to be expected.

EXAMPLE 11.6   Minimum-Wage Legislation

As of 1989, minimum-wage laws in the United States, unlike those of most other advanced nations, specify fixed dollar wage rates that are uniform over the entire country. There are no differentials on the basis of age or experience, though some states impose higher minimum wages than the federal minimum. In contrast, most European countries have youth differentials. In Great Britain, for example, the youth minimum is only about 30 percent of the adult minimum. In Canada, minimum wage schedules are set by the provinces rather than by the central government, which automatically allows for differentials among geographical regions. The absence of differentials in the United States leads us to expect that the brunt of any unemployment effects of minimum wage laws will be suffered by low-wage regions like the South and by low-wage age groups such as youthful workers.

The effects upon youth have been examined by a number of researchers. A study by Y. Brozen[a] found that successive increases in the legal minimum wage indeed raised the teenage unemployment rate. But as productivity and inflation progressed over time, the equilibrium wage for teenagers tended to "catch up" with the legally fixed minimum so as to erode the disemployment effect, until the next round of minimum-wage legislation began the cycle over again.

From 1954 to 1968, a statistical regression analysis by T. G. Moore allowed not only for the level of the minimum wage but also for coverage of the labor force (since, over time, both have tended to increase). The table shows the elasticities of the unemployment rate for various age-sex groups in response to changes in minimum wage coverage and level.

Effect of Minimum Wage upon Younger Age-Group Unemployment (Elasticities)

Rate of Unemployment	Employed Workers Covered by Minimum Wage	Minimum Wages as Proportion of Hourly Earnings
Nonwhites, 16–19	0.26	1.76
Whites, 16–19	0.08	0.58
Males, 16–19	0.08	0.62
Females, 16–19	0.17	0.74
Males, 20–24	0.06	0.05

Source: T. G. Moore, "The Effect of Minimum Wages on Teenage Unemployment Rates," *Journal of Political Economy,* v. 79 (July/August 1971), p. 901.

The data in the table may be interpreted as follows, using the first row as an example. The unemployment rate of nonwhites aged 16 to 19 (1) increased by 0.26 percent for each percent rise in the coverage of the minimum-wage law, and (2) increased by 1.76 percent for each percent increase in the ratio of the legal minimum wage to the average hourly earnings of production workers in private nonagricultural employment. Note that when it comes to unemployment, minimum wage laws bear more heavily upon young nonwhites than young whites, and upon young females more than young males. In contrast, males aged 20 to 24, above the teenage category, were not substantially affected by the minimum-wage legislation.

Using a somewhat different methodology, Mikhail S. Bernstam and Peter L. Swan[b] studied white and black teenagers from 1960 to 1980. They obtained employment elasticities, for changes in minimum wage coverage of −0.26 for whites and −2.14 for nonwhites. That is, a 1 percent increase in coverage would decrease black teenage employment by over 2 percent, but would decrease white teenage employment by only about one-fourth of a percent. The corresponding figures for minimum-wage levels were −0.99 for blacks and −0.13 for whites. Once again, the much heavier impact upon nonwhites is evident. As an interesting point, Bernstam and Swan also found a strong association between the minimum wage laws and the explosive growth of illegitimate births among teenage girls.

COMMENT   These studies provide solid confirmation for the predictions of the competitive model of Figure 11.15.

[a]Y. Brozen, "The Effect of Statutory Minimum Wage Increases on Teen-Age Unemployment," *Journal of Law and Economics,* v. 12 (April 1969).

[b]Mikhail S. Bernstam and Peter L. Swan, "The State as the Marriage Partner of Last Resort: New Findings on Minimum Wage, Youth Joblessness, Welfare, and Single Motherhood in the United States, 1960–1980," Hoover Institution Working Papers in Economics E-86-82 (October 1986).

Regardless of their economic effects, minimum-wage laws have been politically popular. For some explanation, we might look at who is affected and how. Note first that the supposed "beneficiaries"—very low-wage workers previously receiving less than the minimum wage, who are largely teenagers and minorities—may end up worse off. While many of them will remain employed and may receive a substantial wage increase, a good proportion are likely to become unemployed; so for them the effect is mixed. The strongest political pressure in the United States for higher minimum wages comes not from these beneficiaries but from organized labor, in particular the AFL-CIO. This may seem puzzling; unionized employees will not get any direct benefit, since union wages are far higher than the legislated minimum. But a higher minimum wage raises the employer's cost of hiring unskilled workers, thus tending to increase *relative* demand for the skilled workers represented by the AFL-CIO.

11.5 AN APPLICATION: PROTECTION FROM IMPORTS

Suppose there are two competitive industries in the economy, say farming and manufacturing. Let labor be mobile between these two industries, while agricultural land is specific to farming. Consider the effects of a tariff or a quota on manufactured imports. Since this protection from imports shifts the supply curve of manufactured goods to the left, the domestic price of manufactured goods will rise.

What happens to the hire-price of labor? We care here about the purchasing power of a worker, not the nominal wage. The amount of land used in farming is fixed. Because of import protection, less labor will be used in farming and more in manufacturing. This means that the marginal product of labor in farming has increased, and the marginal product of labor in manufacturing has decreased. From equations (11.9) and (11.10) we know that the marginal product of labor in manufacturing equals the hire-price of labor divided by the price of manufactured goods. Thus, import protection allows an hour of labor to purchase less manufactured goods. The increase in the marginal product of labor in farming means that an hour of labor in farming will buy more farm goods. In short, the wages from an hour of labor buy more food and less manufactured goods than before. Whether workers are better or worse off depends, in part, on their taste for food versus manufactured goods.

What about land? With less labor used in farming, the marginal product of land should have decreased (since land and labor are complements). Thus, we would expect the hire price of land to decline.

SUMMARY

This chapter deals with the demand for inputs used in production. A key theme is that the optimal *output* decision and the optimal *input* decision are connected rather than independent choices.

The Factor Employment Condition for any variable input A, in most general form, is Marginal Input Cost of A = Marginal Revenue Product of A. That is, the firm operates where the cost of hiring one more unit is equal to the revenue it generates. If the firm is a price-taker in the product market, then vmp_a (Value of the Marginal Product) can be substituted for mrp_a on the right-hand side of the Factor Employment Condition.

If the firm is a price-taker in the input market, its demand curve for a single input A is simply the downward-sloping branch of the mrp_a curve. Since $mrp_a \equiv MR(mp_a)$, input demand depends both on the marginal physical productivity of the input (mp_a) and on the value to the firm of the additional output produced (MR).

If there are two variable inputs A and B, the Factor Employment Conditions (for a firm that is a price-taker in the input market) are

$$\begin{cases} h_a = mrp_a \\ \\ h_b = mrp_b \end{cases}$$

Inputs are called *complementary* if increased use of either raises the Marginal Product of the other. Inputs are *anticomplementary* if the reverse holds. Complementarity is the normal case. (If there is no interdependence, the inputs are called *independent* in production.) Both complementarity and anticomplementarity make the firm's demand curve for either input more elastic.

The competitive industry's demand for an input is the sum of the demands of the firms in the industry. But there are several complications. As the hire-price h_a falls, the industry will employ more A and thus normally also expand output. This effect will drive down the product price P, and therefore reduce somewhat the industry response to changes in h_a (that is, make the industry demand for A more inelastic). But a reduction in h_a also makes the industry more profitable and thus induces *entry*. The entry-exit effect cuts in the opposite direction and tends to make the industry demand for an input more elastic.

Demand for input A tends to be greater (1) where the employers are product-market competitors rather than monopolists, (2) where the physical Marginal Product mp_a is high, and (3) where the additional output produced by employing A is highly valued by consumers. Demand for A tends to be *more elastic* (1) the more elastic is the consumers' demand for the output, (2) the less powerfully the Law of Diminishing Returns operates as employment of A increases, (3) the greater the normal productive interdependence (complementarity) between A and other inputs, and (4) the greater the exit-entry effect as the hire-price h_a changes.

QUESTIONS

For Review

1. Distinguish the *productivity* and the *revenue* considerations involved in a firm's demand for an input.
*2. a. Does the curve of Marginal Revenue Product for input A, mrp_a, necessarily lie below (to the left of) the curve of Value of the Marginal Product, vmp_a? Explain.
   b. Which is the firm's demand curve for input A?
3. Why is $mrp_a = h_a$ the Factor Employment Condition for a price-taking firm in the *input* market? What if the firm is not a price-taker in the *product* market? Is this condition sufficient, or are there other subsidiary conditions that must be met?

*The answers to starred questions appear at the end of the book.

*4. a. Is it ever rational to employ so much of an input as to be in the region of diminishing marginal returns?
  b. In the region of diminishing average returns?
  c. In the region of diminishing total returns?

*5. With two inputs A and B, explain why the conditions $mrp_a = h_a$ and $mrp_b - h_b$ lead to both the choice of optimal input proportions and to the optimal scale of output.

*6. a. With two factors of production, is the slope of the output isoquant equal (in absolute value) to the ratio of the Marginal Products? Explain.
  b. Interpret the absolute slope of the *isocost* line as a ratio.

  7. Explain why, if two inputs are complementary, the demand curve for either is flatter than the Marginal Revenue Product curves. What if the inputs are anticomplementary?

*8. Is the input demand curve of a competitive industry necessarily less elastic than the summation of the demand curves of the separate firms?

*9, True or false (explain in each case)? The economy-wide demand curve for input A will be more elastic:
  a. The more elastic is consumer demand for products that use input A.
  b. The weaker is the operation of the Law of Diminishing Returns as employment of A increases.
  c. The more elastic is the *supply* of inputs complementary to A.

For Further Thought and Discussion

*1. a. Are there examples in this text providing empirical support for the Laws of Diminishing Marginal and Average Returns?
  b. Would you expect to find any exceptions?

*2. Why might a firm at a given moment hire positive amounts of two inputs that are anticomplementary?

  3. Would you expect, typically, that combinations of different classes of labor (like skilled versus unskilled) are more or less likely to be complementary—in comparison with combinations of labor and machines?

  4. Assuming that labor organizations were interested only in the selfish gains of their members, would you expect them to oppose immigration?

*5. Historically, wages in the United States have been high relative to wages elsewhere. Does the chapter shed light on this phenomenon? Explain.

*6. Would you expect technological progress to raise wage rates, on the average?

  7. How might a consumer boycott of grapes or lettuce work to the detriment of farm workers who specialize in farms raising these crops?

  8. A minimum-wage law raises firms' *relative* demand for skilled labor versus unskilled. Would it tend to raise the *absolute* demand for skilled labor, if skilled and unskilled are complementary? If they are anticomplementary? How does your answer bear upon the attitudes of trade unions toward minimum-wage laws?

CHAPTER 12

RESOURCE SUPPLY AND FACTOR-MARKET EQUILIBRIUM

EXAMPLES

T his chapter completes our trip around the circuit of economic activity (see Figure 1.1). We looked at the demand and supply of consumption goods (the *product market*) in Chapters 3 through 10. Chapter 11 analyzed firms' demands for inputs. This chapter examines the supply of inputs by resource-owners, and then brings supply and demand together to study equilibrium in the *input market* (the market for factors of production).

12.1 THE OPTIMUM OF THE RESOURCE-OWNER

In the analysis of consumption and demand in Chapter 4, the individual was supposed to have a given income I. But income does not come out of thin air. A person earns income by permitting firms to hire the resources he or she owns.

As owner of a resource, an individual must choose between offering it for hire in the factor market or retaining it for his own nonmarket or *reservation* uses. For example, a person must choose between using his time for earning income or for leisure. The word *leisure* suggests the person is just lazing away his time. But leisure to the economist might well include productive activities undertaken outside the market. An important example is homemaking, which produces services that would be costly to buy on the market.

Figure 12.1 shows an individual's indifference curve between income I and leisure R. The arrows for preference directions indicate that income and leisure are both "goods" rather than "bads." Before any exchange takes place, the individual with endowment at E has $\overline{R}$ units of leisure (24 hours per day, let us say) and $\overline{I}$ units (dollars) of non-labor income (from property earnings, perhaps). The bound on the right at $\overline{R} = 24$ says that the individual cannot obtain more than 24 hours of leisure a day; the bound on the left at $\overline{R} = 0$ says that the individual cannot sell more than 24 hours a day of labor.

It is sometimes thought that a job-holder has no choice over the number of hours he works: an 8-hour day requires 8 hours of work, no more and no less. But that is not always true. People can find a job requiring more or fewer hours, or they can moonlight. They can spend time at home reading memos they didn't have time to read at work, or preparing for the next day's meeting. And eight hours at the office does not mean eight hours of work. People can and do engage in personal business on company time, or they can gossip around the water fountain. More generally, then, the number of hours a person works can be quite variable.

Returning to Figure 12.1, the opportunity set is the shaded area lying below the budget line EK. Starting from E, a person who sells an hour of labor (thereby sacrificing an hour of leisure) receives an hourly wage h_L. If the individual is a price-taker with respect to the

List of Notation

ARI	Average resource income	MRS_R	Marginal rate of substitution in
h_L	Hire price of labor = wage rate		resource supply
I	Income	*PEP*	Price expansion path
MRI	Marginal resource income	*R*	Leisure
mrp	Marginal revenue product	*TRI*	Total Resource Income

FIGURE 12.1 **Optimum of the Resource-Owner**   The resource-owner's preferences, as indicated by indifference curves $U_0, U_1, U_2, \ldots$, show that income I and reservation uses (or "leisure") R are both goods. The person with endowment at E has initial income I and leisure $\bar{R}$. The slope of the budget line EK indicates the hire-price or wage at which the individual can obtain income by sacrificing leisure. The tangency point G^* is the resource-owner's optimum position.

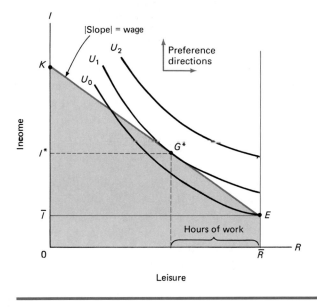

wage rate, the budget line has constant slope $\Delta I / \Delta R = -h_L$.[1] The wage rate h_L can be regarded either as the price to the employer of an hour of labor or the price to the worker of an hour of leisure. The individual's resource-employment optimum (optimal choice of income and leisure) is at the tangency position G^* in Figure 12.1. (Note the similarity between this solution and the optimum of the consumer analyzed in Chapter 4 and pictured in Figure 4.1.)

The equation of the budget line is

$$h_L R + I = h_L \bar{R} + \bar{I} \tag{12.1}$$

The left-hand side of this equation tells us that the value of the individual's endowment is the market value of the leisure "purchased" (by not working), $h_L R$, plus income I. Alternatively, this relation can be formulated in terms of labor or working hours L rather than leisure hours R, where by definition $L \equiv \bar{R} - R$. Subtracting $h_L R$ from both sides of Equation (12.1) yields

$$\bar{I} + h_L L = I \tag{12.1'}$$

---

[1]More explicitly, the slope of the budget line might be expressed as $-h_L/P_I$, where P_I is the price of a unit of income. But P_I is by definition unity, since income is measured in units of *numeraire* (in this case, dollars).

In this form, the budget equation says that the person's income I consists of property earnings $\bar{I}$ plus labor earnings $h_L L$.

At the optimum point G^* two conditions must hold: (1) the resource-owner is on the boundary of his opportunity set and does not throw away either income or leisure and (2) the indifference curve at G^* has the same slope as the budget line. (A person's marginal willingness to trade leisure for income equals the wage the market pays for each unit of time he works.)

The first condition says that the equation of the budget line, in the form either of Equations (12.1) or (12.1′), must hold. Turning to the second condition, the absolute value of the slope of the budget line is h_L. The slope of the indifference curve is called the *Marginal Rate of Substitution in Resource Supply (MRS$_R$)*. This represents the number of units of income (e.g., the number of dollars) the individual is willing to give up per unit increase of leisure R. Thus, the second condition is

$$MRS_R = h_L \tag{12.2}$$

The Marginal Rate of Substitution in Resource Supply can also be interpreted as the ratio of the *Marginal Utilities* of leisure and income—$MRS_R \equiv MU_R/MU_I$. So Equation (12.2) can equivalently be written as follows:[2]

$$\frac{MU_R}{MU_I} = h_L \tag{12.2′}$$

The convex curvature of the indifference curves of Figure 12.1 (the curve gets flatter as we move to the right) is needed to explain why individuals typically choose to have both money income as well as leisure, or why people normally work less than twenty-four hours

---

[2]*Mathematical Footnote:* Using the method of Lagrangian multipliers, the optimization problem of the resource-owner can be expressed as follows:

$$\underset{(I, R, \lambda)}{\text{Max}} \quad K = U(I, R) + \lambda(h_L R + I - h_L \bar{R} - \bar{I})$$

Then

$$\frac{\partial K}{\partial I} = \frac{\partial U}{\partial I} + \lambda = 0$$

$$\frac{\partial K}{\partial R} = \frac{\partial U}{\partial R} + \lambda h_L = 0$$

$$\frac{\partial K}{\partial \lambda} = h_L R + I - h_L \bar{R} - \bar{I} = 0$$

Eliminating λ in the first two equations

$$\frac{\partial U / \partial R}{\partial U / \partial I} = h_L$$

This is the form of (12.2′). And (12.2) follows immediately since

$$MRS_R \equiv -dI/dR \equiv \frac{\partial U / \partial R}{\partial U / \partial I}$$

FIGURE 12.2 Income Expansion Path As endowed income $\bar{I}$ rises, with the hire-price (wage) held constant, the budget line shifts upward parallel to itself. If I and R are both normal (superior) goods, the successive optimum positions G^o, G', G'', . . . show that more income and more leisure will be chosen. Thus, the Income Expansion Path (IEP) has positive slope.

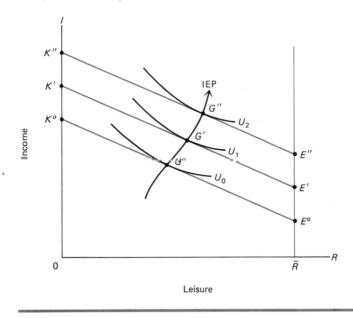

a day, but more than zero per day. Of course, an individual who has abundant property income (has very large $\bar{I}$) may choose not to work at all. Charles Darwin, the founder of evolutionary theory, received such a large inheritance from his father and dowry from his wife that he never worked for pay in his life. In terms of the geometry, an individual would prefer such a "corner solution" if his indifference curve U_0 in Figure 12.1 were steeper than the budget line EK even at the endowment position E.[3]

Exercise 12.1

An individual is endowed with $\bar{R} = 24$ hours of leisure per day and $\bar{I} = 120$ units of income (dollars) per day. His Marginal Rate of Substitution in Resource Supply is $MRS_R = I/R$. His wage rate is $h_L = 10$. How many hours of labor will he supply, and what will be his income from labor?

Answer: His budget constraint in the form of Equation (12.1) is $10R + I = 10(24) + 120 = 360$. Using (12.2), he will set $MRS_R = I/R = h_L = 10$. The solution is $R^* = 18, I^* = 180$. Thus, he works $24 - 18 = 6$ hours per day and earns $6(\$10) = \$60$ per day from labor.

Let us now consider how the optimum of the resource-owner is affected when (1) endowed (non-labor) income $\bar{I}$ varies, and (2) the hire-price (wage) h_L changes.

Figure 12.2 shows increases in property income as shifting the budget line successively upward from E^oK^o to $E'K'$ to $E''K''$. Both income I and leisure R are, it is reasonable to

[3]The analytical condition for a corner solution is that $MRS_R > h_L$ at $R = \bar{R}$.

assume, normal (or superior) goods to the resource-owner. If so, an individual who receives a large inheritance would choose to have both more income to spend on consumption goods, *and* more leisure. The result is a positively sloped Income Expansion Path (IEP).

Figure 12.3 shows the effect of an increase in the wage rate h_L, or a rise in the price of leisure. A higher wage rate is associated with a steeper budget line, pivoted around the endowment position E. The *Price Expansion Path* (PEP) consists of all points of tangency between the budget lines and indifference curves; in the figure some of these points are H^o, H', and H''. Each point describes the individual's utility-maximizing bundle at a different wage rate. For relatively low wage rates the negative slope of the Price Expansion Path indicates that as the wage rate rises an individual would offer more labor (i.e., he will purchase less leisure). But for high wage rates, it is quite possible for the Price Expansion Path to have a positive slope. In Figure 12.3, above point H' a higher wage leads the individual to work *less*.

We saw in Chapter 4 that the substitution effect of a price change (which holds utility constant) always makes a rise in price lead to a fall in quantity purchased. In this case, an increase in the wage rate (say in a lawyer's hourly billing rate) is a rise in the opportunity cost of leisure (each round of golf reduces the lawyer's income by $200 instead of $150), so he purchases less leisure; that is, he works more. So the substitution effect says that the higher the wage, the greater the hours worked.

But there also is an income effect of the increase in the lawyer's hourly billing rate. Since the individual sells labor, an increase in the wage rate makes him richer (he can, for example, afford to buy that new car after fewer hours of work.) And since leisure is a normal

FIGURE 12.3 **Price Expansion Path**   As the wage or hire-price h_L increases, the budget line rotates up around E. In an initial range where the wage rate is still low, increases in h_L will lead to choice of more income but less leisure (that is, more labor will be offered). Thus, the Price Expansion Path (PEP) has negative slope. A range *may* be reached where further increases in h_L lead to less labor being offered—the PEP curve may "bend backward" for sufficiently high h_L.

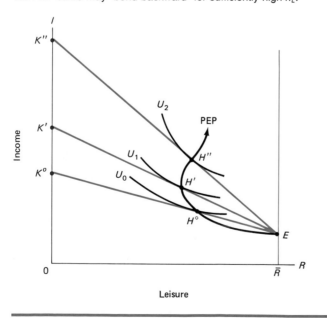

good, enrichment would lead to greater purchases of leisure. Thus, the income and substitution effects of a price (wage) change normally act in opposite directions. (This contrasts with the demand for consumption goods analyzed in Chapter 4, where the substitution effect and the income effect of a price change were normally reinforcing.)

Not only does the income effect act in opposition to the substitution effect in the labor-supply decision, but the magnitude of the income effect associated with a change in the wage rate is relatively large. The reason is the contrast between *diversification in consumption* and *specialization in production*. Since the consumer generally buys a wide variety of products, a rise in the price of any single commodity is not likely to impoverish him substantially. But in terms of input supply, there is one single price that is most important to the lawyer—the wage rate for lawyers. An increase in this wage will typically lead to a big increase in the individual's income.

Nevertheless, at very low wage rates the substitution effect *must always* be more powerful than the income effect. This may be understood as follows. Since the slope of the indifference curve is negative at the endowment position E, there is some wage rate so low that the individual would not work at all. For wage rates only slightly above this, the income effect of a wage change must be very small. The enrichment due to a wage increase is expressed as $L(\Delta h_L)$, where Δh_L is the wage increment and L is the hours worked. A change in the wage rate does not substantially enrich a person who works few hours. Only in the upper regions of the Price Expansion Path is the number of working hours big enough to make the enrichment $L(\Delta h_L)$ substantial, which it has to be to overcome the substitution effect. It follows from this discussion that the Price Expansion Path of Figure 12.3 *must*, starting from the endowment point E, initially move up and to the left. Beyond a certain point, it *may* curve back up and to the right.

CONCLUSION: The income and substitution effects of a change in hire-price h_L work in opposite directions. At low hire-prices the substitution effect must dominate, meaning that the person will choose to work more hours as h_L rises. However, for sufficiently high h_L the income effect may dominate, meaning that as the wage rises the individual chooses to work less.

EXAMPLE 12.1 Retirement Decisions

In recent years the proportion of elderly people who work or seek employment has declined markedly. Of white males aged 65 and over, 46.5 percent participated in the labor force in 1948 but only 22.5 percent in 1974. For non-white males the decline was from 50.3 percent to 21.7 percent.[a] To explain these changes, Michael J. Boskin[b] examined the retirement decisions of white married males in 1968 who were 61 to 65 years old.

The statistical evidence for the period 1968 to 1972 indicated that an increase of $1000 in an elderly person's annual income from assets (equivalent to an upward shift of the endowment point E in Figure 12.2) increased the probability of retirement by 15 percent. An increase of $1000 in net earnings from work (equivalent to a clockwise rotation of the budget line in Figure 12.3) reduced the probability of retirement by about 60 percent. Thus, the income and substitution effects were in the directions anticipated.

Boskin was particularly interested in the effect of Social Security benefits upon these retirement decisions. He found that a $1000 increase in these benefits more than doubled the probability of retirement. This is the effect economic theory predicts, since increased Social Security benefits, like increased income from assets, shifts the endowment point E upward as in Figure 12.2. The Social Security effect, however, was surprisingly large.

The main reason appears to be that receiving Social Security payments limits the income that an individual can earn from working. During the period in question, any income from employment earned by Social Security recipients fell into four ranges. First, there was an initial low level of working income that the recipient could retain without penalty. Above that exemption, the next bracket of earned income was in effect taxed at 50 percent (by a corresponding reduction in Social Security benefits). Above the 50 percent bracket, in the next higher bracket, earned income was taxed at 100 percent. In the top bracket income earned could again be fully retained, since no Social Security benefits remain to be reduced as earnings increase. The key point is that, for many people, an increase in Social Security benefits would be largely taxed away unless they retired (or, at any rate, worked considerably less than before). Since eligibility for increased Social Security benefits depended heavily on the individual not working, increases in benefits encouraged retirement.

[a]From *Manpower Report of the President, 1975* (Washington, D.C.: U.S. Government Printing Office).
[b]Michael J. Boskin, "Social Security and Retirement Decisions," *Economic Inquiry*, v. 15 (January 1977).

12.2 AN APPLICATION: THE INCENTIVE EFFECTS OF WELFARE

Programs to help the poor tend to reduce the incentive to work. Figure 12.4 illustrates a simplified welfare system in which the government guarantees a minimum income of, say, $6000 per year. If an individual's earnings are below this, government welfare payments make up the difference. Notice that this means government benefits are lost, dollar for dollar, for any earnings by the individual up to $6,000.

In the absence of a welfare system the individual's optimum in the diagram would be the tangency point G along the budget line EK. He earns, say, $7,000 per year and spends 115 days a year at leisure (he works $365 - 115 = 250$ days). But if he is guaranteed $6,000 in welfare benefits, the budget line becomes the kinked line MLK. Given the shape of this person's indifference curves, the optimum is now at M, where he does not work at all. (By not working he sacrifices $1,000 of income, but he values the increased leisure at more than the lost income.)

EXAMPLE 12.2 **Interwar Unemployment in Britain**

Between World Wars I and II, British economists were puzzled by the high levels of unemployment in their country (never below 9.5 percent in the period 1921–38). These unemployment rates were much higher than those observed before World War I. (This apparent disequilibrium in markets promoted the development of Keynesian macroeconomic theories in Britain during this period.) A later re-evaluation by the economists D. K. Benjamin and L. A. Kochin[a] suggests that the explanation may have been the liberalization of Britain's unemployment benefits—the *dole*.

After World War I, unemployment compensation was extended to many more workers, payments were increased, and the waiting period was shortened. Using data on the ratio of unemployment benefits to wages, and adjusting for fluctuations in general business conditions, Benjamin and Kochin estimated that the liberalization raised the unemployment rate

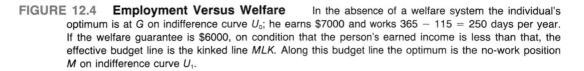

FIGURE 12.4 **Employment Versus Welfare** In the absence of a welfare system the individual's optimum is at G on indifference curve U_0; he earns \$7000 and works $365 - 115 = 250$ days per year. If the welfare guarantee is \$6000, on condition that the person's earned income is less than that, the effective budget line is the kinked line MLK. Along this budget line the optimum is the no-work position M on indifference curve U_1.

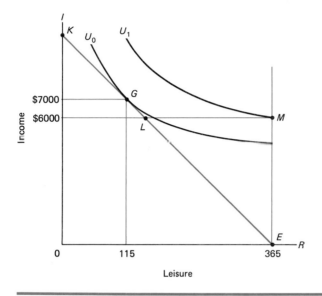

by five to eight percentage points. If unemployment benefits had been no more generous than in the prewar years, they claimed, unemployment in Britain would have been at historically normal levels throughout most of the interwar period.

[a] D. K. Benjamin and L. A. Kochin, "Searching for an Explanation of Unemployment in Interwar Britain," *Journal of Political Economy*, v. 87 (June 1979).

12.3 RESOURCE SUPPLY TO THE MARKET AND EQUILIBRIUM IN THE MARKET FOR INPUTS

Supply and Demand for Labor

The data from the Price Expansion Path (PEP) of Figure 12.3 could be plotted in a separate diagram on R, h_L axes as the individual's demand curve for leisure. It is more usual, however, to present the data on L, h_L axes as the individual's supply curve for labor.

Figure 12.5 shows such an individual supply curve s_L. The hire-prices h_L°, h_L', and h_L'' in Figure 12.5 correspond respectively to the slopes of the budget lines EK°, EK', and EK'' in Figure 12.3. The earlier diagram shows that for low wage rates the Price Expansion Path curves upward and to the left: an increased wage elicits increased labor-hours. Above this range, however, the PEP *may* (as shown in Figure 12.3) curve back up and to the right. That is, an increase in wages may *reduce* the amount of labor supplied. If so, in this range

FIGURE 12.5

Backward-Bending Supply Curve of Labor The supply curve of labor shown here, s_L, has normal positive slope for wage rates up to h'_L but "bends backward" above that wage.

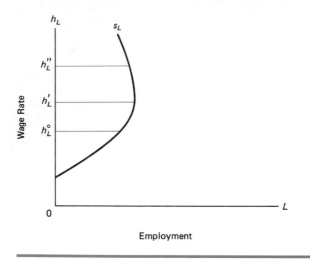

the labor supply curve is said to be backward-bending. In Figure 12.5 such a backward-bending segment is shown for hire-prices above h'_L.

EXAMPLE 12.3   **The Supply of Nursing Service**

Charles Link and Russell Settle[a] examined the labor supply of married professional nurses, using 1970 Census data. They found that the labor supply curve bent backwards, with the bend occurring (depending on race, age, and personal characteristics) at after-tax wage rates between $2.20 and $3.00 in 1970 dollars (between $7.10 and $9.60 in 1989 dollars). Furthermore, most individuals were actually in the backward-bending range. The data also showed that another powerful influence upon nurses' labor supply decisions was husband's income. Among married white registered nurses, for example, a $1 increase in the husband's wage caused the wife to work 140 to 252 fewer hours a year.

Programs such as Medicare and Medicaid have greatly increased the demand for nurses, tending to drive up wage rates. But, the data indicate, at higher wage rates currently employed nurses will supply fewer hours. What helps remedy the situation, however, is that higher wages in nursing will tend to attract newcomers into the nursing profession.

[a]Charles Link and Russell Settle, "Wage Incentives and Married Professional Nurses: A Case of Backward-Bending Supply?" *Economic Inquiry*, v. 19 (January 1981).

Figure 12.6 shows the overall market supply of labor S_L; this is obtained by horizontally summing the supply curves s_L of individuals. Note that even if many or indeed all of the *individual* supply curves bend backward, as in Figure 12.5, the *market* supply curve need not have this shape. At higher wages the existing workers in any industry may work fewer

FIGURE 12.6 Equilibrium in the Labor Market The intersection of the aggregate demand curve for labor D_L and the aggregate supply curve of labor S_L determines the equilibrium wage rate h_L^* and the level of market employment L^*.

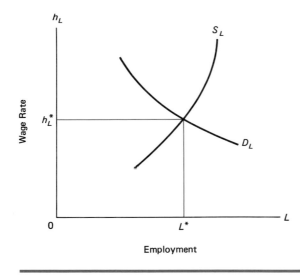

hours, but new workers will be attracted from other industries or from leisure (from nonmarket employments). In fact, the supply of a particular type of labor to a *single industry* will almost never be backward-bending. Imagine, for example, that the wages of supermarket cashiers rise. Existing cashiers may now choose to work fewer hours, but very likely a flood of new applicants will be attracted from other jobs.

EXAMPLE 12.4 Braceros and the Supply of "Stoop Labor"

From 1953 to 1964 the supply of agricultural workers in the United States was supplemented by foreign contract workers from Mexico, known as *braceros*. There was strong domestic political opposition to the bracero program, but employers contended that even at higher wages they could not attract American workers willing to do the "stoop labor" in the fields. In effect, the employers were arguing, the supply curve of American "stoop labor" was vertical or even backward-bending.

Despite these arguments the bracero program was terminated in 1965. The supply curve of labor to the industry proved not to be backward-bending: growers found it possible to attract American labor, though at a much higher wage. A study by Donald E. Wise[a] indicated that for California winter melons, abolition of the bracero program led to a 67 percent increase in the wage rate, a 262 percent increase in employment of American workers (but a 22 percent reduction in *total* employment, since braceros were no longer used), and a 23 percent reduction of output.

[a]Donald E. Wise, "The Effect of the Bracero on Agricultural Production in California," *Economic Inquiry*, v. 12 (December 1974).

EXAMPLE 12.5   **Who Are the Entrepreneurs?**

A person may decide to be self-employed rather than to work for someone else. David S. Evans and Linda S. Leighton[a] studied which individuals were most likely to go into business for themselves by analyzing data from the National Longitudinal Survey of Young Men, which contains detailed information on a sample of almost 4,000 white men who were between the ages of 14 and 24 in 1966, and who were surveyed 12 times between 1966 and 1981.

In 1980, 17.8 percent of labor force participants were self-employed; 13 percent of the self-employed switched that year from self-employment to working for wages. Of all labor force participants, 4 percent switched from being employees to being self-employed; 2.7 percent made the switch in the other direction. New entrepreneurs are not only the young. As the following table shows, the probability of starting a business is rather independent of age after age 25.

New Entrepreneurs

Age	Entry Rate into Self-Employment
21–25	1.7%
26–30	2.9
31–35	2.6
36–40	2.8
41–45	2.7
46–50	2.5
51–55	2.4
56–60	2.3
61–65	3.1

Evans and Leighton found that persons are more likely to switch to self-employment (1) the higher their net worth (there appear to be liquidity constraints for starting a business); (2) the more education they have; (3) the less time they have been at the same job; and (4) the lower their wages (presumably the attraction of self-employment is greater to those who have fared less well on the job market).

[a]David S. Evans and Linda S. Leighton, "Some Empirical Aspects of Entrepreneurship," *American Economic Review,* v. 76 (June 1989).

Changes in Demand and Supply

Competitive equilibrium in the market for inputs is determined by the intersection of the supply and demand curves, as shown in Figure 12.6. Changes in equilibrium, as always, result from shifts in supply or demand, or both.

Following are forces that may alter *demands* for inputs:

1. *Technological change* — Technical progress tends to shift the Marginal Products of some or all inputs upward, and hence their Marginal Revenue Products [since $mrp = MR(mp)$]. This, in turn, increases firms' demand for the resources.[4]

2. *Demand for final products*—An increase in the demand for a product tends to raise its price. The higher price raises *mrp,* and so increases the demand for inputs used in producing that commodity.
3. *Supply of cooperating or competing inputs*—The demand for any one input will be affected by changes in the availability of other inputs that complement it or substitute for it in production. In particular, an increase in the supply of one input raises the demand for inputs complementary to it.

Following are the forces that may shift the *supply* curve for an input:

1. *Increase in wealth*—Wealthier people generally prefer to retain more of their resources for their personal use. This would reduce the supply offered on the market.
2. *Social trends and legislation*—Some societies exclude women from all but domestic activity. Other communities severely restrict the market uses of land. Changes in these customs or laws can affect the market availability of inputs.
3. *Investment and accumulation*—In a growing economy, stocks of produced resources (capital goods) accumulate over the generations. (This topic will be considered further in the next chapter.)
4. *Demography*—The aggregate size of the population and its age-sex composition will obviously affect the supply of labor available to the market.

EXAMPLE 12.6   **The Black Death**[a]

The Black Death (1348–50) is generally believed to have killed between a quarter and a third of the population of Western Europe. Later recurrences of plague in 1360 to 1361, 1369, and 1374 may each have killed perhaps 5 percent of the remaining population. The consequent drastic reduction in labor supply had an immediate effect on wages. "The [wage] increase due to the plague is 32 percent for the threshing of wheat, 38 percent for barley, 111 percent for oats in the eastern counties. In the middle counties the percentages of rise are 40, 69, 111; in the south, 33, 38, 75; in the west, 26, 41, 44; in the north, 32, 43, and 100."[b]

The English government responded to this shock with what we would now call a *wage freeze,* eventually formalized as the Statute of Laborers (1351). This decree froze wages, forbade idleness, and required reasonable prices for necessities. Another ordinance in the same year prohibited emigration of workers. But all these regulations failed. The increased scarcity of labor dictated a rise in wages and in per-capita incomes of the laboring classes. When this occurred, members of the upper classes complained about upstarts and nobodies rising to positions of rank and honor, about the need to recontract or entirely remit feudal dues, and even about the clothing worn by social inferiors. (A Statute of Dress of 1363 forbade the lower classes from imitating upper-class attire.)

COMMENT   The feudal system was about as far removed from the economists' competitive model as can be imagined. Feudal economic relationships are, in principle, dictated solely by custom and status. Nevertheless, competitive forces could not be denied and wages rose. An attempt in the reign of Richard II to reverse the clock and return to the old

[a]This is the normal situation. But consider labor-saving inventions. These raise average productivity, but *may* reduce the demand for labor. The explanation is that demand for an input depends upon *Marginal* Product; an invention can raise an input's Average Product while reducing its Marginal Product (at least over a certain range).

[a]Discussion based upon J. Hirshleifer, *Disaster and Recovery: The Black Death in Western Europe*, RAND Corporation, Memorandum RM-4700-TAB (February 1966).

[b]H. Robbins, "A Comparison of the Effects of the Black Death on the Economic Organization of France and England," *Journal of Political Economy*, v. 36 (August 1928), p. 463.

Efficiency Wages

Labor is not of uniform quality; some persons are especially productive and especially willing to work hard. Here we shall ask whether it might benefit a firm to offer what seems to be an above-market wage, because of the effect on worker quality or effort. One effect of a higher wage is to attract superior workers. A firm is not likely to find Nobel-prize caliber consultants by offering them the minimum wage. But if the higher quality just matches the higher pay, the firm is no better off. If, instead, a slight increase in the wage can greatly increase quality, the firm can increase its profits.

Another effect of higher wages may be to induce employees of a given quality to work harder or to shirk less. Suppose that a firm wants its cashiers to be pleasant to customers, but that some of them would prefer to be rude. To induce better behavior, the firm might offer a worker a premium over the market clearing wage; he loses this premium if he is caught shirking and is fired. For example, suppose the psychic cost to a worker of being nice rather than rude is $1,000 per year, that his current job pays $20,000, whereas his best alternative would pay only $18,000. Then clearly a worker who feared losing his job would prefer not to shirk. And if the damage done to the firm by shirking is anything over $1,000, then the firm would be willing to pay a wage premium of over $1,000 to induce its workers not to shirk. This wage premium, designed to affect the behavior of workers, is an *efficiency wage*.

What is the effect of this wage premium upon the amount of labor the firm will hire? Suppose that initially the firm hired 100 workers, and that the Marginal Revenue Product of the last worker was $10. Now the firm pays the higher wage, and workers therefore work harder. It is convenient to talk of effort levels. Suppose that output depends on the effort level, and that at a wage rate of $10 each worker's effort level was 1, whereas with a wage rate of $11 each worker's effort level is 1.5. To determine the demand for labor, we must determine the effects of efficiency wages on the Marginal Revenue Product *(mrp)* of a worker. Two effects must be considered. First, each worker works harder, so that for a fixed *mrp* per unit of effort, each worker's *mrp* increases. Second, for the same number of workers, the total amount of effort supplied increases; diminishing marginal productivity and decreasing Marginal Revenue cause the *mrp* of each unit of effort to decline. The decline in the *mrp* of a unit of effort, coupled with the increase in the effort of each worker, can thus cause the *mrp* of each worker to either increase or decrease. For example, with 100 workers and 150 units of effort, the *mrp* of an hour worked (that is, of 1.5 units of effort) may be greater than when each worker produced only 1 unit of effort. If the *mrp* of each worker increases by more than the wage premium, each firm will want to hire more workers. If, instead, the *mrp* of a worker declines, or increases by less than the wage premium, the firm will want to hire fewer workers.

EXAMPLE 12.7 **Efficiency Wages at Ford Motors**[a]

In January of 1914 Henry Ford instituted a $5 a day minimum wage in his automobile factory. This doubled the pay of most of his workers. Ford observed the following:

There was no charity in any way involved. . . . We wanted to pay these wages so that the business would be on a lasting foundation. We were building for the future. A low wage business is always insecure. . . . The payment of five dollars a day for an eight hour day was one of the finest cost cutting moves we ever made.

A hallmark of efficiency wage theories is their implication that some firms will pay a wage greater than the minimum necessary to attract labor of the quality they desire.

Did Ford's actions fit the model? Following the introduction of the $5 wage, the *New York Times* reported the following:

Twelve thousand men . . . celebrated the [five dollar day] with a rush on the plant which resulted in a riot and turning of a fire hose on the crowd. . . . The crowd began forming at 10 o'clock last night in spite of a blizzard.

The benefits from the higher wages appear largely in a reduction of turnover. The quit rate fell by 87 percent between March 1913 and March 1914. Absenteeism declined from 10 percent in 1913 to 2.5 percent in 1914.

These changes appeared to have increased productivity, apparently by more than enough to justify the higher wage. Between 1913 and 1914 the Ford Company produced 15 percent more cars per day, with 2000, or about 14 percent fewer workers and a reduction in the number of hours worked per worker. Statistical analysis suggests a substantial productivity increment of between 40 and 70 percent following the introduction of the five-dollar day.

[a]Discussion based on Daniel M. G. Raff and Lawrence H. Summers "Did Henry Ford Pay Efficiency Wages?" Discussion paper no. 1287, December 1986, Harvard Institute of Economic Research.

An increased wage may thus induce a worker to shirk less because he expects that in remaining in his current job he will earn a higher wage than he can elsewhere. This effect may also be achieved by altering the wage stream on the basis of worker seniority. The firm could initially pay a new worker a low wage (lower than his *mrp*), and pay a higher wage (higher than his *mrp*) in later years if the worker performs adequately. The stream of payments can be designed to be equivalent to the worker's *mrp* over his career at the firm. Thus, in contrast to the efficiency wages described earlier, on average the firm pays over time each worker's Marginal Revenue Product.

Since in later years the worker is paid more than his Marginal Revenue Product, he expects to earn more by staying in his current job than in getting a new one. To keep his job, he will want to avoid shirking. One problem with this wage system, of course, is that the firm has an incentive to fire older workers. If, however, the firm has a reputation to keep, or if, perhaps, union rules keep the firm honest, the firm will not be able to do this.

Another problem is that the worker may not want to retire, since he is getting paid so much in his later years; this may require the firm to impose mandatory retirement.[5]

Exercise 12.2

Consider a firm for which labor *(L)* is the only variable factor. The original Total Product function is $q = 100L - L^2$. The hire-price of labor is $w = 10$. The price of the firm's output is 1. (a) How much labor will the firm hire? (b) Now suppose that labor has become more efficient, so that each unit of the newly-efficient labor is the equivalent of two units of the old labor. What is the new production function? How much labor will the firm hire?

Answer: (a) Calculus shows that when the production function is $q = 100L - L^2$, the Marginal Product of labor is $100 - 2L$. Equating vmp_L to the wage rate, 10, yields $L^* = 45$; output is $q = 2475$. (b) Each unit of labor is now the equivalent of two units of the previous labor, so $q = 100(2L) - (2L)^2$, or $q = 200L - 4L^2$. Calculus shows that the Marginal Product of labor is then $200 - 8L$. Solving the equation $200 - 8L = 10$ yields $L^* = 23.75$. Note that the firm will now hire less labor, even at the same wage rate. Total output, however, has increased to 2493.75.

Signaling

The productivity of a given worker can depend not only on individual effort, but also upon innate ability or character. The firm will want to hire productive workers and will be willing to pay them more than it pays less productive workers, but each potential hire will claim to be highly productive. The problem is especially serious if, even after hiring a worker, the firm finds it costly to determine individual productivity. This situation can occur when production occurs in teams—for example, was a sale lost because the salesperson was incompetent, or because the design was defective, or perhaps because the service department has a bad reputation?

The firm's problem, then, is to distinguish between workers of different ability. Suppose half the job candidates have high ability and half have low ability, as measured by Marginal Revenue Product. A worker is offered a wage before being hired and before the firm knows how much the worker will produce once on the job. Though employers do not observe the ability of workers, suppose they can observe levels of education. Suppose education has two levels. Workers choose their education before employers set the wage rates. We make the critical assumption that education is less costly for a worker the greater the individual ability. A person, for example, who is not lazy will enjoy school more, and produce more on a job, than would a lazy person. For expository purposes, let the output of a high ability worker be 10, and his cost of education 3. As shown in Table 12.1, a low-ability worker is less productive and has a higher cost of education. Thus, the average *mrp* for the two classes of workers is $(10 + 6)/2 = 8$.

We wish to determine the wages offered each type of worker and the level of education chosen. We shall show that under the assumptions just made, there is an equilibrium where a high-ability worker gets an education, and a low-ability worker does not. (This is called a separating equilibrium.) The high-ability worker is paid his *mrp,* 10, and the low ability worker is paid his *mrp,* 6. Under these conditions, the high-ability worker clearly wants

---

[5]The discussion here is based on Edward Lazear, "Why Is There Mandatory Retirement," *Journal of Political Economy,* v. 87 (December 1979).

TABLE 12.1   Ability, Education, and Output

	High Ability	Low Ability
Marginal Revenue Product	10	6
Cost of Education	3	5

to get an education; the cost is 3, but he gets a wage of 10 instead of 6. The low-ability worker does not want to incur the costs of additional education; it would cost him 5, but would raise his wage by only $10 - 6 = 4$, which is less than his cost of education. Moreover, competition will force firms to pay these wages: if a firm paid anything less than $10 to a worker with education, say it paid $9, the wage would be less than *mrp*—firms would compete to attract a high-ability worker on whom they make a profit, and therefore the equilibrium wage would have to rise. Similarly, a firm would not pay more than $6 for a worker with no education. Any higher wage would be greater than such a worker's *mrp*, and therefore a firm that paid more than $6 to such a worker would lose money by hiring him.

In such a signaling model, some workers have an incentive to get an education, and workers with high education are paid higher wages than workers with low education. Nevertheless, education does not increase anyone's productivity. By assumption, a high-ability worker's *mrp* is 10, and a low ability worker's *mrp* is 6, regardless of the level of education. Indeed, in demonstrating that some persons would want to incur the cost of an education we did not even have to assume that a person learned anything at all in school! Here is an example of an activity that is privately useful but which may have no social benefit at all.

This strong result about efficiency need not always hold. In particular, for some jobs it may be important to match people with different abilities to different tasks. Perhaps people with high ability should be placed in management positions, and people with low ability in other positions. Here total output could be higher if the firm knew each worker's ability.

Signaling models may have more than one equilibrium. To return to our example, suppose that initially firms cannot distinguish between workers of different ability. The firm's best guess about a worker's ability is therefore the average ability of workers, namely $(10 + 6)/2 = 8$. Now would a high-ability worker have any incentive to get an education? In the best case the firm would believe that any worker who has an education also has high ability, and a firm would therefore be willing to pay him his *mrp*, namely 10. That means that in the best case the worker could increase his salary by $10 - 8 = 2$, but by assumption the cost of his education is 3. Thus, no individual worker has an incentive to get an education, and the equilibrium may have both types of workers get no education and receive a wage of 8. (This is called a pooling equilibrium.)

In contrast, if the cost of education to a high-ability worker were less than 2, then a person with high ability would find it profitable to get an education so as to increase his wage from 8 to 10. A low-ability worker, with a cost of education of 5, would not find it worthwhile to get the education. Therefore, a firm would find it worthwhile to pay almost 10 to a worker with an education.

EXAMPLE 12.8 High School Graduation and Absenteeism

According to signaling theory, high school graduates earn more than persons who do not graduate because graduates differ in some important ways from nongraduates. The graduate may be more tolerant of boring presentations, may be willing to stay in class rather than go to the beach, or may have the character required to stick with an unpleasant task until completion.

Andrew Weiss[a] had access to proprietary data consisting of the personnel files of 2920 newly hired, semi-skilled production workers employed by a high-wage unionized firm. Weiss found that high school graduation is uncorrelated with output per hour (that is, high school graduates do not have a higher marginal product when they are at work), but high school graduates were less likely to be absent or to quit. Since the firm has to incur some cost to hire a replacement, and since absenteeism may require the firm to pay other workers overtime, or to change its production plans for that day, over a year the marginal product of a worker with a low quit or abstention rate is probably higher than that of a typical worker, even though when on the job the workers may have similar output. The data thus appear to support the signaling theory—firms are interested in hiring high school graduates because graduates are more likely to have certain character traits that firms value.

[a]Andrew Weiss, "High School Graduation, Performance, and Wages," *Journal of Political Economy*, v. 96 (1988).

EXAMPLE 12.9 Signaling Among Butterflies

The discussion of signaling in education showed that, given a low enough cost, even a low-ability worker is motivated to obtain an education so that employers could not distinguish him from a worker with high ability. A similar phenomenon is found in nature. Mimicry is a form of protective resemblance in which one species so closely resembles another in external form and coloring as to be mistaken for it, although the two may not really be allied and often belong to distinct families or orders. Alfred Wallace[a], the co-discoverer with Charles Darwin of the theory of evolution by natural selection, described mimicry among butterflies which closely resembles the signaling theory of economists.

The region of the Amazon river in South America has an abundance of brilliantly colored Helicondae with warning coloration. But along with them are butterflies of a totally separate family, the Peridae, which resemble the Helicondae in color, form, and mode of flight. The differences in structure, however, are as large as between pigs and sheep.

The Helicondae, unlike the Peridae, possess an offensive taste and odor, leaving them almost entirely free from attack by insectivores. If any eatable butterflies in the same region should come to resemble any of these uneatable species, they will avoid being eaten. Of special note is that none of these mimicking butterflies were so abundant as the Helicondae they resembled; the proportion is generally one to a thousand. Thus, insectivores found it advantageous to avoid all butterflies with the warning colorations. If the proportions were reversed, insectivores would find it worthwhile to eat butterflies with these striking colors, since most would be edible.

[a]Alfred Wallace, *Darwinism*, 2nd. edition, London: Macmillan and Company, 1889.

12.4 MONOPOLIES AND CARTELS IN THE SUPPLY OF INPUTS

Since no two firms' products are identical, every supplier has *some* monopoly power in the product market. Similarly, although resources differ from each other in some ways, every resource-owner has *some* monopoly power in the input market. But since there are usually close substitutes for any person's owned resources, only in rare situations will an individual have meaningful monopoly power in the sale of his resources (among the important exceptions are motion picture stars and athletic champions). On the other hand, *cartels* of resource-suppliers (e.g., trade unions) are very common.

Optimum of the Monopolist Resource-Owner

The optimizing decision for the resource-monopolist is especially simple if he or she has no reservation uses for the input. Such a monopolist seeks to maximize *Total Resource Income (TRI)*, the revenue he obtains from hiring out the services of his resources. This maximization may dictate holding some units of the resource off the market, not for reservation uses (since by assumption there are none) but solely to obtain a higher price through monopoly power.

Figure 12.7 (p. 336) illustrates such a situation; the total function is shown in the upper diagram and the average-marginal functions are shown in the lower diagram. The monopolist maximizes his revenue by selling L^* units of labor, which generates the maximum point on the *TRI* curve in the upper diagram. The lower diagram shows, equivalently, how L^* is determined at the point where Marginal Resource Income *MRI* is zero. The wage set by the monopolist will be h_L^*, the height of the input demand curve D_L at $L = L^*$. Since $h_L \equiv TRI/L$, the demand curve for the input is also the monopolist's Average Resource Income function, so that this wage equals the slope of the dotted line in the upper diagram.

What if the curve of *TRI* rises throughout the relevant range where $L \leq \overline{R}$? (That is, what if the demand curve for the input is elastic throughout?) In that case Marginal Resource Income remains greater than zero at $L \equiv \overline{R}$, where all of the resource available is employed. Then the monopolist will not find it advantageous to hold any units off the market.

Exercise 12.3

An individual is a monopolist of resource A and has no reservation uses for it. The demand equation is $h_A = 120 - A$. (a) How many units will the monopolist hold off the market if endowed with $R_A = 100$? (b) If endowed with $R_A = 50$?

Answer: (a) The hire-price h_A is also the Average Resource Income *ARI*. Since $ARI = 120 - A$ is the equation of a straight-line, Marginal Resource Income is $MRI = 120 - 2A$. Setting $MRI = 0$, we have $A^* = 60$. The monopolist will therefore hold $100 - 60 = 40$ units off the market. (b) If the endowment is only 50 units of A, then *MRI* remains positive even when the monopolist sells all 50 units. He will not hold any units off the market.

A monopolist with personal reservation uses for a resource must balance this desire with potential earnings from selling the resource in the market. In Figure 12.8, the shaded opportunity set is bounded by a concave curve rather than a straight line. (Recall that a concave, as opposed to a convex, curve, becomes steeper as we move to the right; the wage h_L is *not* constant, but rather is a decreasing function of employment.) The monopolist's optimum position is at the point on the opportunity set that lies on the highest indifference

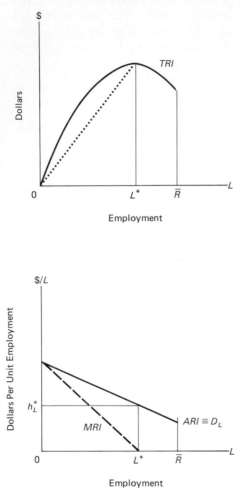

curve, which in turn means the point where an indifference curve is tangent to the opportunity set. This is point G^*; the reservation quantity is R^*, and the corresponding employment quantity is $L^* = \bar{R} - R^*$.

This solution is translated to a price-quantity diagram in Figure 12.9. The Marginal Resource Income *MRI* for any employment level L is the slope, $-\Delta I/\Delta R$, of the budget curve *EK* in Figure 12.8. This is the "Marginal Revenue" in income units of sacrificing an hour of leisure. Corresponding to "Marginal Cost" for the monopolist is the marginal value of reservation uses, which is nothing but the Marginal Rate of Substitution MRS_R as analyzed earlier in "The Optimum of the Resource-Owner." The rising curve MRS_R in Figure 12.9 shows increasing "Marginal Cost" of accepting income in place of leisure. So the tangency

FIGURE 12.8   Factor Monopolist with Reservation Uses, I   On R, I axes a factor monopolist will have a "budget curve" EK bounding the shaded market opportunity set. If he has reservation uses for the resource, the optimum is at G^*, the tangency of EK with the highest attainable indifference curve U. Retained reservation uses are R^*; offered employment is $L^* = \bar{R} - R^*$.

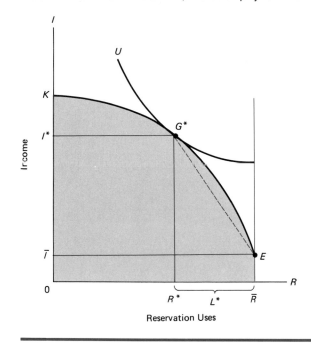

Reservation Uses

FIGURE 12.9   Factor Monopolist with Reservation Uses, II   The curves of Average Resource Income ARI (the demand curve D_L for labor) and of Marginal Resource Income MRI are derived from the budget curve EK of the previous diagram. The curve MRS_R shows the Marginal Rate of Substitution in Resource Supply; it represents the Marginal Cost of supplying labor as the individual's foregone value of reservation uses (leisure). The monopolist supplies L^* units of labor (where MRI and MRS_R intersect), at a unit price of h_L^*.

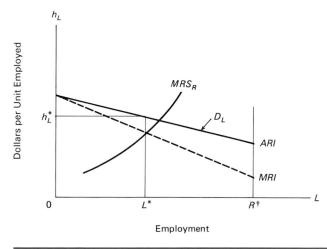

Employment

at $G*$ in Figure 12.8 (where the slope of the budget-curve equals the slope of an indifference-curve) corresponds to the intersection of MRI and MRS_R in Figure 12.9. The monopoly optimum wage h_L^* in Figure 12.9 similarly corresponds to the absolute slope of the dashed line $EG*$ in Figure 12.8.

Exercise 12.4

An individual is endowed with $\overline{R} = 24$ hours of leisure and $\overline{I} = 40$ dollars of income. The Marginal Rate of Substitution between income I and reservation uses of labor, R, is $MRS_R = I/R$. This individual monopolist controls a special type of labor for which the demand is $w = 50 - 4L$, where w is the wage rate and $L \equiv 24 - R$. (a) How much labor should the monopolist offer? (b) At what wage? (c) What is the individual income?

Answer: (a) The individual will want to set MRS_R equal to Marginal Resource Income MRI. Since the demand for labor, $w = 50 - 4L$, is a straight line, $MRI = 50 - 8L$. The equation to solve is $50 - 8L = MRS_R = I/R = I/(24 - L)$. The income earned is $I = 40 + wL = 40 + (50 - 4L)L$. After substituting, we obtain a quadratic equation with two solutions: $L = 5$ and $L = 19.33$. The latter violates economic logic since it implies $I < 0$, so $L = 5$ is the correct result. (b) When 5 hours of labor are put on the market, the wage is $w = 30$. (c) The attained income is $I = 40 + 5(30) = 190$.

CONCLUSION: The monopolist supplier of a resource, like the monopolist supplier of a product, will optimally set Marginal Revenue equal to Marginal Cost. In the input market, Marginal Revenue corresponds to personal Marginal Resource Income (MRI). Marginal Cost corresponds to the owner's Marginal Rate of Substitution between income and reservation uses of the resource (MRS_R). If there are no reservation uses, MRS_R is everywhere zero. Even so, the monopolist input-supplier may still hold some units of the input off the market if Marginal Resource Income falls to zero before the marketed quantity exhausts the owned supply.

Resource Cartels

Trade unions are a labor cartel. Workers who have no monopoly power as individuals may as a group be able to raise wages by collectively restricting the supply of labor.

As explained in Chapter 8, cartels have a major weakness: "chiseling" by their members. Once the union has raised wages, each member has an incentive to accept less than the standard pay or, at least, to work harder or longer than before. A union can survive only if it prevents chiseling. One method is social ostracism or even violence. Another way is to secure pro-union legislation.

Under the National Labor Relations Act in the United States, an election is normally held to choose a collective bargaining agent. Any union that wins a majority of the votes becomes the exclusive bargaining agent for *all* workers in the collective-bargaining unit. ("No union" is also one of the options.) Once a collective-bargaining agent has been officially certified, the firm is forbidden to bargain with individual workers, so that chiseling is effectively made illegal. No single worker can work additional hours by accepting a lower hourly wage, nor can any outsider come in by offering to work for less.

EXAMPLE 12.10 Union Wage Gains

Do unions raise wages? If so, by how much? Surveying several studies by economists, C. J. Parsley[a] found that wage gains varied widely by occupation. A sample is shown in the following table:

Union Wage Gains

Occupation	Union Wage Premium
Industrial	15–20%
Construction	40–50
Teaching	12–14
Firemen	15

In a different study, Freeman and Kleiner[b] examine the effects of unions by comparing wage gains before and after unionization; they compared 203 previously nonunion plants that had union elections in the 1980s with 161 nonunion plants that had no elections.

One year before the election, wages at the nonunion plants that later became unionized were about 3 percent lower than wages at nonunion plants. (It thus appears that low wages give workers an incentive to unionize.) After the union contracts were signed, the unionized plants had wages about 7 percent higher than those at the nonunion plants. Freeman and Kleiner estimate that about 4 of the 7 percentage point change was attributable to unionization. This result differs from the studies summarized in the previous table, which had found wages about 15–25 percent higher for union workers. One reason is that these studies had looked at unions prior to the 1980s, when perhaps unions were more powerful; another reason is that Freeman and Kleiner studied newly organized firms. It seems that such firms do not pay the full union wage premium all at once; instead, wages increase slowly toward the union level.

The major flaw in all this evidence is the failure to adjust for differences in the quality of workers. For example, union wage premiums in construction may be high, in part at least, because union members are better trained or more experienced than nonunion workers.

One way to adjust for differences in worker quality is to look at the wages of the *same* worker as a union and nonunion member. This approach was taken by Wesley Mellow.[c] Using Current Population Survey data from the years 1974 to 1975 and 1977 to 1978, he identified workers who either joined or quit a union during the sample period. Then, adjusting for changes in education and experience, he found that on average a worker's wage rose by 7.5 percent upon joining a union and fell by 7 percent upon leaving.

Another important consideration is the loss of employment as a result of the higher wage. Blanchflower, Milward, and Oswald[d] examined the rate of employment growth at 2019 British establishments over the years 1980–84. The results are shown in the following table:

Employment Growth

Change in Employment 1980–84	Nonunion Establishments	Establishments with at Least 75 Percent of Workers Unionized
Decrease of 20% or more	14%	19%
Decrease of 5% to 20%	19	30
Stable	16	27
Increase of 5% to 20%	17	12
Increase of 20% or more	33	9

Thus, as shown in the last line, 33 percent of establishments with no union saw a growth of at least 20 percent in employment, while only 9 percent of the heavily unionized establishments saw such growth. For a better estimate of the effects of unionization, the researchers estimated a regression equation that controlled for region, industry, county unemployment rate, and establishment characteristics (especially demand, capacity, and financial performance). They found that unionization reduced employment growth by about 3 percent per annum.

[a]C. J. Parsley, "Labor Union Effects on Wage Gains: A Survey of Recent Literature," *Journal of Economic Literature,* v. 18 (March 1980), p. 1.

[b]Richard Freeman and Morris Kleiner, "The impact of new unionization on wages and working conditions: A longitudinal study of establishments under NLRB elections." NBER working paper no. 2563, 1988.

[c]Wesley Mellow, "Unionism and Wages: A Longitudinal Analysis," *Review of Economics and Statistics,* v. 63 (1981), p. 43.

[d]David Blanchflower, Neil Milward, and Andrew J. Oswald, "Unionization and Employment Behavior." Trade Union Institute for Economic Research, Stockholm, Sweden, Paper no. 53, July 1988.

Trade unions are by no means the only resource cartels. Professional associations, such as the American Medical Association (see Example 12.14, "Returns to Medical Education") may engage in cartel-like behavior. Allegedly, one motivation for the American Medical Association to press for increased standards in medical education was to reduce entry into the profession. In general, loosely organized resource-supply cartels find it easier to achieve their ends by restricting entry to the trade. While price-chiseling may be hidden and difficult to control, entry is relatively visible. A sufficiently tight lid on supply, through control of entry, increases the market price even if individual behavior remains competitive. In a supply-demand equilibrium like that of Figure 12.6, entry control could shift the supply curve S_L so far to the left as to achieve a monopoly-like outcome.

EXAMPLE 12.11 Maximum-Hours Laws for Women

A number of jurisdictions in the United States limited the working hours of adult women. Elisabeth M. Landes[a] found that in 1900 only eleven states had such legislation, but by 1920 this had increased to forty states and the District of Columbia.

Landes found that, in 1920, women worked about eight hours less in states with maximum-hours laws. But the effect of this limit was primarily on immigrant women, who had typically been working longer hours. There were also quite significant effects on employment. The employment of foreign-born women fell by as much as 30 percent in the most restrictive states, while employment of native women was largely unaffected. Landes also reported that the greater the manufacturing employment of foreign-born women in a state in 1890, the earlier that state tended to enact a maximum-hours law for women.

This evidence suggests that state maximum-hours laws aimed in part to exclude immigrants from employment, thus increasing the demand for native American workers. The political logic of this is that native American women workers had more political influence than immigrants. Native women were more numerous, and more likely to be voters themselves or to have male family members eligible to vote. (In most states the suffrage had not yet been extended to women even by 1920, but the economic interests of wives and daughters would have influenced the votes of male family members.)

[a]Elisabeth M. Landes, "The Effect of State Maximum-Hours Laws on the Employment of Women in 1920," *Journal of Political Economy,* v. 88 (1980).

One notable exception to tight control over occupational entry is the legal profession. Law schools in the United States have greatly increased their capacity recently, without apparent objection from established lawyers. This exception is, however, understandable. Each additional barber or doctor or accountant competes with his fellows and takes away business. In contrast, an additional attorney who adds to the number of lawsuits, presentments, hearings, trials, or pleadings makes more business for his colleagues.[6] Of course, cartels may be effective over non-labor resources as well, as the following example indicates.

EXAMPLE 12.12   Tobacco Allotments

Under the market order[a] regulating the supply of tobacco, only those specific acres of farmland that carry allotments may be used to grow tobacco. Anyone may become a tobacco grower, but he or she must buy or rent some allotted acres. Thus, the government-sponsored cartel works on behalf of owners of the resource of allotted land, not on behalf of growers as such. One study[b] has estimated the premium paid by growers for land with an allotment (over equivalent land without allotment) as between $962 and $2500 per acre (for land suitable for growing flue-cured tobacco in North Carolina and Virginia counties in the period 1954 to 1957). A later study[c] estimated that by 1962 the premium had risen to $3281 per acre in eastern North Carolina.

[a]See also Example 8.5, "Agricultural Marketing Orders."

[b]F. H. Maier, J. L. Hedrick, and W. L. Givson, Jr., "The Sale Value of Flue-Cured Tobacco Allotments," Agricultural Experiment Station, Virginia Polytechnic Institute, Technical Bulletin no. 148 (April 1960), p. 40.

[c]James A. Seagraves, "Capitalized Value of Tobacco Allotments and the Rate of Return to Allotment Owners," *American Journal of Agricultural Economics,* v. 51 (May 1969).

12.5   THE FUNCTIONAL DISTRIBUTION OF INCOME

The Problem of Classification

Resources have traditionally been classified under the headings of *labor, land,* and *capital.* These were thought to correspond to three categories of functional factor returns, namely, *wages* to labor, *rent* to land, and *interest* to capital. In the emerging period of economic

[6]Old folk saying: "When will a lawyer be poor? When he's the only lawyer in town."

thought, most particularly in England in the late eighteenth and early nineteenth centuries, these groupings corresponded to major social classes of the time. Land was mainly owned by the aristocracy, capital (material assets other than land) was owned by the rising bourgeoisie, labor was provided largely by the working class. Even sociologically speaking, this classification was not very applicable to societies with no feudally based aristocracy. In any case, the claim that these three inputs are functionally distinct in economic terms is not analytically valid.

LAND VERSUS CAPITAL: *Land* is traditionally defined as the "natural and inexhaustible productive powers of the soil" and described by its native fertility, topographical features, and geographical location. *Capital,* in contrast with land, is considered a "produced means of production." But the distinction collapses once it is realized that the actual powers of the soil are as much a human creation as any building or machine. Human effort was needed for the discovery of the vast new lands of America, and, for that matter, for the draining of marshes and clearing of wasteland in the Old World. The fertility of land is maintained by continuing human effort and sacrifice. Most important of all, the original source of any productive power is only of historical, not of economic, significance.

It is sometimes claimed that a useful distinction between land and capital can be made in terms of supply curves. Supposedly, the supply of land is fixed by nature (a vertical supply curve) while the supply of any manufactured resource is responsive to price (a positively sloping curve). But the supply of land is not fixed. More land *will* be provided when the price is right (if necessary, it can be reclaimed from the ocean), while existing land will erode if the reward for maintaining it is insufficient. A waste dump that leaks toxic materials on neighboring land can make that land useless for all purposes; investment in safer disposal methods can therefore increase the supply of productive land. Furthermore, even if the amount of physical land were fixed, as long as there are any reservation uses the supply of land *to the market* responds to price.[7]

LABOR VERSUS CAPITAL: No less problematic is distinguishing between labor and capital. A worker does not sell raw labor power, but rather his trained and educated capacity to apply effort. Training is part of the worker's capital ("human capital"), just as a tool he owns is a part of capital. There is no essential difference between a worker who sacrifices time and effort to acquire training that improves labor skills and a worker who purchases a set of tools to acquire material capital.

EXAMPLE 12.13   **Income Sources of the Wealthy in Britain**

A study by Peter H. Lindert reveals a remarkable change during the past century in the sources of income received by wealthy people in Great Britain. The following table compares the income sources of the upper 10 percent of the population for 1867 versus 1972–73. At the earlier date, profits and interest on investments were by far the major component, labor earnings a distant second, with land rents still substantial. By the 1970s land rents had shrunk. Labor earnings had become the most important source of income for the wealthy, followed by a relatively small share of investment income in the form of profits and interest.

Sources of Income in Britain (top 10 percent of population)

	England and Wales 1867	United Kingdom 1972–73
Land Rents	13%	1%
Investment Income	69	15
Labor Earnings	18	84
TOTAL	100%	100%

Source: Adapted from Peter H. Lindert, "Unequal English Wealth Since 1670," *Journal of Political Economy,* v. 94 (December 1986), p. 1155.

Lindert estimated that the overall shares of national income attributable to human skills rose from around 15 percent in 1867 to 52 percent in the years 1972 to 1973.

COMMENT The main explanation, it appears, is that the vast accumulation of durable capital over the past century has reduced its scarcity value and therefore the rate of earnings on capital. Labor, in contrast, has become relatively scarce. Furthermore, the complexity of modern society has made skills (human capital) increasingly costly to acquire (long years of training and education are required), and these costs must be paid for by markedly higher earnings.

Of course, even if different types of resources are not functionally distinct, there can still be important differences among them. For example, a resource-owner concerned with the threat of confiscation will consider the "portability" of alternative ways of holding wealth. Land is evidently the least portable capital asset. Manufactured capital goods can range from quite immovable buildings to easily transportable light tools. Most portable of all is human capital, which anyone can carry around without much extra cost. So people who fear confiscation might be expected to hold their wealth largely in the form of portable resources, especially human capital.

An Application: Investment in Human Capital

Figure 12.10 (p. 344) illustrates an individual's decision whether or not to add to his human capital by investing in education or training. Suppose that in the absence of such training his optimum position would be at G^* along the budget line EK; his non-wage income is $\bar{I}$ and his wage income is $G^* - G' = I_G - \bar{I}$. Education has two effects. First, it reduces non-wage income because of tuition fees and foregone earnings. Assume this shifts the endowment from E down to E'. Second, education increases the person's wage rate. Thus the new budget line $E'K'$ is steeper than EK. Suppose the individual's new optimum D^* is

[7]The supply curve of land to *all* uses (including reservation uses) will indeed be a vertical line independent of price. But this is true for any resource, including labor. (If "leisure" is counted as a use of labor, the supply of labor is necessarily the entire amount in existence.) Meaningful supply curves always refer to quantities offered for *market* use, excluding reservation uses.

FIGURE 12.10 **Returns to Education**   The individual here is just indifferent as to an investment in
education. With endowment at *E,* along the initial budget line *EK* the optimal position is *G** on indifference
curve *U.* Incurring a cost of education, represented by the vertical distance *EE'*, raises his market wage
so that he has a new steeper budget line *E'K'*. The new tangency optimum *D** along *E'K'* is on the same
indifference curve as *G**. *D** is to the left of *G**; the individual making the educational investment will
thereafter choose higher income but less leisure.

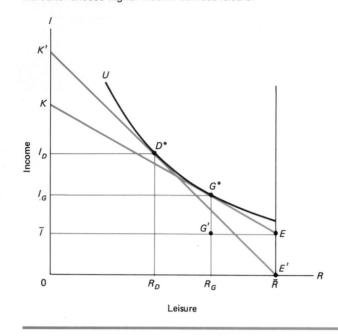

Leisure

on the same indifference curve as *G**. At the new optimum *D**, income I_D is higher than
before, but leisure R_D is less. Note the possibly surprising result: becoming educated means
you should work harder ever after! [*Question for the student:* The analysis above considers
a person who is indifferent between receiving the training or not. But most people who
obtain an education do so with the expectation of living better. Would such a person be
more likely, or less likely, to work longer hours afterward than someone who was just on
the borderline?]

EXAMPLE 12.14 **Returns to Medical Education**

Medical education seems to be exceptionally profitable, suggesting that a cartel may be
limiting entry. C. M. Lindsay has contended, however, that a comparison of income alone
fails to note that, after making human-capital investments such as medical training, individuals will typically enjoy less leisure than before.

In the table, the unadjusted M.D. returns represent the seeming excess value of medical
education ($24,376) in comparison with ordinary college education. This amount is the net
additional income, deducting the cost of medical training, but without any offset for additional
working hours of M.D.s. There are two ways of allowing for the extra hours worked by
M.D.s: adjusting college-graduate hours worked up, or adjusting M.D. hours worked down.
(The correct comparison must lie between the results of these two alternative adjustments.)

Reportedly, M.D.s worked 62 hours per week on the average. For the sake of comparison, alternative assumptions of a 40- and a 45-hour average workweek were used for college graduates. If college graduates work 45 hours per week, the table shows an excess net return to medical education somewhere between the two estimates of $10,830 and $1950. On the 40-hour assumption, however, the two adjustments average close to zero. So if college graduates generally work close to 40 hours per week, there is no evidence of an excess return to medical education—once the M.D.s' loss of leisure is properly taken into account.

Excess Returns to Medical Education

	40-Hour Week	45-Hour Week
Unadjusted M.D. Excess Return	$24,376	$24,376
Adjusted by Raising College Graduate Hours (to 62)	4660	10,830
Adjusted by Lowering M.D. Hours	−4580	1950

Source: C. M. Lindsay, "Real Returns to Medical Education," *Journal of Human Resources,* v. 8 (Summer 1973), p. 338. An interest rate of 10 percent was used to represent the "normal" return from which the "excess" was calculated. (The original source shows the computation in terms of interest rates of both 5 percent and 10 percent).

COMMENT   The 62-hour figure for M.D.s, being self-reported, may be suspect. Physicians (like other people) are apt to report working harder than they really do. If physicians do not in fact work as many as 62 hours per week, the evidence here would tend to support the hypothesis of an excess (cartel-like) return to medical education.

EXAMPLE 12.15   **Which College to Attend?**

The value of an education depends on the quality of the college attended and on the performance of the student. The specific college may be significant because more is learned at some places than others, or for signaling reasons—employers may believe that colleges are very good at selecting the type of people who will later be highly productive.

James Estelle, Nabeel Alsalam, Joseph Conaty, and Duc-Le To[a] used data on males from the National Longitudinal Study of the High School Class of 1972 to examine the effects of education on earnings. The college effects are small. A 100 point increase in the average Scholastic Aptitude Test (SAT) score of the freshman class in the college raises annual earnings by about 3 percent; this applies regardless of the individual's own SAT score. And though private institutions in the East have an advantage of about 5 percent relative to public institutions, expenditure per student at the college has no effect. (This last result is consistent with signaling theory.)

Studying hard appears to help. If a student's grade point average increases from C to B, or from B to A, annual earnings rise about 9 percent. Earnings are also especially high for persons who had majored in engineering, and studied mathematics.

[a]James Estelle, Nabeel Alsalam, Joseph Conaty, and Duc-Le To, "College Quality and Future Earnings: Where Should You Send Your Child to College?" *American Economic Review,* v. 79 (May 1989).

12.6 CAPITAL VERSUS INCOME: THE RATE OF INTEREST

For some purposes, it is essential to distinguish between the *sources* of productive services and the *productive services* themselves. The human being is the source of labor services, but the labor service is the employee-hour (or other unit representing the employment of a worker over some defined period of time). Similarly, land is a source of productive services, but the service itself is measured in units of acre-years. And again, it is necessary to distinguish buildings and machines (both sources) from the services of building and machines.

Sources and their services may both be traded in markets. There is a price for an acre of land, and a hire-price for a year's use of an acre of land. There is a price for a building and a rental for use of the building over some period of time. Labor is a special case. The sources of labor services (the human beings themselves) may not be sold, though labor still can be hired for a periodic wage (the hire-price per employee-hour). The input prices discussed in this and previous chapters have been the hire or rental prices of the productive services not the prices of the resources themselves.

The sources of input services constitute an individual's or a nation's capital. Land is capital, machines and buildings are capital, and the human being's training, strength, and skill are human capital.

EXAMPLE 12.16 **Wages in the Soviet Union**

Paul R. Gregory and Janet E. Kohlase[a] examined a survey of 2793 former Soviet citizens who immigrated to the United States between January 1979 and April 1982; this is before Gorbachev's liberalization of the Soviet economy.

The Soviet adult population largely had freedom of choice of occupations and location. State committees set industry base rates and skill differentials, with adjustments that attempt to compensate for undesirable jobs and locations. Also, plant managers have some flexibility with regard to bonuses, premiums, piece rates, and classification. As a first approximation, the authors concluded, the Soviets use market-clearing wages to allocate labor.

Education and experience are rewarded in the Soviet labor market. On average blue-collar workers with less than 6 years of schooling earned 20-22 percent less than workers with a high school education; workers with 7–8 years of schooling earned 9 percent less. Beyond this point, additional education did not seem to increase wages significantly.

A notable feature of the Soviet system appears to be the importance of political position. With occupation held constant, a person who reported himself as a political leader, organizer, or officer earned 6.1 percent more than persons with no regular political involvement. A person who reported a leadership role in political dissidence earned about 35 percent less than a fellow worker with identical characteristics.

[a]Paul R. Gregory and Janet E. Kohlase, "The Earnings of Soviet Workers: Evidence from the Soviet Interview Project." *Review of Economics and Statistics*, v. 70 (February 1988).

EXAMPLE 12.17 **Capital Value in the Slave-Owning South**

The following table, based on a study by Louis Rose, summarizes the value of various categories of property (capital) in the fifteen states where slaves were emancipated by President Lincoln's proclamation. Slave values varied, of course, with age and other characteristics; the mean was $933. Emancipation constituted an enormous loss to the slave-owners that was balanced by a corresponding economic gain to the slaves (in the form of the transferred ownership of their own persons).

Wealth Data, 15 Southern States, 1860 Millions of Dollars

Value of Real Estate and Personal Property	$8644
Value of Land in Farms	2550
Value of Implements and Machinery in Use	104
Value of Livestock	515
Value of Slaves Emancipated	3685

Source: L. Rose, "Capital Losses of Southern Slaveholders Due to Emancipation," *Western Economic Journal,* v. 3 (Fall 1964), pp. 43, 49.

COMMENT A complete tabulation should also include the labor-power value of the free population. Accounting for both slave and free labor power, it seems likely that the value of the human capital of the 1860 South exceeded all other capital combined. Very likely this remains true today for all modern Western economies. Even though material capital has grown more rapidly than the human population since 1860 (a greater quantity of machines and other productive tools are now available per worker), there has been an enormous increase in the *value* of a labor-hour in comparison with a machine-hour.

The word *capital* is used in two senses that are often confused. *Real capital* refers to the sources themselves—land, buildings, labor power, etc. *Capital value* refers to the market values of the sources, measured in dollars. Similarly, *real income* refers to a flow of actual goods, but when the word *income* is used alone it is usually understood to be in value terms that can be measured by a flow of dollars. The Marginal Product of an acre of land represents real income (bushels of wheat per year), while the Value of the Marginal Product of land is measured in dollars per year.

If a resource is tradable, there will be a market-determined ratio between the *annual value of the service* and the *value of the source*—that is, the ratio of income to capital value. This ratio is called the *rate of return* earned from ownership of the resource. Suppose an acre of land is valued at $1000 and generates real income (has a Marginal Product) of 50 bushels of wheat per year in perpetuity. If the price of wheat is $2 per bushel, the income (Value of the Marginal Product) is $100 per year. Then the rate of return (*r*) earned from the investment in land is $100/$1000, or 10 percent per year. More generally, for any asset

$$\text{Rate of return earned } (r) \equiv \frac{\text{Annual income}}{\text{Value of asset}} \tag{12.3}$$

Of course, any depreciation in the value of an asset during the year should be counted against income. For some asset A, let P_A represent its market value, let ΔP_A be the change in the value (appreciation or depreciation) during the year, and let z_A be the cash flow it generates during the year. Then we can rewrite Equation (12.3) as

$$r_A \equiv \frac{z_A + \Delta P_A}{P_A} \tag{12.3'}$$

There is a fundamental relation between income and capital-value:

PROPOSITION: The proportionate yield (the rate of return earned) on all assets tends to equality.

If asset A has a higher-than-normal rate of return, people will want to buy it, and its price P_A will be bid up. Obviously, as P_A rises in Equation (12.3'), the rate of return r_A falls. This process stops when the rate of return on asset A equals the rate of return on other equivalent assets.

An important implication is that an asset expected to *depreciate* in value during a given time period will yield large cash flows; assets expected to *appreciate* may be attractive despite small cash flows. A land speculator may pay a steep price for a city lot, even if he intends to hold it vacant for some time. Here there would be no positive cash flow at all; the owner may even suffer a negative cash flow due to taxes. But the speculator expects the value of the site to appreciate enough to make the investment worthwhile.

Exercise 12.5

In an economy where the equilibrium rate of return on assets is 5 percent, suppose there are three assets, A, B, and M. A represents acres of land and has an annual cash flow of $z_A = 50$; neither appreciation nor depreciation is anticipated. B, barrels of maturing wine, has a cash flow of $z_B = -30$ (there are no receipts, only storage expenses) and is expected to appreciate 8 percent in value each year. Machines (M) yield a cash flow $z_M = 100$ but are expected to depreciate 5 percent in value each year. Find the asset prices P_A, P_B, and P_M.

Answer: In each case we use the equation $r = (z + \Delta P_A)/P_A$. Land appreciation is $\Delta P = 0$ and so the equation has the simple form $0.05 = 50/P_A$; the solution is $P_A = 1000$. For wine, the expected appreciation is $\Delta P = 0.08P$. Thus the equation becomes $0.05 = (-30 + 0.08P_B)/P_B$, so that $P_B = 1000$ also. For machinery, $\Delta P = -5$ percent and so the equation is $0.05 = (100 - 0.05P_M)/P_M$. Once again the solution is $P_M = 1000$. In this example all three assets have the same value; the numbers are such that for wine anticipated appreciation exactly offsets a negative cash flow, while for machinery a positive cash flow exactly offsets depreciation.

Since rent is the hire-price of land, in equilibrium the *annual rent* on land will equal the rate of return on the price or capital-value of the land. Similarly the additional income due to investment in training would, allowing for loss of leisure, tend to equal the rate of return on the cost of acquiring that training (see Example 12.14, "Returns to Medical Education"). For any input A, then, in equilibrium

$$h_A = rP_A \tag{12.4}$$

CONCLUSION: Interest is not the return to a particular factor called *capital*. Rather, in equilibrium the income earned by any durable resource equals the rate of return on the price or *capital-value* of the resource. Or put another way: the rate of return for any resource is the ratio between its hire-price and its market value.

12.7 ECONOMIC RENT AND PRODUCER SURPLUS

Economists use the term *economic rent* in a rather special way. It must be distinguished from the usual sense of rent as the hire-price of a piece of land or a building. Economic rent is the excess return to an input, meaning the difference between the payment for use of the resource (the hire-price) and the lowest payment the owner would have been willing to accept. Economic rent is therefore very similar to the concept of Producer Surplus introduced in Chapter 7. The only difference is that Producer Surplus refers to a seller's gain from trade in the product market, while economic rent measures the seller's gain from trade in the input market.

Economic rent is shown in Figure 12.11 as the area above the supply curve and below the price. (Note the similarity to the picture of Producer Surplus in Figure 7.7; the difference is that the horizontal axis here is scaled in units of input A rather than units of output Q.) Economic rent exists because the sellers receive h_a^* for each of the A^* units sold, even though sellers would have been willing to sell all but the last unit at a lower hire-price—down to h_a^o for the first unit sold.

Economic rent is a slippery category that must be used with care. Its magnitude depends on the range of alternatives considered. First of all, notice that the size of economic rent in Figure 12.11 is closely related to the shape of the supply curve S_a; the steeper is S_a, the greater the economic rent as a fraction of the income accruing to the input. (In the limit, if S_a were vertical at $A = A^*$, the entire payment $h_a A^*$ would be economic rent.) The slope of the supply curve for a narrowly defined activity, like being a cashier, is likely to be quite flat. This means that the economic rent—the excess return of being a cashier rather than one's next best job as, say, a typist or salesperson—will be small. But a cashier who is getting only a small economic rent as against the alternative of being a typist may be receiving a large economic rent as against the alternative of not working at all.

EXAMPLE 12.18 Economic Rent and the Military Draft

In 1967 Walter Oi[a] analyzed the losses of economic rents that would be suffered, given a continuation of conscription, by suppliers of labor services to the armed forces. For a desired intake of 472,000 recruits annually, it was estimated that the yearly recruitment at the then-current starting wage of $2500 per year would be composed of 263,000 "true" volunteers, 153,700 "reluctant" volunteers (individuals induced to volunteer only to gain some advantages over being drafted), and 55,300 draftees.

The draft viewed as a "tax" affects these groups differently. The true volunteers are those already willing to serve at the $2500 military wage. But if military salaries were raised enough to eliminate any need for reluctant volunteers or draftees, the true volunteers would also receive more pay. Under the most favorable assumption about the elasticity of voluntary supply to the armed forces, Oi estimated that to attract the required numbers the annual wage would have to be $5900. (Under what he regarded as a more realistic assumption, the wage would have to be $7450.) The loss of this benefit (the economic rent that a true volunteer would have received if the wage were $5900) is therefore at least $3400 per true volunteer per year.

The reluctant volunteers, it is reasonable to assume, had better market opportunities than the true volunteers. As a result of enlistment at the $2500 rather than $5900 wage,

Economic rent, and the problems associated with the slipperiness of that concept, have important implications for taxation. Henry George[8] based his famous single-tax proposal on the idea that, since land is in fixed supply (its supply curve is supposedly vertical), practically all of land rent can be taxed without affecting the amount of land made available for productive use. In short, Henry George thought all land rent was economic rent. But this is not the case. As remarked in "The Problem of Classification," land is not in fixed supply. A very heavy tax on land rent would not only discourage reclaiming new land from the ocean, but would rule out the investments needed to prevent erosion and waterlogging on existing land. Also even if the physical supply of land is fixed, its market supply is not. With a sufficiently high tax, landowners would retain their land for reservation uses; they could keep large residential estates or engage in home farming. Finally, a very high tax on land would make it less important for the owner to seek the best use of his land, since he will be able to keep little of its earnings in the highest-paying use.

In general, the flaws in the single-tax proposal all involve a confusion of rent as payment

FIGURE 12.11 Economic Rent   Economic rent is the shaded area lying above the factor supply curve S_a and below the market equilibrium hire-price $h_a{}^*$.

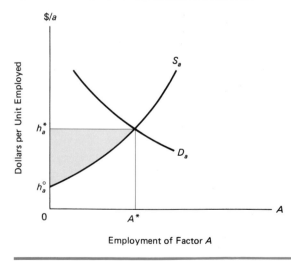

[8]Henry George, 1839–97, American economist and reformer.

to land with true economic rent as an excess that can be taxed away without affecting the way land is directed by the market to its most effective employment.

12.8 CAPITAL, INTERTEMPORAL CHOICE, AND THE CIRCULAR FLOW

We have now studied individuals' choices as *consumers* and as *resource-owners*. But there remains a third dimension of choice, between consumption and increased resource-ownership. Each person has to decide what to consume, how to employ resources he owns, and also how much to save so as to acquire more resources (for himself or his heirs). On some occasions individuals save to physically produce new resources for themselves. More often people save by purchasing claims or titles to resources (for example, by buying stocks or bonds). Savers who buy bonds or shares are not physically producing new resources themselves. But other individuals or firms can thereby obtain the funds needed to manufacture new resources like buildings or machines. *Saving* is refraining from consumption; actually building new real capital is called *investment*.

FIGURE 12.12   The Circular Flow: Consumption and Investment

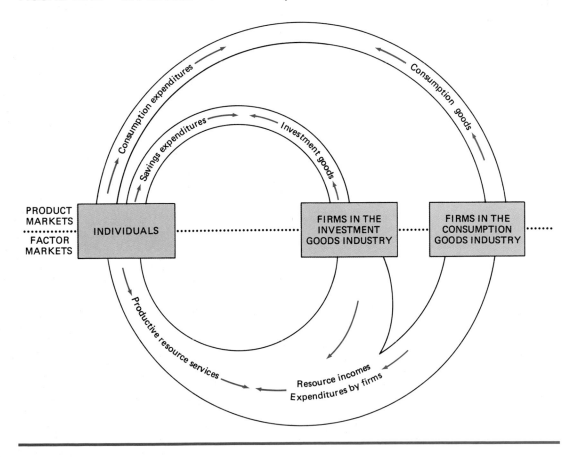

Since saving increases future income, today's consumption-versus-saving decision can also be interpreted as a choice between *present* consumption and *future* consumption. The topic of intertemporal choice will be the subject of Chapter 14.

Figure 1.1, which showed the circular flow of economic activity, can be made more realistic by separating individuals' consumption and saving choices (see Figure 12.12). Imagine there are two types of firms: firms that produce consumption goods and firms that produce real-capital or investment goods (buildings, land, machines, etc.). In the upper portion of the diagram (the product market), individuals purchase the two types of goods by consumption expenditures and savings expenditures, respectively. In the lower part of the diagram (the input market), individuals supply input services to the employing firms. A person who decides to save rather than to consume increases his stock of owned resources so that, in the future, he will be able to supply a larger quantity of productive services and thereby earn more income.[9]

SUMMARY

In the product markets, individuals demand goods; in the input markets they supply resource services. The payments people receive for input services become incomes they can spend on consumer goods.

The owner of any resource must decide between offering it on the market to obtain income or retaining it for personal leisure or reservation uses. The owner maximizes his utility by supplying the quantity of resources that equates his Marginal Rate of Substitution in Resource Supply (the marginal value of the reservation uses) to the hire-price of the resource, $MRS_R = h_a$.

As endowed income (income from other sources) changes, an Income Expansion Path is traced out. If both income and reservation uses of the resource are normal goods, the Income Expansion Path has a positive slope—showing that as income rises more reservation uses are chosen as well (less of the input will be supplied to the market). As hire-price varies, a Price Expansion Path is similarly traced out. In decisions concerning supply of inputs, the income and substitution effects normally work in opposite directions. At very low hire-prices (in the neighborhood of the all-leisure corner solution) the substitution effect must dominate, so that the Price Expansion Path has normal negative slope. But for sufficiently high hire-prices the income effect may dominate; the Price Expansion Path may bend backward.

Corresponding to the possible backward-bending range of the Price Expansion Path is a possible backward-bending range of the input supply curve (so that less is offered as the hire-price rises). However, even if the overall supply curve to the market (as against the alternative of leisure) bends backward, the supply of resource to any limited sector or particular activity is almost certain to have the standard positive slope—since there are so many other alternative input uses to draw supply from as the hire-price rises.

The equilibrium hire-price and quantity for any input in a competitive market is found at the intersection of the supply and demand curves. Demand for inputs tends to rise with

---

[9]The implicit assumption underlying the diagram is that all resources are owned by individuals and rented to firms for productive employment. In actuality, firms themselves may legally own as well as hire resources. But resource-ownership on the part of firms can be regarded merely as a convenient fiction, since ultimately all firms are themselves owned by individuals.

technological progress, with higher consumer demand for final products, and with increased supply of cooperating inputs. On the supply side, greater wealth increases the overall availability of a resource, but at the same time tends to decrease the fraction provided to the market—since suppliers can afford to retain more for reservation uses.

A worker's effort may depend on the wage he is paid. Employers may be able to reduce shirking by offering a worker a wage higher than Marginal Revenue Product, and therefore higher than the wage the worker expects to earn if he is fired from his current job. These high wages may take the form of efficiency wages, or of a wage profile that pays the worker less than his Marginal Revenue Product for an initial period, and more than his Marginal Revenue Product in later periods.

Workers may also differ in their abilities, and thus in their marginal products. In consequence job-seekers may undertake costly signaling. In a separating equilibrium individuals with high abilities incur the cost of signaling and earn a higher wage than workers with low ability. In a pooling equilibrium either all workers or no workers incur the cost of signaling, and all earn the same wage.

A sole supplier of an input (a monopolist) faces a budget curve instead of a budget line in choosing between income and leisure. In deciding how much of the resource to offer on the market, the input-monopolist would balance Marginal Resource Income against the Marginal Cost of providing the input. This Marginal Cost would be the individual's Marginal Rate of Substitution in Resource Supply. In the absence of reservation uses, the input-monopolist's Marginal Rate of Substitution in Resource Supply would be zero and he or she would simply maximize Total Resource Income.

Trade unions and other resource cartels are attempts by smaller suppliers to act as a collective monopolist. As in the case of product-market cartels, there are strong incentives to chisel, which, for the most part, can be effectively countered only by government support of the cartel.

A traditional classification divides inputs into the categories of *land* (resources provided by Nature), *capital* (resources provided by human sacrifice and saving), and *labor* (the human resource itself). This classification is not logically defensible: elements provided by Nature and elements provided by human effort enter into all three of the usual categories.

It is useful, however, to distinguish between *productive services* (such as an employee-hour of labor or an acre-year of land) and the *sources* of these services. These sources, whether in the form of land or machines or human beings, are the "real capital" of the economy. For any resource, the relation between the price of the source and the hire-price of its services involves the rate of return: $h_a = rP_a$; that is, the hire-price equals the rate of return times the price of the asset that generates the services. Put another way, the rate of return is the ratio between the annual net income of any asset (adjusted for depreciation or appreciation) and the value of the asset itself.

Economic rent is the excess of what a resource-seller is paid over what he or she would have been barely willing to accept for supplying a resource to the market. What was called Producer Surplus in Chapter 7 is essentially the same as economic rent. Economic rent is smaller the narrower the range of uses considered. So, even if the owner's economic rent as against the alternative of nonmarket uses or leisure is large, the economic rent received in the best (as against the second-best) market use may be quite small.

The individual's decisions *as a consumer* concern what goods to buy. *As a resource-owner,* the choice is among alternative employments of the owned inputs. A third decision problem is between consuming versus saving or investing so as to acquire more resources. This last is, in effect, a choice between present consumption and future consumption.

For Review

1. *Leisure* is a reservation use of labor. What other resources are likely to have significant nonmarket or reservation uses yielding utility to their owners?

2. Explain, in terms of income and substitution effects, why the market supply curve of a resource service can bend backward.

*3. If leisure were an inferior good, would a backward-bending supply curve of labor be possible?

*4. Why *must* the substitution effect dominate the income effect at very low wage rates?

*5. Is the supply curve of a resource to a particular employment likely to be more or less elastic than the supply to all market uses? Why?

6. In what way does the market opportunity set of an input-monopolist differ from that of a competitive supplier of input services? How will the optimum of the resource-owner be affected?

*7. Physicians commonly work unusually long hours, and are often praised for their dedication to healing the sick and alleviating human suffering. Show why, even if physicians are not exceptionally tenderhearted, they would still be likely to work long hours.

8. Explain the traditional "functional" classification of inputs of production.

*9. How can land and labor power be thought of as capital?

*10. What is the relationship between the hire-price of an input and the purchase price of that input?

11. What causes the rate of return on all material assets to tend toward equality?

*12. What is economic rent? What is its relation to Producer Surplus?

For Further Thought and Discussion

*1. The term *leisure,* in economics, means reservation or nonmarket uses of one's labor. What would be the effect on women's demand for "leisure" of
   a. a decline in the birth rate;
   b. improved household technology (as with the introduction of washing machines, vacuum cleaners, etc.);
   c. a fall in the price of prepared foods? In each case, what would be the effect on men's supply of labor?

2. What would be the effect upon the budget line and the resource-owner's optimum of a progressive income tax on labor earnings? of a time-and-a-half rule for overtime work?

3. Diagram a situation in which a resource-owner devotes all of his or her resource to reservation uses. Does this necessarily imply that income *I* must be a "bad" or a "neuter" commodity at the solution point? Diagram a situation in which the resource-owner's optimum is such that no reservation uses *R* are retained. Does this imply that *R* must be a "bad" or a "neuter" commodity at the solution point? Explain.

*4. There is reason to believe that changes in women's preferences have made reservation uses of their time less attractive than before, in comparison with market employment.

---

*The answers to starred questions appear at the end of the book.

a. What effect would such a change have upon the supply curve of female labor?

b. Upon the relative market wages of male and female workers?

*5. In modern times, real wealth and real wage rates have steadily increased throughout the Western world. But average working hours in market employment have steadily fallen. Would the pure income effect (due to rising per-capita wealth) tend to lead to reduced market employment? Would the pure substitution effect (due to the relative price shift represented by the rising wage rate) tend to have this effect? Comment upon the relative importance of the two in light of the evidence.

*6. Historians generally believe that slave labor is less productive than free labor. Analyze this contention.

7. There have been proposals to base wage rates on comparable worth rather than on supply and demand. A number of states and other political jurisdictions have already accepted this principle for determining salaries of public employees. In fact, there is now a flourishing business of comparable-worth consultants who provide formulas to compute salaries in accordance with the knowledge and skill required, the complexity of the task, physical demands of the job, and so forth. But these various formulas differ drastically from one another. Is there any way of objectively determining comparable worth apart from supply and demand? What consequences would you anticipate if a wage set in accordance with comparable worth diverged from that indicated by supply and demand (see "An Application: Comparable Worth" in Chapter 7)?

8. According to the single-tax movement, a land tax would not affect the productive uses of land since the supply of land is fixed. Is this valid? Distinguish between the consequences of a tax on *market uses* of land, versus a tax on *ownership* of land.

*9. Distinguish between the consequences of a tax upon labor earnings (market uses of labor), versus a tax upon labor capacity (that is, a tax calculated upon the individual's *ability to earn,* whether he or she works or not).

*10. What *supply-side* considerations help explain the relatively high wages received by U.S. workers?

11. Over a century ago Karl Marx, in what is known as the *immiserization hypothesis,* predicted that workers' wages and incomes in the advanced industrial countries would tend to fall—thus bringing on a socialist revolution. This prediction has failed. Some defenders of Marx have argued that immiserization did not occur because in the meantime capitalism has adopted socialistic reforms. Among these might perhaps be classed minimum-wage laws, the forty-hour week, welfare relief for the unemployed, and laws encouraging trade unions and collective bargaining. What effects would you expect each of these reforms to have upon wage rates? upon workers' incomes?

*12. Wage rates are high in New York City, compared to the rest of the United States. But so is the cost of living. Would you conclude that typical New York workers really are, or are not, more productive than workers elsewhere?

CHAPTER 13

EXCHANGE, TRANSACTION COSTS, AND MONEY

EXAMPLES

I n Chapter 7, we introduced the Fundamental Theorem of Exchange which explains how voluntary trade benefits the buyer and the seller. We also discussed how Consumer Surplus and Producer Surplus measure the buyers' and sellers' gains from exchange. Errors of economic reasoning (for example, common arguments for protective tariffs) often arise from ignoring the obvious truth that voluntary trade must benefit both sides.

There are, however, debatable aspects of this theorem. Suppose trickery has taken place: a purchaser paid good money for a beachfront lot that turned out to be a mile out to sea. In this case, there was no actual agreement, no meeting of minds. Also, momentary desires may not represent a person's true considered preferences. Esau sold his birthright to Jacob for a mess of pottage, and regretted the transaction afterward. Still more seriously, individuals may not always benefit from satisfying even their fully considered preferences. What about a person who chooses to consume narcotics? Moralists through the ages argued that a person's desires do not necessarily lead to his true benefit.

While these philosophical questions cannot be studied here, we see that the Fundamental Theorem must be qualified. Nevertheless, it remains the case that participants in an exchange believe that they will gain, even though an outside observer may not think so.

There are two distinct elements in the mutual gain from trade. The first element is the improved allocation of consumption goods among individuals. Suppose John and Kathy are endowed with equal quantities of tea and coffee, but that John prefers tea and Kathy prefers coffee. The potential gain from trade will be obvious. Nor are differences of taste necessary. Suppose John and Kathy have the same preferences for bread and butter, but John initially has all the bread and Kathy all the butter. Again, both can benefit from trade.

The second source of mutual gain arises from a better arrangement of production. If John is superior at baking bread and Kathy at churning butter, the possibility of later trading permits each to specialize in production.

CONCLUSION: Voluntary exchange is mutually beneficial because individuals can (1) trade existing goods so that each consumes a preferred bundle, and (2) specialize in production to increase the totals of goods available.

This chapter probes more deeply into the familiar supply-demand equilibrium of markets to analyze the benefits of exchange. We will also face the fact that exchange is not costless, so that *transaction costs* limit the benefits from trade. The role of *money* in minimizing such costs of transacting is the last topic of the chapter.

List of Notation

MRS_C	Marginal Rate of Substitution in Consumption	**PPC**	Production-Possibility Curve
MRT	Marginal Rate of Transformation in Production		

13.1 PURE-EXCHANGE EQUILIBRIUM: THE EDGEWORTH BOX

This section discusses the first category of benefits: exchange permits each individual to get more of whichever good he or she likes better.

For concreteness, consider international trade. In the nineteenth century the United States exported wheat to Britain in exchange for such manufactured goods as clothing and machines. The situations of typical citizens of the two countries are pictured in Figure 13.1. Notice that for A, the American, the starting point or "endowment" position (E_a) is near the y-axis, where y stands for amounts of wheat. For B, the Briton, the endowment (E_b) is near the x-axis, where x stands for amounts of manufactured goods. Given that A and B both have normal diversified preferences, there is a potential gain from exchange.

Exchange can be analyzed using the "Edgeworth box" of Figure 13.2 (p. 360). The box is constructed by rotating the picture of one of the individuals in the previous diagram. Specifically here, B's preference map has been rotated and superimposed upon A's to make the endowment positions coincide (at point E). A's preference directions remain up and to the right, but B's are now down and to the left. That is, we have constructed the Edgeworth box so that the indifference curves for B show higher utility moving further down and to the left.

If you turn the book upside down, you will see B's indifference curves with the usual shape and origin. Viewed with the book turned upside down, B's utility increases as we move up and to the right. The Edgeworth box thus superimposes two diagrams—the diagram showing A's choices and preferences is depicted with the book in its normal position; B's

FIGURE 13.1 **Differing Endowments and Potential Trade**   At E_a the typical American has a relatively heavy endowment of wheat *(Y)*. At E_b the typical Briton has a relatively heavy endowment of manufactured goods *(X)*. Given normal diversified preferences as indicated by their respective indifference curves U_a and U_b, they can both benefit by trade.

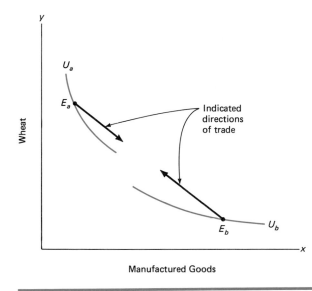

FIGURE 13.2 **Edgeworth Box** *A's consumption of Y and X is measured by distances above and to the right of the origin O_a. For individual B the axes are inverted: his consumption of X is measured by the distance to the left of the origin O_b, and his consumption of Y by the distance below O_b. A's preferences are represented by indifference curves U_a', U_a'', . . . with utility increasing up and to the right; B's preferences are represented by indifference curves U_b', U_b'', . . . with utility increasing down and to the left. The width of the box corresponds to the fixed social total $\overline{X}$, and the height to the fixed social total $\overline{Y}$. Any point in the diagram represents an allocation of these totals between individuals A and B. The allocations preferred by both individuals to E are shown by the shaded Region of Mutual Advantage.*

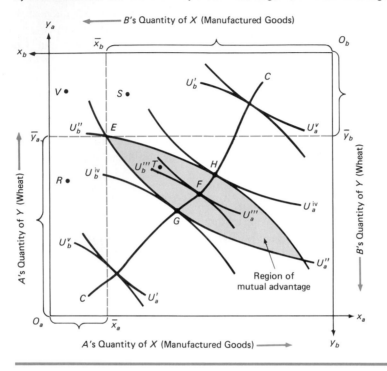

choices are depicted with the book upside down. Thus, the point E depicts A as consuming $O_a\overline{x}_a$ units of good X and $O_a\overline{y}_a$ units of good Y. Point E also shows B consuming $O_b\overline{x}_b$ units of good X, and $O_b\overline{y}_b$ units of good Y. Point G shows consumer B consuming more of both goods X and Y than at point H: the indifference curve that goes through point G must therefore represent a higher utility for B than the indifference curve that goes through point H.

The size of the Edgeworth box is determined by the total quantities of wheat Y and manufactures X available. The American, A, is endowed with $\overline{Y}_a$ units of Y, and the Briton B has $\overline{Y}_b$ units, so the height of the box is $\overline{Y} = \overline{y}_a + \overline{y}_b$. Similarly, the width of the box is determined by the amount of X available: $\overline{X} = \overline{x}_a + \overline{x}_b$.

At the endowment point E, consumer A is on his indifference curve U_a'' and B is on his indifference curve U_b''. If A sells B some wheat in exchange for manufactures, the two parties move in the diagram down and to the right to some point like T where each is on an indifference curve that shows higher utility. So they should be willing to trade from the endowment position E to point T. They would not both be willing to trade to points like R, S, or V, however. [You should verify that moving from point E to point R makes A worse off, that moving to point S makes B worse off, and that moving to point V makes both parties worse off.]

The shaded football-shaped area in the diagram is the *region of mutual advantage*. It consists of all points like T that both persons prefer to the endowment E. Thus, both would want to make any trade that moves them from E to some point in the region of mutual advantage.

Suppose the traders reached a point like F, which is within the region of mutual advantage and where, in addition, their indifference curves just touch, or are tangent to one another. Now A and B can find no mutually advantageous exchange: moving in any direction from point F makes at least one of them worse off. Connecting all points like F that represent mutual tangencies of the indifference curves in the Edgeworth box traces out the *Contract Curve CC*. There will be some region of mutual advantage starting from any point in the Edgeworth box, except for points lying on the Contract Curve.

EXAMPLE 13.1 Economic Exchange and the American Civil War

Before the Civil War the Northern and Southern states had engaged in a mutually advantageous economic exchange. The South produced a vast surplus of cotton that was sold in the North, the proceeds being used to purchase manufactured products. Less than 10 percent of the total prewar (1860) national value of manufactures had been produced in the South.[a]

The war interrupted direct North-South trade. The interruption hit the Confederacy (the South) much harder than the Union (the North). While cotton prices in the North jumped, this was an inconvenience rather than a catastrophe. But the Union blockade largely prevented the South from exporting cotton or importing manufactured products. (The small blockade-running traffic was largely used for the import of luxury goods. "When Captain Hobart Pasha of the *Venus* asked a southern woman in England what was most needed in the Confederacy, she unhesitatingly replied, 'Corsets.'")[b] The South was brought to economic and military collapse by inability to acquire essential manufactured civilian products and implements of war, while huge stocks of unsalable cotton piled up uselessly.

Confederate trade policy was seriously misguided. Export of the cotton crops of 1861 and 1862 would have been possible, since the Union blockade was not effective until later years. The Confederate government discouraged this export. They reasoned that, since "Cotton is king," withholding the crop would force Northern and foreign industrial interests to support the secession. The South's leaders failed to realize how much more vulnerable their own largely one-crop economy was to the interruption of mutually advantageous exchange.

An even more striking error was the policy of the Confederate government that banned trade through the lines with the North, partly on moralistic grounds, partly again to withhold "King Cotton." This was illogical, largely because most of the cotton run through the blockade to Cuba or Bermuda was transshipped to the North anyway. But more important, a strict ban on trade through the lines was, for the Union, a logical complement to the sea blockade that was strangling the Southern economy. In contrast, it was almost as much in the interest of the South to break this overland blockade as to evade the sea blockade. The cotton and tobacco that could have been sent North would, to a minor degree, have helped the Northern war economy. But the Confederacy, its economy collapsing because of inability to finance imports, was more desperately in need of Northern manufactures. (Actually, a substantial amount of illegal trade did pass through the lines, despite the attempts of officials on both sides to stop the practice.) Curiously, even today historians commonly take a moralistic attitude on this question. They fail to appreciate the fundamental asymmetry that made maintenance of the land blockade a wise policy for the Union, but an unwise one for the Confederacy.[c]

[a]Albert D. Kirwan, ed., *The Confederacy* (New York: Meridian Books, 1959), p. 63.

[b]Clement Eaton, *A History of the Southern Confederacy* (New York: Macmillan, 1954), p. 144.

[c]This discussion is based on J. Hirshleifer, *Disaster and Recovery: A Historical Survey*, RAND Corporation, Memorandum RM-3079-PR (April 1963), Section IV.

Figure 13.2 showed that the two parties will trade voluntarily from the endowment position E to some point within the region of mutual advantage. On the assumption that both traders are *price-takers* (neither has any monopoly or monopsony power), and that each is a typical representative of one side of the wheat/manufactures market, Figure 13.3 indicates how the equilibrium price ratio and consumption point are determined.

FIGURE 13.3 **Budget Lines and Competitive Equilibrium** Any price ratio determines the slope of a budget line through the endowment position E. A's opportunity set lies below this line, and B's lies above it. The dashed budget line KL does not correspond to a competitive market equilibrium for these two traders, since along KL individual A's optimum Q_a lies at a different point from B's optimum Q_b. $K'L'$ does correspond to an equilibrium price ratio, since the optimum positions Q_a^* and Q_b^* coincide. The equilibrium must occur at a mutual tangency of the indifference curves.

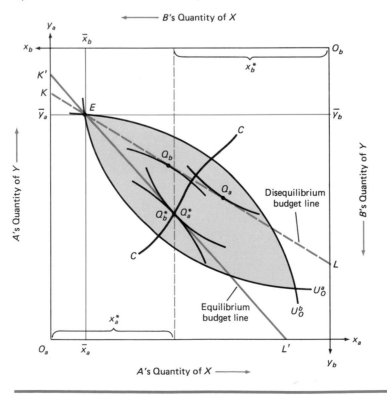

We know from Chapter 4 that the absolute value of the slope of the budget line corresponds to the price ratio—in this case, to the ratio P_x/P_y. Each individual can either consume at point E, or buy and sell at the price ratio P_x/P_y. Suppose for the moment that the absolute slope of the dashed line KL (which goes through point E) is equal to this price ratio. Then line KL is the budget line for both individuals A and B. (But recall that they look at the budget line from different directions. A's opportunity set lies below KL, while B's opportunity set lies above KL.)

With budget line KL in Figure 13.3, individual A would want to consume the bundle shown by Q_a; this is the point on his budget line which gives him the greatest utility. B would want to consume at Q_b. But these two points do not coincide. This means that the quantity of X that A wishes to purchase is not equal to the quantity that B is prepared to supply at that price ratio. The situation is not a competitive equilibrium.

An *equilibrium price ratio* for competitive trading is represented by the steeper line $K'L'$, corresponding to a higher price ratio. At this price ratio individual A wants to consume at Q_a^* and individual B wants to consume at Q_b^*. These two points coincide, so there is neither excess demand nor excess supply. The amount of good X that B wants to sell exactly equals the amount of good X that A wants to purchase. (Correspondingly, of course, the quantity of Y that A wants to sell equals the quantity of Y that B wants to buy.)

PROPOSITION: In the Edgeworth box, the competitive equilibrium allocation of the two commodities (1) lies in the region of mutual advantage, and (2) represents a mutual tangency of both traders' indifference curves with each other and with a common budget line.

Expressed mathematically, the conditions require that A and B consume at a point on their budget lines where their indifference curves have the same slopes (the same Marginal Rate of Substitution in Consumption) as the budget lines. The equations are

$$\begin{cases} P_x x_a + P_y y_a = P_x \bar{x}_a + P_y \bar{y}_a \\ P_x x_b + P_y y_b = P_x \bar{x}_b + P_y \bar{y}_b \\ MRS_C^a = P_x/P_y = MRS_C^b \end{cases} \tag{13.1}$$

Equilibrium for the market as a whole requires that the sum of the individuals' demands for each commodity must equal the totals available. This condition corresponds to the following equations:

$$\begin{cases} x_a + x_b = \bar{X} = \bar{x}_a + \bar{x}_b \\ y_a + y_b = \bar{Y} = \bar{y}_a + \bar{y}_b \end{cases} \tag{13.2}$$

Exercise 13.1

Suppose A's Marginal Rate of Substitution in Consumption is $MRS_C^a = y_a/x_a$; for B let $MRS_C^b = y_b/x_b$. A's endowment is $\bar{x}_a = 10$, $\bar{y}_a = 100$; B's endowment is $\bar{x}_b = 50$, $\bar{y}_b = 20$. Let good Y be the *numeraire* (so that $P_y \equiv 1$). Verify that the competitive equilibrium price is $P_x^* = 2$.

Answer: Individual A would want to consume at the point on his budget line where the Marginal Rate of Substitution equals the price ratio. Expressed mathematically, this means that

$$2x_a + y_a = 2(10) + 1(100) \quad \text{and} \quad y_a/x_a = 2$$

So A's optimum is $x_a^* = 30$, $y_a^* = 60$. For B the corresponding equations are $2x_b + y_b = 2(50) + (20)$ and $y_b/x_b = 2$, leading to the same numerical solution: $x_b^* = 30$, $y_b^* = 60$. Now we need only verify that total demand equals the quantities of the two goods available:

$$x_a + x_b \equiv \overline{X} \equiv \bar{x}_a + \bar{x}_b = 60$$

$$y_a + y_b \equiv \overline{Y} \equiv \bar{y}_a + \bar{y}_b = 120$$

13.2 SUPPLY AND DEMAND IN PURE EXCHANGE

The Edgeworth box makes it easy to visualize the properties of equilibrium once it is reached. To describe how it is reached we must think in terms of supply and demand.

The Price Expansion Path (PEP) in Panel (a) of Figure 13.4 looks very much like the Price Expansion Path of Chapter 4, except for one feature. In Chapter 4 the endowment point E was always on the vertical (Y) axis, so we assumed that the individual initially had no X at all. In Figure 13.4 here, the endowment points are in the interior, meaning that each individual starts out instead with positive amounts of both X and Y. This change has an important result. In Chapter 4 the individual endowed only with good Y would never supply X. But here A's endowment point E lies toward but not quite at the vertical axis; he has a large endowment of Y, and some positive endowment of X. (Thus, America produced lots of wheat, but also some manufactures.) We would therefore expect A to usually supply Y and demand X, but not necessarily always. There is some price ratio P_x/P_y so high (some budget line K^oL^o so steep) that he will want to stand pat with his endowment combination and not make any purchases or sales at all. This is called the *sustaining price ratio*. And for even higher price ratios (even steeper budget lines through E_a), A would supply X to the market; that is, his optimum would lie above and to the left of E_a. Similarly Panel (b) shows that B will usually sell X and buy Y, but at a sufficiently low price ratio P_x/P_y his market behavior would reverse.

The data in the Price Expansion Path curves of Figure 13.4 can be used to generate supply and demand curves in two different ways, which we must be careful not to confuse. The first runs in terms of the whole or full quantities demanded or supplied; the second runs in terms of the net or transaction quantities.

1. An individual's *full demand* for any commodity X (at price P_x) is the total quantity of X he consumes. It is equal to the endowed quantity already in his possession plus the quantity he buys.
2. An individual's *transaction demand* for X is the quantity he buys in the market. It is equal to full demand less the individual's endowed quantity of X.
3. An individual's *full supply* of X is his endowed quantity.
4. An individual's *transaction supply* of X is the quantity he sells. It is equal to the endowed quantity less the amount he retains for consumption.

On the demand side, the full quantity demanded of good X *includes* the endowed quantity $\bar{x}$; this is the demand concept relevant for purposes of consumption. The transaction demand quantity excludes the quantity endowed (the quantity self-supplied); this represents the

FIGURE 13.4 **Price Expansion Paths**   A change in the price ratio tilts the budget lines through the endowment positions [E_a for A in Panel (a) and E_b for B in Panel (b)]. For price ratios leading to points on PEP$_a$ to the right of E_a, individual A will be a net demander of X. At the "sustaining" price ratio (budget line $K^\circ L^\circ$) he will stand pat and not trade; for still higher price ratios he will be a supplier of X (indicated by the range of PEP$_a$ to the left of E_a). A corresponding analysis holds for individual B in Panel (b).

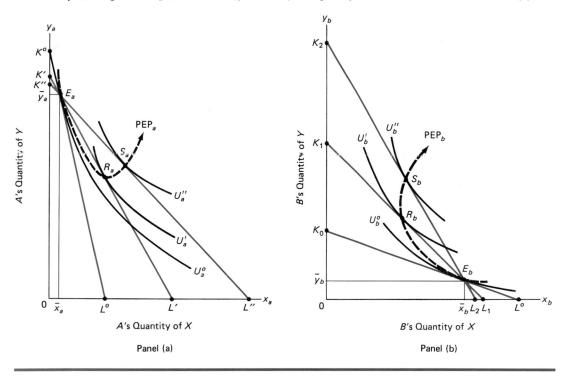

Panel (a)

Panel (b)

demand concept relevant to analyze market trading. On the supply side the full quantity is simply the fixed endowment amount; the transaction quantity is the portion of the endowment sold on the market. Think of the full quantities as those demanded from or supplied to the economy as a whole, while the transaction quantities are the (normally smaller) amounts bought and sold.

The relation between transaction demand and full demands, for any individual i, is given by

$$x_i^t \equiv x_i - \bar{x}_i \qquad\qquad (13.3)$$
Transaction Demands and Full Demands
$$y_i^t \equiv y_i - \bar{y}_i$$

The transaction and full *supplies* are simply the negative of the above (since positive supply is negative demand and vice versa).

In Panel (a) of Figure 13.4, A's full demand for X at any point along the Price Expansion Path curve is simply the x-coordinate of that position. His transaction demand is this horizontal distance less the endowed amount $\bar{x}_a$. It follows that at his sustaining price ratio, A's full demand for X equals $\bar{x}_a$ while his transaction demand for X is zero.

The distinction between full and transaction magnitudes is important in a number of applications, including taxation. A tax on *consumption* is levied on full demands; a tax on *purchases* falls only on transaction demands. Put another way, endowed quantities that are self-consumed escape a transaction tax on purchases, but do not escape a tax on consumption. (A tariff is a transaction tax that burdens international trading but not domestic trading; the latter represents quantities that are self-supplied from the viewpoint of the nation as a whole.) An increase in transaction taxes makes it more attractive for individuals to self-supply their wants rather than deal in the market.

Figure 13.5 traces the supply and demand curves for any individual as the price ratio P_x/P_y varies. (We can set the price of good Y to be the numeraire, so that $P_y \equiv 1$ and the price ratio is simply P_x.) The full demand curve d_i corresponds to the desired consumption quantity x_i; the full supply curve is the fixed endowed quantity $\bar{x}_i$. The transaction demand curve d_i^t is the difference between the two—x_i^t. Note that for prices of X greater than the sustaining price $\bar{P}_x$ it is more convenient to visualize a positive transaction supply (the dashed curve s_i^t) rather than a negative "transaction demand."

Panel (a) of Figure 13.6 shows transaction supply and demand; Panel (b) shows full demand and supply. This figure considers two typical individuals A and B, but more generally many traders would be involved. Panel (a) represents the supply and demand to the market, or the quantities that will be bought and sold; Panel (b) represents the supply and demand to the economy, the quantities individuals want to produce and consume. Notice that the equilibrium price P_x^* can be regarded as determined in either panel. [*Challenge to the reader:* Verify the correspondence between the two panels.]

CONCLUSION: Competitive supply-demand equilibrium can be expressed in two ways. The intersection of the aggregate *transaction* supply curve with the aggregate *transaction* demand

---

FIGURE 13.5   Full and Transaction Supply and Demand Curves (Pure Exchange)   The individual's full demand curve d_i shows, at any price P_x, his or her desired consumption quantity. The full supply curve $\bar{s}_i$ represents the fixed endowment quantity. The transaction demand curve d_i^t shows, at any price P_x, the amount demanded from the market (horizontal difference between d_i and $\bar{s}_i$). In the range where transaction demand d_i^t is negative, it is usually more convenient to speak of a positive transaction supply curve, s_i^t. Transaction demand and transaction supply are exactly zero at the sustaining price $\bar{P}_x$.

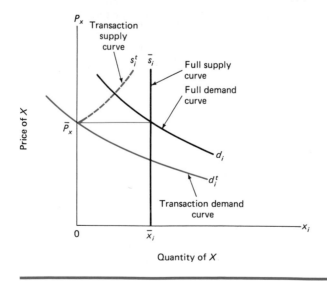

FIGURE 13.6 **Supply-Demand Equilibrium**   Panel (a) shows a demand-supply equilibrium for commodity X in terms of the *transaction* quantities; Panel (b) pictures the same equilibrium in terms of the *full* quantities. The equilibrium in Panel (a) is at the intersection of A's transaction demand curve d_a^t and B's transaction supply curve s_b^t. In Panel (b) the aggregate full supply curve $\bar{S}$ to the economy as a whole is the sum of $\bar{s}_a$ and $\bar{s}_b$. The aggregate full demand curve D is similarly the sum of d_a and d_b. The $\bar{S}$ and D curves in Panel (b) intersect at the same equilibrium price P_x^* as at the intersection of S^t and D^t in Panel (a).

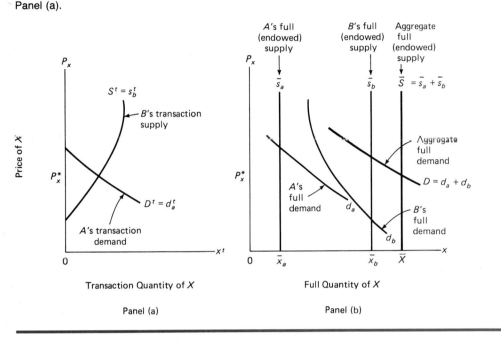

Panel (a)

Transaction Quantity of X

Panel (b)

Full Quantity of X

curve shows the quantity actually traded in the market. The intersection of the aggregate *full* supply curve and the aggregate *full* demand curve shows the entire economy-wide consumption, which must equal the aggregate economy-wide supply of the commodity. The two pictures determine the same equilibrium price.

We should, of course, think not just of two commodities X and Y but rather of all goods simultaneously. The result is a *general* equilibrium of prices and quantities. However, the underlying principles—individuals optimize, and in equilibrium the quantities demanded and supplied are equal—are the same principles illustrated in the two-good world.

Exercise 13.2

Use the data of Exercise 13.1 to find (a) the full supply and demand curves for each individual and for the society, and (b) the corresponding transaction supply and demand curves. Verify the solution $P_x^* = 2$ in each case.

Answer: (a) A's budget equation is $P_x x_a + y_a = 10P_x + 100$. His Marginal Rate of Substitution in Consumption is y_a/x_a. He maximizes utility by choosing to consume at that point on the budget line where $y_a/x_a = P_x$. Solving for y_a, and substituting in the budget equation we obtain the full demand equation $x_a = 5 + 50/P_x$. For B the conditions are $P_x x_b + y_b = 50P_x + 20$ and $y_b/x_b = P_x$, leading to his full demand equation $x_b = 25 + 10/P_x$. The aggregate full demand equation is then $X_d = x_a + x_b = 30 + 60/P_x$. The full supplies are $\bar{x}_a = 10$ and $\bar{x}_b = 50$; the sum of these supplies is $X_s = 60$. Setting $X_s = X_d$, the solution is indeed $P_x^* = 2$. (b) A's transaction demand is $x_a - \bar{x}_a \equiv x_a^t = -5 + 50/P_x$. B's demand is $x_b - \bar{x}_b \equiv x_b^t = -25 + 10/P_x$. In the neighborhood of equilibrium, individual A purchases good X and individual B sells good X. So the aggregate transaction demand is $X_d^t = x_a^t = -5 + 50/P_x$. For the aggregate transaction supply we take the negative of B's transaction demand: $X_s^t = -x_b^t = 25 - 10/P_x$. Setting $X_d^t = X_s^t$, the solution once again is $P_x^* = 2$.

13.3 EXCHANGE AND PRODUCTION

So far this chapter considered trade in a world without production, a world of "pure exchange." Under pure exchange a person can consume a bundle different from his endowment only by buying and selling goods. But in the actual world individuals can also *produce* goods.

In Figure 13.7 the shaded region shows the *production opportunity set*—all the possible baskets of commodities X and Y that a person could produce. The northeast boundary QQ of the production opportunity set is called the *transformation locus* or *Production-Possibility Curve* (PPC). The concave shape, which shows that the slope is flatter as we move to the left, reflects diminishing returns. Suppose an individual or a nation tried to specialize in the production of wheat, that is, tried to produce a combination well toward the Y-axis along QQ. As specialization is pushed further and further, each increment of Y requires a greater and greater sacrifice of manufactures X and increasing opportunity costs are encountered.

FIGURE 13.7 **Productive and Consumptive Optimum: Robinson Crusoe** The shaded region shows a Production-Possibility Curve QQ subject to diminishing returns as the individual specializes in producing either X or Y. Since an isolated Robinson Crusoe must produce what he consumes, the best attainable position is the tangency of QQ with indifference curve U^o at point R^*.

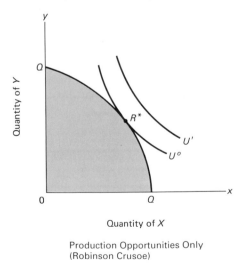

Production Opportunities Only
(Robinson Crusoe)

A Robinson Crusoe with only productive opportunities consumes at $R*$ in Figure 13.7, the point on the Production-Possibility Curve QQ that lies on the highest indifference curve, U^0; equivalently, this is the point where the Production-Possibility Curve is tangent to an indifference curve. Since Crusoe cannot trade, $R*$ is both his consumption optimum and production optimum. The tangency condition can be expressed by the equation

$$MRS_C = MRT \qquad \text{Robinson Crusoe Optimum} \qquad (13.4)$$

Here MRS_C, the Marginal Rate of Substitution in Consumption, corresponds, as in Chapter 4, to the absolute value of the slope of the individual's indifference curve. The new symbol MRT stands for the *Marginal Rate of Transformation. MRT* is $|\Delta y/\Delta x|$, the absolute value of the slope of the Production-Possibility Curve; this is interpreted as the additional amount of Y that can be produced per unit reduction in the quantity of X produced. Observe that this Marginal Rate of Transformation is not a constant, but instead has different values at different points on the Production-Possibility Curve. Note how the opposing curvatures of the Production-Possibility Curve and of an indifference curve guarantee that there will be a unique tangency $R*$.[1]

CONCLUSION: Robinson Crusoe, who can produce but cannot trade, has a productive-consumptive optimum at the point where his Marginal Rate of Substitution in Consumption equals his Marginal Rate of Transformation along the boundary of his production opportunity set.

Robinson Crusoe situations may seem fanciful, but this is not necessarily so. In some historical instances nations did not trade because of geography or sometimes by deliberate choice. A famous example is Japan, which closed itself to trade for over two centuries before Commodore M.C. Perry's visit in 1854.

EXAMPLE 13.2 Animal Robinson Crusoes

Trade is a human invention. Since nonhuman animals do not exchange with one another, they make all their economic decisions under Robinson Crusoe conditions. An example of such a decision is the problem of "optimal diet breadth."[a]

Think of X and Y as two sources of food for a predator—for example, two prey species. Because of diminishing returns the productive opportunity set typically has a shape like the shaded region in the diagram. The more the predator concentrates on consuming prey species X, the scarcer and more difficult it becomes to capture X rather than Y (the Marginal Rate of Transformation becomes steeper towards the right). The predator also has preferences as represented by the indifference curves in the diagram. Each such curve represents a set of equally acceptable diets. The convexity of the indifference curves reflects the fact that diversity in consumption helps provide the many metabolic inputs required by living

---

[1]*Mathematical Footnote:* Using derivatives, the condition can be expressed as

$$\left.\frac{dy}{dx}\right|_U = \left.\frac{dy}{dx}\right|_Q$$

In addition, the individual must be on his Production-Possibility Curve, so that the equation $Q(x, y) = 0$ is satisfied.

organisms. The greater the consumption of food source X, the lower the nutritional benefit of an additional unit of X compared to Y.

The optimal position for the animal is at the tangency point R^*, which will ordinarily represent an interior (mixed-diet) solution.

[a]The discussion here is based on D. J. Rapport, "An Optimization Model of Food Selection," *The American Naturalist*, v. 105 (November–December 1971) and M. L. Cody, "Optimization in Ecology," *Science*, v. 183 (March 22, 1974).

Let us go beyond the isolated individual to consider a world with both production and trade. We can imagine that Robinson Crusoe has been discovered but chooses to remain on his island while trading with the rest of the world. His opportunities to buy and sell goods are shown in Figure 13.8 by the budget line MM, which has slope $-P_x/P_y$ and is tangent to his Production-Possibility Curve QQ. The slope of the budget line reflects the prices of the goods in the world market. The reason for the tangency is as follows. Robinson Crusoe can produce at any point on his Production-Possibility Curve and can trade from that point at the market prices. A budget line that goes through any point other than the tangency Q^* would have the same slope as line MM, but would lie closer to the origin than line MM. Clearly Robinson is better off the further out is the budget line showing his consumption possibilities.

Put differently, the opportunity to trade lets Robinson separate his production and consumption decisions. Specifically, in Figure 13.8 he can produce at Q^* while consuming at C^*. Think of this as a two-step procedure. First, a person moves along QQ to a *productive*

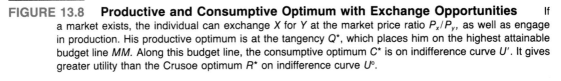

FIGURE 13.8   Productive and Consumptive Optimum with Exchange Opportunities   If a market exists, the individual can exchange X for Y at the market price ratio P_x/P_y, as well as engage in production. His productive optimum is at the tangency Q^*, which places him on the highest attainable budget line MM. Along this budget line, the consumptive optimum C^* is on indifference curve U'. It gives greater utility than the Crusoe optimum R^* on indifference curve U^o.

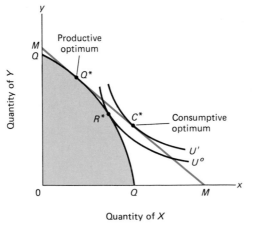

optimum Q*, where the Production-Possibility Curve is tangent to a highest attainable budget line[2] *MM*. Second, by exchanging *Y* for *X* he can move away from *Q**, along the budget line *MM* to a *consumptive optimum* at *C**. A comparison of *C** with the no-trade solution *R** shows the advantages of trade.

The productive optimum position *Q** in Figure 13.8 is described by the equation

$$MRT = \frac{P_x}{P_y} \qquad \text{Productive Optimum Condition} \qquad (13.5)$$

That is, at the productive optimum the absolute values of the slopes of the Production-Possibility Curve *(MRT)* and of the budget line *(P_x/P_y)* must be equal. The familiar consumptive optimum lies at the point where an indifference curve is tangent to the budget line, as at *C**. This condition is expressed by

$$\frac{P_x}{P_y} = MRS_C \qquad \text{Consumptive Optimum Condition} \qquad (13.6)$$

Notice that (13.5) and (13.6) together imply that the Marginal Rate of Transformation in Production equals the Marginal Rate of Substitution in Consumption.

Exercise 13.3

Let Robinson Crusoe's Production-Possibility Curve (PPC) be given by the equation $f^2/2 + g = 150$, where *f* is the amount of fish and *g* the amount of grain he can obtain, depending on the way he divides his time and effort. (Think of *g* as plotted on the vertical axis and *f* as plotted on the horizontal axis.) Robinson's Marginal Rate of Substitution in Consumption (the absolute value of the slope of an indifference curve) is $MRS_C = g/f$. (a) Find Robinson's production-consumption optimum *R**. (b) If Robinson is discovered by a world market in which $P_f = 5$, and $P_g = 1$, determine his productive optimum *Q** and consumptive optimum *C**. (c) Verify that he prefers *C** to *R**.

Answer: (a) *MRT* is the absolute slope along the Production-Possibility Curve. By calculus it can be found that $MRT = f$. (This can be approximately verified by tabulating $\Delta g/\Delta f$ along the Production Possibility Curve.) Setting *MRT* equal to MRS_C, the condition for an optimum becomes $f = g/f$, or $g = f^2$. Substituting in the equation for the Production-Possibility Curve, the *R** solution is $f = 10$, $g = 100$. (b) Robinson finds *Q** by setting $MRT = P_f = 5$. The productive optimum is thus $f = 5$, $g = 137.5$. To find his consumptive optimum, we use the budget condition and Substitution Equivalence Equation: $5f + g = 5(5) + 137.5$ and $g/f = 5$. The *C** solution is therefore $f = 16.25$, $g = 81.25$. (c) We know that Crusoe prefers *C** over *R** because he could obtain the *R** combination by not trading, yet chooses to trade.

Figure 13.9 translates the information pictured in Figure 13.8 into supply and demand curves. Once again it will be useful to distinguish *full* versus *transaction* supply and demand concepts.

Figure 13.9 differs from Figure 13.5 in one important respect. In pure exchange the individual's full supply of *X* to the economy was simply his fixed endowed quantity $\bar{x}_i$ (the vertical line $\bar{s}_i$ in Figure 13.5). But in a world of production and exchange, an individual's

---

[2]We could construct other budget lines, all with slope $-P_x/P_y$, in the diagram. Those lying parallel to *MM* but below it are attainable by the individual, should he choose a production point other than *Q**, but are all obviously inferior to *MM*. Budget lines above *MM* would be superior, but are not attainable.

FIGURE 13.9 **Individual Demand and Supply with Production**   As P_x rises, individual i produces more X, so his full supply curve s_i^q has positive slope. His full demand curve d_i normally has negative slope. His transaction supply and demand for X are exactly zero at his autarky price P_x^o, the price at which the full demand curve and the full supply curve intersect. Above this price his full supply exceeds full demand, so there will be positive transaction supply s_i^t—increasing as P_x rises. Below this price his full demand exceeds full supply, so there will be positive transaction demand d_i^t—increasing as P_x falls.

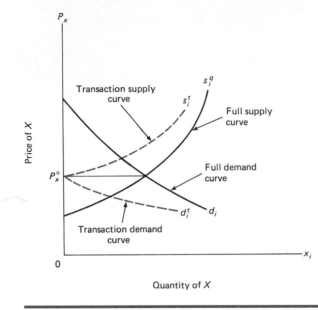

full supply of X varies with price. As P_x rises (with P_y held constant), the market line MM in Figure 13.8 becomes steeper. The point Q^* where the market line MM is tangent with the Production-Possibility Curve QQ therefore shifts down and to the right. This shift corresponds to increased production of X. So the individual's full supply curve s_i^q for commodity X is a rising function of price P_x. The full demand curve d_i of Figure 13.9 similarly represents, for any price P_x, the x-coordinate of the individual's *consumptive optimum* C^* in Figure 13.8.

What about *transaction* demand and supply? Just as in the last section, the individual's transaction demand d_i^t is his net demand in the market (the difference between his full demand and full supply); transaction supply s_i^t is his net supply to the market (the difference between full supply and full demand). At what is known as the *autarky price*[3] the net amount demanded or supplied is zero.

Figure 13.9 applies for a single trader. Equilibrium in the market as a whole is the result of balancing *aggregate* supply with *aggregate* demand. Figure 13.10 shows the solutions for both X^* (the social total of X produced and consumed), and X'^* (the amount of X exchanged in the market). The difference between X^* and X'^* represents the equilibrium amount of X that individuals produce for their own consumption. Note that the transaction

---

[3]The autarky price P_x^o is analogous to the sustaining price $\overline{P}_x$ of pure exchange; each represents the price at which the individual does not trade.

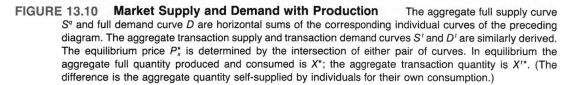

FIGURE 13.10 Market Supply and Demand with Production   The aggregate full supply curve S^q and full demand curve D are horizontal sums of the corresponding individual curves of the preceding diagram. The aggregate transaction supply and transaction demand curves S^t and D^t are similarly derived. The equilibrium price P_x^* is determined by the intersection of either pair of curves. In equilibrium the aggregate full quantity produced and consumed is X^*; the aggregate transaction quantity is X^{t*}. (The difference is the aggregate quantity self-supplied by individuals for their own consumption.)

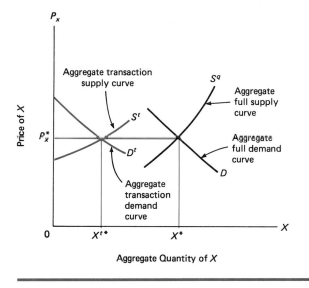

Aggregate Quantity of X

supply and demand curves S^t and D^t intersect at the same price as the full supply and demand curves S^q and D.

The model of pure exchange illustrated one of the advantages of trade: it redistributes existing goods to their highest-valued uses. The model of production and exchange demonstrates the second advantage: it increases the total availability of goods through specialization in production.

In Figure 13.11 (p. 374) the two panels show Production Possibility Curves QQ for a typical American A and Briton B. We continue to assume that A is best at producing wheat Y while B is best at producing manufactures X. Without trade they could only achieve their respective "Robinson Crusoe" solutions R_a^* and R_b^*. Since each of them desires to consume both commodities, in isolation each would have to produce a good that the other could produce more efficiently.

The opening of trade makes budget lines MM (with slope $-P_x/P_y$) available to both parties. Individual A takes advantage of the market by producing at Q_a^*. He now specializes in producing Y, but this does not cause him to reduce his "diversity in consumption," for he will sell off the excess of Y. Correspondingly, B specializes in producing X, and sells the excess to A. The individuals consume at C_a^* and C_b^*. Thus market exchange induces each person (as if led by an "Invisible Hand") to serve the interests of the other.

Trade allows individuals and nations to reach higher levels of preference. Furthermore, thanks to specialization in production the social totals of the traded goods are greater. For these reasons, economists have usually favored free trade among nations.

FIGURE 13.11 **Productive Specialization** In the absence of exchange individuals A and B would produce and consume at R_a^* and R_b^*, respectively. Trade permits each to specialize in producing the commodity favored by his transformation opportunities. A's productive solution Q_a^* involves heavier production of Y, while B's involves heavier production of X. Trade allows each to move along market line MM to consume at C_a^* and C_b^* respectively.

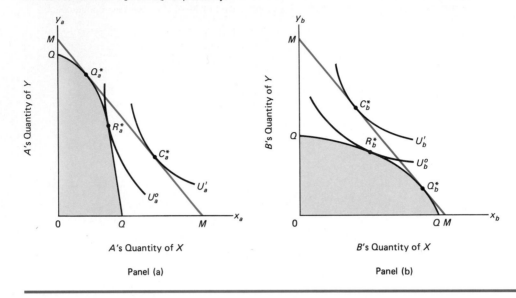

Panel (a)

Panel (b)

EXAMPLE 13.3 International Specialization

Individuals tend to specialize in production but to diversify in consumption. We all work at just one job, or a very few, but consume hundreds of different products. Should we expect the same thing of countries? To some extent, the answer is yes. But the degree of productive specialization should be less for larger countries, which tend to have more highly varied resources and therefore depend less on international trade to diversify consumption.

A study by M. Michaely compared specialization in the exports and imports of 44 countries in the years 1952–64. The table shows, for a number of countries, indexes of specialization in exports and in imports. The measure of specialization employed was the *Gini coefficient*, which in this case has a range of 8.2 to 100.0.[a] The countries in the table are ranked in decreasing order of export (productive) specialization. As can be seen, the highly specialized group at the top tends to be small countries, while the group at the bottom tends to be large countries. No particular pattern is evident in the specialization index of imports, a result consistent with the principle of diversity in consumption.

Indexes of Specialization of International Trade

Country	Exports	Imports
Egypt	84.2	18.6
Colombia	84.0	23.9
Gold Coast	83.5	21.4
Iceland	80.3	19.1

Indexes of Specialization of International Trade (cont.)

Country	Exports	Imports
Finland	38.1	19.2
Mexico	35.0	26.8
Libya	34.1	18.9
Spain	33.9	24.5
Italy	20.5	20.7
United Kingdom	19.2	16.1
United States	18.8	20.5
France	18.0	20.4

Source: Michael Michaely, "Concentration of Exports and Imports: An International Comparison," *Economic Journal*, v. 68 (December 1958), p. 725.

[a]The Gini coefficient for exports is defined as $100 \sqrt{\sum_{i=1}^{N} (x_i/X)^2}$. Here x_i is a nation's annual value of exports of a particular good i, and X is its total annual value of exports. The goods were classified into $N = 150$ categories. If a country exported only a single good, the specialization index would be 100.0. If it exported all 150 goods in equal amounts, the result would be an index of 8.2. The measure of import specialization is similarly defined and has the same range.

13.4 IMPERFECT MARKETS: COSTS OF EXCHANGE

Previous chapters sometimes departed from the assumption of perfect competition (price-taking behavior on both sides of the market)—for example, in the chapters on monopoly and oligopoly. But one assumption has been maintained up to now: *perfect markets*. A market is said to be perfect (even if it is not competitive) if at any moment there is a single price, known to all participants, at which transactions may be executed without further fee or penalty. Elaborating a bit, perfect markets have three main characteristics.

1. *Perfect communication*—The market must be integrated, not segmented by limitations of information. Real-world markets have informational imperfections, as we can see by the efforts made to overcome them: classified newspaper advertising, specialized "middlemen" (such as real-estate brokers), and organized exchanges (such as the New York Stock Exchange).

2. *Instantaneous equilibrium*—A perfect market instantly reaches the market-clearing price. But no such ideal can be achieved in the real world. A farmer bringing vegetables to a city market may (by cleverness or chance) realize a sale at terms higher than the (unknown) true equilibrium price. Or, unluckily, the farmer may accept a price lower than he should have held out for. Thus, in real-world markets there is some "trading at false prices." (*Speculation* can reduce fluctuations of price that lead to false trading, since speculators buy when they believe the price is accidentally too low and sell when price is accidentally too high.)

3. *Costless transactions*—In perfect markets there would be no costs of exchange. In the real world, market middlemen such as wholesalers and retailers, brokers, dealers, and jobbers—although they facilitate exchange—must be paid for their services. Transaction taxes, in which *government* collects "middleman" payments (possibly

reflecting actual services to taxpayers, but possibly not), may also make exchange costly.

EXAMPLE 13.4 **Experiments in Perfect and Imperfect Markets**

An interesting series of economic experiments on the functioning of markets has been conducted by Vernon L. Smith.[a] He proposed the following question: Given that the theoretical conditions of "perfect markets" are never really satisfied, how far can the conditions diverge from "perfection" and still achieve the same essential results? For example, if traders cannot communicate perfectly, or if some trades occur at "false prices," is equilibrium nevertheless quickly attained at a price-quantity outcome close to the theoretical ideal?

In one experiment each participant was informed only of his demand price (the maximum he should be willing to bid if buying) or supply price (the minimum he should be willing to accept if selling). Thus the subjects did not know the *aggregate* supply and demand functions and could not calculate the "true" equilibrium price.

Under the experimental conditions any buyer (or seller) could make an offer at any time, which, if accepted by another trader, became a binding contract. The process was public, so that the terms of any consummated deals became known to as-yet-uncommitted traders. A trading week consisted of five trading days (periods) within which supply and demand conditions remained unchanged. A typical experimental series went as follows. In the first week the supply and demand conditions implied a theoretical equilibrium price of 465; after the end of the third day practically all transactions took place exactly at the correct price of 465. At the beginning of the second week demand and supply conditions were shifted to make the equilibrium price 285. The participants were more experienced, and trading settled down to the correct price by the end of the second day. For the third week a new set of supply-demand conditions made the equilibrium price 735. Convergence to the new equilibrium was so rapid that virtually all trades were made at the equilibrium price, almost from the very beginning.

The model of perfect markets, therefore, provided excellent predictions of actual transaction prices in this experiment. Furthermore, the quantities exchanged were also very close to the theoretical ideal. In short, substantially all the potential advantages of trade (in the form of Consumer Surplus and Producer Surplus) were achieved despite the experimental departure from ideal conditions.

Results such as these suggest that the economist's perfect-market model is robust, in the sense of having a high degree of predictive reliability even though the exact conditions for its validity are not fully met. A similar situation exists in the physics model of a perfect gas that leads to the prediction known as Boyle's Law. No actual gas can meet the requirements of a perfect gas, and yet Boyle's Law is a very reliable predictive equation in physics.

[a]V. L. Smith, "An Experimental Study of Competitive Market Behavior," *Journal of Political Economy*, v. 70 (April 1962); "Effects of Market Organization on Competitive Equilibrium," *Quarterly Journal of Economics*, v. 78 (May 1964); "Experimental Auction Markets and the Walrasian Hypothesis," *Journal of Political Economy*, v. 73 (August 1965).

In the discussion that follows, markets will generally be assumed perfect *except* for transaction costs. This assumption means that middlemen totally eliminate other types of market imperfection—such as limited communication and false trading at nonequilibrium prices. But of course these efficient middlemen must be paid. Costs of exchange, we shall see, have important consequences for the scope of trading and for the degree of specialization in production and consumption.

EXAMPLE 13.5 **Cost of Trading on the New York Stock Exchange**

An organized exchange like the New York Stock Exchange approaches the ideal "perfect" market. Since the exchange guarantees the quality of merchandise delivered and the payment arrangements, the buyer can forego personal inspection of the merchandise and the seller need not be concerned with the credit standing or the character of the buyer. In dealing on the New York Stock Exchange, the buyer does not have to worry about whether the stock certificates acquired are counterfeit and the seller need not fear that the buyer may pay with a bad check.

However, there are costs of trading on the New York Stock Exchange: commission charges and the bid-ask price spread. The commission charges are the explicit fees paid to brokers. These charges are quoted separately from the amounts paid for or received from the securities themselves. The bid-ask spread is a less obvious cost of transacting. At any time the market price to a seller of a stock like General Motors, the *bid price,* is less than the *ask price* that a buyer of GM stock would have to pay. The difference goes mainly to the Exchange's "specialist" in General Motors stock (see Example 8.1) who makes a continuous market in that security. Specialists, like retail or wholesale merchants, must on average buy for less (the bid price) then they sell for (the ask price) if they are to remain in business. (The customer's *broker,* in contrast with the specialist, is normally a pure intermediary who does not buy or sell for his or her own account.)

A study by Harold Demsetz[a] indicated that, on average, in 1965 the bid-ask spread on the New York Stock Exchange was about 40 percent of total transaction costs, and explicit commission charges were about 60 percent. The two together amounted to about 1.3 percent of the value of the securities exchanged. The study also found that the bid-ask spread is normally much lower for frequently traded than for infrequently traded securities. This difference is reasonable if we regard the Exchange's specialist as a merchant who must hold an inventory of securities in order to stand ready to sell. On average the specialist's funds must be tied up longer holding a slow-moving commodity like an infrequently traded stock. Commission charges were also lower in percentage terms for bigger transactions, which is easily understandable in terms of the savings in communications and recording costs.

[a]H. Demsetz, "The Cost of Transacting," *Quarterly Journal of Economics,* v. 82 (February 1968).

A large fraction of national resources appears to be spent on exchange. In 1982 around 22 percent of U.S. nonagricultural employment fell into the occupational category Wholesale and Retail Trade. And many workers classified under other headings—for example, Transportation and Communication, Finance, Insurance, and Real Estate—may also facilitate exchange. This evidence suggests that middlemen are an enormous drain on the nation's resources.

Such an initial impression is misleading. A crucial distinction must be made between (1) the *trading* of goods and services—that is, the social process of market exchange—and (2) the *physical movement* or turnover of commodities between persons. Any economy that integrates the activities of a great number of individuals to take advantage of productive specialization and of the division of labor—whether it be an economy of saints, of ants, or of utility-maximizers under free markets—would still involve physical transfer of commodities. Activities and costs due to the necessary fact of turnover must not be attributed to market trading.

Consider an extreme command economy with a central authority that makes all economic decisions. The economy might be a dictatorship that aims to improve popular well-being. Specialization in production could still be achieved, but by command rather than by an invisible hand. Farmers would be ordered to grow crops and turn them over to railroads; railroads would be ordered to ship them to cities, and turn them over to warehouses; warehouses would be ordered to store food, and turn it over to retail outlets, and so forth. Every transfer of control of goods would involve costs: handling, shipping, storing, record-keeping, and so forth.

The costs associated with these physical movements are *production* costs rather than exchange costs. This accounts for essentially all transportation services. "Adding" transportation to a good brings it to a consumer, and is in principle the same as "adding" baking services to dough to make it into bread, or moving coal from an underground mine to a dump on the ground where it can be used. The consequence is that the costs of market exchange as a process are not nearly so great as might have first been thought. Many of the persons classified under Wholesale and Retail Trade, for example, are really engaged in the physical movement of goods that would still have to take place even in a command economy with no market trading.

What then are the *costs of exchange* proper? These are the costs, in a non-command or free economy that stem specifically from the market process. For voluntary transactions to take place, offers must be communicated and alternatives compared. Contracts must be negotiated, and their execution verified. Fraud or other nonperformance must be guarded against. All these activities involve costs.[4] All the expenses of an institution like the New York Stock Exchange, for example, fall under one or more of these headings. (Without private ownership there would be no need for a stock exchange, since there would be no corporate shares.)

EXAMPLE 13.6   Farmer, Consumer, Middleman

"Consumerists" contend that food prices are too high; farmers complain that the prices they receive are too low. It is natural for both groups to blame the middleman. And, in fact, payments to middlemen form a large share of consumer expenditure on food.

But of course middlemen provide services: processing, transporting, packaging, distributing, and so forth. Over time the amounts of middleman services incorporated into food products have been increasing. We have been choosing to consume food that has traveled further, been processed more elaborately, and is distributed in more complex ways.

One explanation of this phenomenon is that middleman services are a relatively superior or luxury commodity compared to the raw farm products. If so, the income elasticity of demand for off-farm food services is greater than for farm products alone. Confirming this,

---

[4]There might also be severe communication and enforcement problems in any attempt to construct a functioning *command* economy. And in fact such costs of command—the resource wastage in attempting to enforce an economic dictatorship—would almost surely far exceed the costs of market exchange.

Costs of exchange may depend on (1) the volume of goods traded; (2) the frequency of trades; (3) the number of parties involved in a transaction; and (4) the number of distinct commodities per transaction. The next sections will deal only with two-party two-commodity trades, ruling out the third and fourth elements. (Some comments upon costs of multi-party and multi-commodity trading will be made later on.) We look first at costs that depend only on volume (proportional transaction costs), and then at costs that depend only on the frequency of trading (lump-sum transaction costs).

Proportional Transaction Costs

From a trader's point of view, transaction costs are like taxes on exchange (as discussed in Chapter 2). If a tax of $\$G$ per unit were levied upon purchases of a commodity X, then the *gross price* P_x^+ paid by buyers would necessarily be $\$G$ greater than the *net price* P_x^- received by sellers. In Figure 13.12 (p. 380), the shaded area represents the tax collections.

We can apply the same diagram to analyze proportional transaction costs. The *price gap, $G = P_x^+ - P_x^-$*, is the fee per unit charged by middlemen—for example, the bid-ask spread in the New York Stock Exchange. The shaded area represents the aggregate amounts received by middlemen for their services. Note that a proportional transaction charge, like a per-unit tax, reduces the quantities that would otherwise be traded.

Figure 13.13 (p. 380) shows how proportional transaction costs affect a typical trader. Let an individual with endowment E initially face a budget line KL. His market opportunity set is the entire triangle OKL. The slope of the market line is $-P_x/P_y$, or simply $-P_x$ since, as usual, we interpret Y as a *numeraire* (representing "all other goods") with price $P_y = 1$. The dashed line-segments show the effect of a proportional trading charge. A person who wants to buy X (that is, to move below and to the right of his endowment at E) will find that the slope along line-segment EL' is steeper than along EL because P_x^+ is greater than P_x. And a person who wants to sell X (that is, to move above and to the left of his endowment at E) receives only the lower price P_x^- reflected in the flat slope of EK'. Transaction costs therefore shrink the opportunity set, from the triangle OKL to the quadrilateral $OK'EL'$.

Transaction costs reduce the gains from trade. They hinder the redistribution of goods in accordance with people's desires, and decrease specialization in production. In the limiting case, transaction costs may lead individuals to forego trade entirely and to choose *autarky*.

Whether an individual will find trade advantageous depends on the buying and selling prices P_x^+ and P_x^-, on productive opportunities, and on preferences. Point R^* in Figure 13.14 shows the best the individual can do if he cannot buy or sell goods; at point R^* an indifference curve is tangent to the Production-Possibility Curve QQ. Trading opportunities (even with a transaction charge) enlarge the overall opportunity by the two dotted areas

FIGURE 13.12 **Proportional Transaction Costs**   Here there is a proportional transaction charge, in the amount of G per unit of commodity X exchanged. In equilibrium, there must be a price gap of this amount between the price paid by demanders (P_x^+) and the price received by suppliers (P_x^-). The quantity exchanged is X', and the shaded area represents the aggregate transaction costs.

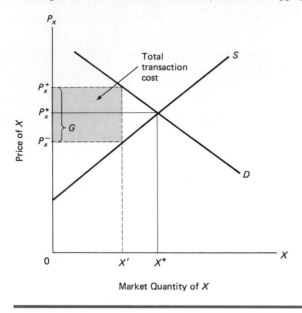

FIGURE 13.13   **Individual Trading Opportunity: Costless Versus Costly Exchange**   Under costless exchange, an individual with endowment at E has a market opportunity set consisting of the entire triangle OKL. A proportional transaction charge implies a flatter budget line for a seller of X (line-segment EK') and a steeper budget line for a buyer of X (line-segment EL'). The market opportunity set is therefore reduced to the shaded area.

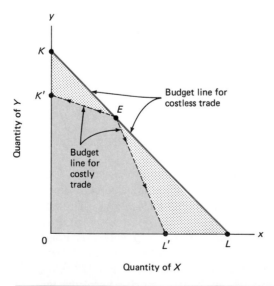

shown. Consider the dotted area at the upper left of the diagram. Let the selling price of good X be P_x^-. Line $K'A$ is drawn to have slope $-P_x^-$; at point A the slope of the Production-Possibility Curve is the same as the slope of $K'A$. Hence, a person who attempts to purchase Y by selling X, and thereby to move above and to the left of R^*, does better along AK' than along QQ. A corresponding argument applies for the dotted area at the lower right, which is bounded by the steeper line-segment BL' whose slope represents the higher buying price P_x^+.

Now if a person's preferences are as shown in Figure 13.14, where the optimum with no trading, R^*, falls between points A and B, then trading does not increase the person's welfare. On the other hand, if R^* falls outside the range AB along the Production-Possibility Curve QQ, the individual will want to trade. Specifically, suppose the tangency point R^* lies above and to the left of A along QQ, as in Figure 13.15 (p. 382). In this range the individual can do better (can reach a higher indifference curve) by trading along the market line-segment AK' than by moving along QQ. The *productive* optimum Q^* is at point A, and the person would sell X for Y to attain a consumptive optimum C^*.

The individual and market supply-demand curves are depicted in Figure 13.16. In Panel (a) the individual's autarky price is P_x^o. An individual who could buy and sell at this price would find no advantage to trade since $-P_x^o$ is equal to the slope of the PPC at R^* of Figure 13.14. (At R^* an indifference curve is tangent to the PPC, so the individual is satisfied to remain at R^*.) If the *net* market price received by sellers, P_x^-, exceeds P_x^o the individual will want to sell X, as shown by the dashed curve labeled $s(P_x^-)$. Similarly, this person will want to buy X only if the *gross* price P_x^+ paid by buyers is lower than P_x^o, as shown by the

---

FIGURE 13.14   Opportunity Set with Proportional Transaction Costs: Autarky Solution

The gross price P_x^+ determines the slope of the line-segment BL'. It is tangent to the Production-Possibility Curve QQ at point B, so that the lower-right dotted area is a portion of the individual's overall opportunity set. Similarly, the net price P_x^- determines the slope of the flatter line-segment AK'. It is tangent to QQ at point A, so that the upper-left dotted area is a portion of the opportunity set. Here the autarky solution R^* remains preferred.

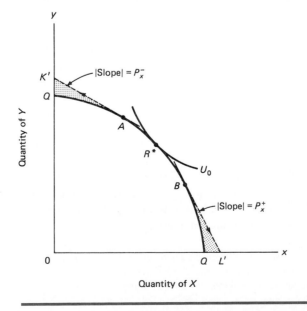

FIGURE 13.15 **Opportunity Set with Proportional Transaction Costs: Trade Optimal**

Here R^* does not lie between the tangency points A and B on QQ. The productive optimum Q^* is at point A. The consumptive optimum C^* lies to the left along AK': the individual sells some of the produced X (at the low selling price P_x^-) to obtain more of Y.

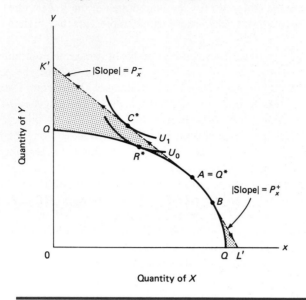

solid curve labeled $d(P_x^+)$. Thus, the individual's market behavior is depicted by the inner pair of curves in Panel (a). It is convenient to also show the supply curve in terms of the gross price, $s(P_x^+)$ (shown solid), and the demand curve in terms of the net price, $d(P_x^-)$ (shown dashed). Each of these differs from its partner by the constant vertical distance G—the price gap.

Summing over all individuals, we have the corresponding pairs of aggregate market supply and demand curves shown in Panel (b). Now we can see why it was convenient to draw the curves in terms of both gross and net prices. The gross or buying price P_x^+ is determined by the intersection of $S(P_x^+)$ and $D(P_x^+)$, the two solid curves. This intersection will be at the same market quantity X^t as the intersection of the two dashed curves $S(P_x^-)$ and $D(P_x^-)$ that determines the net or selling price P_x^-. The two prices differ by the fixed gap G that represents the fee paid to middlemen.

What would happen if the bid-ask spread, the size of the gap G, increased? In Panel (a) of Figure 13.16 the inner pair of curves would not change, since they directly represent individual behavior in terms of the relevant (gross or net) prices. But the outer pair of curves would be pushed further outward as G rises. Since the equilibrium solution determined in Panel (b) necessarily involves an intersection with one or the other of the outer curves, higher transaction costs reduce the volume of transactions.

CONCLUSION: Proportional transaction costs create a gap between buying price and selling price. The higher the transaction charge, the more likely individuals are to choose autarky solutions, and the smaller will be the aggregate volume of market trading.

FIGURE 13.16 **Supply and Demand: Proportional Transaction Costs**   In Panel (a) the inner pair of curves show an individual's transaction supply as a function of the *net* selling price P_x^- (where this exceeds the autarky price P_x^o), and his transaction demand as a function of the *gross* buying price P_x^+ (where this is less than the autarky price). The upper solid curve shows supply as related to the gross price; the lower dashed curve shows demand as related to the net price. Panel (b) pictures the marketwide aggregates of these four curves. The equilibrium transaction quantity X^t is found at the intersection of the two solid curves (which are defined in terms of the gross prices) or else the intersection of the two dashed curves (which are defined in terms of the net prices); the equilibrium gross and net prices are determined accordingly.

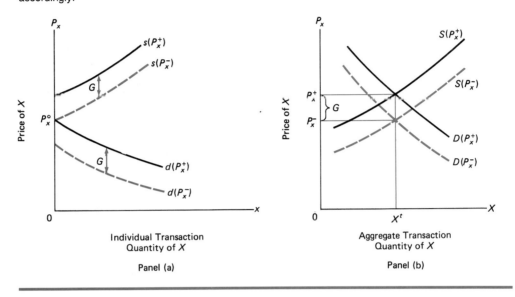

Individual Transaction Quantity of X	Aggregate Transaction Quantity of X
Panel (a)	Panel (b)

Certain markets seem to disappear as a country gets wealthier, for example, the market for used containers or for cigarettes by the unit (rather than by the pack). The market for used clothes has largely vanished in the United States. It has become cheaper to throw used clothes away rather than pay for the middleman services required to make such a market function.

EXAMPLE 13.7   Urban-Farm Food Cost Differentials

In the absence of transaction costs there would be no reason for a heavy producer of commodity X to be a particularly heavy consumer of X. The tailor would not have an unusually ample wardrobe, the candlestick maker would still use electric lights in his home, and the Detroit assembly-line worker would have no special inducement to drive a car rather than use public transit. It follows that where we *do* observe a producer heavily consuming his or her own product, transaction costs are likely to be high.

Urban and farm consumption expenditures for 1960 to 1961 were studied by F. Y. Lee and K. E. Phillips. As can be seen in the table, farmers spend relatively more on "Food prepared at home," and urban-dwellers relatively more on "Food prepared away from home."

There seems little reason to doubt that transaction costs impose more autarky upon farmers, making it more advantageous for them to consume home-prepared food.

On the other hand, costs of exchange are not the sole explanation of the divergence visible in the table. Costs of turnover also play a role. For example, the cost of transporting food from farm to factory and then back to farm might dictate that farmers consume more home-prepared food even under a command economy. It is also possible that farmers are more fond of home-prepared food. Perhaps more important, in the period studied farm families were usually poorer than urban families. Since "Food prepared away from home" has an income elasticity greater than one, the income difference may also provide a partial explanation.

Food Expenditures as Percentage of Total Consumption

	Northeast		West	
Expenditure	Urban	Farm	Urban	Farm
Food prepared at home	21.0	31.0	18.9	27.5
Food prepared away from home	4.8	3.0	4.9	2.9

Source: F. Y. Lee and K. E. Phillips, "Differences in Consumption Patterns of Farm and Non-farm Households in the United States," *American Journal of Agricultural Economics,* v. 53 (November 1971), p. 575.

Lump-Sum Transaction Costs

Proportional transaction costs help us understand certain facts about exchange—in particular, the normal gap between buying and selling prices. But one crucial aspect of exchange remains to be explained: why consumers or producers hold *inventories* (stocks of goods). The reason is that people do not trade continuously; we go to market on specific occasions. Between trips to the market a consumer has to hold inventories; sellers hold them while awaiting the irregular visits of purchasers.

When costs of exchange take the form of a fixed lump-sum *fee per transaction,* consumers have an incentive to reduce the frequency of trades (the number of trips to the market). But the less frequent the transactions, the larger the average inventories the consumer or seller must hold. The cost of holding inventories must therefore be balanced against the cost of frequent trading.

Suppose the transaction cost is a fixed amount F for each trade. Think of it as an entry fee. Consider an individual with constant production and consumption flows of a commodity X, who trades at a regular time-interval of length I. The person produces on his own a flow of good X, at the rate of x^q. (A special case of our analysis applies if x^q is zero.) At discrete times $I, 2I, 3I$, and so on, the individual purchases a quantity k of commodity X. He can thereby maintain a constant consumption flow of $x^c = x^q + (k/I)$. For example, if $x^q = 10$ units per day, k is 140 units, and $I = 7$ days, a consumption rate of $10 + (140/7) = 30$ units per day can be maintained. Figure 13.17 shows this inventory history.

A person who buys X must of course sell some other commodity Y; a similar diagram, showing regular accumulation rather than decrease of inventory between trades, would picture the inventory history for commodity Y.

FIGURE 13.17 **Inventory History for a Consumer**   The individual has a self-supplied continuous production flow x^q and a continuous consumption flow x^c. The difference is made up by discrete market purchases at time-intervals I. At each multiple of I, inventory falls to zero and a new stock quantity k is purchased.

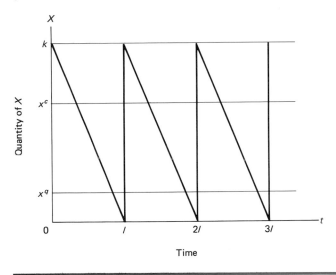

Now let us consider the individual's decision whether to trade at all. Figure 13.18 (p. 386) shows a situation where the person prefers to not trade. In this diagram the person prefers the "Robinson Crusoe solution" R^*, where the Production-Possibility Curve QQ is tangent to indifference curve U_1. With lump-sum transaction costs there are two disadvantages of trading. The first cost is inventory holding costs. In the diagram these costs shrink the Production-Possibility Curve from the solid QQ curve to the dashed $\hat{Q}\hat{Q}$ curve: resources devoted to maintaining inventories cannot be applied to production. The second disadvantage lies in the explicit fee F paid at each transaction. In the diagram, the average fee incurred per unit of time is represented by the vertical distance $\hat{Q}^* - N^*$. This distance is equal to F/I, paid out in units of Y. The key point is that in this model an individual who trades must trade along the market line NN parallel to but below the market line MM. The line NN represents the *effective* trading opportunities, the combinations of X and Y achievable in the market after paying the average lump-sum charges F/I.

Autarky is of course not inevitable. The gap between curves QQ and $\hat{Q}\hat{Q}$ is smaller the lower the costs of holding inventories; the gap between budget lines MM and NN is smaller the lower the transaction charges. The smaller these costs, the less attractive is the autarky solution R^* compared to the trading solution (represented by the point C^* where an indifference curve is tangent to the market line NN). For the trading solution to be superior, C^* would of course have to lie on a higher indifference curve than R^*.

Whether individuals in equilibrium will trade also depends on the market price P_x. A decrease in P_x makes both lines MM and NN flatter. As line MM becomes flatter, the further to the left will be point $\hat{Q}^*$ (the point of tangency between line MM and curve $\hat{Q}\hat{Q}$) and consequently the higher the level of utility that can be reached by trading along line NN which is parallel to MM. There may be a price P_x sufficiently low so that the trading optimum

FIGURE 13.18 Autarky and Lump-Sum Transaction Costs   The autarky solution is at R^* on the (solid) Production-Possibility Curve QQ. To trade, inventories must be held. This reduces the effective production possibilities to the (dashed) $\hat{Q}\hat{Q}$. In addition, each time a transaction is made, a charge of F must be paid. For transactions at intervals of $1/I$ per unit of time, on average a cost of F/I is incurred; this charge is represented by the vertical distance $\hat{Q}^*N^*$. The individual can then trade along the market line NN. In this diagram the autarky solution R^* (on indifference curve U_1) is preferred to the best position C^* (on U_0) that can be attained through trading.

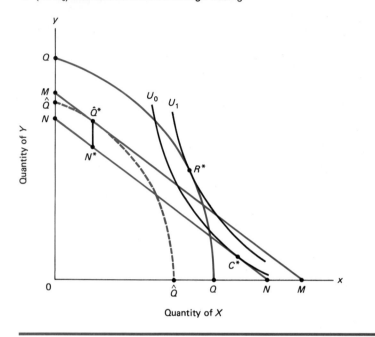

C^* along NN lies on a higher indifference curve than the autarky point R^*—the individual will enter the market as a net demander of X. Similarly, at a sufficiently high price P_x the person may enter the market as a net supplier of X.

If the only transaction cost is a lump-sum fee, there is no gap between the buying and selling price. And as before, for each individual there is an autarky price P_x^o that makes the individual prefer not to trade even if there are no transaction costs. Translating this information into a supply-demand diagram leads to Figure 13.19. There is a *range* of prices around the autarky price within which the individual prefers not to trade. But as the market price increasingly diverges from P_x^o, trade becomes more attractive: it will pay to incur the average trading fee F/I and the inventory costs associated with market exchanges.

Figure 13.19 has the interesting feature that the supply and demand curves start at points J and H rather than at the vertical axis. The price P_x must be sufficiently above or below the autarky price P_x^o before it becomes worthwhile to enter the market. And when trade does become worthwhile, there will also be a minimum positive quantity traded. [Verification of this point is left as a challenge to the reader.]

The individual transaction supply and demand curves can as usual be aggregated into market-wide supply and demand curves. For lump-sum transaction costs, as for proportional

FIGURE 13.19 **Individual Net Supply and Demand: Lump-Sum Transaction Cost**   If there is a lump-sum cost per transaction, the individual will enter the market as a supplier or a demander only if the market price diverges from the autarky price P_x^o by at least a certain discrete amount. If the price divergence is just great enough, the individual will offer or demand a minimal discrete quantity—represented by the point J where the supply curve begins and the point H where the demand curve begins.

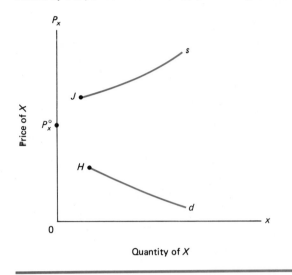

Quantity of X

transaction costs, the market-wide curves may not intersect. If so, the market disappears; at no price will there be trade.

CONCLUSION: Lump-sum transaction costs do not create a price gap. But they induce consumers to exchange only at discrete intervals, so that sellers and consumers hold inventories. Heavy transaction charges and the resulting high inventory costs make individual autarky solutions more likely, reduce the aggregate volume of market trade, and may even eliminate trading.

13.5 THE ROLE OF MONEY

Money is a device that reduces the cost of market trading. But recall that the cost of market trading must be distinguished from the cost of physical turnovers, which are, as we have seen, really costs of production that are unavoidable in *any* economy with specialization and a division of labor. When producers and consumers are far from each other, for example, shipping costs must be incurred even in a perfectly functioning command economy. Money can do nothing to reduce the costs of physically shipping goods. Similarly, when production and consumption cannot be perfectly synchronized, commodity inventories will be required along the manufacturer-wholesaler-retailer-consumer chain. Again, money cannot eliminate this expense.

Money only reduces the costs of bargaining and negotiating by serving as a *medium of exchange* and *temporary store of value*. These functions can be best visualized if we consider three hypothetical social regimes in succession: (1) a pure command economy, with no trading whatsoever but only dictated physical commodity turnovers; (2) a barter economy, with trading but without any monetary commodity; and (3) a money economy.

Money as Medium of Exchange

Suppose an economy has N individuals and N goods, where everyone specializes in producing just one of the commodities. But each person would still like to consume positive quantities of all N goods. Thus, there is specialization in production but diversity in consumption—the normal situation. Since each of the N persons can trade with $N - 1$ others, the number of pairs of possible trades is $N(N - 1)$; for example, with 3 individuals A, B, and C, the 6 possible trades are between A and B, B and A, A and C, C and A, B and C, or C and B.

Imagine that the dictator in a pure command regime is perfectly efficient and benevolent. In such an economy there is no waste due to costs of trading since there is no bidding, negotiating, or contracting. Even so, the costs of turnover, such as transportation expenses, may make some of the $N(N - 1)$ possible commodity movements uneconomic. Suppose oranges are produced in California, and lobsters in Maine. Lobsters could be so expensive to ship that the dictator correctly decides that overall efficiency requires Californians to do without them. But oranges are not so costly to ship, let us suppose, and so the dictator correctly commands that some California oranges be sent to Maine.

Now suppose a revolution displaces the dictator, substituting a regime of barter trade. In this regime, only two-party trade is feasible. (Multi-party barter trades are exceedingly costly to negotiate and enforce and are, therefore, rare.) Then, instead of the $N(N - 1)$ possible commodity movements available to the dictator in a command economy, under bilateral barter only $N(N - 1)/2$ two-way channels of exchange are possible. If shipment of Maine lobsters to California is economically unfeasible due to the high transportation costs, then the two-way channel is blocked. The California oranges cannot go to Maine either, even though it is not as costly to transport oranges, because the lobstermen cannot pay the orange growers. Compared to an ideal command economy, a barter economy not only incurs the costs of negotiating trades, but also leads to an inferior allocation of production and consumption.

We can now see the function of money as a *medium of exchange*. The commodity serving as money can be one of the original goods or else an artificial new commodity like paper currency. In either case, the effect is to make multilateral trading possible through indirect exchanges.

Suppose, to begin with, that one of the initial commodities is chosen as medium of exchange. In the prisoner-of-war situation of Chapter 4, cigarettes served this function. But with knowledge of modern economic history, let us assume that the medium of exchange is *gold*. Then other commodities are no longer traded for one another, but only for gold. This drastically reduces the number of different types of transactions.

In a barter economy the number of possible two-way trading channels is $N(N - 1)/2$. For five goods (four ordinary consumption goods A, B, C, D plus gold G), Figure 13.20 pictures the $(5)(4)/2 = 10$ trading channels required. But if all other commodities are traded only for gold, *four* channels or markets will suffice. In general, a money (gold) economy would need only $N - 1$ types of transactions. As compared with barter, a monetary economy reduces the costs of finding partners and of negotiating, recording, and enforcing trades.

A medium of exchange also allows firms and individuals to specialize in production. Consider the lobster-orange example once again. In a monetary economy the Maine lobsters

FIGURE 13.20 **Trading Channels: Five Goods**   With five commodities, under two-way barter exchange there would have to be ten channels of trade or markets. If commodity *G* is instead the sole medium of exchange, only four markets would be needed.

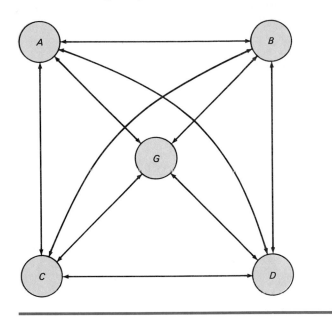

still cannot go to California. The transportation costs are too high, and money cannot change that fact. But the California oranges can now go to Maine! The Maine lobstermen can pay for oranges in gold, which they obtain by selling lobsters to other, non-California customers. Thus, gold makes possible triangular or still more complex exchanges without requiring anything beyond bilateral trades.

One element of cost is likely to be greater in a gold economy than in a barter economy: there will be increased handling and shipping of gold. Clearing arrangements, one aspect of banking, arise to reduce these costs. Also, gold can be replaced by an artificial commodity such as paper money, for which the shipping and handling costs are less. To reduce these handling and shipping costs, modern economies tend to move toward a nonphysical, purely abstract medium of exchange — banking deposits.

Money as Temporary Store of Value

The other important role of money is as a *temporary store of value* (abode of purchasing power). Inventories of money help bridge time intervals between receipts and payments. By carrying an inventory of money, a baker selling bread today can buy meat tomorrow.

To grasp the significance of this, let us think again of the hypothetical pure command economy. Even there, inventories are required for productive purposes. But if a revolution overthrows the dictator in favor of a regime of bilateral voluntary barter exchange, additional trading inventories have to come into existence. Suppose three individuals *1*, *2*, and *3* are the sole specialized producers of commodities *A*, *B*, and *C*, respectively. Imagine that the

FIGURE 13.21 **A Pattern of Barter Trade**   The Busama are producers of taro, which is desired only in certain southern villages. These villagers also desire bowls from Tami Island in the north, but they can pay only in pots. The Busama carry the southerners' pots, in excess of their own needs, to Tami Island to exchange for bowls that will ultimately be carried back to the southern villages. For this trade to be possible, bowls must be more highly valued than pots in the southern villages, and pots more heavily valued at Tami Island in the north.

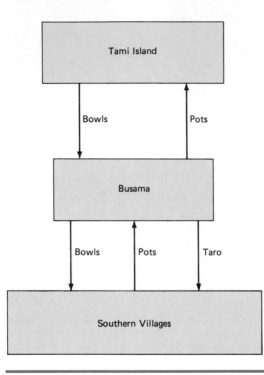

desired pattern of trade is triangular: commodity *A* is to flow from person *1* to *2*, commodity *B* from *2* to *3*, and commodity *C* from *3* to *1*. If multilateral trading is ruled out, we have the "double coincidence" problem of barter. Consider individual *2*, who wants commodity *A* from individual *1* but produces nothing that individual *1* wants from him. Although *2* can provide commodity *B* to individual *3*, the latter produces nothing that *2* desires.

This difficulty is resolved by having some or all individuals hold a trading inventory of the third commodity—that is, of the one they neither produce nor consume. People accept such trade goods in exchange for commodities they produce, in order to have something available to exchange for commodities they do wish to consume.

Rather than hold inventories of many different types of trade goods, it is obviously efficient for everyone to accept in exchange some single store of value commodity. It should be a commodity cheap to produce and cheap to store, and preferably one that is not eroded by consumption over time. Again, there will be a natural tendency to move toward a purely abstract money commodity like banking deposits, which are almost costless to produce and to store and are never actually consumed.

CONCLUSION: The invention of money reduces the costs of market trading, not the costs of physical turnovers that would be required in any economic system with a division of labor. When one commodity is the sole *medium of exchange*, fewer types of transactions are required. A medium of exchange makes possible triangular or even more complex trade patterns that would be impossible under barter. Where inventories of goods must be carried solely for trading purposes, costs of exchange are minimized if everyone agrees on a single monetary commodity that then serves also as *temporary store of value*.

EXAMPLE 13.8 **Barter in the East Indies**

Anthropologist M. Sahlins[a] analyzed a network of exchanges among primitive peoples in the East Indies (see Figure 13.21). He described a puzzling problem. The Busama, who serve as middlemen between the Tami Islanders and certain southern villages, allegedly acquire bowls worth 10 to 12 shillings from Tami Island that they then carry to the south and exchange one-for-one against pots worth only 8 shillings!

The explanation offered was that, while pots and bowls are desired throughout the region, the Busama are producers of taro which is wanted only by the southern villagers. The latter can only pay in pots. Because these exceed the Busama's own requirements, the Busama carry the excess pots to Tami and exchange them against bowls as the only product there available. The quantity of bowls thus acquired again exceeds the Busama's own needs; some are carried back down to the southern villages to be traded along with taro once again for pots.

COMMENT It is clearly not rational for the Busama to carry bowls from Tami—where the bowls are, according to the report, *more* highly valued than pots (10 to 12 shillings against 8)—to southern villages where bowls are relatively *less* highly valued (one against one). Indeed, the logic of the situation strongly suggests that the relative values have been misreported. Surely the pots are relatively less highly valued where they are plentiful, at their origin in the south, and the bowls are relatively less highly valued at their origin on Tami Island. Only if this is the case does the two-way shipping traffic of the Busama become understandable. The Busama must accept pots from the southern villagers, their only customers for taro, but nothing forces the Busama to carry bowls from north to south at a loss.

Note also that since this is a situation of barter exchange, the cited shilling values may lack any real meaning. If shillings are not used as a medium of exchange, reported price quotations may not reflect the terms at which trades take place.

[a]Marshall Sahlins, *Stone Age Economics* (Chicago: Aldine, 1972), Chapter 6.

SUMMARY

Benefits of exchange fall into two main categories: reallocation of existing stocks of goods to the consumers who value them the most, and increased quantities of goods made possible by specialization in production.

The first benefit stands out most clearly in a world of pure exchange, where the society has fixed stocks of all commodities. In a simplified world of two goods X and Y, the Edgeworth box shows how two parties can both increase satisfaction by trading into the region of mutual advantage. At a competitive equilibrium in pure exchange, each trader will exchange X for Y (or vice versa) until his Marginal Rate of Substitution in Consumption MRS_C equals the market price ratio P_x/P_y. This corresponds to achieving a point on the "Contract Curve" in the Edgeworth box.

In a world of production and exchange, the individual's *productive optimum* Q^* will, in general, differ from his *consumptive optimum* C^*. At Q^* the condition satisfied is $MRT = P_x/P_y$, where MRT is the person's Marginal Rate of Transformation; at C^* the condition is $MRS_C = P_x/P_y$ as before. Trade leads to specialization in which each trader concentrates on the activity at which he or she is most productive. The increased output of goods due to this greater division of labor is the second benefit of trade.

Full demand (the desired consumption quantity at any given price) and *full supply* (the total amount endowed or produced at that price) must be distinguished from *transaction demand* and *transaction supply*. The *full* quantities are the amounts supplied to or demanded from the economy; the *transaction* quantities are the amounts traded in markets. The two magnitudes differ by the quantity of goods that individuals retain for their own consumption.

Perfect markets involve perfect communication between buyers and sellers, instantaneous equilibrium with a single price at which all trading takes place, and absence of transaction costs. Actual markets can only approximate these ideal conditions. Middlemen overcome market imperfections, but not costlessly since they must be compensated. The costs of *trading,* properly speaking, are the costs of operating a market system. Not all middleman services represent costs of trading. Services like transportation, warehousing of goods, and retail distribution would persist even in a command economy.

Costs of trading depend, among other things, on the amounts of goods exchanged and on the frequency of trading. Two polar cases were analyzed: transaction costs that are proportional to the quantity of goods changing hands, and transaction costs incurred as a fixed lump sum each time a transaction takes place. Both types of transaction costs reduce specialization in production, and make autarky solutions more likely.

The presence of money as a *medium of exchange* reduces the number of different types of two-way exchanges (in comparison with barter). This lowers the costs of collecting information, keeping records, and shipping goods to settle transactions. Even more important, it opens up triangular or even more complex patterns of trade that would be blocked under two-way barter. As a *store of value,* money economizes the trading inventories that would have to be carried under barter. By facilitating exchange, the institution of money makes possible a better distribution of consumption goods together with increased specialization in production.

QUESTIONS

For Review

1. Explain how the possibility of trade can lead to *consumptive* benefits (improved allocations of given social totals of goods among the different individuals) and to *productive* benefits (larger social totals of desired goods). How is the consumptive

improvement illustrated in the Edgeworth box? Can the productive improvement be illustrated in the Edgeworth box?

*2. a. If two persons have identical preferences (indifference-curve maps), does it follow that they cannot trade to mutual advantage?

b. What if they have identical preferences *and* identical endowments in a world of pure exchange?

c. In a world of production, what if they have identical preferences and identical productive opportunities?

*3. We normally observe specialization in production but diversification in consumption.

a. What shapes of the individuals' Production-Possibility Curves and preference maps lead to this pattern of behavior?

b. Could this pattern be achieved in the absence of trade?

4. What is meant by an individual's sustaining price for a particular good? What happens at higher prices? at lower prices? How does the sustaining price differ from the autarky price?

5. What condition must hold for each individual at competitive equilibrium in a world of pure exchange? What additional condition characterizes the market as a whole?

*6. What are the productive and consumptive conditions that must hold for each individual in a world of production and exchange? What additional conditions characterize the market as a whole?

*7. If market equilibrium takes place at the intersection of the aggregate *transaction* demand and *transaction* supply curves, how can the intersection of the full demand and full supply curves also determine the equilibrium?

8. "For every individual, the s_i^t and d_i^t curves must intersect along the vertical axis, as in Figure 13.9. It is therefore quite impossible for the aggregate S^t and D^t curves to intersect in the interior, as in Figure 13.10." True or false? Explain.

9. What are perfect markets? What is perfect competition?

*10. a. Can autarky occur in costless exchange?

b. Why is autarky more likely the higher are transaction costs?

11. Some markets are illegal (markets for babies, narcotic drugs, government favors, and so on). Law enforcement that is not *totally* effective can be regarded as imposing a transaction cost upon participants. In terms of this chapter's analysis, what effects would you anticipate from increased law-enforcement effort against the narcotic traffic? Would the volume of transactions be affected? What about the gross price paid by buyers in comparison with the net price received by sellers?

12. Illustrate how sufficiently heavy *proportional* transaction costs might make a market nonviable. Do the same for *lump-sum* transaction costs.

*13. Since the existence of markets necessarily involves some burden of transaction costs, wouldn't a command economy dispensing with markets always be more efficient? Explain.

14. Distinguish between turnover costs and exchange costs. How would you class transportation of goods between producer and consumer? What about the costs of negotiating a contract? enforcing a contract?

---

*The answers to starred questions appear at the end of the book.

For Further Thought and Discussion

1. From Omar Khayyam:

   > I often wonder what the Vintners buy
   > One half so precious as the Goods they sell.

   Omar seems to be suggesting that vintners ought not engage in exchange, since wine is more precious than anything else. Where is the fallacy in his reasoning?

*2. Compare the likely effects of taxes levied upon *consumption*, upon *production*, and upon *exchange* of a commodity.

*3. Suppose Robinson Crusoe is superior to Friday in producing *both* fish and bananas. For example, it may take Robinson one hour to catch a fish and two hours to pick a bunch of bananas, while it takes Friday four hours to do either. Show that they still can engage in mutually beneficial exchange. (In international trade this is called the principle of comparative advantage.)

*4. Imagine an initial Edgeworth-box competitive equilibrium, starting from an endowment position where individual i has all of commodity G (grain) and individual j has all of commodity Y *(numeraire)*. Suppose i's endowment of grain doubles, everything else remaining unchanged. Can we be sure that i is better off at the new competitive equilibrium? that j is better off? that at least one of them is better off? [*Hint:* Are wheat farmers necessarily better off if the crop is large? What about consumers of wheat?]

5. Give examples of markets that have existed historically, but do not now exist. Can you explain their disappearance?

6. According to economist K.E. Boulding, a tariff can be regarded as a "negative railroad." Whereas a railroad connects trading communities, a tariff separates them. Is the analogy valid?

*7. The text stated that, in a world of two commodities X and Y, trade would normally lead to greater quantities produced of both goods. Is this *necessarily* the case? Might there possibly be, say, greater production of X but reduced production of Y? Explain. [*Hint:* Consider the case where only trader i has productive opportunities, while j has a fixed endowment.]

*8. Flowers provide bees with nectar, while bees facilitate the pollination of flowers. Is this exchange?

9. Fresh fruits are cheaper at farm roadstands than in city markets. Does the price difference reflect turnover costs or exchange costs, or are there elements of each?

10. Give examples of exchange costs that are reduced by the existence of money as a *medium of exchange*. Of money as a *store of value*.

*11. If rationing is introduced, money is no longer fully effective as a medium of exchange. What types of additional exchange costs emerge in a world where ration coupons and cash are *both* required in order to effectuate a transaction?

*12. According to elementary textbooks, a commodity selected to serve as money should be portable, divisible, storable, generally recognizable, and homogeneous. In terms of the discussion in this chapter, why are these desirable qualities? Can you think of other desirable qualities? [*Hint:* Think of cigarettes serving as money in a prisoner-of-war camp.]

SUPPLEMENTARY
CHAPTER 14
THE ECONOMICS OF TIME

EXAMPLES

S o far we have studied two types of individual decisions: (1) how to spend present income (what consumption goods to purchase) and (2) how to earn present income (what amounts of resource services to offer on the market). This chapter examines a third decision: how to strike a balance, through saving or investment, between the present and the future.

What is meant by "saving" and "investment"? A person who *saves* is simply refraining from current consumption. But *investing* refers to the actual creation of such physical assets as buildings or machines. When Robinson Crusoe takes time off from catching fish by hand in order to weave a fishing net, his own saving (giving up some fish today) makes it possible for him to invest (create the fishing net). In an exchange economy, however, those who save and those who invest need not be the same people. The person who puts money in the bank is not generally the one who builds a new house. Instead, through the financial markets, the savings of some individuals make resources available for the investments made by others.

Why would you save or invest rather than consume today? Only so you, or your heirs, can consume more in the future. A family that builds a house arranges for future shelter; a farmer who plants a tree intends to pick fruit in the future; a business that maintains its machinery expects to increase future earnings.

Section 14.1 analyzes these choices between the present and the future. We will see how the *interest rate* serves as a kind of price in relation to time. Section 14.2 discusses an important practical topic: the criteria used by business firms and by government agencies in deciding upon investments. These concepts are used in Sections 14.3 and 14.4 to determine rules for making the best use of such natural resources as timber and oil. Section 14.5 demonstrates that the interest rate plays a critical role in evaluating projects. The distinction between real interest and monetary interest is introduced in Section 14.6. The role of risk and other factors in determining the interest rate are discussed in Section 14.7. Optimal choices of assets to hold in a portfolio are the topic of Section 14.8.

14.1 CONSUMPTION AND PRODUCTION OVER TIME

For simplicity, let corn *(C)* be the only consumption good. The objects of choice here are *dated* quantities of corn symbolized as C_0 (this year's corn), C_1 (corn one year from now), C_2 (corn two years from now), and so on. We begin by considering elementary two-period choices: whether to consume corn this year or next. (Notice that the analysis is in real units: the choice is between present and future *corn* rather than present and future *dollars*.)

List of Notation

a	Anticipated rate of price inflation	r_A	Rate of return on asset A
d_A	Dividend on stock A	r'	Money interest rate
P_t	The price paid in the current period for a unit of the good to be delivered in period t.	R	Long-term interest rate
		W_0	Endowed wealth
		z_t	Payment from a project in period t
r	Short-term interest rate		

FIGURE 14.1 **Intertemporal Consumptive Optimum** The decision between consumption this year (C_0) and consumption next year (C_1) involves the preference map (indifference curves U', U'', U'''), endowment *(E)*, and budget line *(KL)*. The optimum is C^*. The individual chooses to lend the amount $\bar{c}_0 - c_0^*$ of current claims, receiving in repayment the amount $c_1^* - \bar{c}_1$ of future claims. $\overline{W}_0$ is the endowed wealth measured in units of current claims C_0.

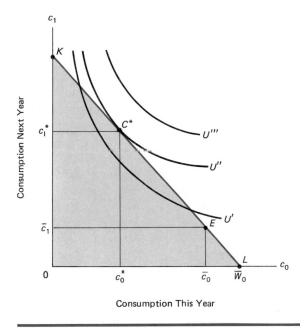

Consumption This Year

Borrowing-Lending Equilibrium

The key to understanding consumption decisions over time (the choice between C_0 and C_1) is to notice that the underlying logic is the same as in choosing between ordinary commodities X and Y within a single period of time. Figure 14.1 closely resembles the "optimum of the consumer" diagrams in Chapter 4. Once again there are indifference curves U', U'', U''', . . . and a budget line *KL*. The tangency point C^* shows the best consumption basket consisting of c_0^* of current corn and c_1^* of future corn.

The individual's endowment is at E, giving him initial entitlements to current consumption ($\bar{c}_0$) and to anticipated future consumption ($\bar{c}_1$).[1] We assume in this section that there is no productive investment—an individual can consume more today only by borrowing from others; he can consume more tomorrow only by lending to others. In the diagram, a person who lends moves from endowment position E to the left along the budget line *KL*—giving up current corn C_0 in exchange for future corn C_1. Someone who moves to the right, obtaining more C_0 at the expense of C_1, is said to borrow. The individual pictured in Figure 14.1 lends $\bar{c}_0 - c_0^*$ of current corn, with an anticipated repayment next year of $c_1^* - \bar{c}_1$. If the endowment position E were to the left of C^* along the budget line, the individual would have been a borrower. Such a person,

---

[1]*Uncertainty* is ruled out here, so anticipations about the future are sure to be realized.

with an endowment mainly in the form of future income, is like the "heir with great expectations" in Charles Dickens' novel. He or she is poor today but has rich prospects for the future.

EXAMPLE 14.1   Savings and the Fear of War

People save to derive benefits in the future. Fear of war can be expected to reduce savings for a variety of reasons. First, the individual and his heirs may all be killed. If so, any current sacrifice in the way of savings may yield little or no future benefit. Second, if war occurs goods may be rationed or otherwise unavailable, which again means that the assets accumulated by savings may not be convertible into consumer benefits. Third, if your nation suffers defeat, your assets may be confiscated by the enemy. However, times of war can be times of great deprivation and this factor operates in the other direction and is likely to cause the marginal utility of additional consumption to be very high. In times of peace $100 may allow you to upgrade from coach to first-class travel; in times of war that amount may provide a loaf of bread that saves your life.

In a 1988 study Joel Slemrod[a] reported the results of a Gallup Poll that asked respondents in 34 countries to estimate the chances of a world war during the next ten years. The differences from nation to nation were surprisingly large. In the United States, 49 percent of those surveyed thought the chance of war was 50 percent or greater. Only 19 percent of the Japanese thought so.

Using these results, Slemrod estimated that an increase of 10 percentage points in the proportion of the population that thinks the chance of a war is 50 percent or greater leads to a decrease of about 4 percent in the fraction of income saved. Thus, the greater the fear of war, the less the saving.

[a]Joel Slemrod, "Fear of Nuclear War and Intercountry Differences in the Rate of Saving." NBER Working Paper No. 2801.

What is the market rate of exchange at which individuals can borrow or lend (that is, at which they can trade current corn against future corn)? This rate corresponds geometrically to the slope of the budget line. Let the price of C_0 be P_0 and let the price of C_1 be P_1. Then the ratio at which the two claims can be exchanged is $-P_0/P_1$. (The minus sign is needed since consumption in one period must be reduced to increase consumption in the other.) We will be assuming that current corn C_0 is the *numeraire* or basis of pricing, so that $P_0 \equiv 1$.

The *interest rate* r is a special kind of price. Specifically, the annual rate of interest r is defined as the premium on the value of a unit of current consumption in comparison with consumption one year in the future—the extra worth of corn today over corn next year. Equivalently, $1 + r$ units of corn delivered in the next period are worth the same as 1 unit of corn delivered in the current period. If P_1 is the price you must pay today to obtain a unit of corn one year from now, then

$$P_1(1 + r) \equiv P_0 \equiv 1 \tag{14.1}$$

We can also use either of the following logically equivalent formulas:

$$\frac{P_1}{P_0} \equiv \frac{1}{1 + r} \tag{14.1'}$$

$$r \equiv \frac{P_0}{P_1} - 1 \tag{14.1''}$$

Consequently, the slope $-P_0/P_1$ of the budget line in Figure 14.1 can also be written as $-(1 + r)$.

Exercise 14.1

(a) If the interest rate is $r = 10$ percent, what is the implied price P_1 of a one-year future claim to corn? (b) What if $r = 100\%$? (c) If future claims become almost valueless (P_1 approaches zero), what would happen to r? (d) Are negative interest rates ($r < 0$) meaningful?

Answer: (a) Using Equation (14.1'), if $r = 0.1$ then $P_1 = P_1/P_0 \equiv 1/(1 + r) = 1/1.1 = 0.9091$. (b) If $r = 1.0$ then $P_1 = 1/2 = 0.5$. (c) As P_1 approaches zero, r goes to infinity. (d) Yes, $r < 0$ means that $P_1 > P_0$: a future claim is worth *more* than a present claim. While unusual, this is not impossible. For example, it might come about if people anticipated great scarcities in the future.

The budget equation $P_x x + P_y y = I$ that we used in Chapter 4 failed to allow people to spend less than their current income (save) or more than their current income (borrow). The analysis of the economics of time here allows us to correct this flaw. It is not *current income* that limits a person's consumption choices, but rather his or her *endowed wealth* $\overline{W}_0$.

DEFINITION: Endowed wealth $\overline{W}_0$ is the value of an individual's endowment of present and future claims.

In terms of the prices P_0 and P_1, endowed wealth is

$$\overline{W}_0 \equiv P_0 \overline{c}_0 + P_1 \overline{c}_1 \tag{14.2}$$

In the alternative "interest" notation, since $P_0 \equiv 1$ and $P_1 \equiv 1/(1 + r)$, Equation (14.2) becomes

$$\overline{W}_0 \equiv \overline{c}_0 + \frac{\overline{c}_1}{1 + r} \tag{14.2'}$$

If $P_0 \equiv 1$, endowed wealth is the horizontal intercept of the budget line KL in Figure 14.1. (The subscript 0 is attached to the symbol for wealth because wealth signifies a *present* market value, the worth *today* of a person's present and future income claims.)

The equation for the budget line KL of Figure 14.1 can similarly be expressed in price notation or interest notation.[2]

---

[2]*Mathematical Footnote:* There is a subtle but important difference between Equations (14.2) and (14.3), or between (14.2') and (14.3'). Equations (14.2) and (14.2') *define* endowed wealth in terms of the endowed current and future income elements $\overline{c}_0$ and $\overline{c}_1$, which are given constants. But c_0 and c_1 in Equations (14.3) or (14.3') are *variables*, representing the current and future consumption amounts achievable out of a given endowed wealth.

$$P_0 c_0 + P_1 c_1 = \overline{W}_0 \qquad\qquad (14.3)$$

$$c_0 + \frac{c_1}{1 + r} = \overline{W}_0 \qquad\qquad (14.3')$$

The market equilibrium here can be determined in the same way as the familiar market equilibrium involving commodities X and Y. Different prices P_1 (or interest rates r) determine different budget lines through the endowment position; the points of tangency between a person's indifference curves and the budget lines determine a Price Expansion Path for each individual. As in Chapter 13, these can then be translated into "full" or "transaction" supply and demand curves—first for the separate individuals, and then for the market as a whole. The final result is shown in Figure 14.2, where lending corresponds to transaction supply and borrowing corresponds to transaction demand. On the vertical axis of the borrowing-lending diagram we put the interest rate r. The L curve is the *market supply of lending;* this is the sum of the transaction quantities of current claims c_0 that individuals are willing to offer on the loan market at each interest rate r. The B curve represents the *market demand for borrowing;* this is the aggregate amount of c_0 that all the individuals together would want to purchase on the loan market at any interest rate r. The intersection of the supply and demand curves determines the equilibrium amounts of borrowing and lending $B_0^* = L_0^*$ and the equilibrium rate of interest r^*.

Exercise 14.2

Suppose John's Marginal Rate of Substitution between C_0 and C_1 is given by c_1^j/c_0^j, and Kathy's by c_1^k/c_0^k. Let the corresponding intertemporal endowments be $(\overline{c}_0^j, \overline{c}_1^j) = (10,100)$ and

---

FIGURE 14.2 Borrowing-Lending Equilibrium   The L curve shows the aggregate supply of current claims offered for lending at each interest rate r. The B curve shows the aggregate demand for borrowing at each r. The intersection determines the equilibrium amount borrowed and lent, and the equilibrium interest rate r^*.

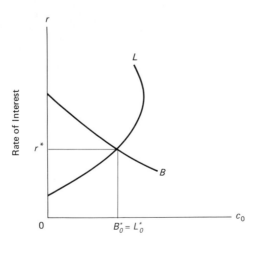

Market Borrowing or Lending

$(\bar{c}_0^k, \bar{c}_1^k) = (50, 20)$. (a) Find John's demand for borrowing b_0 and Kathy's supply of lending l_0. (b) Find the market equilibrium in terms of both the price ratio and the interest rate.

Answer: (a) To find John's consumption optimum, the usual equations are $c_1^j / c_0^j = 1/P_1 \ (\equiv P_0/P_1)$ and $c_0^j + P_1 c_1^j = 10 + 100 P_1$. Eliminating c_1^j we have $c_0^j = 5 + 50P_1$, or $c_0^j = 5 + 50/(1 + r)$. This equation represents John's "full" demand curve for current corn (inclusive of his own consumption). His demand for borrowing is a transaction demand curve, so we must subtract his endowed quantity of current corn: $b_0^j = c_0^j - \bar{c}_0^j = -5 + 50/(1 + r)$. A similar analysis for Kathy leads to $c_0^k = 25 + 10/(1 + r)$, implying $l_0^k = \bar{c}_0^k - c_0^k = 25 - 10/(1 + r)$. (b) In equilibrium $-5 + 50/(1 + r) = 25 - 10/(1 + r)$, so $r = 100$ percent and $P_1/P_0 = 1/2$. Here John borrows $b_0^j = 20$ units of C_0, equal to the amount l_0^k that Kathy is willing to lend.

Saving-Investment Equilibrium

In the borrowing-lending equilibrium just discussed, the savings of lenders equalled the "dissavings" of borrowers. By assumption, no *investment* occurred. We now want to include investment. Since investment is a kind of production, our analysis resembles the discussion of "Exchange and Production" in Chapter 13. When savings and investment are in equilibrium, the net positive supply of individuals' savings and dissavings exactly balances (finances) the actual investment demand in the economy.

To start with the fundamentals, Figure 14.3 (p. 402) shows a Robinson Crusoe isolated from all trade. His endowment at E can be written in consumption units as $(\bar{c}_0, \bar{c}_1)$ or in production units as $(\bar{q}_0, \bar{q}_1)$; these must be the same for him. The productive transformation opportunities are indicated by his Production-Possibility Curve QQ. Robinson's optimum is at R^* where an indifference curve is tangent to the Production-Possibility Curve. Of course, Robinson must produce exactly what he consumes: $R^* = (c_0^*, c_1^*) = (q_0^*, q_1^*)$.

Robinson's *saving* (refraining from consumption) is the horizontal distance $\bar{c}_0 - c_0^*$. Of course, no lending can occur, since there is no one to lend to. Rather, Robinson saves so that he can make physical *investments* (for example, planting seed corn) where $\bar{c}_0 - c_0^* = \bar{q}_0 - q_0^*$. The yield in terms of future corn is shown in the diagram by the vertical distance $q_1^* - \bar{q}_1 = c_1^* - \bar{c}_1$. For an isolated Robinson Crusoe, therefore, plantings of seed (investing) exactly equal his sacrificed consumption of current corn (saving). The same holds for an isolated country: in the absence of foreign trade, a country's saving must equal its own investment.

Once borrowing and lending are possible, an individual or a country's saving and investment may no longer be equal. Figure 14.4 (p. 403) pictures an individual with both productive opportunities and market opportunities. The productive opportunities are represented, as before, by the Production-Possibility Curve QQ. The market opportunities are shown by budget lines of slope $-P_0/P_1 \equiv -(1 + r)$ through attainable points on QQ. Each budget line represents a certain level of wealth according to the following equation:

$$W_0 \equiv q_0 + \frac{q_1}{1 + r} \tag{14.4}$$

One such line, MM, shows possible trades from the endowment position E. But the individual here can do better by producing at Q^*, allowing him to reach the *highest* attainable budget line NN. NN therefore represents the maximum attainable level of wealth, W_0^*:

FIGURE 14.3 **Intertemporal Productive-Consumptive Optimum: Robinson Crusoe**

Robinson Crusoe has no intertemporal exchange (borrowing-lending) opportunities, but can engage in productive transformations between consumption this year and consumption next year. QQ is the Production-Possibility Curve through his endowment E. The Crusoe optimum is at R^*, where QQ is tangent to the highest attainable indifference curve. This is an "autarky" solution: the amounts produced (q_0^*, q_1^*) equal, respectively, the amounts consumed (c_0^*, c_1^*).

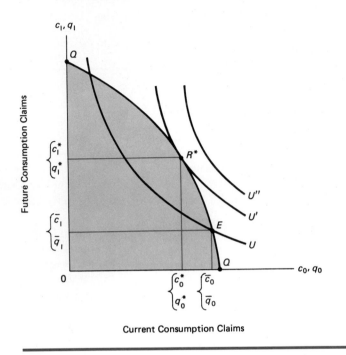

Current Consumption Claims

$$W_0^* \equiv q_0^* + \frac{q_1^*}{1 + r} \tag{14.5}$$

Having maximized his wealth, the person can then engage in market exchange along NN, attaining a consumptive optimum at C^*. (Note that C^* is on a higher indifference curve than R^*.) For someone able to borrow or lend as well as invest, therefore, the effective constraint on consumption is not the Production-Possibility Curve QQ, but the budget line NN. The budget-line equation corresponding to NN is[3]

$$c_0 + \frac{c_1}{1 + r} = W_0^* \tag{14.6}$$

Note that W_0^*, the variable maximized in Equation (14.5), fixes the budget constraint in Equation (14.6).

---

[3]*Mathematical Footnote:* As in the preceding footnote, note the difference between Equations (14.5) and (14.6). Equation (14.5) is an identity in which the maximized wealth W_0^* is *defined*. In equation (14.6) W_0^* is a constant that constrains consumption of C_0 and C_1.

FIGURE 14.4 **Intertemporal Productive-Consumptive Optimum with Exchange** The individual here has intertemporal productive opportunities (shown by the Production-Possibility Curve QQ) as well as exchange opportunities indicated by budget lines like MM and NN of slope $-P_0/P_1 = -(1 + r)$. The productive optimum Q^* involves investment in the amount $\bar{q}_0 - q_0^*$. The consumptive optimum C^* indicates that the individual saves only $\bar{c}_0 - c_0^*$; the remainder of the investment is financed by borrowing in the market.

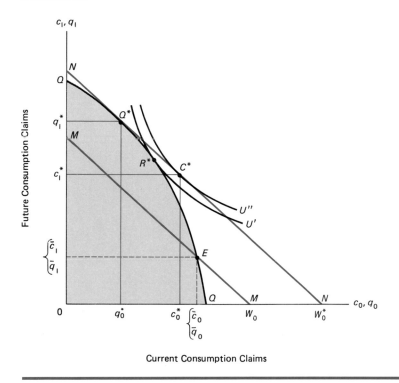

Current Consumption Claims

The individual pictured in Figure 14.4 invests (plants seed corn) in the amount given by the horizontal distance $\bar{q}_0 - q_0^*$. But his *saving* is only the horizontal distance $\bar{c}_0 - c_0^*$. He is reducing his current consumption to gain seed corn, but not enough to cover the full amount planted. The remainder, which he borrows, represents the consumption sacrifices of other individuals.

Market equilibrium is shown in Figure 14.5 (p. 404) in two ways: (1) as a balance between the overall supply of saving S and demand for investment I, and (2) as a balance between the overall supply of lending L and demand for borrowing B. (Recall Figure 13.10 in the preceding chapter that showed equilibrium solutions in terms of full supply and demand versus transaction supply and demand.) The difference between the full magnitude of saving-investment versus the transaction magnitude of borrowing-lending is accounted for by the amount the person invests through his own savings. Note that the aggregate amount borrowed (and lent) can be either greater or less than the amount invested (and saved). An extreme case where borrowing-lending exceeds saving-investment would be in an economy with no opportunities for productive investment at all. Nevertheless, in such an economy some people may borrow or lend to others. At the other extreme, if there were productive opportunities

FIGURE 14.5 **Intertemporal Equilibrium with Productive Investment**   When productive investment takes place, the equilibrium interest rate r^* simultaneously balances: (1) the aggregate supply of saving S with the aggregate demand for investment I, and (2) the aggregate supply of lending L with the aggregate demand for borrowing B. The difference between the two magnitudes, at any interest rate r, is accounted for by the amount of investment self-financed out of investors' own savings.

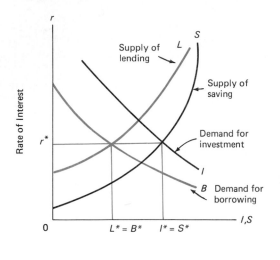

Saving or Investment

and yet all individuals were identical, then they could all save and invest—but no one would borrow or lend.

EXAMPLE 14.2   Growth Versus Investment: International Comparisons

Some nations save and invest more than others. We would expect nations to grow more rapidly the more they invest. The table below indicates that this tends to be the case, where growth is measured in terms of annual changes in Gross Domestic Product (GDP).

Growth, Investment, and Saving (1973–84)*

	Growth Rate of GDP	Investment Rate	Saving Rate
Five Highest Growth Rates			
Egypt	8.5%	25%	12%
Yemen Arab Republic	8.1	21	−22
Cameroon	7.1	26	33
Syrian Arab Republic	7.0	24	12
Indonesia	6.8	21	20
Five Lowest Growth Rates			
Zambia	0.4	14	15
El Salvador	−0.3	12	4

Growth, Investment, and Saving (1973–84)* (cont.)

	Growth Rate of GDP	Investment Rate	Saving Rate
Ghana	−0.9	6	5
Zaire	−1.0	NA	NA
Uganda	−1.3	8	6

*Source: Selected from The World Bank, *The World Development Report* (1986).

COMMENT In interpreting these data, it is important to distinguish between saving and investment. A high saving rate by residents of a country would lead to increases in wealth, but not necessarily to increases in GDP—if, for example, the savings are invested abroad. Conversely, a country can have high investment despite low saving if funds flow in from abroad. Yemen clearly falls into this category; it had a very high investment rate despite a large negative saving rate. (Saudi Arabia provided large financial assistance to Yemen during this period.) Overall, however, there is some correlation between investment and savings, since it is generally easier and safer for people to invest their savings at home rather than abroad. The countries with very low saving and investment rates here were almost all subject to great political disturbances during this period. The countries with extraordinarily high rates were mainly beneficiaries of the oil boom.

CONCLUSION: In the absence of productive investment opportunities, at any given interest rate *r* each individual borrows or lends to achieve a preferred intertemporal pattern of consumption. At the equilibrium interest rate the overall market supply of lending equals the overall market demand for borrowing. In an economy with investment opportunities, each individual chooses the level of investment that maximizes his wealth; each individual also borrows or lends to achieve a preferred time-pattern of consumption. Then the equilibrium interest rate balances the aggregate supply of saving with the aggregate demand for investment, and also balances the aggregate supply of lending with the aggregate demand for borrowing.

The distinction between saving and investment also plays a central role in the example that follows.

EXAMPLE 14.3 Social Security, Saving, and National Income

Before the Social Security program came into effect in the United States, individuals generally provided for their retirement by saving out of income earned in their productive working years. By buying insurance or depositing money in banks, savers helped finance the productive investments that increased the real capital of the nation.

The Social Security program reduced people's need to provide for old age through financial instruments like insurance or bank accounts. Also, Social Security taxes on earnings left people with less income available for saving. So aggregate *private* saving would be expected to decline as a result of the Social Security program. On the other hand, Social Security taxes generated large revenues for the federal government. If the government had "funded" these contributions, the cash inflows would have been used to accumulate a financial reserve in the form of stocks, bonds, real estate, and so on. (Indeed, this is what insurance companies do with premiums paid by individuals for retirement annuities.) Then the collective saving of the Social Security Administration would have balanced the reduction in private savings.

However, a political decision was made not to fund Social Security. No large reserves were accumulated. Instead, Social Security tax revenues were used to support the current expenses of government. Some economists contend that this policy caused savings (and therefore aggregate investment) to decline for the nation as a whole. Martin Feldstein[a] estimated that the Social Security program reduced overall private saving by 38 percent without, as just explained, increasing government saving. The reduced saving and investment over the years has substantially reduced the nation's stock of capital. And since real capital raises the Average Product of labor and other resources, total and per capita national income have also been affected. Feldstein estimated that, by 1972, the Social Security program had reduced GNP by 11 to 15 percent.

A difficulty with Feldstein's estimates lies in his assumption that all private saving was for retirement purposes, whereas in actuality many people save in order to pass on bequests to heirs. Taking account of this and other criticisms, Michael R. Darby[b] produced revised estimates. He concluded that Social Security was responsible for a decrease of between 5 and 20 percent in the capital stock, and between 2 and 7 percent in national income. These results tend to confirm Feldstein's contention that the Social Security program has reduced saving and national income, but the calculated effects are numerically smaller than Feldstein's original estimates.

[a]Martin Feldstein, "Social Security, Induced Retirement, and Aggregate Capital Accumulation," *Journal of Political Economy,* v. 82 (September/October 1974).

[b]Michael R. Darby, *The Effects of Social Security on Income and Capital Stock* (Washington, D.C.: American Enterprise Institute for Public Policy Research, 1979), p. 79.

14.2 INVESTMENT DECISIONS AND THE PRESENT-VALUE RULE

The economics of time has practical implications in the world of affairs. Decisionmakers in government and business have to choose among different investment projects, decide how projects are to be financed, and determine the timing at which benefits will be received. We can now analyze certain of these investment decision problems.

The Separation Theorem

The analysis depicted in Figure 14.4 shows that *the individual's productive optimum position is entirely independent of his or her preferences.* Since the location of Q^* depends only on the shape of the Production-Possibility curve QQ and on the slope of the market line, the indifference curves do not matter for the production decision.

When the conditions underlying this *Separation Theorem* are approximately applicable, important practical results follow. Suppose an owner of a firm delegates production decisions to an agent or manager. The manager would not have to know anything about the time-preferences of the owner. The owner is made as well-off as possible by having the manager simply maximize the firm's wealth. Even more important, a manager could work simultaneously for a number of different owners with different time-preferences, so owners can combine their wealth in a corporation (see Chapter 6).[4]

Strictly speaking, however, the Separation Theorem applies only if the markets for borrowing and lending are perfect and costless (see Chapter 13). What if such transactions were costly, so that (for example) individuals can only borrow at a higher interest rate than at which they can lend? The amount to be invested, the choice of Q^* on the Production-Possibility curve, would then depend in part on preferences—that is, upon the person's willingness to save. Take the extreme case of an isolated Robinson Crusoe, where transaction costs are infinite (there are no market opportunities at all). For Robinson Crusoe the production and consumption choices are identical; *all* his physical investment must be self-financed, and so his time-preferences will surely affect his investment.

The Present-Value Rule

What is the appropriate *investment decision rule* for choosing between projects?

A project generates a sequence of dated income flows or payments. Let z_0 be the payment in the current period, z_1 the payment in the next period, and so on. If z_0 is negative and z_1 is positive, present income is sacrificed for future income and we have an *investment* project. If z_0 is positive and z_1 is negative, we would have a *disinvestment* project.

The *Present Value* V_0 of a two-period project is defined as follows:

$$V_0 \equiv z_0 + \frac{z_1}{1 + r} \tag{14.7}$$

Comparison with the definition of wealth in Equation (14.4) shows that Present Value measures the additional wealth generated by the project. If the Separation Theorem is applicable, all production decisions should be aimed at wealth-maximization: more wealth is always desirable. These considerations lead to two rules.

PRESENT-VALUE RULE 1:   Adopt any project with a positive Present Value V_0; reject any project with a negative Present Value V_0. (Note that this rule has the same form for investment or disinvestment projects.)

Complications arise when projects are *interdependent*. Adopting one project may change the z_0, z_1 payoffs of another. For example, sowing seed corn may increase the benefit of digging an irrigation canal. The obvious implication is to adopt that *set* of projects whose combined payment stream has maximum Present Value. We shall not go through all the possibilities here, but rather state the rule that applies when projects or combinations of projects are *mutually exclusive*.[5]

---

[4]When the Separation Theorem is inapplicable, there is said to be a "clientele effect" in the decisions of the firm. We would expect investors with different tastes to combine in different types of firms, each of which would cater to the particular time-preferences of its owners.

[5]Any list of alternative projects, interdependent or not, can be grouped into mutually exclusive combinations. Thus, the three projects A, B, C can be sorted into the eight mutually exclusive combinations 0, A, B, C, AB, AC, CB, and ABC (where 0 represents adopting no project at all).

PRESENT-VALUE RULE 2:   If two projects (or combinations of projects) are mutually exclusive, adopt whichever has the higher Present Value V_0.

For example, a landowner may have to choose between putting a gas station or an office building on his lot. Since these projects are mutually exclusive, he should pick the one with the higher Present Value.

Exercise 14.3

(a) A project has anticipated cash flows $z_0 = -100$, and $z_1 = 125$. Is this an investment or a disinvestment? What is its Present Value V_0 when the interest rate r is 10 percent? At $r = 20\%$? At $r = 30\%$? What is the highest rate of interest at which the project should be adopted?
(b) The table below shows payment sequences for two interdependent projects M and N. The first two rows show the payments when either project is adopted alone; the third row shows the payments when both are adopted. If the interest rate were 20 percent and you could adopt no more than one project, which (if any) should you choose? If you could adopt both together, would you want to do so?

Project	z_0	z_1
M	-100	125
N	-50	90
MN	-155	205

Answer: (a) This is an investment project. When $r = 10\%$, $V_0 = -100 + 125/(1 + 0.1) = 13.64$. When $r = 20\%$, $V_0 = 4.167$. When $r = 30\%$, $V_0 = -3.85$. To find the highest rate of interest at which the project should be adopted, solve for r in $V_0 = 0 = -100 + 125/(1 + r)$. The answer is $r = 25\%$. The project should be adopted for any r below 25 percent. (b) To determine the optimal investment compare the Present Values of the three mutually exclusive investment alternatives M, N, and MN. At 20 percent, $V_0(M) = -100 + 125/1.2 = 4.17$ and $V_0(N) = -50 + 90/1.2 = 25$. For the combination MN the combined payments are $z_0 = -155$ and $z_1 = 205$, so that $V_0(MN) = -155 + 205/1.2 = 15.83$. The best investment is N alone, even if you could adopt both.

Exercise 14.4

An alternative method of evaluating projects is to compare their *future values:* the amount of money that will be available after all loans are repaid or income receipts reinvested. Suppose a saver has two alternatives: (a) invest \$1,000 at 10 percent for 2 years or (b) invest \$1,000 at 11 percent for the first year, and then reinvest the principal and interest at 9.5 percent for the second year. Which savings plan is better?

Answer: The first plan yields \$(1000)(1.1)(1.1) = \$1210 at the end of the second year. The other plan yields (\$1000)(1.1)(1.095) = \$1204.50. The first plan is therefore better. [*Exercise for the student:* Using the data in Exercise 14.3, part (a), suppose that the \$100 payment at date 0 is borrowed at an interest rate of r. Find the interest rate which makes the future value of the project equal zero. Does the present value calculation lead to the same decision as the future value calculation?]

TABLE 14.1 Interest-Rate Equivalents

Short-Term Interest Rates	Long-Term Interest Rates
$\dfrac{P_1}{P_0} = \dfrac{1}{1 + r_1}$	$\dfrac{P_1}{P_0} = \dfrac{1}{1 + R_1}$
$\dfrac{P_2}{P_1} = \dfrac{1}{1 + r_2}$	$\dfrac{P_2}{P_0} = \dfrac{1}{(1 + R_2)^2}$
$\cdots\cdots$	$\cdots\cdots$
$\dfrac{P_T}{P_{T-1}} = \dfrac{1}{1 + r_T}$	$\dfrac{P_T}{P_0} = \dfrac{1}{(1 + R_T)^T}$

Multi-Period Analysis

Until now we have considered only two periods: "now" (date 0) and "one year from now" (date 1). But the same principles apply for any number of periods. Instead of choosing between only two dates, individuals can plan their consumption choices over all dates from "now" to some future horizon T. We can analyze these decisions by generalizing the concept of Present Value for multiple periods.

The prices of consumption claims at different dates can be written as $P_0, P_1, \ldots, P_T$.[6] As usual, set $P_0 = 1$, so that current income claims continue to serve as the *numeraire*. In translating from *prices to interest rates*, there are two useful formulations. First, consider the successive year-to-year price ratios $P_1/P_0, P_2/P_1, \ldots, P_T/P_{T-1}$. These can be used to define the one-year short-term interest rates $r_1, r_2, \ldots, r_T$ on the left side of Table 14.1 of Interest-Rate Equivalents. Here r_1 is the interest rate for transactions between date 0 and date 1, r_2 is the rate between date 1 and date 2, and so on.

Alternatively, consider the ratios $P_1/P_0, P_2/P_0, \ldots, P_T/P_0$ that are defined so that P_0 appears in all the denominators. These can be used, as on the right side of Table 14.1, to define the long-term interest rates $R_1, R_2, \ldots, R_T$; these rates govern transactions between date 0 and any future date up to T.

The Present Value of a stream of payments from date 0 to date T can be expressed either in terms of the long-term or the short-term interest rates.

$$V_0 \equiv z_0 + \frac{z_1}{1 + R_1} + \frac{z_2}{(1 + R_2)^2} + \ldots + \frac{z_T}{(1 + R_T)^T} \tag{14.8}$$

$$V_0 \equiv z_0 + \frac{z_1}{1 + r_1} + \frac{z_2}{(1 + r_2)(1 + r_1)}$$
$$+ \ldots + \frac{z_T}{(1 + r_T) \ldots (1 + r_2)(1 + r_1)} \tag{14.9}$$

[6]The prices are those quoted in the trading that takes place now. P_1 is the price *today* of a claim to income payable one year in the future, P_2 is the price *today* of a claim payable two years in the future, and so forth.

For some purposes the first formulation is more convenient, for other purposes the second. There is no logical difference between them, since the long-term rate R_T is an average of the short-term rates $r_1, r_2, \ldots, r_T$ between now and date T.

While the "term structure" of the r_T or R_T interest rates is sometimes important, in most practical applications it is assumed that the current rate will maintain itself into the future. Of course, if the r_T are all equal to some common value r then the two formulations (14.8) and (14.9) both reduce to

$$V_0 \equiv z_0 + \frac{z_1}{1 + r} + \frac{z_2}{(1 + r)^2} + \ldots + \frac{z_T}{(1 + r)^T} \qquad (14.10)$$

Let us construct a special case of Equation (14.10), making the following assumptions: (1) the "economic horizon" T is infinite; (2) returns on the project begin at date 1; (3) future receipts $z_1, z_2, \ldots$ are constant forever and equal to z. Then Equation (14.10) reduces to the simple form[7]

$$V_0 \equiv \frac{z}{r} \quad \text{or} \quad r \equiv \frac{z}{V_0} \qquad (14.10')$$

For example, if $r = 0.10$, the Present Value of $10.00 per year forever is $V_0 = 10.00/.10 = 100$. Put another way, if you put $100 in the bank at 10 percent interest, it would yield $10.00 per year forever.

This formulation shows the relation between the annual income from some asset (z) and the current market value of the asset itself (V_0). We can now see a different aspect of the interest rate r. Previously we defined it as a time-premium, the extra market value of earlier over later consumption income. But Equation (14.10') shows that the interest rate is also the ratio between income flow and the value of the source of income. This justifies the discussion in Chapter 12 that described the interest rate as the ratio between the hire-price of an input and the value of the input itself.

Exercise 14.5

(a) If the one-period (short-term) interest rate is $r_1 = 10\%$ and the two-period (long-term) interest rate is $R_2 = 20\%$, what is the implied "forward" short-term rate r_2? Assuming $P_0 \equiv 1$ as usual, what are the implied prices P_1 and P_2 for one-year-future and two-year-future claims,

---

[7]*Mathematical Footnote:* The derivation proceeds from (14.10), under the special assumptions above, as follows:

$$V_0 = z \left[\frac{1}{1 + r} + \frac{1}{(1 + r)^2} + \ldots \right]$$

Let $1/(1 + r)$ be denoted k. Then

$$V_0 = z(1 + k + k^2 + \ldots) - z = \frac{z}{1 - k} - z$$

But

$$1 - k = 1 - \frac{1}{1 + r} = \frac{r}{1 + r}$$

So

$$V_0 = z \left[\frac{1 + r}{r} \right] - z = \frac{z}{r}$$

respectively? (b) Suppose that a three-period project has the cash-flow sequence $-1, 2, 1$, and suppose the interest rate r is constant over time. Over what range of r is this a good project? What if the cash-flow sequence is $-1, 5, -6$?

Answer: (a) Since $P_2/P_0 = (P_2/P_1)(P_1/P_0)$, from the Table of Interest-Rate Equivalents we see that $(1 + R_2)^2 = (1 + r_1)(1 + r_2)$, or numerically here $1.2^2 = 1.1(1 + r_2)$. The solution is $r_2 = 30.9\%$. The implied prices for the future claims are $P_1 = 1/(1 + r_1) = 0.91$ and $P_2 = 1/(1 + R_2)^2 = 0.69$. (b) We want to find the range of r for which $V_0 > 0$. With the first cash-flow sequence the inequality becomes: $-1 + 2/(1 + r) + 1/(1 + r)^2 > 0$. Solving this quadratic equation, the solution (for a positive value of r) is $r = 141.4\%$. Thus the Present Value is positive for any interest rate $r < 141.4\%$. (The quadratic has another root, $r = -141.4\%$, but interest rates less than -100% are impossible.) For the second cash-flow sequence it turns out that V_0 is negative for all allowable interest rates below 100 percent, V_0 is positive in the range between $r = 100\%$ and $r = 200\%$, and V_0 is negative again for still higher r.

EXAMPLE 14.4 Education and Earnings

A study by A. Razin and J. D. Campbell[a] calculated present values of lifetime earnings for holders of bachelor's degrees in various fields, using National Science Foundation 1968 data on yearly incomes of scientific manpower. The authors assumed that earnings begin in the fifth year after admission to college, and terminate in the forty-fourth year, so that Equation (14.10) was applied in the special form:

$$V_0 = \frac{z_5}{(1 + r)^5} + \frac{z_6}{(1 + r)^6} + \ldots + \frac{z_{44}}{(1 + r)^{44}}$$

Calculating with an interest rate $r = 3\%$, the following table indicates some of the results obtained. (The relatively favorable position of the economics degree is consistent with the salary standing of economists reported in Example 1.2.)

Present Values of Earnings for Bachelor's Degrees

Mathematics	$342,068
Economics	339,482
Computer Sciences	306,733
Political Science	300,000
Physics	282,758
Psychology	262,127
Agriculture Science	225,118
Biological Science	215,691
Sociology	213,590

These numbers are not a firm indication of the value of investment in education, since they represent only the added earnings received by holders of the degree. The costs of a college education, such as tuition fees and earnings foregone during the four college years, have not been taken into account.

There is still another difficulty: we cannot assume that the higher earnings of educated individuals are due to their education alone. People who go to college may earn more because they work more hours (see Chapter 12), because they are smart to begin with, come from more affluent families, and so forth. To eliminate some of these biases J. R. Behrman, R. A. Pollak, and P. Taubman[b] compared the earnings of identical twins with different amounts of schooling. They found that the following formula best fitted the observations for men aged 47–57 in 1973:

$$\log(E1/E2) = 0.28 \log(S1/S2) + 0.014$$

Here E_1 and E_2 represent the annual earnings of the two twins, and S_1 and S_2 represent their years of schooling.

With this equation we can estimate that if an individual has a twelfth-grade education and earns $18,400 per year, then his twin with four years of college will earn $20,225 per year—an improvement of $1,825 or only 9.9 percent. Assuming a forty-year working life and an interest rate of 3 percent, the present value of additional earnings attributable to attending four years of college is $42,176. Note how much smaller this figure is than those in the Razin-Campbell study, and recall that neither study makes any allowance for the *costs* of attending college.

This study does not necessarily mean that college is a bad investment. Presumably individuals derive some benefits from college apart from improvement in future earnings. Among the possibilities are intellectual enrichment, new friends, potential marriage partners, and fun and games.

[a]Assaf Razin and James D. Campbell, "Internal Allocation of University Resources," *Western Economic Journal*, v. 10 (September 1972), p. 315.

[b]Jere R. Behrman, Robert A. Pollak, and Paul Taubman, "Parental Preferences and Provision for Progeny," *Journal of Political Economy*, v. 90 (February 1982).

14.3 AN APPLICATION: THE ECONOMICS OF FORESTRY

Suppose it costs $1 to plant a tree. Let the timber value of the tree, if cut at any time t from the date of planting, be $g = \sqrt{t}$, tabulated as follows:

Year of cut (t)	1	4	9	16
Value of timber (g)	1	2	3	4

Considering only the alternative possibilities tabulated (that is, do not interpolate within the table, or extend it beyond 16 years), what is the best time to cut the tree if the interest rate is constant over time and equal to 5 percent?

The problem here is to maximize the present value. We can analyze the possibilities by looking at the following calculations:

Year	Present value		
1	$1/1.05$	=	0.95
4	$2/(1.05)^4$	=	1.65
9	$3/(1.05)^9$	=	1.93
16	$4/(1.05)^{16}$	=	1.83

Clearly, it is best to cut the tree after 9 years.

Now suppose that the cost of planting a tree is \$0.10, and that after a tree is cut down a new one is planted. What is the optimal rule now? We cannot just look at the present value of one cycle, for the earlier a tree is cut down, the earlier the net benefits of second and all following cycles will arrive.

Consider the 1 year cycle. In year 0 the firm incurs a cost of \$0.10; at the end of year 1 it earns \$1 − \$0.10 = \$0.90; at the end of year 2 it earns \$1 − \$0.10 again, and so on forever. The present value is then −\$0.10 + \$0.90/(1.05) + \$0.90/(1.05)^2 and so on; numerical calculation shows the present value to be \$11.12.

If a cycle lasts 4 years, the firm spends \$0.10 in period 0; at the end of year 4 it earns \$2 and pays \$0.10 to plant a new tree, for a net earning of \$2 − \$0.10 = \$1.90. It will have the same net earning in years 4, 8, 12, and so on. Thus the present value of the firm's profits is −\$0.10 + \$1.90/(1.05)^4 + \$1.90/(1.05)^8 + . . . , which is \$8.54.

By similar calculations, it can be shown that the 9-year cycle has a present value of \$5.16, and the 16-year cycle has a present value of \$3.20. The highest Present Value is for the 1-year cycle. Thus, allowing for the possibility of replanting land cleared by cutting, a much shorter cycling time is most profitable.

14.4 AN APPLICATION: THE ECONOMICS OF EXHAUSTIBLE RESOURCES

A resource like petroleum exists in finite quantity. The economic problem is how much to extract in each period. Associated with the *time-path of extraction* there will also be a *time-path of prices*.

To simplify matters, let us assume (unrealistically) that extraction costs are zero: the oil gushes out freely until it is all finally exhausted. The question to be examined is the differences in price and extraction paths chosen by a monopolistic firm and firms in a competitive industry.

Beginning with the competitive case, assume that the demands each year are independent of what happens in other years, and remain the same from year to year. The annual demands are pictured as the (solid) straight-line curve $D^0 = D^1 = D^2 = . . .$ in Figure 14.6 (p. 414). Note the choke-price P^+, which will play an important role in the analysis; demand is zero for any price higher than P^+. The extraction quantity at any date t is q_t, and the price at that date is P^t (where P^t means the price paid t years hence for a barrel of oil delivered in that year).[8]

A price P^1 to be received next year for next year's oil has a Present Value of $P^1/(1 + r)$. In equilibrium oil will be sold in both periods only if the Present Value of next year's price equals today's price, or if

$$P^0 = \frac{P^1}{1 + r} = \frac{P^2}{(1 + r)^2} = . . . \tag{14.11}$$

In Figure 14.6 note the dashed curve $PV(D^1)$ and the dotted curve $PV(D^2)$. As the symbols suggest, the heights of these curves represent the Present Values or (discounted equivalents) of the actual demand curves for dates 1 and 2. For example, if the interest rate

---

[8]Notice that P^1, for example, has quite a different meaning from P_1 as used earlier in the chapter. P_1 is the *price today* of income (corn) to be received at date 1. But P^1 here means the *price at date 1* of oil at date 1.

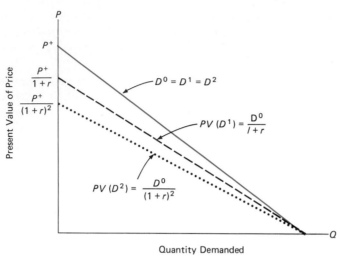

were 20 percent, then for each quantity the height along $PV(D^1)$ is found by dividing the height along the demand curve D^1 by the factor $1 + r = 1.2$. And similarly, the height along $PV(D^2)$ is found by dividing through by the factor $(1 + r)^2 = 1.44$.

To progress further, consider for the moment only two time periods: dates 0 and 1. The width along the horizontal axis in the diagram on the left of Figure 14.7 represents the available fixed stock Q, which is to be distributed between extraction at date 0 (q_0) and extraction at date 1 (q_1). The present value of money received in the current period is simply that amount, so the $PV(D_0)$ curve is identical to the D_0 curve. As can be seen, the directions of the D^1 and $PV(D^1)$ curves are reversed in the diagram. This construction immediately shows that condition (14.11) is met at the intersection of the D^0 and $PV(D^1)$ curves at point C along the horizontal axis, which shows the equilibrium extraction quantities q_0 and q_1 for the two dates. Notice that $q_0 > q_1$, which must necessarily hold if the interest rate r is positive. The price P^0 is read directly from the D^0 curve. The price P^1 is read from the D^1 curve rather than the $PV(D^1)$ curve. The geometry shows also that $P^1 > P^0$, which follows directly from the equilibrium condition (14.11) if $r > 0$. To summarize, for a resource in fixed supply a competitive industry will have a *declining extraction path* and a *rising price path*.

Suppose demand were expected to persist to date 2. Would a competitive industry "conserve" any of the resource for that date? In the diagram on the left of Figure 14.7, note the (dotted) $PV(D^2)$ curve drawn in the normal direction from the vertical axis. The intercept on the vertical axis is the discounted value of the choke price, $P^+/(1 + r)^2$. We have drawn the curve so that this intercept lies *below* the intersection of the D^0 and $PV(D^1)$ curves. This means that even the very first (most highly desired) unit left over for date 2 is not worth as much, in present-value terms, as the marginal unit at dates 0 and 1. Consequently, in this case all of the resource would be extracted in the first two time-periods. But had the discounted

FIGURE 14.7 **Extraction and Prices over Two or Three Dates**   Here extraction is assumed costless. With only two dates, for a competitive industry (upper diagram) the extraction amounts q_0 and q_1 are determined by the intersection above point C of the current-date demand curve D^0 and the present value of the future-date demand curve $PV(D^1)$. Then $q_0 > q_1$ and so $P^0 < P^1$. For the monopoly pictured in the lower diagram, the extractions are determined by the intersection above point M of the current-date Marginal Revenue MR^0 and $PV(MR^1)$. The monopolist extracts somewhat less in the current period, and in fact would reserve some of the resource for a third date.

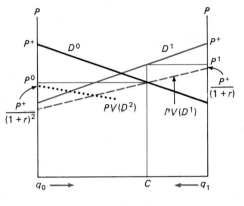

Competitive Industry

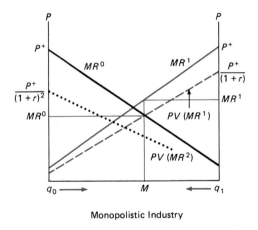

Monopolistic Industry

choke price been *higher* than the equilibrium values of $P^0 = P^1/(1 + r)$, some of the resource would instead have been conserved for extraction at date 2. (And similarly of course for even later dates.) Notice that the lower the interest rate r, the greater will be the amounts retained for future dates.

What if the industry were monopolized? Without explaining the logic in detail, it will be evident that the conditions corresponding to Equation (14.11) are

$$MR^0 = \frac{MR^1}{1 + r} = \frac{MR^2}{(1 + r)^2} = \ldots \qquad (14.12)$$

That is, a monopolist sets the discounted *Marginal Revenues* equal at each date, rather than the discounted *prices*.

In the diagram on the right of Figure 14.7, MR^0 is the Marginal Revenue curve associated with the D^0 demand curve of the previous diagram. (To reduce clutter, the demand curves are omitted from the lower panel.) And similarly $PV(MR^1)$ and $PV(MR^2)$ show the *discounted* Marginal Revenue curves for dates 1 and 2. Here the point where the MR^0 and $PV(MR^1)$ curves intersect (above point M) shows the amounts q_0 and q_1 that a monopolist would extract in a two-period situation.

Will the monopolist reserve anything for date 2? He would do so if the discounted value of Marginal Revenue in year 2 exceeded MR^0 and $PV(MR^1)$. Since Marginal Revenue in year 2 is greatest at $q_2 = 0$, a necessary condition for $PV(MR^2)$ to exceed MR^0 and $PV(MR^1)$ is that the discounted date-2 choke price, $P^+/(1 + r)^2$, is greater than $MR^0 = PV(MR^1)$ at the intersection above point M. In the diagram here, the monopolist would in fact reserve some of the resource for date 2, even though the competitive industry did not.

Exercise 14.6

The annual demand curve for an exhaustible resource is given by $P^t = 100 - q_t$ (for any date t). The total stock of the resource is $Q = 56$, and the interest rate is $r = 25\%$. (a) Find the extraction path and the price path for a competitive industry if there are only two periods (dates 0 and 1). If there is also another period, date 2, to be considered, would any of the resource be conserved for that date? (b) Answer the same questions for a monopolized industry.

Answer: (a) The condition $P^0 = P^1/(1 + r)$ here implies $100 - q_0 = 80 - .8q_1$. The resource constraint is $q_0 + q_1 = 56$. Solving the simultaneous equations, the solution is the extraction path $q_0 = 36$, $q_1 = 20$. The associated prices are $P^0 = 64$, $P^1 = 80$. If some of the resource is to be held for a third date, the discounted choke price $P^+/(1 + r)^2$ would have to exceed $P^0 = P^1/(1 + r) = 64$. But here the discounted choke price is $100/(1.25)^2 = 64$ exactly, so nothing would be conserved for date 2. (b) Under monopoly the condition $MR^0 = MR^1/(1 + r)$ implies $100 - 2q_0 = 80 - 1.6q_1$. The resource constraint is again $q_0 + q_1 = 56$. The extraction quantities are $q_0 = 30.4$, $q_1 = 25.6$; the prices are $P^0 = 69.6$, $P^1 = 74.4$. (The monopoly price path starts higher but ends up lower than the competitive price path.) The monopolist would conserve some of the resource for date 2 if the discounted choke price $100/(1 + r)^2 = 64$ exceeds $MR^0 = 100 - 2q_0 = 39.2$. This condition is indeed met, so the monopolist would distribute the resource over at least the three dates 0, 1, and 2. (This would of course change the previous numerical results that applied when there were only two dates.)

Figure 14.8 illustrates extraction paths and price paths for a competitive versus a monopolistic industry, where time is now assumed to run continuously over many periods. The previous analysis suggests the following:

1. The monopolized industry *extracts less at early dates* and *more at later dates* than a competitive industry: the monopolist is "more conservationist!"
2. It follows that the *prices* for a monopolized industry will be *initially higher* but eventually *lower* at later dates. Specifically, the competitive price path rises at a compound-interest rate, as indicated by condition (14.11). For monopoly, Marginal Revenues rise at compound interest, which implies that the prices will increase somewhat more slowly. Of course, both price paths must eventually approach the same choke price P^+.[9]

FIGURE 14.8 **Extraction Paths and Price Paths**   A competitive industry tends to extract more at early dates and less at later dates in comparison with a monopolist. The corresponding price paths are lower at first for a competitive industry, but ultimately higher.

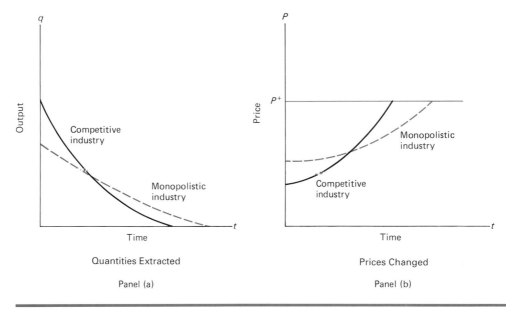

Quantities Extracted

Panel (a)

Prices Changed

Panel (b)

14.5 EVALUATING PROJECTS WITH DIFFERENT INTEREST RATES

Decisionmakers in business or government who compare the Present Values of projects usually find that the numerical interest rate employed has a big effect. This effect is especially true when the annual payments extend over many years into the future. So determining the correct rate of interest to use for purposes of discounting is a very important issue.

EXAMPLE 14.5   **Present Values of the Feather River Project**

The Feather River Project was an enormous undertaking to transport water from northern to southern California. The table here shows the results of an independent assessment (made prior to construction) of the prospective costs and receipts of the project and of the difference between the two, all calculated in terms of Present Values. Three alternative routes then

---

[9]The assumption that there is a finite choke price plays an important role here. It assures, at least for sufficiently high prices, that demand becomes more elastic as price rises. (As would be true, for example, everywhere along a straight-line demand curve.) Without this assumption the conclusion in the text about price paths would not necessarily follow. In the case of a constant-elasticity demand curve, for example, Marginal Revenue will always be a constant fraction of price (see Equation 8.5). Then the monopolist's price will rise over time just as rapidly as the competitive price.

under consideration were evaluated. The Present-Value calculation considered two alternative interest rates, 2.7 percent and 5 percent.

Present Values of the Feather River Project (millions of dollars)

Interest Rate	Costs	Receipts	Net Present Value	Net Present Value, Adjusted*
2.7%				
Route 1	$1241	$1079	$ −162	$ −97
Route 8A	1123	1012	−111	−46
Route 10A	1029	919	−110	−46
5%				
Route 1	1035	515	−520	−502
Route 8A	860	445	−415	−397
Route 10A	799	409	−391	−372

*Adjustment credits an allowance for flood-control benefit and salvage value.

Source: J. C. DeHaven and J. Hirshleifer, "Feather River Water for Southern California," *Land Economics,* v. 33 (August 1957), p. 201. (Some technical footnotes are omitted.)

While all the net Present Values were negative, the higher 5 percent interest rate was associated with relatively lower figures for both costs and receipts. The table shows that a higher value of r has a greater effect upon the Present Value of receipts than upon costs. The reason is that receipts are typically received later, so that a rise in the discount factor $1 + r$ operates more powerfully upon them due to greater compounding over time. In fact, it is a reliable general rule that *the higher the discount rate, the less attractive the project.*

COMMENT The Feather River Project was adopted, despite the showing of negative net Present Value. Thus, the investment decision rule of this chapter was violated. Indeed, the route selected was the one with the most unfavorable receipts-cost balance. (Possible explanations are considered when the political process is analyzed in Chapter 16.)

The next example also illustrates the powerful effect of interest rates upon Present Values.

EXAMPLE 14.6 **Professors and Publications**

Professors devote much of their time to research. The output of successful research usually takes the form of articles published in scholarly journals. Published articles lead to professional recognition and so tend to raise the lifetime earnings of their authors.

H. P. Tuckman and J. Leahey[a] studied the worth of published articles to economics professors in the 1970s. Their results indicate that an Assistant Professor's first article increases the Present Value of lifetime earnings by $12,340, calculated at an interest rate of 5 percent. At a higher 10 percent interest rate, the future earnings gains are discounted more heavily, however, leading to a lower estimate of $7074.

The problem of choosing an interest rate for calculating Present Value may arise in either *normative* or *positive* analysis (as discussed in Chapter 1). From the *positive* point of view we ask: "What interest rates do decisionmakers use in deciding whether to undertake investment projects?" From a *normative* point of view we could ask: "What interest rate should a decisionmaker use in deciding whether to accept or reject an investment project?"

Example 14.4 on the Present Value of a bachelor's degree represented positive analysis: the researchers determined the Present Value of a college degree. Example 14.6 on the worth of a published article also represents positive analysis. Example 14.5, in contrast, represents *normative* analysis. The economists there asked: "Should the Feather River Project have been built by the State of California?" What is the appropriate rate to use for such a normative analysis? In general, the correct rate—the one leading to the decision that would maximize California citizens' wealth—would be the rate used by the market in evaluating investments of comparable risk.

14.6 REAL INTEREST AND MONEY INTEREST: ALLOWING FOR INFLATION

This chapter has so far dealt only with the *real* rate of interest. Following the usual practice in microeconomics we looked behind the "veil of money." But in practice people almost always deal in terms of *money* rates of interest. Suppose a bank advertises that it pays 8 percent. That means if you make a deposit of \$100 you can withdraw \$108 at the end of the year. But, if the cost of living is rising, the \$108 after a year will not buy you as much as \$108 at the beginning of the year; perhaps the end-of-year \$108 will buy only as much as \$103 at the beginning of the year. If so, although 8 percent is the monetary rate of interest, the *real* rate of interest is only about 3 percent. This section analyzes more generally the relation between the monetary rate of interest and the real rate of interest.

The *real* interest rate is the premium on claims to current versus future real goods—for example, the extra amount of future corn that must be offered in the market in exchange for current corn. Let us write this as follows:

$$1 + r \equiv -\frac{\Delta c_1}{\Delta c_0} \tag{14.13}$$

(As usual, the minus sign allows for the fact that market exchange involves getting more of one item and less of the other.) Correspondingly, the *money* interest rate, which we will symbolize as r', is the premium on claims to current money versus future money. Thus, r' is the extra amount of future money that must be returned in exchange for current money.

$$1 + r' \equiv -\frac{\Delta m_1}{\Delta m_0} \tag{14.14}$$

We need to introduce the relation between money and real goods. This is the *price level:* the amount of money required to purchase real goods. The *current* and *future* price levels are

$$P_0^m \equiv -\frac{\Delta m_0}{\Delta c_0} \quad \text{and} \quad P_1^m \equiv -\frac{\Delta m_1}{\Delta c_1} \tag{14.15}$$

Let us now write out the identity

$$\frac{\Delta m_1}{\Delta m_0} \equiv \frac{\Delta m_1}{\Delta c_1} \frac{\Delta c_1}{\Delta c_0} \frac{\Delta c_0}{\Delta m_0}$$

Making the indicated substitutions from the preceding equations we have

$$1 + r' = \frac{P_1^m}{P_0^m} (1 + r) \tag{14.16}$$

We can also define a, the anticipated rate of price inflation

$$1 + a \equiv \frac{P_1^m}{P_0^m} \tag{14.17}$$

It follows immediately that

$$1 + r' = (1 + a)(1 + r) \tag{14.18}$$

Or, simplifying

$$r' = r + a + ar \tag{14.18'}$$

Accordingly, the money rate of interest equals the real rate of interest plus the anticipated rate of price inflation, plus the cross-product of the latter two. When r and a remain in their usual range of percentage points, the cross-product term can, to a good approximation, be ignored. With *compound* interest, the shorter the period of compounding the smaller the error caused by omitting the cross-product. For continuously compounded interest, the cross product drops out entirely and we have exactly

$$r' = r + a \tag{14.19}$$

It is in this simple form that the relation between real and money interest is usually expressed.[10]

PROPOSITION: The money rate of interest equals the real rate of interest plus the anticipated rate of price inflation.

EXAMPLE 14.7   Real and Money Rates of Interest

William E. Gibson[a] examined the effects of inflationary expectations on the rates of interest paid on U.S. Treasury securities in the period 1962–70. In all such studies the practical problem is to evaluate inflationary anticipations, which are not directly visible. Gibson derived a measure from a semiannual survey of economists conducted by Joseph Livingston, a nationally syndicated financial columnist.

Using this measure of anticipated inflation a, and the recorded interest rates as the measure of the money rate r', Gibson statistically estimated an equation in the form

$$r' = H + Ka$$

Here H and K were the parameters of the line of best fit to the observed data. On the assumption that the *real* rate of interest r was constant over this period, comparison with Equation (14.19) shows that the fitted parameter H is an estimate of the real rate r. Also, the fitted parameter K should be 1.

The statistical evidence varied somewhat according to the type of security considered. The estimated H suggests a *real* rate of interest between 2 percent and 3 percent (considerably lower than the money interest rates in this inflationary period, of course). The K estimates were not far from 1 (for example, 0.93 for three-month Treasury bills, 0.90 for three-year to five-year Treasury notes).

One interesting point is that the K estimates were closer to 1 in the later than in the earlier portion of the period. This evidence suggests that the general public gradually adjusted to the prospect of continuing inflation.

[a]William E. Gibson, "Interest Rates and Inflationary Expectations: New Evidence," *American Economic Review*, v. 62 (December 1972).

Equation (14.19) implies that if people expect inflation to be high, the money interest rate r' will be high. Of central concern in macroeconomics is the effect of an increase in the money supply on inflation. On the one hand, expansion of the money supply tends to

---

[10]*Mathematical Footnote:* If i is an annually compounded interest rate, a dollar will grow in value to $1 + i$ dollars at the end of one year. With quarterly compounding, the terminal value will be $(1 + i/4)^4$. Generalizing, with any compounding frequency of f per year, terminal value will be $(1 + i/f)^f$. For continuous compounding, we let f approach infinity. Then $\lim_{f \to \infty} (1 + i/f)^f \equiv \lim_{h \to \infty} [(1 + 1/h)^h]^i$ where $h \equiv f/i$. But the limit within the brackets is e, the base of the natural logarithms. The terminal value of a dollar continuously compounded at interest rate i, at the end of a year, is then e^i. The terminal value of Z dollars at the end of T years is Ze^{iT}.

Expressed in terms of continuously compounded rates, Equation (14.18) becomes:

$$e^{r'} = e^r e^a$$

Taking logarithms, $r' = r + a$ follows directly.

lower money interest rates in the short run. If the government unexpectedly pays some of its bills with newly printed money, people will find themselves with unexpectedly large *current* cash balances. If people do not anticipate correspondingly larger *future* cash balances, they should be willing to trade larger amounts of current money for claims on future money. Then the money interest rate r' in Equation (14.14) must fall. On the other hand, if the government *continually* expands the money supply, an increase in current money may lead people to anticipate that future money balances will be even larger. Thus a *one-time* expansion of the money supply lowers the money rate r', but a *continuing* monetary expansion may generate inflationary expectations that raise r'.

The main lesson to be learned from this discussion is that high monetary or nominal rates of interest do not necessarily imply high real yields to investors. In fact, taking inflation into account the experience of investors over the past half-century has been unimpressive.

EXAMPLE 14.8 **Nominal and Real Yields, 1926–81**

The first column of the following table shows the arithmetic mean of the *nominal* annual returns from holding various types of securities over the 55-year period 1926 to 1981. The second column shows the inflation-adjusted or *real* average annual returns. As can be seen, the real return has been practically zero on both short-term and long-term government issues. Only common stocks show a positive real return. Thus, while there has been some reward for bearing variability risk over this period, savers and investors on average received little or no premium in future real income in return for their current sacrifices of consumption.

Nominal and Real Yields, 1926–81 (arithmetic means)

	Nominal Yield	Real Yield
U.S. Treasury Bills	3.1%	0.1%
Long-term Government Bonds	3.1	0.3
Common Stocks	11.4	8.3

Source: Roger G. Ibbotson and Rex A. Sinquefield, *Stocks, Bonds, Bills and Inflation: The Past and the Future* (Charlottesville, Va.: Financial Analysts Research Foundation, 1982), p. 71.

Furthermore, investors are taxed on their returns from holding securities. The real *tax-adjusted* returns, which vary across individuals depending on tax brackets, will all be smaller than those shown. Finally, in the United States (and in many other nations as well) income tax is levied on the nominal rather than on the real return; this has a damaging effect. Consider an individual who purchases a common stock for $100.00, receives $3.00 in dividends, and sells the stock for $110.00 at the end of the year. Suppose the rate of inflation is 10 percent, and his marginal tax rate is 25 percent. He will pay $0.75 in tax on the dividends, and $2.50 on the capital gain, leaving him with $113.00 − $3.25 = $109.75 after a year. But with 10 percent inflation, the purchasing power of this $109.75 is only $109.75/1.10 = $99.77; his real yield has been negative. U.S. investors have generally incurred negative real after-tax yields over the past half-century, even for securities like common stocks. We should not be surprised, therefore, to learn that the amount of saving in relation to income in the United States has become, in the opinion of many observers, disturbingly low.

14.7 DETERMINANTS OF INTEREST RATES

Interest rates may vary for a number of reasons. First, they change historically, so that Present Values calculated in 1950 or 1960 did not make use of the same interest rates as calculations made in 1970 or 1980. And even at a specific moment of time, there is a "term structure" of interest rates—different rates for discounting near-future versus far-future returns. In November 1989, for example, U.S. Treasury issues (bonds and notes) of different maturities sold at prices representing different net interest yields to purchasers. Issues maturing within 3–6 months typically yielded 7.5 percent; issues maturing in 30 years yielded 7.9 percent.

Interest rates also vary on account of *risk*. Even if maturity and all other elements are the same, bonds of foreign governments or of private corporations are generally considered riskier than U.S. Treasury issues, and so can only be sold at lower prices—implying a higher interest yield to the purchaser. For example, the yield on one-month commercial paper was 8.35 percent in November 1989, which was about 0.8 percent higher than the yield on corresponding Treasury bills. For similar reasons banks require a higher rate for an unsecured loan than for a loan secured by a mortgage or other collateral. (In a secured loan, the lender has the right to repossess the borrower's property, say an automobile or a house. Thus, if the borrower declares bankruptcy, or fails to make his payments, the lender may be able to get some of his money back. In contrast, in an unsecured loan the lender has no such margin of safety.)

Two different aspects of risk should be distinguished.

1. *Default risk*—Suppose a bank makes a one-year $1000 loan at an interest rate of 10 percent. Imagine that the bank has 99 percent confidence in the borrower's performance but believes there is a 1 percent chance of a complete default on both principal and interest. Then the expected or average interest yield for the bank is not 10 percent but only 8.9 percent.[11] It is the 8.9 percent that approximates the "true" interest rate; 10 percent is only the "quoted" interest rate. The difference between 10 percent and 8.9 percent represents an adjustment or premium for default risk.

2. *Variability risk*—Some financial instruments, like common stocks, do not carry any explicit promise of payments. The returns to the investor come in the form of dividends that may vary considerably up or down from the average; this is variability risk. In general, people dislike variability risk. Comparing two securities with the same average yield, most investors prefer the security with a more certain yield. It follows that securities with highly uncertain returns will sell at prices yielding their holders greater average earnings in percentage terms. (We will analyze variability risk more fully in Section 14.8.)

---

[11]The bank anticipates receiving $1100 at the end of the year if all goes well (99 percent probability), but otherwise receiving nothing. Its "expected" or average net interest return is $0.99(\$1100) + 0.01(\$0) - \$1000$, or $89, which is a yield of 8.9 percent on the $1000 principal amount.

EXAMPLE 14.9 Term and Risk Premiums

Roger G. Ibbotson and Rex A. Sinquefield examined the actual yields of different financial instruments over the period 1926–81. In the following table, a difference between the average yield on long-term government bonds versus short-term U.S. Treasury bills would represent a *term premium* offered investors. As you can see, over the period studied this difference was nil. On the other hand, the higher yield on common stocks compared to government bonds indicates that, during this period, investors willing to incur *variability risk* received a substantial premium.

Experienced Average Yields, 1926–81

	Arithmetic Mean	Geometric Mean
U.S. Treasury Bills	3.1%	3.0%
Long-term Government Bonds	3.1	3.0
Common Stocks	11.4	9.1

Source: Roger G. Ibbotson and Rex A. Sinquefield, *Stocks, Bonds, Bills and Inflation: The Past and the Future* (Charlottesville, Va.: Financial Analysts Research Foundation, 1982), p. 71.

The differences between the results calculated in terms of the arithmetic mean versus the geometric mean of the annual experienced yields are also significant. The arithmetic mean answers the question, "On average, what yield can be expected in *any given year* on this type of investment?" The geometric mean answers a slightly different question, "What *average long-term compounded yield* can be expected on this type of investment?" The former average is therefore more relevant for short-term holders of securities, the latter for long-term holders. As can be seen, in this period short-term holders did somewhat better.

EXAMPLE 14.10 Investment in Art and Wine

Though many wines are commonly found to benefit by aging, there is some risk of spoilage. In addition, the quality at the time of sale and the possibly changing tastes of consumers are unpredictable. Investors who hold wines for appreciation must take these risks into account; they must also consider the cost of storing wine. Elizabeth Jaeger[a] examined prices for red Bordeaux and California Cabernet Sauvignon wines produced since 1950 and sold at the Heublein auction over the years 1969–77. As economic theory predicts, Jaeger finds that the average rate of return on wine (a risky asset) exceeded the rate of return on Treasury bills (by an impressive 16.6 percent).

Art as an investment is also subject to various risks, among them fluctuations in price, damage from fire, theft, and the possibility of forgery or mistaken attribution. Bruno Frey and W.W. Pommerehne[b] looked at 1200 art sales, and adjusted prices for inflation and transaction costs (a typical auction fee would amount to more than 10 percent of the value for both the buyer and the seller). They found the average real rate of return on paintings to be 1.5 percent per year for the period 1635–1987. Government securities over this period would have returned a little more than 3 percent a year. For the years 1950 to 1987 art returned 1.6 percent a year; financial assets had a real yield of 2.5 percent. Investment in paintings, though risky, seems to be less profitable than investment in traditional financial assets. One explanation is that investors obtain other benefits, such as the pleasure of viewing the art, so that they do not require as high a financial return.

It may not always be valid to take the rate of return on government securities as riskless. It is only after the fact that we know that U.S. government securities are quite safe; immediately after the American Revolution, for example, the prospect was not so clear.

[a]Elizabeth Jaeger "To Save or to Savor: The Rate of Return to Storing Wine," *Journal of Political Economy,* v. 89 (June 1981).

[b]Bruno S. Frey and Werner W. Pommerehne "Is Art Such a Good Investment?" *The Public Interest,* No. 91 (Spring 1988).

Several other factors explain why interest rates are high in some countries and periods and low in others.

1. *Time-preference*—The more impatient people are, the more they prefer *current* rather than *future* consumption. In Figure 14.1, impatience or high time-preference is reflected in steep indifference curves. At any given interest rate, demand for borrowing will be higher than with flatter indifference curves, and therefore the equilibrium interest rate will be high. Low time preference, or a willingness to invest even at a low interest rate, is associated with personal characteristics such as farsightedness, strong family ties, willingness to defer enjoyment, and the like. The latter years of the Roman Empire were characterized by a decline in such "puritanical" attitudes, and interest rates were accordingly high. A similar shift in values appears to be taking place today, which may help explain the recent tendency of real interest rates to rise.

2. *Time-endowment*—As we have seen, an "heir with great expectations," whose endowment lies mainly in the future, tends to borrow. If most people in an economy expect future income to be much greater than current income, the interest rate will correspondingly tend to be high. A notable example is a community struck by a disaster. A catastrophe usually damages goods relatively close to consumption more drastically than it injures the basic productive powers of the economy. A drought or a hurricane, for example, may destroy crops while leaving long-term productive fundamentals such as fertility of the soil, mineral resources, and human skills unimpaired. Since present incomes are affected more seriously than anticipated future incomes, interest rates tend to rise.

3. *Time-productivity*—Higher time-productivity of investment would be represented by a steeper Production-Possibility Curve in Figure 14.4. If this pattern is typical of a community, investment will be high and interest rates will be high. Thus interest rates have tended to be high in newer and more productive communities—for example, higher in America than in England, and higher in California than in Pennsylvania. Also, technological change works somewhat like new settlement of territory in generating improved opportunities for investment. Thus, interest rates tend to be higher in technologically progressive than in more static countries and eras.

4. *Degree of isolation*—The interest rate in a locality that is financially linked with other regions cannot diverge too far from the more normal rates in the outside world. If the

interest rates do diverge, investments and loans will flow from the low-interest area to the high-interest area. The differences historically observed between interest rates in England and America, or between Pennsylvania and California, have therefore been much smaller than would have been the case had the communities in question been isolated from one another.

EXAMPLE 14.11 **Interest Rates and the Gold Rush**[a]

Gold was discovered in California in 1848, and the gold rush was on. The gold miners (and most other Californians as well) typically thought of themselves as having little current endowed income, but as prospectively very rich. Thus, they were like "heirs with great expectations" who are inclined to be borrowers.

However, until the completion of the first transcontinental railroad in 1869, California was largely isolated from the rest of the world. Californians for the most part could only borrow from one another. Consequently, the interest rate during the period of the gold rush was generally very high; 24 percent per annum was a typical figure. This was far higher than interest rates in the East. After completion of the transcontinental railroad, it became much more feasible to bring in resources from the East, and the interest rate in California dropped to around 6 percent.

[a]See Irving Fisher, *The Theory of Interest* (New York: Macmillan, 1930; reprinted [Fairfield, N.J.: Augustus M. Kelley] 1955), Chapter 18.

14.8 THE CAPITAL ASSET PRICING MODEL

While this section is somewhat difficult, it covers topics in modern corporate finance that many will find exciting and important. The Capital Asset Pricing Model (CAPM) to be described here tells investors how much of each type of stock to buy in order to properly balance their portfolio risks and returns (an optimization problem). It also predicts the relation between the riskiness of different stocks and their prices (an equilibrium problem). The CAPM lies at the heart of the modern theory of finance that is used by professional investors, investment advisers, and corporate treasurers.

Characteristics of Portfolios

In the theory of consumption we asked how a consumer would choose among different *baskets* of goods. Similarly, we ask here how an investor would choose among different *portfolios* of assets. It is very useful to assume that each investor evaluates portfolios on the basis of two characteristics: (1) the expected or average rate of return, and (2) the risk or variability of return.

Assume for simplicity that stocks do not increase or decrease in price, so that the only benefit of owning a stock comes from the dividends it pays. A stock that costs $100 and is expected to pay $5 in dividends each and every year has an expected rate of return of $5/\$100 = 5$ percent. Or more generally, for security A with price P_A and annual dividend d_A expected to continue indefinitely into the future, the rate of return is $r_A = d_A/P_A$ (see Equation 14.10'). If the stock paid $7 in dividends a year, its rate of return would be 7 percent. Investors, however, may be uncertain about the prospects of the firm, and therefore about the dividends. Suppose investors believe there is a one-half chance the dividend will be $5, and a one-half chance that the dividend will be $7. The expected rate of return is then $1/2(5\%) + 1/2(7\%) = 6\%$.

The second characteristic, variability risk, can be measured by the *variance* of this return,[12] or (more conveniently for our purposes) by the *standard deviation* (the square root of the variance). In our example, the variance is $1/2(0.05 - 0.06)^2 + 1/2(0.07 - 0.06)^2 = 0.0001$. The standard deviation is the square root of this variance, 0.01.

Variance and standard deviation are measures of variability risk, that is, dispersion of returns around the mean. For example, suppose that in the previous example the possible rates of return were 4 percent and 8 percent instead of 5 percent and 7 percent. The expected rate of return is the same, 6 percent. But the standard deviation will increase to 2 percent.

The investor does not care about the risk and return of any one asset but about the risk and return on his *portfolio*. It is evident that the characteristics of a portfolio depend on the amounts and characteristics of the different assets held. In particular, as we will see, the relevant asset characteristics are the standard deviation of the rates of return, and the co-variance of those returns.[13]

In Figure 14.9, p. 428, (which closely resembles Figure 3.8 that depicted a bad), the vertical axis measures r, the individual's expected rate of return on a portfolio. The horizontal axis measures the standard deviation, s, of the rate of return on a portfolio. Two indifference curves are depicted in the figure for a particular investor. U_2 represents a higher level of utility than U_1. These curves slope upward because investors like high rates of return but dislike high risk (risk is a "bad"). Consider, for example, a standard deviation of s_1 and an expected rate of return of r_1. These values determine one point on some indifference curve. We want to find another point on the same indifference curve, but with a higher standard deviation, say s_2. To compensate for the higher risk (higher standard deviation) a higher rate of return is needed, say r_2. Thus, (r_2, s_2) lies on the same indifference curve as (r_1, s_1).

---

[12]*Mathematical Footnote:* The variance is calculated by taking the square of the difference between each possible rate of return and the expected rate of return on that asset, multiplying by the probability of that rate of return, and summing these values. Symbolically, for a variable x that can take on values $x_1, x_2, \ldots x_N$ with associated probabilities $p_1, p_2, \ldots p_N$, the expected return $\bar{x}$ and the variance σ_x are

$$\bar{x} = \sum_i^N p_i x_i \text{ and } \sigma_x = \sum_i^N p_i (x_i - \bar{x})^2$$

This is often written as $E(X - \bar{X})^2$, where E is the expectation operator.

---

[13]*Mathematical Footnote:* The covariance describes how the return on one asset varies as the return on another asset varies. Symbolically, let variable X take on values $x_1, x_2, \ldots x_N$, and variable Y take on values $y_1, y_2, \ldots y_N$. The mean of X is $\bar{x}$ and the mean of Y is $\bar{y}$. The probability that $x = x_i$ and that $y = y_j$ is p_{ij}. Then the covariance of these two random variables is

$$Cov(x,y) \equiv \sigma_{xy} = \sum_{i=1}^N \sum_{j=1}^N p_{ij}(x_i - \bar{x})(y_j - \bar{y})$$

This is often written as $E[(X - \bar{X})(Y - \bar{Y})]$. Note that if the value of Y is usually greater than its mean when the value of X is above its mean, then the covariance is positive. If, instead, Y is usually low when X is high, then the covariance will be negative.

FIGURE 14.9 **Preferences over Risk and Return**   The individual views high returns as good, but risk (as measured by the standard deviation) as bad. His indifference curves are upward-sloping, with U_2 representing a higher level of utility than U_1.

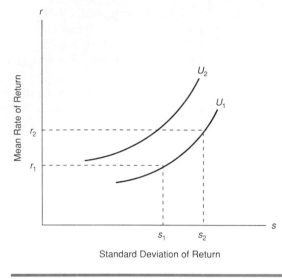

The indifference curves are drawn to become steeper as we move up and to the right. These curves reflect an assumption similar to diminishing marginal rates of substitution: when the risk is high additional risk is increasingly undesired and must be compensated by a larger increase in the rate of return.

We proceed next to the opportunity set. From the point of view of any investor, each asset has a given price, rate of return, and standard deviation (assumed known to the investor). In addition, the covariances of the returns from the different securities are also assumed known. The problem is to calculate the rates of return and standard deviations of portfolios from the characteristics of the individual stocks making up the portfolio.

We shall give an example here. Consider two stocks, A and B, each priced at one dollar. Suppose the dividends on these stocks depend on whether or not there will be an oil shortage. If there is an oil shortage, stock A will pay 5 cents a share, and stock B will pay 7 cents a share (see Table 14.2.) If there is no oil shortage, stock A will pay 10 cents and stock B will pay 4 cents. (Note that there is negative covariance here; the oil shortage makes A do better but B do worse.) Suppose investors think there is a one-third chance of an oil shortage. What are the rate of return and the standard deviation of a portfolio consisting of 400 shares of stock A and 600 shares of stock B?

With probability $1/3$, there will be an oil shortage, in which case the investor will receive 5 cents per share from stock A and 7 cents per share from stock B, or a total dividend payment of $0.05(400) + 0.07(600) = \$62$. Since the initial investment is \$1000, the rate of return is 6.2 percent. With probability $2/3$ there will not be an oil shortage; the total dividend payment will then be $0.10(400) + 0.04(600) = \$64$. The expected, or average, rate of return on the portfolio is therefore $1/3(\$62)/\$1000 + 2/3(\$64)/\$1000 = 6.3$ percent. The standard deviation of the rate of return is the square root of $1/3(0.062 - 0.063)^2 +$

TABLE 14.2 Calculation of Portfolio Rate of Return *(r)* and Standard Deviation *(s)*

	Stock A	Stock B	Portfolio
Price of shares	1	1	—
Number of shares	400	600	—
Value of investment	400	600	1000
Dividend per share if oil shortage (Probability = 1/3)	0.05	0.07	1/1000 [0.05(400) + (0.07)(600)] = 0.062
Dividend per share if no oil shortage (Probability = 2/3)	0.10	0.04	1/1000 [(0.10)(400) + (0.04)(600)] = 0.064
Expected return *(r)*	1/3(0.05) + 2/3(0.1) = 0.083	1/3(0.07) + 2/3(0.04) = 0.05	1/3(0.062) + 2/3(0.064) = 0.063
Standard deviation *(s)*	0.0240	0.014	0.001

$2/3(0.064 - 0.063)^2$, or 0.001. Note that in the example the riskiness of the portfolio (as measured by the standard deviation *s*) is far less than the riskiness of either stock *A* or stock *B*. This occurs in the example because, as mentioned above, the returns on the two stocks have negative covariance. Consequently, when the two securities are combined in a portfolio, their risks offset one another—making the rate of return on the portfolio relatively stable. In fact, though we will not go through the mathematics here, the standard deviation on the portfolio would be smaller than on either stock even if the securities' rates of return were positively (though not perfectly) correlated. This surprising fact is due to the power of *diversification*.

Different portfolios will have different rates of return and standard deviations. Some of these portfolios will be efficient, and others will not be. An efficient portfolio offers an investor the minimum risk *(s)* for a given rate of return *(r)*. Figure 14.10 shows a roughly oval shaped area that encloses all the *r,s* combinations. The efficient set is the upper left-hand boundary of this area which includes points *P* and *M*. You cannot directly tell from the diagram which stocks are held in each portfolio, but each point in the diagram corresponds to a particular portfolio.

Now assume that in addition to stocks, investors can purchase a single risk-free asset—for example U.S. Treasury bills or bonds. Point *T* in Figure 14.10 represents the rate of return and the standard deviation on a portfolio consisting wholly of this risk-free asset. Since the portfolio consisting entirely of this asset is riskless, it lies on the vertical axis.

The availability of such a riskless asset widens the investor's opportunities. If he invests a fraction *f* of his wealth in the stock portfolio shown by point *P*, and a fraction $1 - f$ in Treasury bills, then his expected rate of return is *f* times the rate of return on stocks plus $1 - f$ times the rate of return on Treasury bills. Similar statements hold for the standard deviation: the standard deviation of the portfolio described above is *f* times the standard deviation of portfolio *P* plus $1 - f$ times the standard deviation of Treasury bills. Since, however, the standard deviation of the rate of return on Treasury bills is zero, this simplifies

FIGURE 14.10 **Opportunity Set for an Investor**   Different combinations of stocks yield different returns and risks. The upper left boundary of the oval-shaped area shows efficient portfolios of stocks. If the investor can also invest in a risk-free asset (represented by point T), then he can attain risk-return combinations anywhere along line TM. The portfolio represented by point M is the *market* portfolio. The investor's utility-maximizing portfolio is represented by B, which is a personal portfolio combining the risk-free asset with the market portfolio.

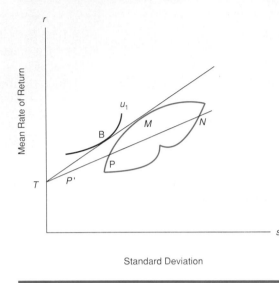

Standard Deviation

to f times the standard deviation of the stock portfolio P.[14] Consequently, the individual's overall opportunity set is no longer just the oval-shaped area of Figure 14.9: he can now attain any linear combination of point T with points on the oval-shaped area.

The Optimal Portfolio

Suppose the investor invests $300 in the stock portfolio shown by point P, and $700 in Treasury bills (so that $f = 0.3$). The expected performance of this portfolio of stocks and Treasury bills is shown by point P'; it lies three-tenths of the distance from T to P. Note that we are now discussing two portfolios: the *stock* portfolio P, and the *personal* portfolio P' that contains both stocks and Treasury bills.

But the investor can do better than the personal portfolio P'. Instead of investing in stock portfolio P, he can invest in stock portfolio M. Then he can attain as a personal portfolio any combination of risk and return shown by line TM. Can he do better yet? No. Consider any other stock portfolio, say N. A person who invests part of his personal portfolio in stock portfolio N and the rest in Treasury bills can obtain risk-return combinations anywhere along line TN. But for any risk-return combination that lies on line TN, there exists a point

---

[14]Let assets X and Y be held in the fractions f and $1 - f$. The variance is symbolized by *Var* and the covariance by *Cov*. Then Var($fX + (1 - f)Y$) = f^2Var(X) + $(1 - f)^2$Var(Y) + $f(1 - f)$Cov(X,Y). Suppose asset Y is Treasury bills with no risk. The last two terms are zero, and the standard deviation of the portfolio is $f\sigma_X$.

on line *TM* that gives the same risk but a higher rate of return. An investor can always do better by choosing a personal portfolio that lies on line *TM* than by choosing a personal portfolio that lies on line *TN*. The special feature of stock portfolio *M* is that a line connecting point *T* (which represents the return and risk of a risk-free asset) to point *M* is tangent to the efficiency set at point *M*. In short, the investor will allocate his funds between the risk-free asset and the stock portfolio *M*, choosing a personal portfolio on line *TM*, at the point where an indifference curve is tangent to the line (point *B* in the diagram). This leads to the following important conclusion: any investor, regardless of his preferences, will want to have a personal portfolio that lies on line *TM*. A remarkable implication is

PROPOSITION: All investors will invest in the same stock portfolio, *M*. Investors will differ only in the total amount they invest, and in the fraction of the total personal portfolio they choose to hold in stocks versus the risk-free asset.

For example, a person who has $1000 to invest may purchase $300 of the stock portfolio *M* and $700 of Treasury bills. If this same person suddenly found that he has $10,000 to invest, he might purchase $8000 of the same stock portfolio, *M*, and $2000 in Treasury bills. When we say that each person holds the same stock portfolio we do not mean that each person owns the same amount of each stock. We do mean that each person holds stocks of different firms in the same ratio, say 1 percent of the value of his stock portfolio is held in stock of firm *A*.

The next step is to notice that since all issued stocks are held by someone, then if all people hold the same stock portfolio the portfolio *M* must simply be a proportionate share of all stocks in the market. If, for example, the market value of the shares of Firm *A* is twice that of firm *B* shares, then in every investor's portfolio the values of *A* and *B* shares will also be in the ratio 2 to 1. For this reason portfolio *M* is called the *market* portfolio.

Equilibrium Stock Prices

Our emphasis now shifts from the analysis of portfolios to the analysis of share prices and rates of return. Any one investor takes the stock prices P_A, P_B, and so forth as constants. But of course, in the market as a whole, the prices are determined by supply and demand. Since $r_A = d_A/P_A$, and the distribution of dividends is assumed fixed, it follows that the rates of return on securities are also variables determined in market equilibrium.

A crucial element in determining the equilibrium per-share rate-of-return is the covariance of the share's dividends with dividends on stocks in general, that is on the market portfolio *M*. (Remember that the dividends and therefore the rate of return on portfolio *M* are not certain, but are subject to some uncertainty, as reflected in the standard deviation of the rate of return.) Suppose that when the dividends on the market portfolio *M* increase by 1 percentage point, the dividend on shares of firm *i* increase by β *(beta)* percentage points.[15] It may be, for example, that when oil prices fall the profits of firms in general increase by 1 percentage point, but that firm *i*, which uses oil to produce plastics, will gain a disproportionate increase of 1.5 percentage points (so that $\beta = 1.5$ for this firm). Some other firm, say a holding company with an oil drilling subsidiary in Texas, will not gain as much,

---

[15]*Mathematical Footnote:* The value of β is defined as σ_{iM}/σ_M^2 where σ_M^2 is the variance of the market portfolio and σ_{iM} is the covariance of stock *i* with the market portfolio.

because its Texas subsidiary is doing poorly. So the value of β for this firm will be less than one.

It turns out that the β's are crucial in determining the prices of the different stocks in market equilibrium. Each personal portfolio on the line *TM* is also characterized by a value of β. For example, a personal portfolio that consists of $700 in Treasury bills and $300 in stocks has a β of 0.3: since only 30 percent of the personal portfolio consists of the stock portfolio, a 1 percent increase in the rate of return on the market portfolio will result in only a 0.3 percent increase in the rate of return on the personal portfolio.

To determine the equilibrium prices of stocks and therefore the rates of return, we shall consider each stock and portfolio as characterized by a value of *r* and β, rather than *r* and the standard deviation *s*. In Figure 14.11, line *TM* shows the combinations of β and *r* available from personal portfolios consisting of the market portfolio and Treasury bills. The market portfolio has a β of 1; Treasury bills have a β of 0.

For an individual stock both β and *r* depend on the price of the firm's shares. The greater the price of the shares of some firm, the lower the rate of return for any given level of dividends. And the higher the price, the greater the market value of the shares of the firm, and therefore the greater the proportion of the market portfolio *M* that consists of these shares. This in turn means that a high price of shares of firm *i* causes a high value of β for those shares.

For simplicity let the market portfolio consist of shares of only two firms, *A* and *B*. In Figure 14.11 suppose tentatively that the prices of the shares of the two firms are such that *r* and β for firm *A* are represented by point *A*, and *r* and β for firm *B* are represented by point *B*.

It can be shown mathematically that the β of any portfolio is simply the weighted average of the βs of the assets making up that portfolio.[16] And, of course, the mean rate of

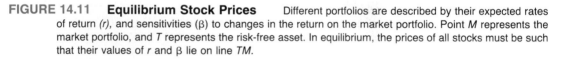

FIGURE 14.11   **Equilibrium Stock Prices**   Different portfolios are described by their expected rates of return *(r)*, and sensitivities (β) to changes in the return on the market portfolio. Point *M* represents the market portfolio, and *T* represents the risk-free asset. In equilibrium, the prices of all stocks must be such that their values of *r* and β lie on line *TM*.

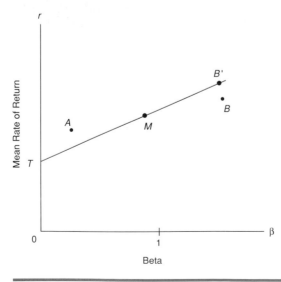

return on a portfolio is necessarily the corresponding weighted average of the r's for the assets in that portfolio. Thus, if the market portfolio consists only of shares of A and B, its r and β must lie at a point on the line connecting points A and B.

The situation pictured in Figure 14.11, however, is not consistent with an equilibrium. For any investor would want to sell some of his shares of B and instead put more of his money into a portfolio that lies along line TM. (He would effectively sell shares in B and buy more shares of A.) In doing so he could obtain the r and β shown by point B' on line TM. Portfolio B' yields a higher rate of return than B, and it has the same β. Moreover, the shares of firm B are riskier than the portfolio B' which has the same β: stock B will, on average, increase or decrease its rate of return to the same extent as portfolio B' following any change in the rate of return on the market portfolio M. But stock B has additional risk: sometimes, when the rate of return on portfolio B' goes up by, say 1 percent, the rate of return on B goes up by more or less than that. Since B thus has greater risk than portfolio B', an investor would prefer to substitute portfolio B' for stock B.

But notice that any combination of stock A and portfolio B' has an r and β that lie on a line connecting A and B', which does not contain point M. That is, for the given prices of shares A and B, the individual would not want to purchase the market portfolio. Since we have seen that in equilibrium all individuals own the market portfolio M, the prices of stocks A and B as depicted in Figure 14.11 cannot be equilibrium prices. Nor can it be that points A and B both lie above line TM. For then again no combination of A and B would give an r and β at point M. We conclude that the only equilibrium prices are those that make both A and B lie *on line TM*.[17] No investor could get a higher return by investing in a portfolio with the same β, and some combination of shares A and B would indeed give the values of r and β represented by the market portfolio M.

Since in equilibrium the r and β of each stock lies on line TM, to find the rate of return on any individual stock we merely determine its β, find a point on the line TM that has that value of β, and read off the rate of return on that portfolio. In other words, the rate of return (or price) of a share is fully determined by its value of β.

EXAMPLE 14.12   A Test of the Capital Asset Pricing Model

A seminal test of the Capital Asset Pricing Model was made by F. Black, M. C. Jensen, and M. Scholes.[a] They grouped different stocks into ten portfolios, each with a different β. They then plotted the β of each portfolio and its average monthly rate of return (above that earned on Treasury bills) for the period 1931–65. They found that these points tightly

---

[16]Consider a portfolio that consists of a fraction f in stock X and a fraction $(1 - f)$ in stock Y. Let r_M be the rate of return on the market portfolio. Then by definition the β of the portfolio is

$$E\ [fX + (1 - f)Y - f\overline{X} - (1 - f)\overline{Y}]\ [r_M - \overline{r}_M]/\sigma_M^2$$

Factoring out f and $1 - f$ we have

$$fE\ [X - \overline{X}]\ [r_M - \overline{r}_M]/\sigma_M^2 + (1 - f)E\ [Y - \overline{Y}]\ [r_M - \overline{r}_M]/\sigma_M^2\ ,$$

which is $f\beta_X + (1 - f)\beta_Y$.

[17]Changes in the prices of shares will also change point M, and thus generate a new line TM. In equilibrium, the prices of shares A and B must yield a line TM and values of r and β for shares A and B so that points A and B lie on TM.

clustered along a line like *TM* in Figure 14.11. The slope of this line (the value of β) was 0.011; the clustering and the positive value of β are both consistent with the Capital Asset Pricing Model.

Another prediction of the model was not verified. The vertical intercept of line TM should show the rate of return on a riskless asset. Instead, the data lie on a line with a vertical intercept significantly above the yield on Treasury bills (taken to represent a riskless asset).

[a]F. Black, M. C. Jensen, and M. Scholes, "The Capital-Asset Pricing Model: Some Empirical Tests." In M. C. Jensen, ed. *Studies in the Theory of Capital Markets* (New York: Frederick A. Praeger Co., 1972).

SUMMARY

Saving is consuming less than income; *investing* is a productive activity that transforms potential current income into future income. The preferences of individuals as to present versus future consumption interact in the market to determine the price ratio between current and future claims, P_0/P_1. This ratio is also defined as $1 + r$, where r is the real rate of interest.

In a world of pure exchange, where investment opportunities are absent, each individual chooses an optimum time-pattern of consumption subject to a fixed wealth constraint. Saving by some people (lending) is necessarily balanced by the dissaving of others (borrowing). The intersection of the aggregate supply curve of lending and the aggregate demand curve for borrowing determines the equilibrium interest rate and the equilibrium amount of borrowing and lending. Where there are real investment opportunities, however, the individual would choose a wealth-maximizing *productive optimum* solution (determining the level of investment) together with a utility-maximizing *consumptive optimum* solution (determining the level of saving). The intersection of the aggregate supply curve of saving and the aggregate demand curve for investment determines the market equilibrium rate of interest and the amount of saving and investment. At this interest rate aggregate borrowing also equals aggregate lending. This analysis generalizes easily to any number of dates, so as to determine the time sequence of short-term and long-term interest rates.

If markets for intertemporal claims are perfect, the Separation Theorem holds. When this is so, production decisions can be aimed solely at maximizing wealth, independently of time-preferences. This feature facilitates the formation of firms. Managers who maximize the wealth of the firm will be making the correct production decisions for all the owners individually, regardless of their possibly differing time-preferences.

A project or set of projects that increases wealth has a positive Present Value V_0. In the simple two-period case, with cash flows z_0 and z_1, Present Value is defined as

$$V_0 \equiv z_0 + \frac{z_1}{1 + r}$$

Any project with positive Present Value should be adopted; any project with negative Present Value should be rejected. The equation defining Present Value can be generalized to the multi-period case, making use of the anticipated stream of payments $z_0, z_1, \ldots, z_T$ and the sequence of either the short-term interest rates $r_1, \ldots, r_T$ or the long-term rates $R_1,$ $R_2, \ldots, R_T$. If the interest rate is expected to be constant at the level r over time, the Present Value formula takes the simple form

$$V_0 \equiv z_0 + \frac{z_1}{1 + r} + \ldots + \frac{z_T}{(1 + r)^T}$$

An important issue is the selection of an appropriate interest rate r for the Present Value calculation. The major problem is to allow properly for risk. Securities promising fixed payments (e.g., bonds) are subject to *default risk;* securities with uncertain returns varying around some expected average level (e.g., stocks) are subject to *variability risk.* For any type of investment there will be an appropriate risk-premium element in the interest rate used for calculating Present Value.

The *real* interest rate r is the extra market value of current real goods over future real goods. The *money* interest rate r' is the extra market value of current money over future money. The relation between the real interest rate and the money interest rate depends on the anticipated rate of price-level inflation, a.

$$r' = r + a$$

The explanation is that someone who borrows money, in order to repay in money, must offer the lender an additional return to cover the expected fall in the real value of money.

The determinants of the real interest rate r in a community include individuals' patterns of *time-preference* (more urgent desires for current goods tend to raise interest rates), *time-endowment* (anticipations of higher future income raise interest rates), and *time-productivity* (better investment opportunities also raise interest rates). Nations and regions that differ in these respects may be characterized by different levels of interest rates, but only to the extent that they are isolated from one another.

The Capital Asset Pricing Model is a useful way of analyzing the decisions of investors and the equilibrium prices of risky assets. It assumes that investors care about the mean rate of return on their portfolio, and on the riskiness of their portfolio as characterized by the standard deviation of its rate of return. A mixed portfolio allows investors to *diversify,* since the risk from one asset partially offsets the risk from others. Two important results were obtained. First, all investors will wish to hold the same portfolio of risky assets, that is, all will wish to hold the *market* portfolio. Second, the rate of return (and therefore the price) of a risky asset will be fully determined by the covariance of its return with the return on the market portfolio; this is often summarized by saying that β is all that matters.

QUESTIONS

For Review

1. Explain the analogy between the intertemporal optimum of the consumer (choice between current consumption C_0 and future consumption C_1) and the optimum of the consumer at a moment of time (choice between consumption of commodity X and commodity Y).

*2. Which is correct?

    a. The annual rate of interest is the ratio P_0/P_1, the price of a current consumption claim divided by the price of a consumption claim dated one year in the future.

    b. The annual rate of interest is the *premium* on the value of current relative to one-year future claims, as given by the expression $P_0/P_1 - 1$.

    Explain.

3. What is *wealth?* How is it related to current and future *incomes?*

*4. The market equilibrium under pure exchange has aggregate borrowing equal to aggregate lending. What can be said about saving and investment?

*5. The market equilibrium in a production economy has aggregate saving equal to aggregate investment. What can be said about borrowing and lending?

6. What is the Separation Theorem? What is its importance? What would tend to happen if it were not applicable?

*7. a. What is the Present-Value Rule?

    b. Will this rule always lead decisionmakers to correct choices of projects when the Separation Theorem holds?

    c. What if the Separation Theorem does not hold?

8. Explain the relation between the rate of interest r as defined in the equation $r = P_0/P_1 - 1$ and as defined in the equation $r = z/V_0$.

9. What is the *money* rate of interest, and how is it related to the *real* rate of interest?

10. Why will investors with different attitudes towards risk all hold the market portfolio?

For Further Thought and Discussion

1. In a two-period preference diagram, illustrate the following endowments. Indicate whether the person is likely to be a borrower or a lender.

    a. A young man with an elderly, wealthy, loving uncle in Australia.

    b. A farmer whose crop has been destroyed by hurricane.

    c. A sugar-*beet* farmer who has just learned that this year's sugar-*cane* crop has been destroyed by hurricane.

    d. A 35-year-old star baseball player.

*2. "Saving need not equal investment for any single individual, but the two must be equal for the market as a whole." Is this necessarily true in equilibrium? Would it be true in a disequilibrium situation, as might result from a floor or ceiling upon interest rates?

*3. In a newly settled country, resources are likely to have great potential but are as yet undeveloped.

    a. Would you expect the real interest rate to be high or low?

    b. Comparing situations in which the new country is or is not in close contact with the rest of the world, in which situation will the interest rate be higher?

    c. In which will more investment take place? Explain.

*4. One country is "stagnant" (i.e., has little investment and economic growth) because productive opportunities yielding a good return on investment are lacking. Another "stagnant" country has excellent investment opportunities, but has little investment because the citizens' time-preferences are very high. Which country would tend to have a high, and which a low, real interest rate? Explain.

---

*The answers to starred questions appear at the end of the book.

5. Money interest rates throughout the world have generally been higher since World War II than they were in the prewar period. Indicate which of the following might provide part of the explanation, and analyze:
   a. Higher rates of time-preference (changes in tastes).
   b. Higher rates of time-productivity (changes in investment opportunities).
   c. Lower ratios of current to anticipated future incomes (increased relative scarcity of current endowments).
   d. Higher rates of inflation (changes in anticipations as to monetary policies of governments).

*6. a. Are negative rates of interest impossible?
    b. Is there a limit upon how negative the interest rate can be?

7. "Annual income twenty pounds, annual expenditure nineteen pounds, result happiness. Annual income twenty pounds, annual expenditure twenty-one pounds, result misery"—Mr. Micawber paraphrased in Dickens' *David Copperfield*. Is this sound economics? Analyze.

*8. *Consumer Reports* raised the question whether a homebuyer might advantageously finance purchase of appliances by an addition to his or her home mortgage. The alternatives considered were (1) purchase of appliances through a retail store for $675, financed by a two-year contract at 15 percent interest; and (2) purchase of the same appliances for $450 through the homebuilder, financed by a mortgage add-on 27-year contract at 7.75 percent interest. The article contended that the first option was superior. The justification offered was that, for the two-year 15 percent contract, the total of interest-plus-principal payments would add up to only $785—whereas, for the 27-year mortgage add-on contract at 7.75 percent, the total payments would eventually sum to $1075. Analyze.

*9. During World War II it was necessary to decide how much of military expenditures were to be financed by taxation and how much by government borrowing. Some economists argued that financing the war by borrowing would "shift the burden to future generations." Is this correct? How would you go about determining how much of the cost of the war was borne by the current generation versus future generations?

*10. In exploiting an exhaustible resource, a monopoly tends to be more "conservationist" than a competitive industry; that is, it tends to stretch out the supply over a longer period of time. Does this mean that, at least with regard to decisions over time, monopoly may be more efficient than pure competition?

11. Suppose that some individuals can invest in assets (such as human capital) that others cannot. Will all investors then hold the same market portfolio of stocks?

CHAPTER 15

WELFARE ECONOMICS: THE THEORY OF ECONOMIC POLICY

EXAMPLES

T his book has emphasized economics as a *positive* science. The intent has been to analyze how the market economy works—regardless of whether the outcomes are judged as socially desirable. But the founders of economics in the eighteenth and nineteenth centuries were also concerned with *normative* issues of public policy, and that remains an important aspect of modern political economy.

How can we decide whether a proposed intervention or reform is good or bad? In other words, what are the theoretical justifications for economic policies that a government might adopt? This area of study, known as *welfare economics,* is the subject of this chapter. The first section of the chapter considers the *goals* of the policy. The second section reviews "The Theorem of the Invisible Hand," a proposition suggesting that attempts to regulate the economy may make things worse rather than better. Such governmental interventions are commonly defended on the grounds that the Invisible Hand fails to guide the economy properly. A discussion of the real or alleged failures of the free market follows in the remainder of the chapter.

15.1 GOALS OF ECONOMIC POLICY

Economists have concentrated attention on only two of the many possible goals of policy: efficiency and distributive equity. We can think of these two criteria as representing, respectively, the *size* of the economic pie (bigger is better) and the *distribution* of slices (fairer is better).

Efficiency Versus Equity and the Possibility of a Social Welfare Function

To begin with, suppose an individual's well-being depends only on income I. For two persons John and Kathy the alternative social allocations of income can be depicted on I^j, I^k axes as in Figure 15.1. The shaded area shows the set of income combinations available.

The curve II' that bounds the social opportunity set, the Social-Opportunity Curve, can have any of a variety of shapes. As drawn it bulges out, (it is concave to the origin) suggesting that total social income $I^T \equiv I^j + I^k$ is larger toward the middle of II' rather than at the corners. In other words, the economy is not a "constant-sum game." If Kathy consumes more, John does not lose the entire amount that Kathy gains.

Consider first *efficiency* as a goal of social policy. It may seem natural to define efficiency as achieving the largest *sum* of income I^T. Geometrically, this maximum is reached at I^* in Figure 15.1. I^* is the point where II' touches the line NN, the highest attainable line of

List of Notation

MC	Marginal Cost	MV_X	Marginal Value of good X
MRT^A	Marginal Rate of Transformation for firm A	PPC	Production-Possibility Curve
MRS_C^A	Marginal Rate of Substitution in Consumption for individual A		

FIGURE 15.1

FIGURE 15.1 **Social Allocations of Income** The shaded region is the social opportunity set, showing the attainable combinations of income for John *(Iʲ)* and Kathy *(Iᵏ)*; its boundary is the Social Opportunity Curve *II'*. Total social income is maximized at *I**, where *II'* is tangent to line *NN* of slope − 1.

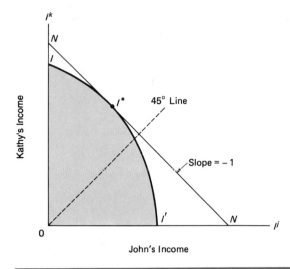

slope − 1 in the diagram. But economists do not define efficiency this way. Treating *I** as some kind of social maximum involves a hidden assumption—that it would be acceptable to deprive John of one dollar if Kathy thereby gets two dollars. Instead, economists use a somewhat weaker concept of efficiency. Any particular income distribution I^j, I^k is called *efficient* if it corresponds to a point on the Social-Opportunity Curve *II'* rather than to a point in the interior of the shaded region.[1]

But income, even if calculated with real rather than money units, does not reliably measure well-being. The effort or risk required to generate the income, and the value of the reservation uses of resources (leisure) that have to be sacrificed, should also be taken into account. In addition, other important sources of satisfaction—such as personal liberty and human companionship—are not factored into measured income. Yet any or all of these can be affected by government policies.

We can get around this problem by using the familiar concept of *utility*. Figure 15.2 (p. 442) shows the social opportunity set in terms of the individuals' achievable utilities U^j and U^k. Utility, we saw in Chapter 3, is an *ordinal* magnitude. A person is assumed to be able to distinguish a more preferred from a less preferred outcome, but there is no basis for measuring the utility difference between them. Also, utility cannot be compared between individuals. For both these reasons the Social-Opportunity Curve in terms of utilities (curve *LL'* in Figure 15.2) has no meaningful shape apart from the ordinal property represented by

---

[1]It might be asked, why not have the parties go initially to *I** and then *redistribute* the maximized total income along *NN* on any basis agreed between them? Moving along *NN*, a point could always be found that is superior for both parties (yields higher income for each) as compared with any point on *II'* that lies below *NN*. But such redistribution is not possible, by the definition of *II'* as the Social-Opportunity Curve. (If it were possible, the line *NN* would be the frontier.)

FIGURE 15.2 Social Allocations of Utility   Since utility has no unique cardinal scaling, only the *ordinal* properties of the Social Opportunity Curve *LL'* are relevant in utility units—that John cannot be made better off without making Kathy worse off, and vice versa. So all we know about *LL'* is that it has negative slope. SW_0 and SW_1 are hypothetical indifference contours of social well-being or "welfare," whose magnitude would be maximized at point *B*. However, if comparisons can be made only in terms of the Pareto criterion, no such contours exist. All that can be said is that distributions to the northeast of any point like *D* (those in the region *DD'BD''*) are preferred to *D*. The Social Opportunity Curve *LL'* is the set of Pareto-efficient distributions; Pareto comparisons cannot be made between points on *LL'*.

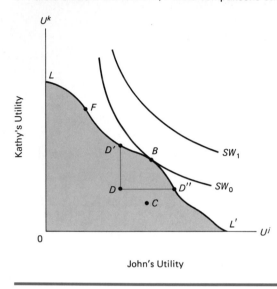

John's Utility

its negative slope. This negative slope tells us only that, once the Social-Opportunity Curve is attained, one person cannot be made better off without making the other worse off.

DEFINITION: An allocation *A* of goods in an economy is "Pareto-preferred"[2] to an allocation *B* if under allocation *A* all persons are at least as well off as under *B*, and at least one person is better off under *A*.

Consider the allocation *D* in the interior of the social opportunity set of Figure 15.2. Comparing *D'* with *D*, Kathy is better off and John is no worse off, so *D'* is Pareto-preferred to *D*. At *D''* John is better off than at *D*, and Kathy is no worse off, so *D''* is also Pareto-preferred to *D*. And for any point between *D'* and *D''* along the boundary *LL'*, John and Kathy are *both* better off, so that any such point is Pareto-preferred to *D*.

Generalizing this reasoning, for any point like *D* in the interior of the social opportunity set there will be points on curve *LL'* that are Pareto-preferred to it. But comparing any two allocations along the boundary *LL'* itself, any gain to one party causes a loss to the other. Hence no point on *LL'* is Pareto-preferred to any other.

The set of boundary points, the Social-Opportunity Curve, is called the set of *Pareto-optimal* allocations. Any of these points can be said to "maximize the size of the economic

[2]Vilfredo Pareto (1848–1923), Italian economist and sociologist (mentioned also in Chapter 3).

pie," in the sense that there is no allocation Pareto-preferred to it. In utility terms, the efficient set of income allocations is the Pareto-optimal set.

What about the goal of distributive equity? Here no single principle seems as compelling as Pareto-optimality.[3] There are two "norms" that do seem to command substantial support: equality and ownership. According to the equality principle, a desirable social outcome has everyone equal. But equal in what sense? Even if opportunities could somehow be equalized we know that—due to differences in skills, work habits, and just plain luck—individuals will end up with different final incomes. As for ownership, the underlying principle is that no one ought to be deprived of property except as punishment for crimes. The ethical problem here is that the present distribution of property, the status quo, may itself largely reflect the fact that some individuals (or perhaps their ancestors) seized the possessions of others in times past.

One tradition in welfare economics "solves" the social optimality problem by using a *social welfare function* that aggregates the utilities of different people. Figure 15.2 shows indifference contours of social utility or "welfare" (SW_0 and SW_1 in the diagram). The social optimum is then at point B, where the boundary LL' touches the highest attainable welfare-indifference contour. One difficulty with this analysis is that people may disagree on which social welfare function to use; most people would be inclined to weigh their own well-being more heavily than others would allow them to.

Moreover, agreement on a social welfare function is more problematic than may at first appear. Suppose someone proposed "Let's rank all social outcomes (that is, each possible size of the pie and each distribution of the slices) on the basis of majority voting." Though appealing, majority voting suffers from the *cycling paradox*.

Consider a society consisting of three individuals, a, b, and c, who must choose among three different social outcomes X, Y, and Z. For majority voting to yield a social welfare function it must satisfy the axioms of comparison and of transitivity (see Chapter 2). Comparison poses no problem, but transitivity does. Thus, for the social outcomes to be ranked in the order *XYZ*, a majority of the voters must prefer X over Y, a majority must prefer Y over Z, and (by transitivity) a majority must prefer X over Z. Suppose Voter a prefers X most, views Y as second best, and Z as third best; Voter c likes Z best, and so on, as tabulated below.

Preferences Subject to Cycling

Voter a	Voter b	Voter c
X	Y	Z
Y	Z	X
Z	X	Y

Consider the choice between alternatives X and Y. Voters a and c prefer X over Y, while Voter b prefers Y over X; X therefore has a 2:1 majority over Y. When Y and Z are the alternatives, voters a and b vote for Y over Z, so that Y has a 2:1 majority over Z. Thus, a majority prefer X over Y, and a majority prefer Y over Z. But when X and Z are the alternatives, then Z has a 2:1 majority over X! In the terminology of Chapter 3, majority-rule choices are not always transitive.

---

[3]There are even objections to Pareto-optimality, as will be seen in the following section.

[*Challenge to the reader:* Consider the alternate set of preferences shown here. Verify that with this set of preferences cycling will not occur. Which alternative is sure to be chosen?]

Preferences Not Subject to Cycling

Voter a	Voter b	Voter c
X	Y	Z
Y	Z	Y
Z	X	X

Where cycling is possible, as with the first set of preferences, the voting sequence (the "agenda") can determine the final outcome. Suppose individual a can determine the order in which votes over pairs of alternatives will be held. He should call first for a vote between Y and Z, the winner to be matched against X. Policy Y would win the first vote, but would be defeated by his favored policy X in the second vote. Any other person as chairman could equally well manipulate the agenda in his or her own favor.

Voting procedures other than majority voting also lead to difficulties. Indeed, Arrow's Theorem states that there exists *no* voting system that can simultaneously satisfy a set of reasonable conditions. Loosely speaking the conditions are (1) completeness (all social outcomes can be ranked); (2) transitivity; (3) the voting method should work with any set of preferences voters may have; (4) the method should not rank alternative X over alternative Y if all individuals prefer Y over $X;$ (5) no person should have dictatorial power, in the sense that the social welfare function should not always mirror the preferences of a specified individual; and (6) the rankings of social outcomes should be immune to manipulation caused by introducing or ignoring alternatives that in any case could never be implemented.

Majority voting, we saw, violates transitivity. A method that ranked alternatives at random would violate condition (4). Point voting (in which individuals can allocate a fixed number of points among the alternatives) violates condition (6) on manipulability. Though Arrow's Theorem does not directly tell us which condition is violated by any particular system, it does tell us that at least one of the six conditions has to be violated. So it is difficult, if not impossible, for individuals to agree on a social welfare function.

Utilitarianism

Turning to somewhat deeper issues, not everyone agrees with the utilitarian philosophy underlying welfare economics.[4] Utilitarians contend that (1) social policies, rules, and institutions are to be judged solely in terms of their *consequences;* and (2) the only relevant consequences are *individuals' gratifications* (pleasures and pains).

The first assertion represents a kind of social pragmatism. For utilitarians all social practices or institutions (e.g., voting, the market, capital punishment, the family, the nation) are mere means or instruments. They should not be adopted or rejected because they agree or disagree with the word of the Bible, or with natural law, or with the dictates of ethical principles. Instead, the only criterion is: Does this arrangement lead to desirable social

---

[4]The terms "utility" and "utilitarianism" were both popularized by Jeremy Bentham mentioned also in Chapter 3.

outcomes? Where others might say "The ends do not justify the means," the utilitarian replies, "What can justify means except the ends attained?"

The second assertion represents radical individualism. Policies may or may not serve the purposes of God, may or may not advance science and learning, may or may not promote the survival of the nation; none of this is relevant for the utilitarian. He asks only whether the results satisfy individual desires. President John F. Kennedy declared "Ask not what your country can do for you, ask what you can do for your country!" A utilitarian would reply, "Why have a country except for what it can do for you?"

A somewhat separate question involves the issue of *hedonism*. In calculating a person's well-being should we count only sensate satisfactions like a warm house or a full belly? What about "higher wants," for example, the desire to do one's duty, or to help others? And, unfortunately, in the world as we know it there are also "lower wants," for example malevolent urges to punish or dominate others. What weight to attach to such wants remains a problem for utilitarians.

The following arguments might be made against the utilitarian position:

1. Social policy should be directed not at giving individuals what they *want*, but what they *ought to have*. As the great moralists and our sacred texts have told us, and as history demonstrates, people should not always get what they want. Efficiency is a goal for raising pigs; it is not a valid criterion for a community of people.
2. Even if satisfying individuals' wants is a legitimate aim, it should not be the only social goal. Liberty, justice, order, community—all these are goals that transcend the satisfaction of individual wants.
3. Apart from *outcomes* is the question of *means*. An allocation of goods and services that is agreed to voluntarily might be better than a perfectly ideal allocation established by dictatorial decree or political trickery.
4. The desires of individuals result from their social conditioning. Much more important than want-satisfaction is want-creation. The main goal of policy should not be to give people what they want, but to get people to desire the proper things.

We cannot resolve these difficult philosophical questions here. Utilitarianism can be criticized from many different points of view: dictatorial or democratic, radical or conservative, ethical or cynical. But recall that economics is the science of the *instrumental,* of the choice of proper means for *given* ends. Economics identifies policies that promote peoples' actual ends, whether or not these ends accord with utilitarian philosophy.

An Application: Efficient Versus "Envy-Free" Allocations

The Edgeworth box of Figure 15.3 (p. 446), based on Figure 13.2, can be used to illustrate efficiency. The shaded area, the football-shaped "region of mutual advantage," is the set of allocations of the two commodities X and Y that are *Pareto-preferred* to the endowment position E. We saw in Chapter 13 that the Contract Curve CC, which consists of the set of points where the indifference curves of the individuals are tangent to each other, is the set of points for which no region of mutual advantage exists. The contract curve CC therefore corresponds to the set of *Pareto-optimal* (or efficient) allocations.

Notice that some allocations that are Pareto-preferred to E are not Pareto-optimal (that is, are not themselves on the Contract Curve). Correspondingly, there are some Pareto-optimal points along the Contract Curve that are not Pareto-preferred to E. Only allocations on the curve in the range DD are *both* Pareto-optimal and Pareto-preferred to E. (Recall

FIGURE 15.3 **Pareto-Preferred and Pareto-Optimal Allocations**   Given an initial allocation of income *E*, the points in the blue football-shaped area are all Pareto-preferred to *E*. The Contract Curve *CC* represents the set of *Pareto-optimal* allocations. Only points within the range *DD* along the Contract Curve are both Pareto-optimal and Pareto-preferred to *E*. At *M*, the midpoint of the diagram, the individuals consume identical amounts of both goods. But, in general, *M* will be neither Pareto-optimal nor Pareto-preferred to *E*.

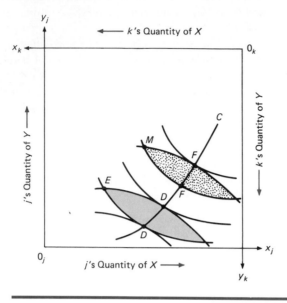

that, as shown in Chapter 13, the competitive equilibrium lies on the Contract Curve within the region of mutual advantage, and so is indeed both Pareto-optimal and Pareto-preferred in comparison with the endowment position.)

What about other possible distributive criteria, in particular equality? In the Edgeworth box there would be material equality at the midpoint *M*, where each person receives exactly the same amount of each commodity. But since in general people's tastes differ, the parties involved would not find material equality very appealing. In fact, since *M* will not ordinarily lie on the Contract Curve *CC*, if the individuals were initially placed at *M* they would voluntarily trade away from it to some "unequal" point lying in the region of mutual advantage (the dotted area in Figure 15.3).

A somewhat subtler interpretation of equality has recently been introduced by economists under the heading of "envy-free" allocations. The idea is that two individuals are effectively equal if neither would prefer to *change places* with the other.

If Individual *A* consumes at point *a*, and individual *B* consumes at point *b*, then "changing places" means that *B* shifts to bundle *a* and that *A* shifts to bundle *b*. Remember, however, that in the Edgeworth box *A*'s consumption bundle is measured from the lower left corner, while *B*'s consumption is measured from the upper right corner. In the Edgeworth box we find the "changing places" allocation that corresponds to a point, say *G*, as follows. Draw the line that contains *G* and *M*, and then find a point *G'* that lies on this line such that the distance *GM* equals the distance *G'M*. Then *A*'s consumption bundle at *G* is the same as *B*'s consumption bundle at *G'*, and vice versa.

FIGURE 15.4   Envy-Neutral and Envy-Free Allocations   *G* and *G'* are diagonally opposite points that lie on one of John's indifference curves. Therefore, John would be just indifferent to "changing places" with Kathy from *G* to *G'*, or vice versa. So *G* and *G'* are *envy-neutral* for John, as are the points *H* and *H'*. Connecting all such points generates John's envy-neutral curve N_jN_j. John's *envy-free* region, the set of points that he prefers to their "changing places" counterparts, lies northeast of N_jN_j. His *envious* region is the set of points southwest of N_jN_j.

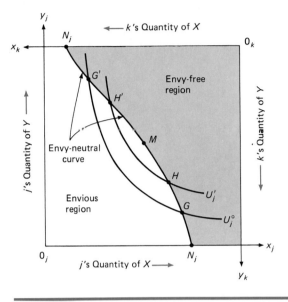

Let us look now for the set of points that are *envy-neutral* for one of the parties, say, for John. This means that John is indifferent between the given position and its "changing-places" counterpart. In Figure 15.4 the points *G* and *G'* are such a pair, since both lie on John's indifference curve U_j^0. Similarly, *H* and *H'* are envy-neutral points for John, since both lie on his indifference curve U_j'. All of John's envy-neutral points will fall on a curve like N_jN_j that generally slopes downward and goes through the midpoint *M*. (The midpoint lies on the curve because it is its own "changing places" image.) [*Query:* Why do all the envy-neutral points lie on a *single* downward-sloping curve? HINT: Suppose *G* and *G'* are "changing places" points between which the consumer is indifferent. Consider a point that lies directly below *G,* so that its "changing places" counterpart lies above *G'*. Show that the consumer cannot be indifferent between these two points as well as between *G* and *G'*.]

Since the curve N_jN_j in Figure 15.4 is drawn to connect all of John's envy-neutral points, the shaded region above and to the right of the curve shows all the points that he actually prefers over their "changing places" counterparts. This shaded area (inclusive of the N_jN_j curve) therefore represents the set of John's "envy-free" allocations. A corresponding envy-neutral curve N_kN_k can be constructed for Kathy, where of course Kathy's envy-free region lies below and to the left of her envy-neutral curve. N_jN_j and N_kN_k are both plotted in Figure 15.5; the dotted region is the set of *mutually envy-free* allocations. The two envy-neutral curves must intersect at the midpoint *M*. While the curves *may* intersect more than once, for simplicity a single intersection is assumed here. On this assumption, the dotted

FIGURE 15.5   Mutually Envy-Free Allocations   Since John's envy-free region lies northeast of N_jN_j and Kathy's envy-free region lies southwest of N_kN_k, the mutually envy-free region is the shaded area. The Contract Curve CC passes through this region, so there will always be allocations that are both efficient and mutually envy-free. But such points are not necessarily Pareto-preferred to the initial endowment E.

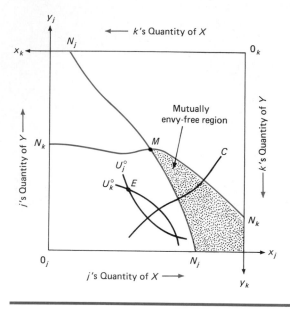

region lies entirely on one side of the midpoint (and, of course, it includes the midpoint itself). Notice also that the Contract Curve CC lies on the same side of the midpoint. [*Query: Why is this the case? HINT:* If the parties are at a mutual indifference-curve tangency along CC, could they ever *both* prefer to change places?]

We see therefore that it is always possible to find allocations that are Pareto-optimal (that lie along the Contract Curve) and that are also mutually envy-free (that fall in the dotted region of Figure 15.5). Thus the conditions of efficiency and of envy-freeness can both be met. However, no point in the envy-free region is Pareto-preferred to an endowment position like E in Figure 15.5. So while it is possible to find allocations that are both Pareto-optimal and envy-free, one of the parties may be made worse off in a move from his endowment to a mutually envy-free allocation.

Exercise 15.1

Suppose Kathy's utility function is $x_k y_k$, and John's is $x_j y_j$. The endowments are $x_k = 1$, $y_k = 1$; $x_j = 4$, $y_j = 4$. Is the competitive equilibrium envy-free?

Answer: The endowment point represents a competitive equilibrium. To see this, note that the MRS_C for John is y_j/x_j, and the MRS_C for Kathy is y_k/x_k. At the endowment point and prices $P_x = P_y = 1$, $MRS_C = P_x/P_y$ for both John and Kathy, and so this is a competitive equilibrium. But this allocation is not envy-free since Kathy is envious of John, who has more of both goods.

15.2 THE THEOREM OF THE INVISIBLE HAND

Adam Smith asserted that the invisible hand of self-interest leads individuals to promote the interests of others. Economists have refined this idea into more precise terms. The Theorem of the Invisible Hand states the following: *Given a number of ideal conditions, optimizing behavior on the part of individuals and firms under pure competition leads to an efficient (Pareto-optimal) outcome.* Here we will discuss the requirements of economic efficiency.

Efficient Consumption

Whatever goods are produced should be distributed so that, on the margin, no one person is more willing to sacrifice Y for X than any other individual. If there were any such difference, they could mutually gain by trade. For example, suppose Susan would gladly give up 1 shirt for 1 dress. Suppose further that Jane would gladly give up 2 shirts for 1 dress. Then they could be made better off if Susan gave Jane 1 shirt, and in return Jane gave Susan 1 dress: Susan is as well off as before, and Jane is better off. The condition for efficiency in consumption is therefore

$$MRS_C^A = MRS_C^B \tag{15.1}$$

We could also interpret the Marginal Rate of Substitution in Consumption MRS_C as the individual's "demand price" or Marginal Value MV for commodity X, in terms of the amount of Y she would be willing to offer. Then Equation (15.1) can be rewritten as

$$MV_x^A = MV_x^B \tag{15.1'}$$

That is, for efficiency in consumption each individual's Marginal Value for the good must be the same.

Efficient Production

In producing goods X and Y, on the margin it should not be possible for one producer to be able to transform Y into X at a different rate from another producer. That is, the Marginal Rates of Transformation MRT between goods X and Y must be equal for all producers. Suppose this were not the case. Suppose Firm A could produce 1 shirt with the material and labor it uses for 1 dress, whereas Firm B could make 2 shirts with the resources it uses to produce 1 dress. If Firm A produced 1 less shirt, the economy would have 1 more dress. Let Firm B then produce 1 less dress (so that the total number of dresses produced by the two firms is unchanged). Firm B could then use these resources to produce 2 shirts, so that in total Firms A and B produce 1 additional shirt and the same number of dresses.

More generally, Firm A should cut back on production of X and Firm B should increase production of X until the Law of Diminishing Returns makes the rates at which the two producers can transform Y and X equal. So the efficiency condition is

$$MRT^A = MRT^B \tag{15.2}$$

If the amount of commodity Y foregone is interpreted as the *cost* of producing X, we can write this condition as follows:

$$MC_x^A = MC_x^B \qquad (15.2')$$

That is, for efficiency in production each producer should operate at the same Marginal Cost.

Efficient Balance Between Production and Consumption

The rate at which producers can convert Y and X should be equal to the rate at which consumers are willing to substitute Y and X in their consumption. In other words the Marginal Rate of Substitution in Production equals the Marginal Rate of Substitution in Consumption, or

$$MRT = MRS_C \qquad (15.3)$$

Once again, if this condition does not hold resources can be reallocated to make at least some consumers better off without making anyone worse off. Thus, suppose a manufacturer with a fixed amount of inputs for production could produce 1 additional shirt by producing 1 less dress. Suppose that Jane would gladly trade 2 shirts for 1 dress. If the firm produced 1 less shirt and 1 more dress, the economy could provide all other consumers with the same amount of goods as before, but give Jane 1 less shirt and 1 more dress; since she would be willing to give up 2 shirts for 1 dress, Jane is clearly better off. That is, Jane can be made better off without making anyone else worse off.

Interpreting the Marginal Rate of Substitution in Production MRT as the Marginal Cost of producing X, and the Marginal Rate of Substitution in Consumption MRS_C as the Marginal Value of X, we can also write

$$MC_x = MV_x \qquad (15.3')$$

Let us now turn to the role of market price. Let commodity Y be the *numeraire,* so that $P_y \equiv 1$. Then the different producers do not directly aim at equating their Marginal Rates of Transformation as in Equation (15.2). Rather, each sets its Marginal Rate of Transformation in Production (which corresponds to the Marginal Cost of producing X) equal to the price P_x. And similarly, the different consumers do not *directly* aim at equating their Marginal Rates of Substitution in Consumption as in Equation (15.1). Rather, each sets her MRS_C (the absolute slope of her indifference curve) equal to the price P_x (the absolute budget-line slope). Thus the market price P_x brings about efficiency by "mediating" everyone's productive and consumptive decisions. We can express this compactly in this equation.

$$MRT = P_x = MRS_C \qquad (15.4)$$

Or

$$MC_x = P_x = MV_x \qquad (15.4')$$

These equations hold over all goods and all individuals.[5] We can portray them pictorially in the following form:

$$\frac{MRT^A}{MRS_C^A} = P_x/P_y = \frac{MRT^B}{MRS_C^B} \quad or \quad \frac{MC^A}{MV^A} = P_x = \frac{MC^B}{MV^B} \tag{15.4''}$$

CONCLUSION: In a free-market economy, the forces of supply and demand will bring about a set of equilibrium prices that lead individuals to meet the conditions of efficienct production, efficient consumption, and efficient balance of production and consumption.

EXAMPLE 15.1 Marginal Excess Burden of Taxation

Taxes impose a "wedge" between buying prices and selling prices, and thus prevent the efficiency conditions (that $MC_x = MV_x$) from being satisfied. Charles L. Ballard, John B. Shoven, and John Whalley estimated this "marginal excess burden" (MEB) of taxation to be generally in the range of 17 to 56 cents per dollar of revenue raised. This means that a government project that produces a marginal benefit of less than $1.17 to $1.56 per dollar collected (depending upon the tax considered) would cause an efficiency loss.

In the following table, notice that the MEB for sales taxes overall is $.39, but for taxes other than those on alcohol, tobacco, and gasoline it is only $.12. It follows that the taxes on these three specific goods must involve extremely high marginal excess burdens. [*Query:* These three goods are taxed at exceptionally high rates. Would you expect a very heavy percentage tax on some particular good to have a larger MEB, *for the last dollar collected,* than a dollar collected from a small percentage tax? Why?]

Marginal Excess Burdens of Specified Taxes*

Tax	MEB ($)
Capital taxes	.46
Sales taxes	.39
Sales taxes (other than alcohol, tobacco, and gasoline)	.12
Income taxes	.31
All taxes	.33

*Assuming elasticities of 0.4 and 0.15 for saving and labor supply, respectively.

Source: Adapted from Charles L. Ballard, John B. Shoven, and John Whalley, "General Equilibrium Computations of the Marginal Welfare Costs of Taxes in the United States," *American Economic Review,* v. 75 (March 1985), p. 136.

[5]This conclusion is subject to certain technical qualifications as discussed in previous chapters, such as the absence of corner solutions, second-order conditions, and so forth.

15.3 WHAT CAN GO WRONG? ALMOST EVERYTHING!

The trouble is, the Theorem of the Invisible Hand is too good to be true. This section will discuss several ways in which things can go wrong.

Monopoly

Any non-price-taking behavior, whether due to monopoly, cartels, oligopoly, or to any of the market-structure situations analyzed in Chapters 8 through 10, implies violation of the efficiency conditions of the preceding section. For convenience, we shall speak here mostly of monopoly.

The profit-maximizing monopoly firm is motivated to set $MC = MR < P$, rather than $MC = P$ as required by Equation (15.4'). So, as previously seen, the monopolist produces too little output. Similarly, a monopolistic resource-supplier would offer too little of the resource on the input market.

CONCLUSION: Under monopoly there is "too little" market exchange. And consequently, there will also be "too little" productive specialization and "too little" market employment of inputs.

Monopoly deprives society of some of the mutual benefits of trade. The violation of the efficiency conditions tells us that if monopoly could somehow be abolished the gain would be great enough to permit compensating the owners of the monopoly while still leaving a net benefit for other persons in the society.

Disequilibrium

Another difficulty is *market disequilibrium*. Section 15.2 on "The Theorem of the Invisible Hand" demonstrated that price-taking behavior leads to satisfaction of the efficiency conditions. But what if the currently quoted price is not the right one for clearing a market? It is true that corrective forces tend to restore equilibrium, as explained in Chapter 2. But in the real world prices are rarely at their exact equilibrium values.

Since prices will sometimes be too high and at other times too low, it might be thought that the effects of disequilibrium would more or less cancel out. That, however, is not the case. Prices that are too high and prices that are too low both reduce the quantities exchanged. Like monopoly, disequilibrium wipes out some of the potential gains from trade.

Figure 15.6 pictures a market with normally sloping supply and demand curves. At the price P' supply is greater than demand, so the quantity exchanged Q' is the *lesser* of the supply and demand quantities, in this case, the demand quantity. It is true that at the high price P' there are unsatisfied sellers, but they cannot find customers. ("It takes two to tango.") The price P'', on the other hand is too low to clear the market, but again here it is the *lesser* (offered) quantity Q'' that governs; there are now unsatisfied buyers, but they cannot find willing suppliers. While price is in the one case above and in the other case below the equilibrium P^*, in both situations the quantity exchanged is *less* than the equilibrium Q^*.

CONCLUSION: Disequilibrium, like monopoly, leads to inefficiency due to the reduced volume of trade.

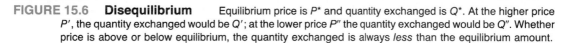

FIGURE 15.6 **Disequilibrium** Equilibrium price is P^* and quantity exchanged is Q^*. At the higher price P', the quantity exchanged would be Q'; at the lower price P'' the quantity exchanged would be Q''. Whether price is above or below equilibrium, the quantity exchanged is always *less* than the equilibrium amount.

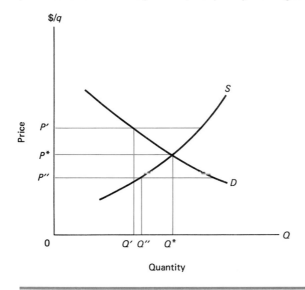

Externalities

"Externalities" are said to arise when some people's actions affect other persons and the decision makers are not penalized for the loss or damage they cause (or rewarded for the benefits they confer). But this definition is too broad for present purposes. Everyone is affected to some extent by actions of people all over the globe that raise or lower the prices of commodities he or she consumes or produces. We here mostly ignore merely "pecuniary" externalities that affect others only through movements in market prices. Rather, we focus on "direct" externalities, which occur when one person's actions have a physical or technological effect upon the consumption or production possibilities available to others.

Consider *pollution*. Chemical pollution may make water undrinkable; heat pollution may make a stream less effective for industrial cooling. *Congestion* is also a kind of pollution. Each additional driver crowds the highways for other drivers; each additional broadcasting station impairs reception of other stations' signals; drilling by one farmer reduces water levels in neighbors' wells.

But a direct externality may also be beneficial. An upstream user's activities could improve the quality of water downstream. Similarly, as discussed in Chapter 7, a farmer in a marshy area who drains his own land lowers water levels and therefore improves the productivity of neighboring land.

Figure 15.7 (p. 454) pictures a harmful externality. A competitive (price-taking) firm maximizes profit by setting perceived Marginal Cost MC equal to price P_x by choosing output x^*. But any increase in the firm's production imposes costs on others—due, say, to pollution. The true social Marginal Cost at any output is then the vertical sum $MC + ME$, where ME may be called the marginal Externality. The output x^{**} at which social Marginal

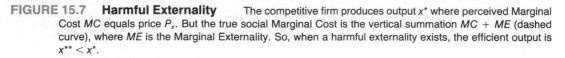

FIGURE 15.7 Harmful Externality The competitive firm produces output *x** where perceived Marginal Cost *MC* equals price P_x. But the true social Marginal Cost is the vertical summation *MC* + *ME* (dashed curve), where *ME* is the Marginal Externality. So, when a harmful externality exists, the efficient output is $x^{**} < x^*$.

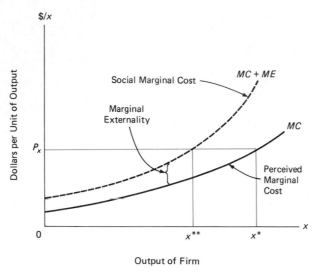

Output of Firm

Cost equals price P_x is evidently less than *x**. (*Query:* What happens in the case of a beneficial externality?)

CONCLUSION: Direct externalities, beneficial or harmful, lead the Invisible Hand astray. In the interests of efficiency, an agent generating a harmful externality ought to reduce output short of the profit-maximizing level. If the externality is beneficial, output should be expanded beyond the profit-maximizing amount.

EXAMPLE 15.2 **Health Costs of Nuclear Versus Coal Power**

A great deal of concern has been expressed about the health consequences of nuclear power. In judging these, a comparison with the health consequences of generating electricity from alternative sources (mostly from coal) is highly relevant.

L. B. Lave and L. C. Freeburg[a] analyzed coal versus nuclear power, taking into account the entire fuel cycle from exploration through extraction, transportation, refining, generation, and recovery. In estimating the health risks to workers involved in the use of coal, the authors concentrated on the mining phase. For nuclear power the costs of mine accidents and chronic diseases were estimated at around 2.4 cents per 1000 kilowatt-hours (kWh) of energy produced; for coal the costs were around 32 cents per 1000 kWh, more than thirteen times as great as for nuclear power. (*Note:* If these occupational health hazards are known to workers and reflected in higher wages, the associated costs would not be externalities; they would be paid for and thus taken into account by producers. On the other hand, to the extent that occupational health costs are borne by others, as when government assists coal-miners suffering from black lung disease, an externality is imposed upon the rest of the community.)

The analysis also examined health effects upon the outside public. These definitely are externalities. Several elements had to be left out of the comparison for lack of generally agreed-upon data, including the risk of nuclear accidents, the chance of terrorist hijacking of nuclear materials, and the long-term environmental effects of coal- and nuclear-waste disposal. Setting these aside, the public-health costs are mainly the result of chronic low-intensity radiation exposure in the case of nuclear power, and pollution of air and water by combustion waste products in the case of coal. For nuclear power the estimated public-health costs were within the range of 0.0003 to 0.03 cents per 1000 kWh; note that even the upper limit is small relative to the already small occupational health costs. For coal, on the other hand, the estimated range for public health costs was $0.10 to $5.00 per 1000 kWh—more than 3,000 times the nuclear costs at the upper limit, and 16,000 times nuclear costs at the lower limit! These results suggest, therefore, that some of the concern about the health hazards of nuclear power might better be redirected toward the very significant health externalities associated with coal power.

COMMENT   The unknown or "unquantifiable" elements might be very large here. The accident record at nuclear plants has on the whole been excellent, and accidental nuclear detonation is considered close to impossible. But, as the 1979 Three Mile Island accident in Pennsylvania indicated, the potential consequences should a major accident occur are truly enormous. While no identifiable health injury ensued from Three Mile Island, the 1986 Chernobyl incident in the Soviet Union caused around 30 direct fatalities (plus much higher estimated long-run deaths due to increased rates of cancer). It is more difficult still to estimate the likelihood or the consequences of a terrorist group's acquiring enough fissionable material to fabricate atomic weapons. So although nuclear power has an enormous advantage with regard to calculable health costs and externalities, we cannot entirely ignore these less quantifiable hazards.

[a]Lester B. Lave and Linnea C. Freeburg, "Health Effects of Electricity Generation from Coal, Oil and Nuclear Fuels," *Nuclear Safety,* v. 14 (September/October 1973).

EXAMPLE 15.3   **Externalities from Smoking**[a]

Smokers impose costs on others. Some of these costs are direct externalities, for example, when a smoker causes a fire that burns down a neighbor's house. Other externalities are pecuniary. For example, suppose a worker has a group health insurance policy that pays 75 percent of his medical bills, and suppose that smoking a pack of cigarettes per day raises medical bills by $6,000. The amount the worker pays (0.25)($6,000) = $1,500 is not an externality. But since the smoker does not pay higher premiums that reflect his or her higher medical costs, the remainder of the cost, $4,500, is a component of pecuniary external costs. On the other hand, since cigarette smokers die at a younger age, there is a pecuniary positive externality when these persons collect less pensions.

Using a zero discount rate, Manning et al. found that each pack of cigarettes increases medical costs by $0.38, but saves $1.82 in public and private pensions because of a 137 minute reduction in life expectancy. Fires cause an externality of $0.02 per pack. At a 5 percent discount rate, the aggregate net externality is $0.15 per pack. This estimate of $0.15 per pack is well below the average (state plus federal) excise and sales taxes of $0.37 per pack. So it appears that smokers do not impose net costs on non-smokers, mainly due to the saving on pensions.

^aDiscussion based on Willard G. Manning, et al. "The Taxes of Sin: Do Smokers and Drinkers Pay Their Way?" Rand Note N-2941-NCHSR, March 1989.

Where direct externalities exist, three types of public policies can be used to achieve efficient production.

1. *Tax-subsidy adjustments*—A tax on externalities motivates firms to reduce the harm imposed on others. An ideal corrective tax would be equal to the Marginal Externality. Then the private Marginal Cost plus the tax penalty would equal the total true social Marginal Cost of production. For a beneficial externality, a corrective *subsidy* would be called for to induce a greater level of the externality-generating activity.

2. *Utilization*—Suppose upstream uses affect the quality of downstream river water. Then if the two types of use were merged or "unitized" under the control of a single economic agent, what was previously an externality would be *internalized*. The single integrated water-using enterprise would now carry on the polluting activity at a socially efficient level; that is, it would pollute only so long as the marginal upstream gain exceeded the marginal downstream loss. Or consider congestion effects in oil fields. Pumping at any well reduces the output of other wells in the same field (by drawing away the oil and by reducing gas pressure). The result is inefficient overdrilling and overpumping. The owner of each well is motivated to pump faster than he otherwise would, to capture oil under others' land and to prevent others from capturing the oil under his land. The owner of land is similarly induced to drill more wells, and to locate them inefficiently along the boundaries of his tract. With unitization of the entire oilfield, the sole ownerships of individual wells are exchanged for pro-rata shares in the overall operation. This eliminates the motivation to overpump or to overdrill.

3. *Property reassignment*—The fundamental source of the externality problem is defective property rights. If property rights were perfectly defined and enforced, externalities would not occur. In the river-water example, the downstream user might ideally be assigned a property right to receive water of some specified quality. An upstream user who degrades the quality below this level would be liable for the damages suffered, and so could not impose harm on others without penalty. But whatever the initial assignment, it is essential that property rights remain exchangeable. If the downstream user was initially entitled to absolutely pure water, for example, in the interests of efficiency the upstream producer should nevertheless be permitted to purchase the other's consent to degrade the river to some agreed degree.[6]

[6]Where the valuable resource takes the form of a "common pool," as in the case of fish in the ocean or underground water or petroleum, it has been proposed to establish a new kind of property right—marketable entitlements to uncaught fish, or to unpumped water or oil. Overexploitation would be discouraged by the fact that anyone extracting a unit of the resource must also purchase an entitlement to do so. The market price of these titles would reflect investors' estimates of the market value of the resource in *future* uses. See Vernon L. Smith, "Water Deeds: A Proposed Solution to the Water Valuation Problem," *Arizona Review,* v. 26 (January 1977).

Coase's Theorem

This last concept has been generalized into what is known as *Coase's Theorem*,[7] which can be stated as follows:

COASE'S THEOREM: Regardless of the specific initial assignment of property rights, the final outcome will be efficient provided that the initial legal assignment is well-defined and that the parties can reach and enforce an agreement at zero cost.

The thrust of Coase's Theorem is that the Invisible Hand is considerably more effective than our previous discussion of externalities may have suggested. There are natural market forces tending to bring the "external" effects into the calculations of the responsible parties. Suppose a firm has the legal right to pollute the air. The victims of the pollution could then pay the firm not to do so. Or perhaps the people in the area have a legal right to clean air. The firm could then pay them a fee in return for their permission to pollute. (In the case of a beneficial externality, of course, the argument applies in reverse.) So long as the legal rights are marketable and well-defined, the Invisible Hand leads the parties to an efficient outcome—that is, to a result that exhausts all possibilities for further mutual gain.

To analyze externalities in consumption between two people, imagine there are two goods: bread, a good that does not generate any externality, and cigarettes, which do cause an externality. Specifically, let John attach positive utility to both bread and cigarettes. Kathy also cares for bread but does not smoke—in fact, she suffers a utility loss from John's smoking.

Figure 15.8 (p. 458) illustrates this situation with a new type of diagram, the "Dolbear triangle,"[8] which in some ways resembles but in other ways differs quite substantially from the Edgeworth box introduced in Chapter 13. In the triangle the lower-left corner, point J, is the usual kind of origin for John. Since bread and cigarettes are both goods for him, his preference directions are upward and to the right, and so his indifference curves (such as U_J^o and U_J') have the normal slope and curvature. For Kathy, bread is again a good but John's cigarettes are a bad. In the diagram, Kathy's origin is along the vertical axis at point K. Her preference directions are downward and to the left (she likes more bread but less smoke), so her indifference curves will be shaped like U_K^o and U_K'.

Let the initial endowment be at point B, meaning that John starts with the amount JB and Kathy with the amount BK of bread. Imagine that John can exchange bread for cigarettes on an outside market at a 1:1 price ratio. So BB' is a budget line for John. He will accordingly move to his consumptive optimum at point A, generating S_A of smoke.

The resulting situation for Kathy has to be interpreted in a novel and rather tricky way. Notice that, in contrast with the Edgeworth box where the social totals of the two commodities were fixed, here as John buys more cigarettes on the outside market in exchange for bread, the social totals available to John and Kathy change. (Equivalently, we can imagine that John is able to produce cigarettes by sacrificing bread one-for-one, i.e., that BB' is a linear Production-Possibility Curve.) Since the original total amount JK of bread will be reduced unit for unit as John exchanges bread for cigarettes, the quantities of the two commodities actually available for John and Kathy together are indicated by the line KK' which parallels John's budget line BB'. So while Kathy's quantity of (involuntarily consumed) cigarettes is

---

[7]R.H. Coase, "The Problem of Social Cost," *Journal of Law and Economics*, v. 3 (October 1960).

[8]S. Trenery Dolbear, "On the theory of optimum externality," *American Economic Review*, v. 57 (March 1967).

FIGURE 15.8 **Externality and the Coase Theorem**   John enjoys both bread and cigarettes; his indifference curves are U_J', U_J°, and U_J''. Kathy views bread as a good, but suffers from the smoke produced by John's cigarettes. Two of her indifference curves are U_K° and U_K', with utility increasing towards the southwest. The competitive equilibrium at point A is not Pareto-optimal—both are better off with an allocation in the shaded area. The efficient allocations lie on the Contract Curve CC'.

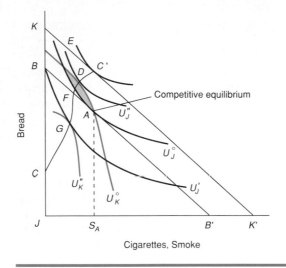

measured in the usual way to the right of the vertical axis, her quantity of bread is indicated by distance *measured downward from the line KK'*. This is consistent, of course, with the fact that her consumption of bread remains the same amount BK while John moves along his budget line BB'. Kathy's indifference curves must therefore be understood as associated with cigarette quantities measured to the right of the vertical axis but bread quantities measured downward from KK'.

The competitive equilibrium is at point A, where John maximizes his utility, and Kathy spends all her income on BK units of bread. It is clear that point A is not Pareto-optimal; any point within the shaded football-shaped area above and to the left of A gives both consumers higher utility. The Pareto-optimal allocations are those where the indifference curves of the two people are tangent, as at points D and G. The Contract Curve CC' shows all the Pareto-optimal points. Notice that point C' is a Pareto-optimal point, but it involves more consumption of the externality-producing good than does point A: Pareto-optimality thus need not require a reduction in the externality. What is true is that all points Pareto-preferred to A involve less consumption of the good that causes the externality.

One way of attaining a Pareto-optimal solution involves assigning property rights. Suppose Kathy is given the right to totally clean air. That is, if John pollutes, then Kathy can go to court and get an injunction stopping him from emitting any pollution whatever. But, and this is critical, suppose also that Kathy can agree not to sue John in return for a sufficiently high payment. Under this rule John would initially consume at point B, which we see is not Pareto-optimal. Kathy, however, would be willing to allow John to consume at point G, where he gives Kathy some bread, so that she consumes more than BK loaves of bread: John is no worse off at G than at B, but Kathy is better off. Similarly, if John has full rights to pollute, he may initially consume at the competitive equilibrium, point A. But Kathy would be willing to pay John to reduce his consumption of cigarettes. The parties may therefore negotiate an agreement to consume at point D where Kathy gives John some of her bread; here Kathy is just as well off as at point A, but John is better off. Points D and G are not the only agreements the two parties may come to. Instead, it is reasonable for them to come to an agreement corresponding to any point on the Contract Curve that is Pareto-superior to point A.

Thus, given any particular assignment of property rights, the parties are motivated to negotiate an agreement that leads them to a Pareto-optimal solution. In accord with Coase's theorem, a Pareto-optimal allocation can come about regardless of how the property rights are initially assigned, provided that the negotiations required are feasible.

EXAMPLE 15.4   **Apples and Bees**

The apple-grower's orchard provides the beneficial externality of nectar for his neighbor's bees—a contribution to the production of honey for which the orchardist receives no reward. The bees in return pollinate the apple blossoms, a valuable service for the apple-grower. These interacting externalities were assumed by earlier economists to represent a clear case in which the Invisible Hand failed. Government action was supposed to be necessary to induce the orchardist to optimally cooperate with the beekeeper, that is, to grow more nectar-yielding apple blossoms than the orchardist's self-interested calculation would dictate. And similarly, it was supposed, something had to be done to induce the beekeeper to provide more pollination benefits to his apple-growing neighbor.

Upon looking into beekeeping in the state of Washington, however, Steven N. S. Cheung found the Invisible Hand alive and well. Beekeepers and orchardists recognize the mutually beneficial externalities of their actions so that active market dealings govern the placement of beehives. The financial arrangements depend upon the relative values of the two interacting external benefits: the honey yield to the beekeeper as against the pollination services gained by the grower. The following table illustrates that where honey yield is great, the beekeeper ordinarily pays an "apiary rent" to buy the right to place his hive on the grower's land. Where the honey yield is small, the grower pays pollination fees for the privilege of having hives placed on his land. (Washington bees are even exported to California to help pollinate the early-season almond crop.) Evidently, as suggested by Coase's Theorem, market transactions bring "externalities" into private economic calculations.

Honey Yields and Pricing Arrangements, Washington 1970–71

Season	Crop	Surplus Honey (Pounds per Hive)	Pollination Fees ($)	Apiary Rent per Hive ($)
Early spring	Almond (California)	0	5–8	—
	Cherry	0	6–8	—
Late spring	Apples and soft fruits	0	9–10	—
	Blueberry (with maple)	40	5	—
(major pollination season)	Cabbage	15	8	—
	Cherry	0	9–10	—
	Cranberry	5	9	—

So far so good. But Coase's Theorem seems to prove too much. Consider a simple monopoly that (by the standard analysis) leads to an inefficient outcome—underproduction of the monopolized good. An inefficiency presents an opportunity for mutually advantageous trade. So, according to Coase's Theorem, a monopolist and his customers would agree on some efficient arrangement that has the monopolist produce more in return for some payment. Monopoly should disappear, along with externalities!

Applying Coase's Theorem to "solve" the problems of monopoly or externalities is difficult if negotiations are costly. Where large numbers of people are involved, it may be impossible to reach agreement. According to Coase's Theorem, *unitization,* for example, should come about by voluntary agreement to solve the externality problem in oil fields. But in practice special legislation has proved to be necessary to compel holdout minority tract-owners to comply with an efficient solution. The "free rider" problem makes unanimity almost impossible: once a substantial majority have agreed to stop overpumping their wells, it pays to be a member of the noncomplying minority.[9]

If the numbers involved are small, on the other hand, the problem becomes one of *strategic behavior* (as discussed in Chapter 10). When a small number of bargainers face one another, the mere possibility of a mutually advantageous agreement does not guarantee that such an agreement will be reached.

EXAMPLE 15.5 **Water Law**[a]

In the eastern part of the United States, state laws governing the use of flowing streams are based mainly upon the "riparian" doctrine; in the West, the "appropriation" doctrine dominates.

Under the riparian principle, every owner of land bordering a stream has an equal right to reasonable use of the flow. Property rights so defined are ambiguous and of limited exchangeability. What is "reasonable" will always be an arguable matter. Water-users are deterred from making costly investments for fear that a later judicial or administrative redetermination of "reasonable" uses may take away the water they counted on having. Nor can any user buy another's water right, since all are equally entitled to the flow.

In the relatively arid western states, this economically unjustifiable doctrine was replaced by the appropriation principle that "first in time is first in right." Subject to qualifications and conditions that vary from state to state, first users were given the right to appropriate specified quantities of flow, sometimes limited also as to time, place, or manner of diversion. Appropriated water was no longer tied to "riparian" uses but could be transferred away from the stream. The appropriation doctrine represented a considerable improvement from the point of view of *certainty* of rights. However, the *exchangeability* of rights has remained subject to erratic legal intervention.

In recent years administrative agencies and courts have tended to revert toward the "reasonable use" philosophy. In consequence, ambiguity has been increasing rather than decreasing. The California Supreme Court, for example, ruled in 1983 that under the "doctrine of public trust" environmentalist groups could challenge diversions of water by the City of Los Angeles from the Mono Basin—despite the fact that the city had long ago purchased the rights to those waters, and had made extensive investments to develop them and to build aqueduct connections to the metropolis. Recent legislation has also tended to be increasingly hostile to market exchanges of water rights. Under the statutes of Colorado, for example, it is illegal to export water to other states. Colorado legislators seem to think that their citizens are too naive to exact an appropriate price from wily out-of-staters.

[a]Discussion based upon J. Hirshleifer, J. C. DeHaven, and J. W. Milliman, *Water Supply: Economics, Technology, and Policy* (Chicago: University of Chicago Press, 1960), Chapter 9.

Public Goods

A commodity is called a *public good* if its consumption by any one person does not reduce the amount available to others. Or put another way, a good is "public" if providing the good to *anyone* makes it possible, without additional cost, to provide it to *everyone*. Public goods thus represent a particular type of beneficial externality. Note that the definition does *not* require that different people get the same enjoyment from the good; people can consume identical quantities of a good without enjoying the same benefits from it.

The traditional example is the lighthouse. If one ship receives the benefit of the light signal, that in no way deprives other ships from doing so. Similarly a radio or television broadcast is available to any and all persons equipped with suitable receivers.[10]

The difference between ordinary goods (which are used *exclusively*) and public goods (which can be used *concurrently* by many people) changes the efficiency conditions. For concreteness, think of Robinson Crusoe and Friday on their island. The ordinary private

[9]The motivation is essentially the same as that of the "chiselers" in a cartel situation. But, it should be noted, absolutely unanimous cooperation is not strictly necessary for a workable degree of agreement in either the unitization or cartel contexts.

[10]Since there are *some* costs to users (stationing a lookout to watch for the lighthouse, buying a receiver for the broadcasts), the goods mentioned are not absolutely "pure" public goods. Many goods lie in the intermediate range of the spectrum between wholly private and wholly public. A stage performance, for example, is "public" to members of a given audience. But the capacity of the theater sets a limit on the number who can be concurrently served, all others being excluded.

FIGURE 15.9   Efficient Provision of Public Good   Wood W is a public good for Robinson and Friday. The social Marginal Cost $\overline{MC}$ of providing the public good is the *horizontal* sum of the individual MC curves; the social Marginal Value $\overline{MV}$ is the *vertical* sum of the individual MV curves. The efficient output of the public good is W^*. Since each individual should produce to the point where his MC is equal to the marginal social value $\overline{P}$ of the public good, Robinson should supply w_s^r and Friday w_s^f. If the value $\overline{P}$ is divided into amounts P^r and P^f to be paid by Robinson and Friday, respectively, each would demand the entire amount of the public good produced.

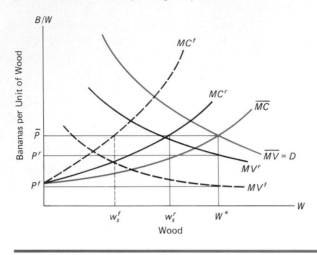

good is bananas B; the public good is wood W. (Since Robinson and Friday share living quarters, they both benefit from wood burnt for warmth.) The efficiency conditions of Equation (15.4), which apply for ordinary private goods, can be written here in the form: $MRT^r = MRT^f = MRS_c^r = MRS_c^f$ (where r stands for Robinson and f for Friday). That is, all the Marginal Rates of Substitution in production and in consumption must be equal for both individuals. In terms of marginal valuations, the conditions are $MC^r = MC^f = MV^r = MV^f$. But when one of the commodities is a public good, the conditions are different. Intuitively, efficiency requires that the Marginal Cost of *either's* production of wood equal the sum of the Marginal Valuations placed on the wood by *both*.

$$MC^r = MC^f = MV^r + MV^f \tag{15.5}$$

PROPOSITION: For a good that can be *concurrently* consumed, the efficiency conditions require that each producer's Marginal Cost equal the *sum* of the consumers' Marginal Values.

Figure 15.9 shows how these conditions may be met. Robinson's rising MC^r curve and falling MV^r (demand) curve are shown as solid, and Friday's corresponding MC^f and MV^f curves as dashed. The crucial point is that the overall or communitywide $\overline{MC}$ curve is the horizontal sum of the curves MC^r and MC^f; the overall demand or $\overline{MV}$ curve is the vertical sum of MV^r and MV^f.[11] The intersection of $\overline{MC}$ and $\overline{MV}$ determines the efficient total W^*

---

[11]In constructing the MV curves in the diagram, the "income effect" has been ruled out. Normally, MV^r, Robinson's marginal willingness to pay for additional wood, should be larger the more wood has been provided by Friday—since any such provision enriches Robinson.

of wood supplied and consumed. Of this quantity, Robinson should supply w_s^r and Friday w_s^f, as determined by the conditions that $w_s^r + w_s^f = W^*$, and that Robinson's and Friday's Marginal Costs be equal. Producers would supply in aggregate the quantity W^* if the price were $\overline{P}$.

The diagram also shows the prices that must be set in order to have Friday and Robinson each want to consume the quantity W^*. Notice that the price charged Robinson (P^r) must exceed the price charged Friday (P^f). For a public good the "price-mediating" conditions required to induce private parties to produce and consume the efficient amounts can be stated as

$$\left.\begin{array}{c} MC^r = \overline{P} \\[2mm] \text{and} \\[2mm] MC^f = \overline{P} \end{array}\right\} \qquad \left.\begin{array}{c} MV^r = P^r \\[2mm] \text{(where } \overline{P} = P^r + P^f) \\[2mm] MV^f = P^f \end{array}\right. \qquad (15.6)$$

Thus a set of prices does exist that would give correct "Invisible Hand" signals to the separate individuals. We now have to consider whether a market process could generate these prices.

A necessary condition for a price system to work at all is *excludability* of nonpayers. Sometimes this may be difficult to achieve. In our example, if Friday refused to pay he might still be able to enjoy the warmth from the wood supplied by Robinson. In the case of radio or television broadcasting the excludability problem has a technical solution: transmission can be scrambled so that only those who pay can decode the message. (Notice that excludability is a question of law and technology, not of the "publicness" or "privateness" of the good. Ordinary private goods may also, in some cases, be non-excludable. For example, the laws of a certain community might say that nonpayers can enter a restaurant and eat on equal terms with those who pay!)

Assuming excludability, two features of Equations (15.6) are of interest: (1) suppliers of the public good must receive a higher price $(\overline{P})$ than what the individual demanders pay $(P^r$ or $P^f)$ and (2) since the prices paid by demanders $(P^r$ and $P^f)$ will generally not be equal to each other, price discrimination will be required. To some extent these conditions could be met by a middleman between the primary producers and consumers. For example, a television station could buy independently produced programs at the price $\overline{P}$ and then sell them to viewers at prices P^r and P^f. And if the intermediary has monopoly power, price discrimination among consumers might be possible (see Chapter 8). But if price discrimination is not possible, the aggregate $\overline{MV}$ seen by firms will be lower than that depicted in Figure 15.9, which would elicit less than the efficient supply of the public good.

CONCLUSION: The efficiency conditions for provision of public goods require that each supplier's Marginal Cost be equal to the *sum* of all the demanders' Marginal Values. If exclusion of nonpayers is possible, a system of prices does exist that would elicit the efficient total supply and would charge enough to demanders to clear the market. But this system of prices requires price discrimination, and so could not be achieved under competition. A competitive industry would tend to undersupply a public good because competitive firms cannot price discriminate; a monopolist would tend to undersupply in order to exploit its monopoly power.

Exercise 15.2 ———

Robinson's demand for the public good is given by $MV^r = 80 - 2W = P^r$ and Friday's by $MV^f = 30 - W = P^f$. The Marginal Cost functions are $MC^r = 2 + 4w^r$ and

$MC^f = 2 + 6w^f$. (a) Find the set of prices that would lead to the efficient production and consumption quantities. (b) What would happen if discriminatory prices could not be charged?

Answer: (a) Adding the demand curves *vertically*, the aggregate $\overline{MV}$ curve is $110 - 3W = P^r + P^f = \overline{P}$. To sum the Marginal Cost curves we determine the levels of w^r and w^f at which $MC^r = \overline{P}$ and $MC^f = \overline{P}$, and find $w^r + w^f$. We have $w^r = (\overline{P} - 2)/4$ and $w^f = (\overline{P} - 2)/6$, so $w^r + w^f = 5/12(\overline{P} - 2)$. From the equations $w = 5/12(\overline{P} - 2)$ and $110 - 3w = \overline{P}$ we obtain $\overline{P} = 50, W = 20$. To clear the market, the respective prices charged the consumers are $P^r = 40$ and $P^f = 10$; these sum to $\overline{P} = 50$. The quantities produced will be $w^r = 12$ and $w^f = 8$; these sum to $W = 20$. (b) In the absence of price discrimination the effective aggregate $\overline{MV}$ curve would be just twice the height of the lower (Friday's) demand curve, so that $MC = 2MV^f = 60 - 2W = \overline{P}$. The equation for the aggregate Marginal Cost (the horizontal sum) is unchanged. Solving simultaneously leads now to the lower equilibrium price $\overline{P} = 33.64$ (approximately). P^r and P^f are half of this, or 16.82. At $\overline{P} = 33.64$ Robinson would produce about 7.91 units and Friday about 5.27; the sum is $W = 13.18$. Given that he is charged the price $P^f = 16.82$, Friday would want to consume exactly the 13.18 units of W produced. Robinson would want to consume even more, but would of course be unable to do so. Evidently, less than the efficient quantity of the public good is produced in the absence of price discrimination.

Voluntary Provision of Public Goods

Even if exclusion of nonpayers is impossible, to some extent public goods may be supplied by self-interested individuals on a strictly voluntary basis to meet their own needs. The amount of the public good voluntarily offered would of course be less than if it were possible to exclude nonpayers: no one wants to incur private costs in producing a public good; everyone wants to free-ride, to let others pick up the tab. Then, the question is, under what circumstances and to what extent will individuals supply any of the public good at all?

Two important propositions will be demonstrated here.

PROPOSITION 1: Wealthy individuals tend to provide *disproportionately* more of the public good.

PROPOSITION 2: As community size increases, provision of the public good will grow, but much less than in proportion to population size.

Why would a self-interested individual ever voluntarily supply any of a public good without payment? Two factors are involved: (1) the individual wants to provide some for his *own* consumption and (2) as others supply him with "free" amounts of the public good he becomes in effect wealthier, which tends to make him want even more of the public good.

Let us return to Robinson Crusoe who chooses between a private good B (bananas) and a public good W (wood) also enjoyed by Friday. Figure 15.10 shows Robinson's initial endowment position at E^o; he has $\bar{b}$ bananas and none of the public good. His Production-Possibility Curve is $E^o K^o$. Evidently, if he were alone on the island the productive-consumptive solution would be R^o, where he provides himself with w_r^o logs of wood. For the sake of the argument, imagine that Friday provides (solely in consideration of his private benefit) the number of logs equal to the vertical distance between E^o and E'. Robinson is then richer by that amount; in effect, his endowment shifts upward from E^o to E'. Since Robinson's productive opportunities are unaffected, his Production-Possibility Curve also shifts upward to become $E'K'$. His new optimum is R'. Since (as we normally assume) both bananas and wood are superior goods for him, Robinson will end up consuming more of both.

FIGURE 15.10   Choice Between Private and Public Good   In Friday's absence, Robinson's endowment is $E°$, where he has zero of the public good W, and the amount $\bar{b}$ of the private good B. His Production-Possibility Curve is $E°K°$, and his productive-consumptive optimum is $R°$. If Friday provides any W, Robinson's endowment position shifts upward by the same amount. As a function of Friday's provision, Robinson's optimum positions trace out an Income Expansion Path *IEP*. If B and W are both normal goods for him, Robinson's IEP curve will have a positive slope, becoming vertical when the limiting quantity $\bar{b}$ is reached.

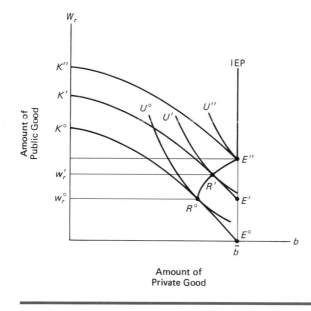

However, and this is a crucial point, Robinson can free-ride on Friday's production, and so Robinson can now consume more wood while producing less, and in fact he will want to do exactly that. Being in effect richer owing to Friday's contribution, he will normally want to consume both more wood and more bananas. But without reducing his own production of the public good, wood, he could not provide himself with any more of the private good, bananas.

As we consider all possible amounts that Friday might supply, Robinson's optimum solutions trace out an Income Expansion Path that includes points $R°$, R', and E'' in the diagram. Eventually, when the amount of wood Friday provides is equivalent to the distance $E'' - E°$, Robinson's Income Expansion Path hits the barrier formed by the vertical line through $\bar{b}$. Beyond this point Friday provides the public good so amply that Robinson would really like to trade wood for bananas, but of course that is impossible.

Using the data summarized by the Income Expansion Path, we can construct in Figure 15.11 Robinson's *Reaction Curve RC_r;* this shows how much of the public good (wood) he provides for each quantity of wood Friday provides. (Compare the duopolists' Reaction Curves in Chapter 10.) Note that RC_r is flatter than the dashed line of slope -1. This indicates that, as Friday produces an additional log of wood, Robinson cuts back his own production but *by less than one unit*. Friday's Reaction Curve RC_f, by similar reasoning, is steeper than the line of slope -1 (due to the reversal of the axes).

The *Cournot solution* (see Chapter 10) is point Q^* at the intersection of the two Reaction Curves. Here each person is satisfied with his own production decision, given the decision

FIGURE 15.11 **Cournot Solution for Supply of Public Good** Robinson's Reaction Curve RC_r shows the quantity of the public good W that he will produce for any given amount provided by Friday. Similarly, RC_f is Friday's Reaction Curve. The intersection Q^* shows Robinson's and Friday's production quantities for the public good, w_r^q and w_f^q. The consumption quantities are the same for each, being the sum $W_r^c = W_f^c = w_r^q + w_f^q$, shown geometrically as the intercepts along the axes of the line through Q^* with slope -1.

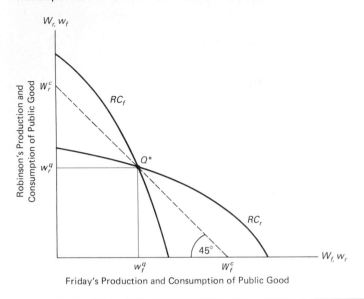

made by the other. The location of Q^* determines the amounts of wood produced by Robinson and Friday. What are the *consumption* quantities? Each individual consumes the total wood produced, $w_r^q + w_f^q$. The consumption quantities W_r^c and W_f^c, which are necessarily equal to each other, are shown geometrically by the intercepts at the axes of the dashed line drawn through Q^*.

Let us now consider Proposition 1 above. As Robinson becomes wealthier he has more resources and so a bigger endowment of bananas in Figure 15.10. Then R^o would shift up and to the right, so Robinson would produce more wood just for his own use. But this would provide Friday with even more of a "free" gift of the public good, wood, so Friday would produce less. In Figure 15.11, if Robinson's Reaction Curve RC_r shifts upward, Q^* shifts to the left and Friday produces less wood. Thus a richer individual will provide *disproportionately* more of the public good.

Exercise 15.3

Suppose Robinson's preferences lead to an Income Expansion Path in the region before the vertical barrier is reached in Figure 15.10 given by the equation $W_r^c = 2b_r$. The equation for his Production-Possibility Curve is $W_r^c + b_r = \bar{b}^r + w_f^q$. (This equation would correspond to a straight-line Production-Possibility Curve in Figure 15.10; notice that it shifts upward as Friday's production w_f^q increases.) Friday is identical to Robinson except for different endowments: $\bar{b}_r = 1800$ while $\bar{b}_f = 900$. Find: (a) the Reaction Curves, (b) the amounts of the public good produced by each, and (c) the consumptive solution.

Answer: (a) Substituting Robinson's Income Expansion Path into his Production Possibility Curve yields $W_r^c + 1/2(W_r^c) = 1800 + w_r^q$, or $W_r^c = 1200 + 2/3(w_r^q)$. But $W_r^c = w_r^q + w_f^q$, and so $w_f^q = 1200 - 1/3(w_r^q)$. This is the equation for Robinson's Reaction Curve. (Notice that Robinson cuts back his production of W by one-third of a unit for each additional unit provided by Friday.) Similarly, Friday's Reaction Curve is $w_r^q = 600 - w_f^q/3$. (b) Solving the Reaction Curve equations simultaneously leads to the results $w_r^q = 1125$ and $w_f^q = 225$. (Thus, as contended in Proposition 1, Robinson provides a disproportionately larger amount of the public good.) (c) The reader should verify that *both* Robinson and Friday consume 1350 of W and 675 of B.

EXAMPLE 15.6 The Economics of Alliance

An *alliance* between independent countries is generally undertaken in the interests of mutual defense. But defense is a kind of public good for allied nations. If your ally destroys an enemy's bombers, that action reduces the threat to your nation as well. So each ally is tempted to free-ride on the efforts of the others. However, the larger nations cannot free-ride to nearly the same degree as the smaller ones.

A study of the North Atlantic Treaty Organization (NATO) defense expenditures in 1964 verified the differential expenditures of larger and smaller participants. The table compares the rankings of NATO nations by their GNP and by the proportion of budget devoted to defense expenditures. The larger and wealthier nations evidently contributed proportionately more. (The most conspicuous exception, Portugal, is explainable on other grounds. That nation, while small in GNP, had large military expenditures in its African colonies.)

NATO Statistics

	GNP, 1964		Defense Budget as Percentage of GNP	
	$ Billion	Rank	Percent	Rank
United States	569.03	1	9.0	1
Germany	88.87	2	5.5	6
United Kingdom	79.46	3	7.0	3
France	73.40	4	6.7	4
Italy	43.63	5	4.1	10
Canada	38.14	6	4.4	8
Netherlands	15.00	7	4.9	7
Belgium	13.43	8	3.7	12
Denmark	7.73	9	3.3	13
Turkey	6.69	10	5.8	5
Norway	5.64	11	3.9	11
Greece	4.31	12	4.2	9
Portugal	2.88	13	7.7	2
Luxembourg	0.53	14	1.7	14

Source: M. Olson, Jr., and R. Zeckhauser, "An Economic Theory of Alliances," Rand Corp. Memorandum RM-4297-IDA (October 1966), p. 26.

Let us turn now to Proposition 2. An intuitive explanation is as follows. Suppose a third person, call her Saturday, joins Robinson and Friday. Robinson's Reaction Curve RC_r in Figure 15.11 is unchanged, since it can be thought to represent his reaction to the *combined* production of Friday and Saturday scaled on the horizontal axis. Friday and Saturday's combined production would surely always be greater than Friday would have produced alone (since Friday will cut back by less than 1:1 in response to any additional units of the public good that Saturday provides). Consequently, the combined Friday plus Saturday Reaction Curve lies further to the right than the previous Reaction Curve RC_f in the diagram; the intersection point Q^* must move down and to the right. Thus, although *total* provision of the public good will increase with community size, as new members enter each of the original citizens will somewhat scale back his or her own individual production.

A third proposition follows directly from the preceding analysis.

PROPOSITION 3: As community size increases, although production rises there will be *increasing underprovision* (shortfall of production of the public good in comparison with the Pareto-efficient amount).

The condition of efficiency for a community of two individuals was derived earlier.

$$MC_r = MC_f = MV_r + MV_f \qquad (15.5)$$

That is, each individual should produce to the point where his or her Marginal Cost equals the *sum* of the Marginal Valuations. As the number of individuals forming the community grows, the sum on the right grows accordingly. Consequently, to achieve efficiency each and every producer should increase his production of the public good. But, we have just seen, each individual producer would in fact cut back production. Hence the shortfall increases, and indeed at an increasing rate, as community size grows.

Exercise 15.4 ———————————————————————————————

Starting with the community of the previous exercise, imagine that the new arrival, Saturday, has exactly the same preferences and endowment as Friday. Compare with the previous result.

Answer: All three individuals have the same Income Expansion Path $W_i^c = 2b_i$ as before. Their Production Possibility Curves now become

$$\text{(Robinson)} \quad W_r^c + b_r = 1800 + w_f^q + w_s^q$$
$$\text{(Friday)} \quad W_f^c + b_f = 900 + w_r^q + w_s^q$$
$$\text{(Saturday)} \quad W_s^c + b_s = 900 + w_r^q + w_f^q$$

Substituting from the respective Income Expansion Path equations

$$W_r^c = 1200 + 2/3(w_f^q + w_s^q)$$
$$W_f^c = 600 + 2/3(w_r^q + w_s^q)$$
$$W_s^c = 600 + 2/3(w_r^q + w_f^q)$$

Since all the consumed quantities on the left of these equations must equal each other and equal the *sum* of the three produced quantities, we obtain:

$$W_r^q = 1200 - 1/3(w_f^q + w_s^q)$$

$$W_f^q = 600 - 1/3(w_r^q + w_s^q)$$

$$W_s^q = 600 - 1/3(w_r^q + w_f^q)$$

These can be solved simultaneously to yield the produced amounts of the public good

$$w_r^q = 1080, \ w_f^q = 180, \ w_s^q = 180$$

The total of W produced is 1440. This is only a little larger than the previous two-person total of 1350 units, since both Robinson and Friday cut back in response to Saturday's production. All three individuals now consume 1440 of W and 720 of B.

To some extent, therefore, public goods can be provided without either markets or government. NATO may perform adequately, for example, even if no super-government coerces its members. But, we have seen, there will be a very considerable shortfall from the ideal, increasingly so as community size grows. So, the larger the population, the stronger the case for coercive government provision of the public good. That is, the government would provide the good and impose the corresponding taxes on citizens.

Some welfare theorists claim that the difficulty of privately supplying public goods dictates that they be "publicly" (i.e., governmentally) provided instead. Indeed, some have thought that the concept of public goods determines the proper scope of government: "private goods" ought to be privately supplied, and "public goods" ought to be publicly supplied. But in fact we do observe private firms supplying public goods. Television broadcasting is the obvious example, but even lighthouse services have at times been privately provided. And on the other hand government agencies, while supplying public goods like national defense, also produce a vast range of private goods. Among the many examples are electric power (TVA), irrigation water (the U.S. Bureau of Reclamation), insurance (Social Security), education (public schools), and postal services (the U.S. Postal Service).

Public Goods and Game Theory

The previous section assumed that the amount of the public good made available is the *sum* of the amounts provided by the separate individuals. In some cases, however, a public good will be provided only if everyone supplies some *minimum* amount (the "weakest link" case) or the level of the public good may depend on the *highest* amount supplied (the "best shot" case). The weakest-link case can arise in the defense of a fortification, where the enemy will break through if any post is not properly defended. The best-shot case can arise in a technological innovation, where the best invention will be adopted. These different situations lead to different results about the free-rider problem.

To illustrate these different cases, let us start with the standard Prisoners' Dilemma situation. Suppose either or both of two individuals may each contribute the amount $a = 3$ or else $a = 0$ to providing a public good that both will enjoy. If only one of them contributes each will receive a benefit $b = 2$. If both contribute, the benefit to each is $b = 4$. These assumptions resemble those made in the previous section. The choices for each individual are to Contribute or Not Contribute. For example, if Row contributes ($a = 3$) and Column does not ($a = 0$), then $b = 2$. Row gets a payoff of $2 - 3 = -1$; Column gets a payoff of $2 - 0 = 2$. (These payoffs are shown in the upper-right cell in Table 15.1 below; the first entry in each cell is the payoff to Row, and the second entry is the payoff to Column.) It is straightforward to verify that the Nash equilibrium here is for both to Not Contribute, which is the Prisoners' Dilemma result. Furthermore, this is the equilibrium whether the parties move simultaneously or in sequence.

TABLE 15.1   Standard Public Good Case (Prisoners' Dilemma)

		COLUMN PLAYER	
		Contribute	Do Not Contribute
ROW PLAYER	Contribute	1,1	−1,2
	Do Not Contribute	2,−1	0,0

Suppose instead that a benefit of $b = 2$ will be received by each if and only if *both* contribute, at a cost of $a = 1$ each. The benefit is zero if either or both do Not Contribute. Now we have the *weakest-link* case, with the revised payoff matrix shown in Table 15.2. Here there are two Nash equilibria under simultaneous play: either both contribute, or else neither does. However, the Pareto-preferred outcome (1,1) is sure to emerge under sequential play. If, for example, Column moves first, then he will do best by choosing to Contribute, since he knows that Row will also choose to Contribute, and Column will have a payoff of 1. If, instead, Column chose to Not Contribute, then neither would Row, and Column would have a payoff of 0. Thus, if either Column or Row goes first, the public good will be provided, and the free-rider problem does not appear.

TABLE 15.2   Weakest-Link Public Good

		COLUMN PLAYER	
		Contribute	Do Not Contribute
ROW PLAYER	Contribute	1,1	−1,0
	Do Not Contribute	0,−1	0,0

In the *Best-shot* case (shown in Table 15.3) each receives the benefit whenever *either* (rather than *both*) contribute. We assume as before that the cost is $a = 1$. The benefit is $b = 2$ if either contribute, and $b = 0$ if neither contribute.

Here there exist two equilibria in the sequential-play game: Row Contributes and Column does not, or Column Contributes and Row does not. Once again, with sequential play there will be an efficient outcome in which the first-mover has payoff 2 and the second-mover has payoff 1. Note here that the first-mover does not contribute, thereby inducing the second-mover to do so.

TABLE 15.3 Best-Shot Public Good

		COLUMN PLAYER	
		Contribute	Do Not Contribute
ROW PLAYER	Contribute	1,1	1,2
	Do Not Contribute	2,1	0,0

15.4 APPROPRIATIVE ACTIVITY OR RENT-SEEKING

Coase's Theorem asserts that market trading will always lead to an efficient outcome—provided, among other things, that property rights are "well defined." What does this condition mean, and what happens when property rights are not "well defined?"

Property rights can be said to be well defined if (1) all resources are appropriated (belong legally to someone), and (2) property rights are perfectly and costlessly enforced.

Consider the second condition. If property rights are not perfectly enforced, then it may become more profitable to steal rather than work. In fact, even without doing anything illegal some people may succeed in taking others' property—for example, by instituting groundless lawsuits or by inducing legislators to change the law in their favor. And on the other side, the present owners of property may respond with defensive measures: patrolling to prevent theft or invasion, hiring expensive lawyers to fight lawsuits, lobbying against new legislation, and so forth. All such proceedings, both offensive or defensive, come under the heading of *appropriative activity*—efforts to impose or to prevent involuntary changes in the ownership of property. (In the special context where individuals or firms compete to acquire legal privileges like licenses or franchises from government, appropriative activity is called *rent-seeking*.) Of course, appropriative efforts are not costless. They absorb resources that could have been devoted to production and exchange instead.

A dramatic historical instance of appropriative activity was the Oklahoma land rush of 1889. When the settlers raced to stake out former Indian territories, the resources devoted to "rushing" to gain possession ahead of others were an efficiency loss.[12] Some of the externality problems discussed earlier in this chapter are also associated with attempts to gain control of unappropriated resources: overpumping of oil occurs because the petroleum is no one's property until brought to the surface. Settling new territories or pumping oil are productive actions in and of themselves; the inefficiency arises from the extra costs of rushing to act before others do.

The efficiency loss due to appropriative activity, it is important to emphasize, is not a consequence of the *existence* of property rights under law. It is a consequence of *imperfections* in their assignment or enforcement. A totally lawless society would not avoid appropriative activity; on the contrary, under anarchy the struggle to acquire and defend control over resources would become everyone's main occupation.

The race to acquire unowned resources has been called *preclusive competition*. Figure

---

[12]The famous Oklahoma "Sooners" were those who cheated by beating the starting gun.

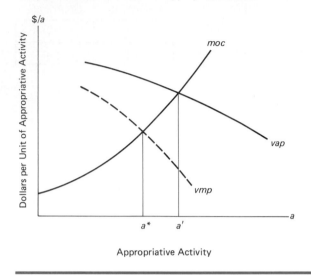

FIGURE 15.12 **Appropriative Activity and Preclusive Competition** The efficient level of appropriative activity for any individual is a^*, where his Marginal Opportunity Cost *moc* equals his Value of the Marginal Product *vmp*. However, if the resource is unowned (like fish in the ocean), the individual will want to set his *moc* equal to the Value of the Average Product *vap* at activity level $a' > a^*$. Thus, preclusive competition leads to excessive appropriative effort.

15.12 illustrates both the efficient level of effort in the attempt to acquire such resources and the extent of inefficient "rushing" that can be anticipated.

For concreteness, think of a community of identical fishermen. If no property rights exist in fish until they are caught, there will be preclusive competition. The typical individual will determine his privately optimal amount of appropriative (fishing) effort, *a,* by balancing the cost and the benefit. The upward-sloping *moc* curve in the diagram is the individual's *Marginal Opportunity Cost* of resources devoted to appropriative effort. This cost is the sacrifice of alternative uses of the resource used up in "rushing." The benefits of appropriative activity are shown by the familiar *Value of the Average Product (vap)* and *Value of the Marginal Product (vmp)* curves.

The efficient level of appropriative activity is a^*, where Marginal Opportunity Cost *(moc)* equals Value of the Marginal Product *(vmp)*. But the crucial point is that in the absence of preassigned property rights the individual would engage in a' of appropriative effort, to the point where *moc* equals the Value of the Average Product *vap*. From his last unit of effort (last hour of fishing) he will do just as well as any other identical fisherman and thus can capture the *Average* Product f/a of hours devoted to fishing. This is greater than the additional catch due to his last unit of effort, which is only his *Marginal* Product $\Delta f/\Delta a$. He can take home more than his true Marginal Product because his fishing effort will haul in not only "new" fish but also fish that would otherwise have been taken by other fishermen anyway.[13]

---

[13]What we have here is a kind of "congestion externality."

An isolated village surrounded by wilderness contains a cultivated banana grove. Bananas *(B)* are the only consumption good; the number of villagers working in the grove is L_g. The grove produces bananas according to the production function $B_g = 12L_g - L_g^2$. Bananas also grow in the wilderness where the production function is $B_w = 2L_w$. The village has 12 identical workers; none of them desires leisure and no other resources or products need be considered. (a) As a benevolent dictator, how would you divide the 12 laborers between grove and wilderness to maximize banana output? (b) Compare the results if the grove were instead "unowned" property, so that any villager can enter and pick what he pleases. (c) What property rights could be assigned to achieve efficiency without a centralized dictatorship?

Answer: (a) Take bananas as the *numeraire* so that $P_B \equiv 1$. Then the Marginal Product is also the Value of the Marginal Product of labor in the grove. This can be found by calculus or by plotting to be $vmp_g = 12 - 2L_g$. The Marginal Opportunity Cost here is the constant return to labor in the wilderness, or $moc = 2$. The benevolent dictator would set $moc = vmp_g$, or $2 = 12 - 2L_g$. The result is the efficient assignment $L_g = 5$ and $L_w = 7$. The banana outputs are $B_g = 35$ and $B_w = 14$, or a total of 49. (b) If the grove is unowned, the villagers will allocate their labor so that average products in the grove and the wilderness are equal. Thus, in equilibrium $(12L_g - L_g^2)/L_g = 2$; there will be 10 workers in the grove and only 2 in the wilderness. The Total Product will be 24, which is the same as if the grove did not exist at all! (c) Each villager could be assigned one-twelfth of the grove as his own to work (or to rent out to others).

Preclusive competition is one type of appropriative activity; rent-seeking is another. The analysis is very similar. Let us suppose that the bureaucracy in a certain community periodically assigns a fixed number of taxicab licenses to drivers. Depending on the detailed arrangements, drivers might compete for the licenses by demonstrating their skills and high character in a public hearing, by hiring accountants or economists to prepare written documented proposals, or even by making private under-the-table payments. As before, each driver will engage in appropriative effort up to the point where his Marginal Opportunity Cost equals the Value of the Average Product.

Rent-seeking differs from the more general case of appropriative activity in that, by definition, there is no true social product from rent-seeking. Regardless of the resources expended in seeking taxicab licenses, there will be the same number of cabs on the streets. (However, if the selection process does find *better-quality* drivers, there could be a social gain.) Notice that if the taxicab licenses were simply auctioned to the highest bidders there would be no waste of resources. The amounts paid to acquire a license would just redistribute wealth between the drivers and the community treasury. If the licenses were auctioned to those willing to pay the highest bribes, there would again be no efficiency loss; only this time the distributive transfers would go to some official personally rather than to the public treasury.

EXAMPLE 15.7 **Rent-Seeking in India**

In nations with pervasive government controls, the overall fraction of national income dissipated by rent-seeking may be very large. In a study of the Indian economy, Sharif Mohammad and John Whalley classified rent-seeking activities under four major headings: those associated with import and export quotas and privileges, with capital market subsidies and controls, with price controls in product markets, and finally with labor markets. Overall, they estimated that rent-seeking losses amounted to the remarkable total of between 30 percent and 45 percent of India's GNP in 1980 and 1981—needless to say, a heavy burden for such a poor nation. Their conclusions are summarized in the table.

Cost of Rent-Seeking in India, 1980–81

Category	Percentage of GNP
Import licenses and export incentives	3.8
Capital market controls	8.2–16.3
Product market controls	16.3–20.2
Labor market controls	2.9
Total	29.9–43.2

Source: Sharif Mohammad and John Whalley, "Rent Seeking in India: Its Costs and Policy Significance," *Kyklos*, v. 37 (1984).

An individual or firm awarded a license to import a good into India, for example, is in a position to buy the commodity at its low world price in international commerce and then resell it (perhaps after some processing) at its high domestic price in the protected Indian economy. Mohammad and Whalley found this premium to be typically about 100 percent of the world price. Needless to say, import licenses are avidly sought. Similarly, firms struggle to obtain tax exemptions and freight concessions that the government grants to approved exporters.

Similar considerations are involved in other important areas of rent-seeking, in India and elsewhere. Licenses may be required for making major investments or for obtaining subsidized credit; price-controlled commodities may be rationed to approved users under a variety of bureaucratic arrangements. One interesting example is the award of high-paid jobs in the government bureaucracy. Here rent-seeking may take the form of acquiring excessive credentials (overinvestment in education) beyond those required for the job.

15.5 WELFARE ECONOMICS: CONCLUSION

Welfare economics is mainly concerned with the problem of *efficiency*—that is, how to reach the Social-Opportunity Curve (as shown, for example, by the curve LL' in Figure 15.2). Any such allocation is efficient, in the sense that there exists no other allocation that is Pareto-preferred to it.

Achievement of efficiency, however, is neither a necessary nor a sufficient criterion for an ideal social policy. The *distribution* of income among individuals and social classes is another important criterion. Even granting the appropriateness of a certain tilt toward distributive *equality*, the question remains how far to go in sacrificing efficiency. And there are, of course, other criteria to be considered: liberty to retain and use lawfully acquired talents or property, community versus individualistic values, and other nonutilitarian considerations.

An older generation of economists tended to think of economic policy as a shotgun with two barrels. The first barrel was a tendency to favor free trade and *laissez faire*, due to the efficiency advantages of a market economy guided by the Invisible Hand. The second barrel was a countervailing tendency to favor government intervention and regulation where needed to remedy recognized imperfections and failures of the market economy, as described in "What Can Go Wrong? Almost Everything!" Neither barrel of the shotgun quite hits the target. Suppose the Invisible Hand worked perfectly. Even so, the efficient allocations of goods and resources thereby achieved by the market economy could violate other desirable ends of public policy, such as distributive equity or preservation of community values. On the other hand, when it comes to remedying the flaws of the market system, we must guard against what has been called "the Nirvana fallacy": the presumption that government intervention will in actual practice improve matters. One must not forget that governments have flaws of their own.

This last point indicates the need for an economic approach to political or governmental decisionmaking. Economists have indeed, though only very recently, turned to serious *positive* analysis of government—that is, to examining the economic consequences of what government *actually* does as opposed to what in some ideal sense it "ought" to do. This will be the topic of the following chapter.

SUMMARY

While there are many possible goals of policy, economists usually concentrate on only two: efficiency and distributive equity. Efficiency is increased by making any change that is Pareto-preferred—that is, that increases the utility of some person or persons without decreasing the utility of any other. An outcome is said to be efficient or Pareto-optimal when there are no other outcomes Pareto-preferred to it. (However, it is not true that an efficient outcome is Pareto-preferred to *every* outcome that is not efficient.) What is regarded as distributive equity may involve a number of norms. Among the most significant are *equality* and *ownership* (that is, the right to retain lawfully held property).

The Theorem of the Invisible Hand states that, under ideal conditions, a *laissez-faire* economy efficiently uses resources. As people respond to prices, efficiency will be attained among producers, among consumers, and in the exchange of goods between consumers and producers.

However, the Invisible Hand may fail to bring about efficiency, to a greater or lesser extent, for several reasons: (1) monopolies of many types exist, all leading to inefficient outcomes if operated for private gain; (2) disequilibrium prices do not give the correct signals to buyers and sellers; and (3) if existing property rights allow some agents to impose direct externalities on others, incentives are distorted. Coase's theorem indicates that there are always market forces at work to overcome inefficiencies. For example, property-owners are motivated to exchange property rights in order to eliminate inefficient externalities. However, this process will be hampered if property rights are poorly defined or if agreements are costly to negotiate and enforce.

Public goods represent a special type of externality: when a public good is provided for one person, there is no additional cost in providing it to others. If a public good is or can be made excludable in the market, it can be privately provided. A pattern of discriminatory prices can achieve efficiency in the private production and use of *excludable* public goods, but in practice such goods are likely to be undersupplied in the market. If a public good is nonexcludable, on the other hand, it can scarcely be provided by the market at all. (But neither could a nonexcludable *private* good.) Finally, where property rights are not well defined, individuals will be motivated to undertake socially wasteful appropriative or "rent-seeking" activities aimed at changing the effective structure of rights (or aimed at preventing such changes).

QUESTIONS

For Review

  1. Explain and justify the normally "concave" shape of the Social-Opportunity Curve in income terms (Figure 15.1). What can be said about the shape of the Social-Opportunity Curve in utility terms (Figure 15.2)?

 *2. Show how a Social-Opportunity Curve in utility terms for two individuals may be derived from the *Contract Curve* in the Edgeworth box diagram of Chapter 13.

 *3. a. What meaning, if any, can be given to the concept of a "social optimum"?
     b. How valid is efficiency or Pareto-optimality as a criterion of social optimality?

  4. Why is it true that in equilibrium all consumers have the same Marginal Rates of Substitution in Consumption purchased even though they differ in tastes and incomes?

  5. What is the Theorem of the Invisible Hand?

  6. What are the conditions of efficiency and are they reached in a free-market economy? Can the conditions be achieved, in principle, without use of the market?

  7. Why does disequilibrium of markets lead to inefficiency?

 *8. a. Explain why a monopolist in the product market is said to hire "too little" of the factors it uses for production.
     b. Does it follow that too large a proportion of the community's resources are employed by competitive firms?

  9. What are public goods? What are externalities? Is a public good a special case of an externality?

 10. How would inability to exclude nonpayers affect the private supply of public goods? the private supply of private goods?

 *11. a. Under what circumstances does the "free rider" problem emerge?
      b. How valid is the assertion that all government is fundamentally a response to the free rider problem?

 *12. a. What is the efficiency condition for optimal provision of a public good?
      b. In the case of public goods why do we sum individual demand curves *vertically*, whereas for private goods we sum *horizontally?*

 *13. Mosquito control at the local level is an example of a pure public good. Suppose that in an economy consisting of two identical persons, each has the following Marginal Value function for mosquito control: $MV = 100 - y$, where y is the quantity of mosquito control. Let the Marginal Cost of mosquito control be $10. What is the socially optimal level of control?

 *14. a. What limits the possibility of private supply of public goods?
      b. Will public provision mean that a more nearly optimal amount will be supplied?

 15. What is Coase's Theorem? Explain the relevance of each of the following conditions for the actual empirical applicability of the theorem:
     a. well-defined property rights.
     b. low costs of negotiating and enforcing agreements.

---

 *The answers to starred questions appear at the end of the book.

16. What is "appropriative activity"? What is "rent-seeking"? What is "preclusive competition"? What are the implications of such activities for economic efficiency?

For Further Thought and Discussion

*1. Analyze the following fragment of a conversation based upon Robert Browning's poem, "My Last Duchess":

> But my dear Dr. H., your own textbook proves that in terms of economic efficiency I was amply justified in taking the life of my last duchess. For, being of not inconsiderable means, I was willing to pay more for her death than she could have afforded to pay to prevent it.

In terms of economic efficiency, was the Duke justified in murdering his wife?

*2. "An efficient allocation of resources maximizes the dollar value of national income." True or false? Explain.

3. In the apples-bees example in the text, the externality is mutually beneficial. Provide an example of a reciprocal relation in which the mutually imposed externalities are harmful. Can there be a case in which in one direction the effect is beneficial but in the other direction harmful?

*4. What sorts of real-world considerations may forestall the working of Coase's Theorem by making property rights ambiguous or uncertain? by raising the costs of negotiating and enforcing contracts?

*5. "An ideal market would achieve a Pareto-efficient outcome, but only one that is Pareto-preferred to the endowment situation; an ideal dictatorship would not be so limited." True or false? Explain.

*6. Steps have been taken in the United States to ban the commercial market in human blood. (One of the arguments given was that commercially provided blood is more likely to be infected with hepatitis than volunteered blood.) Can this ban be justified on efficiency grounds, or any other grounds?

*7. One "market intervention" is the law against polygamy. Historically, many societies have permitted polygyny (multiple wives) and some even polyandry (multiple husbands). It has been contended that the laws banning polygyny work to the *disadvantage* of women as suppliers of wife-services, just as a law forbidding more than one car per customer would be disadvantageous to suppliers of automobiles.
   a. Is this sound?
   b. Who are the main losers and main gainers from monogamy laws?
   c. Can the monogamy laws be defended in terms of efficiency?
   d. Can the same laws be defended in terms of equality?

*8. a. How is it that public goods can sometimes be provided voluntarily, with no market compensation at all?
   b. If a market were feasible would more of the public good be provided with or without a market? Explain.

EXAMPLES

I n 1986 expenditures of local, state, and federal governments in the United States totalled 36 percent of GNP. In a number of other countries these proportions are even higher: about 40 percent in Great Britain and 53 percent in Sweden. So for an overall picture of the economy we must analyze not only how people behave and interact in their market roles as buyers and sellers, but also in their political roles as citizens (demanders of government services) and public officials (suppliers of government services).

Market transactions are voluntary. One person consents to sell and the other consents to buy. But politics largely concerns *involuntary* transactions. A government agency might provide a service like a public road, but some of those taxed to pay for the road may derive no benefit from it, or may even be adversely affected. Governments exercise far more drastic measures when they define certain behaviors as crimes punishable by fines, imprisonment, or death. Or, a government may make war against its enemies, possibly drafting unwilling citizens as soldiers.

Some philosophers contend that while people behave selfishly in the marketplace, they will act in the public interest when it comes to politics. That view is rejected here. Market decisions and political choices are made by the same people, with the same motives. And specifically, we will assume that people are about equally self-interested in both spheres. To explain observed differences between market behavior and political behavior we look not to differences in motives but to differences in the rules of the game.

This chapter first analyzes a hypothetical *public-choice state*. In such a state the government is a creation of citizen-consumers who have voluntarily banded together to provide themselves with certain goods and services—national defense or public roads, for example— that are more effectively secured through a collective-choice arrangement than through markets. The power to vote, like the power to purchase in markets, gives each individual some influence over the final outcome. Just as the market system has its failures and inadequacies, the public-choice state will also only imperfectly achieve individuals' desires. The chapter will analyze some of these imperfections. Perhaps even more important is that a cooperative mechanism like the public-choice state is a very idealized model of how government works. There is also the *coercive* state to consider. In fact, violence and coercion are always close to the heart of politics. Later in the chapter these issues will be taken up under the heading of "Political Conflict."

16.1 THE PUBLIC-CHOICE STATE AND ITS IMPERFECTIONS

Think of political parties as akin to business firms. Just as firms offer goods to consumers at a price, political parties offer packages of government policies, at certain costs in the form of taxes and other burdens, to the citizens. Politicians try to make a "profit" (which might, in some degree, represent satisfactions like power or glory apart from money) by providing citizens with what they want.

Ideal free enterprise in the economy corresponds to ideal democracy in the polity.[1] The forces that push businesspeople to satisfy the desires of consumers are the same forces that push politicians to satisfy the desires of citizens—the pressures of competition. In the ideal market economy, perfect competition among firms drives profits to zero in long-run equi-

---

[1] See Gary S. Becker, "Competition and Democracy," *Journal of Law and Economics,* v. 1 (October 1958).

librium (as discussed in Chapter 7). Then firms have no power to do anything other than what consumers want, since any firm that fails to satisfy consumers will be driven out of business by other firms. In the ideal polity, perfect competition among politicians similarly drives political "profit" to zero. Parties or elected officials would have no power to do anything other than what citizens want, since failing to satisfy the citizens means being voted out of office. Thus, Adam Smith's Invisible Hand—the force that induces individuals, in their own self-interest, to satisfy the needs of others—operates to some degree in the political arena as well as in the market economy.

The preceding chapter analyzed certain imperfections of real-world market systems (monopoly, disequilibrium, externalities, and so on). But, viewed as ways whereby citizen-consumers attempt to achieve their desires, political mechanisms also have important short-comings.

Political Competition

Just as ideal democracy in the polity corresponds to perfect competition in the market, political dictatorship corresponds to monopoly in the market. But political dictatorship is a more drastic matter than market monopoly. Customers can often avoid doing business with a market monopolist who overcharges, but citizens cannot easily escape an oppressive government. Furthermore, the market monopolist wants only our money while the political dictator may want our very lives. Yet even the most absolute dictator faces competition. Possible conquest from outside, or revolution from within, limits a dictator's power.

Democratic political systems are characterized by relatively free entry into the contest for political power. But there appear to be strong economies of scale in the political process. As a result, democratic nations may have only two (or at any rate a very few) effective political parties. So democratic political competition is closer to oligopoly (Chapter 10) than to perfect competition. Furthermore, rare exceptions apart, citizens do not vote directly on policies. They vote only for delegates in the legislative, judicial, and executive branches of government; these delegates supposedly represent the citizens in making policy choices. But elections of delegates are relatively infrequent. Whereas consumers make and reconsider market choices every single day, citizens can choose or recall their political representatives only at election intervals measured in years. And some of the most important political decisionmakers, such as U.S. Supreme Court Justices, are only indirectly "elected" and once chosen are beyond effective recall.

The limited options available further weaken control of delegates by citizens. Many issues are "bundled" together in the election process. A voter may prefer the position of one candidate on one question, of a competing candidate on a second issue, and so forth. But the delegate elected will represent (or misrepresent) the voter in *all* decisions to be made during his or her term of office.

So even in a highly democratic system delegates may have considerable leeway to violate the preferences of their constituents and to pursue their own interests. The clearest evidence of this is the large sums candidates and parties are willing to spend in seeking political office. U.S. Senate and House candidates, for example, were reported by the Federal Elections Commission to have spent about $450 million seeking congressional seats in the 1986 election. And this figure does not include the value of volunteer efforts by sympathizers and party workers, of free publicity from newspapers and other media, of propaganda put out by unions and businesses hoping to win favors, and so on.

EXAMPLE 16.1 **Shirking by Legislators**

An elected legislator may misrepresent constituents by failing to show up and vote when issues come up for decision. Constituents can punish such shirking legislators by not re-electing them, but this type of control will be less effective for those legislators not running for reelection anyway (who are retiring).

John R. Lott, Jr. studied the voting participation rates of retiring and nonretiring members of the 95th U.S. Congress. Some of his results are shown in the following table. As can be seen, retiring members of Congress voted noticeably less often. This remained the case even when an adjustment was made for illness as a possible cause of retirement.

Voting Participation Rates

	Those Retiring	Those Not Retiring
All Congressmen	79.72%	89.36%
Congressmen Not Ill	84.57	89.64

Source: John R. Lott, Jr., "Attendance Rates, Political Shirking, and the Effect of Post-Elective Office Employment," *Economic Inquiry,* v. 28 (January 1990).

Lott also asked whether party leaders could control shirking by offering post-elective political employment to the legislator or to his children. While the evidence was not con-clusive, that factor did seem to have some effect. Also, as a possibly related point, those members of Congress who retired while still relatively young were less likely to shirk in their last session.

EXAMPLE 16.2 **Do Congressmen Represent Their Districts?**

The decennial redistricting of the U.S. House of Representatives carves up districts, reassigns voters from one district to another, creates and eliminates seats, throws some politicians out of work and others into competition with fellow representatives. Though many districts are left intact, a substantial number have their partisan, ethnic, racial, and demographic com-positions altered. In short, redistricting can change the face of the district to which the congressman must appeal for reelection. Evidence that such redistricting leads incumbents to change the way they vote on bills in Congress, to conform to the changes in their constituency, would suggest that democracy does work to some degree.

Amihai Glazer and Marc Robbins[a] used the presidential election of 1980 to measure districts on a liberal versus conservative scale: the greater the vote given Jimmy Carter, the more liberal the district. Consider first the response to constituency change of congressmen elected before 1980 and still in office in 1982. The authors found that for every percentage point increase in the liberalism of the district, the incumbent, based on his roll-call votes, became more liberal by 0.75 points. The responsiveness of congressmen not returned to office in 1982 (either retired or defeated) was positive but lower—only 0.69 instead of 0.75 percentage points.

[a]Amihai Glazer and Marc Robbins, "Congressional Responsiveness to Constituency Change," *American Journal of Political Science,* v. 29 (May 1985).

The Problem of Voting

In a democracy citizens possess the ultimate power to choose their delegates by voting. But the effectiveness of a single vote is tiny, so much so that the ordinary citizen is scarcely motivated to go to the polls at all. Even if the election of the preferred candidate were worth an enormous sum to the voter, it would be fantastically improbable that a single person's ballot would determine the outcome. Or if the citizen simply wants to demonstrate support for a candidate, one vote more or less would scarcely be noticeable. And even if the voter has no selfish aims at all but intends to cast a purely public-spirited ballot, that single vote will no more measurably advance the *public* interest than it would serve the voter's own *selfish* interest.

If a candidate could *buy* votes, on the other hand, there would be no problem of motivating the voter. In fact, a surprisingly good case can be made for allowing politicians to buy citizens' votes at election time. Payment for votes before election would compensate the public for the scarcely controllable power that the delegates possess once elected.

There are other problems with voting, however. In the marketplace you "get what you pay for." In the political arena, it is all too easy to elect a candidate and not get the anticipated results. In view of the difficulties of finding and electing a candidate who supports the whole bundle of your preferred policies, and of ensuring that the elected official abides by his promises, it simply is not worthwhile for you to invest heavily in determining the best policies. Voting is cheap, but voting intelligently can be costly. And so, a subtler flaw of the political process is that citizens typically find it entirely rational to remain ill-informed on the issues.

If the chance of affecting the outcome is negligible, and if policy remains unpredictable even after the election, why do so many people vote? Assuming citizens are rational, it can only be that the costs of casting a ballot are low. And indeed, at least for city-dwellers and when the weather is good, the cost is small. Voting may actually be fun; it provides sociability and a feeling of civic accomplishment to offset the small travel and time cost involved.

EXAMPLE 16.3 Determinants of Voter Turnout

If a citizen rationally considers whether to turn out and vote, his or her decision should depend in part upon (1) the importance of the election, and (2) the probability of affecting the outcome. Y. Barzel and E. Silberberg[a] investigated the effect of these determinants on the proportion of citizens casting ballots in U.S. elections for state governors in the years 1962, 1964, 1966, and 1968 (122 elections).

They found, among other results, the following:

1. *The larger the population, the smaller the percent turnout.* This seems consistent with rational behavior, since the larger the population the smaller is the probability of a single person's vote determining the election. An increase of 1,000,000 in voting-age population of the state was associated with a 6 percent decline in the percent voting.

2. *The more one-sided the election, the smaller the turnout.* Again rational, since if voters had some inkling in advance of the one-sidedness they would place lower credence upon their own single ballot affecting the outcome. Statistically a 10 percent increase in the majority fraction was associated with a 7.7 percent decline in percentage voting.

3. *Coincidence of nongubernatorial with gubernatorial elections increased turnout.* Statistically, a presidential candidacy raised the fraction voting by 11.1 percent; a senatorial

candidacy by 5.5 percent. Obviously, it is more rational to vote if the election is more important.

COMMENT It would have been of interest to see if the difficulty and cost of voting significantly affected turnout. One would anticipate a larger fraction voting the better the weather, the less the average distance to the polls, the more convenient the voting hours, and so on. It is also reasonable to expect a larger turnout on the part of those who expect to be able to cast intelligent ballots.

[a]Y. Barzel and E. Silberberg, "Is the Act of Voting Rational?" *Public Choice,* v. 16 (Fall 1973).

Majority and Minority

Democratic political systems usually operate on the principle of *majority rule*. The necessity of making decisions through delegates poses a problem since a delegate may not faithfully serve constituents' interests. But what if the constituents differ among themselves? Then a delegate need only serve the bare majority that is required for election.

This situation obviously puts the minority at a grave disadvantage. Their most vital interests may be at the mercy of the majority. If 75 percent of the voters approve of abortion and 25 percent oppose it, the delegate is unlikely to divide her roll-call votes on the issues in this proportion. Rather, he or she is motivated to always vote the pro-choice side. In contrast, the market considers both majority and minority preferences in the allocation of resources. If 75 percent of consumers prefer chocolate and 25 percent prefer vanilla, chocolate and vanilla flavors will normally be provided in just about these proportions.

To help protect minority rights, a constitution may limit the laws a majority can pass. Another safeguard for the interests of the minorities is "log-rolling." Suppose minority legislators from farm states feel very strongly about drought relief. Then to swing over votes on this issue they may promise urban legislators to support mass transit or urban renewal. In this way the *intensity* of minority preferences may help counterbalance the mere numbers of the majority. Notice that this process could not work if legislators had to cast secret rather than open ballots on issues.

Log-rolling brings market considerations into politics. Delegates' votes on some issues are "bought" to be "paid for" later by votes on other issues. Log-rolling, though often regarded as an evil, reminds us of the mutual advantage of trade. Indeed, a Pareto-optimal outcome (where it is no longer possible to achieve any further gains to anyone without hurting others) would be attained if the votes of legislators on issues could be openly purchased for money!

We can explain the underlying logic of market considerations in politics as follows. Consider an ideal system of "political exchange" that requires *unanimous* consent for every government action. To achieve unanimity, those who stand to gain from the chosen action would have to purchase the votes of those who lose. Under this procedure all political actions undertaken would be Pareto-preferred over the initial situation (that is, would constitute an improvement for some, and an injury for none). With a majority rather than a unanimity rule, it is true that compensation need not be paid to all those affected— only to a number sufficient to comprise a voting majority. Nevertheless, since *both* sides will try to buy votes, the winning side will be the one that bids higher. Hence under a majority rule with vote-buying the more highly valued alternative would always be chosen. Though some gain and others lose, the benefit to the gainers is greater than the loss to the losers. So the outcome is Pareto-*optimal*, though not necessarily Pareto-*preferred*, over the status quo.

The Median-Voter Theorem and the Cycling Paradox

What is the equilibrium that would come about in a majority-voting system? To start with the simplest case, suppose there is only one issue to be voted on, say, the size of the government budget. In Figure 16.1, voters *a* through *e* are located at positions along a horizontal axis representing their ideal choices for the percent of GNP to be devoted to government. And, we will assume, in moving away from the ideal point in either direction each voter will always prefer an option closer to his or her ideal over one that is farther away. (Notice that this involves only *ranking* of preferences in a given direction. Distance along the line need not be a "cardinal" measure for *scaling* preferences.)

Any choice process, whether it be market dealings or voting, should ideally lead to an outcome that is Pareto-optimal (efficient). In this case the interval from *a* to *e* along the horizontal axis is the set of Pareto-optimal choices. Starting from any point outside the segment, all voters would favor moving to some point within. So the segment $\overline{ae}$ is like the Contract Curve *CC* in the Edgeworth box of Figure 15.3 (p. 446). (It is not necessarily true, however, that *every* point within the segment $\overline{ae}$ is unanimously preferred over any point outside the segment; just as held for the Contract Curve pictured in Figure 15.3, not every *Pareto-optimal* point is *Pareto-preferred* to a given starting position.) Of course, within the Pareto-optimal segment $\overline{ae}$, any move in either direction must necessarily make at least one voter worse off.

Suppose points *V,W,X,Y,Z* represent the alternative proposals (percentages of GNP devoted to government) to be voted on. For there to be a unique equilibrium that is independent of the sequence in which the proposals are offered, some single option must be able to win a majority vote against each and every one of the others. Will there necessarily be such a winner in Figure 16.1? Notice that a majority of voters (namely *b, c, d,* and *e*) prefer *X* over *V* or *W*. Similarly, *Y* wins against *Z* by attracting voters *a, b,* and *c*. So regardless of the order of successive votes between pairs of alternatives (so long as all the options are actually offered), the final winner must be either *X* or *Y*—the options lying just on either side of *c,* the ideal choice of the *median voter*. (Whether *X* or *Y* turns out to be the winner

FIGURE 16.1 **The Median-Voter Theorem: Single Choice Dimension** Voters *a* through *e* choose by majority rule, among proposals *V* through *Z* for the size of the government budget. The segment $\overline{ae}$ is Pareto-optimal. Regardless of the agenda, the ultimate winner will be either *X* or *Y* (the proposals lying on either side of the median voter's preferred position *c*), depending on which of the two the median voter prefers.

% of GNP Devoted to Government Budget

will therefore depend solely on which of the two voter c prefers. The diagram does not show which of the two it will be.)[2]

It would be a mistake to say, however, that the median voter has power to decide on his own what policy will be adopted. Voter c is the median voter in this example only because of the preferences of the other voters. If other voters, for example, all had ideal points to the left of c, then c would no longer be the median voter, and the policy adopted would no longer be the one he prefers most.

If, instead of only the discrete alternatives V through Z, each and every budget from 0 to 100 percent were possible, there is a more precise result: the final outcome will be exactly at the ideal position of the median voter. The outcome will of course still be in the Pareto-optimal interval. Finally, since the median voter's choice will defeat each and every alternative proposal, the cycling problem described in Chapter 15 does not arise.

THE MEDIAN-VOTER THEOREM: In majority-rule voting on a single issue, if voters always prefer proposals that are nearer over those farther from their ideal positions in any given direction, a unique equilibrium will exist regardless of the agenda. (There will be no cycling.) Furthermore, the outcome must be in the Pareto-efficient region. If there is a continuum of options, the result will be exactly at the ideal position of the median voter. With a finite number of options, the outcome will be whichever of the two proposals to either side of the median position is preferred by the median voter.

Cycling did not appear here because of the condition known as *single-peaked preferences:* in each direction each voter prefers an option nearer his ideal position. (It would violate single-peakedness if, for example, a voter for whom the ideal budget was 25 percent of GNP nevertheless prefers 60 percent over 50 percent.) Single-peakedness seems reasonable to assume here, though not necessarily so in all circumstances. Where it holds, we can safely conclude there will be no cycling.

EXAMPLE 16.4   The Median-Voter Theorem in Professional Football

Before 1982, professional football players in the United States negotiated their salaries individually with the team managements of the National Football League (NFL). After a long strike, the National Football League Players Association (NFLPA) signed a contract with the NFL that provided a salary schedule placing considerable weight on years of playing experience in the league.

Since the NFLPA was a democratic organization operating on the principle of majority rule, it might be expected that the interests of the median voters—in this case, players with the median number of years of experience—would tend to be favored by the NFLPA. A study by Michael D. White, which estimated the expected player gains on the basis of the new contract provisions, indicated that this did indeed occur. In the NFL, the median experience was four years of play. As the table shows, while all classes of players were

---

[2]In the diagram, point Y is closer than point X to the median voter's ideal position c, but X and Y lie in different directions from c. Since distance is not a cardinal measure of utility here, distances in different directions cannot be compared.

estimated to gain over the life of the contract, those with four years of experience were on average the biggest gainers.

Predicted Gains over Life of Contract

Experience	Gain
1 yr	9.0%
2	36.3
3	63.5
4	107.4
5	88.1
6	85.4
7	82.7
8	80.0
9	77.3
10	74.6
11	71.9
12	69.2

Source: Adapted from Michael D. White, "Self-Interest Redistribution and the National Football League Players Association," *Economic Inquiry,* v. 24 (October 1986), p. 677.

COMMENT   The data suggest that, moving away from the median, more senior players tended to do better in comparison with junior players. This is understandable in terms of political influence. Junior players are much less likely to have gained the friends and know-how needed for achieving political influence.

Continuing to assume single-peaked preferences, now consider Figure 16.2 (p. 488). Here three voters *a,b,c* face *two* issues (for example, size of the government budget and number of immigrants to be admitted) that are bundled together for simultaneous choice.[3] For example, political candidates might run on platforms representing combined policy positions on the two issues. The *Pareto-optimal set* is the roughly triangular area connecting the three ideal points *a,b,c.* The *ab* boundary of the triangle goes through the mutual tangencies of the (approximately circular) indifference curves of individuals *a* and *b,* and similarly for the other boundaries of the triangle.[4]

Point *X* here represents any arbitrarily selected option within the efficient *abc* region. The different voters' indifference curves through any point like *X* necessarily intersect and determine the three shaded petal-shaped areas. These areas represent policy options that

[3]The discussion that follows is based upon Gordon Tullock, *Toward a Mathematics of Politics* (Ann Arbor: University of Michigan Press, 1967), Chapters 2, 3.

[4]The indifference curves are only approximately circular, since we are not assuming that distance is a cardinal measure for *scaling* utility independent of direction. If distance were a cardinal measure, everyone's indifference curves would be exactly circular around the ideal point, and the Pareto-optimal region *abc* would be exactly triangular.

FIGURE 16.2 **Two Choice Dimensions** The three voters have ideal points at *a, b,* and *c.* The approximately triangular region *abc* is the Pareto-optimal set, whose boundaries are the mutual-tangency points of the (roughly circular) indifference curves. For any point like *X* within *abc,* there are three petal-shaped areas. Each of these areas is a set of proposals that can command a 2:1 majority over *X,* so cycling is inevitable if all possible positions are in contention. Furthermore, the petal-shaped regions include points like *V* that are outside the Pareto-optimal set. But if *X, Y, Z* are the only alternatives offered the voters, *X* is a noncycling equilibrium.

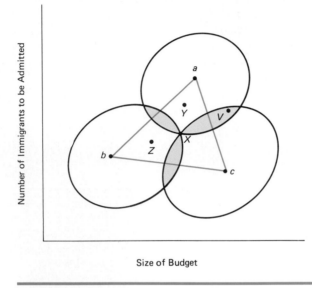

Size of Budget

command a 2:1 majority vote over X. (For example, the petal at the upper left is the policy region that voters a and b both prefer to X.) Since such a petal diagram can be constructed for any point X, cycling is inevitable when every point in the diagram is a possible option. However, when there are only a finite number of alternatives, cycling is possible but not inevitable. For example, if the only options were X, Y, Z as in the diagram, there is no cycling: X would defeat each of the others in majority voting and so be the winner regardless of the agenda. Finally, notice that even a non-Pareto-optimal point (like V) can sometimes command a majority over a Pareto-optimal point (like X). In short, the rather nice results obtained for single-issue majority voting disappear when two or more issues are packaged together.

PROPOSITION: Even with single-peaked preferences, when three voters face two issues and a continuum of options, cycling is inevitable. With a finite set of options, cycling is possible but need not always occur. In either case, outcomes outside the Pareto-optimal region may command a majority against efficient policies within the region.

16.2 SPECIAL INTEREST POLITICS

In Chapter 15 we saw that small groups find it easier than large groups to overcome the free-rider problem. This has an important political implication. Members of a compact "special interest" (for example, businesspeople and workers in a particular industry) are few in number compared to the population at large. Nevertheless, they often obtain political favors like tariffs or subsidies at the expense of the general consuming public. The reason is that the effective influence of the individual citizen-voter upon government is, for the various reasons outlined in the first section of this chapter, extremely weak. Filling the vacuum are "pressure groups," which are subcollectives of individuals interested in pushing particular policies or points of view upon policymakers.

Special interests have two factors on their side in forming pressure groups. First, they are more strongly motivated. Since their financial interest is concentrated (as in the case of a tariff affecting a single industry), they gain far more from appropriate political action than any comparably sized group of the general public stands to lose, even though the *entire* public may suffer in the aggregate a much greater loss. Second, being few in number they are more likely to contribute to and achieve what is for them (but not for the general community) a public good—advantages for their own pressure group.

EXAMPLE 16.5 **Regulated Electricity Rates**

Electricity is a "natural monopoly" now governmentally regulated throughout the United States. The problem of collective action suggests that large consumers of electricity will have an advantage over the multitude of small consumers of electricity in forming a pressure group to influence the political agencies responsible for regulating rates.

This hypothesis was tested by George Stigler and Claire Friedland, making use of data from earlier years when there were still a considerable number of unregulated states. Since it can be presumed that industrial users of electricity are relatively large in scale (and small in number) in comparison with residential users, the ratio of the residential price to the industrial price is a measure of the extent that large users are favored over small. This ratio alone is not a satisfactory criterion, however, since there may well be differences in the cost of service that would warrant some degree of rate inequality between industrial and residential users. But there is no obvious reason for the ratio to differ as between regulated and unregulated states.

The data in the table show that the ratio was indeed substantially higher for the regulated states, consistent with the hypothesis that regulation works to the comparative advantage of large consumers over small consumers.

Average Ratio $\dfrac{\text{Residential Price}}{\text{Industrial Price}}$ for Electricity

	1917	1937
Regulated States	1.616	2.459
Unregulated States	1.445	2.047

Source: G. J. Stigler and C. Friedland, "What Can Regulators Regulate? The Case of Electricity," *Journal of Law and Economics*, v. 5 (October 1962), p. 9.

A related point is that since production is generally more specialized than consumption government interventions often favor producers over consumers. Because we are all both producers and consumers, it might be thought that the effects cancel out. But the political measures that favor producers (for example, permitting formation of a cartel) are often anticompetitive. This leads to a loss of economic efficiency, apart from possibly objectionable effects on wealth distribution.

Of course, the political strength of "special interest" groups is only one side of the picture. It is easier for a small specialized group to organize and bring its weight to bear, but it remains a group small in number. Landlords can organize *against* rent controls more effectively than tenants can organize *for* them, but a politician cannot ignore the fact that there are many more tenant votes than landlord votes.[5]

16.3 BUREAUCRACY

Bureaucrats are responsible not for *making* policies but for *implementing* them. Supposedly impartial and neutral, bureaucrats are not subject to election or recall at the hands of the voters. To the extent that bureaucrats really do determine the actual outcomes of decisions, citizens have even less power to achieve their desires by voting. For all practical purposes, implementation *is* the actual decision. So the bureaucracy surely has substantial power.

What are the interests of the bureaucracy? Apart from high wages for easy work, a critical aim is job security. In modern times, the government bureaucracy has gained extraordinary job security through civil-service regulations that forbid demotion or dismissal except "for cause." While civil-service reform is in many respects preferable to the spoils system, it has nevertheless changed the balance of power within government in favor of the bureaucrats.

Another natural aim of bureaucrats is agency growth. All those involved generally benefit by building empires or by increasing the resources under their control. Following "Parkinson's Law,"[6] even if the Royal Navy diminishes in size, the Admiralty bureaucracy will grow. Let the colonies declare their independence, Her Majesty's Colonial Office in London will still expand. And in the United States the Department of Agriculture will continue to swell in size while the number of farmers shrinks.

Approaching this topic analytically, consider a hypothetical bureaucratic agency of the U.S. government. The Congress, elected by the voters, is in a position to fix the agency's budget and thus determine its size. From the point of view of Congress, agency size is a budgetary cost and so a "bad." But the agency produces an output that Congress regards as a good. A possible indifference-curve map for Congress is pictured in Figure 16.3. (As we saw in Chapter 3, indifference curves between a good and a bad have positive slope.)

However, as a practical matter, the bureaucrats who staff the agency are in a position to determine how the agency produces its output. Suppose that an "efficient" agency would have the production function OQ_1 shown in the diagram. Ideally, Congress should be able to choose the agency size and output indicated by the tangency point G^* on indifference

---

[5]Another factor favoring the political success of residential rent control is that consumers *are* somewhat specialized when it comes to housing. The single rental transaction typically accounts for a large fraction of consumer budgets. This concentration makes it worthwhile to bear the cost of forming a pressure group aimed at getting the government to control rents.

[6]C. Northcote Parkinson, *Parkinson's Law* (Boston: Houghton Mifflin, 1957).

curve U_1. But bureaucrats interested in having a larger agency size are likely, in presenting the agency's budgetary case before Congress, to claim that the production function has a rather different shape.

The curves OQ_2 and OQ_3 represent two alternative agency production functions that the bureaucrats may put before Congress. OQ_2 and OQ_3 are both inefficient, of course; in comparison with OQ_1, each provides smaller output at any agency size. But as between these two, OQ_3 is more advantageous to the agency, though less desirable for Congress. If offered an agency production function OQ_2, Congress would rationally choose point H^* on indifference curve U_2, where both agency size and agency output are quite small. This choice makes sense, since the voters would not want to put a lot of funds into an inefficient activity. But OQ_2 hardly meets the bureaucrats' aims. Instead, the agency is likely to claim that its actual production function is like curve OQ_3. Congress would then prefer point K^* on indifference curve U_3, and would therefore allow the agency to grow substantially. Notice that the trick here is for the agency to claim that its production function exhibits a range of increasing marginal returns. Thus, there will be very little of the desired output, unless the agency gets to be very big.

Though there is some evidence that governmental agencies are less efficient than private firms, which is consistent with the idea that they maximize budgets, we should note that what is loosely called waste may in fact reflect policy choices. Inefficiency in the Veterans Administration may be an implicit subsidy to the handicapped veterans who work there; redundant military bases may be kept open to help the economies of poor regions in the country. Similarly, some excess costs incurred by government represent the price of delivering outputs—such as irrigation water in Arizona or electricity in the Tennessee Valley—that private firms would not provide, but which are nevertheless desirable, at least from the politicians' point of view.

FIGURE 16.3 **Bureaucracy** If the agency convinces Congress that the production function is OQ_3, Congress will rationally choose point K^*, with a large agency size. The agency prefers this outcome over G^* along the true production fuction OQ_i.

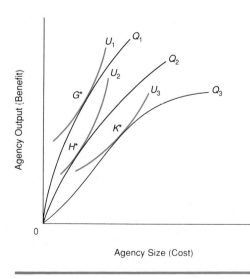

EXAMPLE 16.6   **Government Wages**

Bureaucrats may employ their political power to obtain higher pay for less work.

A study by Steven Benti[a] compared wages of U.S. federal government employees with those in the private sector. Census data from the 1982 Current Population Survey indicated that male workers earn about 33 percent more and female workers about 39 percent more than people in the private sector. However, a substantial portion of this difference may be accounted for by variables such as the special skills and educational background required for federal jobs. On the other hand, federal employment also offers more favorable fringe benefits and employment conditions. Taking these factors into account, Benti concluded that the federal government could attract and retain a labor force of the existing size and quality at average wages of about 16 percent less for men and 42 percent less for women.

COMMENT   These data indicate, as common sense would already have suggested, that bureaucrats' strategic position in government does give them considerable influence over issues of importance to them, notably their own wages. The extra advantage of women in federal employment might be regarded as evidence that the federal wage structure is less discriminatory against women than the private sector; or, alternatively, that women have somewhat more political influence in the process whereby bureaucrats and their organizations extract wage benefits from government.

[a]Steven Benti, *Wages in the Federal and Private Sectors,* National Bureau of Economic Research Working Paper No. 1641 (1985).

16.4   POLITICAL CONFLICT

In the model of the public-choice state, government is merely the instrument through which citizens make collective decisions. We noticed certain imperfections of this process: elected delegates may not represent the desires of constituents, there is a problem of majority versus minority rights, and so on. But a much more drastic real-world "imperfection" arises when rulers do not serve the population at all. A government's leaders may want to fleece and rob their subjects, or perhaps use them as slaves or cannon fodder. What might be called the *exploitation state* is at least as important historically as the public-choice state.

Let us now go to the opposite extreme and develop the idea that *conflict* rather than "public choice" is the essence of politics. Conflict arises in many contexts: among nations, between rulers and subjects within nations, between criminals and victims, and so forth. It is also sometimes useful to think of activities like lawsuits or industrial strikes as instances of conflict, even though bodily violence may not be involved. Conflict may be said to occur when each party involved in an interaction is willing to incur costs in order to impose its will upon the opponent, rather than come to a compromise settlement. From one point of view, conflict is "an agreement to disagree." It is also in a way an educational process: each contender tries to convince the other that it is the one better able to take and to deliver punishment.

Elements of Conflict

Among the important sources of conflict are the following:

1. *Antipathy*—One party may be willing, from hatred or envy, to incur costs in seeking to injure the other. An example was Hitler's war against the Jews.
2. *Rivalry*—If resources are too scarce to meet the requirements of both parties, one or the other may try to improve his position through aggression. While antipathy leads to hot emotion-laden conflict, rivalry may be deadly yet quite cool. ("I got nothing against you, Wyatt Earp, but this town ain't big enough for the two of us.")
3. *Overconfidence*—The stronger the belief in one's own chances of winning the battle, the less the willingness to come to a compromise settlement.
4. *Nonenforceability of agreements*—Sometimes both parties might be happy to come to a compromise settlement. But if there is no way to prevent violation of any agreement made, is useless compromise.

In Panel (a) of Figure 16.4 the curve II' (like the similar curve in Figure 15.1) shows the Social Opportunity Curve—the income combinations attainable by two decisionmakers.[7] We may think of the two sides either as individuals or as groups: let us call them the Blues and the Grays. And "income" may stand for territory, power, or ability to purchase consumption goods.

FIGURE 16.4   Confidence and Conflict   In Panel (a) the Blues anticipate that in the event of conflict their benefit, on average, will be equivalent to an income of I_B^o. The Grays similarly anticipate I_G^o. There is a region of mutual advantage MSS' achievable by a compromise agreement; the efficient solutions lie along the range SS'. In Panel (b) there is no possibility of a compromise solution.

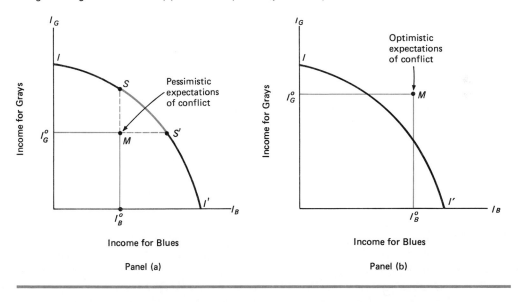

Panel (a)

Panel (b)

[7]The analysis here is based in part upon Donald Wittman, "How a War Ends," *Journal of Conflict Resolution*, v. 23 (December 1979) and David Friedman, "Many, Few, One: Social Harmony and the Shrunken Choice Set," *American Economic Review*, v. 70 (March 1980).

Suppose the Blues believe that a conflict would leave them with an income of I_B^o. Let I_G^o be the corresponding outcome anticipated by the Grays. Then, evidently, the roughly triangular area MSS' represents a "region of mutual advantage" wherein both parties can gain by peaceful compromise—assuming that a compromise settlement would be enforceable. An efficient solution would of course lie somewhere in the range SS' along the opportunity curve.

Panel (b) represents a situation where each party has become more confident of winning in a clash. Here there is no region of mutual advantage, so no compromise is possible. A battle is inevitable since *both* contenders expect to do better by fighting than by settling. (Of course, one or the other must in fact be overestimating its chances of winning the struggle, or very likely both are.)

After having experienced the test of battle, each side will very likely learn the hard truth about its limited strength. This may not lead immediately to a peaceful settlement, however. The loser in battle will likely become more agreeable to compromise, but the winner may be less agreeable. Another factor that more clearly leads to eventual settlement is exhaustion of resources. As both sides become poorer, the wastage becomes more and more painful, while the possible spoils of victory are getting smaller.

Whereas Figure 16.4 highlights the role of *confidence* as a source of *conflict,* Figure 16.5 illustrates the effect of *rivalry.* Panel (a) represents a strongly rivalrous situation; the shape of the Social-Opportunity Curve II' shows that the interests of the two parties are sharply opposed. Here even relatively pessimistic anticipations I_B^o and I_G^o about the outcome of a conflict may not lead to any compromise settlement. Panel (b) represents the opposite situation, where the two parties' interests are strongly complementary; each is highly useful to the other. Accordingly, even if each contender is quite optimistic about his chances in the event of conflict, a compromise settlement might still be preferred by both.

Finally, Figure 16.6 illustrates the role of *antipathy* (and its opposite, sympathy). In

---

FIGURE 16.5 **Rivalry and Conflict** In Panel (a) the two parties are strong rivals, and a compromise settlement is unlikely. In Panel (b) their interests are highly complementary, making a compromise much easier to achieve.

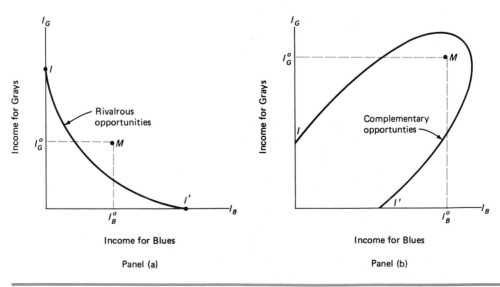

Panel (a)   Panel (b)

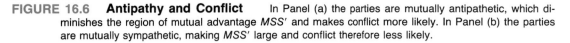

FIGURE 16.6 **Antipathy and Conflict** In Panel (a) the parties are mutually antipathetic, which diminishes the region of mutual advantage *MSS'* and makes conflict more likely. In Panel (b) the parties are mutually sympathetic, making *MSS'* large and conflict therefore less likely.

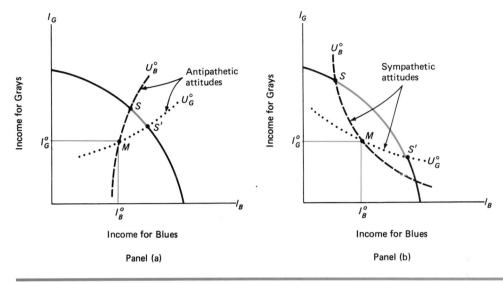

Panel (a) the two parties are antipathetic. The Blues view Gray income I_G as a *bad;* this is indicated by the positively sloping indifference curve U_B^o through point M. Similarly the utility of the Grays declines with the income of the Blues. The effect is to diminish the size of *MSS'*, the region of mutual advantage, and to make peaceful settlement less probable. In Panel (b) on the other hand, the parties are *sympathetic* to each other, making peaceful settlement more likely.

If agreements are not *enforceable,* parties who otherwise could profit from cooperation may not be able to reach a settlement. There are two main ways of persuading people to live up to agreements. The first is through a neutral umpire. Indeed, one of the main services that a government can provide is a judicial system to enforce private agreements. Second, some contracts may be *self-enforcing.* Two parties can so tie themselves to each other that it does not pay either to defect. Usually this happens when there is a profitable continuing relationship between them. If Firm *A* agreed to deliver materials to Firm *B,* one reason for *A* not to cheat on quantity or quality—apart from the possibility of a lawsuit—may be the fear of permanently losing a valuable customer.

Enforceability of agreements is a matter of degree. Going to court is expensive and judges are not infallible. As for "self-enforcing" agreements, they will be adhered to only as long as violating them remains unprofitable to each side.

The possible profitability of conflict raises very serious questions about the validity of Coase's Theorem (as discussed in the preceding chapter). That theorem says essentially that all mutually advantageous agreements will be undertaken and, by implication, adhered to. We saw earlier that Coase's Theorem appeared to "prove too much" in suggesting that monopoly would not permanently exist, that individuals would voluntarily contract with one another to internalize all externalities, and so on. But even more surprising is that the Coase Theorem is inconsistent with the persistence of war, crime, and politics! In fact, the Coase Theorem, along with Adam Smith's Invisible Hand, is valid only under very ideal conditions.

Some of these conditions were already mentioned in the preceding chapter: among them are well-defined property rights and absence of transaction costs. But more important, individuals will be led by self-interest to serve others only to the extent that agreement appears, for each of them, to be more profitable than conflict. Given the sources of conflict just mentioned—antipathy, rivalry, and overconfidence, plus the limited enforceability of compromise settlements—we can be quite sure that war, crime, and politics will be with us for a long time.

Economists have just begun to analyze conflict. We can expect future research to analyze at least five factors: (1) the advantages of offensive versus defensive strategies, (2) the circumstances that sometimes keep conflict limited rather than total, (3) the "production function" that converts resource inputs into likelihood of victory, (4) the additional issues raised by three-sided or even more complex struggles, and (5) the extent to which political developments like the size of nations or the balance of influence among social classes are explainable by coercive strength. But enough has been said to indicate that the *economics of conflict* is just as important as the *economics of exchange and markets*.

EXAMPLE 16.7 Rationality and International Conflict

The political scientist Bruce Bueno de Mesquita explored the implications of assuming that a nation will initiate international conflict only when doing so is advantageous. In effect, he asserted that each nation could be regarded as having a single utility function, which its leader maximized in making decisions about initiating conflict. Among the factors entering into this utility function, according to his analysis, were (1) the relative strengths of the attacker and defender, (2) the significance to the attacker of changing the defender's policies by conflict or the threat thereof, and (3) the prospects and consequences of intervention by third parties.

Using data from 251 cases of conflict, Bueno de Mesquita classified them by degree of severity ranging from outright war to threats short of war. Within each category, the table indicates those which (on his calculations) yielded positive and negative utility to the initiators.

Evidently, most of the time the initiator gained from conflict. Furthermore, the tendency toward positive expected utility increases with increased seriousness of the conflict (upper rows of the table). This is understandable, since a nation might well *threaten* to engage in conflict even at a disadvantage in utility terms, but it is less likely to actually go to war unless there is a gain from doing so.

Expected Utility and Conflict Initiation

	Positive or Zero	Negative
Expected Utility to Initiator:		
Interstate wars	65	11
Interstate interventions	78	24
Interstate threats	50	23
Totals	193	58

Source: Calculated from Bruce Bueno de Mesquita, *The War Trap* (New Haven: Yale University Press, 1981), pp. 128–30.

Conflict and Game Theory

As indicated in Chapter 10, various types of game payoff matrices can be used to distinguish the sometimes subtly different ways in which elements of cooperation and of conflict may be combined. Table 16.1 shows four such patterns. (As in Chapter 10, within each matrix the first number in each cell is the payoff to the Row player, and the second number is the payoff to the Column player.)

TABLE 16.1   **Payoff Matrices for Four Games (larger numbers indicate higher utility)**

LAND OR SEA

	Land	Sea
Land	2,1	1,2
Sea	1,2	2,1

PRISONERS' DILEMMA

	Disarm	Arm
Disarm	3,3	1,4
Arm	4,1	*2,2

HAWK-DOVE

	Dove	Hawk
Dove	3,3	*2,4
Hawk	*4,2	1,1

BATTLE OF THE SEXES

	Patton	Montgomery
Patton	*3,2	1,1
Montgomery	1,1	*2,3

* = Nash solution in pure strategies (see text).

The payoffs here are in rank-ordered form: a higher number for either player represents an *ordinally* preferred outcome. These ranking patterns, in fact, define the "families" of games known as Land or Sea, Prisoners' Dilemma, and so on. Any conclusions that can be drawn solely in terms of the ranked outcomes (i.e., in terms of an *ordinal* measure of benefit or utility to each player) will therefore apply to the entire corresponding "family" of games.

The Land or Sea matrix in the table corresponds to a duel for survival, a "this town ain't big enough for the two of us" situation. Whenever one side is better off, the other is worse off.[8] This is the most rivalrous of the four cases.

In Prisoners' Dilemma the opposition of interests is less total: there is scope for mutual

---

[8]Notice that the elements of each cell, if interpreted as cardinal magnitudes, add up to a constant sum (equal to 3 here). Constant-sum games are necessarily highly rivalrous.

gain from agreement. As applied to an arms race, for example, the Disarm/Disarm strategy-pair (payoffs ranked 3 for each) is mutually preferred to Arm/Arm (payoffs ranked 2 for each). The parties should obviously agree on Disarm/Disarm, except that the agreement may not be enforceable. If not, as will be seen, there are strong pressures leading the two sides toward the Arm/Arm "trap." As we saw in Chapter 10, the Prisoners' Dilemma model also applies to the problem of chiseling in cartels, where each single firm is motivated to expand production.

Hawk-Dove (sometimes called the game of "Chicken")[9] shows another pattern of mixed conflict-cooperation incentives. The idea is that whoever plays Hawk will defeat an opponent playing Dove—but Hawk-Hawk encounters are extremely costly for both sides. The mutual aim to avoid the 1,1 payoffs at the lower-right cell means that the Hawk-Dove pattern involves less intense rivalry than Prisoners' Dilemma (where the non-cooperative "trap" had less adverse payoffs 2,2). Many kinds of negotiation situations correspond to Hawk-Dove, for example, bargaining aimed at avoiding industrial conflicts (strikes and lockouts) or legal conflicts (court trials). Here each side has an incentive to be tough: by playing Hawk it hopes to make the other side give way and play Dove. If both play Hawk, however, the outcome is disastrous to both.

The last matrix in the table—Battle of the Sexes[10]—represents the mildest rivalry of all. Here the two parties really want to coordinate their strategies so as to achieve one of the mutually preferred diagonal cells. The problem is which of the two cells it will be, that is, who will reap the larger share of the mutual gain. This pattern commonly emerges in struggles within an alliance. One such instance occurred during World War II in the early fall of 1944. After breaking out from the Normandy perimeter, American forces under General Patton were approaching the German border from eastern France while British troops in Belgium under Field Marshal Montgomery were nearing Germany from the north. The United States (the Column player) could have provided Patton with supplies for an attack in the south, while the British (the Row player) could have supplied Montgomery's attack in the north. Both agreed that it was better to concentrate the supplies and make only a single attack, but the Americans favored a drive by Patton while the British favored supplying Montgomery. The Allies eventually agreed on the attack by Montgomery.[11]

Having described different types of conflict situations, we can now examine several crucial questions. What is the outcome likely to be? Will an efficient (conflict-minimizing) result be achieved? Which party is likely to gain the advantage?

The outcome in any of the payoff patterns described will depend upon the "rules of the game" that apply. Two possible "rules of the game" are (1) *sequential play:* one party (say, Row) moves first, after which the Column player makes his choice in response,[12] and (2) *simultaneous play:* each player makes his or her decision in ignorance of the opponent's move (for example, a sealed-bid auction).

The solutions or equilibria under these two rules are summarized in Table 16.2. Under sequential-move rules, a discussion of one of the cases, Hawk-Dove, will suffice. Assuming Row moves first, he will surely play Hawk (the lower row of the Hawk-Dove matrix in

---

[9]The traditional story has two teenagers racing their jalopies toward one another on a one-lane road. Whoever turns aside first is the chicken.

[10]This story involves a husband and wife going out for the evening. While they definitely want to be together, the wife prefers the opera while the husband prefers a boxing match.

[11]This strategy turned out to be the wrong decision, which led to the Allied disaster at Arnhem.

[12]The "entry-deterrence game" described in Chapter 10 was an example of a sequential-play situation.

TABLE 16.2   Equilibria for Four Different Payoff Matrices

	Land or Sea	Prisoners' Dilemma	Hawk-Dove	Battle of the Sexes
Degree of Rivalry	Great	Large	Moderate	Small
SEQUENTIAL-MOVE GAME (ROW MOVES FIRST)				
Outcome (payoff)	1,2	2,2	4,2	3,2
(cells)	upper right or lower left	lower right	lower left	upper left
Efficient?	yes	no	yes	yes
Advantage to?	second-mover	neither	first-mover	first-mover
SIMULTANEOUS-MOVE GAME (SYMMETRICAL SOLUTIONS WITH MIXED STRATEGIES)				
Outcome (payoff)	1.5, 1.5	2,2	2.5, 2.5	1.67, 1.67
Probability mix	0.5, 0.5	0, 1	0.5, 0.5	0.67, 0.33
Efficient?	yes	no	no	no
Advantage to?	neither	neither	neither	neither

Table 16.1). Then the best that Column can do is to respond with Dove (the left-hand column). So the solution is the lower-left cell, with payoffs 4 to Row and 2 to Column. (If Column moved first, the outcome would be 2, 4 at the upper-right cell—so that regardless of who goes first, the advantage goes to the first-mover.) This outcome is also efficient, since no other is *unanimously* preferred to it.

Following are some points of interest about the various sequential-move solutions:

1. Except for Prisoners' Dilemma, an efficient outcome is achieved in all cases. (But this is trivial under Land or Sea, where all four cells are efficient!)
2. The advantage lies with the second-mover when the degree of rivalry is greatest (Land or Sea), tending to shift in favor of the first-mover as the rivalry diminishes (Hawk-Dove and Battle of the Sexes).

For games played with *simultaneous-move* rules, the correct solution concept is not so easy to determine. Row's best move may depend upon Column's move, but Column's best choice in turn may depend upon Row's move—so in general there is no strictly rational way of choosing.

This impasse does not apply to Prisoners' Dilemma, however, because here we can appeal to the principle of dominance. In Prisoners' Dilemma Row does better when he chooses the less cooperative strategy *regardless* of the other's move, and similarly for Column. This being the case, each player acts accordingly, and so the inefficient outcome at the lower-right cell remains the solution even for simultaneous play.

Chapter 10 introduced the *Nash solution* and showed it to be the game-theory equivalent of the Cournot solution in duopoly. If the players are at a strategy-pair such that neither would want to unilaterally revise his or her choice, that strategy-pair is a Nash solution. The outcomes meeting this criterion are starred in Table 16.1. As can be seen, in Land or Sea none of the four cells is starred; in Prisoners' Dilemma only the single "trap" is starred;

in Hawk-Dove the two off-diagonal corners are starred; and in Battle of the Sexes, the two diagonal corners are starred. So it would appear that, in general, there are multiple Nash equilibria.

We can push matters further by making use of one additional consideration. In a simultaneous-move game both parties are in exactly the same situation. Consequently, it is reasonable to consider only those solutions that are entirely *symmetrical*—that is, where both players use the same strategies and receive the same payoffs. To arrive at a symmetrical solution requires introducing another important game-theory concept—a *mixed strategy*.

Take Land or Sea. Since one strategy is as good as the other in the simultaneous-play game, a player can plausibly toss a fair coin to select one or the other with equal probability. If both players do this, the payoff to each will be on average $(1/4)(2 + 1 + 1 + 2) = 1.5$. The lower portion of Table 16.2 is constructed on the premise that mixed strategies are indeed used to obtain a symmetrical solution (except, of course, in Prisoners' Dilemma, where we do not need mixed strategies to find the single symmetrical Nash equilibrium). In the Land or Sea game, with the numerical payoffs as shown, we have seen that a .5,.5 mixture is the equilibrium mixed-strategy pair. Given the payoffs shown, .5,.5 is the equilibrium mixture in Hawk-Dove also.[13] But in Battle of the Sexes, in equilibrium, each player chooses the strategy more favorable to himself or herself with 2/3 probability.[14]

Following are some points of interest concerning the simultaneous-move games:

1. Since we have considered only symmetrical solutions, in Table 16.2 neither party ever gains any advantage over the other.
2. While efficient outcomes were achieved for the *sequential-move* game in the case of both Hawk-Dove and Battle of the Sexes, for the *simultaneous-move* game this is no longer the case. In the Hawk-Dove game, so as not to be exploited as a Dove, each player has to be a tough Hawk negotiator a certain fraction of the time. This means that whenever players are tough simultaneously, the adverse 1,1 outcome will occur and so they both suffer. Similarly, under Battle of the Sexes with mixed strategies,

---

[13]Calculation of the optimal mixed strategy for Hawk-Dove proceeds as follows. When Column has chosen his best mixture, Row will be indifferent as between her two possible choices. For Row to be indifferent, Column must have chosen his p (probability of playing the first column) such that

$$3p + 2(1 - p) = 4p + 1(1 - p)$$

The solution is $p = 1/2$. (*Note:* In making these calculations it has been assumed that the numbers in Table 16.1 are actual *cardinal* payoffs rather than only rankings. With the same rankings but different cardinal payoffs, the probability mix will change.) The payoff to Row can then be calculated from either of her strategies:

$$3(.5) + 2(.5) = 4(.5) + 1(.5) = 2.5$$

Of course, the payoff to Column will be the same.

[14]For the Battle of the Sexes matrix, Row will be indifferent if Column has chosen a p (probability of playing the first column) such that:

$$3p + 1(1 - p) = 1(p) + 2(1 - p)$$

The result is $p = 1/3$. Thus, Column will assign 2/3 weight to his second (right-hand) strategy. By a corresponding argument, Row will assign 2/3 weight to her first (upper) strategy. The payoff to Row can be calculated:

$$3(1/3) + 1(2/3) = 1(1/3) + 2(2/3) = 1.67$$

Again, the payoff to Column will be the same.

there will be some positive probability that the players end up at one or the other of the two mutually undesired 1,1 outcomes.

3. Mixed-strategy equilibria have some peculiar properties. As described in a preceding footnote, the optimal mixed strategy is calculated as to make the opponent indifferent over his possible choices. But this means that, if both are at the optimum, either player can deviate without losing thereby. In this sense, all mixed-strategy equilibria are "weak." A Nash equilibrium in pure strategies, in contrast, may be either "strong" (meaning that whichever side deviates will actually suffer a reduced payoff) or "weak" in this sense.

The theory of games is of course by no means limited to the elementary interactions so far examined. There are many important complications and extensions. In *repeated play* the parties do not engage in only a one-time interaction, as assumed here, but expect to be in contact with one another over a long period of time. With *conditional strategies* one or the other player can be in a position to make and execute threats or promises. *Multi-party games* involve not just two but three or more players simultaneously contending with one another. Unfortunately, space does not permit exploring these topics here.

An Application: Should You Pay Ransom?

A kidnapper who has abducted your child threatens to kill her unless a ransom is paid. In terms of game theory, does it make sense to pay?

Your strategies as parent are *Pay* and *Don't Pay*. And the kidnapper has two strategies: *Kill* or *Release* his victim. Since the kidnapper will be observing your choice before he makes his decision, you as parent have the first move and he has the last move.

Naturally you would prefer to pay the ransom if that would assure your child's release. But you fear that the kidnapper may be motivated to kill your child anyway—perhaps to leave no witness alive who can identify him.

Your preference rankings are as shown here; as usual, larger numbers indicate more desired outcomes.

Your ranking is

"I don't pay, he releases"	4
"I pay, he releases"	3
"I don't pay, he kills"	2
"I pay, he kills"	1

You are not sure about the kidnapper's ranking, but suppose they are

"Ransom paid, child released"	4
"Ransom paid, child killed"	3
"Ransom not paid, child released"	2
"Ransom not paid, child killed"	1

These rankings are shown in Matrix 1 of Table 16.3. Note that this kidnapper is "nice": regardless of what you do, he prefers to release the child. (Perhaps he fears that, if caught, he will suffer a more severe penalty for a kidnap-murder than for a kidnap alone.)

With the preferences shown in Matrix 1 of Table 16.3, if these are known to you and

TABLE 16.3 Should You Pay Ransom?

MATRIX 1 ("Nice" kidnapper)

Parent		Kill	Release
	Pay	1,3	3,4
	Don't pay	2,1	4,2

MATRIX 2 ("Nasty" kidnapper)

Parent		Kill	Release
	Pay	1,4	3,3
	Don't pay	2,2	4,1

MATRIX 3 ("Nice" kidnapper if paid)

Parent		Kill	Release
	Pay	1,3	3,4
	Don't pay	2,2	4,1

if you believe the kidnapper is rational, you should clearly choose *Don't pay*. The kidnapper will then choose *Release*. So the equilibrium payoffs are 4 to you and 2 for the kidnapper. Note that this outcome is Pareto-efficient: there is no way of improving the outcome for either side without making the other side worse off.

Alternatively, the kidnapper may be "nasty"—whatever you do he prefers to *Kill*. (He is more concerned about the additional risk of leaving the victim alive to identify him than about the risk of more severe punishment should he be caught.) Then the payoffs would be as shown in Matrix 2 of Table 16.3.

But assuming once again that you know the kidnapper's preferences and believe he will act rationally, your optimal choice remains *Don't pay!* (Your child will be murdered regardless of what you do, so you may as well keep your money.) The equilibrium payoffs are 2,2. Note that this outcome is not Pareto-efficient: both sides could benefit by changing from *Don't pay-Kill* to *Pay-Release,* if an agreement to do so could be reached and enforced.

A "nice" kidnapper would *Release* regardless of your action, and a "nasty" one would *Kill* regardless of your action. And if you don't know whether he is "nice" or "nasty," the best choice remains not to pay. So it might appear that you should never pay ransom. Consider, however, the alternative payoff rankings for the kidnapper shown in Matrix 3 of Table 16.3. Here the kidnapper is "nice" if you *Pay* but turns "nasty" if you *Don't pay*. Of course, this is just what the kidnapper is threatening all along, but is his threat convincing? That is, can such preferences make sense?

Here are two different ways that a kidnapper might attempt to convince you, the parent, that his preferences are really as shown in Matrix 3.

1. Kidnapper: "I am really a 'nice' person. However, only when I have lots of money can I afford to act in accord with my true preferences. Thus, being 'nice' is a normal superior good for me. If you pay the ransom, I'll be rich enough to be 'nice.'"

2. Kidnapper: "I'm not really 'nice' or 'nasty.' I'm just in this business to make money. Obviously, to remain in the kidnapping business, I must convince my customers that, whatever my true preferences might be, my actions will be dictated by the ranking shown in Matrix 3. So you can count on me to release your child if you pay, but kill her otherwise."

In the first scenario, the kidnapper is claiming that he can be "appeased" by meeting his demands. Consider this analogy. In the Munich crisis that preceded World War II, Adolph Hitler claimed that, if appeased by being allowed to take over Czechoslovakia, he would make no more territorial demands. But given his way at Munich, Hitler did not abide by his promise. Almost immediately afterward he started making demands on Polish territory— leading the British and the French to abandon appeasement. [*Question for student:* Under what conditions, if any, does the argument for appeasement make sense?]

In the second situation, the kidnapper says he has a reputation to protect. If parents hear that he releases victims without receiving a ransom, they won't pay. The same holds if people learn that he kills victims even if parents do pay. So, he argues, you can have confidence that he will release the child if you pay, but otherwise he will kill her.

Is this really convincing? Suppose you know that the kidnapper is always "mean" or always "nasty," so that the earlier argument (1) can be set aside. Suppose for the moment that the kidnapper plans to engage in exactly one more crime after this one, and that this is known to all concerned. Then the parent should reason as follows: "The kidnapper, once he commits his next and final crime, will be going out of business. So, for the parent of the next victim, the reputation argument cannot apply. Then the parent of the next victim will rationally refuse to pay ransom. But since that will happen regardless of whether or not I pay ransom now, the effect of my action upon the kidnapper's reputation is irrelevant. Thus, I also should refuse to pay."

Furthermore, this chain of reasoning is valid no matter how many future crimes the kidnapper plans to commit! On the very final crime, we have seen, the parent should not pay ransom. Thus, the kidnapper's reputation will be irrelevant for the parent of the next-to-last victim, and therefore for the next-to-next-to-last, and so on all the way back to the present crime.[15] So you as parent should certainly not pay ransom, unless you think the kidnapper is validly making argument (1) that being nice is a superior good, or if you think the kidnapper is irrational.

SUMMARY

Whereas market transactions are voluntary, the political sphere is characterized by coercive interactions. The individuals who comprise the government are able, with the ultimate backing of force, to dictate to the rest of us.

Two extreme models of government are the *public-choice state* and the *exploitation state*. The public-choice state is merely an instrument whereby citizen-consumers achieve their collective aims. The exploitation state, in contrast, is a government whose rulers are in conflict with their subjects, seeking only to extract resources from them.

In an ideally democratic public-choice state, competition for political leadership acts like competition in the marketplace. Just as competition for sales forces firms to satisfy consumers' desires, competition for office forces political parties to satisfy citizens' wishes.

---

[15]The reasoning would not apply if the kidnapper were planning to engage in an infinite rather than a finite number of crimes, for then there would be no last crime. But since human beings have only a finite life span, this could never be true. Alternatively, it can be shown mathematically that the kidnapper's threat is credible if at any point in the sequence of crimes there is some sufficiently large probability of the sequence continuing—that is, of the kidnapper going on to commit another crime. But this also could not apply for a criminal with a limited life span.

Market competition has serious imperfections, but the imperfections of political competition are even more severe. Citizens vote only at relatively rare intervals; there are few political parties among which to choose (commonly, just two); and many issues are bundled together in the position of each candidate. Another source of imperfection is the fact that a voter has little motivation to incur the informational costs necessary to cast an intelligent ballot. Under majority rule, there is the serious problem of adequate provision for minority desires. "Log-rolling" allows intense minority preferences on some issues to be exchanged for votes on other issues. In principle, log-rolling or even direct purchase of votes will lead to Pareto-optimal outcomes.

Majority rule commonly leads to the paradox of *cycling:* proposal X may be favored by a majority over Y, Y over Z, but Z in turn over X. Where conditions rule out cycling, there is a strong tendency for the winning proposal to be the one favored by the *median voter*.

The individuals comprising the government fall into a number of different categories, with differing motivations. One important category is the bureaucracy, the permanent (non-elected) personnel who actually implement political decisions. Bureaucrats are motivated to seek job security and to increase the size of their agencies.

Models of *conflict,* as between different states or between rulers and subjects, are only beginning to be studied by economists. Conflict is promoted by emotional antipathy, by rivalry for resources, by overconfidence in one's ability to deliver and bear up under punishment, and by lack of enforceability of agreements. Since in the real world all agreements are only imperfectly enforceable, Coase's Theorem (that all mutually advantageous bargains will be achieved) can be valid only to a limited extent. Hence we cannot expect the abolition of war, crime, and politics.

QUESTIONS

For Review

*1. In market competition among firms, economic profit tends to be eliminated (the "zero-profit theorem" of Chapter 7). Does something analogous tend to occur in political competition between parties? Why or why not?

*2. What are some of the major obstacles preventing the expression of the "will of the people" through the political system? How are these analogous to, and how different from, the difficulties of the market system?

3. How may *delegation* of decision-making power to political representatives lead to decisions diverging from the desires of constituents? Considering the corporation as a kind of political system, what protections and escape hatches do stockholders have that may not be available to members of the polity?

4. How do the goals and opportunities of bureaucrats differ from those of elected officials? How do they differ from those of managers of private firms?

*5. a. Is a unanimous consent rule, in which dissident votes must be purchased, an ideal political system—apart from transaction costs?
   b. Does the process of "log-rolling" approximate this result?
   c. What are some objections to log-rolling?

*The answers to starred questions appear at the end of the book.

6. What conditions are necessary for the validity of the Median-Voter Theorem? What types of elections are likely to meet these conditions?

7. Show how emotional antipathy, rivalry for resources, and overconfidence all tend to promote conflict.

8. In a situation where there would be a mutual gain from agreement, show how agreement might not be achieved in the absence of outside enforcement.

*9. What are "self-enforcing agreements"? Give an example.

10. Show how different types of conflict can be represented in game-theory terms. Which are more and which less likely to lead to cooperative solutions?

11. Why do "single-peaked" preferences rule out majority-vote cycling if there is only a single dimension of choice? What happens if there is more than one dimension?

For Further Thought and Discussion

*1. Why is the "public-choice" approach to the problem of political behavior particularly amenable to economic analysis? What other approaches are there?

*2. If votes could be bought for money, would *both* the rich and the poor be better off in accordance with the mutual advantage of trade? What is the objection to buying votes for money?

3. Under what political mechanisms or situations do majorities tend to exploit minorities? Under what mechanisms or situations is it the other way around?

*4. Which is more likely to gain legislative approval: a bill that would simply redistribute cash from the rich to the poor, or one to establish a bureaucracy to provide services to the poor? Explain.

5. How are the administrative decisions of a commissioner with a limited period of office likely to differ from those of a lifetime civil servant?

*6. Would the fidelity of the political system to citizen desires be improved by any or all of the following: more frequent elections, more numerous legislatures, elected rather than appointed judges, the spoils system rather than the merit system in the civil service? Comment.

*7. Suppose there were a sudden unexpected increase in demand for a product now provided through the government sector. Would you expect any systematic differences in the price-quantity response as compared with a product provided through the private sector? What about the response to a decrease in demand? What about responses to increases or decreases in cost of production?

8. Under a system that might be called "open corruption," government officials (including judges) could sell their decisions to the highest bidder. How bad would this be?

ANSWERS

CHAPTER 1

For Review

1. a. Economics consists of theories whose implications provide testable propositions about the real world. These models must stand or fall on the accuracy of their predictions. Such use of evidence makes theories scientific.

   b. Here are some economic predictions. Vegetables will be cheaper in season than out of season. People will seldom be observed throwing money away. Advertisers will claim that their products are better than competitors' products. To take a more extended example: sharply higher gasoline prices will tend to reduce auto travel generally, and also to lower average highway speeds (with a consequent reduction in accidents). It will also encourage sales of smaller cars. In the longer run a trend to more compact cities will be observed. (Of course, all such predictions must be understood in an "other things equal" sense.)

   c. Certainly, economic science cannot predict everything. Economics does not explain why tastes or social attitudes change. We do not understand the determinants of such ideological movements as fascism, Marxism or Christianity, or the full causes of such social trends as growth of government. And even important issues of a more narrowly defined "economic" nature, such as causes of business fluctuations, remain unresolved.

2. a. Behavior may be defined as rational either in terms of method of decision (the choice is made by calculating the costs and benefits of alternative actions) or in terms of results (the action chosen turns out to be well-suited for achieving one's goals).

   b. In terms of method, a prospective wagerer at roulette might calculate the odds and observe the behavior of the wheel before choosing a number. It would be irrational to place a bet on the basis of a dream or heavenly vision. In terms of results, it's probably irrational to bet at all.

   c. Aggregated over many individuals, a limited degree of individual rationality will show up as a tendency toward rational behavior for the group as a whole. Even if the rational element is small, it operates in a consistent and predictable direction.

7. a. In a market economy, self-interested individuals will devote their resources to satisfying others by providing desired goods and services. What others are willing to pay enables the sellers to earn higher income and so better satisfy their own desires.

   b., c., d. No. If their own income is not increased by serving others, self-interested individuals will not do so.

8. a. "Real" flows are flows of goods or services (e.g., lamb chops, labor). "Financial" flows are flows of general purchasing power (money). Each flow represents one side of a class of transaction. Goods or services are traded for general purchasing power.

   b. In the "product market," firms sell to consumers goods and services, and obtain dollars in return. In the "factor market," consumers in their capacity as resource-owners trade their factor services to firms for dollars. The dollars that consumers pay for goods and services must match what they receive for providing factor services. Similarly, the dollars that firms pay for factor services are those which they receive for the goods and services they produce.

For Further Thought and Discussion

1. a. Yes, other things equal. If other things were not equal, a state or nation with capital punishment might also be found to have a high murder rate—if, for example, it was the high frequency of murder that led to the imposition of the death penalty in that jurisdiction.

   b. Yes. Increasing this tax exemption lowers the cost of having children and so should result (other things equal) in an increase in the birth rate.

2. If insurance companies refused to pay for the treatment of "mental illness," and if the government did not finance treatment under Medicare, doctors would be less motivated to diagnose patients' psychological problems as "disease." This would surely lower the reported incidence of "mental illness." Making medical treatment more costly would also induce potential patients to confront their problems rather than accept the dependent status of being "sick." Note that these predicted effects do not depend upon whether Dr. Szasz's theory about mental illness is in fact correct.

5. The principle of the Invisible Hand applies to market interactions, which are both voluntary and mutual. Since the kinds of interactions mentioned in this question (crime, etc.) are not voluntary market exchanges, self-serving behavior may not benefit others.

6. Drivers who wear seat belts would feel safer than before, and might therefore take a little less care to avoid accidents. Thus, pedestrian deaths might rise, though driver deaths would not.

7. Dr. Johnson probably had in mind the Invisible Hand. Charles Baudelaire probably had in mind his publisher's refusal to give him a bigger advance on his royalties.

CHAPTER 2

For Review

1. a. Optimization.
   b. Equilibrium.
   c. Equilibrium.
   d. Optimization.
   e. Equilibrium.
   f. Optimization.

3. The price of a good X is the amount of another good (usually money) that must be given up in order to acquire a unit of X. Consequently, price is a ratio of amounts, or a ratio of quantities (money/X).

6. Yes. Shifting the supply curve up by $T leads to a solution at the intersection of the gross (of tax) supply curve with the original demand curve. Shifting the demand curve down by $T leads to a solution at the intersection of the net (of tax) demand curve with the original supply curve. As the only difference between gross and net supply or demand curves is a vertical displacement of $T, the intersections take place at the same quantity. The intersection of the gross supply curve with the demand curve determines the gross price. The intersection of the net demand curve with the supply curve determines the net (of tax) price. But, of course, it is unnecessary to carry out both constructions; either suffices since the gross price and net price are related by $P^+ = P^- + T$.

8. a. Both.
   b. Raise price paid by consumers.
   c., d. Lower price received by sellers.

10. a. A meaningful price ceiling must be set below the equilibrium price; a meaningful price floor must be set above the equilibrium price.
    b. Because trade is voluntary, the actual quantity traded is the smaller of the desired transaction magnitudes (quantity supplied or quantity demanded). Price ceilings decrease the quantity that sellers are willing to offer. Price floors decrease the quantity that consumers wish to buy. Both decrease the actual quantity traded in the market.
    c. If a "meaningful" price floor, above the equilibrium level, is supported, sellers can make some sales for which there are no demanders (apart from the supporting agency). Transactions then depend solely on the existence of supply at that price. If the floor price is above the equilibrium price, the quantity sold will increase. The supporting agency, however, will accumulate inventories.

13. Each member pays the cost of a can divided by the number of members, or $0.30/40 = 3/4 of a cent. The other 39 members pay the balance, namely 39($0.30)/40. Notice that no member pays the marginal cost to the club of each can he consumes.

14. a. May be true or false.
    b. True.
    c. False.
    d. May be true or false.
    e. True.
    f. May be true or false.

For Further Thought and Discussion

1. a. The tax would have a small effect on quantity exchanged in the market, a small effect on the gross price paid by buyers, but a large effect on net price to sellers. (The result here is seen more clearly if the demand curve is shifted down, rather than the supply curve up.)
   b. The steep supply curve means that suppliers are willing to offer even a slightly larger quantity only at a much higher price. Since the tax reduces quantity sold by lowering the net demand, the net price received by sellers falls sharply. The gross price paid by consumers rises, but only slightly, since the market quantity declines just slightly.

3. a. Since it would be more costly to operate automobiles, the demand curve for cars would shift to the left, leading to a fall in their price.

  b. The price of big, heavy cars ("gas-guzzlers") would fall more.

4. a. As changes in economic conditions affect demand or supply (or both), the new supply-demand equilibrium is attained with no transactions taking place at "wrong" prices. In effect, the new equilibrium is arrived at instantaneously.

  b. In the real world, these conditions are never precisely met. But in a market where traders are well informed, the model may closely approximate reality.

7. a. Wherever the Roman armies marched, the demand for foodstuffs increased because of the addition of military demands to civilian demands. This increase in demand resulted in an increase in equilibrium price.

  b. Diocletian's edict set a price ceiling below the (new) equilibrium price. As a result, there must have been unsatisfied buyers. It is likely that Diocletian's armies made up a large portion of these unsatisfied buyers. So either efforts to evade the edict were successful or Diocletian's armies went hungry, unless indeed they simply confiscated the food they wanted. [See Jacob Burckhardt, *The Age of Constantine the Great* (New York: Pantheon, 1949), Chapter 2.]

8. Total Revenue is Price times Quantity, so at $Q = 0, 3, 6$ the Total Revenues are respectively $R = 0, 60, 72$. The increase from $Q = 3$ to $Q = 6$ provides an estimate of $(72 - 60)/3 = 4$ for the Marginal Revenue at $Q = 4 \ 1/2$. The decrease from $Q = 3$ to $Q = 0$ provides an estimate of $(60 - 0)/3 = 20$ for the Marginal Revenue at $Q = 1 \ 1/2$. Interpolating, we obtain the approximation $MR = (4 + 20)/2 = 12$ at $Q = 3$.

CHAPTER 3

For Review

1. a. Violates the Axiom of Comparison.

  b. Expresses indifference, but does not violate the laws.

  c. Indicates inconsistency, and thus also violates the Axiom of Comparison.

4. Utility is simply an indicator of preference ranking. To say that a consumer prefers one bundle over the other is to say that he gets higher utility from one bundle over the other.

6. Since ordinal utility indicates only direction of preference, only the signs of Marginal Utility can be determined.

8. a. Ordinal.

  b. Cardinal.

  c. Interpersonal comparability.

For Further Thought and Discussion

1. No.

3. Examples of ordinal measures are placement in a horse race, a tennis ladder, or a job seniority list. An interesting scientific example is a measure commonly used for hardness, based on the relation "scratches." Thus, diamond is harder than glass, and glass is harder than chalk, but this measure does not indicate how much harder.

5. Any shape that is symmetrical across the 45° line. This would indicate, for example, that I am indifferent between the combination "His Income is $2,000 while My Income is $1,000" and the combination "My Income is $2,000 while His Income is $1,000."

6. The preference map would take the form of rays out of the origin. Along any single ray, representing a fixed ratio of "My Income" to "His Income," the individual would be equally happy. For such an individual the preference directions would be such that "My Income" is a good, while "His Income" is a bad.

CHAPTER 4

For Review

3. a. The budget line is the northeast boundary of an individual's market opportunity set. It shows the achievable consumption bundles if the individual spends all of his income.

b. The equation of the budget line is $I = P_x x + P_y y$.

c. The slope of the budget line depends upon the relative prices of the goods X and Y. This slope will be $-P_x/P_y$.

4. The optimum of the consumer is found geometrically as the point on the budget line touching the highest achievable indifference curve. If both goods are consumed, this will be an interior solution. If only one good is consumed (if the budget line touches the highest indifference curve at one axis), this will be a corner solution.

6. a. The Consumption Balance Equation is $MU_x/P_x = MU_y/P_y$. The Substitution Equivalence Equation is $MRS_C = MRS_E$ (or, slope of indifference curve = slope of budget line). The Consumption Balance Equation can be reduced to the Substitution Equivalence Equation, but not vice versa. This is because the Consumption Balance Equation requires cardinal utility while the Substitution Equivalence Equation requires only ordinal utility. (Cardinal utility implies ordinal utility, but not vice versa.)

b. Both equations apply to interior solutions. At a corner solution an inequality will ordinarily hold, dictating spending all one's income on one of the commodities.

11. a. If the Income Expansion Path has a positive slope, the Engel Curve for each good will have a positive slope.

b. The Engel Expenditure Curve for each good will have a positive slope, but this slope will not exceed unity (the slope of the 45° line).

c. If X is an inferior good, the Engel Curve will have a negative slope.

14. If the Law of Demand holds, the Price Expansion Path never curls back (to the left).

18. As long as commodity X is a good (rather than a neuter or a bad), those receiving vouchers for purchase of X will consume at least the voucher equivalent. For those previously consuming less than this, the voucher will always increase consumption. For this reason, vouchers are particularly effective (relative to subsidies) in increasing consumption among persons who would otherwise have consumed little or none of a good.

For Further Thought and Discussion

1. a. An experiment could reveal the maximum amount of Y an individual might be willing to pay for a small increment of X. This would be an approximation of the MRS_C.

b. No known experiment could reveal Marginal Utility.

3. a. In the Giffen range, the Price Expansion Path moves toward higher y but lower x. Since utility is increasing along the PEP, it must be that y is increasing fast enough to more than compensate for the decrease in x. But the amount of Y it is possible to acquire is bounded by the horizontal line through the starting-point K. So this process can continue only over a limited range of the PEP, which must eventually turn up and to the right.

   b. This is impossible. Utility is increasing everywhere along the PEP, and the same starting-point cannot have both lower and higher utility.

4. a. An increase in P_x would tend to shift the Income Expansion Path up and to the left.

   b. An increase in income would tend to displace the PEP up and to the right (assuming X and Y are both normal superior goods).

7. The pair of close substitutes is more likely to have a member that is an inferior good. The reason is that complements tend to be consumed together, while substitutes do not. Therefore, increased income is likely to result in increased consumption of both bread and butter (complements). But comparing butter and margarine (substitutes), with increased income an individual is likely to consume less margarine, since he can now better afford the preferred (but more expensive) substitute—butter.

8. With three goods we have to think in terms of a three-dimensional preference diagram. The indifference curves would become "indifference shells," nested like the skins of an onion. And the budget line would become a "budget plane" showing the combinations of the three goods the consumer could purchase. A two-dimensional diagram for goods X and Y, like Figure 4.13, could then be constructed *for each quantity of good Z*. The budget line of that two-dimensional diagram would be the intersection with the budget plane for that amount of Z, and similarly the indifference curves of the two-dimensional diagram are the intersections with the indifference shells. Since a fall in the price of good Z would (normally) lead to increased purchases of Z, in the two-dimensional diagram of Figure 4.13 the budget line would shift up or down (depending on whether expenditures on Z decreased or increased), and the indifference curves would shift positions. If X and Z are complements, the net effect would be that as P_z falls, at any given P_x there would be increased purchases of good X.

9. Since usually only a limited fraction of income is spent on any single good X, the income effect (enrichment or impoverishment) due to a change in P_x will be relatively small.

11. The market price should rise, because increased quantities will be demanded. The effect will be to partially cancel the impact of the subsidy or voucher.

13. a. Coach travel is an inferior good here, since the purchased quantity of coach travel falls as income rises. Specifically, if income were to rise above \$100, more first-class travel and less coach travel would be purchased.

   b. If the traveler's budget is so small that he can complete the trip only by traveling entirely in coach, then he will do so. If the traveler's budget permits the trip to be completed by traveling entirely in first-class, then only first-class travel will be purchased.

14. a. Yes.

   b. If the slope of the budget-line is exactly the same as the slope of the indifference-curve for the two perfect substitutes, then the individual does not care whether he consumes only one of the goods, or only the other good, or any mixture of the two.

15. No, the two Income Expansion Paths curves cannot intersect. Assuming $P_y = 1$ throughout, every point on the original IEP curve represents an indifference-curve tangency with a budget line of slope $-P_x$. Every point on the new IEP' curve represents a tangency with a budget line of slope $-P'_x$. If the two IEP curves crossed, their point of intersection would have to be where an indifference curve is tangent to two budget lines of different slopes, which is impossible.

16. a. Here $P_x = 120$ is the choke price for X; at that price, the quantity demanded falls to zero.

   b. For $P_x > 120$, the demand-curve equation given indicates a negative amount of X demanded, which we rule out as impossible. The correct demand equation, in the range where $P_x > 120$, is simply $x = 0$.

CHAPTER 5

For Review

2. Such Engel Curves (all straight lines through the origin, but with different slopes) depict the same proportionate response of changes in consumption to changes in income. For such curves, greater steepness does not show greater income elasticity but rather that x/I is higher—that is, that the commodity is absolutely more important in the consumer's budget.

5. a. *Elastic demand* means that the absolute value of the price elasticity of demand exceeds one. *Inelastic demand* means that the absolute value of the price elasticity of demand is less than one.

   b. For a linear demand curve, the elasticity at any point is the ratio of two slopes: the slope of a ray from the origin to the point on the curve, divided by the constant slope along the curve.

   c. For a nonlinear demand curve, the slope along the curve is interpreted as the slope of the tangent to the curve at that point.

6. a. Negative infinity.

   b. Zero.

   c. -1.

9. Price elasticity is -1. Income elasticity is $+1$.

10. Permitting the sale of coupons would benefit both the wealthy and the poor. The poor could sell coupons for dollars, shift their income constraint outward, and attain a more preferred position. The wealthy could buy coupons for dollars, shift their ration constraint upward, and also attain a more preferred position.

For Further Thought and Discussion

1. Assuming for simplicity just two goods X and Y, and using expenditure shares as weights, the equation that we want to prove can be written

$$\frac{P_x x}{I}\left(\frac{\Delta x}{\Delta I}\frac{I}{x}\right) + \frac{P_y y}{I}\left(\frac{\Delta y}{\Delta I}\frac{I}{y}\right) = 1$$

After cancellations

$$\frac{P_x \Delta x + P_y \Delta y}{\Delta I} = 1$$

But since $I = P_x x + P_y y$, where P_x and P_y are constants, $\Delta I = P_x \Delta x + P_y \Delta y$. So the numerator and denominator of the fraction above are equal, proving that their ratio does indeed equal unity.

2. a. Since $PX = 100$, expenditure is constant at any price and elasticity is therefore unity. Since expenditure is constant, the share of the budget is also constant.

b. It can be shown with calculus that the (inverse) slope of the demand curve dX/dP is $-200/P^3$. Multiply by P/X to obtain elasticity: $\eta = -200/(P^2X)$. Since $P^2X = 100$ (demand equation), this reduces to $-200/100 = -2$. Elasticity is constant, and each 1 percent fall in price increases quantity by 2 percent. Thus the budget share rises as price falls.

c. Using the same method as in (b), the slope is $-50/P^{1.5}$, and elasticity is $\eta = -50/(P^{.5}X)$. This reduces to $-50/100 = -1/2$. Here a 1 percent fall in price increases quantity by 50 percent, so budget share falls as price falls.

d. "Importance" in the budget may change in either direction as price changes, even when elasticity is constant. In general, there is no necessary relation between importance and elasticity of demand.

3. a. At low incomes consumers are likely to be interested only in nutrition. High-quality and low-quality beef are good substitutes as far as nutrition is concerned. At high incomes other characteristics such as flavor become increasingly important to consumers. Here, low-quality beef is not a good substitute for high-quality beef. Higher indifference curves would therefore have greater curvature.

b. Because high-quality beef is a luxury (it has a stronger positive income effect than low-quality beef), the price elasticity of demand for high-quality beef should be high relative to the price elasticity for low-quality beef.

5. The secretary is mistaken. The professor would be willing to pay more in total for three tickets than for two. But if the price is only $10, he does not have to pay more for three tickets than he would have paid for two at a price of $20 each. Looking at this another way, the $10 is the worth of a third ticket to the professor, not the worth of each of three tickets. (If the objection were valid, it would never make sense for a consumer to have an inelastic demand for a good.)

6. This is indeed possible, though opinions may differ about how likely it is. Consumers seeking snob appeal gain utility from exclusiveness. At a high price, they get not only the commodity but also the exclusivity. The fact that the price is high guarantees that not many people can afford the commodity, and therefore makes "snobbish" consumers more willing to buy than at a low price. But if the exclusiveness were provided in some other way (as by the medieval Statute of Dress that made it illegal for the lower orders to wear upper-class clothes), presumably the Law of Demand would hold.

7. This is very much like the previous question, but here the consumer believes the high-price good is of higher quality. There is of course nothing paradoxical about someone preferring high quality at a high price over low quality at a low price. Again, if the quality were guaranteed in some other way than by high price (perhaps by a consumer organization's rating of the product), presumably the Law of Demand would hold—a high-quality product at a low price would be chosen over the same high-quality product at a high price. Chapter 9 discusses this issue in greater depth.

8. a. The usual justification is that rationed commodities tend to be those that are "essential" to life or health. If ration allowances were exchangeable, rich people might end up with more than "their fair share" of these essential commodities. Note that this assumes that the poorer people who sell their allowances are foolish in giving up some "essentials" for nonessentials—or else possibly that poorer people have to be forced to remain in good working condition for the sake of the war effort, though they themselves might prefer otherwise!

b. The adverse consequences include the loss of the gains from trade, plus the diversion of resources into black-market activities and the policing efforts required to minimize such activities.

CHAPTER 6

For Review

3. a. Economic profit is the difference between revenues and economic costs.

   b. Since owners receive profits, maximization of profit (owner wealth) is an appropriate goal for owners. Managers, if they are not also owners, have no claim on profits and so would be uninterested in maximizing profit. Managers might be interested in power, growth, stability, and a favorable corporate image as well as in larger salaries and more pleasant working conditions.

   c. Owners tend to develop mechanisms to impose their profit-maximizing goal upon managers. Lawsuits and proxy fights can punish managers who are not pursuing owners' goals. Similarly, profit-sharing and stock-option plans reward managers for pursuing owners' goals. These mechanisms are imperfect, though, so the likely result is that the firm will pursue some mixture of owner and manager goals.

6. a. Recall that total cost is fixed cost F plus variable cost VC. Since $AVC = 10 + 2.5q$, $VC = (AVC)(q) = 10q + 2.5q^2$; and total cost is $F + VC = 250 + 10q + 2.5q^2$.

   b. The firm maximizes profits at that output where $P = MC$, or numerically $50 = 10 + 5q$; the solution is $q = 8$.

   c. Profits are total revenue R minus total cost C. $R = pq = 50(8) = 400$. Substituting in the equation $C = 250 + 10q + 2.5q^2$, we obtain $C = 490$. The firm is therefore losing $90. Nevertheless, price is greater than $AVC = 10 + 2.5(8) = 30$, so in the short run the firm will continue producing.

7. a. Yes. At the vertical axis, AC is greater than or equal to MC. (If there are Fixed Costs, AC is infinite.) As MC falls from its initial level along the vertical axis, it makes AC fall as well.

   b. No. By proposition 2.2a, when AC is falling, MC lies below AC; but MC can be less than AC and still not be itself falling.

9. A firm will make short-run adjustments to changes in economic conditions if such changes are viewed as temporary. A firm will make long-run adjustments to changes in economic conditions if such changes are viewed as permanent.

For Further Thought and Discussion

3. Taking on additional traffic at a price lower than Average Cost would be financially advantageous if the price exceeds Marginal Cost. But even if Average Variable Cost is only one-third of Average Cost, Marginal Cost might not be low enough to warrant taking on the new traffic. (Indeed, Marginal Cost could then be larger than Average Cost.)

4. a. If changing conditions are viewed as temporary, some inputs may be held fixed in the face of a contraction of output; this avoids the transaction costs incurred in selling the inputs and then buying them back when conditions return to normal—or, for an expansion of output, avoids the costs of buying inputs and then selling them back. A similar result holds to the extent that the firm's operations involve specializing resources to the firm. Such specialized resources can only be sold at a low price to others, yet must be purchased at a high price. Then these resources may be held fixed during temporary changes in output.

   b. The inputs that are held fixed are those which are highly specialized to the firm, or for which transaction costs are high.

8. The short-run Marginal Cost is the additional cost of temporarily increasing output. Whether these costs are paid immediately (overtime wages, increased usage of power, etc.) or at a later time (deferred maintenance), they are all costs. The factory manager is confusing short-run costs with costs that must be paid immediately. They are not the same.

10. a. The Marginal Cost of providing service to more passengers when trains are running empty is quite low. Another passenger can be transported at a very little additional cost. When trains are running full, however, the Marginal Cost of providing service is much higher. Additional trains must be run, or further unpleasant crowding must be imposed on passengers. Since Marginal Cost is very low in off-hours, the transit line should encourage off-hour business, not discourage it. The management consultant is confusing Marginal Cost with Average Cost.

   b. Commutation tickets will increase ridership at rush hours, but it is during these times that the trains are already full. If the cost of running additional trains or of imposing crowding on customers is high, then the transit line is likely to be worse off by selling commutation tickets. Discount tickets for off-hour riders, on the other hand, would likely increase revenues without a commensurate increase in cost. This type of discount would be a good idea.

CHAPTER 7

For Review

1. Yes. Steepness and elasticity of supply, at a given point, must be inversely related.
2. While the issue of whether or not doubling all inputs would always double output is arguable, it is not economically relevant. In the real world, it is never possible to double all relevant inputs.
4. Where there are no "external" effects, the industry supply curve will be less steep than the firm supply curve but will have the same elasticity (the *proportionate* response of output to price will be the same).
6. a. In long-run equilibrium, the marginal firm is on the borderline between staying in the industry and leaving. The value of its opportunities elsewhere practically equals what it can earn in this industry. Consequently, the *economic* profit of the marginal firm will be (only negligibly above) zero.

   b. Infra-marginal firms have access to some special resources particularly suited to producing in this industry. Other firms will bid for the right to use these special resources. When the infra-marginal firm charges itself the opportunity cost—what it could get by offering the special resources to these other bidders—it is also left with zero economic profit.

For Further Thought and Discussion

1. True. A competitive firm will produce positive output only if Marginal Cost exceeds Average Variable Cost (in the short run) or Average Cost (in the long run). So *AVC* in the former case, or *AC* in the latter case, must be rising.
4. No. All firms may be earning zero economic profit, and yet some may be able to survive even if product price falls. These will be the "infra-marginal" firms (see For Review Question 6).
6. a. If all coupons were used initially, allowing resale would only redistribute coupons.

Only if some coupons were initially unused would sale of coupons tend to raise the price of petroleum and elicit more supply.

b. Salability, though, would cause a redistribution of coupons to those consumers having the highest demand prices for gasoline—at least as high as the sum of the product price and the price paid for a coupon.

c. Without the sale of coupons, some buyers may receive little or no Consumer Surplus from their purchases of gasoline, while others who would receive great Consumer Surplus may be unable to make purchases. Salability will allow those previously unable to make purchases to bid away the coupons from those currently receiving little Consumer Surplus from gasoline.

7. If the nonsalable ration coupons are all assigned to consumers who are unwilling to pay even the low ceiling price, then it might seem that trading of the good will be entirely blocked because no one would want to buy at the ceiling price. But this is not correct, since, as a consequence of the reduced demand, the market price could fall below the ceiling price. In fact, unless all the nonsalable ration tickets went to individuals unwilling to pay even the choke price for supply, the new market equilibrium price would be below the ceiling price but above the choke price for supply, and so trade would take place. On the other hand, if the coupons were salable they would be resold to those who value them the most. Then there would be trading at the ceiling price.

10. No. The output from existing wells is based, even in the short run, on a calculation of the price received for oil versus the cost of pumping. The higher the price, the more it pays to pump. In the longer run, the higher the price, the more profitable it will be to extend the life of an existing well by heating, flooding, redrilling, etc.

12. a. By reversing the analysis pictured in Figure 7.10, it can be seen that Consumer Surplus will increase (rather than decrease) because of the lower price to consumers, and Producer Surplus will increase (rather than decrease) because of the higher price to sellers.

b. No. A tax leads to inefficiency due to reduced exchange; a subsidy leads to inefficiency due to excessive exchange. Since the price received by sellers exceeds the price paid by consumers, there will be units produced and sold whose value to consumers does not cover the Marginal Cost of production. It may seem puzzling that Consumer Surplus and Producer Surplus both increase in this market and yet there is inefficiency. The explanation is that the subsidy here reduces Consumer Surplus and Producer Surplus elsewhere. Other industries must be taxed to finance the subsidy.

CHAPTER 8

For Review

1. To maximize profit, a monopolist will set $MR = MC$. Since Marginal Cost is always positive, the monopolist will always produce where Marginal Revenue is positive. $MR > 0$ implies $|\eta| > 1$.

2. If the firm continued to produce 1,000 panes, then its savings would be $10(1,000) = $10,000. But the reduction in Marginal Cost means that the firm will choose to produce more than 10,000 panes, so that (before paying for the machine) its profits increase by more than $10,000. Thus, the firm should be willing to pay more than $10,000.

4. In comparison with pure competition, monopoly results in a smaller rate of output. Because less is produced and traded, some of the gains from specialization and trade are lost; the sum of Consumer Surplus and Producer Surplus is smaller.

6. Owners of monopolies may not be any more interested in nonprofit goals than owners of competitive firms, but reduced competitive pressure allows indulging such goals. As another matter, they may be less successful in imposing the goal of profit maximization upon managers, since owners of monopolies cannot measure their managers' performances by comparing them to competitors. Also, antitrust policy may act as a threat. (If profits are too large, perhaps an antitrust suit will be forthcoming.) Finally, many monopolies are regulated and so prevented from maximizing profits. For any of these reasons, monopolies may not pursue profits as vigorously as do competitive firms.

8. In deriving the supply curve of the competitive industry, we assume that each separate firm sets output where Marginal Cost equals price. The height of the point on the supply curve therefore shows the Marginal Cost of each firm for that level of industry output. Consequently, that point on the supply curve also shows what the Marginal Cost would be if that industry were monopolized.

For Further Thought and Discussion

1. Yes, there is a contradiction. An effective monopolist always operates in the range of elastic demand (see For Review Question 1). But if demand is elastic, higher prices will have a big effect on quantity demanded.

3. a. At the simple monopoly optimum $MR = MC$, price exceeds Marginal Cost. A perfectly discriminating monopolist, on the other hand, will expand output until *price* equals Marginal Cost. A perfectly discriminating monopolist, then, might be expected to produce more than a simple monopolist. However, if the income effect is very strong, this conclusion may not hold. The discriminating monopolist extracts more income from consumers at each level of output, which tends to reduce demand for additional units.

   b. A market-segmentation monopolist will charge a price higher than the simple monopoly price to some market segments, and so sell less in those segments; but he will also charge a price lower than the simple monopoly price to the other segments and so sell more there. The total produced and sold by a market segmentation monopolist, then, may be more or less than that of a simple monopolist.

   c. While a multi-part pricing monopolist will charge a price higher than the simple monopoly price for small purchases, he will charge a price lower than the simple monopoly price for purchases beyond a certain size. Some customers will buy less because they purchase too little to receive the lower marginal price. Other customers will purchase enough to receive the lower marginal price and so will purchase more (in the absence of a strong income effect) than if faced with a single monopoly price. The multi-part pricing monopolist, therefore, also may or may not produce more than a simple monopolist.

4. Price discrimination is effective only if resale of the commodity is difficult. Resale of services is more difficult than resale of manufactured goods.

5. a. It is probably not too difficult for a theater to price discriminate in favor of the young. Many persons clearly look too old, and in questionable cases the theater may ask for a student identification card, driver's license, or other proof of age. In general, it is easier to price discriminate when the seller sees who receives the service, than when he sells a good which can later be resold.

b. It is probably true that the young, having less money, are less willing to pay for a movie ticket. That does not necessarily mean, however, that the young have a more elastic demand for movies.

6. a. Yes. The markets are divided between customers who are willing and customers who are not willing to take the trouble of collecting and using coupons.

b. There should be little or no "leakage," since those not using coupons (and so paying higher prices) are unwilling to take the time and trouble needed to shift to the lower-price market.

c. Yes, the consumers with more elastic demands will find it more worthwhile to go to the trouble of using coupons.

10. Yes. Consider theft, for example. The marginal yield to the "industry" as a whole is probably less than that perceived by the individual competitive thief. One thief may steal on Tuesday what another thief wanted to steal on Wednesday. Also, any increase in the scale of thievery tends to raise the intensity of defensive actions by potential victims, thereby reducing the returns to thieves in the aggregate. A monopolized theft industry would take all this into account and therefore engage in fewer (but more remunerative, on the average) crimes.

Chapter 9

For Review

4. The monopolist is really interested in producing services S desired by consumers, where the service amount is $s = qz$ (quantity of physical product times "quality" in terms of service provided by each unit of physical product). Normally, there will be increasing Marginal Cost of expanding S either by increasing quantity or by increasing quality. So, a monopolist who wants to produce a smaller service output will normally cut back on both quantity and quality.

5. a. A monopolist would obviously not suppress an invention that lowered costs.

b. If consumers are fully informed, it would not pay to suppress an invention that raised quality at a given cost. (The only possible exception would be if the invention somehow destroyed the monopoly.)

c. Consumers would not necessarily be better off. It is conceivable that adoption of a cost-reducing invention would lead the monopolist to produce a smaller amount than before, at a higher price. A similar result may come about for a quality-increasing invention.

For Further Thought and Discussion

1. No, monopolistic competition emerges when consumers' tastes for different varieties provide each supplier with a degree of monopoly power over a "clientele" for its product. In contrast, if a single generally recognized quality attribute is desired by all consumers, they will purchase from whichever firm offers this attribute at the lowest price. If there are many firms, each can survive only by offering the same price as the others, per unit of quality attribute. As price-taking suppliers of the single quality attribute, the firms are engaging in pure competition.

3. Hospitals usually engage in oligopolistic or monopolistic competition rather than pure competition. Nevertheless, the analysis in the text suggests that a shift toward monopoly is unlikely to increase efficiency. The analysts making the assertion about "excessive

competition" probably have in mind certain special features of the hospital market, notably the subsidies to medical care provided by governmental or private agencies. To the extent that medical care is subsidized, of course, the demand will be greater. And, as follows from the discussion in the text, a competitive industry would make a greater response to the increased demand both in terms of quantity and quality of service provided. But the fault, if any, is not in the competitive response, but with the amount or the type of subsidy offered users of medical services.

5. The discussion of "Suppression of Inventions" showed that an invention lowering Total and Average Cost at every level of output might conceivably raise Marginal Cost in some ranges of output. If so, even for a competitive industry, a cost-reducing invention might reduce the quantity offered at some prices. (This could happen only over a limited range, and even so seems a rather unlikely possibility.) Since a quality-improving invention is logically equivalent to a cost-reducing invention (in terms of the cost of producing the attribute desired by consumers), a corresponding analysis applies: the invention might conceivably (though this seems improbable) reduce consumer welfare.

6. Think of oranges as providing various amounts of a desired attribute, flavor. High-quality oranges contain more attribute than low-quality oranges. But it costs no more to ship a high-quality than a low-quality orange. Then shipping costs per unit of quality attribute will be less if high-quality oranges are shipped. Consequently, oranges shipped to distant locations tend to be of higher quality.

7. This is similar to the situation with oranges. The tax makes it relatively cheaper than before to supply high-quality (high-mileage) gasoline. Some firms that previously found it more advantageous to produce a lower grade of gasoline are likely now to shift over to a better grade.

9. Since there is some tradeoff between quantity and quality, any program that restricts only the number of acres planted motivates farmers to enlarge output at the expense of quality. So in this period American tobacco farmers specialized in high-yield but low-quality varieties. The reformed program had exactly the opposite effect. Since the restriction was only upon the number of pounds produced, it paid farmers to make each pound of tobacco a more valuable product. So American farmers shifted over to high-quality strains of tobacco. See J. A. Seagraves, "The Life Cycle of the Flue-Cured Tobacco Program," Department of Economics and Business, North Carolina State University, Working Paper No. 34 (March 1983).

CHAPTER 10

For Review

2. The "Prisoners' Dilemma" is a type of social interaction where each participant is motivated to adopt a shortsightedly selfish strategy, with the result that all parties lose. The source of the difficulty is that an individual who cooperates cannot induce or compel the others to do the same, so the unselfish player ends up worse than the others. Evidently there is an unexploited mutual gain from exchange here, due to inability to make binding agreements.

3. Monopolistic competition is a market structure in which each firm's product is differentiated from the others, but the relatively large number of firms rules out strategic

behavior. In contrast, the essence of oligopoly is that the behavior of any one firm will noticeably affect the behavior of others.

4. In the Nash solution of game theory, each party does the best it can given the strategies of the others. The Cournot solution for oligopoly similarly assumes that each firm chooses the profit-maximizing quantity, given the choices made by the others.

8. a. If the demand curve is "kinked," the Marginal Revenue curve has a vertical gap at the rate of output at which this kink exists. To maximize profit the firm sets $MR = MC$. Assuming that MC initially cuts through the gap in MR, moderate changes in MC will still leave MC cutting through this gap in MR. As long as this is the case, the firm will not change its rate of output or price. Moderate shifts in the demand curve to the left or right may also leave MC cutting through the gap in MR—now at a greater or smaller rate of output. Again, price will tend to be rigid.

   b. One method of enforcing a collusive agreement is for "loyal" firms to match any price cut by a defecting firm, but to refrain from matching any price increase. This leads to each potential defector viewing its demand curve as kinked at the agreed level of prices.

For Further Thought and Discussion

2. "Learning" by firms opens up many new possibilities, and the final outcome is not easily predictable. Suppose first that at each output of the other firm, the "learned" duopolist produces more than the simple duopolist. If both firms "learn," the Reaction Curve of each will shift to the right relative to the Reaction Curves of simple duopolists. As a consequence, the outcome approaches the competitive solution—both firms are worse off than before! So they may "learn" by this to behave more cooperatively, holding back on output so as to approach the monopoly solution instead. But if one firm learns that the other is inclined to hold back, the first is tempted to "free-ride" and produce more. So the final result is unclear.

3. Even though the monopolist might find it more profitable to share the market with any single new entrant, once he establishes that precedent many new competitors are likely to try to enter. So the monopolist would want to build a reputation for always being a ruthless price-cutter against new entrants. He can then point out to a potential new competitor that his threat is credible, since otherwise his reputation for toughness would be ruined and he would lose his monopoly position. See "An Application: Should You Pay Ransom?" in Chapter 16 for a further discussion of reputation effects.

4. Yes. The kink would have a more extreme form under homogeneous oligopoly. A firm that raised its price, while other firms kept their prices constant, would lose all its business—so above the kink the demand curve would be flat (perfectly elastic). A firm that lowered price would find that other firms follow, so its demand below the kink would be no more elastic than the overall industry demand.

6. a. Table 10.3 shows that the symmetrical Collusive solution is not generally better than the Threat solution for both parties. If the threat can be made effective without having to be enforced very often, the "predatory price-cutter" can do better than under collusion.

   b. Predatory price-cutting is more likely to emerge where one firm is much more powerful or aggressive than the other, so that the threat is highly credible.

CHAPTER 11

For Review

2. a. For a monopolist in the product market, Marginal Revenue is always less than product price. Consequently, for such a monopolist mrp_a lies below (to the left of) vmp_a. For a competitor in the product market, Marginal Revenue equals product price. For such a competitor, mrp_a is identical to vmp_a. So only for a monopolist in the product market does mrp_a lie to the left of vmp_a.

   b. Whether the firm is a monopolist or a competitor in the product market, mrp_a is the firm's demand curve for factor A (within the relevant range of the curve).

4. a. mrp_a must be declining for $mrp_a = h_a$ to be an optimum. For a competitor in the product market, price is a constant, so that $mrp_a = P(mp_a)$ has the same sign as mp_a. Thus, the competitor will always produce in the region of diminishing marginal returns (where mp_a is declining). For a monopolist in the product market, MR is also declining, so it may be possible to achieve declining $mrp_a = MR(mp_a)$ even with rising mp_a.

   b. The equation $mrp_a = h_a$ can be satisfied in the region of diminishing marginal returns but rising average returns (where mp_a lies above ap_a). But then $h_a = mrp_a \equiv MR(mp_a) > MR(ap_a)$. Then for a competitive firm, $h_a > P(q/a)$, or $h_a a > Pq$. This means that the expenditure on input A alone exceeds Total Revenue! So a competitive firm would always operate in the region of diminishing average returns.

   c. $mrp_a = h_a$ could never hold in the region of diminishing total returns, where mp_a is negative; since a firm will always produce where $MR > 0$, $mrp_a \equiv MR(mp_a)$ would also be negative. Since factor hire-price h_a can never be negative, the condition $mrp_a = h_a$ cannot hold when $mp_a < 0$.

5. The conditions $mrp_a = h_a$ and $mrp_b = h_b$ imply that $mp_a/h_a = mp_b/h_b$. This equation states that an extra dollar spent on either input A or input B will increase output by the same amount. Consequently, input proportions are optimal. And $mrp_a/h_a = mrp_b/h_b = 1$ is also implied, which is equivalent to $MR/MC = 1$. Consequently, the scale of output is also optimal.

6. a. Yes. The slope of the output isoquant shows the rate at which input B can be substituted for input A while maintaining output. If one unit less of input A is employed, the fall in output will be (approximately) mp_a. The number of units of input B which must be hired to maintain output will be (approximately) mp_a/mp_b. The approximation approaches exactness for very small changes. So the absolute value of the slope at a point on the output isoquant is mp_a/mp_b.

   b. The absolute value of the slope along an isocost line is the rate at which input B can be traded for input A in the market—equal to h_a/h_b.

8. No, because firms can enter or leave the industry. The entry-exit effect tends to make the industry's demand for a factor more elastic.

9. a. True. A drop in the hire-price of input A will lead to an increase in the employment of input A and so normally to an increase in output. If the demand curve for the product is inelastic, this will induce a relatively large fall in product price. So the industry will respond to a fall in the hire-price with only a small increase in the employment of A (and a small increase in output). The demand curve for input A will be steep and so tend to be inelastic.

   b. True. The weaker the operation of the Law of Diminishing Returns, the more gradual the decline in mp_a as more A is hired. When this decline is more gradual, firm demand curves for factor A and the resulting market demand curve will be relatively flat and so tend to be elastic.

c. True. As the hire-price of input A falls, more A will be hired and so the demand for complementary inputs will increase. The more elastic the supply curves of inputs complementary to A, the greater the increase in employment of these inputs when the demand for them increases. The large increase in the quantity of complementary inputs leads to a large upward shift in mrp_a and so to a relatively large increase in the quantity of factor A employed. Consequently, each firm's demand curve (and so the market demand curve) for input A will be flatter and so tend to be more elastic, the more elastic the supply of complementary inputs.

For Further Thought and Discussion

1. a. See Examples 11.1 through 11.3.
   b. This is a question of fact. The Laws of Diminishing Returns appear to be founded upon general physical aspects of the world. Note, however, that economists admit a range of exceptions when they say that Marginal or Average or Total returns eventually diminish as employment of one input increases relative to others. It is possible that in a practical situation the "eventual" point may not be reached, so increasing returns apply in the relevant range.

2. Even if two inputs are anticomplementary, it is quite possible that each has positive Marginal Product. For each factor mp enters into the value of $mrp = MR(mp)$, which is compared to the hire-price in making the employment decision.

5. This chapter examines aspects of the demand for labor. Supply considerations (to be studied in the next chapter) also have a bearing upon whether wages are high or low. Demand for labor has been high in the United States as a result mainly of the presence of large amounts of complementary factors. In the early years these took the form of rich natural resources (fertile land, mineral wealth, navigable rivers). In more recent years, accumulations of complementary manufactured resources (machines, roads) have contributed to the demand for labor. Other possible sources of high demand for labor in the United States include rapid technological progress (see next question), and relatively strong competition in product markets (so that mrp does not diverge very much from vmp for labor).

6. Technological progress by definition tends to raise the Average Product of labor. It will tend to raise wages if the Marginal Product of labor increases. While the effects on Average Product and Marginal Product are usually parallel, there are exceptions. A "labor-saving" invention may raise the productivity of the first few workers employed so much that the Marginal Product for larger numbers falls. There is another line of causation, however, associated with the general enrichment that technological progress brings about. With higher wealth, there will be more demand for products involving labor of all types. So wages will tend to rise as a result of "revenue" considerations (see For Review Question 1) even if the "productivity" considerations are affected adversely.

CHAPTER 12

For Review

3. No. The supply curve can bend backward only if the income effect opposes the substitution effect. If leisure were an inferior good, the enrichment due to a wage increase

would lead to less consumption of leisure (more supply of labor), thus reinforcing the substitution effect of the wage increase.

4. At very low wage rates, few hours are being worked. A wage increase, multiplied by only a small number of hours, will have only a small enrichment effect compared with the substitution effect.

5. The supply curve to a particular employment is likely to be much more elastic. Different employments of labor are probably, from the worker's point of view, close substitutes. Then a relatively small change in the wage differential between two employments will induce a relatively large shift in labor supply from the less attractive to the more attractive employment.

7. At a high wage, a physician will tend to consume less leisure. Indeed, if the investment in medical training leaves the individual only as well off as before (on the same indifference curve), that person will surely work more, as shown in Figure 12.10. Here only the substitution effect of the wage increase is effective; the income effect is exactly canceled by the income loss due to the cost of training. If the individual ends up on a higher indifference curve as a result of the investment, however, then there will be a net income effect which may lead to working less.

9. Each is a source of productive services, and thus is a portion of society's real capital.

10. This relationship is $h_a = rP_A$. The hire-price of the factor is equal to the interest yield on the capital value or purchase price of the factor. This is an equilibrium relation. The purchase price of the factor will be bid up or down until the relation holds.

12. Economic rent is that portion of payment to a factor in excess of the amount required to call it into employment. Economic rent is a measure of the resource-owner's (seller's) net gain from trade in the factor market. It is, then, analogous to Producer Surplus, which is a measure of the seller's net gain from trade in the product market.

For Further Thought and Discussion

1. a. A decline in the birth rate would reduce demand for "leisure"—that is, for nonmarket uses of women's time. Note that "leisure" does not imply idleness.
   b. Here again, reduced time required for housework will reduce demand for "leisure" time.
   c. Same as b. above.

4. a. Such a change in taste would lead to an outward shift in the market supply curve of female labor. More labor would be offered at each wage rate.
   b. If males and females make up at least partially distinguishable types of labor, the outward shift in the supply of female labor would lead to a decrease in the equilibrium wage rate for female workers relative to male workers.

5. As long as leisure is a normal good, rising per-capita wealth in the form of non-labor income will lead to an increase in leisure and so to a decrease in the number of hours worked. Rising real wages embody both an income and a substitution effect. The pure substitution effect always implies a decrease in leisure and an increase in hours worked, but the income effect works in the opposite direction. Since hours worked have been steadily falling as real wages have risen, the pure substitution effect of rising real wages appears to have been overwhelmed by the sum of the two income effects: that due to rising per-capita wealth (property income), and the income effect of rising real wages.

6. Given the choice, a slave would prefer all leisure (working less than a free person would), while the master would choose no leisure, with the slave working more than a free person would. Thus, a master with strong control may be able to make his slave more productive than a free worker. However, it is costly to control a slave, so the

master's control will not be absolute. The productivity of slave versus free labor is thus a question of circumstances. Where monitoring and negative incentives (punishments) are not too costly, slave labor may turn out to be very productive. But on the whole, the rewards (positive incentives) that free persons can achieve by working have been more effective, especially where motivation and intelligent effort are needed for doing a good job.

9. A tax on earnings generates a substitution effect (work less) and an income effect (normally work more, on the assumption that leisure is a normal good). The tax therefore has an ambiguous effect. A tax on labor capacity would generate only an income effect, and therefore (if leisure is a normal good) would increase the supply of labor.

10. Any decrease in the supply of labor will cause an increase in the equilibrium wage. Strong unions may cause such a reduction in supply. More importantly, if leisure is a normal good, then high income makes workers supply less labor. An abundance of recreational opportunities, and the opportunity to spend time in relatively large homes, also increases the desire to consume leisure.

12. From equations 11.9 and 11.10 of the previous chapter we know that in a competitive market $h_a = P(mp_a)$. The high wages in New York can therefore be the result either of a high marginal product of labor, or else of high prices for produced goods.

CHAPTER 13

For Review

2. a. No. Mutually beneficial trade can occur as long as their MRS_C's differ at their endowed positions (or at their Crusoe optimum positions, if production is possible).
   b. If individuals have identical preferences and endowments in a world of pure exchange, each individual's MRS_C will be the same and no mutually beneficial trade can occur.
   c. Similarly, if they have identical preferences and identical productive opportunities, each individual's MRS_C at the Crusoe optimum will be the same and no mutually beneficial trade can occur.

3. a. Asymmetrical Production-Possibility Curves lead to specialization in production. (Another possibility would be a range of increasing returns.) An individual who is relatively well-suited to producing one good will tend to specialize in producing that good. Symmetrical indifference curves tend to lead to diversification in consumption.
   b. No. In the absence of trade an individual's degree of specialization in production and in consumption would have to be identical. Trade allows the simultaneous existence of productive specialization and consumptive diversification.

6. In a world of production and exchange (assuming interior solutions), at the productive optimum each individual produces at a point along his Production-Possibility Curve such that MRT equals the ratio of market prices. Similarly, at the consumptive optimum, each individual's MRS_C equals the ratio of market prices. Additionally, for each good, the sum over all individuals of the produced quantities must equal the sum of the consumed quantities.

7. The intersection of the full demand and supply curves determines the point at which the total quantity desired for consumption just equals the total quantity available for consumption. The intersection of the transaction demand and supply curves determines the point at which the quantity desired in exchange equals the quantity offered for

exchange. Since the two pairs of curves differ only by the nontraded amounts of the good (endowed and self-consumed quantities in pure exchange, or produced and self-consumed quantities in a world of production), the price that brings desired transaction quantities into equilibrium must also bring desired full quantities into equilibrium.

10. a. Yes, but only in a very special case. Autarky will occur under costless exchange if for every individual the ratio of market prices exactly equals the MRS_C and MRT at his or her Crusoe solution.

   b. Transaction costs create a gap between the gross and net price ratios. Any time an individual's MRS_C and MRT at the Crusoe solution fall inside this gap, the individual will choose an autarky solution. The higher the transaction costs, the greater this gap and the more likely the autarky solution.

13. A command economy could avoid transaction costs by dispensing with markets, but the associated enforcement costs may be larger than the transaction costs saved. While market economies must use resources to integrate individual decisions, command economies must use resources to enforce central decisions. At least as important, the commanders would need an enormous amount of information to make the economy function rationally—information automatically provided by price signals in market economies. Most important, the command economy will aim at "efficiency" in carrying out the desires of the commanders, which may be quite different from the desires of consumers.

For Further Thought and Discussion

2. A tax on consumption will reduce the incentive to acquire the taxed good either by production or by exchange. There will be less consumption and less production, whether for self-supply or for the market. A tax on production will have quite similar effects. A tax on exchange, in contrast, will diminish production for the market but increase production for self-supply. On balance, consumption of the good will also be less since some of the cost-reducing advantages of specialization will be lost.

3. For Robinson, a bunch of bananas has an opportunity cost of two fish, while for Friday a bunch of bananas costs only one fish. Robinson has an absolute advantage in both activities, but Friday has a comparative advantage in picking bananas. Robinson could, for example, pick one less bunch of bananas and use the time to catch two fish. He could then sell one fish to Friday for one bunch of bananas and have the other fish left over to eat. In total, the community thus gains one fish from this specialization in production.

4. Clearly, at least one of the two parties must be better off, since there is more of G and no less of Y available. But i (the seller of good G) might end up worse off. If the demand for grain is inelastic, i will get less revenue in Y-units as he sells more G. More surprisingly, j (the buyer of G) might alternatively end up worse off—if Y is an inferior good for i. (Work this out!)

7. If j has a fixed endowment, he cannot revise his production plans after the opening of trade with i. Individual i, on the other hand, will almost always revise his production plans to produce more X and less Y, or vice versa. Either way there will be less total production of one of the two commodities. Thus, we cannot say that trade necessarily leads to larger production of all goods.

8. A Martian observer, unfamiliar with the mental limitations of flowers and bees, might indeed fail to appreciate the difference as compared with human exchange. Perhaps we're kidding ourselves, but we like to think that our exchanges are the result of choice. Presumably, the behavior of the bees is governed entirely by blind instinct, while the

flowers are even further from having any choice as to whether or not to offer their nectar to bees.

11. Where both ration coupons and cash are required for trade, traders must maintain inventories of coupons as well as cash. In addition, traders must transport, authenticate, and physically transfer ration coupons as well as cash. If coupons can be bought and sold, there is also the cost of the coupon market. If coupons cannot be bought and sold, there are the costs of enforcing (and the costs of evading) the restrictions on the sale of coupons.

12. All these qualities reduce the cost of using money as medium of exchange or as store of value. A somewhat less obvious but very important quality, illustrated by the prisoner-of-war example, is that the monetary commodity should not also be a consumption good. And, of course, the money should be cheap to produce.

CHAPTER 14

For Review

2. b. is correct. The ratio P_0/P_1 is the rate at which current consumption claims can be traded for one-year future consumption claims. If a current consumption claim is foregone, the market will pay back that claim plus interest next year. So $P_0/P_1 \equiv 1 + r$. Consequently, $r \equiv (P_0/P_1) - 1$. The annual rate of interest is the premium on the relative value of current over one-year future consumption claims.

4. Investment must always equal zero in a world of pure exchange. So, at equilibrium, aggregate saving and aggregate investment are both zero.

5. At equilibrium with production, aggregate saving equals aggregate investment. It is also true that aggregate borrowing equals aggregate lending. The total of borrowing or lending can be greater or less than the total of saving or investment. For example, in some economy there may be no net investment; but individuals may nevertheless lend or borrow if different consumers have different preferences or different endowments.

7. a. The Present-Value Rule directs decisionmakers to adopt any incremental project for which the Present Value is positive, and to reject projects for which Present Value is negative.

   b. As long as the Separation Theorem holds, productive optimization is equivalent to wealth maximization. Since the Present-Value Rule is a wealth-maximizing rule, decisionmakers will then be led to the productive optimum.

   c. If the Separation Theorem does not hold, however, wealth maximization and productive optimization are not identical. Here, not only wealth but its distribution over time becomes important, and so the Present-Value Rule will not necessarily lead to a productive optimum.

For Further Thought and Discussion

2. At equilibrium it must be true that—even though saving need not equal investment for any individual—both actual and desired saving equal actual and desired investment in the aggregate. If this were not the case, the interest rate would adjust to bring about the equality. If a floor or ceiling were placed upon the interest rate, it will still be true that actual aggregate saving equals actual investment. Here, the *smaller* of desired aggregate saving and desired aggregate investment will determine the actual quantity of saving and investment. It will not be true, in general, that desired aggregate saving equals desired aggregate investment at the "frozen" market interest rate.

3. a. Because time-productivity will be relatively great in such a newly settled country, the real interest rate will tend to be high.
   b. The real interest rate will be higher if the country is isolated.
   c. Close contact with the rest of the world will lead to an inflow of resources that will increase total investment and decrease the real rate of interest in the new country.

4. If little investment is taking place because of low time-productivity, real interest rates will be low. If little investment is taking place because of high time-preference, interest rates will be high.

6. a. Negative rates of interest are possible. As Equation (14.1) indicates, all that is required is that future claims exchange at a premium against current claims ($P_0 < P_1$). Negative interest rates are rarely observed, however. In most situations there are attractive investment opportunities that increase the investment demand for current funds, while time-preference (impatience) raises the consumptive demand for current funds. The combination assures that current funds will almost always exchange at a premium against the future funds.
   b. Yes. In Equation (14.1″), since P_0/P_1 cannot be less than zero, r cannot fall below -1. In terms of percentages, the interest rate cannot be less than -100 percent.

8. The present worth of a stream of payments is not found by adding up the simple total of the interest-plus-principal installments over the years. This mistakenly assumes that a future payment is worth as much as one today. In fact, at 7.75 percent a dollar payment deferred 27 years is worth today only about 13 cents. At 7.75 percent interest, the payments required by the two-year contract ($392.50 one year from now, and an equal amount two years from now) have present worth of $702.34. But the 27 annual payments (of $39.81 each) of the other contract have a present worth of only $445.21! So the consumer advice provided was seriously off the mark. (Note that the quoted "price" of the appliances is irrelevant for these calculations; only the actual payments matter.)

9. Financing a war by borrowing does not "shift the burden to future generations" any more than financing a war by taxation. Borrowing and taxing are only intermediate processes. The extent to which the burden is shifted to future generations depends upon the degree to which the war reduces consumption or reduces investment. If consumption is reduced, the burden falls on the current generation; if investment is reduced, more of the burden falls upon future generations, since there will be less to eat in the future. So what matters is the extent to which citizens cut back on consumption or on investment when they lend or pay taxes to government.

10. No. "Conservation" is not necessarily economically efficient. For each resource there is an efficient pattern of use over time, not too fast and not too slow. Unless there are "externalities" (discussed in Chapter 15), competition leads to the most efficient pattern of resource use.

CHAPTER 15

For Review

2. The Contract Curve of the Edgeworth-box diagram shows all those allocations from which no mutually beneficial trade can occur. Consequently, the utilities of the two individuals at a point on the Contract Curve become the coordinates for a point on the utility Social Opportunity Curve.

3. a. Given a social criterion, the "social optimum" is simply that allocation which best achieves the criterion. Currently, there seems to be no agreement as to a social

criterion, and so the term "social optimum" lacks agreed meaning. For example, some people regard free abortion as social progress, others see it as social calamity.

    b. Efficiency seems a valid goal, but there are many reasons why it should not be the only element in a social criterion. For one thing, considerations of equity may indicate some sacrifice of efficiency. Also, efficiency is based upon the satisfaction of individual wants as the measure of well-being. It might be argued that individuals are poor judges of what will actually benefit them, or that wants are not autonomous but really socially determined, or that supra-individualistic policy goals (liberty, justice, community) are also important.

8. a. The monopolist violates the efficiency condition $vmp_a = h_a$. It sets $h_a = mrp_a < vmp_a$, and so produces "too little" since $vmp_a > h_a$. This causes an efficiency loss because the firm could, by producing more, convert units of resource A into a larger product value than competitive firms satisfying the condition $vmp_a = h_a$.

    b. Yes, it follows that "too much" of resource A is used by competitive firms. Also "too much" A is retained for reservation uses that could more efficiently be devoted to market employment in the monopolized industry.

11. a. A free-rider problem in the provision of goods will tend to arise whenever it is difficult to exclude nonpayers from the benefits of group action—as when public goods are provided even to those who do not contribute to defray the costs.

    b. Not very valid. While much of government activity appears to be concerned with the provision of public goods—defense, law, and redistribution can all be viewed as having public-good characteristics—governments are also heavily involved with the provision of private goods. And to the extent that the "exploitation" model is valid, government may not be interested in serving the citizens at all.

12. a. This efficiency condition is $MC^i = \Sigma MV^j$; that is, the Marginal Cost for each supplier of providing the public good must equal the sum of all the consumers' Marginal Values for the public good.

    b. For a public good, since every consumer can receive the same unit, the vertical summation of individual demand curves for a public good shows the marginal social valuation. For a private good, only one consumer receives each unit. So the marginal social valuation of the private good is simply the marginal valuation of the consumer receiving the marginal unit. It is, however, incorrect to view the vertical summation of individual demand curves for a public good as a *demand curve* for the public good. This vertical summation does not indicate the quantity that would be purchased at any price; all it shows is the marginal social valuation of the public good.

13. These functions represent each person's marginal valuation schedule for mosquito control. Summing them we obtain $200 - 2y$. Equating this to Marginal Cost, 10, we obtain the solution $y^* = 95$.

14. a. The private supply of public goods is limited, first, by the difficulty and cost of exclusion. Nonpayers would have to be excluded for private provision to be feasible, and this may be impossible or quite costly. Where exclusion costs are sufficiently low, a private firm may provide a public good but will still not likely provide an efficient quantity. For efficient provision, firms would have to charge different prices to different individuals. Such price discrimination might be illegal or simply too costly.

    b. Public provision may result in a quantity closer to the optimum. Where exclusion is impossible or very costly, private provision is unlikely, and so public provision may be inevitable.

For Further Thought and Discussion

1. The Duke did not read the text carefully enough. If the Duchess were initially endowed with a property right to her own life, a Pareto-preferred movement toward an efficient solution would have to be mutually beneficial. It seems unlikely that the Duke could have paid enough to have the Duchess agree to her own death. If the Duke initially possessed the right to take the Duchess's life, on the other hand, his argument would be valid on efficiency grounds. Even then, however, he was not necessarily morally "justified."

2. False. First of all, conventional national income measures fail to allow for a whole variety of sources of utility and disutility: for example, homemakers' services are not counted, nor is the value of leisure, nor degradation of the environment. But the statement would not be true even if there were a perfect national income measure. Monopolization of a good, for example, might raise the market value of national income while reducing efficiency.

4. Property rights will be ill-defined when laws or court rulings are ambiguous and where legal precedents are conflicting or in a state of flux. Also, if it is costly to learn about one's rights, subjective uncertainty may persist even if the underlying legal theory is settled. The costs of transacting (negotiating and enforcing contracts) will tend to be high when multilateral contracting is required, or when individuals have incentives to behave strategically in order to capture more of the gains from an agreement. Some potential trades are hampered by the difficulty of describing the good or service in advance, or of measuring delivery performance thereafter. For example, contracts for labor service cannot generally guarantee in advance how devotedly the worker will perform, and this may even be hard to measure afterward. Another example is the used-car business, where a buyer finds it difficult to determine quality prior to purchase, and where writing a level of agreed quality into the contract is almost impossible.

5. True, since market reallocations of resources must be mutually beneficial. A dictator, in contrast, might achieve a Pareto-efficient outcome that was not Pareto-preferred to the original situation.

6. A ban on trade in blood is certainly inefficient. The hepatitis problem is not a sufficient reason for a ban, since buyers are at liberty to use whatever method they deem appropriate in screening commercial donors. (As might have been anticipated, the prohibition of blood sales has caused dangerous blood "shortages.")

7. a. Yes, the analogy is sound. Laws banning polygyny reduce the demand for wife-services. Since only women can provide those services, the laws work to the disadvantage of women in general (for exceptions, see b.).

   b. Women in general lose, and especially those who would rather be one of the wives of a desirable husband than remain unmarried or be an only wife of a less desirable spouse. Those men who would have been willing and able to acquire multiple wives also lose. The gainers from monogamy laws include women who are exceptionally desirable wives, assuming they prefer to be the sole wife. If polygyny were legal, any such woman could still contract with her husband to be the sole wife but might have to pay a high price for that privilege. But the biggest gainers from the monogamy law are undoubtedly those men who would otherwise have been unable to obtain wives.

   c. Monogamy laws cannot be defended in terms of efficiency.

   d. Monogamy laws tend to increase equality among men, since males who are less attractive husbands have better chances of acquiring wives. They probably increase inequality among women, however, since they improve the ability of more-desirable wives to monopolize the best husbands.

8. a. Since each individual is a member of the "public," he will want to provide some of the public good simply for his own consumption. Furthermore, when others do the same he will become effectively richer, making him want to consume more of the public good than before. So he will not cut back his own contribution 1:1 as others increase theirs. When the public good is of the weakest-link type, voluntary private provision is more likely to approach the efficient level.

   b. If a market were feasible (if it were possible to collect a price from consumers of the public good), firms would enter to supply the public good. While fully efficient provision of the public good can occur only when different prices can be charged to different classes of users (price discrimination), nevertheless we can be confident that—if any supplying firms survive at all—there will be more of the public good provided than in the absence of a market. There will always be more supplied when the motivation to do so is not only to provide for one's own consumption but also to receive payment from others. Furthermore, the surviving firms in the market are likely to be the most efficient suppliers. So there will be more specialization in production of the public good.

CHAPTER 16

For Review

1. Yes, while a political party in office might capture a "profit" by looting the taxpayers, or more subtly by carrying out ideological programs in opposition to voters' desires, its ability to do so is limited by competition from other parties. Ideally, new parties would enter the politics "industry" until no such profit opportunity remained: the surviving parties would have to follow what the voters desire. However, political competition is less effective than market competition (see the following question), and so political profit may not be driven to zero.

2. The imperfections of the democratic political system in serving citizen desires are analogous to, but more severe than, the imperfections of the market. First, in the political system citizens almost never make choices directly on substantive issues; decisions are made by imperfectly controllable delegates. Second, citizens have only a very narrow range of choice even of delegates. They must select from a limited number of candidates (i.e., political competition is highly imperfect) at widely separated election intervals, whereas in the market individuals select almost continuously from a vast menu of choices. Third, even democratic majority rule is likely to override minority desires. Fourth, the cost of acquiring information is much higher for political choices.

5. a. Unanimous consent, involving the purchase of dissident votes, would permit only those decisions that improve the welfare of each and every voter. In terms of Pareto-efficiency, this would be an ideal political system.

   b. Log-rolling allows voters to trade votes on one issue for votes on another issue, and so would often lead to Pareto-preferred outcomes—a series of decisions which together leave everyone better off.

   c. The objections to log-rolling are due primarily to the fact that delegates, not citizens, actually vote on policies. When the delegate is better off, that does not mean the constituents are necessarily better off.

9. An agreement is "self-enforcing" when neither party to the agreement can gain by defecting. For example, a physician and her patient might have invested significant effort in getting to know one another. In order to maintain the relationship, the patient may pay his bills and the physician may provide good service even in the absence of legal enforcement.

For Further Thought and Discussion

1. The public-choice approach views politics as a kind of exchange process. Citizens shop for the type of government that provides them the highest utility. Political parties compete to become the government and so to capture the "profit" of being in power. Since utility maximization, exchange, and competition are all involved, this approach is particularly amenable to economic analysis. An alternative approach views politics as a conflict process, in which some individuals and groups attempt to exploit others.

2. Any voluntary trade is mutually beneficial. So if the poor traded votes to the rich for money, both would gain in comparison with the initial situation. Objections to this practice are probably based on objections to the fact that the rich have more money to begin with.

4. Cash redistributions are not unknown. Social Security comes close to falling into this category, being a redistribution from the working age-group to the retired age-group. But politicians generally prefer to establish service programs to "help" the poor by health care, job training, education, etc. Legislators gain by giving jobs to political supporters and bureaucrats get larger agencies.

6. More frequent elections, more numerous legislatures, and elected judges would allow citizens to more closely control government officials. However, the more frequent are elections and the more numerous the legislatures, the less important is any single vote and so the less informed will voters typically be. So it is not clear whether or not any of these proposals would improve the fidelity of the political system to citizen's desires. Replacing the merit system in civil service by the spoils system would give citizens more control over bureaucrats. The spoils system would therefore make the governmental mechanism more accountable to citizen desires, but might reduce the quality of personnel in government.

7. When government is viewed in a public-choice framework, changes in demand or costs should have somewhat similar effects upon price and output for a governmentally provided good as for a privately provided good. The strength of the effects, however, will differ. Bureaucrats tend to have an interest in larger output and so in keeping prices low to users. An increase in demand will lead to a larger increase in quantity and a smaller increase in price than in the case of private provision. For a decrease in demand, government provision will probably result in a smaller decrease in quantity and a larger fall in price than private provision. Analogous conclusions apply for changes in costs.

INDEX OF NAMES

Rachlin, H., 93
Radford, R. A., 88
Raff, D. M. G., 331
Rapport, D. J., 10, 370
Razin, A., 411–2
Rhodes, V. J., 298
Robbins, H., 330
Robbins, M., 482
Rose, L., 347
Ruback, R. S., 152
Rubin, P. H., 8
Russell, L. B., 190

Sahlins, M., 391
Salop, S. C., 278
Schelling, T., 265
Scholes, M., 434
Schoney, R. A., 287
Seagraves, J. A., 341, 520
Settle, R., 326
Shoven, J. B., 451
Shubik, M., 267
Siegel, S., 270
Siegfried, J. J., 130
Silberberg, E., 484
Simon, J. L., 62, 275
Sinquefield, R. A., 422, 424
Slemrod, J., 398
Smith, A., 12, 13
Sobell, L. C., 105
Sobell, M. B., 105
Stackelberg, H., 270
Stigler, G. J., 181, 199, 221, 275, 489
Stiglitz, J. E., 278
Summer, M. T., 37
Summers, L. H., 331

Swan, P. L., 312

Taubman, P., 412
Tinic, S. N., 215
To, D., 345
Toda, M., 70
Tuckman, H. P., 419
Tullock, G., 487
Turner, J. E., 10
Tyrrell, T., 125

Vroman, S. B., 190

Wallace, A., 334
Ward, R., 37
Weil, D. N., 74
Weinstein, A. A., 57
Weiss, A., 221, 334
Weiss, L., 278
Welch, F., 69
West, J. G., 298
Whalley, J., 451, 474
White, M. D., 487
Whiting, G. C., 12
Wimmer, L. T., 12
Wise, D. E., 327
Wittman, D., 493
Wolfe, L. L., 46
Wolpin, K., 10
Woolf, A. G., 30
Worcester, D. R., Jr., 221

Zardoshty, F., 130
Zeckhauser, R., 467
Zuckerman, S., 188

INDEX OF TOPICS

long-term, 409
prices, 398, 409
real vs. monetary, 419–22
relation to capital value, 346–48
risk, 423–24
short-term, 409
Inventions, 252–54
Inventory, 384–87
Investment, 351 (*see also* Present value):
art, 423
borrowing-lending equilibrium, 397–401
Capital-Asset Pricing Model (CAPM),
426–34
education, 411–12
exhaustible resource, 413–18
forestry, 412–13
human capital, 343–45
intertemporal, 396–419
national growth, 404–05
saving-investment equilibrium, 401–09
Separation Theorem, 406–07
wine, 424
Invisible Hand, 12, 449–51
Isocost line, 300
Isoquant, 295

K

Kinked demand curve, 273–76

L

Labor supply (*see also* Inputs):
backward bending, 325–26
black death, 329
braceros, 327
entrepreneurs, 328
Income Expansion Path (IEP), 94–99, 321–
22, 352
Marginal Rate of Substitution in Resource
Supply, 320, 352
minimum wage, 311–12
monopoly, 335–41
nurses, 326
Price Expansion Path (PEP), 322, 352
resource cartels, 338–41
retirement, 323–24
supply, 318–30, 335–41
welfare, 324–25
Labor unions, 338–40
Lagrangian, 85, 302, 320
Land, 342–3 (*see also* Inputs)
Law of Diminishing Returns, 285
Leisure, 318–22

Lending (*see* Investment)
Logrolling, 484
Long run:
costs, 163–67, 171
shutdown, 159, 180
supply, 176–84
Luxuries, 131

M

Macroeconomics, 15–16
Management:
compensation, 151
effectiveness, 147
Marginal Cost, 47, 156–60, 176, 180, 288
Marginal Product, 285, 288, 296
Marginal Rate of Substitution in Consumption,
87–88, 368, 449–51
Marginal Rate of Substitution in Exchange, 87–
88
Marginal Rate of Substitution in Resource
Supply, 320, 352
Marginal Rate of Transformation, 368, 449–51
Marginal Resource Income, 335–36
Marginal Revenue, 43, 44, 123, 127, 155, 171,
209–10
Marginal Revenue Product, 292, 333 (*see also*
Inputs)
Marginal tax, 49
Marginal traffic flow, 50
Marginal Utility, 62, 85
Marginal Value, 87
efficiency conditions, 449–50
public goods, 452–53
Market portfolio, 430
Market segmentation, 227–29
Marketing orders, agricultural, 235
Median voter, 485–88
Minimum wage, 311–12
Money, 387–91
interest rate, 419–23
medium of exchange, 388–89
source of happiness, 62
store of value, 389–90
Monopolistic competition, 208, 242–47
compared to monopoly, 245
Monopoly, 207–40 (*see also* Marginal Revenue,
Marginal Revenue Product):
cartels, 233–38
compared to competition, 213–14
compared to monopolistic competition, 243
discriminatory pricing, 227–33
efficiency, 219–23, 271, 452